THE LIFE AN[D]

FREDERICK DOUGLASS

PHILIP S. FONER

The Life and Writings
of Frederick Douglass

VOLUME II

Pre-Civil War Decade
1850-1860

INTERNATIONAL PUBLISHERS
NEW YORK

ISBN (4 Vol. Set) 0-7178-0119-5; 0-7178-0118-7 (pbk.)
ISBN (Volume 2) 0-7178-0435-6; 0-7178-0436-4 (pbk.)
Library of Congress Catalog Card Number 50-7654

 209

Printed in the United States of America

Contents

PREFACE

In the first volume of *The Life and Writings of Frederick Douglass,* we traced the career of the great Negro leader from his childhood and youth in slavery through the year 1849. Only twelve years after his escape from bondage, he had already become a world celebrity, one of the great orators of his day, a distinguished editor, a tribune of his people. In 1849 Douglass was still a Garrisonian Abolitionist. He still adhered to the Garrisonian doctrines that moral suasion was the only effectual instrument for the extermination of slavery; that the North should secede from a Union which protected slavery; that the United States Constitution was a pro-slavery document, and that consequently no sincere Abolitionist could vote or hold public office.

But Douglass was always rounding out his knowledge and learning from day-to-day experience in the struggle. In the early 'fifties, he saw the need to rescue the anti-slavery movement from the Garrisonian sectarianism which hung like an albatross around its neck. Soon his eloquence and fire were matched by a political understanding unequalled by his contemporaries in the anti-slavery movement.

In the present volume, we see how Douglass discarded the Garrisonian swaddling clothes, became a leading champion of militant Abolitionism, and the greatest organizer and agitator for political Abolitionism during the ten crucial years preceding the Civil War. While Douglass did not oppose moral suasion, he took a firm stand against the Garrisonian doctrine that it was the *only* weapon in the battle against slavery. More than any other figure in the anti-slavery crusade, he saw the necessity of conducting a many-sided struggle to mobilize the American people into action to destroy slavery. More than any other anti-slavery leader, Douglass insisted that the Negro people, slave and free, must play a decisive role in this struggle. And to white and Negro America alike, Douglass emphasized that "without struggle there is no progress." He likewise stressed the interrelation of the struggle for his people's liberation with all movements for human liberty.

Frederick Douglass' editorials, speeches, and letters in the ten-year period covered by this volume are among the most penetrating and eloquent of any American. They stamp him as one of the greatest minds of his time, a master strategist and tactician, and a people's leader of superb statesmanship. Here is the mature Douglass, seasoned in ten years of activity in the two-front struggle against slavery in the South and against every form of prejudice and discrimination in the North.

Croton-on-Hudson   Philip S. Foner
March, 1950

FREDERICK DOUGLASS

The Universal Reformer

When Frederick Douglass wrote to Garrison in 1846 that he could not allow himself "to be insensible to the wrongs and sufferings of any part of the great family of man," he struck a theme which he was to carry out during the rest of his life. Six months after the founding of *The North Star,* he announced in the journal:

"Standing as we do upon the watch-tower of human freedom, we can not be deterred from an expression of our approbation of any movement, however humble, to improve and elevate the character of any members of the human family."[1]

The editorial columns of Douglass' paper are replete with such expressions of approbation. Douglass spoke favorably of the temperance cause, although he was critical of the fact that many of the organized societies were cool to Negro membership.[2] He called himself a Chartist, and announced that he was "even in favor of more radical [re]forms than they have yet proposed." He hailed the movement to abolish "the bloody and inhuman practice of flogging in the Navy."

"Of course," he editorialized, "we hate the whole naval system, and would sign a petition to have it utterly blotted out of existence . . . and if we cannot abolish the navy, let us do what we can to abolish the barbarous inhumanity of subjecting the soft flesh of man to the cursed and bloody scourge."[3]

Douglass enthusiastically supported the universal peace movement sponsored by Elihu Burritt which enlisted workingmen in the crusade to outlaw war. He endorsed the land reform movement, declaring that "the welfare of the world demands the abrogation of monopolies." "What justice is there," he asked, "in the general Government giving away, as it does, the millions upon millions of acres of public lands, to aid soulless railroad corporations to get rich?" He was convinced that through the distribution of free land to the people, many of the evils of society could be abolished. "Multiply the free homes of the people," he argued, "let each man have around him the blessed influence

of family and home, and the rampant vice and rowdyism of our country
will disappear."[4]

Douglass' paper featured many calls for the abolition of capital
punishment, and offered prayers that the day would come when "throughout the Union and throughout the world, this barbarity will be forever
cancelled."[5] But Douglass did not confine himself to pious utterances
in behalf of the cause. In the fall of 1858 he took part in a pioneer effort
in which he suffered bitter discrimination but showed his moral courage.
That year he joined Susan B. Anthony, Isaac and Amy Post, Samuel
D. Porter, and others in an effort to prevent the execution of one, Ira
Stout, who was about to be hanged for murder. Douglass drew up a
call for a mass meeting which Susan B. Anthony circulated.

"The undersigned, citizens of Rochester, and others, believing Capital
Punishment to be unfriendly to the progress of civilization, hostile to a true
religion, repulsive to the best instincts of humanity, and deprecating the effects of executions on the public mind, do respectfully invite a general attendance of the public at a meeting to be held at City Hall, Thursday Evening, October 7th, at 7 o'clock, with a view of securing, in the case of Ira
Stout, condemned to be hung for the crime of murder, commutation of the
sentence of death to imprisonment for life."

A counter handbill was immediately distributed by the more conservative citizens of Rochester calling upon the public to assemble
in the City Hall and "rescue the meeting from the hands of the fanatics
and save the city from the disgrace of being supposed in favor of the
abolition of the gallows." Fully aware that trouble was brewing, the
adherents of the abolition of capital punishment went ahead with
their plans, and Douglass prepared a set of resolutions to be read to the
meeting for approval.[6]

When the person designated to serve as chairman failed to make
an appearance at the meeting, Douglass was chosen to replace him. "We
all felt that a man of *power* must be obtained for chairman," explained
one of the sponsors of the gathering, "or the meeting was lost. Such
a man is Frederick Douglass; he yielded his own feelings to serve, in
this most trying hour, the cause of humanity." A storm of hisses greeted
Douglass when he mounted the platform. The mob yelled: "Put in a
white man!" "Down with the n——r!" "Whitewash him!" Douglass
lashed into the crowd.

"Seldom," wrote an observer, "have we heard such earnest eloquence as
fell from the lips of Mr. Douglass, as he stood before the maddening crowd,

and defended the right of Free Speech. Insulted almost beyond parallel, and ... beyond endurance, not once did he forget the dignity of his position or the responsibility of the office with which he was invested. Much of his speech, so happily did he use his rich and powerful voice, was distinctly heard above the terrible noise of the mob."

Douglass read his resolutions denouncing capital punishment and asking Governor King to commute Ira Stout's punishment to imprisonment for life. But it was impossible to act on them. Yells, groans, hisses, stamping of feet, whistling, and vile epithets greeted the reading. When some of the rowdies attempted to attack Douglass, the mayor came to the platform and asked the chairman to adjourn the meeting. Douglass, with his daughter upon his arm and his sons by his side, left the hall, "surrounded by a gang of ruffians, heaping all measure of sayings upon him, for the simple and only reason that 'he wore a skin not colored like their own.' "[7]

Next to Abolition and the battle for equal rights for the Negro people, the cause closest to Douglass' heart was woman's rights. In the anti-slavery agitation women took an active and significant part, and no one knew better than Douglass how deeply the Negro people were indebted to the tireless efforts of the women's anti-slavery societies. In reports from communities he was visiting, Douglass regularly devoted space in his paper to descriptions of the work of the anti-slavery women. He constantly stressed the unique contribution of the annual fairs conducted by these women.

"In bringing together persons who stand aloof from anti-slavery meetings," he wrote, "attracting attention to the subject of slavery, acquainting the community with our mode of operating upon public opinion, removing the green-eyed monster—prejudice against color, and demonstrating the industry, taste, skill and disinterestedness of those engaged in the anti-slavery movement, the Anti-Slavery Fairs thus held are pre-eminently successful."[8]

For the women themselves who organized the fairs he had only the highest words of praise:

"We never feel more ashamed of our humble efforts in the cause of emancipation [he wrote in *The North Star* of January 8, 1848], than when we contrast them with the silent, unobserved, and unapplauded efforts of those through whose constant and persevering endeavors this annual exhibition is given to the American public. Anti-slavery authors and orators may be said to receive compensation for what they do, in the applause which must, sooner or later, redound to them; but not so with the thousands whose works of use and beauty adorn this fair. It is for them to work, unnoticed and unknown, and sometimes unenquired for; and many of them unable to see the good that results from their efforts."

While Douglass believed that the anti-slavery movement was doing much "for the elevation and improvement of women," he understood fully the need for an independent, organized movement to achieve equal rights for women. On July 14, 1848, *The North Star*, which featured the slogan, "Right is of no sex," carried an historic announcement:

"A Convention to discuss the Social, Civil and Religious Condition and Rights of Women, will be held in the Wesleyan Chapel at Seneca Falls, New York, on Wednesday and Thursday, the 19th and 20th of July instant.

"During the first day, the meetings will be exclusively for women, which all are earnestly invited to attend. The public generally are invited to be present on the second day, when Lucretia Mott, of Philadelphia, and others, both ladies and gentlemen, will address the Convention."

Thirty-five women and thirty-two men, courageous enough to run the risk of being branded "hermaphrodites" and "Aunt Nancy Men," responded to the call for the world's first organized gathering for woman's rights. Douglass was the only man to play a prominent part in the proceedings.

A "Declaration of Sentiments" adopted by the convention proclaimed: "The history of mankind is a history of repeated injuries and usurpations on the part of man toward woman, having in direct object the establishment of an absolute tyranny over her." Sixteen facts were "submitted to a candid world" by way of proof, after which the Declaration demanded that women "have immediate admission to all the rights and privileges which belong to them as citizens of the United States." Eleven resolutions were then introduced which made such demands as the right of women to personal and religious freedom, the right to vote and to be elected to public office, to testify in courts, equality in marriage and the right to their own children, the right to own property and to claim their own wages; the right to education and equality in trades and professions.[9]

The only resolution that aroused controversy and was not unanimously adopted was the ninth, asserting that it was "the duty of the women of this country to secure to themselves their sacred right to the elective franchise." Many of the delegates, even Lucretia Mott, felt that the demand for the right to vote was too advanced for the times and would only heap ridicule on the entire movement. But Elizabeth Cady

Stanton who had introduced the proposal was determined to press the issue, and looked about the Convention for an ally. "I knew Frederick, from personal experience, was just the man for the work," she told an audience of suffragists years later. Hurrying to Douglass' side, Mrs. Stanton read the resolution and asked him to speak on the question. Douglass promptly arose, and addressed the delegates. He argued convincingly that political equality was essential for the complete liberation of women. The resolution was adopted by a small majority.[10]

In 1888, a few years before his death, Douglass recalled his role at the Seneca Falls Convention, and told the International Council of Women:

"There are few facts in my humble history to which I look back with more satisfaction than to the fact, recorded in the history of the Woman Suffrage movement, that I was sufficiently enlightened at the early day, when only a few years from slavery, to support your resolution for woman suffrage. I have done very little in this world in which to glory, except this one act—and I certainly glory in that. When I ran away from slavery, it was for myself; when I advocated emancipation, it was for my people; but when I stood up for the rights of woman, self was out of the question, and I found a little nobility in the act."[11]

In *The North Star* of July 28, 1848, Douglass praised the action taken by the Seneca Falls Convention, announced his support of the "grand movement for attaining the civil, social, political, and religious rights of women," and bade the women engaged in the crusade his "humble Godspeed." Two weeks later, on August 2, he attended a series of meetings in Rochester to ratify the program of the Seneca Falls Convention. Again he was called upon to argue the merits of the suffrage resolution, and, "in a long, argumentative and eloquent plea," convinced many delegates who were hesitant about demanding the ballot. Not only was the proposal adopted, but the women of Rochester, persuaded by Douglass' arguments, voted to petition the state legislature to grant them the ballot and dedicated themselves to continue the appeal year after year until it was granted. Douglass hailed their stand, declaring "that the only true basis of right was the capacity of individuals."[12]

At the anti-slavery meeting held in Boston in 1850 an invitation was extended from the speaker's desk to all those who were interested in a plan for a National Woman's Rights Convention to meet in the anteroom. Nine women responded and entered the dank and dingy room. From this little meeting came the plans which resulted in a call signed by many prominent men and women for the first National Woman's Rights Convention to meet in Brinley Hall, Worcester, on October 23, 1850.

Douglass was in Massachusetts at this time, organizing opposition to the Fugitive Slave Act. He read the call for a national convention to consider "the question of Woman's Rights, Duties and Relations," and arranged his schedule so that he could be in Worcester on October 23. The attendance at the convention was large, representatives from nine states being present. Douglass, Garrison, Wendell Phillips, S. S. Foster, and Sojourner Truth were a few of the many Abolitionists who served as delegates. The motto of the convention, "Equality before the law without distinction of sex or color," was evidence of their influence.

The convention voted to petition the legislature of eight states to grant the ballot to women. A national committee was appointed to achieve this goal as well as to seek the repeal of property laws discriminating against women, and the opening to women of all government and professional positions. Wendell Phillips was made treasurer of the committee.

Over in England the *Westminster Review* in an elaborate article by Mrs. John Stuart Mill noted the Worcester convention and endorsed the proceedings. But in America the newspapers pelted it with abuse. It was "the Hen Convention," and its members "ismizers of the rankest stamp." "Woman's office," shrieked the New York *Mirror,* "are those of wife, mother, daughter, sister, friend—Good God, can they not be content with these?"[13]

In spite of this cheap ridicule the woman's movement gained momentum. Douglass continued to lend it his active support. Few indeed were the woman's rights conventions held during the 'fifties at which Douglass was not a featured speaker and whose proceedings were not fully reported in his paper. Susan B. Anthony even advised Gerrit Smith to look in Douglass' weekly for regular notices of woman's rights gatherings. Invariably the notice would be accompanied by an editorial comment hailing the meeting and expressing the editor's hope that the proceedings "will have a powerful effect upon the public mind." In 1853 when Douglass was thinking of changing the name of his paper, he rejected the proposed title, *The Brotherhood,* because it "implied the exclusion of the sisterhood."[14]

Douglass was a prominent figure at several conventions which pioneered in condemning discrimination because of sex. He was the presiding officer at the national convention of Colored Freemen at Cleveland in 1848 when a resolution was passed affirming a belief in the equality of the sexes and inviting the women present to participate in the proceedings. Two months later, at Philadelphia, Douglass was one of the organizers of a convention of Negro people at which a similar invitation was extended to women, white as well as Negro. Lucretia Mott decided to accept the liberal invitation:

"We are now in the midst of a convention of the colored people of this city," she wrote to Elizabeth Cady Stanton. "Douglass & Delany—Remond & Garnet are here—all taking an active part—and as they include women & *white* women too, I can do no less, with the interest I feel in the cause of the slave, as well as of woman, than be present & take a little part—So yesterday, in a pouring rain, Sarah Pugh & self, walked down there & expect to do the same today."[15]

At the Colored National Convention at Rochester in July, 1853, Douglass, chairman of the Committee on Declaration of Sentiments, wrote to Gerrit Smith: "We had one Lady Delegate—Mrs. Jeffrey of Geneva—strange to say we had good sense to make no *fuss* about it."[16]

Douglass was a member of the executive committee of the Radical Abolitionists which met in Worcester in 1860 to consider the feasibility of establishing a political party on strict anti-slavery grounds. The gathering invited women to participate in the proceedings, an invitation which marked the first effort made "to organize a political party upon a basis of absolute justice and perfect equality."[17] The stand was in keeping with Douglass' role as a reformer. To the powerful appeal he had made for freedom from chattel slavery, he had added the demand for the broadest liberty for all people.

Douglass and the Negro Convention Movement

Although Douglass' best work in the battle against slavery and prejudice was done on the platform and in his newspaper, he made notable contributions in the organized movement of the Negro people, especially as a leading figure in the ante-bellum Negro conventions. Here he joined forces with other Negroes in public life to protest, petition, and carry into operation a program of, by and for the Negro people of the United States.

The Negro convention movement started long before Douglass became actively involved in the anti-slavery struggle. Beginning with 1817, the year of Douglass' birth, local and state-wide meetings of Negro people were held in many northern communities in protest against the American Colonization Society. The agitation increased during the 1820's when the Colonization Society purchased Liberia and began its propaganda campaign throughout the nation. Through this agitation, thousands of American Negroes for the first time felt a sense of communication with groups from other sections of the nation. It was inevitable that this development would lead to a realization among the Negro people that their ultimate victory lay in an integrated program representing a national viewpoint.

Events during the late 1820's hastened the movement for a national organization of the Negro people. In 1829, the Ohio courts declared that the Black Laws adopted in that state in 1804-1807 were still constitutional. These laws restricted the freedom of Negro people and demanded of each a $500 bond for good behavior. Unwilling to wait for officials to enforce the decisions, groups of white citizens in the southern part of the state took matters into their own hands and gave notice that the Negro people either post the bond within a limited time or get out of the state. When the Negroes disregarded these warnings or were slow to act, mobs fell upon them, on one occasion killing a number and destroying the property of the others. Overnight, Negro communities in Ohio were emptied as the Negro people fled into Canada, into western Pennsylvania, or into other states in the Great Lakes region.[1]

Fearing that legislators and mobsters in the East would follow the pattern set by Ohio, Negro leaders decided to plan concerted action on a nation-wide scale to stem the tide of repression. A circular issued by five Negro leaders in Philadelphia called for a convention of Negro delegates from the several states "to meet on the 20th Day of September, 1830, to devise plans and means for the establishment of a colony in upper Canada, under the patronage of the General Convention. . . ." Forty delegates met under President Richard Allen of Philadelphia,[2] organizer and first bishop of the African Methodist Episcopal Church, and concurred upon a proposal to buy extensive Canadian land with a view to establishing a colony of free Negroes. But their most significant achievement was the recommendation of formation of a parent society, to be called the National Negro Convention, with auxiliaries in different towns and cities.

In the six years following 1830, the National Negro Convention met annually and adopted programs for the security and elevation of the Negro people.[3] In addition, the convention founded a series of organizations, known as the Phoenix Societies, in the urban areas of the North.

Under the direction of Rev. Christopher Rush, Rev. Theodore S. Wright, and Rev. Peter Williams, Jr., these local societies made proposals to improve the moral welfare of the Negroes, and to instruct them in literature and mechanical arts.

A series of dissensions which had been brewing since 1831 split the National Convention after its 1836 meeting. Some of the delegates were convinced that Canadian colonization was still the most urgent business at hand. Others felt that it was necessary to concentrate upon building a better social order in the United States. Some were beginning to support political action while others clung to the Garrisonian doctrine of moral suasion. One group doubted the efficacy of associating with any set of white Abolitionists and advocated restricting the convention to Negro membership. Another, convinced of the inability to achieve equality for Negroes in existing institutions, favored continuing the establishment of separate schools and churches for the Negro people. The latter was opposed by a group of Pennsylvania Negroes under the influence of the wealthy Robert Purvis, William Whipper, and James Forten, Sr., who refused to recognize any special needs and problems of the Negro people requiring separate organizations, and called for their immediate and complete integration into American life.

In 1836, the Pennsylvania-dominated American Moral Reform Society, organized a year before to extend the work of the Phoenix Societies, withdrew from the National Convention, set up its own constitution and published its official organ, *The National Reformer,* edited by William Whipper. Meeting annually from 1836 through the early 1840's, the society endorsed the platform of Garrisonianism, and proclaimed that the Negro people attend only those schools and churches open to both races. The Garrisonians through the *National Anti-Slavery Standard* and the *Liberator* supported this point of view.

Opposition to the Moral Reformists grew as it became clear to many of the 500,000 free Negroes in the United States that the white people were not anxious to share their institutions with Negroes. In 1840 a demand arose for the holding of a new National Negro Convention and so Committees of Correspondence and local and regional bodies were established. In September, 1840, the National Reformed Convention of the Colored People met in New Haven, under the leadership of David Ruggles. The delegates emphasized two points in their proceedings: the importance of Negro initiative in "extricating themselves from the tyrant's yoke," and the degrading influence of slavery upon the free Negro population. Through the efforts of Ruggles, William C. Nell, Rev. Pennington, and John B. Vashon, the American Reform Board of Disfranchised Commissioners was organized and met in New York City in 1841.[4]

Although the American Moral Reform Society and the Reformed Convention were shortlived, the state conventions and local auxiliary societies progressed rapidly during the 1830's and early 1840's despite the unfortunate factionalism in the national movement. Innumerable Negro organizations sprang up throughout New England and the Middle States. Societies of free Negroes appeared in the great western centers of Detroit, Chicago, and Cincinnati. State conventions were held annually in the western states of Ohio, Illinois, Michigan, Indiana, and in the border state of Maryland.[5]

After a lapse of seven years, the National Negro Convention reconvened in Buffalo in 1843. Fifty-eight delegates were present, thirty-six of whom were from New York state; ten states, including Virginia, North Carolina, and Georgia were represented. Amos Gerry Beman, a New Haven clergyman, was elected president, and Douglass served as one of the vice-presidents. But the outstanding figure at the convention was Henry Highland Garnet, pastor of the Liberty Street Negro Presbyterian Church. In the most savage indictment of slavery delivered by a Negro since David Walker's *Appeal*, Garnet stirred the assembly:

"Brethren, arise, arise! Strike for your lives and liberties. Now is the day and the hour. Let every slave throughout the land do this, and the days of slavery are numbered. You can not be more oppressed than you have been —you cannot suffer greater cruelties than you have already. Rather die freemen than live to be slaves. Remember that you are four millions."

Still under the influence of the Garrisonian principles of non-resistance and moral suasion, Frederick Douglass took issue with Garnet. He observed that there was "too much physical force both in the address and remarks of Garnet; that the address, could it reach the slaves, and the advice . . . be followed, while it might not lead the slaves to rise in insurrection, for liberty, would nevertheless, and necessarily be the occasion for insurrection. . . ." And that, Douglass concluded, was what he wished "in no way to have any agency in hurrying about and what we were called upon to avoid."

For several days, the convention debated Garnet's proposal, and finally, by the narrow majority of one vote, 18 in favor of Garnet's measure and 19 against it, Douglass' position was sustained.

Later in the convention, Douglass proposed a plan of moral suasion to induce the slave-owners to release their slaves from bondage. Garnet objected bitterly to reliance on such tactics, and asked that the plan be rejected. Douglass resumed the floor in defense of his report, and won a majority vote at the final count.[6]

The proceedings revealed that important sections of the Negro population were definitely breaking away from Garrison's moral suasion doctrine. By still adhering to this doctrine, Douglass, at this stage, was not as advanced as the most militant section of the Negro people. But, as we shall shortly see, Douglass soon recognized the futility of relying on moral suasion as a chief weapon to end slavery.

Although they rejected Garnet's proposal, the delegates were so aroused by his address that they attacked the problems confronting the Negro people with renewed determination. They voted to send capable Negro speakers into northern communities to inform whites and Negroes about "the claims, disabilities, sentiments, and wishes of the colored people," to impress the free Negroes with the importance of education, of improvement in science and literature, and of applying themselves to the mechanical arts. The convention also went on record as favoring the circulation of petitions to Congress for the abolition of slavery in the territories and opposing the annexation of Texas.[7]

Meeting in Troy, New York, in 1847, the National Colored Convention was attended by sixty-eight delegates from nine states, forty-six of whom were from New York and fourteen from Massachusetts. Nathan Johnson of New Bedford, who had befriended Douglass a decade previously, was elected president. Vice-presidents included Rev. J. W. C. Pennington and Dr. James McCune Smith.

Douglass took a prominent part in the debates, creating "some excitement" among the delegates by urging the Negro people "to come out from their pro-slavery churches; exclaiming that his right arm should wither before he would worship at their blood-stained altars; they were not the places for colored men." As chairman of the committee to draft a report on the best means of abolishing slavery and destroying caste in the United States, Douglass revealed that he was still under the influence of the Garrisonian wing of anti-slavery thought. The committee condemned "any attempt to lead our people to confide in brute force as a reformatory instrumentality," and endorsed moral suasion—"a faithful, earnest, and persevering enforcement of the great principles of justice and morality, religion and humanity"—as the "only invincible and infallible means within our reach to overthrow this foul system of blood and ruin."[8]

The convention laid plans for a national press with committees in six states appointed to gather pertinent information and opinion. In the meantime, *The Ram's Horn, The National Watchman, The North Star,* and *The Mystery* were considered papers worthy of support. Among other business, Gerrit Smith presented the delegates with 120,000 acres of New York state farming and timber land to which about three thousand Negro people of that state could lay claim if they wished to settle upon the property and put small farms into operation.[9]

Douglass' stand on the question of establishing a national Negro press disappointed many of the delegates. Garnet introduced the resolution calling for a press "solely under the control of the people of color." The suggestion was submitted to a special committee, headed by Dr. James McCune Smith, which endorsed the proposal.

"Of the means for the advancement of a people placed as we are," went the report, "none are more available than a press. . . . Among ourselves we need a press that shall keep us steadily alive to our responsibilities, which shall constantly point out the principles which should guide our conduct and our labors, which shall cheer us from one end of the land to the other, by recording our acts, our sufferings, our temporary defeats, and our steadily approaching triumph, or rather the triumph of the glorious truth 'Human Equality,' whose servants and soldiers we are."

The report paid tribute to the services rendered by newspapers edited and published by Negroes, then pointed out that because of the poverty of their owners their influence was limited. No one man, it declared, among five hundred thousand free Negro people was "yet set apart with a competence for the purpose of advocating our cause and the cause of our brethren in chains." Hence the committee called for setting up:

"In these United States, a printing press, a copious supply of type, a full and complete establishment, wholly controlled by colored men; let the thinking, writing man, the compositors, pressmen, printers' help—all, all, be men of color; then let there come from said establishment a weekly periodical and a quarterly periodical, edited as well as printed by colored men; let this establishment be so well endowed as to be beyond the chances of temporary patronage; and then there will be a fixed fact, a rallying point, towards which the strong and the weak amongst us would look with confidence and hope. . . ."[10]

To the surprise of the delegates, Douglass led the opposition to the report. He favored Negro newspapers, he told the convention, but believed that a national Negro press at that time was a visionary scheme since it could not be successfully sustained. More important, "a paper started as a national organ, would soon dwindle down to be the organ of a clique," and in the end would mean the control of the editor by the group. He was in favor of sustaining the present newspapers instead of killing them off by a national press which was doomed to a brief existence.[11]

The delegates were not impressed by Douglass' reasoning and voted 27 to 9 for the national Negro press. Strangely enough, Douglass published the entire text of the report on the press in his paper, and, at the same time, called on the Negro people to support *The North Star* and make it a real national Negro paper.[12] Evidently his opposition to a national Negro press stemmed basically from his reluctance to relinquish control of his own paper. He was convinced that a paper sponsored by the National Convention and edited by a group of people would prove cumbersome in operation and would create constant dissensions.

While nothing came of the plan to establish a national Negro press, a number of Negro leaders were critical of Douglass for his stand on this issue. They accused him of permitting his own interests to interfere with a program which promised to achieve advances for his people. Douglass' decision in 1851 to call his journal *Frederick Douglass' Paper* also evoked criticism for the same reason. While none of the leaders questioned the outstanding qualities of the paper, they believed it was somewhat inconsistent for the editor to urge the Negro people to support it as their own journal while he insisted on conducting it as his personal organ. These critics overlooked the fact that they were living in an era of personal journalism, and that one of the chief reasons for the attention accorded Douglass' paper was precisely because it was the paper of a man who was recognized as the outstanding American Negro. Moreover, Douglass always insisted in editorials and speeches that the paper was not his personal organ but rather the tribune of the Negro people, both the enslaved and the free.

In September, 1848, between sixty and seventy delegates met in Cleveland and chose Douglass as president of the National Negro Convention. Douglass was delighted to discover in examining the delegates' credentials that they represented a cross-section of the free Negro people—printers, carpenters, blacksmiths, shoemakers, engineers, dentists, gunsmiths, editors, tailors, merchants, wheelwrights, painters, farmers, physicians, plasterers, masons, clergymen, barbers, hairdressers, coopers, livery stable keepers, bath-house keepers, and grocers.

Reversing the position adopted a year before on the national Negro press, the convention anounced that *The North Star* answered the needs and purposes of such a press and urged its support by all Negro people. The delegates also endorsed the Free Soil Party, but declared that they were "determined to maintain the higher stand and more liberal views which heretofore characterized us as *abolitionists.*" This meeting recommended "a change in the conduct of colored barbers who refused to treat colored men on a basis of equality with the whites." Committees were appointed in different states to organize vigilante groups, "so as to enable them to measure arms with assailants without and invaders within."[13]

Douglass' voice was heard throughout the proceedings. He opposed the preamble to the seventeenth resolution "inasmuch as it intimated that slavery could not be abolished by moral means alone." He moved to amend the thirty-third resolution, declaring that the word "persons" used in the resolution designating delegates be understood "to include *women.*" The motion was seconded, and carried "with three cheers for woman's rights."[14]

Douglass' role at the Cleveland Convention won him nationwide attention. The proceedings were printed in the press, and special comments on the presiding officer appeared in the editorial columns. The pro-southern papers exhausted their vocabulary in slandering Douglass, but other journals were extravagant in their praise. Answering an attack by the *Plain Dealer* of its city, the Cleveland *Daily True Democrat* declared: "Frederick Douglass is a man, who if divided into fifty parts would make fifty better men than the editor of the *Plain Dealer.*" Gerrit Smith was so delighted with Douglass' conduct at the convention that he ventured the opinion that "he has the talents and dignity that would adorn the Presidency of the nation."[15]

But there were serious weaknesses in the movement which Douglass was convinced had to be eliminated if the cause was to progress. Basic differences among those adhering to moral suasion and those who believed strongly in political action, differences between various religious sects, and numerous petty jealousies and feuds prevented the adoption of a co-ordinated program that would present the viewpoint of the Negro people to the nation. Furthermore, the absence of a truly functioning organization between conventions resulted in a failure of the delegates to implement the work during the intervening period. Nor was there in existence a national body with sufficient authority to call meetings of the Negro people to take action on the vital issues of the day. Even the conventions themselves were brought into being by groups of individuals acting solely on their own initiative. Consequently, the movement lacked continuity and authority.

To create harmony and unity among the Negro people and to give the National Convention movement a permanent organizational structure, Douglass projected the idea of a National League of Colored People. In *The North Star* of August 10, 1849, he placed the motto, "The Union of the oppressed for the Sake of Freedom," at the head of the editorial column, and published an outline of a constitution for the "National League." The preamble went:

"Whereas, the voice of reason, and the admonitions of experience, in all ages alike, impress us with the wisdom and necessity of combination; and that union and concert of action are highly essential to the speedy success of any good cause; that as in division there is weakness, so in union there is strength; and whereas, we have long deplored the distracted and divided state of the oppressed, and the manifold evils resulting therefrom, and desiring as we do to see an union formed which shall enable us the better to grapple with the various systems of injustice and wrong by which we are environed, and to regain our plundered rights, we solemnly agree to unite in accordance with the following."

The object of the League was the abolition of slavery, and the elevation and improvement of the free Negro people of the United States. It would seek to achieve these goals by means of lectures and the press, "and all other means within their power, consistent with christian morality." The League would have a president, secretary, treasurer, and a council of nine.

For several weeks after this initial announcement, Douglass' paper featured the constitution of the proposed league and the call for a convention which was scheduled to meet in Philadelphia on September 21. The editor waited anxiously for the reaction of his "colored brethren in different parts of the country on the subject of *union*."[16]

The response was disappointing. Among white Abolitionists, the *Anti-Slavery Bugle* hailed the project, and wished it well, observing that it "has long been a source of grief to Abolitionists that the Free Colored People of this country are so widely separated from each other by sectarian and party lines as to impair their efficiency in the work of their own elevation and in breaking the chains of the enslaved."[17] But the Negro leaders themselves displayed little interest in the proposed organization, and the Negro press did little to publicize it. One Negro correspondent voiced his regret to Douglass that there was "so much apathy manifested on the part of our leading men to your noble and philanthropic scheme," and attributed it to personal jealousy and to the opposition of colored clergymen to a plan sponsored by one who had "attacked the proslavery character of the church, and told them that they should not let slaveholders and their abettors preach in their pulpit."[18] The bitter attack against Douglass launched by Rev. Henry Highland Garnet at the time the National League was projected would bear out this conjecture. Garnet accused Douglass of having spoken lightly and contemptuously of the religious convictions of the Negro people, and of having denied "the inspiration of the Bible." Although Douglass denied the charges and the *Anti-Slavery Bugle* denounced Garnet for echoing the cries of the "pro-slavery church," the attack was influential in turning Negro clergymen against Douglass' League.[19]

Despite the indifference of the Negro leaders and press, Douglass was determined to proceed with the organization of the National League. If only thirty persons could be found who were willing to form the League, he was convinced that "from this small beginning, an institution may be erected, fraught with untold good to ourselves and to posterity." Unfortunately, the organization meeting at Philadelphia was so poorly attended that even Douglass was forced to admit that his proposal had been premature. Criticizing Negro leaders sharply for their refusal to join in the founding of a national organization for improving the condition of their people, he abandoned the project. Yet even as he dropped the plan, Douglass expressed confidence that eventually the Negro would create an organization such as he envisaged:

"It is impossible to keep a people asunder for any long time, who are so strongly and peculiarly identified together, when there is a vigorous effort made to unite them. We shall never despair of our people—an union shall yet be effected—our ranks cannot always be divided. The injuries which we mutually suffer—the contempt in which we are held—the wrongs which we endure, together with a sense of our own dignity as men, *must* eventually lead us to combine."[20]

For five years after the Cleveland convention, the National Convention movement lay dormant. Following the passage of the Fugitive Slave Act in 1850, many Negroes were too terrified to attend public gatherings. Any Negro who was unable to produce proof of his freedom satisfactory to a southern deputy was in danger of being returned to slavery. Hundreds of Negro families from Ohio, Pennsylvania, and New York fled to Canada, abandoning their homes and work. Professor Fred Landon estimates that approximately twenty thousand Negroes, the greater percentage of whom were probably former slaves, fled to Canada during the decade 1850-1860.[21]

The very intensity of the drive against the Negro population in the North compelled the revival of the National Convention. In July, 1853, a hundred and forty delegates from nine states gathered in Rochester, New York, in what was the most important of all conventions. The call for the gathering indicated some of the major problems which made the reconvening of the National Convention necessary:

"The Fugitive Slave Act, . . . the proscriptive legislation of several States with a view to drive our people from their borders—the exclusion of our children from schools supported by our money—the prohibition of the exercise of the franchise—the exclusion of colored citizens from the jury box—the social barriers erected against our learning trades—the wiley and vigorous efforts of the American Colonization Society to employ the arm of the government to expel us from our native land—and withal the propitious awakening to the fact of our condition at home and abroad, which has followed the publication of 'Uncle Tom's Cabin'—calls trumpet-tongued for our union, co-operation, and action. . . ."

Reverend J. W. C. Pennington was elected president of the Rochester Convention and the vice-presidents included Douglass, William C. Nell, and John B. Vashon.

Douglass was also chairman of the committee on Declaration of Sentiments and drew up the "Address of the Colored Convention to the People of the United States." This remarkable "Address" set forth the basic demands of the Negro people for justice and equality. Today, one hundred years afterward, it may still be read, not only for the clarity and grace of its prose but also for its significance.

The "Address" demanded that "the doors of the school-house, the work-shop, the church, the college, shall be thrown open as freely to our children as to the children of other members of the community"; that "the white and black may stand upon an equal footing before the laws of the land"; that "colored men shall not be either by custom or enactment excluded from the jury-box"; that "the complete and unrestricted right of suffrage, which is essential to the dignity even of the white man, be extended to the Free Colored Man also," and that laws "flagrantly unjust to the man of color . . . ought to be repealed." These demands were justified on the simple principle that the Negro people were American citizens "asserting their rights on their own native soil."

Realizing that this claim of citizenship was denied by the national government, Douglass presented a masterly historical analysis to buttress his argument, quoting extensively from state Constitutional Conventions, from congressional debates, and from Andrew Jackson's proclamation to the free colored inhabitants of Louisiana during the Battle of New Orleans.

"The case is made out," Douglass concluded. "We and you stand upon the same broad national basis. Whether at home or abroad, we and you owe equal allegiance to the same government—have a right to look for protection on the same ground. We have been born and reared on the same soil; we have been animated by, and have displayed the same patriotic impulses; we have acknowledged and performed the same duty; we have fought and bled in the same battles; we have gained and gloried in the same victories; and we are equally entitled to the blessings resulting therefrom."[22]

"No nobler paper was ever put forth by any body of men," commented the reporter for the *New York Tribune*.[23]

One of the most important and controversial issues before the Rochester Convention was the question of founding a manual labor college for colored youth. As in the case of almost every problem discussed by the delegates, it was by no means a new idea. Samuel Cornish had outlined a plan for a Negro Manual Labor College in *Freedom's Journal* as early as 1827. Four years later, at the National Negro Convention in Philadelphia, the idea, proposed by Garrison and his colleagues, won the support of the delegates. Cornish was elected the agent to collect the necessary funds for the institution, and auxiliary committees to assist him were set up in the important centers of free Negroes.

New Haven was chosen for the site, and plans for the college, with a board of trustees consisting of a majority of Negroes, were drawn up. Arthur Tappan purchased several acres of land in the southern part of New Haven with the intention of presenting it to the Negro Convention for the school campus, but so much opposition arose from the townspeople that, on September 8, 1831, the mayor issued an order prohibiting the proposed school within the city limits. On September 10, the "best citizens" of New Haven, led by the mayor and a number of Yale professors and students, staged riots before the homes of supporters of the college. Many Negroes wished to proceed in the face of this hostility, but some timid white Abolitionists withdrew their support, and the college was abandoned.

Still the idea persisted. The New England Anti-Slavery Society, at its first annual meeting in January, 1833, announced that it was making "strenuous exertions for the establishment of a manual labor school for colored youth, and will probably soon attain its object." The Society appointed Garrison its agent to collect funds for the school, and the Abolitionist leader decided to visit England for the purpose of raising money.[24] England at this time was in the midst of a campaign to abolish slavery in the British West Indies, and the people would extend a hearty welcome to any mission from the United States seeking financial aid against slavery in this country.

Negroes in the United States not only endorsed Garrison's mission to Europe, but provided a large part of the funds for his trip. At the National Negro Convention in June, 1833, the delegates approved Garrison's mission, and, on the basis of the hopes aroused by this new venture, abandoned their efforts to colonize extensively in Canada.[25]

In the *Liberator* of July 5, 1834, Garrison announced that more than fifteen hundred dollars had been subscribed for the manual labor school, and pledged himself to carry on a consistent campaign until the institution was established. But nothing came of the movement, and gradually Garrison lost interest in the project. Negroes themselves, moreover, began to be divided on the issue. Douglass, for example, was at first opposed to a Negro college, contending that it was based upon the principle of segregation and tended to perpetuate prejudice against color.

Events themselves compelled Douglass to change his viewpoint. Negroes were increasingly being shut out from all lucrative employment and compelled to do only the most menial work. Even in firms owned by white Abolitionists a colored man found it impossible to get a job higher than a porter, no matter what his capabilities.[26] What was equally if not more alarming was the influx of immigrants from Ireland who in the 'forties and 'fifties threatened the Negro's position even in the lowliest employments. Negro workers were being displaced as porters, barbers, cab-drivers, wood-sawyers, stevedores, and common laborers. Unable to secure employment as skilled craftsmen and finding themselves pushed out of menial jobs, the Negro workers faced a serious crisis.

As he traveled about the country visiting Negro communities, Douglass became familiar with the economic problems of his people. "Learn Trades or Starve," he wrote in 1853. "We must find new methods of obtaining a livelihood, for the old ones are failing us very fast." He appealed to white anti-slavery men and women to employ Negro boys and girls as apprentices "and teach them trades, by which they can obtain an honorable living." Funds raised to send Negro students to

European colleges were all very well, but it was more important for the Negroes to learn how to make a good living than to learn Latin and Greek. Anti-slavery men who called themselves friends of the Negro people but refused to hire Negro workers for anything but the most menial jobs were hypocrites.[27]

In March, 1853, Douglass visited Harriet Beecher Stowe at her home in Andover, Ohio, to consult with the author of *Uncle Tom's Cabin* "as to some method which should contribute successfully, and permanently, to the improvement and elevation of the free colored people in the United States. . . ." Mrs. Stowe asked Douglass to propose the best plan to achieve that goal. He replied:

"What can be done to improve the condition of the free people of color in the United States? The plan which I humbly submit in answer to this inquiry—and in the hope it may find favor with you, and with many friends of humanity who honor, love and co-operate with you—is the establishment in Rochester, N. Y., or in some other part of the United States equally favorable to such an enterprise, of an *industrial college* in which shall be taught several branches of the mechanical arts. This college is to be opened to colored youth. . . ."[28]

Anxious to secure approval of his plan, Douglass read his reply to Mrs. Stowe to the Rochester National Negro Convention. A number of delegates, Charles L. Remond and George T. Downing among them, were hostile to the proposal. They argued that the college would be too costly; that the Negro people would not be interested in the institution. The old contention that a Negro college was a capitulation to prejudice against color was also raised.

Douglass, Dr. James McCune Smith and James W. C. Pennington led the battle for the industrial college. They pointed out that there were few Negro apprentices since there were not many Negro craftsmen and most white craftsmen were opposed to taking a Negro into service. An industrial college would produce skilled workers, and the presence of an "industrious, enterprising, upright, thrifty and intelligent free black population would be a killing refutation of slavery." Since the college would be open to all students regardless of color, it could hardly be considered a segregated institution.

The majority of the delegates concurred with the arguments in favor of the industrial college, and voted to sponsor the institution.

To implement its program and provide for its operation before the next national meeting, the Rochester Convention organized a National

Council of the Colored People consisting of two members from each of ten northern states. Aided by state councils, the popularly elected members of which were to have direct control of local affairs, the National Council set up four committees: the Committee on a Manual Training School which was to procure funds, select the location and establish the school complete with dormitories and a farm; the Committee on Business Relationships which was to establish a large-scale employment office; the Committee on Publication which was to compile records, statistics, and the history of every phase of Negro life, a collection which was to be made available to the public; and the Committee of Protective Union which was to establish a kind of co-operative at which Negroes could buy and sell staples.[29]

Thoroughly satisfied with their work, the delegates left Rochester imbued with a determination to translate their deliberations into action. They had reason for feeling elated. The Convention had received favorable comments from a large section of the press. A citizen of Rochester, who had never before attended an anti-slavery meeting, wrote a glowing letter to the *New York Tribune* describing his reactions to the sessions:

"Throughout, it has been conducted by colored men, and their debates as well as proceedings generally have been equal to any of the white men who have heretofore espoused their cause as abolitionists or philanthropists of any kind. . . . I have never heard more chaste and refined dictum from any class of men, neither have I seen better oratorical powers displayed. . . . I have never seen delegates come in cleaner apparel, and more dignified manner than have the colored men."[30]

The letter was typical. Douglass informed Gerrit Smith that the deliberations had improved "the current of feeling toward the colored people" in Rochester. The *Rochester Democrat* pointed out that the impressions left upon the minds of many "Anglo Saxon spectators" was "highly favorable." It added:

"What is equally important, it has convinced the colored people themselves, that they have many able and practicable minds among them, and they are resolutely engaged in devising schemes for their own moral, ...ental and physical improvement. . . . Had *Wm. Lloyd Garrison, Gerrit Smith,* and other able champions of their cause, been present and prominent in their proceedings, they, and not the *Remonds, Douglasses* and others would have received the praise for all that was wisely done, while the colored people would have shared the odium of all that might have been wrong. There can be no doubt that these people have the ability to devise and carry out measures for their own social advancement, and for the general improvement of their condition. . . . Let them have the sympathy and pecuniary aid of others, but let their plans be devised and executed by themselves. . . ."[31]

Inspired by the great success of the Rochester Convention, dozens of local and regional Negro people's conventions were held throughout the North during the closing months of 1853. Numerous mass meetings were held in churches and schools to endorse the proceedings at Rochester, and many leaders of the National Convention visited Negro leaders to help them establish local groups. On October 6, 1853, the Illinois State Negro Convention met in Chicago, heard Douglass discuss the Rochester Convention, voted to support the movement, and adopted the slogans of the 1853 convention in mobilizing the fight against the black laws.[32] As in the case of the Rochester Convention, the sessions made a deep impression upon the community. A letter in the *Chicago Tribune* of October 11, 1853, describes the reaction of a spectator at the sessions:

"During the recent meeting of the convention of colored men in this city, I have several times looked in, to witness their proceedings—and I must be allowed to say, that if the colored men there assembled are to be taken as an example of that race, they have been hitherto very much underrated and abused.

" . . . I have been very much in the habit of mingling with political bodies of men, and taking part in public meetings of a political character, and I do not hesitate to say, that for courtesy, urbanity and kindness towards each other I never saw the members of this colored convention outdone.

"And I have seen many white conventions that would much improve by emulating the conduct of the members of this convention of wronged, despised, abused, and down trodden people. . . .

"To say the speech of Frederick Douglass on Friday evening was good would be too tame an expression to convey to the reader an idea of its real merits. . . .

"As a whole, the colored convention just held must greatly tend to elevate the colored people in the estimation of [the] community generally, and to satisfy many that the estimate usually made of the colored man is much too low; that this branch of the universal brotherhood are capable of high elevation in the moral and intellectual scale; that as men they are entitled to protection, and not oppression by our laws as to equal privileges under those laws."

Unfortunately, most of the plans laid down at Rochester and ratified at local conventions never went beyond the paper stage. At the first meeting of the National Council in January, 1854, not enough delegates were present to constitute a quorum. The second, the last meeting, at Cleveland was disrupted by factional disputes shortly after it got under way.

A combination of factors was responsible for the failure to carry out the program of the 1853 convention. Although defeated at Rochester, the colonizationists increased their efforts to convince the Negro people that emigration was the only solution to their problems. Shortly after the Rochester Convention, a call was issued for a convention in Cleveland on August 24, 1854, to discuss the emigration question. Douglass criticized the move as a deliberate attempt to sabotage the program set up in Rochester for ameliorating the condition of the Negro people. He appealed to the colonizationists to abandon their schemes, and to put all their efforts behind the program of the National Convention.[33]

Douglass' criticism of the call for a colonization convention in Cleveland was justified. A dismal failure, the endless debates and factional disputes preceding and following the convention created confusion among Negro leaders and diverted their attention from the pressing problem of implementing the program of the National Convention.[34]

Little progress was made in the campaign to establish a manual labor college. As chairman of the committee to establish the school, Douglass drew up a detailed plan for the institution, which was to be known as the "American Industrial School." It was to be located within one hundred miles of Erie, Pennsylvania, on a site of at least two hundred acres of land, one hundred and fifty of which would be used as a farm for agricultural instruction. Teachers would be selected and students admitted to the school "without reference to sex or complexion," and special efforts would be made "to aid in providing for the female sex, methods and means of enjoying an independent and honorable livelihood." For every course in literature, there would be a course in handicraft. Each student would occupy half his time while at school working at some handicraft or on the farm, and all handicrafts produced would be sold at a market within easy access of the school.

It was an ambitious program, one which anticipated the curriculum and organization of most of the manual labor schools established since the Civil War. But its fulfillment hinged upon the raising of a fund sufficient to launch the institution. The committee proposed a foundation fund of thirty thousand dollars, two-thirds of which was to be raised through the sale of two thousand shares of stock, at ten dollars a share, and one-third in outright contributions from friends of the cause. As soon as three thousand dollars came into the fund, the site would be selected; when ten thousand dollars was received, construction of the school building and work-shop would start; with fifteen thousand dollars, the school would open its doors.

Designated as agent to raise the foundation fund, Douglass entered upon his duties with his customary enthusiasm, lecturing and writing appeals for funds. But the appeals went unheeded. The Negro people themselves were too poor to contribute. A good deal had been expected from Harriet Beecher Stowe, but she reconsidered her offer and, for reasons not divulged, decided against the project.[35] The Garrisonians not only did not aid the project but Garrison himself criticized the proposal for an industrial school and accused the Negro advocates of laboring under a *"morbid state of mind."*

By June, 1855, two years after the Rochester Convention, Douglass had collected only a pitiful amount of money and the project had to be abandoned. But his conviction that the institution was essential for his people was as strong as ever. On March 21, 1856, Douglass wrote:

"I am yet of the opinion that nothing can be done for the free colored people—remaining in their present employment. These employments—such as waiting at hotels, on steamboats, barbering in large cities, and the like—contribute to no solid character. They require servility, beget dependence, destroy self-reliance, and furnish leisure and temptation to every possible view—from smoking cigars to drinking whiskey. What we want is steady employment at respectable trades, or on the land. To this end if I had money I would establish an industrial school to begin with, where the education of the hands and heart should be the main feature."[36]

The collapse of the program for the elevation of the Negro people outlined at the Rochester Convention practically spelled the end of the ante-bellum Negro convention movement. On October 16, 1855, one hundred and twenty-four delegates representing six states and Canada met in Philadelphia and conferred for three days. The most spirited discussion centered about the manual labor college question. A committee, dominated by the Philadelphia delegates, denounced the college as "a complexional institution" designed to further separate the Negro youth from the population. It declared that there were a number of institutions already in existence which could be utilized by the Negroes, and which could give them proper training. Furthermore, the Negro people could not provide a school which would furnish adequate training; nor would the masses of the Negro people avail themselves of the opportunity to use such a school, even if it were established. A substitute plan was offered whereby a central bureau would be established to collect funds and promote the mechanical arts among Negro youth.

Dr. James McCune Smith led the opposition to the report against the industrial college, and, with Douglass' aid, influenced the convention to have the report amended to include his own recommendations which called for the establishment of industrial associations in communities with large Negro populations. The associations were to correspond and cooperate with one other, and hold a national convention in October, 1857. Douglass warmly endorsed Smith's proposal.[37]

Despite the spirited discussion, the delegates had few illusions concerning the possibility of continuing the National Convention. When they left Franklin Hall on October 18, the majority knew that they had participated in the last National Convention for years to come.

Factional disputes, personal jealousies, fears of disclosure, lack of finances, the exodus of Negroes to Canada and Europe after the passage of the Fugitive Slave Act were among the major reasons for the failure of the Negro Convention movement to maintain a stable existence and to convert large parts of its program into reality. Yet the movement was one of great significance for the Negro people. The auxiliary conventions directed by officers of the National Convention were able to improve the conditions of Negro people living in northern rural sections and remote villages. Throughout all the northern cities, the local Negro meetings organized benevolent societies to provide essentials for needy persons, to create mutual insurance funds for their members, to provide teachers and social workers for the communities, to extend loans, and to furnish jobs and markets for goods. Sponsoring itinerant speakers, the National Convention emphasized the importance of rudimentary education and advanced study in arts and sciences even where public education facilities were restricted. Particularly did the convention address itself to the courage, the self-reliance of the Negro people to counteract the propaganda of white newspapers and speakers. It urged the Negro to apply himself to trades and to respectable daily tasks. At the same time, the convention exposed merchants and industrialists, including white Abolitionist employers, who refused to hire Negro help or insisted on placing them only as porters. The convention's opposition to emigration was influential in dooming the colonization movement to failure. The efforts and accomplishments of the convention stimulated the frank praise of incredulous whites, and did more than any agent to refute the widespread theory of Negro inferiority.

The National Convention and its state and local auxiliary societies created among the Negro people a feeling of confidence and self-respect. It was to these groups that the free Negro turned to voice his opinion. For these bodies were his own organizations; he spoke, wrote, and petitioned not as an individual but as a member of the convention of American Negroes. The convention brought northern Negroes together as no other body did and provided them with an opportunity to arrive at a common perspective of problems and solutions. It developed local and national leaders of the Negro people and prepared the ground for those men who were to play a prominent role during the Civil War and later would go into the old slave areas and co-operate with the freedmen in the struggle to achieve a new life.

Although he entered the movement long after it had been launched, Douglass' contributions to the convention were of major significance. True, he was criticized by other Negro leaders for failing sufficiently to integrate his ideas with the movement. But his position as the outstanding spokesman of and for the Negro people was recognized by the delegates. His newspaper was adopted as the official organ of the National Convention. Twice (1843 and 1853) he was elected a vice president and once (1848), its president. He was the author of the most important document issued by the movement, the "Address of the Colored Convention to the People of the United States." He served on numerous committees and freely contributed his time and energy toward the full implementation of its program. His work in the movement won him nationwide recognition as the leading champion of freedom and equality for the Negro people.

Anti-Slavery Activity in Rochester

"I have now been at home about one week," Douglass wrote from Rochester on March 21, 1856, "and am resting a little from my winters labors. I have travelled this winter between four and five thousand miles, visited communities as far east as Bangor, and as far west as Cincinnati, delivered about seventy lectures, been in snow drifts oft, but have reached this season, always very trying [to] my health with nothing more serious than a soar [sic] throat which is now on the mend."[1]

The letter described a fairly typical aspect of Douglass' life during the 'fifties when he spent about six months of the year on the road. He would return from his tours exhausted, but within a week would fling himself into the local anti-slavery activities.

Under the sponsorship of the Rochester anti-slavery group, Douglass spoke frequently in Corinthian Hall, the city's most popular auditorium. Here, during the winter of 1850-51, he taught a course on slavery. The aim of the course, which consisted of seven lectures, was to counteract the influence of the local press and the pulpit in creating among the people of Rochester "an indifference and coldness" toward the enslavement of their fellowmen "which might be looked for only in men hardened by the most atrocious and villainous crimes."[2] The lectures were well attended and they contributed to the growth of anti-slavery sentiment in the community; several were reported in full in the local press and reprinted in pamphlet form.

It was in the Corinthian Hall, too, that Douglass delivered his famous address on July 5, 1852, commemorating the anniversary of the signing of the Declaration of Independence. In bitter, eloquent prose, he told his audience that had he the ability and could he reach the nation's ear he would "pour out a fiery stream of biting ridicule, blasting reproach, withering sarcasm, and stern rebuke"; for it was not light that was needed but fire. He asked his listeners if they had meant to mock him when they invited him to speak on such an occasion; to him the fourth of July was not a day for rejoicing, but for mourning. Then followed what is probably the most moving passage in all of Douglass' speeches:

"What, to the American slave, is your 4th of July? I answer; a day that reveals to him, more than all other days in the year, the gross injustice and cruelty to which he is the constant victim. To him, your celebration is a sham; your boasted liberty, an unholy license; your national greatness, swelling vanity; your sounds of rejoicing are empty and heartless; your denunciation of tyrants brass fronted impudence; your shouts of liberty and equality, hollow mockery; your prayers and hymns, your sermons and thanksgivings, with all your religious parade and solemnity, are to him, mere bombast, fraud, deception, impiety, and hypocrisy—a thin veil to cover up crimes which would disgrace a nation of savages. There is not a nation on the earth guilty of practices more shocking and bloody than are the people of the United States, at this very hour."[3]

An important phase of the anti-slavery activity in Rochester was the struggle for the abolition of segregated schools for Negro children.

Douglass, the leader of the movement, felt a personal interest in the outcome. The Rochester Board of Education refused to allow his children to enter Public School 15 near his home, and insisted that they travel to the other side of the city to attend the school for Negro children.

Refusing to accept the system of segregated schools, Douglass, in August, 1848, arranged for his daughter, Rosetta, to attend Seward Seminary, a fashionable school for girls in Rochester. He was overjoyed to learn that the principal was an Abolitionist, and left for a visit to Cleveland happy in the thought that his child "was about to enjoy advantages for improving her mind, and fitting her for a useful and honorable life." What was his rage to discover on his return that Rosetta had been isolated in a room by herself and was being taught separately. He promptly protested to the principal "against the cruelty and injustice of treating [my] child as a criminal on account of her color." The principal weakly replied that the trustees of the school had objected to the admission of a Negro girl, and to overcome their prejudices by gradual stages she had hit upon the idea of having the child taught separately until such time as she could be admitted to the regular classes.

Upon Douglass' protest, the principal of the school submitted the question of Rosetta's status to the pupils and then to their parents. "How many of you are willing to have this colored child be with you?" the principal asked. All of the children held up their hands. "The children's hearts were right," Douglass told Mark Twain several years later.

Only one parent objected, but Rosetta was asked to leave the school. Douglass had already decided to withdraw his daughter from the seminary, but he did not permit the incident to pass over quietly. In a scathing letter to H. G. Warner, the single parent who objected to Rosetta's presence, he promised that he would use all his powers to proclaim this "infamy" to the nation. Scores of papers reprinted the letter with its blistering conclusion:

"We are both worms of the dust, and our children are like us. We differ in color, it is true (and not much in that respect), but who is to decide which color is most pleasing to God, or most honorable among men? But I do not wish to waste words or argument on one whom I take to be as destitute of honorable feeling, as he has shown himself full of pride and prejudice."[4]

Publicly announcing that *"in no emergency"* would he send any child of his to a segregated school, Douglass dispatched Rosetta to a private institution in Albany for two or three years; in 1851, he secured the services of a governess for her and the other children. Meanwhile, he worked unceasingly with Samuel D. Porter and other citizens of Rochester to abolish the separate school system which he called "the question of questions for the colored people of this place."[5]

For eight years Douglass pressed the issue of separate schools in Rochester. In 1857 the campaign bore fruit; the separate schools were abolished and Negro children were permitted to attend the public schools.

It was in the capacity of superintendent of the Underground Railroad in Rochester that Douglass made some of his most important contributions to the anti-slavery cause. He took more pride in his work for the Underground than in most of his other activities.

Although the Underground Railroad originated in the seventeenth century, it did not achieve full importance until after 1831 when restrictions upon the slaves were increased. The Underground was a network of routes, stretching northward from the border states and the Appalachian country into Canada. In nearly every important town and city throughout the North, organizations existed, known as Vigilance Committees, ostensibly organized for the purpose of preventing the arrest of a fugitive or of furnishing aid in the case of an apprehension. But in addition to these activities, the members of the committees were nearly always agents of the Underground. Among them Negroes played a distinguished part. The New York Vigilance Committee included David Ruggles, Rev. Theodore S. Wright, and Rev. Samuel Cornish; in Philadelphia, Robert Purvis, William Still, and Charles L. Reason served on the committee. Many of the agents along the 450 to 1,000 mile route, from isolated mountain districts in the South to the great terminals in the North, were unknown to one another, each intent upon his particular job in the chain and depending upon the "grapevine" to keep informed of events in the Underground.

Beginning in the upland country of North Carolina, Tennessee, Virginia, or Kentucky, an escaped Negro found refuge in remote farmhouses or pasture sheds. He was hidden in a cellar or in lofts and cared for until it was time to move on, disguised, or concealed under a load of hay or grain, to another farmhouse where, perhaps, several more fugitives had been smuggled. Divided into pairs, the fugitives traveled northward, always under cover, usually at night. They went from agent to agent, from one remote house and crossroad to others, along infrequently traveled byways. Along all large rivers, ferrymen were stationed to transport the fleeing pairs or small bands. Reaching the North, the first and most dangerous lap of the journey was completed. But now another danger loomed. Throughout the border counties were scattered southern agents whose duty it was to capture the slave, present an affidavit before a justice, and transport the fugitive back to slavery. While great numbers of northern whites hated these officers who enforced the unpopular Fugitive Slave Law, there were others who were opposed to the sudden influx of unskilled fugitives, or were anxious to prove to the slaveowners that they were reliable friends and worthy of their trade and patronage, and would turn the fleeing Negroes over to the authorities. So the journey through the free states had to be marked with caution until the fugitive reached the area along the Great Lakes or until he arrived in southern Ontario or Quebec.[6]

Rochester was the last main stop on the Underground. To this city came the fugitive slaves by railroad, by wagon, or on foot, exhausted from the harrowing weeks en route to freedom. They needed money, food, clothing, rest, and encouragement. By word-of-mouth direction, they found their way to the homes of the Posts, the Blosses, the Porters, and other "forwarders" in the community. In the winter of 1847, Douglass' house on Alexander Street became an important station. By 1850 Douglass was the leader of the Railroad in Rochester, superintending all the activities and having contact with agents in the rest of the country.

The very first issue of *The North Star* carried the news that its editor was already involved in the operations of the Underground:

"A SISTER RESCUED FROM SLAVERY

"There has just left our office, an amiable, kind, and intelligent looking young woman, about eighteen years of age, on her way from slavery."[7]

Horace McGuire, one of Douglass's newspaper employees, recalled that it was not an unusual thing for him to find fugitives sitting on the office stairs in the early morning. As soon as Douglass arrived, he went into action, and the fugitives were escorted either to the Post's cellar, Edward C. Williams' sail loft, Lindley Moore's barn, William Bloss's woodshed, or to Douglass' own attic. Throughout the day Douglass visited trusted sympathizers, passing the word that funds were needed to "ship a bale of Southern goods," and collecting money, food, and clothing. When night fell, the escaped slaves were usually sent on to Oswego or Lewiston. Some, too exhausted to travel, remained during the night, and were put aboard the morning train to Canada. "They usually tarry with us only during the night," Douglass wrote, "and are forwarded to Canada by the morning train. We give them supper, lodging, and breakfast; pay their expenses, and give them a half dollar over."[8]

In 1850 the underground was confronted with new problems. The newly strengthened Fugitive Slave Act provided for the appointment of special federal commissioners to aid in slave catching, and compelled all United States marshals and deputies whom they might designate to aid in the search. Furthermore, all citizens were subject to call to aid in the prosecution of the statute. The decision of the commissioner as to the Negro's identity was final. His fee was five dollars if he discharged the victim, and ten dollars if he decided he was a fugitive slave! Only a white person's testimony was acceptable in determining the status of the Negro.[9]

During the months when the Fugitive Slave Bill was under discussion, Douglass let it be known that he had no intention of abiding by any act of Congress which would facilitate the restoration of fugitives to slavery. He was a member of the committee which drafted the resolution for a mass meeting held at Corinthian Hall on April 5, 1850:

"Resolved, compromise or no compromise, constitution or no constitution . . . no testimony short of a bill of sale from Almighty God can establish the title of the master to his slave, or induce us to lift a finger to aid in his return to the house of bondage."[10]

On August 21, 1850, four weeks before the Fugitive Slave bill became law, Douglass presided at a convention at Cazenovia, New York, known as the "Fugitive Slave Convention." Over 2,000 people attended the meeting among whom were thirty fugitives. An "Address of Fugitive Slaves to Brethren in the South" was drawn up urging the slaves to escape to freedom. The convention pledged itself to raise funds for the defense of William Chaplin, who had been imprisoned in Maryland for assisting in the escape of the slaves of Robert Toombs and Alexander H. Stephens. A week later at an "Anti-Fugitive Slave Bill Meeting" at Syracuse, Douglass and J. C. Hathaway raised three hundred and fifty dollars for Chaplin's defense.[11]

When the news of the passage of the infamous measure reached Rochester, Douglass was again at Corinthian Hall "hurling out anathema" against the Act. A few weeks later, on October 14, he delivered one of the main addresses at a gigantic meeting at Faneuil Hall in Boston. Describing the terror the new law had struck in the hearts of thousands of escaped slaves in the North, he declared that it was the universal feeling of his Negro brethren "to die rather than be returned into slavery."[12]

Douglass became increasingly militant as he saw many of the Negro inhabitants of Rochester fleeing to Canada because they feared capture by slave-hunters.[13] In 1852 he told a Pittsburgh audience: "The only way to make the Fugitive Slave Law a dead letter is to make a half a dozen or more dead kidnappers. . . . The man who takes the office of a blood-hound ought to be treated as a bloodhound. . . ." In his journal he expounded this theme. Raising the question, "Is it Right and Wise to kill a kidnapper?" Douglass presented a long analysis to prove that any person who assisted in restoring fugitives to slavery "labelled himself the common enemy of mankind," and that his slaughter would be "as innocent, in the sight of God, as would be the slaughter of a ravenous wolf in the act of throttling an infant." He urged the Negro people to arm themselves and prepare to fight back. "Every colored man in the country," he cried, "should sleep with his revolver under his head, loaded and ready for use. Fugitives should, on their arrival in any Northern city, be immediately provided with arms, and taught at once that it is no harm to shoot any man who would rob them of this liberty." Such defiance was not only justified but necessary for the vindication of the Negro people against the charge that they were "an inferior race."

"This reproach must be wiped out, and nothing short of resistance on the part of colored men, can wipe it out. Every slave-hunter who meets a bloody death in his infernal business, is an argument in favor of the manhood of our race. Resistance is, therefore, wise as well as just."[14]

In September, 1851, Douglass came to the assistance of three fugitive Negroes who had fought back against the slave-catchers. The leader of the group, William Parker, a free Negro in Sadsbury, Pennsylvania, had sheltered a fugitive slave. The slaveowner, one Gorsuch, together with United States marshals, arrived in Sadsbury to claim the fugitive. Warned by the Philadelphia Vigilance Committee the people of Sadsbury were prepared.

When Gorsuch demanded the fugitive, he was refused. His home attacked, Parker sounded a horn and up sprang a large body of Negroes armed with clubs, axes, and guns. A battle ensued, the slave catchers were routed, several were wounded, and Gorsuch himself was killed.

Parker and two fugitives fled, and, after an exciting journey on the Underground, arrived in Rochester. Douglass, aware that the authorities were hot on their trail, took them into his home and gave them shelter.[15] While the men remained in hiding, Julia Griffiths drove to the boat landing on the Genesee River and made arrangements for their shipment to Canada. When the fugitives boarded the boat, Parker handed Douglass the gun with which he had killed Gorsuch.[16]

"I could not look upon them as murderers," Douglass wrote years later, "to me they were heroic defenders of the just rights of men against men-stealers and murderers."[17]

Douglass did not participate in the exciting Jerry Rescue at Syracuse on October 1, 1851, in which Gerrit Smith and other Abolitionists had forcibly rescued the fugitive, Jerry McHenry, who had been seized and imprisoned by a deputy United States marshal. But at the 1854 celebration of this event, Douglass read a series of resolutions to the gathering which asserted that the rescue had demonstrated "the wisdom and entire rightfulness of forcible resistance to the Fugitive Slave Bill," and declared:

"That the peculiar glory of this day, is not that one man has escaped from slavery, for there have been many such escaped—not that freedom has gained a victory through the blunders of lawyers, or through the faulty network of the law:—but that it consists in the fact, on this day three years ago, the people of Syracuse, and of Western New York, were wrought up to the point of open resistance to what they deemed a cruel, monstrous and inhuman enactment of Congress."[18]

Douglass continually raised money to aid escaped slaves. Frequently his fees from lectures would augment the fund which was used to "help such of our unfortunate countrymen who deem it no longer safe to remain in the United States," to aid fugitives to move on to Canada, and to assist slaves to ransom themselves from slavery. Contributions to the fund came from England and Ireland. In this country, the Negro people themselves, in spite of their limited resources, were the most frequent contributors. "The colored citizens," wrote William C. Nell from Rochester in February, 1852, "have systematically aided their hunted brethren, and have just held a donation festival, exclusively for the benefit of the fugitive." Three months later, Douglass observed: "The colored people of this city have acted well in this matter. They have contributed, heretofore, liberally, but the last meetings held for raising funds among them, show that their resources are nearly exhausted. . . ."[19]

Contributions were regularly listed in Douglass' journal and subscribers were urged to forward their mite. "Gerrit Smith, with his characteristic benevolence," went a notice in *The North Star* of January 9, 1849, "has kindly sent us his check for ten dollars, to aid John White, the fugitive slave of whom we spoke in last week's *North Star*. This leaves the sum of thirty dollars remaining to be paid to complete the ransom of this brother bondman. We will gladly be the medium of other sums for this truly deserving man.—F.D." During the next two weeks the thirty dollars came in to the paper, John White's freedom was purchased, and the Negro people of Rochester met to celebrate the rescue of another brother from bondage.

The secrecy of the Underground Railroad makes it impossible to determine the number of slaves Douglass aided. But it was a figure which easily ran into the hundreds.[20] "Fugitives are constantly passing through here," William C. Nell wrote from Rochester in 1852, "giving no rest to their feet nor slumber to their eyelids, until the protecting aegis of Queen Victoria makes them welcome freemen on Canada's shore. A party of fifteen thus rid themselves of republican slavery on Thanksgiving day!!!"[21] In 1854 Douglass stated that in two weeks he had aided over thirty fugitives on their way to Canada. In June, 1857, he informed his subscribers that four fugitives "passed through our hands to the Queen's dominions." On January 8, 1858, he wrote to the Ladies' Irish Anti-Slavery Association: ". . . you will be glad to know that the number escaping from Slavery has latterly been unusually large. We have passed over our section of the underground railroad about forty within the last sixty days." The *Rochester Express* of October 25, 1859, reported that in one day "not less than fifteen thousand dollars worth of 'property' passed through this city, on the 'underground,'" in the shape of "a dozen smart, intelligent, young and middle-aged men and women." In May, 1860, ten fugitives found "food and shelter, counsel and comfort," under Douglass' roof, and during the following month he sped ten more on the road to Canada and freedom.[22]

Rochester had only one case of a fugitive being returned to his master. This was in 1827.[23]

Douglass' services as an agent and "forwarder" of the Underground Railroad were of great importance to the anti-slavery movement, but he was the first to recognize the superior contribution made by Harriet Tubman, the heroic woman who fearlessly "carried the war into Africa." In his letter to the Ladies' Irish Anti-Slavery Association, Douglass referred to "one coloured woman, who escaped from Slavery eight years ago, has made several returns at great risk, and has brought out, since obtaining her freedom, fifty others from the house of bondage. She has been spending a short time with us since the holidays. She possesses great courage and shrewdness, and may yet render even more important service to the Cause."[24] Many years later, Douglass wrote to the "Moses of her people":

"Most that I have done has been in public, and I have received much encouragement. . . . You on the other hand have labored in a private way. . . . I have had the applause of the crowd. . . . While the most that you have done has been witnessed by a few trembling,. scared and footsore bondmen. . . . The midnight sky and the silent stars have been the witnesses of your devotion to freedom and of your heroism."[25]

Douglass realized that the activities of the Underground Railroad could no more free all the slaves than "a teaspoon could bail out the ocean," but the freedom of one slave was worth any risk, and the increasing number of runaways created a strong repugnance in the North to the entire slave system and so strengthened the anti-slavery cause.

In every phase of his work in Rochester, Douglass had the valuable assistance of his close friend, "Dear Julia." Miss Griffiths arranged the series of lectures in Corinthian Hall, read and corrected Douglass' speeches, collected the funds for their publication in pamphlet form, assisted in the campaign to abolish separate schools for colored children, and was a constant companion in the work of the Underground.

Much as they valued her ability in organizational work and understood her contributions to Douglass' full development as a writer and thinker, Abolitionists in Rochester were concerned over the effect upon public opinion of the unusual relationship between the Negro leader and this white woman. People had recovered from their first shock of seeing Douglass walk down the street with Miss Griffiths on his arm, but they never quite accepted the fact that a white woman should live in the same household with a colored man and his wife. The long hours Douglass and Miss Griffiths spent together in the newspaper office caused the rumor to spread that their friendship went beyond the bounds of intellectual companionship. By 1849 the rumors were so persistent that Douglass, without referring to Miss Griffith, editorially denounced those "who maliciously (and without even the shadow of provocation), artfully and deliberately manufacture lies and insidiously circulate them with no other motive than to blast the fair name of another."[26]

The article had no effect on the scandalmongers. In January, 1852, Samuel D. Porter, Douglass' close associate in the anti-slavery movement, advised his friend that Rochester was "full of scandalous reports" implicating him and Miss Griffiths. Douglass' spirited reply is the only statement we have from him on the subject of the relationship between himself, his family and Miss Griffiths.[27] "I am a husband and a father," he reminded Porter, "and withal a citizen,—honorably, and to the best of my ability, endeavouring to discharge the duties of this three fold relation. When the city, which you allege to be full of scandalous reports implicating Miss G and me, shall put those 'reports' in a definite shape, and present a responsible person to back them, it will be time enough for me to attempt to refute them." Miss Griffiths, he went on, had decided to leave his household two months before and was living with another family. "When she was in my family, I was necessarily much in her society. Our walking and riding together was natural. Now we are separate and only meet at my office at business hours and for business purposes, where we are open to the observation of my printers and the public, from ten o'clock or earlier in the morning until four o'clock in the afternoon." How long she intended to remain in Rochester he did not know, but the decision was entirely hers. And, under no circumstance, would he permit rumors to blind him to the fact that she had "a just claim upon my gratitude, respect and friendship."[28]

It is unfortunate that this letter was not made public for the matter did not die in 1852. The following year the question of Douglass' relations with Miss Griffiths became an important issue in the conflict between the Negro leader and the Garrisonians.

The Split with the Garrisonians

Douglass' relations with the Massachusetts Abolitionists after he left Lynn in the fall of 1847 to establish his residence in Rochester remained cordial. The Massachusetts Anti-Slavery Society expressed regret that he would be working in a region so far from New England, but assured him that he would be "followed to his new home and new sphere of usefulness by the most good wishes of his many friends in this his first home of freedom."[1] Douglass maintained close contact with the Garrisonians during the next three years, and at the annual meetings of the American Anti-Slavery Society, he spent much time in the company of his old friends. With Garrison, however, he was not entirely at ease. He knew that the Abolitionist leader had neither forgotten what he regarded as

Douglass' lack of solicitude during his illness in Cleveland, nor forgiven him for the decision to publish his paper. The two men shared the same platform at the annual meetings, but their courteous references to each other lacked the old warmth.[2]

Within a few years this strained relationship turned into bitter antagonism, and the anti-slavery press, much to the dismay of its subscribers and to the delight of its enemies, was treated to a unique spectacle as charges and counter-charges were hurled against each other by the participants in the conflict. Personal antagonisms, often of the most petty character, were so deeply intertwined with ideological issues that it became almost impossible to separate the two. Yet fundamentally the conflict emerged out of a sharp difference of opinion over questions of vital importance to the anti-slavery movement.

During the first ten years of his work as an Abolitionist, Douglass had accepted all of the doctrines of the Garrisonian school. In his speeches, letters, and early editorials in *The North Star,* he reiterated his belief that the Constitution was wholly a pro-slavery document, called for the destruction of the American Union, reaffirmed his opposition to the use of the ballot against slavery and again asserted his conviction that moral suasion was the major instrumentality for ending slavery. "I am willing at all times to be known as a Garrisonian Abolitionist," he wrote on September 4, 1849.[3]

But as he moved outside the orbit of the Massachusetts Abolitionists and came into contact with anti-slavery men who differed with the Garrisonian school, Douglass began for the first time to examine his beliefs critically. After considerable study and extensive reading in law, political philosophy, and American government, he concluded that there were serious flaws in the Garrisonian doctrines. Gradually he formulated a new anti-slavery creed.

The weakening of Douglass' faith in the Garrisonian principle of non-resistance came first. It was John Brown who led Douglass to doubt the value of relying mainly on "moral suasion." Late in 1847, while on a lecture tour in New England, Douglass met Brown, then a merchant in Springfield, Massachusetts. In his editorial correspondence to *The North Star,* he wrote of having a "private interview" with Brown who "though a white gentleman, is in sympathy a black man, and as deeply interested in our cause, as though his own soul had been pierced with the iron of slavery." Douglass did not reveal the nature of the interview, merely reporting Brown's joy at the appearance of men "possessing the energy of head and heart to demand freedom for their whole people," the result of which "must be the downfall of slavery."[4] Years later he filled in the details. After dinner at Brown's simple home, his host expounded his views on slavery. Brown not only condemned the institution, but added that the slaveholders "had forfeited their right to live, that the slaves had the right to gain their liberty in any way they could." "Moral suasion" could never liberate the slaves nor political action abolish the system. Brown outlined a plan to establish five bands of armed men in the Allegheny Mountains who would run off slaves in large numbers.[5]

Douglass thought that Brown's plan had "much to commend it," but was still convinced that "moral suasion" would succeed in converting the entire nation, including the slaveholders, to the anti-slavery position. None the less, Brown's belief that slavery was actually a state of war profoundly impressed him. "My utterances," Douglass wrote later, "became more tinged by the color of this man's strong impressions." A year after his visit he was echoing Brown's language, writing editorially that slaveholders had "no rights more than any other thief or pirate. They have forfeited even the right to live, and if the slave should put every one of them to the sword to-morrow, who dare pronounce the penalty disproportionate to the crime, or say that the criminals deserved less than death at the hands of their long-abused chattels?" In June, 1849, he astonished a Boston anti-slavery audience in Faneuil Hall with the announcement:

"I should welcome the intelligence tomorrow, should it come, that the slaves had risen in the South, and that the sable arms which had been engaged in beautifying and adorning the South, were engaged in spreading death and devastation."

Noticing the alarm his remark had caused, Douglass swept on with lashing irony and bitter criticism:

"Why, you welcomed the intelligence from France, that Louis Phillipe had been barricaded in Paris—you threw up your caps in honor of the victory achieved by Republicanism over Royalty—you shouted aloud—'Long live the republic!'—and joined heartily in the watchword of 'Liberty, Equality, Fraternity'—and should you not hail with equal pleasure the tidings from the South that the slaves had risen, and achieved for themselves, against the iron-hearted slaveholder, what the republicans of France achieved against the royalists of France?"[6]

The fury of his language did not mean that Douglass had entirely abandoned his faith "in the operation of moral force." But more and more he began to justify the right of the slaves to revolt "on the ground that it is consistent with the conduct of the revolutionary patriots." Step by step he abandoned his belief in the efficacy of moral instrumentalities, and by the late 'fifties was one of the leading exponents of "militant abolitionism." In 1856 he wrote that while it was still necessary to use "persuasion and argument" and every means that promised "peacefully" to destroy slavery, he was convinced "that its peaceful annihilation is almost hopeless. . . ." Four years later he no longer had any doubts.

"I have little hope of the freedom of the slave by peaceful means," he wrote on June 29, 1860. "A long course of peaceful slaveholding has placed the slaveholders beyond the reach of moral and humane considerations. They have neither ears nor hearts for the appeals of justice and humanity. While the slave will tamely submit his neck to the yoke, his back to the lash, and his ankle to the fetter and chain, the Bible will be quoted, and learning invoked to justify slavery. The only penetrable point of a tyrant is the *fear of death.*"[7]

As Douglass abandoned sole reliance on moral power for the overthrow of slavery, he was forced to re-examine his attitude toward political action. During 1841-1848 he had placed his hopes in the non-political activities of the anti-slavery societies. In a speech at the Higham Anti-Slavery Convention in November, 1841, he ridiculed political action, exclaiming that the slaveholders "care nothing about your political action, they don't dread the political movement; it is the *moral* movement, the appeal to men's sense of right, which makes them and all our opponents tremble."[8]

The belief in non-political action Douglass maintained consistently during the next few years. Like all Abolitionists under the influence of the Garrisonian wing of anti-slavery thought, he would have nothing to do with a government and a constitution framed and administered by men who "were and have been until now, little better than a band of pirates." Until the government and the Constitution were replaced by institutions which would "better answer the ends of justice," no true friend of liberty in the United States could vote or hold office.[9]

The key to Douglass' anti-political views was his interpretation of the Constitution "as a most foul and bloody conspiracy against the rights of three millions of enslaved and imbruted men." As a Negro, he knew at first hand the farce that history had made of the Declaration of Independence; his personal suffering made him only too ready to accept the Garrisonian doctrine that the Constitution was "a Covenant with death and an agreement with hell." If slaveholders appealed to the Constitution, he would appeal to a higher law, to divine morality. The founders of the American Union, he told an audience in England, while proclaiming liberty throughout the land, were themselves trafficking in their fellow men, and since then American government and society had been dedicated to defending the great lie of slavery. Slavery, he claimed, was not a southern but an American institution, a system that derived its support as much from the non-slaveholding states as from those where slavery was accepted. By swearing to uphold the American Constitution and the American Union, the people of the North had sworn before high heaven that the slave would be kept a slave. As long as they accepted the Constitution and its compromises in favor of the slaveholders, they were responsible for the existence of slavery in the United States and must share the guilt for that great crime.[10]

It required two years of study and discussion for Douglass to change his attitude toward the Constitution. The first indication he gives that he was beginning to re-examine his thinking is the brief comment in *The North Star* of February 9, 1849: "On a close examination of the Constitution, I am satisfied that if strictly 'construed according to its reading,' it is not a pro-slavery instrument. . . ." Six weeks later he wrote that if he could be convinced that the Constitution was essentially anti-slavery in its origins and purposes, he would be quick to use the ballot box against slavery, and to urge others to do likewise. He doubted, however, that he could be easily persuaded that such were the origins and purposes of the document.

Operating in central New York among men who adhered to an anti-slavery constitutional interpretation, Douglass was constantly being called upon to justify his view that the Constitution was a pro-slavery instrument. The more he discussed this question with Gerrit Smith and William Goodell and the more he studied their writings the more difficult it became for him to uphold his theory. Through these discussions and readings, Douglass became convinced that the preamble to the Constitution—that the national government had been formed to establish a more perfect union, promote the general welfare and secure the blessings of liberty—governed the meaning of the document in all its parts and details. The Constitution was thus, by its avowed purpose, anti-slavery.

Slavery was not, nor could it become legalized, and it was the duty of the federal government to eradicate it. Political action to secure that end was both warranted and necessary.

As Douglass saw it, national necessity compelled him to accept an interpretation of the Constitution which might not be evident in the document itself. Realizing the importance of having the Constitution fight for him, he interpreted it in a way most convenient for the anti-slavery crusade. The Garrisonians, by their insistence on an interpretation which the slaveholders shared, no matter how apparently correct that interpretation might be, not only played directly into the hands of their enemies, but created enmity for themselves. Whatever the average Northerner felt about slavery, he did not believe that his country was built upon falsehood and iniquities. While the Garrisonians announced their determination to destroy the Constitution and the Union to end slavery, Douglass decided to use both in the struggle against "a system of lawless violence; that never was lawful and never can be made so."

Step by step Douglass arrived at the conclusion that there was no need to dissolve the Union. He saw clearly that disunion would isolate the slaves and leave them at the mercy of their masters. For the North to secede, as the Garrisonians advocated, would relieve it of its share of responsibility for slavery and deny the slaves their most important allies. For the Garrisonian slogan, "No union with slaveholders," Douglass substituted "a more sensible motto, namely, 'No union with slaveholding.' "[11]

The change in Douglass' anti-slavery creed had been developing for a number of years but it did not become public until 1851.[12] At the eighteenth annual meeting of the American Anti-Slavery Society held in Syracuse in May, 1851, a resolution was submitted by Edmund Quincy proposing that the *Anti-Slavery Standard*, the *Pennsylvania Freeman*, the *Anti-Slavery Bugle*, and *The North Star* receive the recommendation of the society. When Samuel J. May suggested that the *Liberty Party Paper* be added to the list, Garrison opposed this motion on the ground that this journal did not stand for the dissolution of the Union and believed that the Constitution was an anti-slavery document. This in turn led to a resolution that no paper should be endorsed which did not assume the Constitution to be a pro-slavery document. Douglass thereupon announced that he could not consider his paper eligible for endorsement since he had "arrived at the firm conviction that the Constitution, construed in the light of well-established rules of legal interpretation, might be made consistent in its details with the noble purposes in its preamble," and that in the future he would insist that the Constitution "be wielded in behalf of emancipation." His changed attitude had not been suddenly or impulsively arrived at, and he attributed it to "a careful study" of the writings of Lysander Spooner, Gerrit Smith, and William Goodell. His opinions had "recently changed materially in relation to political action," and he now believed that it was "the first duty of every American citizen, whose conscience permits him so to do, to use his political as well as his moral power for its [slavery's] overthrow."

These words created a stir. Enraged, Garrison cried out: "There is roguery somewhere." He moved that *The North Star* be stricken from the list and this was promptly voted by the convention.[13]

Douglass never forgot Garrison's "insulting remark," though in his paper he wrote that he could "easily forgive" the man for whom he still cherished "a veneration only inferior in degree to that we owe to our conscience and to our God." What really concerned him was that his former associates greeted the union of *The North Star* and the *Liberty Party Paper* in June, 1851, with the cry that he had sold out his principles to gain financial support from Gerrit Smith and other political Abolitionists.[14]

Douglass hotly denied that this change had been sudden and unheralded or that he had been primarily influenced by his financial dependence upon Smith. He offered proof that he had gradually altered his attitude toward political action and had reached the conclusion that the Constitution was an anti-slavery document long before the question of uniting his paper with the *Liberty Party Paper* was broached. But neither his protests nor his evidence convinced his former associates. Samuel J. May voiced the sentiments of the Garrisonians when he wrote: "It would be a strange thing, indeed, if a mind so acute as that of Mr. D. could not find plausible reasons for the change he has made."[15]

For almost a year after the 1851 convention, the conflict between Douglass and the Garrisonians lay dormant. To be sure, the *Liberator,* early in 1852, carried a critical article charging that party spirit had "made some havoc of the character of Frederick Douglass," but adding that "his genius had placed him at the head of the colored race, and that his magnificent oratory and powerful writings have demonstrated the natural intellectual equality of his race with that of the Caucasian tyrants by whom even he is trampled upon and degraded in the United States."

Douglass continued publishing speeches of the leading Garrisonians in his weekly, and praised the American Society for "doing a great and good work."[16]

But this was only the calm before the storm. At the next annual meeting of the American Society, held in Rochester, May 11-13, 1852, the feud between Garrison and Douglass flared up again. Garrison again called for the dissolution of the Union and charged that "never had any political constitution in this country taken the colored race as equal to the white." Douglass proceeded to defend his position on the Union as opposed to that of Garrison. At once, he was regarded "as an enemy." Taking the bull by the horns, he asked why he was "treated as an alien." To which Phillips, Remond, Foster, and Robert Purvis listed more than ten reasons. These boiled down to four basic charges: that Douglass had changed his opinion about the Constitution; that he had aided in forming an anti-slavery society in central New York not affiliated with the American Society and had become friendly with its *"deadliest* enemies"; that his journal was "a political and not an anti-slavery paper," and that he had attacked George Thompson. Douglass answered the charges. Evidently he was sufficiently impressive for he was later in the session elected to the Board of Managers of the American Society. But the rupture had been seriously widened by the barrage of accusations let loose at the convention. In December, 1852, Phillips informed Elizabeth Pease that "Douglass is completely estranged from us."[17]

But the worst was still to come. The differences led to personal attacks and by the fall of 1853 the conflict reached a stage of vituperation unparalleled in the entire history of the anti-slavery movement. In reporting the 1853 convention of the American Anti-Slavery Society, Douglass threw out the remark that Pillsbury, Wright, and Foster "had been induced to absent themselves on this occasion because their presence might give new force to the charge of infidelity, which is brought against the Anti-Slavery Society." The remark went unanswered for two months. Then at the celebration of West India Emancipation at Framingham, Massachusetts, Wendell Phillips publicly lashed Douglass for daring to attend the ceremonies after his diatribe, and demanded that Douglass justify his slur "upon the integrity of the American Anti-Slavery Society." Unprepared for the severity of the attack, Douglass, who had arrived in Framingham during a storm and was "shivering with cold, wet to the skin, tired and hungry," offered a feeble defense. He denied that he had said that the three men had been subjected to pressure to prevent them from attending the annual meeting, asserted his right to criticize in his paper "the character of any anti-slavery effort or any anti-Slavery Society in existence," and protested that it was improper to turn a celebration of the first of August into a discussion of relations between himself and the Massachusetts Abolitionists.[18]

Aware that his rejoinder had not been too convincing, Douglass wrote a long editorial on the Framingham incident which he entitled, "Something Personal." It closed with a quotation from the Apostles: "If it is possible, as much as lieth in you, live peaceably with all men." But Douglass must have been under no illusions as to the effects of the article. He refused to retract the charge of "infidelity" he had leveled against the three Garrisonians, maintaining that they gloried in their disbelief in the Bible. He denied that his charge was the invention of the pro-slavery church and its allies; he said that it arose from their statements ridiculing the recognition of any book as of divine authority. Furthermore, he contended that "Messrs. Foster, Pillsbury and Wright might have been induced to remain away to screen the Society from the odium of their infidel opinions."[19]

Douglass moved next to a denunciation of the Negro Garrisonians, referring to Remond, Nell, and Purvis as *practical* enemies of the colored people." Nell was also a "contemptible tool," and Purvis' inherited wealth was described as "blood-stained riches."[20]

The Garrisonians were stunned momentarily by the vituperative nature of Douglass' offensive, but they were too well versed in the give-and-take of such battles to remain silent for long. Soon after the appearance of Douglass' "Something Personal" editorial, the entire Garrisonian press hit back. Douglass had torn off the mask and revealed himself as an ally of "the whole pro-slavery press and pulpit in the United States," went the general refrain in column after column of denunciation. He had become so clearly the victim of "the curse of worldly ambition" that he could only be regarded as a deadly foe of the entire anti-slavery cause.[21]

Heretofore Garrison himself had refrained from engaging in the controversy with his former co-worker. But convinced that "with Douglass the die seems to be cast," he now joined in the attack. Not satisfied with using his bitter pen to demolish the Negro leader, he published extracts from Douglass' articles in his "Refuge of Oppression" column in the *Liberator,* a place usually reserved for material from pro-slavery papers.[22]

This was a notification to his fellowers that their leader regarded Douglass as among the worst enemies of the slave.

Nor did Garrison halt here. One of his followers had reacted critically to the attacks on Douglass. He had just heard the Negro orator deliver several addresses in Chicago, and was convinced that he was completely sincere in advocating political action and an anti-slavery interpretation of the Constitution. Douglass was "faithful to the cause of the slave and to the highest convictions of his soul," and was still "bestowing upon that cause all the energies of his mind, his pen, his God-given genius, and his powerful eloquence." Hence he asked Garrison:

"Why is he ostracized from the sympathies of yourself and of the Society which acknowledges you as its exponent and head? Why do you characterise his course as wayward and hostile? Why do you place his articles in the 'Refuge of Oppression,' side by side with the vilest pro-slavery venom from the vilest sheets in the land? Is it on account of his change of opinion on the constitutional question? Shall it be said with truth that you and your particular coadjutors cannot tolerate an honest difference of opinion?"[23]

Garrison made short shrift of his critic. He denied that the conflict with Douglass was the result of differing opinions on anti-slavery issues, blaming it entirely on the latter's selfish spirit. Douglass had not been expelled; he had "ostracized" himself. "He has lost much of moral power, and will finally lose what yet remains, if he persists in defaming those whose infidelity to the anti-slavery cause has never been impeached." Having attacked Douglass' integrity and his motives, Garrison plunged on to attack even his family life:

"For several years past, he has had one of the worst advisers in his printing-office, whose influence over him has not only caused much unhappiness in his own household, but perniciously biased his own judgment; who, active, futile, mischievous, has never had any sympathy with the American Anti-Slavery Society, but would doubtless rejoice to see it become extinct; and whose sectarianism is manifestly paramount to any regard for the integrity of the anti-slavery movement."[24]

The reference, of course, was to Julia Griffiths, Douglass' able assistant in his newspaper office. This was by no means the first attack on Miss Griffiths during the controversy (the *Anti-Slavery Standard* had already referred to her as "a Jezebel whose capacity for making mischief between friends would be difficult to match")[25], but no one heretofore had publicly raised the question of domestic discord in the Douglass household.[26]

Mrs. Douglass immediately sent a short note to Garrison stating: "It is not true, that the presence of a certain person in the office of Frederick Douglass causes unhappiness in his family. . . ." Garrison printed the letter, but commented that it was "evasive in its language, as our charge had reference to the past and not to the present." A bit later he denied that he had intended to imply anything immoral in his charge and expressed regret that he had ever raised the question of relations between Douglass and his wife.[27] But by that time the damage had already been done.

So many charges had been leveled against him in the Garrisonian press that Douglass decided to devote almost the entire issue of his weekly to a final answer. On December 9, 1853, *Frederick Douglass' Paper* carried six columns of denunciatory articles from the *Liberator*, the *Anti-Slavery Standard,* and the *Pennsylvania Freeman*.[28] The next twelve columns were devoted to Douglass' rejoinder. He calmly defended his position and injected a minimum of personal charges or bitterness in his reply. He was under attack only because he dared differ from the American Anti-Slavery Society and its leaders as to how he should exercise his powers "for the promotion of the anti-slavery cause, and the elevation of the Free People of color in the United States." For four months, since the celebration at Framingham, he had been systematically "pursued, misrepresented, traduced and vilified, with a bitterness ever increasing and a steadiness and violence only characteristic of malice, deep, broad, lasting, and in its worst form." He had been silent through all this, but he could remain silent no longer.

Douglass was especially furious at Garrison for the personal character of his attacks. "He has seen fit to invade my household," he wrote bitterly, "despite the sacredness of my home, break through the just limits of public controversy, and has sought to blast me in the name of my family." He refused to discuss his family relations in the press, arguing that it involved "considerations wholly foreign to the present controversy," and that "a man's wife and children should be spared the mortification involved in a public discussion of matters entirely private. . . ." But he did get back at Garrison, charging him with harboring contempt for the contributions of the Negroes in the struggle against slavery. Quoting Garrison's observation that "the Anti-Slavery cause, both religiously and politically, has transcended the ability of the sufferers from American Slavery and prejudice, *as a class,* to keep pace with it, or to perceive what are its demands, or to understand the philosophy of its operations," Douglass commented caustically:

"The colored people ought to feel profoundly grateful for this magnificent compliment (which does not emanate from a Colonizationist) to their high, moral worth, and breadth of comprehension so generously bestowed by William Lloyd Garrison!—Who will doubt, hereafter, the natural inferiority of the *Negro,* when the great champion of the Negroes' rights, thus broadly concedes all that is claimed respecting the Negro's inferiority by the bitterest despisers of the Negro race."

Douglass' reply to the charge that he was more concerned about his own interests than about those of the anti-slavery cause was both moving and effective:

"Was it *selfish,* when in England, surrounded by kind friends, and strongly invited by them, to make my home among them, with every provision made for my comfort and security in a land where my *color* was no crime—I say, was it selfish in me to *quit* the shores of that country, and return to this, to endure insult, abuse, and proscription, with the rest of my oppressed people? Was it selfish in me, when my English friends gave me more than two thousand dollars, leaving the disposal of the Testimonial to my own option, whether to appropriate it to my own personal wants, or to devote it to the establishment of a paper to advocate the cause of my enslaved fellow countrymen and to promote the elevation of the free colored people—I say, was it *selfish* in me to prefer the latter to the former? Was it selfish in me to refuse a donation of five hundred dollars, raised in Finsbury Chapel, London, at one meeting; simply because that sum had been raised with a view of taking my family over to England, and not having been devoted to that object, I refused to receive it for my *personal benefit?*"

Douglass' defense made little impression upon Garrison and his associates. Oliver Johnson, who had specifically accused Douglass of selfishness, called the reply "an exhibition of moral perversity, blindness and malice." He was thankful that Douglass was now "an avowed enemy instead of a secret, stealthy foe," but was apprehensive that "of all the seceders and apostates from our ranks, he will prove the most malignant in spirit, the most efficient and sleepless in his hostility."[29]

To attempt, almost a century later, to evaluate the relative merits of the contentions of all parties in a controversy which raked the anti-slavery movement during the closing months of 1853 is scarcely a pleasant task. The men involved were all sincere people who honestly believed that their critics were inspired by unworthy motives and that they were the ones sinned against. All lamented the schism, but regarded it as unavoidable, believing that their opponents were the aggressors. As tempers flared, judgment suffered and with it the entire cause.

Unquestionably the Garrisonians had good reason to resent Douglass' charge of infidelity against many anti-slavery men who had made great sacrifices for the movement. Douglass may have been perfectly correct as to the facts, but he must have been aware from personal experience of the use to which the pro-slavery forces could put his charge.

There is, however, a broader issue involved in this controversy between Douglass and the Garrisonians that cannot be ignored. During his early years as an Abolitionist, Douglass had been unsparing in his criticism of the American churches. He had charged that slavery had been "made part of the religion of the land," and that he would have nothing to do with any church which remained indifferent to the existence of slavery or actually supported the slaveholders. "I . . . proclaim myself an infidel to the slaveholding religion of America," Douglass had declared.[30]

The Garrisonians had good cause for their hostility to the church. Many ministers defended slavery, more gave their support to political candidates of the slavocracy, and a great majority assailed the anti-slavery men as "dangerous radicals," not even excluding fellow ministers who opposed slavery. Nevertheless, the Garrisonian attitude toward organized religion was basically unwise, for it ignored the strong anti-slavery sentiment within the churches which was growing in influence and authority. In the 'forties, a series of events occurred that changed the entire picture of American religion. The South had been completely victorious in keeping any discussion of slavery out of national conventions of religious groups, and, from 1826 to 1836, even succeeded in excluding Abolitionists from the Methodist conventions. Elon Galusha was dismissed from the Board of Managers of the Baptist convention in 1841 for his anti-slavery sentiments and was replaced by a man sympathetic to the slaveowners. But gradually, the northern anti-slavery men gained strength, and succeeded in defeating their southern opponents on the crucial issue of whether or not religious leaders, from preacher to bishop, could own slaves—in other words, whether or not slavery was *morally* acceptable. In 1845, after this defeat, southern Baptists formed their own independent society, while, about the same time, southern Methodists formed the Methodist Episcopal Church, South. These breaches became wider as the Civil War approached, and were not healed untill well into the present century. The Old School Presbyterian Church alone remained firm in its defense of slavery, for the church was entirely in the control of the southern leaders.[31]

The schism between northern and southern churches showed clearly that the former were not as reprobate and willing to serve the southern slaveholders as the Garrisonians had charged. New tactics consequently had to be devised to gain the support of these churches. But the Garrisonians continued to battle the churches as if nothing had happened, alienating many people who should have been their allies, and earning for themselves the epithet, "infidel." Douglass understood the weakness of the Garrisonian approach to the churches, and as the importance of the separation between northern and southern churches became clear to him, he began to reconsider his views on the issue. When he refused to defend the agnostics centered about Garrison (men such as Wright, Foster, and Pillsbury) from the charge of infidelity so insistently leveled against them, it was not because he opposed their right to their opinions, but because he was determined to dispel all doubts in the minds of anti-slavery religious leaders that he adhered to these views. While criticizing every manifestation of pro-slavery and anti-Negro tendencies in the churches, he also let it be known that he was prepared to co-operate with the anti-slavery groups in the northern churches. Thus the charge of the Garrisonians that he had been motivated by pure malice toward Wright, Foster, and Pillsbury is ill-conceived. To gain support for the cause, it was necessary for Douglass as a Negro leader to disassociate himself from the dogmatic and narrow attitude of many of the Garrisonians toward the church.

Douglass' attack upon Garrison for his slur on the Negro people in the anti-slavery struggle was, in the opinion of one contemporary observer, "highly discreditable to him in every respect."[32] Yet it is significant that large sections of the Negro population supported Douglass' position. At a mass meeting of the Negro people in Chicago on December 26, 1853, a report was unanimously adopted denouncing Garrison's remarks as "an insult to the intelligence of the colored people," and condemning the "vile crusade" conducted by the Garrisonians to destroy Frederick Douglass, "the voice of the colored people." A similar stand was adopted at the Rhode Island Convention of the

People of Color late in 1853, where Douglass was hailed as "our acknowl-edged leader."[33]

Douglass' most violent blasts against Garrison came only after the anti-slavery leader had dragged Douglass' domestic relations into the controversy and had continued harping on them even after Anna Doug-lass' letter of denial. Granted that there were reports that the letter "was concocted by Frederic & Julia"[34] (to which the knowledge that Anna was illiterate gave credence), the fact remains that it was un-principled for Garrison to resort to such tactics. Mrs. Jane Swisshelm, a western female reformer, was thoroughly justified in asking: "How can any man, professing to know anything of the common courtesies of life, dare drag a woman before the public as the enemy of her own husband, and persist in holding her in such a position, despite her protest?" James B. Vashon, a Negro leader in Pittsburgh, denounced Garrison for his "savage attack" upon Julia Griffiths, "an innocent female, whose humanity caused her to leave her native country," and who had consistently proved to be a "true fighter against oppression."[35]

The side issues and personal recriminations disposed of, the basic fact remains that however much the Garrisonians protested that their hostility did not stem from Douglass' conversion to new anti-slavery principles, their words revealed how bitterly they resented his in-dependent thinking as to what constituted the best policies for the move-ment. The efforts made to prove that Douglass was simply the puppet of Gerrit Smith and other political Abolitionists and that he echoed the opinions of Julia Griffiths, were simply manifestations of this re-sentment. Certainly the fact that his paper was located in Rochester where the Liberty Party had its largest support influenced Douglass' views; certainly he was influenced by Gerrit Smith; certainly he was indebted to Julia Griffiths for clarification of his views. But fundamen-tally Douglass' differences with the Garrisonians came after careful study of every facet of the anti-slavery movement. On the basis of this study, having decided that the approach of his colleagues was unrealistic, narrow, and detrimental to an effective struggle against slavery, Douglass showed great courage in upholding his principles in the face of terrific opposition.

If Douglass had been mainly concerned with advancing his own selfish interests, he could, as he pointed out, have taken advantage of many opportunities to do so. It would have been much easier for him to have remained with the Garrisonians as an anti-slavery lecturer than to move to a new community, start a new career and become involved in the heart-breaking struggle to publish a newspaper. But Douglass believed that the most important contribution he could make to the struggle was to demonstrate that the Negro people were active participants in the battle, had their own spokesmen and were not simply passive bystanders watching the white humanitarians relieve them of their burdens. It was Gerrit Smith's sympathy and understanding of this that drew the Negro close to his benefactor; it was Douglass' knowledge that Julia Griffiths shared his belief that played such an important part in their successful collaboration.

For all their sincerity and good-will, it was this emphasis on the important contribution that the Negro himself should make through his own independent efforts that Garrison and his closest associates resented most, and explains why they were a good deal kinder in their treatment of others who had left their ranks than they were of Douglass.[36]

What was certainly the shrewdest comment on the chain of events during the summer and fall of 1853 was offered by Harriet Beecher Stowe in a letter to Garrison. Despite its length, it merits quotation in full:

"Cabin, Dec. 19 [1853]

"Mr. Garrison
"Dear Sir:

"After seeing you, I enjoyed the pleasure of a personal interview with Mr. Douglass & I feel bound in justice to say that the impression was far more satisfactory, than I had anticipated.

"There does not appear to be any deep underlying stratum of bitterness— he did not seem to me malignant or revengeful. I think that it was only a temporary excitement & one which he will outgrow.

"I was much gratified with the growth & development both of his mind & heart. I am satisfied that his change of sentiments was not a mere political one but a genuine growth of his own conviction. A vigorous reflective mind like his cast among those holding new sentiments is naturally led to modified views.

"At all events, he holds no opinion which he cannot defend, with a variety & richness of thought & expression & an aptness of illustration which shows it to be a growth from the soil of his own mind with a living root & not a twig broken off other men's thoughts & stuck down to subserve a temporary purpose.

"His plans for the elevation of his own race, are manly, sensible, comprehensive, he has evidently observed carefully & thought deeply & will I trust act efficiently.

"You speak of him as an apostate—I cannot but regard this language as unjustly severe—Why is he any more to be called an apostate for having spoken ill tempered things of former friends than they for having spoken severely & cruelly as they have of him?—Where is this work of excommunication to end—Is there but one true anti-slavery church & all others infidels? —Who shall declare which it is.

"I feel bound to remonstrate with this—for the same reason that I do with slavery—because I think it, an injustice. I must say still further, that if the first allusion to his family concerns was unfortunate this last one is more unjustifiable still—I am utterly surprised at it—as a friend to you, & to him I view it with the deepest concern & regret.

"What Douglass *is* really, time will show—I trust that he will make no further additions to the already unfortunate controversial literature of the cause. *Silence* in this case will be eminently—*golden*.

"I must indulge the hope you will reason at some future time to alter your opinion & that what you now cast aside as worthless shall yet appear to be a treasure.

"There is abundant room in the antislavery field for him to perform a work without crossing the track or impeding the movement of his old friends & perhaps in some future time meeting each other from opposite quarters of a victorious field you may yet shake hands together.

"I write this letter because in the conversation I had with you, & also with Miss Weston I admitted so much that was unfavorable to Mr. Douglass that I felt bound in justice to state the more favorable views which had arisen to my mind.

"Very sincerely your friend,

"H. B. Stowe"[37]

Mrs. Stowe, a friend of both, was earnestly trying to arrange a reconciliation between Garrison and Douglass. But her words were wasted on the leader of the American Anti-Slavery Society. Garrison met Douglass at various anti-slavery functions but refused to speak to him, still regarding him as one of the "malignant enemies of mine" and as being "utterly unscrupulous in carrying out his own designs." Characteristic of Garrison's attitude was his rejection of an invitation to attend a celebration in Syracuse in October, 1860. After indicating that he was in poor health and had been advised by his doctor not to travel, he wrote:

"But, were I 'in speaking order,' the fact that Frederick Douglass is to be present at the celebration, and to participate therein, would powerfully repel me from attending. I regard him as thoroughly base and selfish, and I know that his hostility to the American Anti-Slavery Society and its leading advocates is unmitigated and unceasing. . . . In fact, he reveals himself more and more to me as destitute of every principle of honor, ungrateful to the last degree, and malevolent in spirit. He is not worthy of respect, confidence, or countenance."[38]

This, at the very same time that the Negro leader was telling his audiences:

"No difference of opinion, no personal assaults, shall ever lead me to forget that some who, in America, have often made me the subject of personal abuse, are, at the same time, in their own way, earnestly working for the abolition of slavery."[39]

Even during the Civil War, when all groups of Abolitionists joined forces in their struggle to achieve emancipation, Garrison and Douglass remained apart. In principle, however, the war brought them closer and Douglass had the satisfaction of seeing the Garrisonians adopt several of the doctrines whose espousal had led to his condemnation. A month after Fort Sumter he announced that he felt "a personal, if not a little malicious pleasure" in learning that Garrison and his associates had abandoned their slogans condemning the American Union and, instead, were calling for the preservation of the Union against rebels and traitors. Ten years before, he reminded his readers, he had concluded that "the battle of freedom should be fought within the Union, and not out of it; that instead of leaving the Union on account of slavery, we should stand by the Union, and drive out slavery." The avowal of these beliefs had led to his being branded an "apostate" and to his expulsion "from the fellowship of those whom he had long loved and venerated as the chosen champions of the cause of the slave."

"We spoke ten years too soon," he concluded, "or rather the slaveholding rebellion came just ten years too late, else today we might have been a member, in good and regular standing, in the Garrisonian anti-slavery church, instead of being, as now, a worker for the slave as a single individual."[40]

In later years, as the anti-slavery struggle faded into the background, Douglass repeatedly praised the contributions of the Garrisonians. "It was they," he said, speaking of Garrison and Phillips, "who made Abraham Lincoln and the Republican party possible. What abolished slavery was the moral sentiment which had been created, not by the pulpit, but by the Garrisonian platform."[41] Looking back on the bitter controversy between himself and the Garrisonians, Douglass observed in 1885, in a letter to Oliver Johnson:

". . . I sincerely do assure you, that, while I cannot pretend to forget some differences which arose between us years ago, I have still no other than feelings of respect, gratitude, and love to you and the noble band of abolitionists led by William Lloyd Garrison, and with whom from first to last you faithfully cooperated.

"Like yourself, I grow less a partizan as I grow older and find it easy to make little of mere personal differences as to methods and even as to estimates of character growing out of such differences. These were but the dust and smoke of the fierce battle with slavery, and now that the enemy is vanquished, I joyfully recognize every instrumentality by which this grand result was attained."[42]

The break with the Garrisonians marked the end of one phase of Douglass' career and the beginning of another. After 1853, when the break was complete, Douglass fully emerged as an Abolitionist leader in his own right. From that year until the end of the Civil War he occupied a place in the anti-slavery movement second to none.

Anti-Slavery Political Action

The first gun fired at Fort Sumter was the climax of the inevitable conflict between two antagonistic systems in the United States—one in the North based upon free farming and free labor, the other in the South, based upon chattel slavery. During the seven years preceding the shot at Fort Sumter this conflict had been reaching the point of explosion. Harbingers of the gathering storm were the passage of the Kansas-Nebraska Bill which repealed the Missouri Compromise and opened northern territory to slavery, the battle between the pioneer farmers and the slaveholders for the possession of Kansas, the Dred Scott decision with its pronouncements that the black man had no rights that the white man was bound to respect, and that Congress had no power to abolish or prevent slavery in any of the territories, the hanging of John Brown from the gallows in a Virginia prison yard, the birth of the Republican Party, and the election of Abraham Lincoln on a program calling for the restriction of slavery to its then existing boundaries. Each of these events, as Frederick Douglass so aptly put it, was "one necessary link in the chain of events preparatory to the complete overthrow of the whole slave system."

By the time the Kansas-Nebraska Bill was passed by Congress, Douglass had already become an influential figure in the American political scene. As a political tactician he ranked far above many of his famous contemporaries.

During most of his political career before the Civil War Douglass was allied to the Liberty Party. The vast majority of American historians have underestimated the Liberty Party since it never carried a state, or even came close to carrying it, in any election. Yet the significance of this party cannot be estimated from the number of votes cast for its candidates at any given time. Its newspapers and propaganda went into the homes of Whigs and Democrats alike; its lecturers spoke to hundreds of people whose sense of party loyalty prevented them from voting the Liberty Party ticket. The Liberty Party men helped to shape the principles, forge the arguments, and train the leaders who in 1854 formed the Republican Party.

The Liberty Party was organized in April, 1840, by an anti-slavery convention representing six states. The chief driving force behind its organization was Myron Holley, the noted Abolitionist from Rochester, New York. The platform of the party, adopted three years later at a convention at Buffalo, added to its denunciation of slavery an announcement of the purpose of the Abolitionists "whether as private citizens or as public functionaries sworn to support the Constitution of the United States, to regard and to treat the third clause of the fourth article of that instrument [relating to the return of fugitive slaves], whenever applied to the case of a fugitive slave, as utterly null and void, and consequently as forming no part of the Constitution of the United States, whenever we are called upon or sworn to support it."

Negroes were active in the Liberty Party from its very inception in April, 1840.[1] Samuel Ringgold Ward allied himself with the Liberty Party as soon as it was formed; Henry Highland Garnet proudly proclaimed himself "a Liberty Party man," and J. W. Loguen and William Wells Brown took the stump for the party. The Buffalo Convention of Colored Citizens in August, 1843, passed a resolution endorsing the principles of the Liberty Party. Two dissenting votes were cast, one by Douglass and the other by Charles L. Remond, both Garrisonians. At the National Convention of the Liberty Party in Buffalo in 1843, Negroes, for the first time in American history, were active participants in a national political gathering. Ward led the convention in prayer; Garnet was appointed on the nominations committee, and Charles B. Ray was elected one of the convention secretaries.[2]

By the time Douglass joined its ranks, the Liberty Party had passed its peak. In the election of 1844 the party, headed as in 1840 by James G. Birney, increased its vote from less than 7,000 in 1840 to 63,324. This was the high mark. After 1844 it rapidly lost strength as the majority of political Abolitionists left the organization, and, merging with practical politicians, labored to build a political mass movement directed against slavery. Dissension among those who remained further weakened the organization. The advocates of the "one idea" policy insisted that the only program to be presented to the voters was a call for the overthrow of slavery "within the limits of national jurisdiction." Another group, aware that the voters wanted to know the party's stand on the tariff, the bank, the distribution of the public lands, called for a broad platform.

The division over issues in the Liberty Party inevitably led to a split. Early in June, 1847, about forty prominent Liberty Party men, all calling for a fuller program, met at Macedon Locke, Wayne County, New York, and, under the leadership of Gerrit Smith, adopted a program of nineteen articles. Separating itself from the Liberty Party, the Macedon Convention nominated Smith and Elihu Burritt, "the Learned Blacksmith," for President and Vice President of the United States.[3]

In October, 1847, the Liberty Party held its national convention in Buffalo. Ignoring the platform and candidates of the seceders, the delegates reaffirmed the "one idea" policy, and chose John P. Hale of New Hampshire and Leicester King of Ohio as their candidates. Not so easily downed, Gerrit Smith issued a call for another convention to be held in Buffalo on June 14, 1848.

The Buffalo Convention of the National Liberty Party, the name assumed by the group to distinguish it from the "one idea" Liberty Party, was the first official political gathering Douglass ever attended. He was impressed by the proceedings, and listened intently as Gerrit Smith read "An Address to the Colored People of the Northern States" urging them "to prove their superiority to the whites in industry, economy, temperance and education, in order to disprove the frequently repeated charge that Negroes were only fit for slavery," and advising them to withdraw "from pro-slavery political parties and churches." Douglass was pleased that the convention went on record for free public lands to actual settlers, for woman's political rights, for the ten-hour system of labor, and the right of workers to organize into trade unions. Suffering from a severe attack of "tonsil inflammation," Douglass was finally prevailed upon to speak and supported vigorously the Garrisonian position on the Constitution and the Union. Despite sharp rebuttal by several delegates, Douglass held his ground, arguing that the Constitution was designed to protect the interests of the slaveholders.[4]

His initial contact with a political convention made no dent in Douglass' confidence in the Garrisonian creed.

"Our attendance at this Convention," he informed his readers, "while it has done much to remove prejudices from our mind respecting some of the prominent men engaged in it, has also deepened our conviction that the only true ground for an American Abolitionist is, *No Union with Slaveholders.*"

But he was irritated by the objections raised by some Garrisonians to his attendance at the Buffalo Convention on the ground that it indicated a willingness "to give his influence" to further the objects of the National Liberty Party. He reminded his critics that he was still a Garrisonian and could well do without a "diplomatic reproof."[5]

But national events were compelling Douglass to revise his thinking regarding political action. In the summer of 1846, when the war with Mexico was only a few months old, President Polk asked Congress for two million dollars to be used in the acquisition of new territory. Thereupon Judge David Wilmot of Pennsylvania offered his famous amendment which became known as the Wilmot Proviso. The essential language of the Proviso was that neither slavery nor involuntary servitude ever exist in any territory acquired from the republic of Mexico. The House of Representatives passed the bill twice, but it failed each time in the Senate.

The idea embodied in the Proviso, however, did not die. Out of the furor aroused over the Wilmot Proviso rose the Free Soil Party.

On May 22, 1848, the Democratic National Convention nominated Lewis Cass of Michigan for President upon a platform framed to suit the South. Cries of anger and disappointment came from the free states. "Had a bombshell fallen into our quiet city yesterday," commented the *Chicago Journal,* "it could not have created more consternation."

On June 10, the Whig National Convention nominated Zachary Taylor, a Louisiana slaveholder, for President, and howled down the Wilmot Proviso. Immediately anti-slavery Whigs, especially in the Western Reserve, rose as one man to repudiate him.

"As we anticipated," declared the Cleveland *True Democrat,* "the Whigs have nominated Zachary Taylor for president. And this is the cup offered by slaveholders for us to drink. We loathed the sight. We will neither touch, taste, nor handle the unclean thing."[6]

Awakened by the controversy engendered by the Wilmot Proviso, Douglass began to see that, valuable as moral suasion was, a basic struggle for the freedom of the slave would take place in Congress, where the attention of the entire people could be focused. Hailing the "Great Uprising of the North," he wrote in his paper: "We look upon the Wilmot Proviso and its supporters as indications of the presence of a great principle in the national heart, which by patient cultivation will one day abolish forever our system of human bondage." Although the true radical principle for him was not opposition to the extension of slavery, but complete extirpation of every vestige of human bondage throughout the entire nation, nevertheless Douglass fully understood how important was the struggle for the Wilmot Proviso.

"It serves to keep the subject before the people—to deepen their hatred of the system—and to break up the harmony between the Northern white people and the Southern slaveholders, which has so long been the safeguard against an uprising of slaves against their cruel masters. . . . To limit slavery where it now is," argued Douglass, "if it does not abolish it, will at least fix upon it the nation's reprobation. Should the North gain in this contest, it will be the first victory gained since the formation of the Government."[7]

Thus while he still considered himself a Garrisonian, Douglass showed an un-Garrisonian delight and enthusiasm for the new political movement which was arising in the summer of 1848 pledged to support the Wilmot Proviso.

Douglass was present at the historic convention held in Buffalo on August 29, 1848, in which discontented members of the Whig and Democratic parties as well as Liberty Party men, not overly rigid in their approach to anti-slavery political action, united to form the Free Soil Party on a platform of opposition to the extension of slavery in the territories. The Democrats were represented by the Barnburners of New York who favored the Wilmot Proviso, had refused to accept Lewis Cass, and had already nominated Martin Van Buren as their standard-bearer. Among the Conscience Whigs were men like Charles Francis Adams and Charles Sumner who could not stomach their party's candidate. These anti-slavery men from all parties were united by their determination to secure the adoption of the Wilmot Proviso.

Eighteen states were represented and there were 465 delegates. As many as ten thousand persons attended some of the large mass meetings. Martin Van Buren, already nominated by the best organized group in the convention, was chosen to head the ticket and Charles Francis Adams was nominated for the second highest office. The platform proposed no interference with slavery in the states, but demanded that Congress halt its advance into the territories—"No more slave States, no more slave territory, no more compromises with slavery; and freedom for Oregon, California and New Mexico." The slogan of the new party was: "Free Soil, Free Speech, Free Labor and Free Men."[8]

Douglass was seated in the convention hall, when a Mr. Husbands of Rochester, addressing the delegates, announced that he saw "Frederick Douglass here." The delegates responded with three cheers. The next day there were loud calls for Douglass to speak. He took the stand and stated that he was grateful for the opportunity to address the delegates, but deeply regretted his inability to speak since he had only recently had an operation on his throat. "One thing, however, I want to say, God speed your noble undertaking." The official reporter added: "The audience appeared to feel a great disappointment when they learned that Mr. Douglass could not address them."[9]

In his first editorial discussions, Douglass placed his stamp of approval on the Free Soil discussions, and argued that as the Free Soilers were the only openly anti-slavery party, it was the duty of the Abolitionists to support Van Buren. The Constitution might be pro-slavery, but the tactical exigencies of the struggle made it necessary that every possible weapon be utilized. The adherents of slavery were gathering around Taylor and Cass, while the forces of freedom were hesitant and disunited. What should the friends of the slave do in this crisis? Douglass' answer reveals his profound grasp of the correct strategy to be used by the Abolitionists:

"... We may stand off and act the part of fault finders—pick flaws in the Free Soil platform, expose the weakness of some persons connected with it—suspect and criticize their leaders, and in this way play into the hands of our enemies, affording the sticks to break our own heads. Or we may consign ourselves to oblivion ... remain silent as if we were speechless, and let things take their own course, and thus morally to commit suicide. In neither of these ways can we go. We feel it our duty to pursue the course which will make us in some degree a terror to evil doers, and a praise to all that do well . . . to be a worker on the anvil now before us—that whatever influence we may possess, it shall be given in the right direction."[10]

Douglass' endorsement of the Free Soil Party came in conflict with his Garrisonian beliefs, and he gradually withdrew from the advanced position he had set forth in his first editorials. A month after the Free Soil Party was organized, he announced editorially that "it would be a violation of anti-slavery principles for us to vote." At the Colored Convention in Cleveland, on September 6, 1848, he opposed the adoption of a resolution which hailed "with delight this great movement as the dawn of a bright and more auspicious day." The resolution was defeated.[11]

Despite his reluctance to abandon his faith in the Garrisonian doctrines, Douglass could not refrain from endorsing the new party. He realized that the Free Soil Party had brought the struggle against slavery to the attention of hundreds of thousands whom the Abolitionists had been unable to reach. True, the new party was not to be regarded as "the real anti-slavery movement of the country," but it decidedly was "a noble step in the right direction." It was still necessary for the anti-slavery movement to be kept "mainly a moral one"; the slogan "No Union with Slaveholders in Church or State" must still be inscribed on the banners of those concerned with the wrongs of the slave. But the Free Soilers had already done some good and could do more in the future. On September 10, 1848, *The North Star* editorially recommended the Free Soil candidates, Van Buren and Adams.

It is interesting to note that even before Douglass had left the Garrisonians, he was already ahead of Gerrit Smith in his understanding of the fundamental issues involved in the political campaign. For while Douglass wished the Free Soilers every possible success even though he was not prepared to abandon his Garrisonian principles, Smith declared the new party to be entirely inadequate and refused to support Van Buren. Smith understood the necessity for political action but lacked Douglass' insight into the methods necessary for obtaining the largest popular support for each measure to restrict slavery. Douglass understood that this was the beginning of a great movement which would finally split the Democrats, destroy the Whig Party, and create a new political anti-slavery movement with a mass following.[12]

Douglass was excited by the colorful campaign. Free Soilers sang themselves hoarse up to election day:

The North is ripe for the Proviso
Hurrah! Hurrah! Hurrah!
She'll back the names from Buffalo
Hurrah! Hurrah! Hurrah!

Whigs, Democrats, we'll all unite
And Liberty boys—for our cause is right,
Hurrah! Hurrah! Hurrah![13]

Although Van Buren did not carry a single state, the Free Soil Party received 291,678 votes out of the 2,882,120 which were cast, and elected five men to Congress. The *Liberator* sought to interpret this large vote for the new party as an evidence of the influence of Garrisonian principles:

"The Slave Power is beginning to falter—fresh adherents are daily rallying around the standard of Liberty, and the cry of 'No Union with Slaveholders' is causing the knees of the oppressor to tremble."[14]

While Douglass was bitter over Taylor's election, he was encouraged by the vote cast for the Free Soil candidates. He was convinced that it was the duty of all anti-slavery men to promulgate their principles among the Free Soilers so that gradually "a true Free Soil Party" could be established. "We must go on and lead the Free Soilers," he told the audience at the Thirteenth Annual Meeting of the Rhode Island Anti-Slavery Society a month after the election.[15]

Had the Free Soil Party continued to fulfill his bright hopes, Douglass might have allied himself with the movement. But he was disappointed by the failure of the party's leaders to maintain an active organization after the national elections, and by their formation of coalitions with various conservative political groups, thus abandoning independent political action.[16] On March 23, 1849, he inquired editorially, "What Good has the Free Soil Movement Done?" and answered that it had "promised much and has performed little." It had proved to be "a dull and indolent concern, gone to sleep and refusing to wake, until roused by the thunders of another political campaign." Instead of moving closer to Abolitionism and winning the approval of anti-slavery men, it had sought alliances "with the enemies of that holy cause." It had "swallowed up the Liberty Party press . . . and weakened its once powerful testimony against slavery." It had increased the burdens of the Abolitionists by creating the impression in the public mind that it was unnecessary to deal with slavery in the South as long as it could be kept out of the territories. "No abolitionist," cried Douglass, "who is truly such, will be gratified with, or encourage any measure or doctrine that does not contemplate slavery everywhere as marked out for destruction." Disillusionment bit deeply.

Even the belief expressed by the *Providence Transcript* that he would be nominated by the Free Soil Party in 1852 as its Vice-Presidential candidate did not change Douglass' attitude toward the movement. Instead, as he began "wielding the Federal Constitution for the abolition of American Slavery," and decided to use both moral and political power, he turned in another direction and allied himself with the Liberty Party, associating himself with the Gerrit Smith wing of the organization. On May 15, 1851, he wrote that he knew "of no one principle of that party that I should oppose." The following autumn he attended the convention of the Liberty Party in Buffalo and was appointed to the National Committee and to the Committee on Nominations. And in the fall elections he assured anti-slavery voters that there was "no way in which the cause of the slave can be better promoted than by voting the Liberty Party ticket."[17]

In the meantime, the Free Soilers had not given up hope of winning Douglass to their cause. At the Whig Convention in Rochester in October, 1851, the Free Soil delegates proposed Douglass as representative for the Second Assembly District in the State Legislature and secured twenty-two votes on the first ballot for their candidate. The convention finally nominated another candidate, but the press generally admitted that if the "Free Soilers had been in a majority," Douglass would have secured the nomination.[18]

Douglass, however, rebuffed all overtures from the Free Soilers. Even when a number of Liberty Party members prepared early in 1852 to enter the Presidential campaign under the Free Soil banner, he continued his support of an independent Liberty Party. "I think we ought to stand by and maintain the Liberty Party with all its great principles and purposes," he wrote to Smith on February 19, 1852. Early in April he carried an editorial in his paper, headlined "Stand by the Liberty Party." He reminded the political Abolitionists who were flirting with the Free Soilers that the aim of the Free Soil Party was "to denationalize and sectionalize and not to abolish slavery," whereas the Liberty Party, whether followed "by many or by few," would continue to call for the eradication of slavery everywhere. As for himself he could not see "how a not less comprehensive or a less elevated platform can be occupied by those who would radically oppose slavery at the ballot box."[19]

But in spite of all this, not many months later Douglass was in the ranks of the Free Soil Party. As he marked the busy preparations of the Free Soilers for the national campaign and noted the enthusiasm evoked by this growing mass movement, he realized the futility of the isolationist policy he had been advocating. Recalling his original position that it was the duty of the Abolitionists to lead the Free Soilers, he wrote to Smith on July 15, 1852, that it was their political responsibility to attend the approaching Pittsburgh convention of the Free Soil Party. The gathering could be "made to occupy such a position as the 'Liberty Party' may properly vote for its candidates." The masses who would be present in Pittsburgh were far ahead of their leaders, and were quite prepared to support a program in advance of "mere *Free Soil.*" It remained for men like Smith to bring up the issues around which the delegates would rally.[20]

On August 11, 1852, two thousand persons crowded into the Masonic Hall in Pittsburgh to attend the second national convention of the Free Soil Party. Douglass and Smith sat in the New York section. Soon after convening, Douglass was nominated as a secretary of the convention by Lewis Tappan, was elected by acclamation, and took his seat "amid loud applause." Barely had the next speaker started to address the delegates, when loud calls for Douglass drowned out his voice. Amid cheers Douglass moved to the platform. Taken by surprise, he had no prepared address. But he launched immediately into what reporters described as "an aggressive speech."[21]

"The object of this Convention is to organize a party, not merely for the present, but a party identified with eternal principles and therefore permanent," he began. He had come to Pittsburgh "not so much of a Free Soiler as others." He stood, of course, with the delegates "for circumscribing and damaging slavery in every way." But his motto was for exterminating slavery everywhere, not only in California but in New Orleans. He assured them that in making their party platform nothing could be gained by "a timid feeling." The Constitution was directed against slavery since "human government is for the protection of rights." Even if the framers of the document had asserted the right to enslave human beings, it would not have the binding authority of reasonableness.

"Suppose you and I had made a deed to give away two or three acres of blue sky; would the sky fall—and would anybody be able to plough it? You will say that this is an absurdity, and so it is. The binding quality of law, is its reasonableness. I am safe, therefore, in saying, that slavery cannot be legalized at all. I hope, therefore, that you will take the ground that this slavery is a system, not only of wrong, but is of a lawless character, and cannot be christianized or legalized."

The audience applauded Douglass throughout and cheered as he concluded with the advice that "numbers should not be looked to as much as right." As the afternoon session drew to a close, the delegates again called on Douglass to speak, but he declined with the brief statement that his throat was sore from his previous exertion.[22]

The reception of Douglass at the Free Soil Convention aroused comment in Europe as well as in this country. In London *The Anti-Slavery Reporter* viewed it as one of the brightest signs of the time.

"The appointment of Frederick Douglass as one of the secretaries of the convention," it observed, "is a cheering indication of the advance of anti-slavery sentiment in the United States. That a colored man should be called upon to act as an officer in a large political meeting is a sign of progress in that country, where to belong to the enslaved race has been to be proscribed and neglected."[23]

Douglass informed his readers that he had been favorably impressed by the "spirit" displayed at the Free Soil Convention "no less than with its principles" and candidates. John P. Hale of New Hampshire was "a large-hearted philanthropist . . . a dreaded foe to slavery," and George W. Julian of Indiana was "one of the truest and most disinterested friends of freedom whom we have ever met." He urged the Liberty Party convention about to assemble at Canastota, New York, to endorse the Free Soil nominations.

Early in September the Liberty Party convened. The movement to support Hale and Julian ran into opposition when a number of delegates called for the selection of Presidential candidates from the Liberty Party. Outvoted, the faction opposing the endorsement of the Free Soil nominations withdrew and selected William Goodell and Charles C. Foote as their candidates for President and Vice-President.

Douglass was critical of the seceders. He was convinced that it would be unwise for the Liberty Party to "array itself against Free Soilery." Nor did he believe that he was sacrificing a basic principle in supporting Hale and Julian. What was "morally right" was "not, at all times, politically possible." "Our rule of political action is this: the voter ought to see to it that his vote shall secure the highest good possible, at the same time that it does no harm."[24]

The masthead of Douglass' journal carried the names of Hale and

Julian inscribed on an American flag. But the editor's main concern in the autumn of 1852 was in the campaign for representative from the twenty-second Congressional district of New York. His friend and mentor, Gerrit Smith, had been nominated for the office by the Liberty or Free Democrat's Party. Douglass campaigned through the state even though he doubted that Smith, being "too far in advance of the people and of the age," could possibly be elected. He could not believe his ears when people said they were "going to vote for Gerrit Smith" and expressed confidence in Smith's election.

"This however, I deem unreasonable," he wrote to Smith from Chittenango Falls on October 21. "How could such a thing be? Oh! if it could only be so, the cup of my joy would be full. It is too good to be true. Yet *I* am the only man whom I have heard speak disparagingly in private about the matter."[25]

The Free Soil vote of 1852 was about one-half of what it had been in 1848, but Douglass' disappointment was speedily forgotten with the announcement of the election of Gerrit Smith to Congress by an overwhelming majority. The "grand event," which even Garrison admitted was "among the most extraordinary political events of this most extraordinary age," completely filled his "cup of joy." "The election of *Gerrit Smith*—what an era!" he exulted. He was especially overjoyed by the fact that Smith went to Congress "a *free man,*" and "not by the grace of a party caucus, bestowed as a reward for party services; not by concealment, bargain or compromise. . . ." As his excitement mounted, he predicted that "with men and money," the Liberty Party could carry New York state "for freedom" in 1856.[26]

Douglass placed great hope in Smith's congressional career. On August 18, 1853, four months before the session convened, he wrote to his co-reformer advising him to master the parliamentary rules of Congress so as "to defy all the mantraps which they will surely set for your feet." Unfortunately Smith did not remain in Washington long enough to put this sound advice to much use. After joining in the attack on the Kansas-Nebraska Bill, introduced into Congress early in 1854, and leading the movement to strike out the word "white" from the bill granting land to actual settlers in New Mexico, he decided he had had enough of life in the nation's capital and returned to Peterboro. On August 7, 1854, Smith resigned his seat in Congress. The only explanation he gave was the "pressure of my far too extensive business."[27]

Many Abolitionists felt let down by Smith's return to private life after an eight months congressional career. They believed that he had accepted a sacred trust when he entered Congress, and that he had no right to permit personal considerations to interfere with his work for the cause. Douglass probably shared the disappointment of his anti-slavery colleagues, but he criticized those who viewed Smith's resignation as evidence of "treachery and meanness." It required courage, he reasoned, for a man to give up "place and power at a point when that place was every hour becoming more honorable, and when that power was becoming more and more widely felt."[28] By the same token, of course, it made Smith's resignation all the more difficult for the anti-slavery men to swallow. Unquestionably Douglass' friendship for Smith caused him to overlook the demoralizing effect the resignation had upon those voters who, like himself, had expected great things of the Liberty Party congressman.

For a few weeks there was some discussion in the press over the possibility of Douglass succeeding Smith in Congress. The *New York Tribune* started the ball rolling with an editorial making the proposal, and several papers immediately took it up. The *Massachusetts Spy* was convinced that "Frederick Douglass would make an admirable member of Congress," and expressed the wish that "we could have the privilege of voting for him." The *Cincinnati Commercial* not only agreed, but ventured the opinion that the Negro would do better in Congress than the white Douglas who was Senator from Illinois.[29]

The discussion caused a terrific outcry in the press friendly to the South, and shrieks arose that the "plot" to place Douglass in Congress proved the real design of the Abolitionists.

"It is time for the people of the North," the *Philadelphia Argus* cried, "to look at the acts and purposes of these abolition traitors who . . . agree to elect, if possible, a Negro to the House of Representatives—are they willing that a Negro should be sent to Congress for an army of avant couriers to shield them in their designs upon the Union."[30]

The furor died as quickly as it was born. No political group took up the *Tribune's* suggestion, nor did Douglass indicate any political ambitions. He did, however, write a prophetic editorial discussing the significance of the proposal:

"The possibility of electing a Negro to the American Congress, is a modern suggestion. The idea is a new one, as little hoped for by the despised colored people, as dreamed of by their white friends. We accept it simply as an indication of a slighly altered state of mind in the country, but without the slightest belief that the idea will ever be realized in our person, tho' we do hope and expect to see it realized in some competent colored man before we shall have done with the journey of life. The thing is in itself reasonable, and, therefore, probable. It is consistent with all the elementary principles of the American government, though it is in conflict with our national prejudices and practices. It is evident of some progress that the subject has called forth an expression so general and so decided at this time—and this is the only importance we feel at liberty to allow it. We certainly do not believe in the existence of any serious intention to offer us or to accept us, as a candidate for Congress, or for any other office in this government, State or National."[31]

The passage of the Kansas-Nebraska Act produced a general re-alignment in American political life. Democrats who refused to stay in their party now that it was dominated by slave owners, Whigs who were fed up with their party's straddling on the slavery question, were looking for a new political organization. Together with Abolitionists, Free Soilers, German-American Communists and other reformers, they organized in the summer and fall of 1854 a political movement dedicated to fight the further extension of slavery. The name of the newly formed coalition was the Republican Party.

The Republican Party attracted the support of all but a small group of diehard political Abolitionists. Some three hundred Liberty Party members remained outside the new coalition, contending that "the signs of the times forbid the dissolution" of their organization. They were the only party, they argued, willing to fight the battle of freedom on the ground that "slavery cannot be legalized" anywhere on the earth; the only party calling for "the utter annihilation of slavery." In September, 1854, thirty Liberty Party men met in Syracuse and nominated William Goodell for Governor on a platform calling upon the federal government to abolish slavery. Douglass attended the convention as a delegate and took the stump for Goodell.[32]

Douglass was not blind to the significance of the rapidly growing Republican movement. "We rejoice in this demonstration," he wrote in July, 1855. "It evinces the fact of a growing determination on the part of the North, to redeem itself from bondage, to bury party affinities, and predilections, and also the political leaders who have hitherto controlled them; to unite in one grand phalanx, and go forth, and whip the enemy."

But he could not abandon the Liberty Party and ally himself with the Republican movement. The Republican Party did not go far enough; it gave aid and comfort to the slaveholders by its willingness "to let Slavery where it is." Yet this was precisely where slavery should be attacked. There was need for a party which calls for "a clean sweep of slavery everywhere," and which "by its position and doctrines, and by its antecedents, is pledged to continue the struggle while a bondman in his chains remains to weep." Such was the Liberty Party, and on its platform "must the great battle of freedom be fought out. . . ." While it could not boast of mass support, the Liberty Party could fulfill an important function by keeping alive the demand for the abolition of slavery throughout the nation until such time as events themselves compelled other political parties with greater numerical support to incorporate this program in their platforms. Douglass was confident that this would come to pass; he was convinced that the Republican Party "as it grows in numbers, will also grow *in the knowledge of the Truth.*"[33] Meanwhile, until this happy event was realized he believed that he could best make his contribution to the political battle against slavery by galvanizing the Liberty Party into life.

With this in mind, Douglass, in March, 1855, urged Gerrit Smith to go forward with plans for a National Liberty Party Convention. A month later, he joined with Lewis Tappan, William Goodell, Gerrit Smith, and James McCune Smith in issuing a call for a convention of the party supporters to be held in Syracuse in June. The call opened: "We are few—but we are not, therefore, to cease from our work. Work for a good cause, be that cause popular or unpopular, must be work to the end." The purpose of the new political movement was toward the removal of slavery from the territories and the states "by means of our national political power." The existing parties were incapable of achieving this goal, the call asserted, the Whig, Democratic, and Know-Nothing parties being dominated by their slaveholding members while the Free Soil Party, although "an anti-slavery party," denied the right of the national government "to touch slavery in the States."[34]

After a three-months preparation, the convention met on June 26-28, 1855. James McCune Smith was elected chairman and Douglass was designated to serve on the Business Committee. A "Declaration of Sentiments," an "Exposition of the Constitutional Duty of the Federal Government to Abolish Slavery," and an "Address to the Public" were drawn up and adopted. The body also endorsed a program calling for the use of the political power of the nation "to overthrow every part and parcel of American Slavery."[35] Following the issuance of a call for a national convention to assemble in October, the meeting adjourned.

Douglass left the convention optimistic. On August 15 he departed on a four-week lecture tour in up-state New York during which he planned "to uphold the great principles of freedom as laid down . . . at the radical abolition convention." At the end of the trip he attended the Liberty Party Convention at Ithaca. Douglass was nominated for the office of Secretary of State of New York, the first time such an honor was bestowed upon an American Negro. But the Liberty Party failed to designate a slate for national offices, as it was awaiting the action of the Radical Abolitionists which, of course, was simply the Liberty Party by another name.[36]

Late in October Douglass traveled to Boston to attend the convention of the Radical Abolitionists. Smith, Beriah Green, and Abram Pyne, a Negro editor, were also present. A terrific downpour and the simultaneous opening of the National Agricultural Fair accounted for the small attendance. Under these circumstances the body decided to take no definite action. Still Douglass was not discouraged. He was as confident as ever in "the ultimate triumph" of the views of this handful of Liberty Party men and Radical Abolitionists. Sooner or later those interested in the struggle against slavery would come to see that these views were correct. "We shall, therefore, contribute our mite toward effecting this desirable consummation," he wrote editorially in mid-November.[37]

The American political scene during the opening months of 1856 was full of confusion and change. The Whig party had practically disappeared. The American Party (Know-Nothings) was in the throes of dissolution over the slavery issue. The Republican Party, carrying a majority in nearly half the states in its first election, was assuming ever increasing importance.

On February 22, 1856, Republican leaders met at Pittsburgh, planned a national convention for June and drew up an "Address to the People of the United States." The document was a severe disappointment to the political Abolitionists who still clung to the ideals of the skeleton Liberty Party. They had expected the Republican leaders to move closer to the radical Abolitionist position. Instead, these leaders, believing that even their limited anti-slavery program was unacceptable to many in the North, had actually retreated. In the entire document, said Douglass, only the demand of freedom for Kansas reflected the influence of the anti-slavery forces in the Republican Party. "Nothing said of the Fugitive Slave Bill—nothing said of Slavery in the District of Columbia —nothing said of the slave trade between States—nothing said of giving dignity of the nation to Liberty—nothing said of securing the rights of citizens from the Northern States, in the constitutional right to enter and transact business in the slave states." He saw only one argument that might influence Abolitionists to follow the Republican Party and that argument was "the grand corrupter of all reforms . . . that the only thing needful, the thing to precede all else, is a large party; and in order to do this, we are at liberty to abandon almost everything but a name." With such a philosophy he would have nothing to do. He looked toward the convention of the Radical Political Abolitionists to be held in Syracuse on May 28 rather than toward the Republican convention scheduled to meet in Philadelphia in June.[38]

On March 21, 1856, Garrison wrote somewhat gleefully:

"I see that Lewis Tappan, Douglass, McCune Smith, Goodell and Gerrit Smith have called a convention for the purpose of nominating candidates for the Presidency and Vice Presidency of the United States!! Can anything more ludicrous than this be found inside or outside of the Utica Insane Asylum?"[39]

Indifferent to such caustic comments, Douglass addressed the convention on the afternoon of its first day. He admitted that he was tempted to join the Republican Party, but was dissuaded by the realization that "they do not give a full recognition to the humanity of the Negro," that they sought to limit slavery only in Kansas and Nebraska. "Liberty must cut the throat of slavery or have its own cut by slavery," he concluded.[40]

The convention nominated Gerrit Smith for President and Samuel McFarland for Vice President. Douglass had been named for Vice President but an objection was made because Smith and he came from the same state. Douglass announced that he soon planned to move from New York to Ohio and therefore "avoid that objection." Although

McFarland was finally nominated, reports arose that Douglass had been the convention's choice. On June 21, 1856, almost a month late, the *New York Herald* declared that "the Abolitionists pure and simple have designated as their standard bearers for the succession, Gerrit Smith (white man), Frederick Douglass (black man)."[41] At the very same time the names of Gerrit Smith and Samuel McFarland appeared at the head of the leading editorial column of *Frederick Douglass' Paper.*[42]

On August 15, Douglass withdrew these names and informed his readers of his purpose "to support, with whatever influence we possess, little or much, John C. Frémont, and William L. Dayton, the candidates of the Republican Party for the presidency and vice-presidency of the United States, in the present political canvass." Coming after his continuous denunciations of the Republican Party and especially after his characterization of it in June as "a heterogenous mass of political antagonism, gathered from defunct Whiggery, disaffected Democracy, and demented, defeated and disappointed Native Americanism," Douglass knew that his political somersault would arouse consternation among his readers. So he accompanied his announcement with a careful explanation of this new course which apparently seemed so inconsistent with the policies he had hitherto advocated. He was not concerned with consistency as commonly understood, for "anti-slavery consistency" required of the anti-slavery voter only that he deliver the severest blow against slavery at any given moment. Such action was "always consistent, however different may be the forms through which it expressed itself." His support of the Republican candidates, he went on, did not signify that he had abandoned his anti-slavery principles. He would continue to contend for the extinction of slavery in every part of the republic, but he could best do this in the ranks of the Republican Party, using his voice and pen to teach and influence the vast numbers who were flocking to its banner. The fact that the Republican Party did not go as far as he wished on the slavery question was no reason for withholding his support for its candidates.

[A man was not] "justified in refusing to assist his fellow-men to accomplish a good thing, simply because his fellows refuse to accomplish some other good things which they deem impossible. Most assuredly, that theory cannot be a sound one which would prevent us from voting with men for the Abolition of Slavery in Maryland simply because our companions refuse to include Virginia. In such a case the path of duty is plainly this; go with your fellow-citizens for the Abolition of Slavery in Maryland when they are ready to go for that measure, and do all you can, meanwhile, to bring them to whatever work of righteousness may remain and which has become manifest to your clearer vision."[48]

In subsequent editorials Douglass enlarged on reasons for his action and in cogent, well-defined arguments set dowⁱ the correct role for any vanguard reform group. Instead of isolating itself from a mass movement which was not ready to accept a more advanced program, the duty of the vanguard was to work inside the movement, gradually bringing to its membership the understanding that would result in the adoption of an advanced position. In September, 1856, he expressed his conception of political strategy in an editorial entitled "The Republican Party" which showed the genius of a true political organizer, one who knew how to fight on all fronts, to use all avenues of advance:

"From our political philosophy, we are at liberty to consider the state of the public mind, and to look at immediate results, as well as remote consequences. We are at liberty to inquire how far our vote, at a given time, will forward what we conceive to be the highest interests of society; and having considered this, we are at liberty,—nay it is our indispensable duty to cast our vote in that direction, which, upon a survey of the whole facts in the case, will best promote that great end."

Turning directly to the bitter attacks on him for his endorsement of Frémont, he continued:

"That man is a fool," says Mr. L. D. Campbell, "who expects the Republican party to stop with restricting Slavery"; the enlightened public sentiment will stop its onward progress, only when Slavery is abolished, and not till then.—But we must hold back, say some of his friends, we must not join ourselves to this party until they declare for the Abolition of Slavery; to circumscribe it is not enough. . . . We will not refuse our neighbor's aid in breaking the soil and planting our crops, even though he will not pledge himself to aid us in harvesting. We plant the crop, and when it is ready for harvest, there is no fear but that the laborers will be found. Even so with the Republican party. The rescue of our Government from the hands of slaveholders; curbing the mad career of the slave-power, must precede the establishment of liberty wherever the laws of the Republic extend. He who votes the Republican ticket gives no pledge of peace toward Slavery in the future. It is simply a vote for the non-extension to which the party is pledged. When this much is accomplished, invite the party to a higher ground; if they fail to come up, sound the alarm: 'To your tents, O Israel'; and the Republican leaders will see, that while they were true to liberty, they could carry the masses with them, but when they undertake to impede the advancing hosts of freedom, the power will depart from them."[44]

Buchanan won the election with an electoral vote of 174 and a popular vote of 1,838,169. But the Republicans showed that they had gained enormous strength. Frémont received 114 electoral votes and 1,341,264 popular votes.

Douglass summed up all of the arguments in defense of his support of the Republican candidates in a brief note to Gerrit Smith. "We have turned Whigs and Democrats into Republicans and we can turn Republicans into Abolitionists."[45] He was soon to see his prediction fulfilled.

Douglass' support of Frémont did not mean that he had become a member of the Republican Party; six weeks after the election he announced that he was still a Radical Abolitionist.[46] He participated in the demise of the Liberty Party when it met in Syracuse on September 30, 1857, and, as its final official act, nominated James McCune Smith as Secretary of State.[47] A year later he campaigned for Gerrit Smith for governor of New York, candidate of the "People's State Ticket" and the Radical Abolitionists. The insignificant vote cast for Smith, despite an active campaign,[48] was an indication of how completely isolated were these diehard political Abolitionists. With the Negro voters throwing their support to the Republican Party, there were very few to whom the Radical Abolitionists could appeal. Little wonder that by the summer of 1859 the party had all but ceased to exist. "Where is its committee? where its paper, its lecturers and patrons?" asked Douglass in July, 1859. "All gone!"[49]

Douglass was determined to make a final effort to revive the Radical Abolition Party. But before he could do much, he became involved in the chain of events surrounding John Brown's historic raid on the arsenal at Harpers Ferry, Virginia.

Douglass and John Brown

On October 17, 1859, Douglass lectured in the National Hall at Philadelphia on "Self-Made Men." A capacity audience listened to his recital of men who had risen to fame "from the depths of poverty" as a result of "patient, enduring, honest, unremitting work, into which the whole heart is put. . . ." One of them was Benjamin Banneker, a Negro slave born in Maryland, who became a learned mathematician, an outstanding surveyor, who assisted in the laying out of the city of Washington, "and compelled honorable recognition from some of the most distinguished scholars and statesmen of that early day of the Republic." Douglass quoted Jefferson's letter to Banneker of August 30, 1790, in which the author of the Declaration of Independence praised the Negro's almanac, describing it as "a document to which your whole colour had a right for their justification against the doubts which have been entertained of them."

"This was the impression," Douglass declared, "made by an intelligent Negro upon the father of American Democracy, in the earlier and better years of the Republic. I wish that it were possible to make a similar impression upon the children of the American Democracy of this generation. Jefferson was not ashamed to call the black man his brother and to address him as a gentleman."[1]

At that very moment, a man who not only regarded the Negro slave as his brother but was willing to sacrifice his life for his brother's freedom, was attempting to capture the federal arsenal at Harpers Ferry. The raid was part of a more ambitious plan conceived by John Brown whose ultimate aim was the emancipation of the slaves throughout the South.

Douglass' relations with John Brown, it will be recalled, began more than ten years before the raid on Harpers Ferry. It was at Brown's home in Springfield that Douglass first learned of the former's plan to aid the slaves, a project which embraced the setting up of an armed force which would function in the very heart of the South. At that time Brown pointed to a large map of the United States. These Allegheny mountains stretching from the borders of New York State into the South, he told Douglass, afforded an excellent "pathway for a grand stampede from the Slave States, a grand exodus into the Free States, and, through the latter, into Canada." The mountains were full of hiding places and once the slaves were brought there and scattered among the glens, deep ravines, and rocks, it would be difficult to find them and even more difficult to overpower them if they were found. "I know these mountains well," said Brown, "and could take a body of men into them and keep them there in spite of all the efforts of Virginia to dislodge me, and drive me out. I would take at first about twenty-five picked men and begin on a small scale, supply them arms and ammunition, post them in squads of fives on a line of twenty-five miles, these squads to busy themselves for a time in gathering recruits from the surrounding farms, seeking and selecting the most restless and daring." Once he had gathered a force of a hundred hardy men and drilled them properly, they would run off slaves in large numbers, keeping the braver ones in the mountains, and sending the others north by the underground railroad. Gradually the operations would be enlarged to cover the entire South, and in due course the movement would seriously weaken slavery in two ways—first, by destroying "the money value of slave property," by making it insecure, and second, by keeping alive anti-slavery agitation and thereby compelling the adoption of measures to abolish the evil altogether.

From eight o'clock in the evening until three in the morning, Douglass and Brown discussed this plan. Douglass pointed to serious flaws in the project. Once the plan went into operation, the slaveowners would sell their slaves further South or would use bloodhounds and armed forces to track down and overpower Brown and his band. Again, it would be almost impossible to keep the group in the mountains provided with supplies. Brown brushed aside these objections. If the slaves were removed to the lower South he would follow them; even to drive them out of one county would be a victory. Regardless of difficulties he would persevere in his attempt, for some startling event was necessary to prevent the agitation over the slavery question from dying out. If he should die in the effort he would be giving his life for the cause closest to his heart.[2]

Despite his original skepticism, Douglass came to think favorably of Brown's plan. The more he examined the project, the more convinced he became that it might contribute to undermining slavery, for "men do not like to buy runaway horses, nor to invest their money in a species of property likely to take legs and walk off with itself."[3] At the very least, the plan would reawaken the slumbering conscience of the nation. His sympathy for Brown's project grew as his confidence in the efficacy of moral suasion waned.

Douglass and Brown discussed the project many times after their first meeting in 1847. On several occasions Brown stopped at Douglass' home in Rochester,[4] and spent the night outlining the project for a chain of hide-outs in the Maryland and Virginia mountains from which men could go down to the plantations and encourage the slaves to escape. What Brown did not tell his friend, however, was that in the meantime in Kansas he had added a significant detail to his original plan. He now believed that it would be possible, given a few sound men, to establish a base in the mountains, to which slaves and free Negroes would come, and where, after beating off all attacking forces, whether state or federal, a free state would be set up.

On February 1, 1858, Brown arrived at Douglass' home. He would not stay long, he assured his host, and insisted upon paying for his accommodations. He remained several weeks, spending most of the time in his own room writing to numerous friends for financial assistance for his venture, the nature of which he did not reveal. At other times Brown would talk at length of his plan for mountain strongholds, even explaining them to Douglass' children and illustrating "each detail with a set of blocks."[5] Before he left Rochester he had secured a recruit in the person of Shields Green, a runaway slave who was staying at Douglass' home. Brown had also drawn up a constitution for his projected free state. Consisting of a preamble and forty-eight articles, the document provided a framework of government, under a military commander-in-chief, which was to go into operation after his forces had gained power.

Brown and Douglass were to meet again in Philadelphia on March 5, 1858, but the latter had to postpone the meeting. Writing from Syracuse on February 27, 1858, Douglass expressed the hope that Brown "would find work enough in and about New York" until his arrival. On March 11, Brown and his son John, Jr., conferred with Douglass, Garnet, and William Still, the latter a leading agent in the Underground Railroad. His funds exhausted, Brown appealed to them for men and money. He did not, however, divulge the wide reach of his new plans. Nor did Brown add to Douglass' knowledge of the project when he and his son spent the night at the Negro leader's home early in April.[6] All Douglass knew was that Brown was still proceeding with his original plan of setting up hide-outs in the mountains.

In April, 1858, Brown wrote to Douglass: "I expect to need all the help I can get by the first of May."[7] As this letter indicates, Brown had intended to strike in 1858 instead of 1859. The year's delay was made necessary by the treachery of Hugh Forbes, an Englishman who had fought with Garibaldi and had joined Brown after they had met in Kansas. Forbes had agreed to drill Brown's men and to recruit army officers. But Forbes was primarily interested in the project in order to line his own pocket. After getting as much money as he could from Brown, he began to mulct his leader's friends. When that source of income dried up, he threatened to expose the conspiracy if further funds were not forthcoming.

Douglass had reluctantly assisted Forbes in November, 1857, with "a little money" and with letters of introduction to friends.[8] But he had reacted unfavorably to the adventurer, was unimpressed by his tale of family woes, and so was not surprised when he learned that Forbes was threatening to disclose Brown's plans. He relayed this information to Brown. At the same time a committee of Brown's backers, Samuel Gridley Howe, Gerrit Smith, Theodore Parker, George L. Stearns, and Thomas Wentworth Higginson, met in secret at the Revere House in Boston and counseled Brown to postpone his operations and leave for Kansas. Assured that he would receive additional funds in the spring, Brown eventually traveled to Kansas.[9]

Douglass met Brown soon after his return from the Kansas region. En route to Peterboro during the second week of April, 1859, Brown stopped off for a few hours in Rochester. Horace McGuire, one of the employees in Douglass' printing office, recalled that "a tall, white man, with shaggy whiskers, rather unkempt, a keen piercing eye, and a restlessness of manner" called at the shop "several months prior to October 16, 1859," and asked for Douglass. The visitor gave the appearance of one whose "interview was by appointment." When Douglass returned, "the greeting between the white man and the former slave was very cordial." The two men "talked freely."[10]

In the early summer of 1859, Brown fixed upon Harpers Ferry as the base of his operations in Virginia and rented a farm about five miles from there to collect his arms and his band of followers. By mid-summer he had recruited a little army of twenty-one men, including several Negroes, and was almost ready to strike. In August, Brown decided to reveal the full details of his plan to Douglass in the hope of enlisting him as a member of the company preparing to attack Harpers Ferry. Douglass received a letter from Brown asking him to be present at Chambersburg, Pennsylvania, and to bring Shields Green along. The meeting took place on the night of August 20, in a stone quarry near Chambersburg. Brown, his lieutenant Kagi, Douglass and Green were present. It was in the old quarry that Douglass for the first time learned of Brown's plan to seize Harpers Ferry, capture the leading citizens and hold them as hostages while his band rounded up the slaves in the surrounding areas.[11] Brown was dismayed by the emphatic disapproval registered in Douglass' reaction to this plan. Douglass assured Brown that he was still prepared to join with him in carrying out the original plan of running slaves through the Alleghenies, but the raid on Harpers Ferry was an attack on the national government and was doomed to failure. But no amount of argument could dissuade Brown. The seizure would dramatize the evils of slavery, he argued, capture the attention of the nation and arouse the people to action.[12]

Brown's eloquence and his burning enthusiasm for the cause moved Douglass tremendously, but he remained adamant to all entreaties to participate in the enterprise. As he was preparing to leave, Brown made a final appeal: "Come with me, Douglass! I will defend you with my life, I want you for a special purpose. When I strike, the bees will begin to swarm and I shall want you to help me hive them." Douglass shook his head sadly, and turning to Shields Green he asked him if he had made up his mind. The former slave indicated his decision with the now famous reply that he would go with the "old man."[13]

Brown did not give up hope of recruiting Douglass. With sufficient pressure, he was convinced, the latter would reconsider his decision. A few weeks later, Douglass received a letter signed by a number of Negro men inviting him to represent them at a convention to be held "right away" in Chambersburg. The signers pledged themselves to see that his family would be "well provided" during his absence "or until your safe return to them." They also offered to "make you a remittance." Douglass suspected that Kagi had instigated the letter, but not without Brown's approval.[14] The appeal went unanswered.

The Chambersburg meeting between Douglass and Brown marked the last time these good friends were to see one another. On the night of October 16, Brown gave the order to march on Harpers Ferry. When the morning dawned, Brown and his men were in possession of the United States armory and the bridges leading to the Ferry. A few slaves had been persuaded to join them. The following night a company of United States marines, under the command of Colonel Robert E. Lee, arrived; at dawn the building was taken by assault. Brown fought with amazing coolness and courage, but was finally overpowered. Amid popular excitement, he was tried for treason and found guilty. On December 2, 1859, Brown was hanged at Charlestown.

Douglass received the startling news of Brown's capture while lecturing in the National Hall at Philadelphia. He was informed that letters had been found in Brown's possession implicating him, among others, of knowledge of the plot.[15] He knew at once that with the mounting hysteria his life was in extreme danger. At the advice of his friends he left Philadelphia and hastened to New York City, pausing at Hoboken to wire to B. F. Blackball, telegraph operator in Rochester: "Tell Lewis to secure all the important papers in my high desk."[16] Later Douglass learned how fortunate he had been in following the advice of friends in Philadelphia. John W. Hurn, a telegraph operator, and an admirer of Douglass, suppressed for three hours the delivery of a message to the sheriff of Philadelphia ordering him to arrest Frederick Douglass.[17]

Douglass' alarm increased as he read the New York papers. The *New York Herald* headlined a report of Brown's alleged confession to Governor Wise of Virginia: *"Gerrit Smith, Joshua Giddings, Fred Douglass and Other Abolitionists and Republicans Implicated."* "Enough it seems has been ascertained to justify a requisition from Governor Wise of Virginia, upon Governor Morgan, of New York, for the delivery over to the hands of justice of Gerrit Smith and Fred. Douglass, as parties implicated in the crime of murder and as accessories before the fact." From Richmond came an announcement that one hundred Southerners were offering rewards for the heads of "Traitors" among whom Douglass' name was prominently featured.

On his arrival in Rochester, several friends warned Douglass that the New York Governor would probably surrender him to the Virginia authorities upon request. As most citizens of Rochester would resist the attempt to return Douglass to the South and bloodshed and rioting would follow, he was advised both for his own safety and for the peace of the community, to cross over the border to Canada.[18] Aware that President Buchanan would employ the full power of the federal government to achieve his arrest, Douglass took the advice of his friends and fled to Canada.

Douglass barely evaded his pursuers. He had already been charged in Virginia with "murder, robbery and inciting to servile insurrection in the State of Virginia." Moreover, Govenor Wise had asked President Buchanan and the Post-Master General of the United States to grant two agents from Virginia authority to serve as detectives for the post-office department for the purpose of delivering Douglass to the Virginia courts.[19] On October 25, 1859, the Rochester *Union and Advertiser* reported:

"It is understood that United States Attorney Ould of Washington, and other federal officers, were here yesterday. It is supposed they came hither for the purpose of arresting Frederick Douglass for his alleged participation in the organized scheme against the slaveholding states, of which the Harper's Ferry insurrection was one of the appointed results."[20]

Had Douglass been arrested by federal authorities at that time the chances are that in the prevailing tense atmosphere he would have followed Brown to the gallows. Despite its facetious tone, the *New York Herald* knew whereof it spoke when it commented: "The black Douglass having some experience in his early life of the pleasures of Southern society had no desire to trust himself again even on the borders of the Potomac."[21] No evidence would have been required to sentence a Negro Abolitionist to death in Virginia during the weeks following the attack on Harpers Ferry.

Douglass has been severely criticized for his refusal to join Brown's expedition and for having fled to Canada after the raid.[22] John E. Cook, one of the men captured with Brown, even blamed Douglass for the failure of the expedition, charging that the latter had been assigned to bring a large body of men to reinforce Brown. In a letter to the editor of the Rochester *Democrat* from Canada on October 31, Douglass denied the charge. It was a brilliant document, opening with the caustic observation that Cook was "now in the hands of the thing calling itself the Government of Virginia, but which in fact is but an organized conspiracy by one party of the people against the other." Douglass admitted that "tried by the Harpers Ferry insurrection test," he was "deficient in courage," but denied that he had ever at any time encouraged the taking of Harpers Ferry or promised to join the expedition. This denial was motivated more by "a respectful consideration of the opinion of the slave's friends, than from my fear of being made an accomplice in the general *conspiracy* against Slavery." He was willing to support any movement against slavery, when there was "a reasonable hope of success," and he believed that any effort to overthrow the system of human bondage was basically moral. He had not joined Brown because he did not believe that this was the way in which he could best work for the abolition of slavery. "The tools to those who can use them," was the way Douglass put it. No shame could be attached to him, he added, for keeping out of the way of the United States marshals. Would a government that recognized the validity of the Dred Scott decision be likely "to have any very charitable feelings" toward a Negro Abolitionist?[23] The question answered itself.

There is not the slightest evidence that Douglass at any time indicated his intention of joining Brown's expedition. The very fact that he had made plans to leave for Europe in November, 1859, long before the attack on Harpers Ferry, is proof that he had made no commitments to Brown and his band.[24]

Douglass felt justified at his decision not to join Brown's company. The venture, as he had told Brown, was doomed to fail, and he believed that there was more work for him to do than to end his life at this stage of his career on the gallows in Virginia. "It is gallant to go forth single-handed," he later observed, "but is it wise?"[25]

All this did not mean that Douglass failed to grasp the significance of John Brown's raid. Two weeks after Harpers Ferry, Douglass wrote an editorial on John Brown which cut through the hysterical outpourings of the press and predicted the course the nation would soon follow:

"Posterity will owe everlasting thanks to John Brown for lifting up once more to the gaze of a nation grown fat and flabby on the garbage of lust and oppression, a true standard of heroic philanthropy, and each coming generation will pay its installment of the debt. . . .

"He has attacked slavery with the weapons precisely adapted to bring it to the death. Moral considerations have long since been exhausted upon slaveholders. It is in vain to reason with them. . . . Slavery is a system of brute force. It shields itself behind *might,* rather than right. It must be met with its own weapons. Capt. Brown has initiated a new mode of carrying on the crusade of freedom, and his blow has sent dread and terror throughout the entire ranks of the piratical army of slavery. His daring deeds may cost him his life, but priceless as is the value of that life, the blow he has struck, will, in the end, prove to be worth its mighty cost. Like Samson, he has laid his hands upon the pillars of this great national temple of cruelty and blood, and when he falls, that temple will speedily crumble to its final doom, burying its denizens in its ruins."[26]

On November 12, 1859, Douglass, in line with previously laid plans, sailed from Quebec for Liverpool. In his farewell note to his "Readers and Friends" in America, he cautioned them against losing heart because, owing to the frenzy aroused by Brown's raid, slavery seemed "to have gained an advantage" for the moment, and created "a more active resistance to the cause of freedom and its advocates." But this, he assured them, was only "transient." The "moment of passion and revenge" would pass away, and "reason and righteousness" would grow stronger. "Men will soon begin to look away from the plot to the purpose—from the effect to the cause." Then would come the reaction, "and the names now covered with execration will be mentioned with honor, or, as noble martyrs to a righteous cause. . . . The benumbed conscience of the nation will be revived and become susceptible of right impressions." The ultimate victory had been made more certain than ever by the "battle of Harpers Ferry."[27]

On his return to Rochester in May, 1860, Douglass found that sentiment around John Brown and those associated with him had changed. In December, 1859, a Senate Committee, headed by James M. Mason of Virginia, had been appointed to investigate the attack on Harpers Ferry. On June 14, 1860, the committee submitted an innocuous report which stated that while Brown had planned "to commence a servile insurrection" which he hoped to extend "throughout the entire South," he did not appear to have intrusted even his immediate followers with his plans. After much consideration, the committee announced that it was "not prepared to suggest any legislation."[28]

In a letter to a group of Abolitionists assembling at North Elba, in the Adirondacks, on July 4, 1860, to do honor to the memory of John Brown, Douglass wrote:

"To have been acquainted with John Brown, shared his counsels, enjoyed his confidence, and sympathized with the great objects of his life and death, I esteem as among the highest privileges of my life. We do but honor to ourselves in doing honor to him, for it implies the possession of qualities akin to his."[29]

The Eve of the Civil War

The news that Frederick Douglass was on the high seas bound for England aroused considerable excitement in British anti-slavery circles. Here was the one man who could revive the drooping spirits of anti-slavery forces and inspire the English people into vigorous activity for the cause of abolition. His talents and reputation were enough, but the report of his implication in the Harpers Ferry affair and his narrow escape from imprisonment were additional guarantee that he would address capacity audiences. The British *Anti-Slavery Reporter* was confident that Douglass' visit would do much "to stimulate the energy and increase the efficiency of the existing Societies, and to lead to the formation of many new ones."[1]

As in his previous visit thirteen years before, Douglass did much to strengthen the British anti-slavery movement. His lectures, dealing mainly with the significance of John Brown's raid and the anti-slavery interpretation of the Constitution, were not only well-attended but were widely distributed in pamphlet form. "His *powerful* and eloquent appeals," wrote James Walker, secretary of the Leeds Young Men's Anti-Slavery Society, "deepen our detestation of slavery, and have imparted to us a stronger impulse for, and led us more actively and devotedly into anti-slavery work than ever."[2] The impetus Douglass gave the British anti-slavery forces during his five months' visit in 1859-1860 became evident during the Civil War and was in some measure responsible for the tremendous support of the English masses for the Union cause.

Douglass' tour of England was cut short by the tragic news of the death of his youngest daughter, Annie, "the light and life of my house." Very devoted to her father, the ten-year-old child had grieved since his abrupt departure for Canada. She had been a constant companion of John Brown during the weeks he had spent in Rochester, and Douglass was convinced that her death in March, 1860, resulted from her anxiety over her father's safety, and "deep sorrow" for the death of the old man upon whose knee she had so often sat.

Although he was urged to continue his tour into Ireland and the south of England, Douglass decided "to fly to my sorrow-stricken family." He promised to resume his tour in the fall but this was not to be. He did not return to England until long after the Civil War. In the September, 1860, issue of his monthly he announced that he was giving up his plan to return to British soil where he breathed "freer . . . than elsewhere." "Were we to consult our own pleasure," he told his British friends, "our freedom from insult, proscription, social ostracism and oppression on account of color, we should be back to England in the next steamer. But we have something better than personal ease and security to live for, and that is the cause of our enslaved and oppressed people. That cause seems to make it our duty to stay here for the present." A presidential election was confronting the American people, and the public mind was "peculiarly awake. He who speaks now may have an audience. We wish to avail ourselves of the opportunity to strike while the iron is hot."[3]

When Douglass returned to this country, he found that the Presidential campaign was already under way. At their national convention at Charleston in April, the Democrats had split into two separate factions with Stephen A. Douglas heading one and John C. Breckenridge the other. Early the following month, the Constitutional Union Party had selected James A. Bell and Edward Everett as their candidates for President and Vice-President. In mid-May, the Republicans, in high glee over the dissension in the Democracy, assembled at Chicago and nominated Abraham Lincoln to head their national ticket.

The readers of *Douglass' Monthly* for June, 1860, were treated to a masterly analysis of the significance of Lincoln's nomination. Douglass did not share the prevailing opinion among eastern journalists that "the Rail-Splitter candidate" for President was an absolute nonentity whose nomination was the result of pure accident plus vote-swapping, logrolling and wirepulling. "Mr. Lincoln," he wrote, "is a man of unblemished private character; a lawyer, standing near the front rank at the bar of his own State, has a cool well balanced head; great firmness of will; is perseveringly industrious; and one of the most frank, honest men in political life. . . . His political life is thus far to his credit, but it is a political life of fair promise rather than one of rich heritage." Lincoln merited the support of the more radical elements among the Republicans. "In his debates with [Stephen A.] Douglas, he came fully up to the highest mark of Republicanism, and he is a man of will and nerve, and will not back down from his own assertions."

Douglass criticized the Republican Party for its slogan in the campaign "No more Slave States" instead of "Death to Slavery." He conceded, however, that the people were not yet ready for the more advanced slogan, and announced that as between the Democrats and the Republican Party, "incomplete as is its platform of principles," he could not hesitate to choose the latter. "While we should be glad to co-operate with a party fully committed to the doctrine of 'All rights, to all men,' in the absence of all hope of rearing up the standard of such a party for the coming campaign, we can but desire the success of the Republican candidates."[4]

When this was written, the Radical Abolitionist movement was quite dead. But in the excitement engendered by the Presidential campaign the political anti-slavery men felt that they could stage a comeback. On August 29, they met in convention at Syracuse. Douglass attended this meeting and was appointed to the Business Committee which presented the resolutions to the gathering. These resolutions condemned the Democratic Party, but also indicted the Republican Party for its "almost infinitesimal amount of anti-slavery professions" which were "inadequate

. . . to 'quiet the agitation' upon the subject of the slave's right to liberty."⁵ Unwilling to go along with the Republicans, the convention nominated Gerrit Smith and Samuel McFarland on a strong anti-slavery platform. Douglass was chosen as one of two presidential electors-at-large, the first time a Negro was nominated for such a position.

Three weeks after the Radical Abolition National Convention, Douglass went to Worcester to attend an adjourned meeting of a Political Anti-Slavery Convention called by Stephen S. Foster and John Pierpont "to consider the propriety of organizing a *Political Party* upon an Anti-Slavery interpretation of the U. S. Constitution, with the avowed purpose of abolishing slavery in the states, as well as the Territories of the Union."⁶ For some time he had hesitated to attend the gathering in Worcester as he did not want to be snubbed by the Garrisonians scheduled to be present. But, dissatisfied with the inadequacies of the Republican platform, he was anxious to co-operate with Foster in the endeavor "to re-unite the scattered anti-slavery elements of the country, and produce one solid abolition organization, who will use all the powers of the Federal as well as State Governments of the country for the abolition of slavery."⁷ So he attended the convention.

Douglass served on the Executive Committee, and introduced a resolution extending "earnest sympathy and their hearty God-speed for the little band of faithful Abolitionists which has nominated Gerrit Smith as their candidate to be supported for the Presidency in the coming election." Despite the opposition of the Garrisonians who still clung to their non-voting beliefs, the resolution was adopted.⁸

In October, Douglass advised his readers that ten thousand votes for Gerritt Smith would accomplish more for the abolition of slavery than two million for Lincoln, "or any man who stands pledged before the world against the interference with slavery in the slave states and who is not opposed to making free states a hunting ground for men under the Fugitive Slave Law."⁹ What part Douglass played in the Presidential campaign during the next few weeks is difficult to decide. In his autobiography Douglass stated that he worked actively for Lincoln's election during the closing month of the campaign.

"Against both Douglas and Breckenridge," he wrote, "Abraham Lincoln proposed his grand historic doctrine of the power and duty of the National Government to prevent the spread and perpetuity of slavery. Into this contest I threw myself, with firmer faith and more ardent hope than ever before, and what I could do by pen or voice was done with a will."¹⁰

Knowing how suddenly Douglass had switched to Frémont in 1856, it is not at all unlikely that, as the campaign developed, he decided it was wiser to use whatever influence he could wield to secure a Republican victory rather than waste it on a fruitless effort for Gerrit Smith. It is certain that in October he agreed with Smith that the weaknesses in the Republican Party were such as made it "unworthy the support of all genuine Abolitionists," but at the same time he criticized his fellow-reformers for lumping the Republican Party with the Democrats and indicating indifference as to which party triumphed. Douglass argued that the Republican Party was "now the great embodiment of whatever political opposition to the pretensions and demands of slavery is now in the field," and that "a victory by it in the coming contest must and will be hailed as an anti-slavery triumph."[11]

Actually, most of Douglass' energy in the closing weeks of the campaign was directed toward securing the repeal of the New York state law requiring that Negro citizens own real estate valued at two hundred and fifty dollars as a condition for voting.[12] Some idea of the hysteria whipped up in the press over the proposed measure which would place Negro citizens on an equal footing with others in the exercise of the right of suffrage, can be gleaned from the following appeal in the *Brooklyn Daily Times:*

"Give the Negroes an unlimited suffrage, and the logical and inevitable result is a Negro alderman, a Negro representative on the county ticket, and so forth.

". . . If [the Negro] Alderman officiates in places of civil honor, with his badge and staff of office, can you deny him the entree to your semi-public assemblies—can you keep him from meeting even the ladies of your family, on many semi-public occasions, as a social equal?

". . . It needs no prophetic eye to foresee that ere long, the countless millions of Asiatic barbarians, Chinese and Japanese—will overflow the narrow limits in which these fecund hordes have been confined—and spread through the Pacific states, all over this continent. Gladly will the Negro voters of this State welcome these allies. The unrestricted franchise which we are now asked to extend to Negroes, may be a fearful weapon when turned against us."[13]

In the face of such vicious outpourings, Douglass dedicated himself to the battle for an unrestricted franchise. For almost twelve weeks prior to November 6, he toured the western part of the state, distributing twenty-five thousand tracts on the *Suffrage Question in relation to colored voters* issued by "The New York City and County Suffrage Committee of Colored Citizens."[14] On election day, Douglass remained at the polls in Rochester from dawn to dusk to prevent fraudulent ballots from being cast. The defeat of the equal suffrage measure by a two-to-one majority[15] was a bitter pill to swallow.

What, asked Douglass, had the anti-slavery cause gained by Lincoln's election? His answer was:

"Not much, in itself considered, but very much when viewed in the light of its relations and bearings. For fifty years the country has taken the law from the lips of an exacting, haughty and imperious slave oligarchy. The masters of slaves have been masters of the Republic. Their authority was almost undisputed, and their power irresistible. They were the President makers of the Republic, and no aspirant dared to hope for success against their frown. Lincoln's election has vitiated their authority, and broken their power. It has taught the North its strength, and shown the South its weakness. More important still, it has demonstrated the possibility of electing, if not an Abolitionist, at least an *anti-slavery reputation* to the Presidency of the United States. The years are few since it was thought possible that the Northern people could be wrought up to the exercise of such startling courage. Hitherto the threat of disunion has been as potent over the politicians of the North, as the cat-o'-nine tails is over the backs of the slaves. Mr. Lincoln's election breaks this enchantment, dispels this terrible nightmare, and awakes the nation to the consciousness of new powers, and the possibility of higher destiny than the perpetual bondage to an ignoble fear."[16]

What next? The duty of the Abolitionists was clear. It was to revitalize their activities; organize, lecture, hold meetings, build the spirit manifested in the earlier stages of the anti-slavery movement; make this spirit the watch-dog of the Republican Party, preventing them from yielding to the demands of slavery and pushing them forward toward the total annihilation of the accursed system. For that goal, Douglass announced, he was prepared to work with any group, few or many.

It was no simple task, however, to revive the old spirit of the anti-slavery movement in the weeks following Lincoln's election. As threats of secession of the southern states mounted, northern conservatives tried to convince the slaveholders that they had nothing to fear from remaining in the Union. Personal liberty laws to prevent the return of fugitive slaves were repealed, resolutions condemning the Abolitionists were adopted by Union-Saving gatherings, and paid hoodlums were hired to disrupt anti-slavery meetings. Northern newspapers fanned the flames of hysteria, calling for demonstrations wherever Abolitionists gathered.[17]

Douglass was once again the special target for attack. At a meeting in Boston on December 3, 1860, to commemorate the anniversary of John Brown's execution, ruffians, hired by merchants engaged in the southern trade, invaded the hall, disrupted the proceedings, and singled out Douglass for attack. Fighting "like a trained pugilist," the Negro Abolitionist was thrown "down the staircase to the floor of the hall."[18]

The meeting was adjourned to a church on Joy Street. As the audience poured into the street, Negroes were seized, knocked down, trampled upon, and a number seriously injured. "The mob was howling with rage," Douglass recalled years later. "Boston wanted a victim to appease the wrath of the south already bent upon the destruction of the Union."[19]

A few days later, Douglass spoke in Boston's Music Hall and presented one of the most stirring pleas for free speech in American history. He described at length the attack on the meeting by both respectable gentlemen and rowdies. The right of free speech was basic to all other rights. No other right "was deemed by the fathers of the Government more sacred than the right of speech." "Liberty is meaningless," cried Douglass, "where the right to utter one's thoughts and opinions has ceased to exist." Nor did the right of free speech belong only to the rich and powerful. In words that have never lost their meaning, Douglass concluded:

"There can be no right of speech where any man, however lifted up, or however old, is overawed by force and compelled to suppress his honest sentiments. . . . When a man is allowed to speak because he is rich and powerful, it aggravates the crime of denying the right to the poor and humble. . . .

"A man's right to speak does not depend upon where he was born or upon his color. The simple quality of manhood is the solid basis of the right—and there let it rest forever."[20]

As the secession movement progressed, Douglass saw only one ray of hope for the cause—Lincoln's inauguration. His admiration of Lincoln had increased in the weeks following the election. He observed with satisfaction the President-elect's determination not to capitulate to the demands for a compromise policy that would appease secessionists and "his refusal to have concessions extorted from him under the terror instituted by thievish conspirators and traitors. . . ." The Negro leader shared Lincoln's attitude toward the pro-compromise advocates, pointing out: "All compromises are now but as new wine to old bottles, new cloth to old garments. To attempt them as a means of peace between freedom and slavery, is as to attempt to reverse irreversible law."[21]

Together with the entire nation Douglass looked forward to Lincoln's inaugural address. Late in February, 1861, a convention of slave owners had set up a provisional government at Montgomery, Alabama, with Jefferson Davis as President of the Confederate States of America. How would Lincoln meet this unprecedented crisis?

Douglass was bitterly disappointed by the inaugural address. Lincoln had pledged himself not to interfere directly or indirectly with slavery in the states where it then existed; promised to support the enforcement of the fugitive slave law; and declared he would maintain the Union. Douglass saw little in this message to gladden the hearts of the Negro people.

"Some thought we had in Mr. Lincoln the nerve and decision of an Oliver Cromwell," he wrote bitterly, "but the result shows that we merely have a continuation of the Pierces and Buchanans, and that the Republican President bends the knee to slavery as readily as any of his infamous predecessors."

Further analyzing the address, Douglass admitted that Lincoln's announcement "that the laws of the Union shall be faithfully executed in all the United States," was a significant advance over Buchanan's "shuffling, do-nothing policy." But he doubted whether the President had the courage to carry out his program. "It remains to be seen," he concluded, "whether the Federal Government is really able to do more than hand over some John Brown to be hanged, suppress a slave insurrection, or catch a runaway slave—whether it is powerless for liberty and only powerful for slavery."[22]

Viewing events following Lincoln's election, Douglass, for the first time since he had joined the anti-slavery movement, began to feel some doubt about the ultimate triumph of the cause. For years he had announced his conviction that forces of history were on the side of the Abolitionists, and that while they might suffer setbacks the final victory was theirs.

"In the spirit of the age," he had told an audience in Canandaigua in 1847 at a celebration of West India Emancipation, "in the voice of civilization, in the improvement of steam navigation, in every bar of railroad iron, I read the approach of that happy period, when, instead of being called upon to celebrate the emancipation of eight hundred thousand persons in the West Indies, we shall be summoned to rejoice over the downfall of Slavery in our own land."

Up to now, almost every speech and editorial contained some reference to the inevitability of emancipation. "The hour which shall witness the *final struggle,* is on the wing," he had assured Abolitionists in 1855. "Already we hear the *booming* of the bell which shall yet toll the death knell of human slavery." Anti-slavery men must not allow temporary discouragements to cause them to forget that "the Principles which form the basis of the Abolition movement . . . must triumph. . . ."[23] Precisely because he was convinced that the cause would triumph, he had used his pen and voice against all emigration schemes, believing that the free Negro people must remain in the land where they lived, where their brothers and sisters were held in slavery, and where they could contribute to the liberation of their people.

But events since the election of Lincoln—the repeal of the Personal Liberty Laws by the Republican legislatures and the attacks upon innocent Negro people by northern mobs—made Douglass doubt whether his confidence had been justified. He began to look with some favor on the emigration movement of Haiti.[24]

Early in April, 1861, Douglass made plans to visit Haiti so that he could investigate conditions for himself and report back to the people in the United States. His steamer, chartered by the Haitian Bureau of Emigration at Boston, was scheduled to sail on April 25. Douglass notified his readers that his trip would take about ten weeks.

Following this announcement was a paragraph which revealed that Douglass had fully recovered from his momentary feeling of despair:

"Since this article upon Haiti was put into type, we find ourselves in circumstances which induce us to forego our much desired trip to Haiti, for the present. The last ten days have made a tremendous revolution in all things pertaining to the possible future of the colored people in the United States. We shall stay here and watch the current of events, and serve the cause of freedom and humanity in any way that shall be open to us during the struggle now going on between the slave power and the government. When the Northern people have been made to experience a little more of the savage barbarism of slavery, they may be willing to make war upon it, and in that case we stand ready to lend a hand in any way we can be of service. At any rate, this is no time for us to leave the country."[25]

The events referred to were the firing on Fort Sumter by the Confederates, the call for volunteers by President Lincoln, and the outbreak of the Civil War.

WRITINGS AND SPEECHES OF FREDERICK DOUGLASS

Pre-Civil War Decade, 1850-1860

Let me give you a word of the philosophy of reform. The whole history of the progress of human liberty shows that all concessions yet made to her august claims, have been born of earnest struggle. The conflict has been exciting, agitating, all-absorbing, and for the time being, putting all other tumults to silence. It must do this or it does nothing. If there is no struggle there is no progress. Those who profess to favor freedom and yet deprecate agitation, are men who want crops without plowing up the ground, they want rain without thunder and lightning. They want the ocean without the awful roar of its many waters.

This struggle may be a moral one, or it may be a physical one, and it may be both moral and physical, but it must be a struggle. Power concedes nothing without a demand. It never did and it never will. Find out just what any people will quietly submit to and you have found out the exact measure of injustice and wrong which will be imposed upon them, and these will continue till they are resisted with either words or blows, or with both. The limits of tyrants are prescribed by the endurance of those whom they oppress. In the light of these ideas, Negroes will be hunted at the North, and held and flogged at the South so long as they submit to those devilish outrages, and make no resistance, either moral or physical. . . .

WEST INDIA EMANCIPATION SPEECH, AUGUST, 1857

HENRY CLAY AND SLAVERY

Long and assiduously have the derided and contemned advocates of emancipation labored in the work of disseminating their principles and opinions at the North; and anxiously have they looked forward to the period when these opinions and principles should be brought before the entire nation. That time has now arrived. Notwithstanding that the slaveholders of the South, with equal assiduity have been active in originating schemes, with a view to stay the progress of these opinions and principles, and in fortifying the system of slavery against attack, by trampling upon the right of petition, by suppressing free discussion, by fettering the American press, by gagging the American pulpit, and by enlarging their borders,—the judgment-day of slavery is dawning—the devices of the oppressor, thanks to the God of the oppressed, have most signally failed—the "wisdom of the crafty" has been confounded, and the "counsels of the ungodly have been brought to nought;" the great movement for freedom has rolled onward with a speed accelerated in proportion to the amount of opposition arrayed against it. This should be a time of rejoicing with the humble laborers in the cause. We speak advisedly, and in no canting spirit, when we term this cause holy; for if to have triumphed over foes mighty and multitudinous—to have removed mountains of difficulty,—if to have, with one, "chased a thousand," and with two, to have "put ten thousand to flight," be any evidence of the guardianship of Heaven, we can say, with one of old, "Truly the Lord is with us." This dreaded agitation, so feeble in its commencement, now rocks the land, from end to end. The vexed question of slavery has forced itself into the councils of the nation; and, like the rod of the Hebrew deliverer, it has swallowed up all other topics. Scarcely a day has passed since the meeting of the present Congress, but that the hated subject has been the theme of fiery discourse. Our entire exchange comes to us laden with leaders and speeches on this once obscure and strictly avoided topic. The public mind has reached a point of interest and excitement unprecedented. The South demands the extension of slavery into the new territories; while the North sternly insists upon its exclusion; but words pass on both sides, and the waves of agitation rise higher and higher. It is at this juncture that the crafty Clay, with his characteristic temper and skill, has thrown himself on the turbid waters of debate. He comes, as he is wont to do, with that soft and gentle diction, and in that spirit of conciliation and compromise, for which he has been so long and so highly distinguished. He wishes, as usual, to revive the expiring embers of patriotism—to soothe all asperities—to allay all sectional jealousies, and to knit the nation into a firmer bond of union. He has presented a string of resolutions to the Senate, for the purpose, (to use his own language,) of making *an amicable arrangement of all questions in controversy between the free and the slave States, growing out of the subject of slavery.* [1] This object, it must be admitted, is a comprehensive one; and it displays no small ambition that any one man should essay to accomplish it. But let this pass. Will he succeed? is the question. We think not. The plan which Mr. Clay proposes, like all Southern compromises, gives everything to Liberty, *in words,* and secures everything to Slavery, *in deeds.* He is most generous in giving away that which he does not possess; but is never betrayed into the weakness of bestowing that which he has the power to retain. The first Resolution of his compromise goes the enormous length of proposing the admission of California into the Union, without forcing her to open her golden domain to the foul and corrupting system of slavery. What a magnificent concession is here! Ought not every Northern man to bow, with grateful emotion, to the magnanimous man by whom it is proffered? This liberal and generous concession, to be fully appreciated, must be viewed in the light of certain notorious facts. The first fact is, that California has already, with singular unanimity, adopted a constitution which excludes for ever the foul system of bondage from her borders. The next fact is, that she has already received, from the present Administration of the United States government, especial marks of its approbation. Another fact is, with the growing population of California, her vast extent and boundless wealth, she is, of herself sufficiently strong to command respect, without asking the favor of any; and the last and most important fact of all is, that the North has the disposition and power to admit her into the Union, with or without the generous compromise, so nobly and complacently presented by that father of compromises, Henry Clay. Mr. Clay's proffered liberality is about as noble as that of a highwayman, who, when in the power of a traveller, and on his way to prison, proposes a consultation, and offers to settle the unhappy difficulty which has occurred between himself and the latter, by accepting the half of the contents of his purse, assuring him, at the same time, that IF his pistol had NOT missed fire, he might have possessed himself of the whole. This assuming to concede, as a mark of liberality, the right of a State to enter this Union, without being compelled to have the foul curse of slavery fastened upon her, would be about as ridiculous as it is disgraceful; but that the slightest token of concession, on the part of the South to the North, is hailed by so many doughfaces with marks of humble gratitude! The impudence of slaveholders exceeds everything! They talk about *the rights* (*!!*) of slavery, just as if it were possible for slavery to have rights. The *right* to introduce it into the new territories! the constitutional right, &c. Shame on such insolent pretensions! Slavery has NO RIGHTS. It is a foul and damning outrage upon all rights, and has no right to exist anywhere, in or out of the territories. "The earth is the Lord's," and "righteousness" should "cover it;" and he who concedes any part of it to the introduction of slavery, is an enemy to God, an invader of his dominion, and a rebel against his government.

The next resolution of Mr. Clay adopts practically, the non-intervention doctrine so universally held up to ridicule by the Whig press of the North, as the offspring of that prince of sycophants, Gen. Cass. They are as follows:

"Resolved, that the western boundary of the State of Texas, ought to be fixed on the Rio del Norte, commencing one marine league from its mouth, and running up that river to the Southern line of New Mexico; thence with that line eastwardly, and so continuing in the same direction, to the line established between the United States and Spain, excluding any portion of New Mexico, whether lying on the east or west of that river.

"Resolved, That it be proposed to the State of Texas, that the United States will provide for the payment of all that portion of the legitimate and *bona fide* public debt of that State, contracted prior to its annexation to the United States, and for which the duties on foreign imports were pledged by the said State to its creditors, not exceeding the sum of $——, in consideration of the said duties so pledged having been no longer applicable to that object, after the said annexation, but having thenceforward become payable to the United States; and upon the condition, also, that the State of Texas shall, by some solemn and authentic act of her Legislature, or of a Convention, relinquish to the United States any claim which it has to any part of New Mexico."

No comments on the foregoing resolutions, are needed from us. We put them on record merely as links in the chain of this compromise. It will be seen that Mr. Clay does not concede the justice of the claims which Texas has recently set up, for a large portion of New Mexico. So far so good.

The fifth and sixth resolutions are as follows:

"Resolved, That it is inexpedient to abolish Slavery in the District of Columbia, while that institution continues to exist in the State of Maryland, without the consent of that State, without the consent of the people of the District, and without just compensation to the owners of slaves within the District.

"But, Resolved, That it is expedient to prohibit within the District the slave-trade, in slaves brought into it from States or places beyond the limits of the District, either to be sold therein as merchandize, or to be transported to other markets without the District of Columbia."

If the abolition of slavery is to depend upon the assent of the slave-holders of Maryland, and the other contingencies specified, it is easy to see that slavery in the District of Columbia cannot be reached until the last vestige of slavery has disappeared from the State of Maryland. When that event takes place, there will be no necessity for compromise. And so far as these resolution have any bearing at all, their effect will be to clog the wheels of emancipation.

What is said about abolishing the slave-trade in the District of Columbia, is a mere *ruse:* since the slavetraders of Maryland can easily reside in Washington, and sell their slaves out of that city, under the very management which pretends to obstruct the trade. While slavery remains in the District, and the right to buy and sell is retained by the slaveholders, it will be impossible to suppress the slave-trade there.

The seventh resolution in the series is as follows:

"Resolved, That more effectual provision ought to be made by law, according to the requirement of the Constitution, for the restitution and delivery of persons bound to service or labor in any State who may escape into any other State or territory in the Union."

Hardened as we have had reason to believe Mr. Clay to be, and inconsistent as he always is, we scarcely expected such a resolution from him as the foregoing, at this time, and in such a connection. When the sympathy of the nation has, by his eloquence and that of others, just been wrought up to the greatest intensity for the Hungarian fugitives from oppression, that he should propose *such* a resolution, at *such* a time, for hunting down fugitives *in our own land,* who are fleeing from a bondage and tyranny far more terrible than that of Austria, is almost as shocking to our sense of consistency and propriety, as it is revolting to our moral perceptions of right and wrong.

But we give Mr. Clay's eighth and last resolution, that the reader may judge for himself as to the benefit which freedom will derive from this mis-named compromise. To us, the whole seems like the handle of a jug—all on one side.

"Resolved, That Congress has no power to prohibit or obstruct the trade in slaves between the slaveholding States; but that the admission or exclusion of slaves brought from one into another of them, depends exclusively upon their own particular laws."

This resolution declares what is not true.—If there be any meaning in words, the Constitution of the U. S. does confer upon Congress full powers to abolish the slave trade between the States. Having already extended this article beyond the limits we had prescribed, we bring it at once to a close.—F. D.

The North Star, February 8, 1850

WEEKLY REVIEW OF CONGRESS

Great speakers, rather than great speeches, have signalised the proceedings of Congress during the past week. John C. Calhoun, of South Carolina, and Daniel Webster, of Massachusetts, the former representing truly the slaveholding spirit of his State, and the latter as truly *misrepresenting* the anti-slavery sentiment of Massachusetts, have presented to the Senate and the country their views on the all-engrossing subject of slavery;[2] and neither of them, in our judgment, has added anything tending towards its final adjustment.

Of the two speeches, that of Mr. Calhoun, though exceedingly defective, is the more creditable and praiseworthy. It is plain, straightforward and consistent, and it shows that the object aimed at, infernal though it be, is devoutly wished for by its author. But, while it possesses these qualities, the speech will, doubtless, disappoint and mortify many of Mr. Calhoun's friends at the South, by the hopelessness of its spirit, the tameness of its tone, and the staleness of the material of which it is composed. On listening to its delivery, his ultra Southern friends must have felt, as Webster once said, under a slight disappointment, "This is not the entertainment to which we were invited." Something brilliant and powerful was expected; and something dim and weak was given.

The master-spirit of the South, the great champion of human bondage, upon whom, at the present crisis, all eyes are turned, and in whose movements the whole nation is profoundly interested, speaks, and the magic charm is broken! The mighty man of slavery is found to be mightier in his silence than in his eloquence. While he could shroud himself in mystery, he seemed a giant; but—his voice heard, his views expressed, his measures proposed—and he at once shrinks into a pale, feeble and deathly skeleton! So lifeless and powerless has this lion become, that even hangman Foote, the common buffoon of the Senate, dares to withstand him to the face. We repeat, and repeat gratefully, *the tyrant power of Calhoun, in this nation, is broken;* the great object of his life has been attacked by an overwhelming force; and he has no arm to defend it. Amen! even so let it be with all the defenders of slavery and oppression!

We can do no more in our present number, than give a synopsis of the most striking features of this long looked-for, much-dreaded, but really harmless speech of Mr. Calhoun.

His exordium shows that the speaker had, from the first, a clear insight into the nature of the whole anti-slavery movement at the North; and that he clearly foresaw what would be its effect upon the public mind, if it were allowed to proceed. It was plain to him, that a thoroughly anti-slavery conscience, a deep conviction of the sin of slavery, could not long rest under the restraints, nor long abide by what are called the compromises of the Constitution. It was easy for such a mind as his to see the ultimate conclusion, from the premise that "Slavery is a sin;" that that granted, all things by which it is upheld, must fall or flourish with it; that war cannot be made upon slavery, without also attacking the arrangements that uphold it; that the demand urged by William Lloyd Garrison, for a dissolution of the Union, is simply the legitimate inference from the principle that "slaveholding is sin."

In describing the disease of, or the cause of weakness to the Union, Mr. Calhoun is far more successful than in prescribing a remedy for its removal. The South is discontented, alarmed and excited. Religious ties between the North and the South, have been broken. Powerful and influential denominations, which once formed a strong bond of union between the two sections, have been riven by the explosive force of anti-slavery discussion. Political ties have yielded to the same power. The North has rapidly increased in population and in political strength. The equilibrium between the North and the South, which existed at the commencement of the government, has been seriously disturbed, and is still further threatened, by the restless progress of freedom; and general apprehension and alienation prevail. This is a brief description of the disease of the body politic, and which, according to Mr. Calhoun, endangers the stability of the Union.

Now, to remedy these evils, to allay discontent, to remove unfriendly feeling, to dispel fears, and to produce harmony and union, Mr. Calhoun proposes an amendment of the Constitution! "Most lame and impotent conclusion!" He must amend, or rather deform the constitution of human nature; he must make wrong equal to right—cruelty equal to kindness—and injustice equal to justice, in loveliness and good report among men, before he can hope to establish a permanent equilibrium between Slavery and Liberty. It is idle for statesmen to legislate against the anti-slavery sentiment. God has legislated in its favor; and, in the language of Brougham, "while men loathe rapine and hate fraud, they shall reject with indignation the wild and guilty fantasy that man may hold property in man." No! Mr. Calhoun; melancholy as the truth may be to the dealers in human flesh, no constitutional change, no legislative enactment, no human contract nor agreement, can save the accursed system of human bondage from the decay and death to which God and Nature have doomed it. Within or without the Union, Slavery must fall; the long-crushed Negro *must rise;* Ethiopia must stretch out her hands unto God; and not all the enactments of human codes can prevent this Heaven-ordained consummation.

Abolitionists can desire no stronger evidence of the efficiency of their measures for the accomplishment of their object, than is given them in the speech of the great South Carolinian. His testimony is full, clear and unequivocal. He has traced the movement through its various stages of progress; from the time when it was spoken of with contempt, to the present period, when it compels respect. We regret to say, that he has over-estimated the number of those at the North, who are really hostile to slavery, and who are actively seeking its abolition. The genuine friends of Freedom are comparatively few and poor in purse. They are, however, under God, "the little leaven that shall leaven the whole lump."

And now to Mr. Webster. We have read his speech through—a heavy task, truly; and we breathe more freely, since we have completed it. Sydney Smith once said, that "whatever question might arise, as to the usefulness of middle men, in the letting out of estates, no one could doubt their utility in standing between Jeremy Bentham and the public." We think the same true, as regards the long speeches of Webster and Cass. They both need the services of a faithful friend, to abridge and compress their tedious productions, that the public may not be deterred from bestowing upon them the distinction which they really merit.

Mr. Webster is eloquent; Mr. Webster is grand; Mr. Webster is patriotic; but neither his eloquence, his grandeur nor his patriotism, can save this speech of his from the overwhelming condemnation of all liberal and high-minded men. It was not the speech for the occasion. An oppor-tunity was presented for the display of the orator's great powers, in a manner which would have done essential service to the cause of human freedom, and have carried his name down with blessings to posterity. But he has occupied his time to no good purpose. His sketch of the rapid settle-ment of California, and of the manner in which that territory and New Mexico, were acquired by this Government, are familiar to all; and being, like his history of Slavery in all countries and ages, destitute of moral feel-ing, and not even having the merit of an apparent end or aim, need not be repeated in our columns. His remarks, too, on the separation of the Methodist Episcopal church, which divided on the question of slavery, show that a man, how largely soever endowed with intellect, may yet be wholly devoid of that higher quality, moral integrity.

Upon this subject, Mr. Webster presents us with a specimen of his skill, in the art of substituting darkness for light, and bitter for sweet, and of the manner in which he can confound ignorant bigotry with uncom-promising and intelligent fidelity to principle.

The following was, doubtless, intended as a thrust at those Abolition-ists from whom he has received no small share of honest rebuke, for his inconsistent and temporising course on the subject of slavery:

"They deal with morals as with mathematics, and they think what is right, may be distinguished from what is wrong, with the precision of an algebraic equation. They have, therefore none too much charity toward others who differ with them. They are apt, too, to think that nothing is good but what is perfect, and that there are no compromises or modifications to be made in submission to difference of opinion, or in deference to other men's judgment. If their perspicacious vision enables them to detect a spot on the face of the sun, they think that a good reason why the sun should be struck down from Heaven. They prefer the chance of running into utter darkness to living in heavenly light, if that heavenly light be not absolutely without any imperfection. There are impatient men—too impatient always to give heed to the admonition of St. Paul, 'that we are not to do evil that good may come'—too impatient to wait for the slow progress of moral causes in the improvement of mankind."

Why is it that men may not ascertain with certainty, as to what is right, and what is wrong? The only reason is, that they allow their own fancied interest to warp their judgments. There is no real difficulty in arriving at right conclusions, in a case so plain as that of slavery; for with respect to this giant sin, if "a man's eye be single, his whole body may be full of light."

Mr. Webster refers to the state of feeling which pervaded this country, before, and at the adoption of the United States Constitution; but how? For what purpose? *Not* with a view to inspire the present generation with a similar feeling. *Not* to kindle in the bosoms of the sons, a desire to carry into practice the views and sentiments of their ancestors, by destroying what *they* pronounced an evil, but, sad to say, for the low purpose of excusing and palliating the freedom with which the system of slavery is now denounced in the southern section of the Union. Instead of summoning the spirits of the departed, to aid in the defence of Liberty, he invokes them merely to propitiate the dark embodiment of Slavery.

Mr. Webster reviews the annexation of Texas to the Union, and the motives which prompted its annexation; and, in order to be faithful to the history of that transaction, he was compelled to charge Mr. Calhoun, as one of the prominent actors in it, with seeking, in the consummation of that measure, to strengthen the slave interests of the country. The New England orator here complimented the champion of slavery for his boldness and manliness. This was a blunder which a man of Mr. Webster's wit and sagacity might have been expected to avoid; since it was well calculated to provoke comparisons, and perhaps even to call forth rebuke, that he honored in another the virtue of which he himself is most destitute.

Calhoun is open and candid, as we have elsewhere said. He is a statesman of whose position no doubt need be entertained. He uses language to declare, and not to conceal his sentiments and designs. In this the dark orator of the North might well learn of Calhoun. But we are digressing.

On the question of the exclusion of slavery from the territories acquired from Mexico Mr. Webster stands, practically, upon the ground of General Cass, General Taylor and the Cabinet. The difference between them, (if any exist) is merely theoretical. The former would excuse his unfaithfulness to Liberty, and his treachery to the North, by demonstrating the unfitness of those countries for slavery, and by solemn assurances against the possibility of its introduction into those territories; and the latter would plead the same assumption as an apology to slaveholders and the South, for refusing a positive enactment for its introduction. There seems to have been a general understanding among the old politicians, on this subject—a regular combination to defeat the rising spirit of freedom. Nothing is heard now in the Senate, of the Wilmot Proviso. Messrs. Webster, Clay, Cass, Benton, Berrian, and other leading men, have united in denouncing it, as unnecessary, irritating and injurious. Webster has the honor, thus far, of giving the last stab to this youthful agent of Liberty. He claimed it once as his child, and charged Mr. Wilmot with "stealing his thunder." If he has not murdered his own child, it has been from no want of disposition so to do. He ridicules the Proviso, and derides its advocates in a manner far more calculated to irritate and to provoke resentment from the North, than the speeches of Cass, Benton, and Clay.

From the subject of the Wilmot Proviso, the speaker passes to the alleged grievances of the two sections of the Union. These, however, are mainly set down to the account of the North; and the chief of them he attributes to the bad faith of the free States, in their action on the subject of returning fugitive slaves to bondage. He has the hardihood and cold-blooded villainy to openly advocate the return of slaves to bondage, as a duty which the Free States are solemnly and religiously bound to discharge. His views on this subject, concur with those of Clay, Meade, and the most obdurate slavecatcher and man-trapper of the South. He does not even intimate the necessity of guarding the rights of the free colored citizens of his own State; but he avows his intention to vote for the bill of Mr. Meade, with all its horrid peculiarities. Like Clay, he goes beyond the decision of the Supreme Court, in the case of Prigg *vs*. Pennsylvania,[3] and would take the work of slave-hunting and slave-capturing from the general Government, and bind it upon the shoulders of the Free States.

He next considers the grievances of the South; that there are Abolition Societies at the North. He thinks that they have not produced anything good or valuable; that they have put back the cause; that they have spent money enough to purchase all the slaves in Maryland; that they have bound the slaves more firmly, &c. &c. Having denounced the Abolition Societies, and apologised for the violence of the Northern Press, he eulogises the Union and ridicules the idea of its peaceful dissolution. He then avows himself a colonizationist, and closes his lengthy speech with the following appropriate, significant and humiliating application to his Southern masters, for the office of President:

"And now, Mr. President, I draw these observations to a close. I have spoken freely, and I meant to do so. I have sought to make no display; I have sought to enliven the occasion by no animated discussion; I have sought only to speak my sentiments fully and at large, being desirous once, and for all, to let the Senate know, and to let the country know, the opinions and sentiments which I entertain on all these subjects. These opinions are not likely to be suddenly changed. If there be any future service that I can render to the country, consistently with these sentiments and opinions, I shall cheerfully render it. If there be not, I shall still be glad to have any opportunity to disburden my conscience from the bottom of my heart, and to make known every political sentiment that therein exists."

Well done, Daniel! you've done the work, and it's proper to ask for the pay. You have betrayed "innocent blood"—why should you be denied the "thirty pieces of silver"?—F. D.

The North Star, March 15, 1850

OATH TO SUPPORT THE CONSTITUTION

The present is a peculiarly fitting time to examine the nature of, and the obligations imposed by, an oath to support the Constitution of the United States. The recent speech of the Hon. W. H. Seward[4] has attracted the public mind, with much interest, to this particular point, and has called forth a torrent of conflicting opinions on the subject, from the presses of the two great political parties. His recognition in that speech, of authority higher than the Constitution, of obligations not to be repealed

by human enactments, has carried intense alarm into the foremost ranks of each political organization. They stand appalled—terror-stricken, at the approach of this heavenly truth—and howl under its touch. . . .*
Gen. Cass, the head of American Democracy, has pronounced the speech in question the most *dangerous* of any he ever listened to in the Senate. The Taylor party are said to repudiate it. "Doughfaces" [5] at the North and Slaveholders at the South, have been alike stunned by it, and even the political friends of Mr. Seward cannot wholly endorse it. They bestow upon his masterly effort a large amount of *general* praise, but it is *"general."* It is declared by them to speak the sentiment of the North, but they do not come to particulars. Meanwhile the Democratic press is pouring out its vials of wrath upon the head of the distinguished Senator. Now why is this timidity on the part of friends, and this bitterness on the part of enemies? The answer is—Wm. H. Seward has, (in the face of this Christian country!) intimated a belief that the Authority of the Most High God is greater than the authority of man!

> *The very head and front of his offending,*
> *Hath this extent; no more.*

It must be confessed, that, while Mr. Seward has said many other excellent things, the idea to which we have above referred, constitutes the chief peculiarity of his speech, and forms the chief ground of offense. But for *this,* he might have passed unscathed. Calhoun would not have denounced him as a cut-throat, nor would the Republic have repudiated him as a member of the Whig party. For the utterance of that sentiment he is to be visited with political excommunication, and to be branded as a political heretic. All this may be inferred from what is transpiring around us; and the mind naturally inquires, what is to be the result of such a course? To us it seems clear, that a more suicidal policy could not be adopted by the Northern Whigs, than to oppose and make Wm. H. Seward the object of attack. If the Whig party wish to cover itself with odium, and to encounter a storm more terrible than the whirlwind itself, let it come out and declare before all Israel and the sun, that there is no God higher than the Constitution, and let it further pronounce political annihilation on every man who will not receive upon his brow their mark of rank atheism. Such a course might for a time cover the party with a blaze of glory; but the day of retribution would come at last; and "Ichabod" would certainly be written upon the walls of Whiggery. For,

*One line illegible in the original copy of the paper.—*Ed.*

dark and depraved on this subject as the great majority of the people of the free States are, they are not yet so sunken in atheism, nor so lost to all sense of consistency, as to permit such foul blasphemy to pass without their reprobation. We say again—let Whigs and Democrats make war on Wm. H. Seward; let them seek to inflame the public mind against him; and they will have, for their pains, the creation of a new and powerful Northern party, which will not leave "the Hunkers" of either a leg to stand upon. The man who could calmly and distinctly advance such sentiments as did W. H. Seward in the American Senate, the very stronghold of slavery, is a man who will not be easily silenced nor subdued. His native manliness will command respect, and his high endowments will draw round him the better portion of the American people. He has already given form, force and expression to the latent thoughts and feelings which have long groaned and sighed for utterance in the bosoms of Northern religious men; and should he become the object of general attack, this class would rally around him; and their love for him, and their adherence to him, would increase, just in proportion to the intensity and bitterness of the assaults made upon him.

But it was not our purpose to defend, nor to eulogise Mr. Seward. That we feel a warm gratitude to him, and to other Senators and Representatives, who have stood forth in defense of justice, is most true. We think that Mr. Seward shares the grateful regard of every colored man in the land; and yet, it becomes us to state, that even with him we cannot fully agree. While we thank him for extending to us all the legal protection which the Constitution—strained to its utmost tension—will allow; while we thank him for demanding the Rights of *Habeas Corpus* and Jury Trial, for the fugitive from bondage, we submit that no such trial can be rightfully had, as the trial of a man for his freedom. To be arrested for being at large, even before a jury, is a hardship too great to be quietly endured by any man. We therefore think, that no arrest should be made, no trial should be had, on the ground that a man is alleged to have been held in bondage. The slaveholders of the South should be made to know that Northern ground cannot be polluted; and that Northern people will not submit to be shocked and insulted by any such atrocious proceedings in their midst. But then, we are asked, what becomes of the Constitution and of the oath to support it? We answer, that the oath requires that which is morally impossible.

Among the many truths which have been elicited during the present discussions, we have been impressed with none more than this; that the whole framework of the American government is radically at fault; that it is founded on a gross and scandalous fraud; that in it are comprised two distinct and hostile elements; and that no Jesuitism can ever reconcile and render them consistent.

Liberty and Slavery—opposite as Heaven and Hell—are both in the Constitution; and the oath to support the latter, is an oath to perform that which God has made impossible. The man that swears to support it vows allegiance to two masters—so opposite, that fidelity to the one is, necessarily, treachery to the other. If we adopt the preamble, with Liberty and Justice, we must repudiate the enacting clauses, with Kidnapping and Slaveholding. It is this radical defect in this Constitution—this war of elements, which is now rocking the land. There is a deep reason for the singular attitude in which the straight forward opponents of slavery are now placed, contending as they are for the very measure as a means of preserving freedom, which the Slaveholders threaten to adopt as the last resort to uphold slavery. Garrison sees in the Constitution precisely what John C. Calhoun sees there—a compromise with Slavery—a bargain between the North and the South; the former to free his soul from the guilt of slaveholding, repudiates the bond; and the latter, seeing the weakness of mere parchment guarantees, when opposed to the moral scope of the parties to meet, seeks a dissociation of the Union as his only means of safety. This fundamental contradiction in the Constitution is the real cause of the present storm-tossed condition of the public mind. The South have looked to the Constitution, from the ramparts of Slavery, and have seen in it their highest power of defense. Slaveholders have sworn to support it as such, and have never sworn to support the whole Constitution. On the other hand, Northern men have recognised in the instrument the principles of liberty and justice; and have scarcely observed the pro-slavery principle cunningly wrought into the instrument. The opposite view, therefore, of the Constitution and its requirements, is the primary cause of the present agitation.

The question arises, as to who is right in this contest? We answer, so far as the Constitution is concerned, that all are wrong; and necessarily so; since neither party, North nor South, could, if they would be faithful to the requirements of the oath to support the Constitution of the United States. Every slaveholder in the land stands perjured in the sight of Heaven, when he swears his purpose to be, the establishment of justice—the providing for the general welfare, and the preservation of liberty to the people of this country; for every such slaveholder knows that his whole life gives an emphatic lie to his solemn vow. And how stands the case with our Free Soil friends, who swear to promote the Constitution! Why, they differ from the slaveholder only in motive. They swear to promote the Constitution, as a means of promoting beneficent measures; and under a certain system of reasoning, based on alleged necessity, they justify their oath. They have our sympathies, but not our judgment. They have a theory of human government, which makes it necessary to do evil, that good may come. We are not convinced that that theory is correct; and we must continue to hold, for the present, that the Constitution, being at war with itself, cannot be lived up to, and what we cannot do, we ought not to swear to do; and that, therefore, the platform for us to occupy, is outside that piece of parchment.—F. D.

The North Star, April 5, 1850

COLORED MEN SPEAKING OUT

But for our absence from home last week, we should have accompanied the spirited account of the meeting in Shiloh Presbyterian church, New York, with some remarks of our own. It is always gratifying to us to observe any public demonstration on the part of our white friends in favor of our rights but for many reasons, it is far more cheering to observe such movements among ourselves. We may be grateful that British benevolence has distributed millions to feed the Irish poor, but a higher and happier emotion is awakened, when we learn that those destitute millions are, in the spirit of a manly independence industriously laboring to supply their own wants. In like manner do we look upon the efforts of our own people, as compared with those made by others. It is evident, that in such a crisis the colored man has a duty to perform. His voice cannot now be deemed impertinent. The measures maturing at Washington are not only intended to fasten the chains of slavery more firmly upon the limbs of the slave, and to make the North less secure for the fugitive; but they strike a fatal blow at the liberty of every free colored man in the North.

We are therefore happy, that at such a time, the colored citizens of New York and Boston have come forth with their views on the subject. Philadelphia should speak. Its citizens are peculiarly exposed to the incursions of rapacious slavehunters; and in the event of the passing of Mason's

Bill,[6] we have no doubt that a vigorous slave-catching business will be driven in Philadelphia.

There are those who think that the proposed law, if passed, will become a dead letter. We differ from such persons. If there be not sufficient moral power arrayed against it, to defeat its adoption, from whom can we expect the moral power to defeat its execution? There are those in our large cities who would delight in a slave-hunt, were they protected in the infernal chase by the sanction of law. Let us not be deceived. Those editors who stand by Webster and his slaveholding wickedness, afford no assurance that they are too virtuous to reduce their profligate theory to practice. The apology which they make for their position, is the Constitution; and that is broad enough to shelter any abomination.—F. D.

The North Star, April 12, 1850

TO HON. S. P. CHASE

Rochester, May 30, 1850

My dear Sir:

I feel honored by the receipt of your favor of 4th May and should have replied to it sooner, but for my absence from home. Please accept my thanks for the donation of five dollars as well for its moral as for its intrinsic value. On the subject on which you have done me the honor to ask my views, I have taken the liberty to enclose two articles from my pen originally published in my paper, the *North Star.* The article under the caption, "The Destiny of Colored Americans,"[7] although not as elaborate or as well supported as it might have been, contains my present opinion as to the possibility of our remaining in this country. You will observe that in my speculations I make no reference to climate and its influence in determining the question of our destiny. It is my humble opinion that this is a question with which climate and geography have but little to do. Experience, I think, has demonstrated beyond all reasonable doubt that the black man's constitution as readily adapts itself to one climate as another. I think that the causes likely to influence or affect our destiny are wholly moral and political, and although these do not appear very favorable to our remaining here viewed unconnected with the past, yet I think there has been no time in the history of our country when there were more favorable indications than are to be seen at this day.

Most gratefully yours,

Frederick Douglass

Samuel P. Chase Papers, Library of Congress

SHAMEFUL ABANDONMENT OF PRINCIPLE: inequality sanctioned.—Colored men degrading themselves.—Selling the cause of freedom for popular applause, and playing into the hands of their oppressors.

It becomes my duty, as an humble advocate of equal rights—as defender of the principle of human freedom—to record my earnest testimony at this crisis, against what appears to me to be a most disgraceful concession to the venomous hatred so strongly cherished in this city by the *white* against the *colored* people. When principle is sacrificed in high places—when high and important trusts have been scandalously abused—it becomes those who suffer from such apostasy to repudiate both the traitors and the treachery. This is their duty: to do boldly and earnestly, and at whatever cost of popular applause. To perform this duty I have thus promptly sent forth the *North Star Extra,* hoping that it may be the means of opening the eyes of many, who might else remain in darkness, and perhaps be allured from the cause of our common liberties. Should this good result be secured, it will be high compensation for all the abuse and misrepresentation to which I shall probably be subjected. But, without further preface, I lay before the reader a complete copy of a handbill which has been widely circulated in this city, and under which a large meeting has been held:

"THE FEDERAL CONSTITUTION *versus* NEGRO SLAVERY

"A Committee of White Citizens having been appointed, at the meeting at Franklin Hall, on Tuesday evening last, to request the Rev. Samuel R. Ward to address the citizens on the subject of Constitutional Slavery, have labored to procure a Hall for that purpose, but in vain—such is the prejudice against the Negro race. The Trustees of the Second Presbyterian Church in St. Mary Street, below Lombard, between Sixth and Seventh, have kindly tendered the use of their Church for that purpose. *The Lower Saloon will be appropriated exclusively to our White fellow citizens,* who are respectfully requested to attend, this evening, May 16th, at half-past seven o'clock, and listen to one of the most eloquent and powerful men in this country, whether White or Black. We are convinced that those having a prejudice against the race, after hearing him, will surrender the same."

You have read the handbill, and you already see in it that upon which I beg to offer a few remarks, and against which I would bear my humble, but not the less honest testimony. You have it here first stated that a *white* committee was appointed at Franklin Hall, to secure a place of meeting for Mr. Ward. Now, why was a *white* committee selected from a meeting composed of both white and colored persons? Was it because a committee composed in part of colored persons, would favor too much the idea of social equality?—or was it merely an act of courtesy towards the whites, and a mark of humility on the part of the colored people there assembled? For whatever reason the measure was adopted, I am opposed to all such measures, and of course heartily repudiate this. Away with all compromises to secure good-will, when the only condition upon which it can be attained is a sacrifice of self-respect and acknowledgment of our own inferiority! In the very first announcement, then, in this handbill, I find cause of complaint; and although the basis of that complaint, standing alone, might pass without animadversion, standing, as it does, in connection with other and more abnoxious features, I have felt fully justified in bestowing upon it this word of comment.

The reader is next informed by the authors of this handbill, that they have labored in vain to secure a Hall in which Mr. Ward might hold a meeting; and allege, as the reason of their failure, *"the prejudice against the Negro race."* This was undoubtedly the true reason—the "prejudice against the Negro race"—aye, the PREJUDICE! This unnatural, unreasoning and malignant prejudice is the secret of most of our social troubles and misfortunes. By it we are proscribed, plundered and oppressed. This it is that has shut us out not only from halls, from hotels, from steam-boat cabins, from the ballot-box, from lyceums, from place of amusement, from churches, from almost every honorable employment—but even from decent burial grounds in this city. Yes, it is this venomous prejudice that stands, as if armed with a thunderbolt, to strike dead any black man who dares to seek his own and the *true* elevation of his race. This prejudice it is which we are to meet, encounter and subdue, before any essential change for the better can take place in our condition. This is the Goliath which at present defies all the armies of Israel. And, alas! at the very moment when the colored people of this city had reason to hope that an effective blow would be dealt upon the head of this arch enemy, the very principle for which we are bound to contend, has been most cowardly and shamefully abandoned.

Here it is in these significant lines: read it again. "The Lower Saloon will be appropriated exclusively to our white fellow citizens!!! Who are respectfully requested to attend."

It is not easy to conceive of a more shameful concession to the spirit of slavery and prejudice than this. It is colonization sanctioned by the very men who profess to loathe and detest it. Separated from the circumstances, it is a violation of the very first principles of human brotherhood—for which the friends of freedom have contended for more than twenty years—it is the wholesale adoption of the mean and unchristian *"Negro pew"* system—which has been everywhere regarded as the strong bulwark of slavery and oppression. But taken in connection with the declared object of the meeting, the well known character of the gentleman for whom the meeting was convened, and the complexion of the people who own the Church in which the meeting was held—it is the most cowardly, contemptible and servile specimen of self-degradation which has ever come under my notice. It is literally admitting that all that has been said by our enemies, of our unfitness for the possession of equal rights and privileges in the relations of life, is true, and that it ought to be reduced to practice. What use will the revilers and slanderers of our people make of this concession? Why this, and none else than this:—that we are sensible of our own inferiority; that we know our place; that we are conscious of our own unfitness for the society of white people; that it is quite proper we should be separated from them in the house of prayer; that the two varieties of the same family ought not to be allowed to occupy an equal footing; that the lower and commodious part of the church—the house of *worship*—*should be reserved* for white people *exclusively,* and that colored people should be separated and sent up stairs—colonized. Such, then, are the inferences which our oppressors may naturally draw from this open and palpable abandonment of the doctrine and practice of human equality, into which the colored people of this city have been wantonly and scandalously betrayed. Let me ask those colored men who have sanctioned this disgraceful transaction, to show, if they can, what difference there is in the principle of *caste* and *exclusiveness* involved in this case—and the principle upon which Mr. Ward and colored men in general are excluded from the Chinese Museum? Is there any? Are not the two things founded on the same basis? Mr. Ward was excluded from the Chinese Museum because he was a "colored man." Colored men, by *this notice*, were *excluded* from the lowest part of St. Mary's Street Church—because of their color. The principle was the same in the one case as in the other and it is equally to be reprobated in both cases. He who approves the one has no right to condemn the other. "Out of thine own mouth will I condemn thee. Thou that sayest a man shalt steal, dost thou steal?" Thou that sayest that God is *impartial,* art thou partial? Will you condemn in others that which you justify in yourself? How long will it take you to convince [the] world of human equality and brotherhood by preaching, while you openly violate the principle in your practice? Is precept stronger than example? Will men reduce to practice that which the preacher himself tacitly admits to be impracticable? Alas! for human weakness and the spirit of compromise, which is here displayed!—purchasing the oppressor's favor by selling our birthright to liberty. This seeking our elevation in the very pathway to self-gradation will end only in disappointment, shame and confusion.

The question will naturally arise, as to how Mr. Ward and his friends will dispose of this handbill, and justify his speaking, and their assembling under its provisions. Upon this subject I cannot speak positively. I have understood from respectable sources, that Mr. Ward denies being the author of the handbill. This is good—so far as it goes—but to my apprehension it falls far short of exculpating him from just and severe censure. He does not, and cannot, deny that he was apprized of the infamous arrangement before the meeting took place. He knew all about the matter beforehand. His answer to one friend was, "that white men wrote the bill, and if there was anything wrong in it, white men must make it right."

Now this answer is anything than creditable to the honesty, consistency and good sense, of him who made it. It is evasive, unsatisfactory, and a mere quibble, which will only sink its author deeper in disgrace, than the act which he designed to shield from condemnation. In a matter of this sort, a man like Mr. Ward cannot be allowed neutral ground. He is here as an apostle of liberty and equality. He is jealously to watch over, and boldly to defend the cause of human freedom. What if Mr. Ward should throw off all responsibility in the matter of Slavery, and give up the contest, under the ridiculous pretext "that if there be any wrong in it, white men have committed the wrong, and white men must mend it." Would any man regard him in any other light than as an apostate?

The answer in question shows to what vile and paltry shifts, a man in a false position will resort. He was reminded of the nature of this "bill," by another friend who pointed out the objectionable feature which it contained, and made no answer at all. Now why was this course pursued by the eloquent Samuel R. Ward? Where was his sense of justice? Where was his impartiality? Where was his manly indignation? Why did he not denounce the whole transaction at once, and declare either that he would not speak under such a call, or that he would take this handbill as the basis of his discourse, and show the impropriety of sending forth such a handbill? But he made no such declaration, he manifested no sense of the insult offered to colored citizens, and worse still, attended the meeting, made an eloquent speech, treated his hearers to any quantity of fun, and never raised a whisper against the infamous handbill.

Now this leaves Mr. Ward without excuse. His silence at such a time was a sanction of the whole proceedings. He is responsible for the insult and degradation, offered to the colored citizens of Philadelphia. He might have cleared himself of all blame in the matter, by disclaiming the contents of that handbill, in the presence of the *"white committee,"* who are supposed to have framed it. This it seems he lacked the manliness to do. He could not so far test the sincerity of his new converts, and risk their applause, as to tell them that they were yet in the darkness of Slavery, and under the influence of prejudice; but glazed the whole matter over in silence. Now if this be fidelity, what is treachery? It is now no time to mince matters—no time to "run with the hare, and hold with the hound." The colored people of this city and country, have had enough of this playing fast and loose, and the time has come, unless I mistake the signs of the times, when they will demand of those who stand forth as their advocates, an inflexible adhesion to the principle of equal and impartial freedom.—F. D.

The North Star, May 30, 1850

AT HOME AGAIN

Having been, during the past few weeks, the special object of attack, marked out by a corrupt and fiendish Press, for assassination, the victim of a continuous train of almost unprecedented abuse—harassed and dogged from day to day by the furious blood-hounds of American Slavery,—I should be something more than a Stoic, if I did not feel and acknowledge a sense of profound gratitude to the God of the oppressed, that I am again permitted safely to occupy my editorial chair. Never since the day I entered the field of public effort in the cause of my enslaved brethren, have I been called to endure persecution more bitter, insults more brutal, violence more fierce, scorn and contempt more malicious and demoniacal, than that heaped upon me in the city of New York, during the past three weeks. I have been made to feel keenly that I am in an enemy's land—surrounded on all sides by hardships, difficulties and dangers—that on the side of the oppressor there is power, and that there are few to take up the cause of my deeply injured and down-trodden people. These things grieve, but do not appal me. Not an inch will I retreat—not one jot of zeal will I abate—not one word will I retract; and, in the strength of God, while the red current of life flows through my veins, I will continue to labor for the downfall of slavery and the freedom of my race. I am denounced as an offender. I am not ignorant of my offences. I plead guilty to the worst of those laid to my charge. Amplified as they have been, enormous as they are alleged to be, I do not shrink from looking them full in the face, and glorying in having committed them. My *crime* is, that I have assumed to be a man, entitled to all the rights, privileges and dignity, which belong to human nature—that color is no crime, and that all men are brothers. I have acted on this presumption. The very "head and front of my offending hath this extent—no more." I have not merely talked of human brotherhood and human equality, but have reduced that talk to practice. This I have done in broad open day, scorning concealment. I have walked through the streets of New York, in company with white persons, not as a menial, but as an equal. This was done with no purpose to inflame the public mind; not to provoke popular violence; not to make a display of my contempt for public opinion; but simply as a matter of course, and because it was right so to do. The right to associate with my fellow worms of the dust, on terms of equality, without regard to color, is a right which I will yield only with my latest breath.

My readers will have observed, in the *North Star* of last week, an account of a most cowardly assault made upon me in the Battery at New York. Like most other statements which emanate from the American press, this one (though partly true) is false in several particulars. It is not true that I walked down Broadway with two white females resting on my arm, in the case alluded to, although I *insist* upon the right to do so. It is not true that the ladies in company with me placed themselves under the care of the gentleman (ruffian?) who assaulted me, nor any of the villainous party, nor of anybody else. It is not true that I sneered or spoke to the loafing assailants. The facts briefly are these. Myself and friends were going to Philadelphia, and supposing that the "John Porter" departed from New York at twelve o'clock, we rode down a quarter before twelve but found on our arrival, that we had been mistaken; the time of starting being half-past one o'clock. The interval, therefore, we passed in the Battery. When about to leave for the Steamer, five or six men surrounded us, assailing us with all sorts of coarse and filthy language, and two of them finally struck the ladies on the head, while another attacked me. I warded off the blows with my umbrella, and the cowardly creatures left without doing any personal harm. Thinking that we should not be disturbed by them again we walked slowly toward the Steamer, one of the mob observing that I was off my guard, ran up behind me and before I could put myself in a position to ward off the assassin's blow, I was struck in the face. These are the whole facts in the case. I never was more calm or self-possessed than when under his beastly assault. I felt no indignation towards the poor miserable wretches who committed the outrage. They were but executing upon me the behests of the proslavery church and the clergy of the land; doing the dirty work of the men who despise them, and who have no more respect for them in reality than they have for me.

F.D.

The North Star, May 30, 1850

PREJUDICE AGAINST COLOR

Let no one imagine that we are about to give undue prominence to this subject. Regarding, as we do, the feeling named above to be the greatest of all obstacles in the way of the anti-slavery cause, we think there is little danger of making the subject of it too prominent. The heartless apathy which prevails in this community on the subject of slavery—the cold-blooded indifference with which the wrongs of the perishing and heart-broken slave are regarded—the contemptuous, slanderous, and malicious manner in which the names and characters of Abolitionists are handled by the American pulpit and press generally, may be traced mainly to the *malign* feeling which passes under the name of prejudice against color. Every step in our experience in this country since we commenced our anti-slavery labors, has been marked by facts demonstrative of what we have just said. The day that we started on our first anti-slavery journey to Nantucket, now nine years ago, the steamer was detained at the wharf in New Bedford two hours later than the usual time of starting, in an attempt on the part of the captain to compel the colored passengers to separate from the white passengers, and to go on the forward deck of that steamer; and during this time, the most savage feelings were evinced towards every colored man who asserted his right to enjoy equal privileges with other passengers.—Aside from the twenty months which we spent in England, (where color is no crime, and where a man's fitness for respectable society is measured by his moral and intellectual worth,) we do not remember to have made a single anti-slavery tour in any direction in this country, when we have not been assailed by this mean spirit of caste. A feeling so universal and so powerful for evil, cannot well be too much commented upon. We have used the term prejudice against color to designate the feeling to which we allude, not because it expresses correctly what that feeling is, but simply because that *innocent* term is usually employed for that purpose.

Properly speaking, *prejudice against color* does not exist in this country. The feeling (or whatever it is) which we call *prejudice,* is no less than a *murderous, hell-born hatred* of every virtue which may adorn the character of a *black man.* It is not the black man's color which makes him the object of brutal treatment. When he is drunken, idle, ignorant and vicious, *"Black Bill"* is a source of amusement: he is called a good-natured fellow; he is the first to [give] service in holding his horse, or blacking his boots. The white gentleman tells the landlord to give "Bill" *"something to drink,"* and actually drinks with "Bill" himself!—While poor black "Bill" will minister to the pride, vanity and laziness of white American gentlemen—while he consents to play the buffoon for their sport, he will share their regard. But let him cease to be what we have described him to be—let him shake off the filthy rags that cover him—let him abandon drunkenness for sobriety, industry for indolence, ignorance for intelligence, and give up his menial occupation for respectable employment—let him quit the hotel and go to the church, and assume there the rights and privileges of one for whom the Son of God died, and he will be pursued with the fiercest hatred. His name will be cast out as evil; and his life will be embittered with all the venom which hate and malice can generate. Thousands of colored men can bear witness to the truth of this representation. While we are servants, we are never offensive to the whites, or marks of popular displeasure. We have been often dragged or driven from the tables of hotels where colored men were officiating acceptably as waiters; and from steamboat cabins where twenty or thirty colored men in light jackets and white aprons were frisking about as servants among the whites in every direction. On the very day we were brutally assaulted in New York for riding down Broadway in company with ladies, we saw several white ladies riding with *black servants*. These servants were well-dressed, proud looking men, evidently living on the fat of the land—yet they were servants. They rode not for their own, but for the pleasure and convenience of white persons. They were not in those carriages as friends or equals.—They were there as appendages; they constituted a part of the magnificent equipages.—They were there as the fine black horses which they drove were there—to minister to the pride and splendor of their employers. As they passed down Broadway, they were observed with admiration by the multitude; and even the *poor* wretches who assaulted us might have said in their hearts, as they looked upon such splendor, "We would do so too if we could." We repeat, then, that color is not the cause of our persecution; that is, it *is not our color* which makes our proximity to white men disagreeable. The evil lies deeper than prejudice against color. It is, as we have said, an intense hatred of the colored man when he is distinguished for any ennobling qualities of head or heart. If the feeling which persecutes us were prejudice against color, the colored servant would be as obnoxious as the colored gentleman, for the color is the same in both cases; and being the *same* in both cases, it would produce the *same* result in both cases.

We are then a persecuted people; not because we are *colored,* but simply because that color has for a series of years been coupled in the public mind with the degradation of slavery and servitude. In these conditions, we are thought to be in our place; and to aspire to anything above them, is to contradict the established views of the community—to get out of our sphere, and commit the provoking sin of *impudence.* Just here is our sin: we have been a slave; we have passed through all the grades of servitude, and have, under God, secured our freedom; and if we have become the special object of attack, it is because we speak and act among our fellow-men without the slightest regard to their or our own complexion;—and further, because we claim and exercise the right to associate with just such persons as are willing to associate with us, and who are agreeable to our tastes, and suited to our moral and intellectual tendencies, without reference to the color of their skin, and without giving ourselves the slightest trouble to inquire whether the world are pleased or displeased by our conduct. We believe in human equality; that character, not color, should be the criterion by which to choose associates; and we pity the pride of the poor pale dust and ashes which would erect any other standard of social fellowship.

This doctrine of human equality is the bitterest yet taught by the abolitionists. It is swallowed with more difficulty than all the other points of the anti-slavery creed put together. "What, make a Negro equal to a *white* man? No, we will never consent to that! No, that won't do!" But stop a moment; don't be in a passion; keep cool. What *is* a white man that you do so revolt at the idea of making a Negro equal with him? Who made . . .* an angel of a man? "A man." Very well, he is a man, and nothing but a man—possessing the same weaknesses, liable to the same diseases, and under the same necessities to which a black man is subject. Wherein does the white man differ from the black? Why, one is white and the other is black. Well, what of that? Does the sun shine more brilliantly upon the one than it does upon the other? Is nature more lavish with her gifts toward the one than toward the other? Do earth, sea and air yield their united treasures to the one more readily than to the other? In a word, "have we not all one Father?" Why then do you revolt at that equality which God and nature instituted?

The very apprehension which the American people betray on this point, is proof of the fitness of treating all men equally. The fact that they fear an acknowledgment of our equality, shows that they see a fitness in such an acknowledgment. Why are they not apprehensive lest the horse should be placed on an equality with man? Simply because the horse is not a man; and no amount of reasoning can convince the world, against its common sense, that the horse is anything else than a horse. So here all can repose without fear. But not so with the Negro. He stands erect. Upon his brow he bears the seal of manhood, from the hand of the living God. Adopt any mode of reasoning you please with respect to him, he is a man, possessing an immortal soul, illuminated by intellect, capable of heavenly aspirations, and in all things pertaining to manhood, he is at once self-evidently a man, and therefore entitled to all the rights and privileges which belong to human nature.—F. D.

The North Star, June 13, 1850

   *Several words are illegible in original copy of the paper.—*Ed.*

TO THE EDITOR OF THE LONDON *TIMES*

Rochester, June 29, 1850

Sir,

Although I fear it may be an unwarranted intrusion upon your time and attention on my part, I must yield to the strong desire which moves me to thank you, in the name of justice and humanity, for your timely remarks in *The Times* of June 11, on the subject of American slavery,[8] and more especially for your animadversions on the brutal assault made upon me by a mob while I was quietly and inoffensively walking on the Battery at New York.

The influence exerted upon the more intelligent class of the American people by the judicious expression of British sense of justice and humanity is immense, and, I believe, highly beneficial.

The outrage committed upon me in New York was the work of low and vicious people. Yet, Sir, you were perfectly right in taking that outrage, as a fair illustration of the bitter antipathy which is entertained here, even by the better class of white people, against coloured persons. Polished American gentlemen would applaud a deed of ruffianism like the one in question, although they might shrink from the performance of the deed itself. My offence is alleged to be that of walking down Broadway in company of "two white women." This, however, is not a fair statement of that offence. My offence was that I walked down Broadway, in company with white persons, on terms of equality. Had I been with those persons simply as a servant, and not as a friend, I should have been regarded with complacency by the refined and with respect by the vulgar class of white persons who throng that great thoroughfare. The clamour here about human equality is meaningless. We have here an aristocracy of skin, with which if a man be covered, and can keep out of the state prisons, he possesses the high privilege of insulting a coloured man with the most perfect impunity. This class of aristocrats are never more displeased than when they meet with an intelligent coloured man. They recognize in him a contradiction to their ungenerous and unsound theories respecting the Negro race, and, not being able to reason him down to a level with the brute, they use brute force to knock him down to the desired level. I am, perhaps, trespassing too long upon your time, and although it may be a small matter to you as to how I may feel with respect to your noble defence of injured and insulted humanity, I could not be satisfied with myself without expressing in my humble way my sincerest gratitude for that defence.

Very respectfully yours,

Frederick Douglass

London *Times,* July 18, 1850

LECTURE ON SLAVERY, NO. 1, delivered in Corinthian Hall, Rochester, N. Y., on Sunday evening, December 1, 1850

I come before you this evening to deliver the first lecture of a course which I purpose to give in this city, during the present winter, on the subject of American Slavery.[9]

I make this announcement with no feelings of self-sufficiency. If I do not mistake my own emotions, they are such as result from a profound sense of my incompetency to do justice to the task which I have just announced, and have now entered upon.

If any, then, demand of me why I speak, I plead as my apology, the fact that abler and more eloquent men have failed to speak, or what, perhaps, is more true, and therefore more strong, such men have spoken only on the wrong side of the question, and have thus thrown their influence against the cause of liberty, humanity and benevolence.

There are times in the experience of almost every community, when even the humblest member thereof may properly presume to teach—when the wise and great ones, the appointed leaders of the people, exert their powers of mind to complicate, mystify, entangle and obscure the simple truth—when they exert the noblest gifts which heaven has vouchsafed to man to mislead the popular mind, and to corrupt the public heart,—*then* the humblest may stand forth and be excused for opposing even his weakness to the torrent of evil.

That such a state of things exists in this community, I have abundant evidence. I learn it from the Rochester press, from the Rochester pulpit, and in my intercourse with the people of Rochester. Not a day passes over me that I do not meet with apparently good men, who utter sentiments in respect to this subject which would do discredit to savages. They speak of the enslavement of their fellow-men with an indifference and coldness which might be looked for only in men hardened by the most atrocious and villainous crimes.

The fact is,—we are in the midst of a great struggle. The public mind is widely and deeply agitated; and bubbling up from its perturbed waters, are many and great impurities, whose poisonous miasma demands a constant antidote.

Whether the contemplated lectures will in any degree contribute towards answering this demand, time will determine.

Of one thing, however, I can assure my hearers—that I come up to this work at the call of duty, and with an honest desire to promote the happiness and well-being of every member of this community, as well as to advance the emancipation of every slave.

The audience will pardon me if I say one word more by way of introduction. It is my purpose to give this subject a calm, candid and faithful discussion. I shall not aim to shock nor to startle my hearers; but to convince their judgment and to secure their sympathies for the enslaved. I shall aim to be as stringent as truth, and as severe as justice; and if at any time I shall fail of this, and do injustice in any respect, I shall be most happy to be set right by any gentleman who shall hear me, subject, of course, to order and decorum. I shall deal, during these lectures, alike with individuals and institutions—men shall no more escape me than things. I shall have occasion, at times, to be even personal, and to rebuke sin in high places. I shall not hesitate to arraign either priests or politicians, church or state, and to measure all by the standard of justice, and in the light of truth. I shall not forget to deal with the unrighteous spirit of *caste* which prevails in this community; and I shall give particular attention to the recently enacted fugitive slave bill. I shall keep my eye upon the Congress which is to commence to-morrow, and fully inform myself as to its proceedings. In a word, the whole subject of slavery, in all its bearings, shall have a full and impartial discussion.

A very slight acquaintance with the history of American slavery is sufficient to show that it is an evil of which it will be difficult to rid this country. It is not the creature of a moment, which to-day is, and to-morrow is not; it is not a pigmy, which a slight blow may demolish; it is no youthful upstart, whose impertinent pratings may be silenced by a dignified contempt. No: it is an evil of gigantic proportions, and of long standing.

Its origin in this country dates back to the landing of the pilgrims on Plymouth rock.—It was here more than two centuries ago. The first spot poisoned by its leprous presence, was a small plantation in Virginia. The slaves, at that time, numbered only twenty. They have now increased to the frightful number of three millions; and from that narrow plantation, they are now spread over by far the largest half of the American Union. Indeed, slavery forms an important part of the entire history of the American people. Its presence may be seen in all American affairs. It has become interwoven with all American institutions, and has anchored itself in the very soil of the American Constitution. It has thrown its paralysing arm over freedom of speech, and the liberty of the press; and has created for itself morals and manners favorable to its own continuance. It has seduced the church, corrupted the pulpit, and brought the powers of both into degrading bondage; and now, in the pride of its power, it even threatens to bring down that grand political edifice, the American Union, unless every member of this republic shall so far disregard his conscience and his God as to yield to its infernal behests.

That must be a powerful influence which can truly be said to govern a nation; and that slavery governs the American people, is indisputably true. If there were any doubt on this point, a few plain questions (it seems to me) could not fail to remove it. *What* power has given this nation its Presidents for more than fifty years? *Slavery.* What power is that to which the present aspirants to presidential honors are bowing? *Slavery.* We may call it "Union," "Constitution," "Harmony," or "American institutions," that to which such men as Cass, Dickinson, Webster, Clay and other distinguished men of this country, are devoting their energies, is nothing more nor less than American slavery. It is for this that they are writing letters, making speeches, and promoting the holding of great mass meetings, professedly in favor of *"the Union."* These men know the service most pleasing to their master, and that which is most likely to be richly rewarded. Men may "serve God for nought," as did Job; but he who serves the devil has an eye to his reward. "Patriotism," "obedience to the law," "prosperity to the country," have come to mean, in the mouths of these distinguished statesmen, a mean and servile acquiescence in the most flagitious and profligate legislation in favor of slavery. I might enlarge here on this picture of the slave power, and tell of its influence upon the press in the free States, and upon the condition and rights of the free colored people of the North; but I forbear for the present.—Enough has been said, I trust, to convince all that the abolition of this evil will require time, energy, zeal, perseverance and patience; that it will require fidelity, a martyr-like spirit of self-sacrifice, and a firm reliance on Him who has declared Himself to be *"the God of the oppressed."* Having said thus much upon the power and prevalence of slavery, allow me to speak of

the nature of slavery itself; and here I can speak, in part, from experience—
I can speak with the authority of positive knowledge....

First of all, I will state, as well as I can, the legal and social relation of
master and slave. A master is one (to speak in the vocabulary of the
Southern States) who claims and exercises a right of property in the person of a fellow man. This he does with the force of the law and the sanction of Southern religion. The law gives the master absolute power over
the slave. He may work him, flog him, hire him out, sell him, and, in certain contingencies, *kill* him, with perfect impunity. The slave is a human
being, divested of all rights—reduced to the level of a brute—a mere
"chattel" in the eye of the law—placed beyond the circle of human brotherhood—cut off from his kind—his name, which the "recording angel" may
have enrolled in heaven, among the blest, is impiously inserted in a *master's ledger,* with horses, sheep and swine. In law, the slave has no wife, no
children, no country, and no home. He can own nothing, possess nothing,
acquire nothing, but what must belong to another. To eat the fruit of his
own toil, to clothe his person with the work of his own hands, is considered
stealing. He toils that another may reap the fruit; he is industrious that
another may live in idleness; he eats unbolted meal, that another may eat
the bread of fine flour; he labors in chains at home, under a burning sun
and a biting lash, that another may ride in ease and splendor abroad; he
lives in ignorance, that another may be educated; he is abused, that another
may be exalted; he rests his toil-worn limbs on the cold, damp ground,
that another may repose on the softest pillow; he is clad in coarse and
tattered raiment, that another may be arrayed in purple and fine linen;
he is sheltered only by the wretched hovel, that a master may dwell in a
magnificent mansion; and to this condition he is bound down as by an arm
of iron.

From this monstrous relation, there springs an unceasing stream of
most revolting cruelties. The very accompaniments of the slave system,
stamp it as the offspring of hell itself. To ensure good behavior, the slaveholder relies on *the whip;* to induce proper humility, he relies on *the whip;*
to rebuke what he is pleased to term insolence, he relies on *the whip;* to
supply the place of wages, as an incentive to toil, he relies on *the whip;* to
bind down the spirit of the slave, to imbrute and to destroy his manhood,
he relies on *the whip,* the chain, the gag, the thumb-screw, the pillory, the
bowie-knife, the pistol, and the blood-hound. These are the necessary and
unvarying accompaniments of the system. . . .

Nor is slavery more adverse to the conscience than it is to the mind.

This is shown by the fact that in every State of the American Union, where slavery exists, except the State of Kentucky, there are laws, *absolutely* prohibitory of education among the slaves. The crime of teaching a slave to read is punishable with severe fines and imprisonment, and, in some instances, with *death itself*.

Nor are the laws respecting this matter, a dead letter. Cases may occur in which they are disregarded, and a few instances may be found where slaves may have learned to read; but such are isolated cases, and only prove the rule. The great mass of slaveholders look upon education among the slaves as utterly subversive of the slave system. I *well* remember when my mistress first announced to my master that she had discovered that I could read. His face colored at once, with surprise and chagrin. He said that "I was ruined, and my value as a slave destroyed; that a slave should know nothing but to obey his master; that to give a Negro an inch would lead him to take an ell; that having learned how to read, I would soon want to know how to write; and that, bye and bye, I would be running away." I think my audience will bear witness to the correctness of this philosophy, and to the literal fulfilment of this prophecy.

It is perfectly well understood at the South that to educate a slave is to make him discontented with slavery, and to invest him with a power which shall open to him the treasures of freedom; and since the object of the slaveholder is to maintain complete authority over his slave, his constant vigilance is exercised to prevent everything which militates against, or endangers the stability of his authority. Education being among the menacing influences, and, perhaps, the most dangerous, is, therefore, the most cautiously guarded against.

It is true that we do not often hear of the enforcement of the law, punishing as crime the teaching of slaves to read, but this is not because of a want of disposition to enforce it. The true reason, or explanation of the matter is this, there is the greatest unanimity of opinion among the white population of the South, in favor of the policy of keeping the slave in ignorance. There is, perhaps, another reason why the law against education is so seldom violated. The slave is *too* poor to be able to offer a temptation sufficiently strong to induce a white man to violate it; and it is not to be supposed that in a community where the moral and religious sentiment is in favor of slavery, many martyrs will be found sacrificing their liberty and lives by violating those prohibitory enactments.

As a general rule, then, darkness reigns over the abodes of the enslaved, and "how great is that darkness!"

We are sometimes told of the contentment of the slaves, and are entertained with vivid pictures of their happiness. We are told that they often dance and sing; that their masters frequently give them wherewith to make merry; in fine, that that they have little of which to complain. I admit that the slave *does* sometimes sing, dance, and appear to be merry. But what does this prove? It only proves to my mind, that though slavery is armed with a thousand stings, it is not able entirely to kill the elastic spirit of the bondman. That spirit will rise and walk abroad, despite of whips and chains, and extract from the cup of nature, occasional drops of joy and gladness. No thanks to the slaveholder, nor to slavery, that the vivacious captive may sometimes dance in his chains, his very mirth in such circumstances, stands before God, as an accusing angel against his enslaver.

But *who* tells us of the extraordinary contentment and happiness of the slave? What traveller has explored the balmy regions of our Southern country and brought back "these glad tidings of joy"? Bring him on the platform, and bid him answer a few plain questions, we shall then be able to determine the weight and importance that attach to his testimony. Is he a minister? Yes. Were you ever in a slave State, sir? Yes. May I inquire the object of your mission South? To preach the gospel, sir. Of what denomination are you? A Presbyterian, sir. To whom were you introduced? To the Rev. Dr. Plummer. Is he a slaveholder, sir? Yes, sir. Has slaves about his house? Yes, sir. Were you then the guest of Dr. Plummer? Yes, sir. Waited on by slaves while there? Yes, sir. Did you preach for Dr. Plummer? Yes, sir. Did you spend your nights at the great house, or at the quarter among the slaves? At the great house. You had, then, no social intercourse with the slaves? No, sir. You fraternized, then, wholly with the *white* portion of the population while there? Yes, sir. This is sufficient, sir; you can leave the platform.

Nothing is more natural than that those who go into slave States, and enjoy the hospitality of slaveholders, should bring back favorable reports of the condition of the slave. If that ultra republican, the Hon. Lewis Cass could not return from the Court of France, without paying a compliment to royalty simply because King Louis Phillippe patted him on the shoulder, called him "friend," and invited him to dinner, it is not to be expected that those hungry shadows of men in the shape of ministers, that go South, can escape a contamination even more beguiling and insidious. Alas! for the weakness of poor human nature! "Pleased with a rattle, tickled with a straw!"

Why is it that all the reports of contentment and happiness among the slaves at the South come to us upon the authority of slaveholders, or (what is equally significant,) of slaveholder's friends? *Why* is it that we do not hear from the slaves direct? The answer to this question furnishes the darkest features in the American slave system.

It is often said, by the opponents of the anti-slavery cause, that the condition of the people of Ireland is more deplorable than that of the American slaves. *Far* be it from me to underrate the sufferings of the Irish people. They have been long oppressed; and the same heart that prompts me to plead the cause of the American bondman, makes it impossible for me *not* to sympathize with the oppressed of all lands. Yet I must say that there is no analogy between the two cases. The Irishman is poor, but he is *not* a slave. He *may* be in rags, but he is *not* a slave. He is still the master of his own body, and can say with the poet, "The hand of Douglass is his own." "The world is all before him, where to choose," and poor as may be my opinion of the British Parliament, I cannot believe that it will ever sink to such a depth of infamy as to pass a law for the recapture of Fugitive Irishmen! The shame and scandal of kidnapping will long remain wholly monopolized by the American Congress! The Irishman has not only the liberty to emigrate from his country, but he has liberty at home. He can write, and speak, and co-operate for the attainment of his rights and the redress of his wrongs.

The multitude can assemble upon all the green hills, and fertile plains of the Emerald Isle—they can pour out their grievances, and proclaim their wants without molestation; and the press, that "swift-winged messenger," can bear the tidings of their doings to the extreme bounds of the civilized world. They have their "Conciliation Hall" on the banks of the Liffey, their reform Clubs, and their newspapers; they pass resolutions, send forth addresses, and enjoy the right of petition. But how is it with the American slave? *Where* may he assemble? *Where* is his Conciliation Hall? Where are his newspapers? Where is his right of petition? Where is his freedom of speech? his liberty of the press? and his right of locomotion? He is said to be happy; happy men can speak. But ask the slave— *what* is his condition?—*what* his state of mind?—*what* he thinks of his enslavement? and you had as well address your inquiries to the *silent dead*. There comes no *voice* from the enslaved, we are left to gather his feelings by imagining what ours would be, were our souls in his soul's stead.

If there were no other fact descriptive of slavery, than that the slave is dumb, this alone would be sufficient to mark the slave system as a grand aggregation of human horrors.

Most who are present will have observed that leading men, in this country, have been puting forth their skill to secure quiet to the nation. A system of measures to promote this object was adopted a few months ago in Congress.[10]

The result of those measures is known. Instead of quiet, they have produced alarm; instead of peace, they have brought us war, and so must ever be.

While this nation is guilty of the enslavement of three millions of innocent men and women, it is as idle to think of having a sound and lasting peace, as it is to think there is no God, to take cognizance of the affairs of men. There can be no peace to the wicked while slavery continues in the land, it will be condemned, and while it is condemned there will be agitation; Nature must cease to be nature; Men must become monsters; Humanity must be transformed; Christianity must be exterminated; all ideas of justice, and the laws of eternal goodness must be utterly blotted out from the human soul, ere a system so foul and infernal can escape condemnation, or this guilty Republic can have a sound and enduring Peace.

The North Star, December 5, 1850

LECTURE ON SLAVERY, NO. 2, delivered in Corinthian Hall, Rochester, on Sunday evening, December 8, 1850

In my lecture of Sunday evening last, I strove to impress those who kindly gave me their attention, with a slight idea of the all-controlling power of American slavery in the affairs of the nation.

I briefly unfolded the nature of the relation between master and slave; the cruel, arbitrary and despotic authority of the slaveholder; and I portrayed the deplorable ignorance and the deep debasement of the enslaved.

This evening I shall aim to expose further the wickedness of the slave system—to show that its evils are not confined to the Southern States; but that they overshadow the whole country; and that every American citizen is responsible for its existence, and is solemnly required, by the highest convictions of duty and safety, to labor for its utter extirpation from the land.

By some who will hear me, these propositions will be, perhaps, re-garded as far too tame for the basis of a lecture on slavery at this exciting period. But I would beg such persons to remember that they are the few, not the many; and that being the exception, they afford no criterion for the course I ought to pursue on the present occasion. By them, the anti-slavery alphabet was learned perhaps twenty years ago; but the great mass of the American people, I am sorry to say, have that simple lesson yet to learn. I design, therefore, to speak to opponents, rather than to friends, and although I may not be able to entertain the latter by the utterance of new truths, I may afford them the satisfaction of hearing those truths enforced which they have so long cherished.

Indeed, I ought to state, what must be obvious to all, that, properly speaking, there is no such thing as *new* truth; for truth, like the God whose attribute it is, is eternal. In this sense, there is, indeed, nothing new under the sun. Error may be properly designated as *old* or *new,* since it is but a misconception, or an incorrect view of the truth. Misapprehensions of what truth is, have their beginnings and their endings. They pass away as the race moves onward. But truth is "from everlasting to everlasting" and can never pass away.

Such is the truth of man's right to liberty. It existed in the very idea of man's creation. It was *his* even before he comprehended it. He was created in it, endowed with it, and it can never be taken from him. No laws, no statutes, no compacts, no compromises, no constitutions, can abrogate or destroy it. It is beyond the reach of the strongest earthly arm, and smiles at the ravings of tyrants from its hiding place in the bosom of God. Men may hinder its exercise, they may act in disregard of it, they are even permitted to war against it; but they fight against heaven and their career must be short, for Eternal Providence will speedily vindicate the right.

The existence of this right is self-evident. It is written upon all the powers and faculties of man. The desire for it is the deepest and strongest of all the powers of the human soul. Earth, sea, and air—great nature, with her thousand voices, proclaims it.

In the language of Addison, we may apostrophize it:
> *Oh, Liberty! thou Goddess, heavenly bright,*
> *Profuse of bliss, and pregnant with delight!*
> *Thou mak'st the glowing face of nature gay,*
> *Giv'st beauty to the sun, and pleasure to the day.*

I have said that the right to liberty is self-evident. No argument, no researches into moldy records, no learned disquisitions, are necessary to establish it. To assert it, is to call forth a sympathetic response from every human heart, and to send a thrill of joy and gladness round the world. Tyrants, oppressors and slaveholders are stunned by its utterance; while the oppressed and enslaved of all lands hail it as an angel of deliverance. Its assertion in Russia, in Austria, in Egypt, in fifteen States of the American Union, is a crime. In the harems of Turkey, and in the Southern plantations of Carolina, it is alike prohibited; for the guilty oppressors of every clime understand its *truth,* and appreciate its electric power.

Slavery is a sin, in that it comprehends a monstrous violation of the great principle of human liberty, to which I have endeavored thus to draw your attention. In this respect, it is a direct war upon the government of God. In subjecting one man to the arbitrary control of another, it contravenes the first command of the decalogue; and as upon that command rests the whole superstructure of justice, purity and brotherly kindness, slavery may be justly regarded as a warfare against all the principles of infinite goodness. It is not, however, merely with slavery as a system that I propose to deal. It has been well characterized by the faithful John Wesley as *"the concentration of all crime."* I prefer to speak of the villains in connection with the villainy, and of the criminals in connection with the crimes. I like the pure and stern testimony of John Wesley. It expresses the sense of a true heart in respect to the foul abomination. Adam Clarke is no less emphatic. To the traffickers in the souls and bodies of men, this great commenator says, "Oh! ye most flagitious of knaves, and worst of hypocrites! Cast off at once the mask of religion, and deepen not your endless perdition by professing the faith of our Lord Jesus Christ, while you continue in this traffic."

In contemplating the sin of slavery, and the guilt of slaveholders, I have marvelled at the coolness and self-complacency with which persons at the North often speak of having friends and relatives who are slaveholders at the South. They speak of the fact without a blush of shame, and even as though honor were conferred upon them by their slaveholding friends and relatives. What a commentary is this on the state of morals among us! Why, if the moral sentiment of the North were what it ought to be, a lady would as soon tell of an abandoned sister or a pirate brother, as boast of having slaveholding relatives, for there is nothing in piracy, nothing in lewdness, that is not to be found in the slave system—indeed, slavery is a system of lewdness and piracy. Every slaveholder is the legalized keeper of a house of ill-fame; no matter how high he may stand in Church or in State. He may be a Bishop Meade or a Henry Clay—a reputed saint or an open sinner—he is still the legalized head of a den of infamy.

As a nation we profess profound respect for chastity and the marriage institution. A violation of either is looked upon (and very properly so) with feelings of absolute horror. A maddened husband, or an outraged father, is almost justified by public opinion in taking the law into his own hand, and executing summary vengeance upon the guilty creature who, by studied arts, covers his family with shame. The laws of this commonwealth, like those of other Northern States, have thrown around innocence the most stringent protection. Our pulpits are keenly alive to the importance of the marriage institution, and the press is not a whit behind the pulpit. These things indicate, I say, a profound respect for moral purity. I will not controvert the genuineness of this seeming virtue of the community. But if it be genuine, the State of New York must be an emancipation State, and that speedily. I hold myself ready to prove that more than a million of women, in the Southern States of this Union are, by the laws of the land, and through no fault of their own, consigned to a life of revolting prostitution; that by those laws, in many of the States, if a woman, in defence of her own innocence, shall lift her hand against the brutal aggressor, she may be lawfully put to death. I hold myself ready to prove, by the laws of the Slave States, that three millions of people of those States, are utterly incapacitated to form marriage contracts. I am also prepared to prove that slave-breeding is relied upon by Virginia as one of her chief sources of wealth. It has long been known that the best blood of old Virginia may now be found in the slave markets of New Orleans. It is also known that slave women who are nearly white, are sold in those markets, at prices which proclaim, trumpet-tongued, the accursed purposes to which they are to be devoted. Youth and elegance, beauty and innocence, are exposed for sale upon the auction block; while villainous monsters stand around, with pockets lined with gold, gazing with lustful eyes upon their prospective victims. But I will not go behind the scene further. I leave you to picture to yourselves what must be the state of society where marriage is not allowed by the law, and where *woman* is reduced to a mere *chattel*. To the thoughtful I need say no more. You have already conceived a state of things equalling in honor and abomination, your worst conceptions of Sodom itself.

Every slaveholder is a party, a guilty party, to this awful wickedness.

He owns the house, and is master of the victims. He is therefore responsible. I say again, no matter how high the slaveholder may stand in popular estimation—he may be a minister of religion, or an Honorable Member of Congress; but so long as he is a slaveholder, he deserves to be held up before the world as the patron of lewdness, and the foe of virtue. He may not be personally implicated in the wickedness; he may scrupulously maintain and respect the marriage institution for himself and for his family, for all this can be done selfishly; but while he robs any portion of the human family of the right of marriage, and takes from innocent woman the protection of the law, no matter what his individual responsibility may be, he is to be classed with the vilest of the vile, and with the basest of the base. To boast of relationship or friendly association with these infamous men—to fellowship with such men as good Christians, is a sad commentary on the morals and the religion of those who do it. It implies that their professions of purity are conventional and artificial; that there is no real soundness in them; that their virtue is seeming rather than real; that their reverence for the marriage institution is the merest affectation, and has no higher nor stronger support than that afforded by public opinion; and that their horror at its violation depends wholly upon the complexion of the parties involved, and not upon the sin committed.

I have now spoken plainly, but not more so than the nature of the case requires. If any have been shocked at my plainness of speech, I beg them to remember that true delicacy does not consist in a squeamish ear. In the language of the eloquent Fox, I would remind them "that true humanity does not consist in shrinking and starting at such recitals, but in a disposition of the heart to remedy the evils they unfold. True virtue belongs rather to the mind than to the nerves, and should prompt men to charitable exertion in correcting abuses. To shudder at enormities, and do nothing to remove them, is little better than to stamp ourselves with the most pitiful and contemptible hypocrisy." To quote another author, I would say,

> *True modesty is a distinguished grace,*
> *And only blushes in the proper place.*
> *But counterfeit is base, and skulks through fear*
> *Where 'tis a shame to be ashamed t'appear.*

I pass now to the consideration of another feature of slavery. I allude to its cruelty. Much is said among us, both by the press and the pulpit, of the kindness of the slaveholders to their slaves, and of their natural attachment. The relation of master and slave has been called patriarchal, and only second in benignity and tenderness to that of the parent and child. This representation is doubtless believed by many northern people; and this may account, in part, for the lack of interest which we find among persons whom we are bound to believe to be honest and humane. What, then, are the facts? Here I will not quote my own experience in slavery; for this you might call one-sided testimony. I will not cite the declarations of abolitionists; for these you might pronounce exaggerations. I will not rely upon advertisements cut from newspapers; for these you might call isolated cases. But I will refer you to the laws adopted by the legislatures of the slave states. I give you such evidence, because it cannot be invalidated nor denied. I hold in my hand sundry extracts from the slave codes of our country, from which I will quote.*

Now, if the foregoing be an indication of kindness, *what is cruelty?* If this be parental affection, *what is bitter malignity?* A more atrocious and blood-thirsty string of laws could not well be conceived of. And yet I am bound to say that they fall short of indicating the horrible cruelties constantly practiced in the slave states.

I admit that there are individual slaveholders less cruel and barbarous than is allowed by law; but these form the exception. The majority of slaveholders find it necessary, to insure obedience, at times, to avail themselves of the utmost extent of the law, and many go beyond it. If kindness were the rule, we should not see advertisements filling the columns of almost every southern newspaper, offering large rewards for fugitive slaves, and describing them as being branded with irons, loaded with chains, and scarred by the whip. One of the most telling testimonies against the pretended kindness of slaveholders, is the fact that uncounted numbers of fugitives are now inhabiting the Dismal Swamp, preferring the untamed wilderness to their cultivated homes—choosing rather to encounter hunger and thirst, and to roam with the wild beasts of the forest, running the hazard of being hunted and shot down, than to submit to the authority of *kind* masters.

I tell you, my friends, humanity is never driven to such an unnatural course of life, without great wrong. The slave finds more of the milk of human kindness in the bosom of the savage Indian, than in the heart of his *christian* master. He leaves the man of the *bible,* and takes refuge with

* See *Life and Writings of Frederick Douglass,* Vol. I, pp. 211-12, for extracts from the Slave Codes.—*Ed.*

the man of the *tomahawk*. He rushes from the praying slaveholder into the paws of the bear. He quits the homes of men for the haunts of wolves. He prefers to encounter a life of trial, however bitter, or death, however terrible, to dragging out his existence under the dominion of these *kind* masters.

The apologists for slavery often speak of the abuses of slavery; and they tell us that they are as much opposed to those abuses as we are; and that they would go as far to correct those abuses and to ameliorate the condition of the slave as anybody. The answer to that view is, that slavery is *itself* an abuse; that it lives by abuse; and dies by the absence of abuse. Grant that slavery is right; grant that the relation of master and slave may innocently exist; and there is not a single outrage which was ever committed against the slave but what finds an apology in the very necessity of the case. As was said by a slaveholder, (the Rev. A. G. Few,) to the Methodist conference, "If the relation be right, the means to maintain it are also right"; for without those means slavery could not exist. Remove the dreadful scourge—the plaited thong—the galling fetter—the accursed chain—and let the slaveholder rely solely upon moral and religious power, by which to secure obedience to his orders, and how long do you suppose a slave would remain on his plantation? The case only needs to be stated; it carries its own refutation with it.

Absolute and arbitrary power can never be maintained by one man over the body and soul of another man, without brutal chastisement and enormous cruelty.

To talk of *kindness* entering into a relation in which one party is robbed of wife, of children, of his hard earnings, of home, of friends, of society, of knowledge, and of all that makes this life desirable, is most absurd, wicked, and preposterous.

I have shown that slavery is wicked—wicked, in that it violates the great law of liberty, written on every human heart—wicked, in that it violates the first command of the decalogue—wicked, in that it fosters the most disgusting licentiousness—wicked, in that it mars and defaces the image of God by cruel and barbarous inflictions—wicked, in that it contravenes the laws of eternal justice, and tramples in the dust all the humane and heavenly precepts of the New Testament.

The evils resulting from this huge system of iniquity are not confined to the states south of Mason and Dixon's line. Its noxious influence can easily be traced throughout our northern borders. It comes even as far north as the state of New York. Traces of it may be seen even in Rochester;

and travelers have told me it casts its gloomy shadows across the lake, approaching the very shores of Queen Victoria's dominions.

The presence of slavery may be explained by—as it is the explanation of—the mobocratic violence which lately disgraced New York, and which still more recently disgraced the city of Boston.[11] These violent demonstrations, these outrageous invasions of human rights, faintly indicate the presence and power of slavery here. It is a significant fact, that while meetings for almost any purpose under heaven may be held unmolested in the city of Boston, that in the same city, a meeting cannot be peaceably held for the purpose of preaching the doctrine of the American Declaration of Independence, "that all men are created equal." The pestiferous breath of slavery taints the whole moral atmosphere of the north, and enervates the moral energies of the whole people.

The moment a foreigner ventures upon our soil, and utters a natural repugnance to oppression, that moment he is made to feel that there is little sympathy in this land for him. If he were greeted with smiles before, he meets with frowns now; and it shall go well with him if he be not subjected to that peculiarly fitting method of showing fealty to slavery, the assaults of a mob.

Now, will any man tell me that such a state of things is natural, and that such conduct on the part of the people of the north, springs from a consciousness of rectitude? No! every fibre of the human heart unites in detestation of tyranny, and it is only when the human mind has become familiarized with slavery, is accustomed to its injustice, and corrupted by its selfishness, that it fails to record its abhorrence of slavery, and does not exult in the triumphs of liberty.

The northern people have been long connected with slavery; they have been linked to a decaying corpse, which has destroyed the moral health. The union of the government; the union of the north and south, in the political parties; the union in the religious organizations of the land, have all served to deaden the moral sense of the northern people, and to impregnate them with sentiments and ideas forever in conflict with what as a nation we call *genius of American institutions*. Rightly viewed, this is an alarming fact, and ought to rally all that is pure, just, and holy in one determined effort to crush the monster of corruption, and to scatter "its guilty profits" to the winds. In a high moral sense, as well as in a national sense, the whole American people are responsible for slavery, and must share, in its guilt and shame, with the most obdurate men-stealers of the south.

While slavery exists, and the union of these states endures, every American citizen must bear the chagrin of hearing his country branded before the world as a nation of liars and hypocrites; and behold his cherished national flag pointed at with the utmost scorn and derision. Even now an American *abroad* is pointed out in the crowd, as coming from a land where men gain their fortunes by "the blood of souls," from a land of slave markets, of blood-hounds, and slave-hunters; and, in some circles, such a man is shunned altogether, as a moral pest. Is it not time, then, for every American to awake, and inquire into his duty with respect to this subject?

Wendell Phillips—the eloquent New England orator—on his return from Europe, in 1842, said, "As I stood upon the shores of Genoa, and saw floating on the placid waters of the Mediterranean, the beautiful American war ship *Ohio,* with her masts tapering proportionately aloft, and an eastern sun reflecting her noble form upon the sparkling waters, attracting the gaze of the multitude, my first impulse was of pride, to think myself an American; but when I thought that the first time that gallant ship would gird on her gorgeous apparel, and wake from beneath her sides her dormant thunders, it would be in defense of the African slave trade, I blushed in utter *shame* for my country."

Let me say again, *slavery is alike the sin and the shame of the American people;* it is a blot upon the American name, and the only national reproach which need make an American hang his head in shame, in the presence of monarchical governments.

With this gigantic evil in the land, we are constantly told to look *at home;* if we say aught against crowned heads, we are pointed to our enslaved millions; if we talk of sending missionaries and bibles abroad, we are pointed to three millions now lying in worse than heathen darkness; if we express a word of sympathy for Kossuth and his Hungarian fugitive brethren, we are pointed to that horrible and hell-black enactment, "The Fugitive Slave Bill."

Slavery blunts the edge of all our rebukes of tyranny abroad—the criticisms that we make upon other nations, only call forth ridicule, contempt, and scorn. In a word, we are made a reproach and a by-word to a mocking earth, and we must continue to be so made, so long as slavery continues to pollute our soil.

We have heard much of late of the virtue of patriotism, the love of country, &c., and this sentiment, so natural and so strong, has been impiously appealed to, by all the powers of human selfishness, to cherish the viper which is stinging our national life away. In its name, we have been called upon to deepen our infamy before the world, to rivet the fetter more firmly on the limbs of the enslaved, and to become utterly insensible to the voice of human woe that is wafted to us on every southern gale. We have been called upon, in its name, to desecrate our whole land by the footprints of slave-hunters, and even to engage ourselves in the horrible business of kidnapping.

I, too, would invoke the spirit of patriotism; not in a narrow and restricted sense, but, I trust, with a broad and manly signification; not to cover up our national sins, but to inspire us with sincere repentance; not to hide our shame from the world's gaze, but utterly to abolish the cause of that shame; not to explain away our gross inconsistencies as a nation, but to remove the hateful, jarring, and incongruous elements from the land; not to sustain an egregious wrong, but to unite all our energies in the grand effort to remedy that wrong.

I would invoke the spirit of patriotism, in the name of the law of the living God, natural and revealed, and in the full belief that "righteousness exalteth a nation, while sin is a reproach to any people." "He that walketh righteously, and speaketh uprightly; he that despiseth the gain of oppressions, that shaketh his hands from the holding of bribes, he shall dwell on high, his place of defense shall be the munitions of rocks, bread shall be given him, his water shall be sure."

We have not only heard much lately of patriotism, and of its aid being invoked on the side of slavery and injustice, but the very prosperity of this people has been called in to deafen them to the voice of duty, and to lead them onward in the pathway of sin. Thus has the blessing of God been converted into a curse. In the spirit of genuine patriotism, I warn the American people, by all that is just and honorable, to beware!

I warn them that, strong, proud, and prosperous though we be, there is a power above us that can "bring down high looks; at the breath of whose mouth our wealth may take wings; and before whom every knee shall bow;" and who can tell how soon the avenging angel may pass over our land, and the sable bondmen now in chains, may become the instruments of our nation's chastisement! Without appealing to any higher feeling, I would warn the American people, and the American government, to be wise in their day and generation. I exhort them to remember the history of other nations; and I remind them that America cannot always sit "as a queen," in peace and repose; that prouder and stronger governments than this have been shattered by the bolts of a just God;

that the time *may* come when those they now despise and hate, may be needed; when those whom they now compel by oppression to be enemies, may be wanted as friends. What has been, may be again. There is a point beyond which human endurance cannot go. The crushed worm may yet turn under the heel of the oppressor. I warn them, then, with all solemnity, and in the name of retributive justice, *to look to their ways;* for in an evil hour, those sable arms that have, for the last two centuries, been engaged in cultivating and adorning the fair fields of our country, may yet become the instruments of terror, desolation, and death, throughout our borders.

It was the sage of the Old Dominion that said—while speaking of the possibility of a conflict between the slaves and the slaveholders—"God has no attribute that could take sides with the oppressor in such a contest. I tremble for my country when I reflect that God *is just,* and that his justice cannot sleep forever." Such is the warning voice of Thomas Jefferson; and every day's experience since its utterance until now, confirms its wisdom, and commends its truth.

Lectures on American Slavery, by Frederick Douglass. Delivered at Corinthian Hall, Rochester, N. Y., Buffalo, 1851

TO GERRIT SMITH, ESQR.

Rochester, Jan. 21st, 1851

My Dear Friend:

I thank you sincerely for your donation, and feel much pleased that amid the multitudinous demands made upon your purse, you yet find the means of encouraging me in my humble labors in the cause of human redemption.

I have thought much since my personal acquaintance with you and since hearing your reasons for regarding the Constitution of the United States an Anti-Slavery instrument, and although I can not yet see that instrument in the same light in which you view it, I am so much impressed by your reasoning that I have about decided to let Slaveholders and their Northern abettors have the Laboring *oar* in putting a proslavery interpretation upon the Constitution. I am sick and tired of arguing on the slaveholders' side of this question, although they are doubtless right so far as the intentions of the framers of the Constitution are concerned. But these intentions you fling to the winds. Your legal rules of interpretation override all speculations as to the opinions of the Constitution makers and these *rules* may be sound and I confess I know not how to meet or refute them on *legal* grounds. You will now say I have conceded all that you require, and it may be so. But there is a consideration which is of much importance between us. It is this: may we avail ourselves of legal rules which enable us to defeat even the wicked intentions of our Constitution makers? It is this question which puzzles me more than all others involved in the subject. Is it good morality to take advantage of a legal flaw and put a meaning upon a legal instrument the very opposite of what we have good reason to believe was the intention of the men who framed it? Just here is the question of difficulty with me. I know well enough that slavery is an outrage, contrary to all ideas of justice, and therefore cannot be law according to Blackstone. But may it not be law according to American legal authority?

You will observe by reading the resolutions adopted at the Annual meeting of the Western N. Y. Anti-Slavery Society, that I have already ceased to affirm the pro-slavery character of the Constitution. In drawing up the resolutions for that meeting, I purposely avoided all affirmation of the pro-slavery "Compromises," as they are termed.

My good friend, Julia Griffith, forwarded to your address one copy of my two first lectures in Rochester this morning. I hope it will reach you. I am greatly pleased by your good opinion of these lectures. I sometimes fear that being delivered by a fugitive slave who has never had a day's school constitutes the only merit they possess. Yet I am so much encouraged by my friends here, and elsewhere, that I am seriously intending, if I can command the money, to publish them in Book form.[12] Your generous offer of 25 dollars for that purpose, was timely and very thankfully received. I shall give four or five more lectures to complete the course. The fact that Negroes are turning Book makers may possibly serve to remove the popular impression that they are fit only for Bootblacking, and although they may not *shine* in the former profession as they have long done in the latter, I am not without hope that they will do themselves good by making the effort. I have often felt that what the colored people want most in this country is character. They want manly aspirations and a firm though modest self-reliance, and this we must have, or be like all other worthless things swept away before the march of events.

I see now that a strong effort is being made to get us out of this country. The speech of Mr. Clay in the Senate the other day, an article in the New York *Tribune* now before me on the subject, the starting up of a new Colonization paper in New York,[13] are facts which all point the way, and that is "Out with the Negroes," and I really fear that some whose presence in this country is necessary to the elevation of the colored people will leave us, while the degraded and worthless will remain to help bind us to our present debasement.

But I have already trespassed upon your time long enough. I know how closely your time is occupied. Miss Griffiths unites with me in kind regards to yourself and Mrs. Smith.

Very gratefully yours,
Frederick Douglass

I would say excuse my writing, but that your own *writing* suggests that consideration so often that I do not wish to weary you by such a reminder. I am however rapidly getting over the difficulty of reading letters from your pen and am always glad to get one at any rate.

Gerrit Smith Papers, Syracuse University

TO GERRIT SMITH

Rochester May 1st, 1851

My Dear Friend:

I feel honored and pleased by the contents of your favor of 27th April. It is not impossible that I am too much elated with the plan you propose, to consider of it as calmly as its great importance plainly demands.[14] I am grateful to you that you have thought of me in such a connection. As well as I have known your generous character and as much as you had taught me to expect at your hands, I never expected such an offer as that which you have now suggested. I agree with you as to the character of the *National Era*.[15] It is most attractive and fair seeming to the eye, but it is as cold and lifeless as marble. Were it but half as faithful as it is beautiful, it would shake this guilty land. But alas! it is dead. No living heart throbs beneath its pure white ruffles. It is powerless for good, and only remains to taint the anti-slavery atmosphere.

But let the *Era* pass. Let the dead bury their dead. You want a good looking as well as good paper, established in western N. Y. and have a plan to accomplish that object. *I like the plan.* You may rely upon me to answer the part you have assigned for me, in the mode of attaining such a paper. I am in favor of such a union of papers and talents of which you speak. What we want is a good paying subscription list. But in order to get this we must send forth a sheet such as will take the eyes of friends, and such as they will not be ashamed to solicit subscribers for, even among foes. To get such a sheet, money is necessary. We must have money to buy good clear white paper. It must not be so flimsy as that upon which the *North Star* and [the] "Liberty party paper" are published. We must have good paper as that upon which the *National Era* is printed. Money we must have or fail to command the needful talent to make our columns full rich and fresh. Money must be at hand or the Editor will have his brains more puzzled by the means than about the end. Now I believe that by uniting the "Liberty party paper" and [the] *North Star*—saying nothing of the *Citizen* we shall have a very good start, and with your donation monthly for two years, be able to move forward firmly.

The *North Star* sustains itself, and partly sustains my large family. It has just reached a living point. Hitherto the struggle of its life has been to live. Now it more than lives, and was just as your letter came to hand about to make some little improvement in the quality of the paper upon which it is printed. I have now decided to pause. The first two years of the *Star* spent the whole two thousand dollars sent to me from England by my dear friends there, and stript me of all but a very valuable experience in managing money in connexion with a newspaper.

The condition of the *Star* is not such as to make me anxious to seek a union with any other paper, and yet I see that a great gain will flow to me and to the cause by the union which you have kindly proposed and I go for it. In regard to the place of publication, I think Rochester the place. Besides general reasons in its favor, I have private ones. My house, home and family are here. My house will be paid for in the course of a few months. My family are averse to moving, and I am unprepared too for living at a distance from them. If I should leave Rochester I should leave an important work incomplete—the breaking down of prejudice. I wish to live here and cheer the hearts of those who have stood by me, and silence opposition. But I will not be too strongly wedded to Rochester.

As to principles, mine are well expressed in the admirable address submitted by you to the Anti-Fugitive Slave Law Convention held in Syracuse.[16] I am prepared to treat Slavery as a system of *"Lawless violence"* incapable in its nature of being legalized. I am prepared to contend for those rules of interpretation which when applied to the Constitution make its details harmonize with its declared objects in its preamble. I am satisfied on those points, and my heart is strong. The change in my views on this question has not been sudden, nor brought about with reference to any emergency. I have arrived at my present position after months of thought and investigation. I am therefore free from embarrassment in accepting this part of your proposal. This is the only point that has separated me from you for the last three years. But to the practical part.

I find it almost impossible to get my paper printed without errors and inaccuracies which greatly mortify me. The reason is, that we are compelled to get our paper printed in another office on a steam press. In an unfriendly office, that press once in motion, they will not stop it for corrections. Now should our plan work, I purpose to build a printing office on my own lot. It will not cost more than three hundred dollars, and shall set up a good press. I should need about one hundred and fifty dollars worth of type. This would do quite well with what I now have, and enable me to produce a beautiful sheet. *All sorts of horse medicines would be swept from our columns, and my advertising type might be used for items and quotations.*

The money matters of the paper might well be left to the care of my industrious and vigilant friend and co-worker Julia Griffiths. With her eye on the subscription list, I think very little would go wrong in that quarter. Had she had the management of my books at the commencement, I feel sure that I should have had double the number of subscribers I now have. To her the credit belongs that the *Star* is now out of debt. In twelve months, she paid off a debt of between seven and eight hundred dollars. She ought to have this credit for you need not be told that she has had much to annoy and at times to weigh down her spirit. I shall count much upon her assistance in any event.

As to the name of the paper—I am willing that the paper should take my own if that shall be thought best. Frederick Douglass will be rather a long name to precede paper, but we will think of it.

I wish to make a remark which I hope will meet your approval. I have an impression that there are many abolitionists who have very narrow views, and some who have a share of meanness in their composition. There are some who would not feel free to aid a paper if they knew that Gerrit Smith had set his heart on making it successful. They will gladly stand by and subscribe for a single copy, but they have no idea of doing more. They say Gerrit Smith is rich, and he will not let the effort fail for want of funds. Now the thought has struck me that your financial help to the paper should not at once be made public, but that the paper should be flung out among the people as needing their help. This is policy, and it may be sound policy. Then again it would disarm evil surmisers, until we get in a position to cope with them. I only fling out the thought.

The motto which you have suggested is good, very good.[17] Now then for a paper, the right sort of a paper—a paper which shall be highly respectable in appearance, warm and sound in heart, generous and free in spirit, demanding for universal humanity all the rights of human nature.

Hoping soon to see you and hear you further,

I am your grateful friend,

Frederick Douglass

Gerrit Smith Papers, Syracuse University

TO GERRIT SMITH, ESQR.

Rochester, May 15th, 1851

My Dear Sir:

I am obliged by your favor of Saturday, and it should have been immediately answered, but that it came to hand when I was in the midst of getting out the present number of the *Star*. I saw Mr. Thomas as you desired me, on the morning yourself and Mrs. Smith left Syracuse for Peterboro. We had a pleasant talk about the union of papers, but came to no definite agreement. I assured him of my acceptance of your proposal to the fullest extent—that he need have no fears that in writing for the proposed paper, he would at all feel himself fettered—told him of the amounts of compensation which it was thought would be sufficient to secure his services, in fine read your letter to him, and told him I was ready to comply with it. He thought that the sum proposed for his services was too small; he should have to give his whole time to it, and four dollars would not be sufficient to support him. Thought he should be in the office and that he could not be of much service if he were not, etc. He evidently desires to keep up the "Liberty party paper," and nothing else. I think in this that Brother Thomas is unreasonable. While I would [not] have the paper known as the organ of the L.P., I know of no one principle of that party that I should oppose. He might advocate the claims of the [slave] with all the power and earnestness which he ever exercised in his own paper, and have the satisfaction of feeling that he is speaking to thousands where before he spoke only to hundreds.

I shall leave this matter just where it ought to be left, in your own hands. I shall stand ready at any moment to unite the papers in the manner you have prescribed, and to make the paper such as I think your taste and judgment will approve.

The sooner the arrangement is made the better. A knowledge of the fact that such a paper has come into existence will have a good effect.

I think a great deal of female influence in all great moral undertakings, and I venture to suggest that a warmhearted, earnest and intelligent woman correspondent would be a great accession to *our paper*. I think Sally Holly such a person as I have described and I think her services might be secured. You I think would be the person to speak to her on the subject. Will you do so?

Please remember me kindly to your dear family. Tell Mrs. Smith that I am expecting much from her counsels in the matter.

I am most sincerely your grateful Friend,
Frederick Douglass

Gerrit Smith Papers, Syracuse University

CHANGE OF OPINION ANNOUNCED

The debate on the resolution relative to anti-slavery newspapers [at the annual meeting of the American Anti-Slavery Society[18]] assumed such a character as to make it our duty to define the position of the *North Star* in respect to the Constitution of the United States. The ground having been distinctly taken, that no paper ought to receive the recommendation of the American Anti-Slavery Society that did not assume the Constitution to be a pro-slavery document, we felt in honor bound to announce at once to our old anti-slavery companions that we no longer possessed the requisite qualification for their official approval and commendation; and to assure them that we had arrived at the firm conviction that the Constitution, construed in the light of well established rules of legal interpretation, might be made consistent in its details with the noble purposes avowed in its preamble; and that hereafter we should insist upon the application of such rules to that instrument, and demand that it be wielded in behalf of emancipation. The change in our opinion on this subject has not been hastily arrived at. A careful study of the writings of Lysander Spooner, of Gerrit Smith, and of William Goodell, has brought us to our present conclusion. We found, in our former position, that, when debating the question, we were compelled to go behind the letter of the Constitution, and to seek its meaning in the history and practice of the nation under it—a process always attended with disadvantages; and certainly we feel little inclination to shoulder disadvantages of any kind, in order to give slavery the slightest protection. In short, we hold it to be a system of lawless violence; that it *never was lawful, and never can be made so;* and that it is the first duty of every American citizen, whose conscience permits so to do, to use his *political* as well as his *moral* power for its overthrow. Of course, this avowal did not pass without animadversion, and it would have been strange if it had passed without some crimination; for it is hard for any combination or party to attribute good motives to any one who differs from them in what they deem a vital point. Brother Garrison at once exclaimed, "There is roguery somewhere!" but we can easily forgive this hastily expressed imputation, falling, as it did, from the lips of one to whom we shall never cease to be grateful, and for whom we have cherished (and do now cherish) a veneration only inferior in degree to that which we owe to our conscience and to our God.

The North Star, reprinted in *The Liberator,* May 23, 1851

TO GERRIT SMITH, ESQR.

Rochester, May 21st, 1851

My Dear Sir:
    It needs no ghost to assure me, that I am to be made for a time, an object of special attack. I am not afraid of it and am not pained in view of it. I know too well the temper of very old companions to hope to escape the penalty which all others have paid who have ventured to differ from them. The leaders in the American Anti-slavery Society are strong men, noble champions in the cause of human freedom, and yet they are not after all the most charitable in construing the motives of those who see matters in a different light from themselves. Insinuations have already been thrown out and will be again.
    There are two ways of treating assaults from that quarter and that character. They can be replied to or be allowed to spend their force unanswered. Judgment is needed here. A word of advice from you will at

any time be most welcome. You will do me the kindness and the cause of truth and freedom the service, of giving a little attention to any controversy which may arise between my old friends and me, in regard to my present position on the *Constitutional* question. That my ground is correct I am satisfied, and can easily, I think, defend it against the strongest. But I am persuaded that the war will be waged, not against opinions but *motives,* especially if the union of papers which we contemplate shall go into effect. If in this, time shall prove me correct, I shall need a word from you which I am sure you will generously give. You can prove that even in the *North Star* more than two years ago, I gave up the ground that the Constitution, when strictly construed, is a pro-slavery document,[19] and that the only points which prevented me from declaring at that time in favor of voting and against the disunion ground related to the intentions of the framers of the Constitution. I had not made up my mind then, as I have now, that I am only in reason and in conscience bound to learn the intentions of those who framed the Constitution *in the Constitution itself.*

You yourself do know that before I could have had the slightest hope of affecting the union of papers which we now contemplate, that I distinctly assured you of the change in my opinion which I have now publicly avowed. For months I have made no secret of my present opinion. I talked the matter over with S. S. Foster. I told him soon after leaving your house this spring that I no longer hewed to the no voting theory. I assured S. J. May of the same thing. The only reason which I had in not publicly avowing before the change in my mind, was a desire to do so in open court. I espoused the doctrine among my old companions. I wished to reject it in their presence. I write from the office or I am sure that my wife would unite with Miss Griffiths (who is industriously wielding her pen at another desk) in sending love to yourself and Dear Lady.

Yours most truly,
Frederick Douglass

Gerrit Smith Papers, Syracuse University

"F. D."

We have during the last three years signed our editorials with the above initials. The custom originated in a desire to remove certain doubts which were most liberally entertained by the pro-slavery public as to who wrote the leading editorials of the *North Star*. It had been repeatedly denied that an uneducated fugitive slave could write the English language with such propriety and correctness as those early editorials evinced. Well, we pocketed the compliments to our skill, although at the expense of our veracity; and having won the former, we set about to establish the latter by affixing our initials. We have followed the custom now more than three years, and hope we have removed all doubts which our signature can possibly remove in this line. We shall now, therefore, dispense with them, and assume fully the right and dignity of *an Editor*—a Mr. Editor if you please!

Frederick Douglass' Paper, June 26, 1851

TO GERRIT SMITH, ESQR.

Rochester, Sept. 3rd, 1851

My Dear Friend:

I thank you sincerely for your response to the appeal of my friend Miss Griffiths. I regretted that you should be so soon called upon for a helping hand especially in view of the very large drain which the Chaplin case has made upon your purse,[20] but necessity, my friend, would listen to no regrets. I was under the hammer and my friend Julia seeing it cried out in my behalf. You came to my help and I am on my legs again. I bless you for it, and that God, the friend of whose poor you are, will ever bless you.

Have you seen Judge Conklin's decision in the case of the man Daniel?[21] As a whole it is a cheering affair. The Judge has appealed to principles in that decision which leaves Slavery—*property in the souls and bodies of men*—without a single Constitutional leg to stand upon. It is an important sign of progress of sound views on this subject when a judge of such standing falls back upon such principles of legal interpretations as have made you regarded as a dangerous man.

I have received your circular in behalf of my paper. You are a little more than just to me in your estimate of my ability.

With the aid of this circular and my own efforts in the lecturing field, I hope to be able to pass through the autumn into the New Year free from debt.

A Female Anti-slavery Society has been formed in Rochester from which I am expecting much aid. The Ladies who compose it are persons upon whom I can rely. They are intelligent and sound in our views of Anti-slavery action. The constitution of the Society with the names of the officers will appear in the paper of this week. Julia Griffiths is highly pleased with the results of her labors in forming this Society. I am glad on her account that she has surrounded herself with such friends.

Please remember my Love to Mrs. Smith.

Most truly your grateful friend,
Frederick Douglass

Gerrit Smith Papers, Syracuse University

CUBA AND THE UNITED STATES

Our voracious eagle is whetting his talons for the capture of Cuba. This beautiful Island has long been a coveted treasure, and, at last, has so excited our national cupidity that we are no longer able to restrain it. The value of the prize, and the probability of success in securing it, alike conspire to sharpen our ever-keen and almost insatiable appetite for that which can only be attained by plunder.

Our gallant sons have their eyes turned thither as the theatre for the display of those brilliant qualities which have given the American soldier such *enviable* renown throughout the world since the Florida bloodhound war, and the still more glorious one waged against Mexico. From present indications, the history of Cuba may be read in the past history of Texas, New Mexico and California. What their fate has been, hers must be. She must prepare to go down into the same remorseless maw with them.— Lions may rise in the path, but what are lions against the indomitable spirit and bravery of our rapacious eagle? All difficulties will be encountered, all dangers braved, and though it may cost millions of treasure and rivers of blood, Cuba will be conquered and severed from the Spanish crown, and sooner or later annexed to the United States. So, at least, we read passing events with respect to the destiny of that island.

We arrive at this conclusion, not merely from the fact that hundreds, and perhaps thousands, of American citizens have now landed on that island, and that many more are on their way; but more especially from the tone of the press, north as well as south, and from the present attitude of the American government towards the government of Cuba. The whole scene presents an aspect similar to that which existed just prior to the revolution in Texas, which finally resulted in the severance of that State from Mexico, and its annexation to the United States.—Then, as now, the rotten end of this Republic was literally alive with sympathizers with the rebels, and, as usual, Liberty was the watchword and disguise of freebooters, pirates and plunderers. Great meetings were held then, as now, in almost all southern cities, and in many northern ones, with a view to cheer on *the oppressed* in the struggle for their rights. Slaveholders, slave-traders, and cold-blooded tyrants of every grade, poured forth their swelling words of sympathy with the oppressed and execration of the oppressor. Help, in the way of men and money, was sent to strengthen the hands of the insurgents, and to render them victorious in the fraudulent work of wresting that State from Mexican authority.

The government then, as now, was loud in its professions of neutrality, and was high in its pretensions to honor, good faith, and to its scrupulous regard for the solemn stipulations of existing treaties. We doubt not that Andrew Jackson was as sincere in his proclamations and professions against the interference of American citizens in Mexican affairs, as Millard Fillmore now is, in making similar proclamations and professions.—The attempt, on the part of the Government, then, to restrain and hinder the mobocratic and piratical desperadoes of the States, from their plundering designs upon a friendly power, was attended with precisely the same results that we see transpiring with respect to Cuba. It is, perhaps, true that the sham now, has less power to deceive the simple than in the case already specified. Republican rapacity and perfidy had not then reached their present, gigantic proportions, nor attained their present shameless audacity. These propensities have grown rapidly of late. It is laid down as a truth in phrenology, that an organ of the mind increases, both in size and activity, by exercise; and we are told by moralists, that the first step in the broad road of transgression, is taken with more reluctance than any on this side of the last dread leap into ruin. If this be so, a career of high-handed villainy, is opening to our Republic, and we may expect great things in this line from our freedom-loving nation; for the leaven of tyranny, hypocrisy, and cruelty, is rapidly penetrating American society to the core. Man-stealing and man-hunting are preparing the way to bloody war and national ruin. We have got Texas, New Mexico, and California, and we are still a prosperous nation, young, robust, and strong. This is enough to satisfy our popular theologians, that God is still with us, and smiles approvingly upon the great actions of the Republic. Indeed such divines may be expected to see the hand of Providence as well in a war with Spain as in a war with Mexico: for both of which they will not fail, through the misty mazes of theology, to trace responsibility to the throne of Heaven.

> *There is a Divinity that shapes our ends,*
> *Rough hew them how we will.*

What shall oppose *"the destiny"* of the American people? And is it not *"the destiny"* of this Republic to give laws to this whole continent, and the adjacent isles of the sea? Is it not plain as the sun in the heavens, that European despots should be thoroughly routed from this continent, and that the broad, benevolent principles of our free, Republican Institutions, should be established instead? Is there anything in American morality, humanity, or religion, (all of which are on the side of man-stealing, man-hunting, and man-imbruting,) which cannot withstand this reasoning? There is nothing. We are, therefore, prepared to see this nation madly rushing into a war, which may end in the utter destruction of the present government, or in the consolidation under its form of a slaveholding oligarchy of fearful magnitude, imperilling the freedom and happiness of every nation on the globe.

The fact that the American Government has reminded American citizens of the duty of neutrality, proves nothing against our speculations as to the future. We have not forgotten the lie so greedily swallowed, that war had commenced by the act of Mexico; nor have we forgotten a fact more remote, but still more important, as a means of arriving at sound views, in respect to the future course and conduct of this Government. At the very time when General Jackson was issuing his proclamation against the gangs of marauders which were pouring out of the States into Texas, to aid in the revolt, there his sympathies were known to be on the side of the rebels; and subsequent events show that his professed determination to enforce neutrality, was a mere *ruse*. Under his authority, General Gaines, Commander-in-chief of the army of the Southern department of the United States, penetrated, with his troops, the revolted province, and placed them in a position to take actual part in the revolt. To be sure, this was not done without a pretext; it was alleged to be in fulfilment of a duty, imposed on each party, to prevent Indians on the one side of the boundary line from committing depredations on the other: and this lie was swallowed by the nation, notwithstanding that the common sense of all saw the absurdity of troops being sent thirty miles into Mexico, to watch the movements of Indians, who were, perhaps, thirty miles on the U. S. side of the boundary.

But it may be said that the present government will not be able to plead any such pretext for interfering in the affairs of Cuba and will not now pursue the course of its predecessor. The answer is, the fray once begun and blood once heated, "trifles light as air" will be sufficient to bring Spain and the United States into collision. Indeed the incipient steps towards this result have already been taken. Fifty-two American freebooters and pirates, with arms in their hands and bullets in their pockets, have been apprehended and shot by order of the Cuban government, and the news of this transaction scarcely reaches us before we learn that an United States' ship of war is dispatched to Havana to demand explanation, as if any explanation were needed!

But this is not all. The Spaniards have been saucy to Lieutenant Rogers, and have actually compelled him to heave to. This is a grave offense, and it serves well to inflame the passions of our people and to provoke resentment, although everybody knows that were hostile troops landing upon our shores from a neighboring country, for the avowed purpose of revolutionizing our government, we should have been far less decorous than the Spaniards to any vessel suspected of aiding in such design.

Here, then, are two points upon which to hinge a quarrel. The first thing to be done in all dignified fights is to demand an explanation; not that explanation is ever necessary, far otherwise. No one needs to be told whether an insult offered him is intended or not; these things generally speak for themselves. It is simply a polite preliminary to the fight. It is part of the fight.—We do not believe that there is a man in the country, who, for one moment, thinks that any other motive than that of preserving the peace and stability of the government of Cuba induced either one or the other of these acts on the part of the authorities. As to the fifty-two Americans who were shot, we can only say of them, *they died as the fool dieth;* they were not in Cuba at the call of duty! They had assumed the name of liberators, the better to disguise their characters as plunderers. They had abandoned their own country for a profession which made them outlaws. They went abroad to shoot, and to run the chance of being shot. They staked their lives upon a desperate game, and they lost; that is all that need be said of them. This Government has no more business to demand an explanation in the case of these American outlaws, than it has to demand an explanation on account of the execution of any class of offenders under any Government of Europe. The man who quits these shores with the view to a hostile demonstration on the shores of any country with which we are at peace as a nation, forfeits all claim to protection, on the part of his Government, and becomes an outlaw.

It is, however, answered that, among these fifty-two, there might have been those shot who were entirely innocent of promoting revolt, but, we put it to every reflecting mind, if it is at all likely that the authorities of Cuba, under all the circumstances, would seize unoffending American citizens, and subject them to instantaneous death? The presumption evidently is, that they would not.

Spain is not so desirous to incur the displeasure of the United States, as to disregard the rights of American citizens. Her very weakness forbids such an idea, but what if, in the exasperation occasioned by the fact that armed thousands are permitted by the American Government to leave American ports, notoriously for the purpose of invading Cuba, and of stirring up revolt against the Government of that island, the authorities thereof should confound the innocent with the guilty in a particular instance? Even such case would not, we think, justify the belligerent tone adopted by the Press, and especially by the organs of the present administration.

The true explanation of the present tone of the press, in regard to this occurrence is, that the ruling power of this nation which is slavery, wants a pretext for the Conquest of Cuba, and for the final annexation of that country to the United States, and the deed will be done.

Frederick Douglass' Paper, September 4, 1851

TO SAMUEL D. PORTER

Sept. 1851

There are three men now at my house who are in great peril. I am unwell, I need your advice. Please come at once.

F. D.

Samuel D. Porter Papers, University of Rochester

ROCHESTER AND SLAVE-CATCHING

It is a source of much gratitude that Rochester continues to be spared the guilt and shame of returning to slavery, torture and death any one of its humblest and least regarded inhabitants. It is something to the credit of this community that, while nearly every other important city of the North has experienced incursions of the greedy hunters of men, Rochester has thus far been exempted. It implies a state of feeling in the community hostile to the barbarous practice; and we are happy in the belief that this feeling really exists, affording, as it does, a degree of security and repose to our unfortunate people. But, while this is the case, there are a thousand reasons which should place every colored man on his guard, and keep him in constant readiness for this species of assault. There are two presses, at least, vigorously at work to induce a sentiment in the public mind favorable to slave-catching. They virtually invite slave-hunters to Rochester, and assure them of a cordial welcome, and a patriotic co-operation in hunting their prey. Both the *Advertiser* and the *American* are openly insisting upon the execution of the murderous law. The *Advertiser* is especially active in this work. Articles appear in its columns, which, for baseness and brutality, cannot be exceeded by the most obdurate slave-driver that ever wielded the lash upon the slave's quivering flesh. Here is a specimen:

"ARMING OF 'YOUNG AFRICA.'

"A correspondent writes us, that 'for a few days past it has been observed that colored persons are pricing and buying fire arms, such as pistols, revolvers, &c., with the avowed intention of using them against the ministers of the law, and our orderly citizens, should they be called upon to aid in executing the fugitive law, in our city.' And the writer suggests that some measures should be adopted to put a stop to these premonitory symptoms of treason.

"Whether what our correspondent apprehends be fully justified by the facts or not, we are unable to say. But we have no apprehensions of the sort—let the Negroes buy as many revolvers as they please—but they may rest assured that the first one that is used by them against our citizens, will be the signal for the extermination of the whole Negro race from our midst. If they wish to provoke *a war of the races,* by re-enacting the bloody scenes of Christiana,[22] they will find our civil and military authorities, and our citizens at large, prepared to defend themselves, and to put down their murderous assaults, with an avenging arm that will carry retributive justice home to such vile traitors and assassins. If the issue is to be forced upon us, to decide whether the white races are to maintain their rights and their position, or whether

Negro mob law is to govern, and ride rampant over our laws, constitution and liberties, let it be known at once, that our people may be prepared for the enemy."

"*If they wish to provoke a war of the races.*" How absurd, in a community where there is but about *one* fugitive to *one thousand* white citizens! Can any *sane* man suppose that there is any such wish on the part of the handful of colored people in this city? The thing is utterly preposterous. There is not a colored man in the city, however enthusiastic, courageous, brave, and ambitious he may be, but who would scout the idea of a wish such as that imputed by "the Editor of the *Advertiser.*" "*If the issue is to be forced upon us.*" Can villainy exceed this? There are a handful of Negroes, for the most part, poor, and uneducated, and comparatively, friendless; encountering every hour of their lives, a stern and bitter prejudice, and only desiring to get leave to live—held up as daring the whites to a conflict—*forcing* the issue of a bloody war. Then *mark* again, it is said, "if"—(we are glad that it admits of some doubt,)—"*the issue is forced upon us,*" (the whites)—why? "*Our citizens at large are prepared to defend themselves, and to put down their murderous assaults with an avenging arm that will carry retributive justice home to such vile traitors and assassins!*" Citizens of Rochester! Here you have a field of glory spread out before you! The enemy dares you to the assault! He forces the issue upon you! He wishes to provoke you to a war of the races! And it is said that he is already armed for the battle!

Laurels await you more rich and glorious than ever entwined the victorious brow of the most illustrious conquerors, from the days of Alexander the Great, to those of Napoleon. We would rouse you, citizens of Rochester! We put it to you sternly, can you, with any credit to yourselves, omit an opportunity so inviting, and so grand, for signalizing your bravery, and sending your names down to posterity encircled with a halo of imperishable glory! Think of your numbers! You are *a thousand to one;* but do not let that deter you. There is no reason to apprehend that, in the conflict "*forced* upon you," the prophetic declaration will be fulfilled, that "*one shall chase a thousand;*" for remember that "*the issue is forced upon you,*" and that the Negroes are the aggressors. You are vindicators of insulted *justice;* and your enemies are "*traitors and assassins!!!*"

To insult a preacher, to mislead a blind man, to trip up a man with one leg, to beat a beggar, or to flog a woman, is brave, manly, heroic, honorable, gallant, magnanimous and humane, compared with this dastardly attempt to kindle up the vengeance of our forty thousand white fellow-citizens against the few straggling, harmless, inoffensive colored people who have here sought and found a home.

Frederick Douglass' Paper, October 23, 1851

TO S. D. PORTER, ESQR.

Rochester, Jan. 12th, 1852

My dear Sir:

I am in receipt of yours dated 8th January. It is not necessary to tell you with what feelings I read it—or to attempt a long reply to its contents. I am a husband and a father, and withal a citizen, honorably and to the best of my ability endeavouring to discharge the duties of this three-fold relation. When the city, which you allege to be full of scandalous reports implicating Miss G and me, shall put those *"reports"* in a definite shape, and present a responsible person to back them, it will be time enough for me to attempt to refute them.

Individuals have rights not less than society, and while I do not wish to trench upon the rights of society, I am as little disposed to admit any unjust claims which any individual may set up in the name of society. You and I have been friends during the last two or three years, and on as intimate terms as can well subsist between the rich and the poor. I say this last not reproachfully. It seems to me that a friendly word might have been, ere this, whispered to me, apprising me of these "scandalous reports," and advising me how to allay them. In not doing this you have acted more delicately than faithfully. Miss Griffiths is a free woman, and of her own free will preferred to board in a nobler family than mine nearly two months ago. She is in a respectable family. I am in no way responsible for her words, her deeds, or her dress, nor indeed, for her thinking me a *"God"*—if she is so foolish or wicked as to think so. Still I do feel that she has a just claim upon my gratitude, respect and friendship. Were she an unworthy person I might feel, perhaps, like joining with you in speaking lightly of her. When she was in my family, I was necessarily much in her society. Our walking and riding together was natural. Now we are separate and only meet at my office at business hours and for business purposes, where we are open to the observation of my printers and the public, from ten o'clock or earlier in the morning until four o'clock in the afternoon. I know not how long she will feel it her duty or for her interest to act as my clerk, and work for the circulation of my paper, as she has seriously thought lately of returning to England, but whether her stay shall be long or short, shall be a matter for her own discretion, uninfluenced by any interference of mine. But I am doing what I had no intention of doing, when I took up my pen, and therefore bring this letter to a close at once.

Believe me to be very truly yours,
Frederick Douglass

Samuel D. Porter Papers, University of Rochester

HON. HORACE GREELEY AND THE PEOPLE OF COLOR

There is not, perhaps, a single public man in all the United States, unconnected with the Anti-Slavery movement, who has, at any time, evinced a more generous and manly spirit towards the Free People of color, nor indicated the entertainment of a more genuine desire for their welfare and happiness than Horace Greeley of the *New York Tribune.* He has often defended our people from the brutal attacks of the press, *far* more effectively than ever our technical friends could do; for while they speak to tens, Greeley speaks to thousands. Regarding us in the light of a misunderstood, under-estimated, and oppressed people, struggling against immense odds, to be men and citizens, he has, at times extended to us a helping hand, almost fraternal. Did a colored man rise up among his brethren, and by industry, perseverance and talents, make himself master of a position among men of high moral and intellectual worth, Mr. Greeley was among the first of all American Editors to recognize and to proclaim the fact with apparent satisfaction. There is not a colored public man in the United States who has signalized himself, either by his devotion to liberty, or by his ability, who is not, to some extent, indebted to Mr. Greeley for a friendly word of encouragement. Even within the last two years, he has poured such a torrent of denunciation upon the slave system; attacked with such boldness the slave power; portrayed with such faithfulness, the disgraceful and shocking slave hunts; despised with such hearty good will, the demagoguism of Webster and Fillmore; as displayed in their pretended alarm for the safety of the Union; battled so earnestly against the new doctrine of treason as almost to win for himself the unpopular yet enviable title of being the Negro's friend. What black man did not feel grateful to the *Tribune,* a few months ago, for the gallant manner in which it exposed the frauds and falsehoods practiced upon this nation in respect to the true character of Haiti? *Who* among us did not feel a thrill of gratitude when he read, in September last, the defense of the heroic colored men at Christiana? Why, every one of us. But while we do not forget all this, we must nevertheless, recognize Mr. Greeley as being among the most effective and dangerous of our foes. We say this more in sadness than in bitterness of spirit. We may misapprehend his motives: they are between himself and the Searcher of all hearts; yet we repeat, that by his present position he is, practically, among our deadliest enemies. He is the advocate of Colonization, which, to us, means *ultimate extermination;* and in this advocacy, Henry Clay himself, whose olfactory nerves are disturbed by the most distant allusion to *"Free* people of color," does not assume a more haughty, imperious, and over-bearing spirit towards us than this same Horace Greeley. In urging our departure from our native land to Africa, this gentleman appeals more to our fears than to our hopes. He paints our ignorance, degradation and wretchedness in the darkest colors and warns us that *worse,* not better, days await us in this country. He points us to the inhuman, barbarous, and unconstitutional legislation of Indiana,[23] and without pouring forth a true man's abhorrence of such legislation, he complacently asks us what such legislation means; and intimates that this is but the beginning of the "Reign of Terror." He does not call upon the people of Indiana to wipe out its disgraceful Statute; but he calls upon the free people of color to *take the hint from such legislation,* and *clear out to Africa.* He has even become so averse to our remaining here of late, as to frown upon all efforts of ours to obtain our civil and political rights. He held up the Committee who signed the call for the "Colored State Convention," to the ridicule of his readers last week, for proposing such a convention, and stated that he had always advised Negroes to refrain from agitating for the right of suffrage. If his advice were taken, he would probably point to our inertness as an evidence of our unfitness for the exercise of that right. A queer and incomprehensible man is Mr. Greeley. For the poverty and misery of the poor white man in this country, his mind is fruitful of remedies. "Working men's union," "Co-operative associations" have his hearty concurrence and advocacy. At their conventions and congresses, he is prophet, priest, and philosopher—soothing their poverty by his sympathy, increasing their courage by his counsel, and stimulating them to exertion by the fruits of his own example. But for the poor black man, he has neither sympathy, prophecy, nor plan. His advice to us may be stated in two words, and is such as is commonly addressed to dogs— "*Be gone.*"

Mr. Greeley is called a benevolent man; and, as such, we ask him, how he reconciles his course towards the Free Colored People with the spirit of benevolence? Does he not know that the certain effect of urging them to depart, and alarming them with the idea that it is impossible for them to remain here, is to damp their aspirations, to fill them with doubt, and to paralyze their energies for improvement and elevation? To us, this circumstance constitutes one of the strongest objections to the Colonization discussion.—Slaveholders will not emigrate with their slaves to New Mexico, while there are doubt and uncertainty of their ability to hold them when they get there; and colored people will not exert themselves to acquire property, and settle down as good citizens of the State, while they are alarmed and terrified by the prospect of being (ultimately) driven out of the country. This truth is *well* known by our oppressors; and it is, doubtless, one motive for the constant agitation of the Colonization scheme.

Frederick Douglass' Paper, January 29, 1852

TO GERRIT SMITH, ESQR.

Rochester 19th Feb., 1852

My dear Sir:

You have not time to write nor to read long letters. I shall therefore come at once to the point. I have noticed (and the fact cannot have altogether escaped your observation), namely, that certain gentlemen of the Liberty Party are either prepared to abandon or to have that organization absorbed by another less radical, less stringent [party], and I think less comprehensive in its character; a party which will command more votes. If I have not misread and misunderstood certain recent articles from our friend Thomas, he fully approves this policy, and is quite ready to unite on the platform of the Free Democracy of Ohio. I have been informed that James C. Jackson, Wm. L. Chaplin and J. C. Hathaway are quite willing to go into the next presidential election under Free Soil and antifugitive Slave bill leaders. I write not to condemn this policy. These are wise and honorable men, and what they propose may be for the best. But so it does not now strike me. I know not your mind concerning it. But my own conviction is that the policy is unwise and if adopted will be followed by mischievous results. I think we ought to stand by and maintain the Liberty Party with all its great principles and purposes. I do confide much in your judgment as to all matters touching the cause of human freedom. I therefore solicit a few lines to let me know your opinion of this matter. I cannot promise that I could follow if you should go for disbanding the Liberty Party, but I will promise to stand by that party if you say *stand!* One thing more, my dear Sir, you *must, yes* you must (if you possibly can) attend the Convention in this city on the 18th and 19th March.

You quite encouraged me about my chirography. My hand is a picked up one, gathered from different sources, and therefore lacks consistency. How different with yourself. I should know your hand, I had almost said although you should make but a straight mark.

Please remember me kindly to Mrs. Smith.

Your faithful and affectionate friend,

Frederick Douglass

Sallie Holley lectures here this evening. She now wears the bonds that I have thrown off, being a pupil of Mrs. Foster and as I fear goes it *blind*. She will, however, see her way out in the end.

Gerrit Smith Papers, Syracuse University

LETTER TO KOSSUTH, Concerning Freedom and Slavery in the United States, in behalf of the American Anti-Slavery Society

He who comes to this country, hoping to escape *"entanglements"* on the slavery question, (as it is called by those who shrink from it,) must not only keep his mouth shut and his ears closed, but must actually put his eyes out, or cover them with bandages too thick to allow him to catch the lineaments of our national face; and in choosing one to lead him, must be sure to select an individual as blind as himself; for so sure as these conditions are not complied with, he will find his fond hopes blasted.—

The line between Freedom and Slavery, in this country, is tightly drawn; and the combatants on either side are in earnest and fight hand to hand. He who chances to be on one side or on the other, if it be but in the estimation of a single hair, must fight, or die. There is no neutral ground here for any man. Father Mathew looked for such ground, but he looked with his eyes open; and this is the secret of his bad luck.[24] Had he been deaf, dumb, and blind, he might have, peradventure, stumbled on the weak side; but he saw the strongest, and consulting his fears, he threw himself in the arms of the oppressor, because on his side was power. Kossuth has tried it, and although, backed by his non-intervention doctrine; and being, perhaps, the greatest tactician of modern times, the result has been the same, and worse than the same. A tourist may visit Austria, Russia, France, Spain and the Barbary States, and perhaps escape committal or controversy; but so he may not do in the United States. Entanglement is certain. We allow no man to enter here without conflict. He must show his hand, try his strength, prove his metal; and there's no escape.

Who are to blame for these bad manners which so annoy and perplex the stranger?—Some say the abolitionists; and they are abused on all sides soundly for the same.—Their impertinent intermeddling with foreigners, is a source of the utmost pain and mortification to the decent, well-behaved, conservative class of our citizens, many of whom would be glad to banish them to Africa with "the n——rs" if they could; for you know in this case the innocent have to suffer with the guilty. Our reputation, as a nation, is the thing that is injured; and patriotism cherishes nothing more dearly than national reputation. According to high authority, men will seek this bauble in the cannon's mouth. It is not strange, then, that our *"potent, grave* and *reverend seniors,"* of Hunker standing, frown upon the abolitionists as an ill-mannered and mischievous set, who must be put down at all hazards.—"What," say they, "has it come to this, that a minister cannot come here from another country to preach the gospel, without being insulted by a request from these impertinent mad-caps to remember the American slave in his prayers!—that Father Mathew, the apostle of temperance, cannot come here without being *bothered* by an invitation to attend an anti-slavery meeting!—that the noble Kossuth cannot come here to address our citizens on the great doctrines of independence, the rights of man and universal liberty, without being pestered with deputations and addresses, exhorting him to be true to himself, to his position, to his history at home and abroad, to the great doctrine of

universal freedom which he preaches! Why! the bad manners of this set
are intolerable!"

Such are the sentiments of our pro-slavery noodles. It is they, not we,
who are at fault in this manner. They have got a foul, unnatural, loath-
some abomination, to uphold against all the noble instincts of human
nature; and bowing themselves before this huge and bloody idol, they
call upon all men, of every land and nation, who venture within its pre-
cincts, to "do likewise;" or at any rate, to padlock their lips, and be dumb,
in regard to the monstrosity. They, not we, are the aggressors. They
throw themselves athwart the current of nature, of conscience, of truth, of
justice, and of the spirit of the living God. *They* make war on man, as
well as on manners, and when we cry out against it, and call upon others
to do so, we, forsooth, are meddlesome and indecorous!

We have been induced to make the foregoing remarks, in anticipation
of the reception which awaits the pamphlet containing the letter to Kossuth, the title of which is given at the head of this article. The subject is
a fruitful one, and we would gladly say more, but our space will not
permit us to do so. The letter to Kossuth, is a most searching production;
and if he be not insensible to the claims of that justice he so eloquently
advocates, he must be convinced by it, that he has bestowed eulogies on
this nation, *not* deserved; that he has been playing into the hands of
tyrants, worse than Austria ever knew; and that he has inflicted a wound
on the cause of freedom, which he cannot too speedily do his utmost to
heal.

Frederick Douglass' Paper, February 26, 1852

HORACE GREELEY AND COLONIZATION

Frederick Douglass' Paper is requested to take notice that the *Tribune*
is quite as willing that the blacks should colonize in this country as out of it.
Our opinion is that the work of civilizing and Christianizing Africa is one
which especially commends itself to the civilized and Christianized blacks of
this country; but we would like to see them buy out a township in Southern
Jersey, or a county in Nebraska for a beginning, and see what work they
would make of colonizing that. What we mean to make them do, even at
the expense of incurring their deadliest hatred, is to stop currying horses,
blacking boots and opening oysters for a living and go to plowing, hoeing

and harvesting their own fields, where the world can see what they do and who does it. Hitherto the great mass of them have acted as if their race were made for servitude and unfit for anything else.—We don't believe that, but they act as if they did, and we mean to make them act differently if we can.—*Tribune.*

We are glad to know that the *Tribune* is *"willing"* that the blacks should colonize in this country; for, however indifferent such *willingness* may seem, when viewed from the stand-point of right and justice, it is magnified into a shining virtue, when compared with the cruel and bitter spirit which would drive every freeman of color off this continent. But we differ from the *Tribune,* even in its more innocent notion of colonization. We say to every colored man, *be a man where you are;* neither a "township in Southern Jersey," nor a "county in Nebraska," can serve you. You must be a man here, and force your way to intelligence, wealth and respectability. If you can't do that here, you can't do it there. By changing your place, you don't change your character. We believe that contact with the white race, even under the many unjust and painful restrictions to which we are subjected, does more toward our elevation and improvement, than the mere circumstance of being separated from them could do. The truth is sometimes acknowledged by Colonizationists themselves. They argue (for a diabolical purpose it is true) that the condition of our race has been improved by their situation as slaves, since it has brought them into contact with a superior people, and afforded them facilities for acquiring knowledge. This position is sound, though the hearts that gave it birth, are rotten. We hold, that while there is personal liberty in the Northern States for the colored people, while they have the privilege to educate their children, to speak and write out their sentiments, to petition, and in some instances, and with some qualifications, to exercise the right of suffrage, the time has not come for them to emigrate from these States to any other country, and last of all, to the wilds of Africa. The *Tribune* need not, we think, apprehend the "deadliest hatred" of the colored people, by urging them to "stop currying horses, blacking boots, and opening oysters for a living." Numbers of them are taking this advice, and urging it upon others. Be patient, Mr. Greeley, a nation may not be born in a day, without a miracle.

Frederick Douglass' Paper, February 26, 1852

TO GERRIT SMITH, ESQR.

Rochester, March 24th, 1852

My Dear Sir:

I thank you warmly for attending our festival. Your visit to Rochester has done good both to the cause of temperance and to Anti-slavery. The festival was highly successful, and has left a good impression. The receipts amount to more than four hundred dollars, and I believe that the expenses do not exceed one hundred dollars. You may well suppose that Julia Griffiths is highly pleased with the result.

I regret that you could not have remained to witness the scene which occurred the morning you left for home. The constitution of the *"New York State Anti-slavery Society,"* drawn up by our friend Goodell, was submitted at ten o'clock that morning to a large meeting, and before a single article of that constitution could be adopted, the indefatigable Stephen [Foster] was on his legs with a motion and speech in favor of making the Society auxiliary to the *American Anti-slavery Society,* telling us that he had come to test us and to compel us to show cause for not uniting with the American Society, etc. The next objection to the constitution by Mr. Foster was the assertion of the impossibility of legalizing Slavery. I need not tell you that these objections were all overcome. The constitution was adopted very heartily and almost unanimously. In the account which I have given of the Convention in my paper, I have thought proper to leave out all mention of the Fosters. I am persuaded that there is a desire to provoke me into a controversy with them. They accuse me now, openly, of having sold myself to one Gerrit Smith, Esq., and to have changed my views more in consequence of your purse than your arguments! These things are disagreeable but they do not move me. A consciousness of my own rectitude affords me abundant repose and enables me heartily to despise these assaults.

I wait for their accusations to appear in some of their papers. I may then make a reply. One handle they have against me is that I told you of the change in my views before I told the public. This, they think, is proof positive of corruption.

But I will pester you no longer with these slanders. I am content to bide my time.

In haste, most truly yours,
Frederick Douglass

Gerrit Smith Papers, Syracuse University

TO MRS. S. D. PORTER, PRESIDENT OF THE ROCHESTER LADIES ANTI-SLAVERY SOCIETY

Rochester, March 27, 1852

Dear Madam:

It is with sentiments of profound gratitude I acknowledge the receipt of *two hundred and thirty-three dollars* from the Treasurer of the "Ladies Anti-Slavery Sewing Society," and I beg that you will accept, for yourself, and for the excellent Ladies composing the Society, my heartfelt thanks, not more for the valuable donation, than for the kind appreciation of my labors which it implies. Like most other anti-slavery journals, mine continues to need pecuniary support, over and above that, which is derived from its subscription lists. But for such aid, coming often in the moment of extreme want, my enterprise must have long since perished, and the pro-slavery world would have again, had occasion to rejoice, at the failure of another press, under the management of a colored man.

Thank God! my journal yet continues, and there is still a witness of the Sable race in the field, humbly asserting emancipation for the Slave and progress for the free. It is gratifying to know that the Society which you represent, look kindly on this effort in behalf of my enslaved, slandered, and persecuted people, and that they do not, in a sectarian spirit, withdraw all support from my paper, because I am a "Liberty Party" man and think I can give a more direct vote against slavery by acting with that party than by voting with any other.

Allow me to say that my spirit has been greatly cheered by observing your enlightened liberality, and your self-denying labors, and I rejoice to know that, neither you nor the Society over which you preside, are weary in well doing; and that you and they are resolved to press forward in the holy cause which you have espoused so earnestly and have labored for so successfully.

It is to the Rochester "Ladies Anti-Slavery Sewing Society" that I look for improving the moral sense of this community, in the subject of human freedom, [which] seems, providentially, committed to your Society. It is for you to call conventions, secure the attendance of eloquent speakers, and make all the needful arrangements for the spread of Anti-Slavery truths here. Should you fail to do this, the work must fail, or others will take it up. At present you have the field to yourselves; and it is meet that you should occupy it. Should we stand firm, always cultivating the truly Catholic spirit which has thus far, so beautifully characterised the proceedings of your Society, you may hope to unite with you, all the useful friends of Anti-Slavery in the community. Such an union of strength would be none too great for the work required to be done, since we, who feel for those "in bonds as bound with them," are yet but a handful when compared with our whole population. The friends of this cause are sometimes told, by those who know not the happiness that flows from disinterested and self-denying labors that their efforts are useless—that the Nation is, even now, more impenitent than ten years ago. Little do such persons know of the true mission to which we are called, and of the spirit and power by which we are supported. What, to them, is a reason for giving up our efforts in this cause, is to us, a reason for clinging more firmly to that cause, and increasing our efforts for its triumph.

We are only called upon to do "our duty" and to leave, with the Eternal Father, the honor and glory of all our endeavors.

Hoping, Dear Madam, ever to remain worthy of the kind cooperation of the Society over which you preside, I beg you to believe me, very truly your grateful friend.

Frederick Douglass

Samuel D. Porter Papers, University of Rochester

TO GERRIT SMITH, ESQR.

Rochester, April 15th, 1852

My dear Sir:

I am not unmindful of the favor you did me, nor of the debt I owe you for giving me the chance of seeing James G. Birney as he passed through Rochester. I had seen Mr. Birney once before. I saw him in New York in the "Apollo Saloon," and altho' the day was bright the Hall was dark and, owing to that darkness, or the darkness of my own prejudices, I did not get a good *daguerreotype* of the man. It is true that I was struck with the honest expression, calm and dignified bearing of the man, even then, and that glance at him though made in a dark place, left me in doubt if he had not had great wrong in the bitter assaults made upon him by particular friends. I, however, at that time, lived in the whirl and excitement of a lecturing life, and soon forgot the meeting with Mr. Birney, and the meeting with him here seemed like meeting one I had not seen before. I have a large share of veneration for great *men;* and will go further to see one than I would to see all other sights besides. I was glad to find Mr. Birney's speech so little impaired. I could understand him well, and the interview left upon me the impression that he has never been overestimated, even by his best friends. This is saying a great deal for Mr. Birney. For, of whom has more been said than of him? I have not time to give you a detailed account of my visit to Mr. B. I spent about one hour with him and, on rising to leave, both Mr. B. and Mrs. Talman invited me to dine there—and there, let me tell you, I did dine. Now, what is the world coming to! Besides, I was not treated with a mere formal courtesy but with evident kindness such as I should receive under your own comprehensive roof. The dear little daughter of Mrs. T.—a lovely child—came to me, smiled, and played willingly with my *sable* hand, seeing apparently nothing in my color, form or features to repel her. "Except ye become as little children, ye cannot enter into the kingdom of Heaven." I take Mrs. Birney to be one of the happiest of women, just the spirit to throw light and joy all around her. I saw her but for a few minutes as I was called away (to assist a colored man who had got into trouble,) before dinner was over, but in that time, I became so well acquainted as to feel if ever I should visit Michigan, I should go to Saginaw with an assurance of welcome.

I am now preparing for my journey to Cincinnati. I should go to that Convention with a firmer tread, were I sure of meeting you there. There are three subjects upon which I should like for you to speak before the abolitionists of the West—1st, the true sphere of human or civil government, 2d, the unconstitutionality of Slavery everywhere in this Republic, 3d, the right, power, and duty of this government to abolish Slavery in every State in this Union. Such an exposition as you might give of these subjects, could not fail to open up new trains of thought among the men and women of the West, who will assemble at that Convention. I see that Friend C. C. Burleigh is to be there, and will, doubtless, press his *non voting theory.* He has talents of a superior order, and eloquence as fervid and showy as that of any orator of the no-voting school. He will make an impression doubtless, at this Convention and it does seem to me, considering the importance of the occasion, there ought to be some strong man on the ground to stand up for the *truth.* Men should not, under the guidance of a false philosophy, be led to fling from them such powerful instrumentalities against Slavery as the Constitution and the ballot. Should you be there our cause would be safe. I should really like to see you rise there—after one of Burleigh's arguments—and in one-half the words used by him, break every link of his non-voting logic. I shall take with me a number of copies of your arguments, and should you be absent, I will try to give tongue to them. I have received the *Non-Conformist* bearing the mark of Peterboro. I thank you for that paper, also for the *Banner* you have several times sent to me. I get the latter regularly in exchange. I see by the *Non-Conformist* that G. Thompson attaches some importance to politics in England, however he may scout that subject or science in America. The address, read by him before the Reform Conference is quite a political document.

I have been asked *why* I never replied to the nine columns of Mr. Farmer.[25] My answer is, that Mr. Farmer conceded all I said of Mr. Thompson to be true. He admitted that Mr. Thompson swore to support the Queen as the rightful Sovereign. Now what is this, but to support the Queen as the head of the Church, as well as of the State? I found that his friends looked upon every thing that I said of Mr. Thompson as a personal quarrel and that the pro-slavery papers were exulting in the controversy. I, therefore, felt willing to remain buried under *nine heavy columns* rather than do harm to a good cause.

You will, I am sure, be pleased with the able Address from the Executive Committee of the New York State Anti-slavery Society, published in this week's paper. It is from the pen of Wm. Goodell, one of the soundest reasoners in this country. There are those who think him prosey, and so he may be to some minds. But to my mind he is always interesting and at times rises to lofty strains of purest eloquence—of eloquence, not of foaming torrents, gentle showers, or beautiful flowers, but the eloquence of the sturdy bark which, after outriding the pelting storms of a perilous ocean, brings cargo and crew safely into port.

Since beginning this letter, I have seen yours to Julia Griffiths. I am glad that I was able to behave like a *"gentleman"* with Mr. Birney. The fact of my having been a slave made him overlook any awkwardness on my part. Please remember me kindly to Mrs. Smith, and believe me affectionately and gratefully yours,

Frederick Douglass

Gerrit Smith Papers, Syracuse University

TO GERRIT SMITH, ESQR.

Rochester, May 7th, 1852

My dear Sir:

I am at home again and am none the worse for my jaunt to Cincinnati, although somewhat hoarse from constant speaking. The Convention was said to have been the best ever held west of the Alleghenies.

The Convention was not quite as radical as I desired it should be in regard to the duty of this government to abolish slavery, but I think the resolution asserting that duty, would have been adopted could you have been there to have set forth its truth. I am quite satisfied with the proceedings of the Convention in every respect, aside from its treatment of the resolution asserting that duty.

You were expected at the Convention till the last. I do wish we had a few more *Gerrit Smiths*—say about 16—one for every free State. The cause of human progress hath need of just that number. Anti-slavery is quite timid in the neighborhood of Kentucky, and it needs somebody from the bracing atmosphere in which Jerry was rescued[26] to give it courage. Your friend *Fee* is a noble man and is doing a good work in Kentucky, but a few months in the North would be of service to him. Mr. *Julian* is a *whole* man. He is an abolitionist and something more—a reformer. I think he is far in advance of his party in the west and is more in harmony with the Liberty Party than with free-soilers. Your old Friend Sam'l Lewes came out bravely on the wicked position of the American Church in regard to Slavery, and firmly maintained the *"higher law"* which by the way, makes slavery *illegal* everywhere although Friend Lewes would not perhaps, go that doctrine. You left me to reply to my friend C. C. Burleigh. I trembled as I looked forward to the performance of the task, but I was less perturbed when the work was to be done. The subject was not, however, discussed at length. The resolutions adopted were for the most part drawn up by myself. You will see them in this week's paper.

In haste, very truly yours in the fulfilment of all righteousness,

Frederick Douglass

Gerrit Smith Papers, Syracuse University

TO GERRIT SMITH, ESQR.

Rochester, 15th May, 1852

My dear Sir:

I was unable last week to write such an article as I wished to have accompany my call upon you, for your view in respect to the mission and course of Louis Kossuth. The call shall appear next week. The American Anti-Slavery Society closed its annual meeting here Thursday night. I am hardly qualified to give an opinion of its proceedings, for the reason that I have been pretty roughly handled by some of the "choice and master spirits" of the Society. Taken as a whole, the meeting was far from a happy one and has done little to strengthen the Society in the good opinion of the friends of the slave in this vicinity. The first morning of the meeting was very properly devoted to the memory of the humane I. T. Hopper, tidings of whose death had first reached us. The afternoon meeting was mainly occupied by a speech from Friend Garrison, defending the position of the Am. So. towards the *world* at large and to its own members in particular. I was pleased with his exposition, but while the theory was sound, I felt that the practice of the Society had not been according to its theory. I found myself treated as an enemy to the American Society, a deserter from its fold, and I was bound to know the cause. I therefore took occasion to place myself before the Society the next morning in such a manner as to enable my fellow abolitionists to *search* me and to probe me to the bottom. I inquired *why* I was treated as an alien here? You may depend this was enough. They were all ready, and *more* than ready to meet me and to show cause for coldness towards me. My accusers stood full *seven men deep*. There were many things alleged against me. My whole course was brought under review, and my old friends were far from mealy mouthed. My *spirit* and *acts* were criticized fully, and I am happy to be able to say that, for the most part, I was strengthened to bear it without perturbation. I have time only to set down a few of the points made against me.

1st. I had changed my opinion in respect to the U. S. Consti[tution].

2d. I had acquainted Gerrit Smith with that change before I said anything about it in my paper.

3d. I had joined in forming a Society in this State, not aux[iliary] to the American Society.

4th. I had allowed myself to be patted on the shoulder by John Scoble at our Buffalo Convention.

5th. I had accepted a bribe from Benjamin Coates, a Colonizationist.

6th. I had been in fellowship with the *deadliest* enemies of the American Society.

7th. My paper was no longer anti-slavery but a Liberty Party paper.

That John Thomas had used its columns to uphold Louis Kossuth.

That he had said that slavery was a matter of less importance than land reform.

That Gerrit Smith had virtually made the same declaration in Corinthian Hall.

That my paper is a political and not an anti-slavery paper, in the same sense that the *Tribune* is.

Two of the agents—Mr. and Mrs. Foster—said that they had and should continue to labor, to have my paper supplanted by the *Standard* just as they would have abolitionists to drop the *Tribune* or any other paper, partly an Anti-slavery paper, for one wholly so.

9th. That I had attacked George Thompson, etc.

You must know that these naked points were urged with any amount of side blows, innuendo, dark suspicions, such as avarice, faithlessness, treachery, ingratitude, and what not.

I will not tell you *how* I met the onset. Suffice it to say, that I stood it all, with spirit unruffled, and have now the pleasing satisfaction to know that I was elected a manager in the Society with but one dissenting vote, and that was the vote of my old jealous friend, *Remond*.

You will see some further account of this meeting in my next paper.

Ever truly your grateful and affectionate friend,

Douglass

Gerrit Smith Papers, Syracuse University

THE MEANING OF JULY FOURTH FOR THE NEGRO, speech at Rochester, New York, July 5, 1852

Mr. President, Friends and Fellow Citizens:

He who could address this audience without a quailing sensation, has stronger nerves than I have. I do not remember ever to have appeared as a speaker before any assembly more shrinkingly, nor with greater distrust of my ability, than I do this day. A feeling has crept over me quite unfavorable to the exercise of my limited powers of speech. The task before me is one which requires much previous thought and study for its proper performance. I know that apologies of this sort are generally considered flat and unmeaning. I trust, however, that mine will not be so considered. Should I seem at ease, my appearance would much misrepresent me. The little experience I have had in addressing public meetings, in country school houses, avails me nothing on the present occasion.

The papers and placards say that I am to deliver a Fourth of July Oration. This certainly sounds large, and out of the common way, for me. It is true that I have often had the privilege to speak in this beautiful Hall, and to address many who now honor me with their presence. But neither their familiar faces, nor the perfect gage I think I have of Corinthian Hall seems to free me from embarrassment.

The fact is, ladies and gentlemen, the distance between this platform and the slave plantation, from which I escaped, is considerable—and the difficulties to be overcome in getting from the latter to the former are by no means slight. That I am here to-day is, to me, a matter of astonishment as well as of gratitude. You will not, therefore, be surprised, if in what I have to say I evince no elaborate preparation, nor grace my speech with any high sounding exordium. With little experience and with less learning, I have been able to throw my thoughts hastily and imperfectly together; and trusting to your patient and generous indulgence, I will proceed to lay them before you.

This, for the purpose of this celebration, is the Fourth of July. It is the birthday of your National Independence, and of your political freedom. This, to you, is what the Passover was to the emancipated people of God. It carries your minds back to the day, and to the act of your great deliverance; and to the signs, and to the wonders, associated with that act, and that day. This celebration also marks the beginning of another year of your national life; and reminds you that the Republic of America is now 76 years old. I am glad, fellow-citizens, that your nation is so young. Seventy-six years, though a good old age for a man, is but a mere speck in the life of a nation. Three score years and ten is the allotted time for individual men; but nations number their years by thousands. According to this fact, you are, even now, only in the beginning of your national career, still lingering in the period of childhood. I repeat, I am glad this is so. There is hope in the thought, and hope is much needed, under the dark clouds which lower above the horizon. The eye of the reformer is met with angry flashes, portending disastrous times; but his heart may well beat lighter at the thought that America is young, and that she is still in the impressible stage of her existence. May he not hope that high lessons of wisdom, of justice and of truth, will yet give direction to her destiny? Were the nation older, the patriot's heart might be sadder, and the reformer's brow heavier. Its future might be shrouded in gloom, and the hope of its prophets go out in sorrow. There is consolation in the thought that America is young.—Great streams are not easily turned from channels, worn deep in the course of ages. They may sometimes rise in quiet and stately majesty, and inundate the land, refreshing and fertilizing the earth with their mysterious properties. They may also rise in wrath and fury, and bear away, on their angry waves, the accumulated wealth of years of toil and hardship. They, however, gradually flow back to the same old channel, and flow on as serenely as ever. But, while the river may not be turned aside, it may dry up, and leave nothing behind but the withered branch, and the unsightly rock, to howl in the abyss-sweeping wind, the sad tale of departed glory. As with rivers so with nations.

Fellow-citizens, I shall not presume to dwell at length on the associations that cluster about this day. The simple story of it is, that, 76 years ago, the people of this country were British subjects. The style and title of your "sovereign people" (in which you now glory) was not then born. You were under the British Crown. Your fathers esteemed the English Government as the home government; and England as the fatherland. This home government, you know, although a considerable distance from your home, did, in the exercise of its parental prerogatives, impose upon its colonial children, such restraints, burdens and limitations, as, in its mature judgment, it deemed wise, right and proper.

But your fathers, who had not adopted the fashionable idea of this day, of the infallibility of government, and the absolute character of its acts, presumed to differ from the home government in respect to the wisdom and the justice of some of those burdens and restraints. They went so far in their excitement as to pronounce the measures of government unjust, unreasonable, and oppressive, and altogether such as ought not to be quietly submitted to. I scarcely need say, fellow-citizens, that my opinion of those measures fully accords with that of your fathers. Such a declaration of agreement on my part would not be worth much to anybody. It would certainly prove nothing as to what part I might have taken had I lived during the great controversy of 1776. To say now that America was right, and England wrong, is exceedingly easy. Everybody can say it; the dastard, not less than the noble brave, can flippantly discant on the tyranny of England towards the American Colonies. It is fashionable to do so; but there was a time when, to pronounce against England, and in favor of the cause of the colonies, tried men's souls. They who did so were accounted in their day plotters of mischief, agitators and rebels, dangerous men. To side with the right against the wrong, with the weak against the strong, and with the oppressed against the oppressor! here lies the merit, and the one which, of all others, seems unfashionable in our day. The cause of liberty may be stabbed by the men who glory in the deeds of your fathers. But, to proceed.

Feeling themselves harshly and unjustly treated, by the home government, your fathers, like men of honesty, and men of spirit, earnestly sought redress. They petitioned and remonstrated; they did so in a decorous, respectful, and loyal manner. Their conduct was wholly unexceptionable. This, however, did not answer the purpose. They saw themselves treated with sovereign indifference, coldness and scorn. Yet they persevered. They were not the men to look back.

As the sheet anchor takes a firmer hold, when the ship is tossed by the storm, so did the cause of your fathers grow stronger as it breasted the chilling blasts of kingly displeasure. The greatest and best of British statesmen admitted its justice, and the loftiest eloquence of the British Senate came to its support. But, with that blindness which seems to be the unvarying characteristic of tyrants, since Pharaoh and his hosts were drowned in the Red Sea, the British Government persisted in the exactions complained of.

The madness of this course, we believe, is admitted now, even by England; but we fear the lesson is wholly lost on our present rulers.

Oppression makes a wise man mad. Your fathers were wise men, and if they did not go mad, they became restive under this treatment. They felt themselves the victims of grievous wrongs, wholly incurable in their colonial capacity. With brave men there is always a remedy for oppression. Just here, the idea of a total separation of the colonies from the crown was born! It was a startling idea, much more so than we, at this distance of time, regard it. The timid and the prudent (as has been intimated) of that day were, of course, shocked and alarmed by it.

Such people lived then, had lived before, and will, probably, ever have a place on this planet; and their course, in respect to any great change (no matter how great the good to be attained, or the wrong to be redressed by it), may be calculated with as much precision as can be the course of the stars. They hate all changes, but silver, gold and copper change! Of this sort of change they are always strongly in favor.

These people were called Tories in the days of your fathers; and the appellation, probably, conveyed the same idea that is meant by a more modern, though a somewhat less euphonious term, which we often find in our papers, applied to some of our old politicians.

Their opposition to the then dangerous thought was earnest and powerful; but, amid all their terror and affrighted vociferations against it, the alarming and revolutionary idea moved on, and the country with it.

On the 2d of July, 1776, the old Continental Congress, to the dismay of the lovers of ease, and the worshipers of property, clothed that dreadful idea with all the authority of national sanction. They did so in the form of a resolution; and as we seldom hit upon resolutions, drawn up in our day, whose transparency is at all equal to this, it may refresh your minds and help my story if I read it.

"Resolved, That these united colonies are, and of right, ought to be free and Independent States; that they are absolved from all allegiance to the British Crown; and that all political connection between them and the State of Great Britain is, and ought to be, dissolved."

Citizens, your fathers made good that resolution. They succeeded; and to-day you reap the fruits of their success. The freedom gained is yours; and you, therefore, may properly celebrate this anniversary. The 4th of July is the first great fact in your nation's history—the very ring-bolt in the chain of your yet undeveloped destiny.

Pride and patriotism, not less than gratitude, prompt you to celebrate and to hold it in perpetual remembrance. I have said that the Declaration of Independence is the ringbolt to the chain of your nation's destiny; so, indeed, I regard it. The principles contained in that instrument are saving principles. Stand by those principles, be true to them on all occasions, in all places, against all foes, and at whatever cost.

From the round top of your ship of state, dark and threatening clouds may be seen. Heavy billows, like mountains in the distance, disclose to the leeward huge forms of flinty rocks! That bolt drawn, that chain broken, and all is lost. Cling to this day—cling to it, and to its principles, with the grasp of a storm-tossed mariner to a spar at midnight.

The coming into being of a nation, in any circumstances, is an interesting event. But, besides general considerations, there were peculiar circumstances which make the advent of this republic an event of special attractiveness.

The whole scene, as I look back to it, was simple, dignified and sublime. The population of the country, at the time, stood at the insignificant number of three millions. The country was poor in the munitions of war. The population was weak and scattered, and the country a wilderness unsubdued. There were then no means of concert and combination, such as exist now. Neither steam nor lightning had then been reduced to order and discipline. From the Potomac to the Delaware was a journey of many days. Under these, and innumerable other disadvantages, your fathers declared for liberty and independence and triumphed.

Fellow Citizens, I am not wanting in respect for the fathers of this republic. The signers of the Declaration of Independence were brave men. They were great men, too—great enough to give frame to a great age. It does not often happen to a nation to raise, at one time, such a number of truly great men. The point from which I am compelled to view them is not, certainly, the most favorable; and yet I cannot contemplate their great deeds with less than admiration. They were statesmen, patriots and heroes, and for the good they did, and the principles they contended for, I will unite with you to honor their memory.

They loved their country better than their own private interests; and, though this is not the highest form of human excellence, all will concede that it is a rare virtue, and that when it is exhibited it ought to command respect. He who will, intelligently, lay down his life for his country is a man whom it is not in human nature to despise. Your fathers staked their lives, their fortunes, and their sacred honor, on the cause of their country. In their admiration of liberty, they lost sight of all other interests.

They were peace men; but they preferred revolution to peaceful submission to bondage. They were quiet men; but they did not shrink from agitating against oppression. They showed forbearance; but that they knew its limits. They believed in order; but not in the order of tyranny. With them, nothing was "settled" that was not right. With them, justice, liberty and humanity were "final"; not slavery and oppression. You may well cherish the memory of such men. They were great in their day and generation. Their solid manhood stands out the more as we contrast it with these degenerate times.

How circumspect, exact and proportionate were all their movements! How unlike the politicians of an hour! Their statesmanship looked beyond the passing moment, and stretched away in strength into the distant future. They seized upon eternal principles, and set a glorious example in their defence. Mark them!

Fully appreciating the hardships to be encountered, firmly believing in the right of their cause, honorably inviting the scrutiny of an on-looking world, reverently appealing to heaven to attest their sincerity, soundly comprehending the solemn responsibility they were about to assume, wisely measuring the terrible odds against them, your fathers, the fathers of this republic, did, most deliberately, under the inspiration of a glorious patriotism, and with a sublime faith in the great principles of justice and freedom, lay deep, the corner-stone of the national super-structure, which has risen and still rises in grandeur around you.

Of this fundamental work, this day is the anniversary. Our eyes are met with demonstrations of joyous enthusiasm. Banners and pennants wave exultingly on the breeze. The din of business, too, is hushed. Even mammon seems to have quitted his grasp on this day. The ear-piercing fife and the stirring drum unite their accents with the ascending peal of a thousand church bells. Prayers are made, hymns are sung, and sermons are preached in honor of this day; while the quick martial tramp of a great and multitudinous nation, echoed back by all the hills, valleys and mountains of a vast continent, bespeak the occasion one of thrilling and universal interest—a nation's jubilee.

Friends and citizens, I need not enter further into the causes which led to this anniversary. Many of you understand them better than I do. You could instruct me in regard to them. That is a branch of knowledge in which you feel, perhaps, a much deeper interest than your speaker. The causes which led to the separation of the colonies from the British crown have never lacked for a tongue. They have all been taught in your common schools, narrated at your firesides, unfolded from your pulpits, and thundered from your legislative halls, and are as familiar to you as household words. They form the staple of your national poetry and eloquence.

I remember, also, that, as a people, Americans are remarkably familiar with all facts which make in their own favor. This is esteemed by some as a national trait—perhaps a national weakness. It is a fact, that whatever makes for the wealth or for the reputation of Americans and can be had cheap! will be found by Americans. I shall not be charged with slandering Americans if I say I think the American side of any question may be safely left in American hands.

I leave, therefore, the great deeds of your fathers to other gentlemen whose claim to have been regularly descended will be less likely to be disputed than mine!

My business, if I have any here to-day, is with the present. The accepted time with God and His cause is the ever-living now.

> *Trust no future, however pleasant,*
> *Let the dead past bury its dead;*
> *Act, act in the living present,*
> *Heart within, and God overhead.*

We have to do with the past only as we can make it useful to the present and to the future. To all inspiring motives, to noble deeds which can be gained from the past, we are welcome. But now is the time, the important time. Your fathers have lived, died, and have done their work, and have done much of it well. You live and must die, and you must do your work. You have no right to enjoy a child's share in the labor of your fathers, unless your children are to be blest by your labors. You have no right to wear out and waste the hard-earned fame of your fathers to cover your indolence. Sydney Smith tells us that men seldom eulogize the wisdom and virtues of their fathers, but to excuse some folly or wickedness of their own. This truth is not a doubtful one. There are illustrations of it near and remote, ancient and modern. It was fashionable, hundreds of years ago, for the children of Jacob to boast, we have "Abraham to our father," when they had long lost Abraham's faith and spirit. That people contented themselves under the shadow of Abraham's great name, while they repudiated the deeds which made his name great. Need I remind you that a similar thing is being done all over this country to-day? Need I tell you that the Jews are not the only people who built the tombs of the prophets, and garnished the sepulchers of the righteous? Washington could not die till he had broken the chains of his slaves. Yet his monument is built up by the price of human blood, and the traders in the bodies and souls of men shout—"We have Washington to *our father*."—Alas! that it should be so; yet so it is.

> *The evil that men do, lives after them,*
> *The good is oft interred with their bones.*

Fellow-citizens, pardon me, allow me to ask, why am I called upon to speak here to-day? What have I, or those I represent, to do with your national independence? Are the great principles of political freedom and of natural justice, embodied in that Declaration of Independence, extended to us? and am I, therefore, called upon to bring our humble offering to the national altar, and to confess the benefits and express devout gratitude for the blessings resulting from your independence to us?

Would to God, both for your sakes and ours, that an affirmative answer could be truthfully returned to these questions! Then would my task be light, and my burden easy and delightful. For *who* is there so cold, that a nation's sympathy could not warm him? Who so obdurate and dead to the claims of gratitude, that would not thankfully acknowledge such priceless benefits? Who so stolid and selfish, that would not give his voice to swell the hallelujahs of a nation's jubilee, when the chains of servitude had been torn from his limbs? I am not that man. In a case like that, the dumb might eloquently speak, and the "lame man leap as an hart."

But such is not the state of the case. I say it with a sad sense of the disparity between us. I am not included within the pale of this glorious anniversary! Your high independence only reveals the immeasurable distance between us. The blessings in which you, this day, rejoice, are not enjoyed in common.—The rich inheritance of justice, liberty, prosperity and independence, bequeathed by your fathers, is shared by you, not by me. The sunlight that brought light and healing to you, has brought stripes and death to me. This Fourth July is *yours,* not *mine. You* may rejoice, *I* must mourn. To drag a man in fetters into the grand illuminated temple of liberty, and call upon him to join you in joyous anthems, were inhuman mockery and sacrilegious irony. Do you mean, citizens, to mock me, by asking me to speak to-day? If so, there is a parallel to your conduct. And let me warn you that it is dangerous to copy the example of a nation whose crimes, towering up to heaven, were thrown down by the breath of the Almighty, burying that nation in irrevocable ruin! I can to-day take up the plaintive lament of a peeled and woe-smitten people!

"By the rivers of Babylon, there we sat down. Yea! we wept when we remembered Zion. We hanged our harps upon the willows in the midst thereof. For there, they that carried us away captive, required of us a song; and they who wasted us required of us mirth, saying, Sing us one of the songs of Zion. How can we sing the Lord's song in a strange land? If I forget thee, O Jerusalem, let my right hand forget her cunning. If I do not remember thee, let my tongue cleave to the roof of my mouth."

Fellow-citizens, above your national, tumultuous joy, I hear the mournful wail of millions! whose chains, heavy and grievous yesterday, are, to-day, rendered more intolerable by the jubilee shouts that reach them. If I do forget, if I do not faithfully remember those bleeding children of sorrow this day, "may my right hand forget her cunning, and may my tongue cleave to the roof of my mouth!" To forget them, to pass lightly over their wrongs, and to chime in with the popular theme, would be treason most scandalous and shocking, and would make me a reproach before God and the world. My subject, then, fellow-citizens, is American slavery. I shall see this day and its popular characteristics from the slave's point of view. Standing there identified with the American bondman, making his wrongs mine, I do not hesitate to declare, with all my soul, that the character and conduct of this nation never looked blacker to me than on this 4th of July! Whether we turn to the declarations of the past, or to the professions of the present, the conduct of the nation seems equally hideous and revolting. America is false to the past, false to the present, and solemnly binds herself to be false to the future. Standing with God and the crushed and bleeding slave on this occasion, I will, in the name of humanity which is outraged, in the name of liberty which is fettered, in the name of the constitution and the Bible which are disregarded and trampled upon, dare to call in question and to denounce, with all the emphasis I can command, everything that serves to perpetuate slavery—the great sin and shame of America! "I will not equivocate; I will not excuse";[27] I will use the severest language I can command; and yet not one word shall escape me that any man, whose judgment is not blinded by prejudice, or who is not at heart a slaveholder, shall not confess to be right and just.

But I fancy I hear some one of my audience say, "It is just in this circumstance that you and your brother abolitionists fail to make a favorable impression on the public mind. Would you argue more, and denounce less; would you persuade more, and rebuke less; your cause would be much more likely to succeed." But, I submit, where all is plain there is nothing to be argued. What point in the anti-slavery creed would you have me argue? On what branch of the subject do the people of this country need light? Must I undertake to prove that the slave is a man? That point is conceded already. Nobody doubts it. The slaveholders themselves acknowledge it in the enactment of laws for their government. They acknowledge it when they punish disobedience on the part of the slave. There are seventy-two crimes in the State of Virginia which, if committed by a black man (no matter how ignorant he be), subject him to the punishment of death; while only two of the same crimes will subject a white man to the like punishment. What is this but the acknowledgment that the slave is a moral, intellectual, and responsible being? The manhood of the slave is conceded. It is admitted in the fact that Southern statute books are covered with enactments forbidding, under severe fines and penalties, the teaching of the slave to read or to write. When you can point to any such laws in reference to the beasts of the field, then I may consent to argue the manhood of the slave. When the dogs in your streets, when the fowls of the air, when the cattle on your hills, when the fish of the sea, and the reptiles that crawl, shall be unable to distinguish the slave from a brute, *then* will I argue with you that the slave is a man!

For the present, it is enough to affirm the equal manhood of the Negro race. Is it not astonishing that, while we are ploughing, planting, and reaping, using all kinds of mechanical tools, erecting houses, constructing bridges, building ships, working in metals of brass, iron, copper, silver and gold; that, while we are reading, writing and ciphering, acting as clerks, merchants and secretaries, having among us lawyers, doctors, ministers, poets, authors, editors, orators and teachers; that, while we are engaged in all manner of enterprises common to other men, digging gold in California, capturing the whale in the Pacific, feeding sheep and cattle on the hill-side, living, moving, acting, thinking, planning, living in families as husbands, wives and children, and, above all, confessing and worshipping the Christian's God, and looking hopefully for life and immortality beyond the grave, we are called upon to prove that we are men!

Would you have me argue that man is entitled to liberty? that he is the rightful owner of his own body? You have already declared it. Must I argue the wrongfulness of slavery? Is that a question for Republicans? Is it to be settled by the rules of logic and argumentation, as a matter beset with great difficulty, involving a doubtful application of the principle of justice, hard to be understood? How should I look to-day, in the presence of Americans, dividing, and subdividing a discourse, to show that men have a natural right to freedom? speaking of it relatively and positively, negatively and affirmatively. To do so, would be to make myself ridiculous, and to offer an insult to your understanding.—There is not a man beneath the canopy of heaven that does not know that slavery is wrong *for him*.

What, am I to argue that it is wrong to make men brutes, to rob them of their liberty, to work them without wages, to keep them ignorant of their relations to their fellow men, to beat them with sticks, to flay their flesh with the lash, to load their limbs with irons, to hunt them with dogs, to sell them at auction, to sunder their families, to knock out their teeth, to burn their flesh, to starve them into obedience and submission to their masters? Must I argue that a system thus marked with blood, and stained with pollution, is *wrong?* No! I will not. I have better employment for my time and strength than such arguments would imply.

What, then, remains to be argued? Is it that slavery is not divine; that God did not establish it; that our doctors of divinity are mistaken? There is blasphemy in the thought. That which is inhuman, cannot be divine! *Who* can reason on such a proposition? They that can, may; I cannot. The time for such argument is passed.

At a time like this, scorching irony, not convincing argument, is needed. O! had I the ability, and could reach the nation's ear, I would, to-day, pour out a fiery stream of biting ridicule, blasting reproach, withering sarcasm, and stern rebuke. For it is not light that is needed, but fire; it is not the gentle shower, but thunder. We need the storm, the whirlwind, and the earthquake. The feeling of the nation must be quickened; the conscience of the nation must be roused; the propriety of the nation must be startled; the hypocrisy of the nation must be exposed; and its crimes against God and man must be proclaimed and denounced.

What, to the American slave, is your 4th of July? I answer; a day that reveals to him, more than all other days in the year, the gross injustice and cruelty to which he is the constant victim. To him, your celebration is a sham; your boasted liberty, an unholy license; your national greatness, swelling vanity; your sounds of rejoicing are empty and heartless; your denunciation of tyrants, brass fronted impudence; your shouts of liberty and equality, hollow mockery; your prayers and hymns, your sermons and thanksgivings, with all your religious parade and solemnity, are, to Him, mere bombast, fraud, deception, impiety, and hypocrisy—a thin veil to cover up crimes which would disgrace a nation of savages. There is not a nation on the earth guilty of practices more shocking and bloody than are the people of the United States, at this very hour.

Go where you may, search where you will, roam through all the monarchies and despotisms of the Old World, travel through South America, search out every abuse, and when you have found the last, lay your facts by the side of the everyday practices of this nation, and you will say with me, that, for revolting barbarity and shameless hypocrisy, America reigns without a rival.

Take the American slave-trade, which we are told by the papers, is especially prosperous just now. Ex-Senator Benton tells us that the price of men was never higher than now. He mentions the fact to show that slavery is in no danger. This trade is one of the peculiarities of American institutions. It is carried on in all the large towns and cities in one-half of this confederacy; and millions are pocketed every year by dealers in this horrid traffic. In several states this trade is a chief source of wealth. It is called (in contradistinction to the foreign slave-trade) *"the internal slave-trade."* It is, probably, called so, too, in order to divert from it the horror with which the foreign slave-trade is contemplated. That trade has long since been denounced by this government as piracy. It has been denounced with burning words from the high places of the nation as an execrable traffic. To arrest it, to put an end to it, this nation keeps a squadron, at immense cost, on the coast of Africa. Everywhere, in this country, it is safe to speak of this foreign slave-trade as a most inhuman traffic, opposed alike to the laws of God and of man. The duty to extirpate and destroy it, is admitted even by our doctors of divinity. In order to put an end to it, some of these last have consented that their colored brethren (nominally free) should leave this country, and establish themselves on the western coast of Africa! It is, however, a notable fact that, while so much execration is poured out by Americans upon all those engaged in the foreign slave-trade, the men engaged in the slave-trade between the states pass without condemnation, and their business is deemed honorable.

Behold the practical operation of this internal slave-trade, the American slave-trade, sustained by American politics and American religion. Here you will see men and women reared like swine for the market. You know what is a swine-drover? I will show you a man-drover. They inhabit all our Southern States. They perambulate the country, and crowd the highways of the nation, with droves of human stock. You will see one of these human flesh jobbers, armed with pistol, whip, and bowie-knife, driving a company of a hundred men, women, and children, from the Potomac to the slave market at New Orleans. These wretched people are to be sold singly, or in lots, to suit purchasers. They are food for the cotton-field and the deadly sugar-mill. Mark the sad procession, as it moves wearily along, and the inhuman wretch who drives them. Hear his savage yells and his blood-curdling oaths, as he hurries on his affrighted captives! There, see the old man with locks thinned and gray. Cast one glance, if you please, upon that young mother, whose shoulders are bare to the scorching sun, her briny tears falling on the brow of the babe in her arms. See, too, that girl of thirteen, weeping, *yes!* weeping, as she thinks of the mother from whom she has been torn! The drove moves tardily. Heat and sorrow have nearly consumed their strength; suddenly you hear a quick snap, like the discharge of a rifle; the fetters clank, and the chain rattles simultaneously; your ears are saluted with a scream, that seems to have torn its way to the centre of your soul! The crack you heard was the sound of the slave-whip; the scream you heard was from the woman you saw with the babe. Her speed had faltered under the weight of her child and her chains! that gash on her shoulder tells her to move on. Follow this drove to New Orleans. Attend the auction; see men examined like horses; see the forms of women rudely and brutally exposed to the shocking gaze of American slave-buyers. See this drove sold and separated forever; and never forget the deep, sad sobs that arose from that scattered multitude. Tell me, citizens, where, under the sun, you can witness a spectacle more fiendish and shocking. Yet this is but a glance at the American slave-trade, as it exists, at this moment, in the ruling part of the United States.

I was born amid such sights and scenes. To me the American slave-trade is a terrible reality. When a child, my soul was often pierced with a sense of its horrors. I lived on Philpot Street, Fell's Point, Baltimore, and have watched from the wharves the slave ships in the Basin, anchored from the shore, with their cargoes of human flesh, waiting for favorable winds to waft them down the Chesapeake. There was, at that time, a grand slave mart kept at the head of Pratt Street, by Austin Woldfolk. His agents were sent into every town and county in Maryland, announcing their arrival, through the papers, and on flaming *"hand-bills,"* headed cash for Negroes. These men were generally well dressed men, and very captivating in their manners; ever ready to drink, to treat, and to gamble. The fate of many a slave has depended upon the turn of a single card; and many a child has been snatched from the arms of its mother by bargains arranged in a state of brutal drunkenness.

The flesh-mongers gather up their victims by dozens, and drive them, chained, to the general depot at Baltimore. When a sufficient number has been collected here, a ship is chartered for the purpose of conveying the forlorn crew to Mobile, or to New Orleans. From the slave prison to the ship, they are usually driven in the darkness of night; for since the anti-slavery agitation, a certain caution is observed.

In the deep, still darkness of midnight, I have been often aroused by the dead, heavy footsteps, and the piteous cries of the chained gangs that passed our door. The anguish of my boyish heart was intense; and I was often consoled, when speaking to my mistress in the morning, to hear her say that the custom was very wicked; that she hated to hear the rattle of the chains and the heart-rending cries. I was glad to find one who sympathized with me in my horror.

Fellow-citizens, this murderous traffic is, to-day, in active operation in this boasted republic. In the solitude of my spirit I see clouds of dust raised on the highways of the South; I see the bleeding footsteps; I hear the doleful wail of fettered humanity on the way to the slave-markets, where the victims are to be sold like *horses, sheep,* and *swine,* knocked off to the highest bidder. There I see the tenderest ties ruthlessly broken, to gratify the lust, caprice and rapacity of the buyers and sellers of men. My soul sickens at the sight.

> *Is this the land your Fathers loved,*
> *The freedom which they toiled to win?*
> *Is this the earth whereon they moved?*
> *Are these the graves they slumber in?*

But a still more inhuman, disgraceful, and scandalous state of things remains to be presented. By an act of the American Congress, not yet two years old, slavery has been nationalized in its most horrible and revolting form. By that act, Mason and Dixon's line has been obliterated; New York has become as Virginia; and the power to hold, hunt, and sell men, women and children, as slaves, remains no longer a mere state institution, but is now an institution of the whole United States. The power is co-extensive with the star-spangled banner, and American Christianity. Where these go, may also go the merciless slave-hunter. Where these are, man is not sacred. He is a bird for the sportsman's gun. By that most foul and fiendish of all human decrees, the liberty and person of every man are put in peril. Your broad republican domain is hunting ground for *men. Not* for thieves and robbers, enemies of society, merely, but for men guilty of no crime. Your law-makers have commanded all good citizens to engage in this hellish sport. Your President, your Secretary of State, your *lords, nobles,* and ecclesiastics enforce, as a duty you owe to your free and glorious country, and to your God, that you do this accursed thing. Not fewer than forty Americans have, within the past two years, been hunted down and, without a moment's warning, hurried away in chains, and consigned to slavery and excruciating torture. Some of these have had wives and children, dependent on them for bread; but of this, no account was made. The right of the hunter to his prey stands superior to the right of marriage, and to *all* rights in this republic, the rights of God included! For black men there is neither law nor justice, humanity nor religion. The Fugitive Slave *Law* makes mercy to them a crime; and bribes the judge who tries them. An American judge gets ten dollars for every victim he consigns to slavery, and five, when he fails to do so. The oath of any two villains is sufficient, under this hell-black enactment, to send the most pious and exemplary black man into the remorseless jaws of slavery! His own testimony is nothing. He can bring no witnesses for himself. The minister of American justice is bound by the law to hear but *one* side; and *that* side is the side of the oppressor. Let this damning fact be perpetually told. Let it be thundered around the world that in tyrant-killing, king-hating, people-loving, democratic, Christian America the seats of justice are filled with judges who hold their offices under an open and palpable *bribe,* and are bound, in deciding the case of a man's liberty, *to hear only his accusers!*

In glaring violation of justice, in shameless disregard of the forms of administering law, in cunning arrangement to entrap the defenceless, and in diabolical intent this Fugitive Slave Law stands alone in the annals of tyrannical legislation. I doubt if there be another nation on the globe having the brass and the baseness to put such a law on the statute-book. If any man in this assembly thinks differently from me in this matter, and feels able to disprove my statements, I will gladly confront him at any suitable time and place he may select.

I take this law to be one of the grossest infringements of Christian Liberty, and, if the churches and ministers of our country were not stupidly blind, or most wickedly indifferent, they, too, would so regard it.

At the very moment that they are thanking God for the enjoyment of civil and religious liberty, and for the right to worship God according to the dictates of their own consciences, they are utterly silent in respect to a law which robs religion of its chief significance and makes it utterly worthless to a world lying in wickedness. Did this law concern the *"mint, anise, and cummin"*—abridge the right to sing psalms, to partake of the sacrament, or to engage in any of the ceremonies of religion, it would be smitten by the thunder of a thousand pulpits. A general shout would go up from the church demanding *repeal, repeal, instant repeal!*—And it would go hard with that politician who presumed to solicit the votes of the people without inscribing this motto on his banner. Further, if this demand were not complied with, another Scotland would be added to the history of religious liberty, and the stern old covenanters would be thrown into the shade. A John Knox would be seen at every church door and heard from every pulpit, and Fillmore would have no more quarter than was shown by Knox to the beautiful, but treacherous, Queen Mary of Scotland. The fact that the church of our country (with fractional exceptions) does not esteem "the Fugitive Slave Law" as a declaration of war against religious liberty, implies that that church regards religion simply as a form of worship, an empty ceremony, and *not* a vital principle, requiring active benevolence, justice, love, and good will towards man. It esteems sacrifice above mercy; psalm-singing above right doing; solemn meetings above practical righteousness. A worship that can be conducted by persons who refuse to give shelter to the houseless, to give bread to the hungry, clothing to the naked, and who enjoin obedience to a law forbidding these acts of mercy is a curse, not a blessing to mankind. The Bible addresses all such persons as "scribes, pharisees, hypocrites, who pay tithe of *mint, anise,* and *cummin,* and have omitted the weightier matters of the law, judgment, mercy, and faith."

But the church of this country is not only indifferent to the wrongs of the slave, it actually takes sides with the oppressors. It has made itself the bulwark of American slavery, and the shield of American slave-hunters. Many of its most eloquent Divines, who stand as the very lights of the church, have shamelessly given the sanction of religion and the Bible to the whole slave system. They have taught that man may, properly, be a slave; that the relation of master and slave is ordained of God; that to send back an escaped bondman to his master is clearly the duty of all the followers of the Lord Jesus Christ; and this horrible blasphemy is palmed off upon the world for Christianity.

For my part, I would say, welcome infidelity! welcome atheism! welcome anything! in preference to the gospel, *as preached by those Divines!* They convert the very name of religion into an engine of tyranny and barbarous cruelty, and serve to confirm more infidels, in this age, than all the infidel writings of Thomas Paine, Voltaire, and Bolingbroke put together have done! These ministers make religion a cold and flinty-hearted thing, having neither principles of right action nor bowels of compassion. They strip the love of God of its beauty and leave the throne of religion a huge, horrible, repulsive form. It is a religion for oppressors, tyrants, man-stealers, and *thugs.* It is not that *"pure and undefiled religion"* which is from above, and which is *"first pure, then peaceable, easy to be entreated,* full of mercy and good fruits, *without partiality, and without hypocrisy."* But a religion which favors the rich against the poor; which exalts the proud above the humble; which divides mankind into two classes, tyrants and slaves; which says to the man in chains, *stay there;* and to the oppressor, *oppress on;* it is a religion which may be professed and enjoyed by all the robbers and enslavers of mankind; it makes God a respecter of persons, denies his fatherhood of the race, and tramples in the dust the great truth of the brotherhood of man. All this we affirm to be true of the popular church, and the popular worship of our land and nation—a religion, a church, and a worship which, on the authority of inspired wisdom, we pronounce to be an abomination in the sight of God. In the language of Isaiah, the American church might be well addressed, "Bring no more vain oblations; incense is an abomination unto me: the new moons and Sabbaths, the calling of assemblies, I cannot away with; it is iniquity, even the solemn meeting. Your new moons, and your appointed feasts my soul hateth. They are a trouble to me; I am weary to bear them; and when ye spread forth your hands I will hide mine eyes from you. Yea! when ye make many prayers, I will not hear. Your hands are full of blood; cease to do evil, learn to do well; seek judgment; relieve the oppressed; judge for the fatherless; plead for the widow."

The American church is guilty, when viewed in connection with what it is doing to uphold slavery; but it is superlatively guilty when viewed in its connection with its ability to abolish slavery.

The sin of which it is guilty is one of omission as well as of commission. Albert Barnes but uttered what the common sense of every man at all observant of the actual state of the case will receive as truth, when he declared that "There is no power out of the church that could sustain slavery an hour, if it were not sustained in it."

Let the religious press, the pulpit, the Sunday School, the conference meeting, the great ecclesiastical, missionary, Bible and tract associations of the land array their immense powers against slavery, and slave-holding; and the whole system of crime and blood would be scattered to the winds, and that they do not do this involves them in the most awful responsibility of which the mind can conceive.

In prosecuting the anti-slavery enterprise, we have been asked to spare the church, to spare the ministry; but *how,* we ask, could such a thing be done? We are met on the threshold of our efforts for the redemption of the slave, by the church and ministry of the country, in battle arrayed against us; and we are compelled to fight or flee. From *what* quarter, I beg to know, has proceeded a fire so deadly upon our ranks, during the last two years, as from the Northern pulpit? As the champions of oppressors, the chosen men of American theology have appeared—men honored for their so-called piety, and their real learning. The Lords of Buffalo, the Springs of New York, the Lathrops of Auburn, the Coxes and Spencers of Brooklyn, the Gannets and Sharps of Boston, the Deweys of Washington, and other great religious lights of the land have, in utter denial of the authority of *Him* by whom they professed to be called to the ministry, deliberately taught us, against the example of the Hebrews, and against the remonstrance of the Apostles, *that we ought to obey man's law before the law of God.*[28]

My spirit wearies of such blasphemy; and how such men can be supported, as the "standing types and representatives of Jesus Christ," is a mystery which I leave others to penetrate. In speaking of the American church, however, let it be distinctly understood that I mean the *great mass* of the religious organizations of our land. There are exceptions, and I thank God that there are. Noble men may be found, scattered all over these Northern States, of whom Henry Ward Beecher, of Brooklyn; Samuel J. May, of Syracuse; and my esteemed friend (Rev. R. R. Raymond) on the platform, are shining examples; and let me say further, that, upon these men lies the duty to inspire our ranks with high religious faith and zeal, and to cheer us on in the great mission of the slave's redemption from his chains.

One is struck with the difference between the attitude of the American church towards the anti-slavery movement, and that occupied by the churches in England towards a similar movement in that country. There, the church, true to its mission of ameliorating, elevating and improving the condition of mankind, came forward promptly, bou᾽ up the wounds of the West Indian slave, and restored him to his lioerty. There, the question of emancipation was a high religious question. It was demanded in the name of humanity, and according to the law of the living God. The Sharps, the Clarksons, the Wilberforces, the Buxtons, the Burchells, and the Knibbs were alike famous for their piety and for their philanthropy. The anti-slavery movement *there* was not an anti-church movement, for the reason that the church took its full share in prosecuting that movement: and the anti-slavery movement in this country will cease to be an anti-church movement, when the church of this country shall assume a favorable instead of a hostile position towards that movement.

Americans! your republican politics, not less than your republican religion, are flagrantly inconsistent. You boast of your love of liberty, your superior civilization, and your pure Christianity, while the whole political power of the nation (as embodied in the two great political parties) is solemnly pledged to support and perpetuate the enslavement of three millions of your countrymen. You hurl your anathemas at the crowned headed tyrants of Russia and Austria and pride yourselves on your Democratic institutions, while you yourselves consent to be the mere *tools* and *body-guards* of the tyrants of Virginia and Carolina. You invite to your shores fugitives of oppression from abroad, honor them with banquets, greet them with ovations, cheer them, toast them, salute them, protect them, and pour out your money to them like water; but the fugitives from your own land you advertise, hunt, arrest, shoot, and kill. You glory in your refinement and your universal education; yet you maintain a system as barbarous and dreadful as ever stained the character of a nation—a system begun in avarice, supported in pride, and perpetuated in cruelty. You shed tears over fallen Hungary, and make the sad story of her wrongs the theme of your poets, statesmen, and orators, till your gallant sons are ready to fly to arms to vindicate her cause against the oppressor; but, in regard to the ten thousand wrongs of the American slave, you would enforce the strictest silence, and would hail him as an enemy of the nation who dares to make those wrongs the subject of public discourse! You are all on fire at the mention of liberty for France or for Ireland; but are as cold as an iceberg at the thought of liberty for the enslaved of America. You discourse eloquently on the dignity of labor; yet, you sustain a system which, in its very essence, casts a stigma upon labor. You can bare your bosom to the storm of British artillery to throw off a three-penny tax on tea; and yet wring the last hard earned farthing from the grasp of the black laborers of your country. You profess to believe "that, of one blood, God made all nations of men to dwell on the face of all the earth," and hath commanded all men, everywhere, to love one another; yet you notoriously hate (and glory in your hatred) all men whose skins are not colored like your own. You declare before the world, and are understood by the world to declare that you *"hold these truths to be self-evident, that all men are created equal; and are endowed by their Creator with certain inalienable rights; and that among these are, life, liberty, and the pursuit of happiness;* and yet, you hold securely, in a bondage which, according to your own Thomas Jefferson, *"is worse than ages of that which your fathers rose in rebellion to oppose,"* a *seventh part* of the inhabitants of your country.

Fellow-citizens, I will not enlarge further on your national inconsistencies. The existence of slavery in this country brands your republicanism as a sham, your humanity as a base pretense, and your Christianity as a lie. It destroys your moral power abroad: it corrupts your politicians at home. It saps the foundation of religion; it makes your name a hissing and a bye-word to a mocking earth. It is the antagonistic force in your government, the only thing that seriously disturbs and endangers your *Union.* It fetters your progress; it is the enemy of improvement; the deadly foe of education; it fosters pride; it breeds insolence; it promotes vice; it shelters crime; it is a curse to the earth that supports it; and yet you cling to it as if it were the sheet anchor of all your hopes. Oh! be warned! be warned! a horrible reptile is coiled up in your nation's bosom; the venomous creature is nursing at the tender breast of your youthful republic; *for the love of God, tear away,* and fling from you the hideous monster, and *let the weight of twenty millions crush and destroy it forever!*

But it is answered in reply to all this, that precisely what I have now denounced is, in fact, guaranteed and sanctioned by the Constitution of the United States; that, the right to hold, and to hunt slaves is a part of that Constitution framed by the illustrious Fathers of this Republic.

Then, I dare to affirm, notwithstanding all I have said before, your fathers stooped, basely stooped

> *To palter with us in a double sense:*
> *And keep the word of promise to the ear,*
> *But break it to the heart.*

And instead of being the honest men I have before declared them to be, they were the veriest impostors that ever practised on mankind. This is the inevitable conclusion, and from it there is no escape; but I differ from those who charge this baseness on the framers of the Constitution of the United States. It is a slander upon their memory, at least, so I believe. There is not time now to argue the constitutional question at length; nor have I the ability to discuss it as it ought to be discussed. The subject has been handled with masterly power by Lysander Spooner, Esq., by William Goodell, by Samuel E. Sewall, Esq., and last, though not least, by Gerrit Smith, Esq. These gentlemen have, as I think, fully and clearly vindicated the Constitution from any design to support slavery for an hour.

Fellow-citizens! there is no matter in respect to which the people of the North have allowed themselves to be so ruinously imposed upon as that of the pro-slavery character of the Constitution. In that instrument I hold there is neither warrant, license, nor sanction of the hateful thing; but interpreted, as it ought to be interpreted, the Constitution is a glorious liberty document. Read its preamble, consider its purposes. Is slavery among them? Is it at the gateway? or is it in the temple? it is neither. While I do not intend to argue this question on the present occasion, let me ask, if it be not somewhat singular that, if the Constitution were intended to be, by its framers and adopters, a slaveholding instrument, why neither slavery, slaveholding, nor slave can anywhere be found in it. What would be thought of an instrument, drawn up, legally drawn up, for the purpose of entitling the city of Rochester to a tract of land, in which no mention of land was made? Now, there are certain rules of interpretation for the proper understanding of all legal instruments. These rules are well established. They are plain, common-sense rules, such as you and I, and all of us, can understand and apply, without having passed years in the study of law. I scout the idea that the question of the constitutionality, or unconstitutionality of slavery, is not a question for the people. I hold that every American citizen has a right to form an opinion of the constitution, and to propagate that opinion, and to use all honorable means to make his opinion the prevailing one. Without this right, the liberty of an American citizen would be as insecure as that of a Frenchman. Ex-Vice-President Dallas tells us that the constitution is an object to which no American mind can be too attentive, and no American heart too devoted. He further says, the Constitution, in its words, is plain and intelligible, and is meant for the home-bred, unsophisticated understandings of our fellow-citizens. Senator Berrien tells us that the Constitution is the fundamental law, that which controls all others. The charter of our liberties, which every citizen has a personal interest in understanding thoroughly. The testimony of Senator Breese, Lewis Cass, and many others that might be named, who are everywhere esteemed as sound lawyers, so regard the constitution. I take it, therefore, that it is not presumption in a private citizen to form an opinion of that instrument.

Now, take the Constitution according to its plain reading, and I defy the presentation of a single pro-slavery clause in it. On the other hand, it will be found to contain principles and purposes, entirely hostile to the existence of slavery.

I have detained my audience entirely too long already. At some future period I will gladly avail myself of an opportunity to give this subject a full and fair discussion.

Allow me to say, in conclusion, notwithstanding the dark picture I have this day presented, of the state of the nation, I do not despair of this country. There are forces in operation which must inevitably work the downfall of slavery. "The arm of the Lord is not shortened," and the doom of slavery is certain. I, therefore, leave off where I began, with hope. While drawing encouragement from "the Declaration of Independence," the great principles it contains, and the genius of American Institutions, my spirit is also cheered by the obvious tendencies of the age. Nations do not now stand in the same relation to each other that they did ages ago. No nation can now shut itself up from the surrounding world and trot round in the same old path of its fathers without interference. The time was when such could be done. Long established customs of hurtful character could formerly fence themselves in, and do their evil work with social impunity. Knowledge was then confined and enjoyed by the privileged few, and the multitude walked on in mental darkness. But a change has now come over the affairs of mankind. Walled cities and empires have become unfashionable. The arm of commerce has borne away the gates of the strong city. Intelligence is penetrating the darkest corners of the globe. It makes its pathway over and under the sea, as well as on the earth. Wind, steam, and lightning are its chartered agents. Oceans no longer divide, but link nations together. From Boston to London is now a holiday excursion. Space is comparatively annihilated.— Thoughts expressed on one side of the Atlantic are distinctly heard on the other.

The far off and almost fabulous Pacific rolls in grandeur at our feet. The Celestial Empire, the mystery of ages, is being solved. The fiat of the Almighty, "Let there be Light," has not yet spent its force. No abuse, no outrage whether in taste, sport or avarice, can now hide itself from the all-pervading light. The iron shoe, and crippled foot of China must be seen in contrast with nature. Africa must rise and put on her yet unwoven garment. "Ethiopia shall stretch out her hand unto God." In the fervent aspirations of William Lloyd Garrison, I say, and let every heart join in saying it:

> God speed the year of jubilee
>   The wide world o'er!
> When from their galling chains set free,
> Th' oppress'd shall vilely bend the knee,

And wear the yoke of tyranny
  Like brutes no more.
That year will come, and freedom's reign,
To man his plundered rights again
  Restore.

God speed the day when human blood
  Shall cease to flow!
In every clime be understood,
The claims of human brotherhood,
And each return for evil, good,
  Not blow for blow;
That day will come all feuds to end,
And change into a faithful friend
  Each foe.

God speed the hour, the glorious hour,
  When none on earth
Shall exercise a lordly power,
Nor in a tyrant's presence cower;
But to all manhood's stature tower,
  By equal birth!
That hour will come, to each, to all,
And from his prison-house, to thrall
  Go forth.

Until that year, day, hour, arrive,
With head, and heart, and hand I'll strive,
To break the rod, and rend the gyve,
The spoiler of his prey deprive—
So witness Heaven!
And never from my chosen post,
Whate'er the peril or the cost,
  Be driven.

Oration delivered in Corinthian Hall, Rochester, by Frederick Douglass, July 5, 1852, Rochester, 1852

TO GERRIT SMITH, ESQR.

Rochester, July 14th, 1852

My dear Sir:

Your notes of this and yesterday morning cheer me. You not only keep life in my paper but keep spirit in me. I owe you much every way for my people and for myself. Your letter to my friend Miss Griffiths in which you send 25 dollars to be used in publishing my 4th July speech makes me uneasy. The zeal of my friend is great and I fear she sometimes seems too urgent on my behalf. I must tell you however that I really am desirous to make some money as well as do some good with that speech. I am intending to do considerable lecturing, and I must have something to carry with me to sell. I rely mainly on this method for the means of living and travelling. Every town has not a Gerrit Smith in it to slip a five *"dollar bill"* in the hand of the Anti-Slavery lecturer to enable him to pay his way. I must have something to sell. Your pamphlets which you generously gave me are now nearly exhausted, and I must have something to fill their place. Yet my dear sir, I would not, in view of what I know to have been your expenses in the Chaplin case, have called upon you for one cent to help me publish my lecture here on the 4th or 5th July.

You shall not be called upon further to aid in publishing my lectures, and yet I do not doubt if I should very much need your friendly aid, you would give it. Since on this point, I may say, that I am not looking for one cent more from you, in the support of *"Frederick Douglass' Paper"* than you kindly offered to give at the first. And should the paper not be able to live when that sum is exhausted, I will submit with resignation to its death. Not that I sit lightly by it for so I do not. I have nursed it too long not to love it and to desire long life and usefulness to it. But that feeling must be subject to proper limits. I ought not to strip myself of all I have to sustain my paper. I have already given the half of my worldly goods, and the whole of my time for five years with the incidental support which friends like you at heart but unlike you in *purse* have been able to give me. Now I am unwilling to tax my friends for my support, unless with their fresh consent. I am fully able to work and to get a living and if after a fair trial, I find that my paper shall not be deemed of sufficient use to be sustained, I will freely give up and go to work.

With sincere gratitude and warm affection

Yours to the end
Frederick Douglass

Gerrit Smith Papers, Syracuse University

TO GERRIT SMITH, ESQR.

Rochester, July 15th, 1852

My dear Sir:

A word in regard to the Pittsburgh Convention. Cannot that Convention be made to occupy such a position as that the "Liberty Party" may properly vote for its candidates? I believe it can, and I believe moreover, that could you attend that Convention, you would stamp upon it the great principle of Righteous Civil Government and give effect to many of the doctrines of the Liberty Party.

I want to attend that Convention, and to attend with you and to have the aid of your intelligent judgment in shaping my course. Mere *Free Soil,* I am sure, will not satisfy the masses who will attend that Convention. The abolitionists of the west are in advance of their leaders. They are ready for a more certain sound than that which has of late called them out to battle. Can you not go and give them that sound?

Yours most truly, and to the end,

Frederick Douglass

Gerrit Smith Papers, Syracuse University

THE FUGITIVE SLAVE LAW, speech to the National Free Soil Convention at Pittsburgh, August 11, 1852

Gentlemen, I take it that you are in earnest, and mean all you say by this call, and therefore I will address you. I am taken by surprise, but I never withhold a word on such an occasion as this. The object of this Convention is to organize a party, not merely for the present, but a party identified with eternal principles and therefore permanent. I have come here, not so much of a free soiler as others have come. I am, of course, for circumscribing and damaging slavery in every way I can. But my motto is extermination—not only in New Mexico, but in New Orleans— not only in California but in South Carolina. No where has God ordained that this beautiful land shall be cursed with bondage by enslaving men. Slavery has no rightful existence anywhere. The slaveholders not only forfeit their right to liberty, but to life itself.—[Applause.] The earth is God's, and it ought to be covered with righteousness, and not slavery. We expect this great National Convention to lay down some such principle as this. What we want is not a temporary organization, for a temporary want, but a firm, fixed, immovable, liberty party. Had the old liberty party continued true to its principles, we never should have seen such a hell born enactment as the Fugitive Slave Law.

In making your Platform, nothing is to be gained by a timid policy. The more closely we adhere to principle, the more certainly will we command respect. Both National Conventions acted in open contempt of the anti-slavery sentiment of the North, by incorporating, as the corner stone of their two platforms, the infamous law to which I have alluded— a law which, I think, will never be repealed—it is too bad to be re-pealed—a law fit only to trampled under foot, (suiting the action to the word). The only way to make the Fugitive Slave Law a dead letter is to make half a dozen or more dead kidnappers. [Laughter and applause.] A half dozen more dead kidnappers carried down South would cool the ardor of Southern gentlemen, and keep their rapacity in check. That is perfectly right as long as the colored man has no protection. The colored men's rights are less than those of a jackass. No man can take away a jackass without submitting the matter to twelve men in any part of this country. A black man may be carried away without any reference to a jury. It is only necessary to claim him, and that some villain should swear to his identity. There is more protection there for a horse, for a donkey, or anything, rather than a colored man—who is, therefore, justified in the eye of God, in maintaining his right with his arm.

A Voice.—Some of us do not believe that doctrine.

Douglass.—The man who takes the office of a bloodhound ought to be treated as a bloodhound; and I believe that the lines of eternal justice are sometimes so obliterated by a course of long continued oppression that it is necessary to revive them by deepening their traces with the blood of a tyrant. [Much applause.] This Fugitive Slave Law had the support of the Lords, and the Coxes, the Tyngs, the Sharps and the flats. [Laughter.] It is nevertheless a degradation and a scandalous outrage on religious liberty; and if the American people were not sunk into degradation too deep for one possessing so little eloquence as I do to describe, they would feel it, too. This vile, infernal law does not interfere with singing of psalms, or anything of that kind, but with the weightier matters of the law, judgment, mercy, and faith. It makes it criminal for you, sir, to carry out the principles of Christianity. It forbids you the right to do right—forbids you to show mercy—forbids you to follow the example of the good Samaritan.

Had this law forbidden any of the rites of religion, it would have been a very different thing. Had it been a law to strike at baptism, for instance, it would have been denounced from a 1000 pulpits, and woe to the politician who did not come to the rescue.—But, I am spending my strength for nought; what care we for religious liberty? what are we— an unprincipled set of knaves. [Laughter.] You feel it to be so. Not a man of you that looks a fellow Democrat or Whig in the face, but knows it. But it has been said that this law is constitutional—if it were, it would be equally the legitimate sphere of government to repeal it. I am proud to be one of the disciples of Gerrit Smith, and this is his doctrine; and he only utters what all law writers have said who have risen to any eminence. Human government is for the protection of rights; and when human government destroys human rights, it ceases to be a government, and becomes a foul and blasting conspiracy; and is entitled to no respect whatever.

It has been said that our fathers entered into a covenant for this slave-catching. Who were your daddies? [Laughter.] I take it they were men, and so are you. You are the sons of your fathers; and if you find your fathers exercising any rights that you don't find among your rights, you may be sure that they have transcended their limits. If they have made a covenant that you should do that which they have no right to do themselves, they transcended their own authority, and surely it is not binding on you. If you look over the list of your rights, you do not find among them any right to make a slave of your brother. [Many cries of "no, no, no—and so say we, all of us."]

Well, you have just as good a right to do so as your fathers had. It is a fundamental truth that every man is the rightful owner of his own body. If you have no right to the possession of another man's body your fathers had no such right. But suppose that they have written in a constitution that they have a right, you and I have no right to conform to it. Suppose you and I had made a deed to give away two or three acres of blue sky; would the sky fall—and would anybody be able to plough it? You will say that this is an absurdity, and so it is. The binding quality of law, is its reasonableness. I am safe, therefore, in saying, that slavery cannot be legalized at all. I hope, therefore, that you will take the ground that this slavery is a system, not only of wrong, but is of a lawless character, and cannot be christianized nor legalized. [Applause.]

Can you hear me in that end of the hall now? [Laughter and applause.] I trust that this Convention will be the means of laying before the country the principles of the Liberty Party which I have the honor to represent, to some extent, on this floor. Slavery is such a piracy that it is known neither to law nor gospel—it is neither human nor divine—a monstrosity that cannot be legalized. If they took this ground it would be the handwriting on the wall to the Belshazzars of the South. It would strip the crime of its legality, and all the forms of law would shrink back with horror from it. As I have always an object when speaking on such subjects as this, I wish you to supply yourselves with Gerrit Smith's pamphlet on civil government, which I now hold in my hand. I thought you doubted the impossibility of legalizing slavery. [Cries of no.]

Could a law be made to pass away any of your individual rights? No. And so neither can a law be made to pass away the right of the black man. This is more important than most of you seem to think. You are about to have a party, but I hope not such a party as will gather up the votes, here and there, to be swallowed up at a meal by the great parties. I think I know what some leading men are now thinking. We hear a great deal of the independent, free democracy—at one time independent and another time dependent—but I want always to be independent, and not hurried to and fro into the ranks of Whigs or Democrats. It has been said that we ought to take the position to gain the greatest number of voters, but that is wrong.

We have had enough of that folly. It was said in 1848 that Martin Van Buren would carry a strong vote in New York; he did so but he almost ruined us. He merely looked at us as into the pig-pen to see how the animal grew; but the table was the final prospect in view; he regarded the Free Soil party as a fatling to be devoured. [Great laughter.] Numbers should not be looked to so much as right. The man who is right is a majority. He who has God and conscience on his side, has a majority against the universe. Though he does not represent the present state, he represents the future state. If he does not represent what we are, he represents what we ought to be. In conclusion, this party ought to extend a hand to the noble, self-sacrificing patriot—glorious Kossuth. But I am a voting delegate, and must now go to the convention. You will excuse me for breaking off so abruptly.

Frederick Douglass' Paper, August, 1852

TO HON. CHAS. SUMNER

Rochester, Sept. 2d, 1852

My dear Sir:

Accept my thanks for your note of Aug. 31st. The speech of Mr. Watkins found its way into my columns simply as the production of a colored man. I dissent from its spirit and its philosophy. It evinced the possession of talent by its author, and for this it was published.

I saw your speech on the militia question, and marked it for publication, but I am so much on the wing, so much from home, and withal have so little order, that the paper containing your speech slipped through my fingers, and is gone. You will, therefore, do me a service by sending the speech. It shall be published at once. I understand your views and feelings on the subject of peace and war exactly, and am prepared with every disposition to do you justice fully.

Mr. Watkins is a young man, a man of some promise I should think. He is now in a school of reformers, a school through which I have passed, a school which has many good qualities, but a school *too* narrow in its philosophy and too bigoted in spirit to do justice to any who venture to differ from it. I am at this moment assailed with more bitterness by that school than from any other quarter. I need much of your self-possession and patience. I am often tempted to strike back and I am not sure that I will not do so at some future time. For the present, however, I propose for myself silence under every provocation. Especially do I wish to maintain silence under whatever Mr. Garrison may say. I stand in relation to him something like that of a child to a parent.

But not so in relation to any other man of the party.

You will bear with me if I take this occasion to explain the cause of much ill feeling in that quarter towards me. My first offense was starting my paper against their advice. My 2d offense, was refusing to make it the organ of their Society. My third offense [was] the abandonment of the non-voting theory.

It will be news to you when I tell you that Mr. Garrison and Mrs. Chapman, upon the starting of my paper, wrote immediately to my friends in England, counselling the withdrawment of all support from it, on the ground that there was no need for such a paper and that the *Standard* and *Liberator* were quite sufficient. They wrote in various directions predicting the failure of the paper, complimenting me as a speaker, and decrying me as a writer, and regretting the loss of me in the lecturing field. This was the best possible way to undermine and destroy my paper. Yet the attempt failed and ought to have failed. Not that I can boast of the power they deny me—I mean the power to write—but they might have given me a fair opportunity to try my hand without their volunteer disparagement. They might have allowed my friends to ascertain for themselves, how far I was capable of serving the Anti-Slavery cause with my pen.

But I am taking up too much of your precious time. Pardon the freedom of this note, and believe me, your sincere and grateful friend,

Frederick Douglass

Charles Sumner Papers, Harvard University

OUR POSITION IN THE PRESENT PRESIDENTIAL CANVASS

We shall, perhaps, surprise some and grieve others when we declare now, our fixed purpose to support with whatever power we possess, John P. Hale for President and George W. Julian for Vice-President of the United States—the candidates unanimously nominated by the "Free Democratic" party at Pittsburgh. We promise to the free Democracy the aid of our pen, voice and vote, and that if their candidates are not elected it will be from no fault of ours. This pledge, however, is given with the distinct understanding, that, should these gentlemen in accepting their nomination write letters of a compromising character, we shall drop them and take up such as are already in the field, by the action of a small division of the Liberty Party.

That this course of ours will be condemned in some quarters, and by some persons with whom we have of late acted, we have no doubt. Valuing the good opinion of these friends, and happy to find ourselves at agreement with them, we beg to state with some distinctness, and at length the reasons for thus taking our stand with the "Free Democracy." Convinced ourselves of the wisdom of this policy, we find it easy to believe that others can be so convinced.

In dealing with this subject we cannot address ourselves to any such as have made up their minds to vote for either General Scott, or for *General* Pierce.[29] These gentlemen are out of the controversy for the present. We address ourselves to voting abolitionists, those who hold themselves bound to carry their moral convictions into the government, and to do all they can to establish "an every-way-righteous civil government." *"We speak unto wise men; judge ye what we say."*

1. *Slavery* is, beyond all comparison, the first and greatest evil in this country. It not only rests with crushing weight on the troubled bosoms of the helpless millions, whose claims to sympathy and relief alone are quite overwhelming; but it involves the whole country in a common guilt and shame, and stands directly in the way of all righteous progress, making true liberty impossible. It pollutes and must pollute while it continues, press, pulpit, and people, and render them unfit and unwilling to attend to moral considerations in connection with their political duties and responsibilities. In proof of this position, argument is needless. The evidence is as broad as the country, and extends through every part of it. We have but to open our eyes to see it, and our ears to hear it. The lesson taught by this, is, that slavery is the first great evil to be removed, and liberty the first great good to be attained by the American people.

2. It is not less the voice of reason and nature, than it is the voice of the sacred scriptures, that freedom is a fundamental condition of accountability and the foundation of all manly virtue. Moses was charged by the Almighty to tell Pharoah to let the Hebrews go free, as the first condition to religious obedience. *"Let my people go free, that they may serve me."* Such is the voice of God, and such is the deduction of reason. It was not said, let my people *serve me,* that they may go *free;* but emancipation was demanded as the first condition needful to render service to God. We commend this consideration to our Bible-reading and Bible-voting friends, feeling that it may help to relieve them on a point upon which they entertain scruples against casting a merely anti-slavery vote.

3. *To guard against misunderstanding.*—While we hold that slavery is emphatically the *first* great evil which concerns the people of this country, and that liberty is the first great interest to be secured and preserved, we would not be understood as being indifferent to other interests. No evil should go unopposed, and no good should go unsought. This is our meaning, there is a natural order of things, and in this order the abolition of slavery in this country stands first, and is for the time being sufficiently important to be the first object of political action.

4. It will be objected that this theory limits a man's political duties, and destroys the significance of a vote. "I want my vote," says one, "to represent fully all my moral convictions of what should be politically

done;" and a vote that does less than this is a compromising vote, doing but part of what it ought to do, and leaving undone a part of that which it ought to do. The fallacy here is in the assumption that what is *morally* right is, at all times, equally politically possible. One man may see nineteen applications of the principles of justice, another twenty; but, on the principle stated above, the man of the twenty would be bound to separate from him of the nineteen, altho' in the nineteen points they are perfectly agreed. Again, the absurdity of the objection is seen in the fact, that the principle would make party action, or combined effort impossible, by requiring complete identity of opinion, and failing to recognize (as it does) those differences which result from location, education, habits of thought, temperament, and mental development, it leaves no ground for a minority to stand upon.

To differ with them is to be divided, not merely in opinion, but in action. We heard one of this class say that he would vote for the candidates of the Liberty Party, or that he would not vote at all. Before he would vote for John P. Hale, he would stay away from the polls. Now, what would be thought of a man who should see a thousand men drowning, and should quietly fold his hands on the shore, declaring, that inasmuch as he could not save *all,* he would not save any?—Further, he might say, "If I save that man yonder, who is battling with the waves for life, may not that perishing woman, with her babe in her arms, justly feel herself neglected, and pierce my soul with her reproachful glance?" This reasoning would be quite as much entitled to respect as his, who would not vote to attain one or more great political blessings, or to move one or more great political wrongs, because such a vote would not accomplish all that he might desire to have accomplished by his vote. Yet this is, as we understand it, the very ground taken by those of the Liberty Party at Canastota, last week, who left the party because they were outvoted, and nominated candidates for themselves.

5. Having shown thus briefly, and we think conclusively, the unsoundness of that philosophy of political party action, adopted by our friends at Canastota, for whom, by the way, we entertain sentiments of high respect and warm affection, they may very well call upon us to indicate a rule or principle of political party action, which is free from all valid objection. Very well. It is evident that all reforms have their beginning with ideas, and that for a time they have to rely solely on the tongue and pen for progress, until they gain a sufficient number of adherents to make themselves felt at the ballot-box. The idea of "Free

Trade," "Direct Taxes," "Land-Reform," "Right of Suffrage," "Women's Rights," together with "opposition to Capital Punishment," to "secret societies," and "intervention," may all, in certain circumstances, receive due attention, while yet remaining within the region of ideas, and about which there may be a difference of opinion, and yet those who differ may very properly unite *in political action* for some one great and good end. We ask no man to lose sight of any of his aims and objects. We only ask that they may be allowed to serve out their natural probation. Our rule of political action is this: the voter ought to see to it that his vote shall secure the highest good possible, at the same time that it does no harm.

6. According to this rule, we may vote in many instances with perfect propriety; for men, who, in regard to many things, entertain ideas totally different from ours. We can vote for a man who affirms, and will carry out one important truth, even though he should be totally blind in respect to others that we might deem important, provided, of course, he does not require us to deny any part of the truth which we hold; or, in other words, we can affirm his truths just so far and so long as he does not require us to negative ours. It seems to us, there can be no valid objection against this rule of action, or the philosophy by which it is sustained, especially when it is remembered that, often the very best way of promoting one cause, is by promoting the triumph of another.—Draw out the old tooth and give place to the new one. One thing at a time, or, at least, only so many as at the time being, strongly commend themselves as proper to be done. Abolish slavery; remove this stupendous system of iniquity, under whose death-like shade moral feeling is deadened, and intellect languishes, and you have done a double good. You have helped forward a thousand good causes, by promoting the triumph of one. We repeat, do all the good you can, and do no harm.

7. It may be said that these arguments do not apply to the case under consideration; that they lose their force, in the fact that the Free Democracy cannot do more in the struggle for the Presidency than bear its own testimony in favor of certain rights, and against certain wrongs; and that, therefore, *"the Liberty Party"* really stands upon an equal footing with the Free Democracy. Indeed, it may possibly be contended that, based on broader principles, and animated by higher aspirations, "the Liberty Party" holds decided advantage over *"the Free Democracy."* We admit the pertinency of this objection, and it deserves to be met. We assume what we believe to be true, that in point of fundamental principles, *"the Liberty Party"* and *"the Free Democracy"* occupy common ground; the

difference between them, on the subject of slavery, is exceedingly slight. Verbal, rather than real. It is plain, therefore, that reasons for preferring the one to the other, must be sought in something aside from the moral superiority of the one over the other. The advantage of *"the Free Democracy"* over *"the Liberty Party,"* is to be found in the superiority of its circumstances. It has the power to unite a very influential minority on a sound principle of universal application. It can give to the good cause the energy derived from complete organization, and animate and encourage, by the power of sympathy.—It can give us the wisdom of two heads instead of one; and the might of a multitude instead of a few. "United we stand, divided we fall," will apply to the case in hand; and should only be forgotten when the object for which we are united is worth less than the good to be obtained by separation. We repeat, assuming that there is, really, no moral difference between the two organizations on the question of slavery, we are led by a fair view of the advantages of a united army against slavery, to rally under one standard in the coming election.

8. But if this be sound argument, it may be asked, why may we not abandon "the Free Democracy," and go over to the Whig party, and General Scott? The reason is obvious, neither the Whig party nor General Scott aim at the regeneration, or reformation of the American Government. Both stand pledged against all reformation; both are quite content with things as they are; both are wedded to the slave power, and neither purposes to do anything to blot out the foul disgrace and scandal of slavery, or for the repeal of that most shocking of all human enactments, the fugitive slave act. They cherish slavery as a blessing, and stand by it as its special friends and guardians.

The Democratic party is equally unworthy, equally to be shunned and deserted with the Whig party. They stand on one common footing of wickedness, their only struggle is for place and power. Without ringing the changes here, it is enough to say that the cases supposed have no likeness, and that therefore the argument based upon the premises has no force or application. The whole matter is settled, by the fact that the Free Democracy is a party of progress and reform, while the other parties are anti-progress, anti-reform, and are such from the very nature of their organizations.

9. It is feared by some, that *"the Free Democratic Party"* will by-and-by retrograde, and finally sell out to one or the other of the great political parties. It would be idle not to admit such a thing to be possible; but the

probabilities are strongly against such a supposition. *"The Free Demo-cratic Party"* has disencumbered itself of the causes which have dragged down both the old parties to their present depth of degradation, and has grasped with decisive energy the principles which are at the bottom of all political progress, to wit, "Justice, Liberty, and Humanity." It asks no support of those who would corrupt it, and gathers its friends from the shrine of truth and freedom. But what if in an evil hour that party should fall, as others have done before, there is still a God in Israel. The remedy is at hand. Abandon it and build another house. Out of the wisdom gained by experience, organize a better party. Fealty to party has no claims against fidelity to truth.

10. It is objected to *"the Free Democracy,"* that it does not deny the possibility of legalizing slavery; but is this so? We understand *"the Free Democracy"* to admit, what it would be folly to deny, that *"property in man"* can be asserted and maintained by force, under the forms of legisla-tion. We suppose every one will admit this. We understand, at the same time, that *"the Free Democracy"* deny the validity of such legislation, as being destitute of any authority over the slave, or over the conscience of any class of men. We believe that even Gerrit Smith regards the Free Democracy as going this length; but he objects, that in another part of the platform, there are admissions which militate against this doctrine; such, for instance, as the following resolution:

"That no permanent settlement of the Slavery question can be looked for except in the practical recognition of the truth, that Slavery is sectional and Freedom national, by the total separation of the General Government from Slavery, and the exercise of its legitimate constitutional influence on the side of Freedom, and by leaving to the States the whole subject of Slavery and the extradition of fugitives from service."

Now, admitting that this is an unsound plank in the Pittsburgh platform, there is an explanation by which, in truth, this resolution does not belong at all to the platform. The fact is, that a resolution asserting precisely what this resolution now asserts, at least asserting that which makes this resolution objectionable, was almost unanimously voted down, and cast out of the platform; it must therefore be plain that the present resolution holds its place in the series of resolutions purely by accident or oversight, not by design. Any other supposition would stamp the Pitts-burgh Convention as meanly paltering in a double sense. Nevertheless, there are persons in *"the Free Democracy"* whose sentiments are expressed in this resolution; and it will, in the circumstances, be claimed by all such, as a part of the platform; but in the light of the explanation we have given, it does seem that it ought not to be made a barrier against the union of *Liberty Party* men and *Free Democrats;* certainly not, when it is remembered that the right of discussion is secured, and the means of enlightenment are at hand.

Now let us see the principles laid down by the Free Democracy. Here are their resolutions on slavery:

"Having assembled in National Convention as the delegates of the Free Democracy of the United States, united by a common resolve to maintain Right against Wrongs and Freedom against Slavery; confiding in the intelligence, the patriotism and the discriminating justice of the American People; putting our trust in God for the triumph of our cause, and invoking his guidance in our endeavors to advance it, we now submit to the candid judgment of all men the following declaration of principles and measures:

"1. That Governments deriving their just powers from the consent of the governed, are instituted among men to secure to all those inalienable rights of life, liberty and the pursuit of happiness, with which they are endowed by their Creator, and of which none can be deprived by valid legislation, except for crime.

"2. That the true mission of American Democracy is to maintain the Liberties of the People, the Sovereignty of the States and the perpetuity of the Union, by the impartial application to public affairs, without sectional discriminations, of the fundamental principles of equal rights, strict justice, and economical administration.

"3. That the Federal Government is one of limited powers, derived solely from the Constitution, and the grants of power therein ought to be strictly construed, by all departments and agents of the government, and it is inexpedient and dangerous to exercise doubtful constitutional powers.

"4. That the Constitution of the United States is ordained to form a more perfect union, to establish justice, and secure the blessings of liberty, or property, without due process of law; and therefore, the government, having no more power to make a slave than to make a king, and no more power to establish slavery than to establish a monarchy, should at once proceed to relieve itself from all responsibility for the existence of slavery, wherever it possesses constitutional power to legislate for its extinction.

"5. That to the persevering and importune demands of the Slave Power for *more Slave States, new Slave Territories, and the nationalization of Slavery,* our distinct and final answer is no more Slave States, no Slave Territory, no nationalized Slavery, and no legislation for the extradition of Slaves.

"6. That slavery is a sin against God and a crime against man, which no human enactment nor usage can make right, and that Christianity, Humanity and Patriotism alike demand its abolition.

"7. That the Fugitive Slave Act of 1850 is repugnant to the Constitution, to the principles of the common law, to the spirit of Christianity, and to the principles of the civilized world. We, therefore, deny its binding force upon the American people, and demand its immediate and total repeal.

"8. That the doctrine that any human law is a finality and not subject to modification or repeal, is not in accordance with the creed of the founders of our government, and is dangerous to the liberties of the people.

"9. That the acts of Congress known as the Compromise measures of 1850, by making the admission of a sovereign State contingent upon the adoption of other measures by the special interest of Slavery by their omission to guarantee freedom in Free Territories; by their attempt to impose unconstitutional limitations on the power of Congress and the people to admit new States; by their provisions for the assumption of five millions of the State debt of Texas, and for the payment of five millions more, and the cession of a large territory to the same State, under menace, as an inducement to the relinquishment of a groundless claim; and by their invasion of the sovereignty of the States and the liberties of the people, through the enactment of an unjust, oppressive and unconstitutional Fugitive Slave Law—are proved to be inconsistent with all the principles and maxims of Democracy, and wholly inadequate to the settlement of the questions of which they are claimed to be an adjustment."

11. These resolutions speak for themselves, and need no comment. They are broad and comprehensive in their scope, clear in their aim, cover the whole ground of anti-slavery principle, and the party adopting them is pledged to unceasing warfare against slavery, and all its pretentions.

Other resolutions were adopted at Pittsburgh, in respect to other matters which commend themselves to our judgment; but, considering that the first work to be done is the abolition of slavery, we have waived other considerations in discussing the merits of the Free Democracy.

12. We confess ourselves pleased with the spirit of *"the Free Democracy,"* not less than with its principles. It has passed through a trying ordeal. Defeated in its first great purpose, by the treachery of those who, under the pretended pressure of danger to the union, gave up the struggle and joined the enemy; deserted by States that had avowed themselves favorable to the ends sought by the Buffalo Convention, with ranks thinned by repeated defection; their organization rudely broken up, where it at one time seemed strongest; the two great parties sallying forth to battle against them under one banner and in one cause; scattered and disjointed, yet they gather at the ancient trumpet call of freedom, and with undaunted spirit they meet and arrange themselves for a renewal of the conflict as if confident of a final victory. There is evidence

here of an unconquerable spirit, and a firm resolve to fall or flourish with their convictions.

No man with proper feeling could behold without admiration the Pittsburgh Convention, a body of intelligent men thoroughly in earnest, scorning to remain with party and power, when their principles had been put under the ban—"great, glorious and free," though small in numbers and held in derision by the proud and the prudent. A noble, manly, independent, yet sympathizing spirit, diffused throughout their ranks without question drew us to their company, and compelled us to cast in our lot with them. *"These are the friends of God's suffering poor,"* came upon us with irresistible force, silencing all cavil.

Let the candidates then speak the same word, and breathe the same spirit, and the men of New York will stand by them, and for them, and against all who oppose them. Liberty will again be united against slavery, the friends of the slave will then join hands and present an undivided front, not merely defending the sacred cause of liberty, but boldly assailing the stronghold of the enemy.

Frederick Douglass' Paper, September 10, 1852

TO GERRIT SMITH, ESQR.

Rochester, Nov. 6th, 1852

My dear Sir:

The cup of my joy is full. If my humble labors have in any measure contributed (as you kindly say they have) to your election, I am most amply rewarded. You are now, thank heaven, within sight and hearing of this guilty nation. For the rest, I fear nothing. You will do the work of an apostle of Liberty. May God give you strength. Your election forms an era in the great Anti-Slavery struggle. For the first time, a man will appear in the American Congress completely imbued with the spirit of freedom. Heretofore, virtue has had to ask pardon of men. Our friends who have nobly spoken great truths in Congress, on the subject of Slavery, have all of them found themselves in straits where they have been compelled to disavow or qualify their abolitionism so as to seriously damage the beauty and force of their testimony. Not so will it be with you. Should your life and health be spared (which blessings are devoutly prayed for), you will go into Congress with the "Jerry Level" in your hand, regarding Slavery as "naked piracy." [30] You go to Congress, not by the grace of a party caucus, bestowed as a reward for party services; not by concealment, bargain or compromise, but by the unbought suffrages of your fellow citizens acting independently of, and in defiance of party! The odds against you were not insignificant. The *Dixes*, the *Woodburys*, the *Stantons*, the *Seymours*, and the *Conklings*, the very flower of your opponents were pitted against you. You are elected and they are defeated. "Nough said." You go to Congress, not for quiet nor seclusion, shut out from the eye of the world, where your thoughts and feelings had to be imagined, but you go from the very whirlwind of agitation, from "rescue trials," from womans' rights conventions and from "Jerry celebrations," where your lightest words were caught up and perverted to your hurt. You go to Congress a *free man*. I will not weary you with congratulations. My friend Julia, is even more ecstatic than myself about your election.

Please remind, favourably, Mrs. Smith, of your faithful friend,

Frederick Douglass

Gerrit Smith Papers, Syracuse University

A CALL TO WORK

The mission of the political abolitionists of this country is to abolish slavery. The means to accomplish this great end is, first, to disseminate anti-slavery sentiment; and, secondly, to combine that sentiment and render it a political force which shall, for a time, operate as a check on violent measures for supporting slavery; and, finally, overthrow the great evil of slavery itself.—The end sought is sanctioned by God and all his holy angels, by every principle of justice, by every pulsation of humanity, and by all the hopes of this republic. A better cause never summoned men to its support, nor invoked the blessings of heaven for success. Its opponents (whether they know it or not) are fighting against all that is noble in man—all that is best in society; and if their principles shall prove uneradicable, and their measures successful, then, just so sure as there is a God in the universe, the hope of this republic will go out in blood. Men may laugh—they may scoff—they may wrap themselves in heedless indifference; but every fact of history, every sentiment of religion, every indication of Providence proclaims, trumpet-tongued, that a day of reckoning will come. If this guilty country be saved—if it be made a blessing to mankind, that result will be accomplished, under God, by the faithful and self-sacrificing labors of the abolitionists. The work is great—very great. There has been a great deal done; but there is much more to do. There never was a time when we should advance to that work with a lighter heart or a firmer tread. The anti-slavery sentiment of the country has just made its mark on the public records in a manner not to be despised, and well calculated to inspire confidence in final success. The means are at hand to carry that mark higher still. Whoever lives to see the year 1856, will see anti-slavery in the field, with a broader front and loftier mien than it ever wore before.

Causes are in operation greatly calculated to concentrate the anti-slavery sentiment, and to bring it to bear directly against slavery. One of these causes is the complete overthrow of the Whig party,[31] and the necessity which it imposes upon its Northern anti-slavery members to assume an attitude more in harmony with their convictions than they could do on the Baltimore platform. The Southern wing of this party (never very reliable) will naturally become fused into the Democratic party, with which it is now more in sympathy than it can be with Northern Whigs. It is evident, that the Whigs of the North must stand alone or stand with us. It is equally evident that they cannot, and do not, desire to array themselves against the only living sentiment of the North, since they would, by such a course, only commit political suicide and make themselves of no political consequence. The danger now to be apprehended is, not that our numbers will not increase, and increase rapidly and largely, but that we shall be tempted to modify our platform of principles and abate the stringency of our testimonies, so as to accommodate the wishes of those who have not hitherto distinctly acted with us, and who now wish to do so.

Now the way to swell our vote for freedom and to prevent the evil, thus briefly hinted at, is, to spread anti-slavery light, and to educate the people on the whole subject of slavery—circulate the documents—let the anti-slavery speaker, more than ever, go abroad—let every town be visited, and let truth find its way into every house in the land. The people want to do what is best. They must be shown that to do right is best. The great work to be done is to educate the people, and to this work the abolitionist should address himself with full purpose of heart.—This is no time for rest; but a time for every one to be up and doing. The battle, though not just begun, is far from being completed. The friends of freedom, in their various towns and counties, should, without waiting for some central organization to move in the matter, take up the work themselves—collect funds—form committees—send for documents—call in lecturers, and bring the great question of the day distinctly and fully before their fellow-citizens. We would not give the snap of our finger for one who begins and ends his anti-slavery labors on election day. Anti-slavery papers are to be upheld—lecturers are to be sustained—correspondence is to be kept up—acquaintances are to be formed with those who sympathize with us, and a fraternal and brotherly feeling is to be increased, strengthened and kept up. Here, then, is work—work for every one to do—work which must be done if ever the great cause in which we have embarked is brought to a happy consummation. Let every one make this cause his own. Let him remember the deeply injured and imbruted slave as bound with him. Let him not forget that he is but a steward, and that he is bound to make a righteous use of his Lord's money. Let him make his anti-slavery a part of his very being, and God will bless him and increase him an hundred fold. Now is the time for a real anti-slavery revival. The efforts to silence discussion should be rebuked. We *ought* not, we must not be "hushed and mum" at the bidding of slave power conventions, or any other power on earth.

Frederick Douglass' Paper, November 19, 1852

TO HON. GERRIT SMITH

Rochester, Jan. 14th, 1853

I have troubled you so little with my pen since you were elected to Congress,[32] that I fear you will begin to think that your elevation has desolved [sic] the bonds of my grateful affection. It is not so however. A thoughtful regard for your precious time, and a knowledge of the fact that you are increasingly occupied, is my apology. I am impatient to meet you at the rescue trials. I want to see and hear you on that great occasion—for great it will be—and I mean to have a string of appointments which will bring me up at Albany on the 29th. Our paper is getting on well. Subscribers are renewing their subscriptions, and a career of usefulness seems to unfold before it. My health was never better than during this winter and my spirits—though subject to some clouds—are quite bright. Mrs. Smith intended to have called yesterday at the office, but feeble health prevented. My friend Miss Griffiths has twice called upon her at Mrs. Talman's and once to tea. She was much delighted with the kind reception given her by Mrs. T. But what kind of news is this to be telling one, now burdened with the "affairs of State"? Well, I know that Gerrit Smith the man, is before Gerrit Smith the "honorable member."

A very unpleasant controversy is springing up among the fugitives in Canada. Mr. Ward and Miss Shadd on the one side, Mr. and Mrs. Bibb on the other. The question is whether "The Refugees Home Society" ought, or ought not be supported. Bibb thinks it ought. Ward thinks it not. Both sides shall be heard in our paper.

I think of changing the name of my paper, or in other words giving my paper a name, for as friend Garrison clearly proved, my paper is without a name. Will you not suggest one? I shall lose my reputation for being unstable if I don't change soon.

How would this do *"The Black Man"*
or this *"The Agitator"*
or this *"The Jerry Level"*
or this *"The Brotherhood"*

The black man is good but common. The agitator is good but promises too much. The brotherhood implies the exclusion of the sisterhood. Upon the whole I like the *"Jerry Level"* best. That's distinctive, smooth, and conveys the true anti-slavery idea. But I shall wait your suggestion and shall doubtless adopt it when it comes.[33]

My family are all well, except colds. Of these they have all had aplenty.

Yours most truly,
Frederick Douglass

Gerrit Smith Papers, Syracuse University

LEARN TRADES OR STARVE!

These are the obvious alternatives sternly presented to the free colored people of the United States. It is idle, yea even ruinous, to disguise the matter for a single hour longer; every day begins and ends with the impressive lesson that free negroes must learn trades, or die.

The old avocations, by which colored men obtained a livelihood, are rapidly, unceasingly and inevitably passing into other hands; every hour sees the black man elbowed out of employment by some newly arrived emigrant, whose hunger and whose color are thought to give him a better title to the place; and so we believe it will continue to be until the last prop is levelled beneath us.

As a black man, we say if we cannot stand up, let us fall down. We desire to be a man among men while we do live; and when we cannot, we wish to die. It is evident, painfully evident to every reflecting mind, that the means of living, for colored men, are becoming more and more precarious and limited. Employments and callings, formerly monopolized by us, are so no longer.

White men are becoming house-servants, cooks and stewards on vessels—at hotels.—They are becoming porters, stevedores, wood-sawyers, hod-carriers, brick-makers, white-washers and barbers, so that the blacks can scarcely find the means of subsistence—a few years ago, and a *white* barber would have been a curiosity—now their poles stand on every street. Formerly blacks were almost the exclusive coachmen in wealthy families: this is so no longer; white men are now employed, and for aught we see, they fill their servile station with an obsequiousness as profound as that of the blacks. The readiness and ease with which they adapt themselves to these conditions ought not to be lost sight of by the colored people. The meaning is very important, and we should learn it. We are taught our insecurity by it. Without the means of living, life is a curse, and leaves us at the mercy of the oppressor to become his debased slaves. Now, colored men, what do you mean to do, for you must do something? The American Colonization Society tells you to go to Liberia. Mr. Bibbs tells you to go to Canada. Others tell you to go to school. We tell you to go to work; and to work you must go or die. Men are not valued in this country, or in any country, for what they *are;* they are valued for what they can *do.* It is in vain that we talk about being men, if we do not the work of men. We must become valuable to society in other departments of industry than those servile ones from which we are rapidly being excluded. We must show that we can *do* as well as *be;* and to this end we must learn trades. When we can build as well as live in houses; when we can *make* as well as *wear* shoes; when we can produce as well as consume wheat, corn and rye—then we shall become valuable to society. Society is a hard-hearted affair.—With it the helpless may expect no higher dignity than that of paupers. The individual must lay society under obligation to him, or society will honor him only as a stranger and sojourner. *How* shall this be done? In this manner: use every means, strain every nerve to master some important merchanical art. At present, the facilities for doing this are few—institutions of learning are more readily opened to you than the work-shop; but the Lord helps them who will help themselves, and we have no doubt that new facilities will be presented as we press forward.

If the alternative were presented to us of learning a trade or of getting an education, we would learn the trade, for the reason, that with the trade we could get the education, while with the education we could not get the trade. What we, as a people, need most, is the means for our own elevation.—An educated colored man, in the United States, unless he has within him the heart of a hero, and is willing to engage in a life-long battle for his rights, as a man, finds few inducements to remain in this country. He is isolated in the land of his birth—debarred by his color from congenial association with whites; he is equally cast out by the ignorance of the *blacks*. The remedy for this must comprehend the elevation of the masses; and this can only be done by putting the mechanic arts within the reach of colored men.

We have now stated pretty strongly the case of our colored countrymen; perhaps some will say, *too* strongly; but we know whereof we affirm.

In view of this state of things, we appeal to the abolitionists, What boss anti-slavery mechanic will take a black boy into his wheelwright's shop, his blacksmith's shop, his joiner's shop, his cabinet shop? Here is something *practical;* where are the whites and where are the blacks that will respond to it? Where are the anti-slavery milliners and seamstresses that will take colored girls and teach them trades, by which they can obtain an honorable living? The fact that we have made good cooks, good waiters, good barbers, and white-washers, induces the belief that we may excel in higher branches of industry. *One thing is certain: we must find new methods of obtaining a livelihood, for the old ones are failing us very fast.*

We, therefore, call upon the intelligent and thinking ones amongst us, to urge upon the colored people within their reach, in all seriousness, the duty and the necessity of giving their children useful and lucrative trades, by which they may commence the battle of life with weapons commensurate with the exigencies of the conflict.

Frederick Douglass' Paper, March 4, 1853

A DAY AND A NIGHT IN "UNCLE TOM'S CABIN"

It was our pleasure and privilege, during our recent visit to Massachusetts, to pass a day and a night in *"Uncle Tom's Cabin,"* at Andover. The house is known through the town by this designation. It was only necessary to inquire at the railroad station for *"Uncle Tom's Cabin,"* to be at once directed to the door of Mrs. Stowe's dwelling—an edifice, by the way, bearing little resemblance to slave cabins, as we have seen them, either in the size, in the materials of which it was constructed, in the character of its architecture, or the style of its furniture; but it is just such a dwelling, in all these particulars, as befits the exalted genius which it shelters.

The house is plain, large and substantial—built of solid granite, of sombre hue, and looks as if it might abide the blasts of ages. The site on which the dwelling stands is well chosen, fronting, as it does, the college buildings, and the beautiful public square, which is filled with trees, and must, in summer, be a charming spot.

We have seen it when it was thronged with the youthful flowers of New England orthodoxy; young gentlemen sent hither to the school of the puritan prophets, to fathom the mysterious depths of the theology of their fathers.

As we looked on *"Uncle Tom's Cabin,"* and the grand old college, we could not help thinking that the cabin would, in history, outshine the college, illustrious though the latter may be. Already, the dazzling fame of "the Cabin" has transcended, and thrown into the shade that of the college. The name of its occupant is known among nations, whose men of learning have not heard of Andover. How happens this? Here is the explanation. The word of Mrs. Stowe is addressed to the soul of universal humanity. That word, bounded by no national lines, despises the limits of Sectarian sympathy, and thrills the universal heart. *God bless her for that word!* The slave in his chains shall hear it gladly, and the slaveholder shall hear it; *both* shall rejoice in it, and by its light and love learn lessons of liberty and brotherhood.

Our reception, at the Cabin, by Mr. and Mrs. Stowe, was free from all ostentation; and, though kindly, very quietly managed. No high-sounding phrases of welcome to cover the lack of cordiality. Dr. Stowe himself was quite unwell, and the excellent authoress had to be master as well as mistress, of ceremonies, which, by the way, not being very complicated, cost very little effort.

So much has been said and written about Mrs. Stowe, that it is hardly worth while for us to give our daguerreotype impression of her. Yet, everybody wants to know how persons of her eminence look; how they speak; how they act at home? Whether they're pretty or homely? Whether they are quiet or boisterous? Whether they are loquacious or reserved? We are all looking out for examples, and we look for them among the great ones; if we cannot imitate them in their great works we can, at least, imitate them in their manners and bearing.

Well, in respect to Mrs. Stowe, as might be supposed, she has a way and a manner of her own; having more points of resemblance, perhaps, with the sisterhood of American women than most persons; yet, peculiar, marked, original. Sitting at the window of a milliner's shop, no one would ever suspect her of being the splendid genius that she is! She would be passed and repassed, attracting no more attention than ordinary ladies. She would appear simply as a thoughtful, industrious manager of household affairs; nothing more.

It is only when in conversation with the authoress of *"Uncle Tom's Cabin"* that she would be suspected of possessing that deep insight into human character, that melting pathos, keen and quiet wit, powers of argumentation, exalted sense of justice, and enlightened and comprehensive philosophy, so eminently exemplified in the *master book* of the nineteenth century.

The object of our visit was to consult with the authoress, as to some method which should contribute successfully, and permanently, to the improvement and elevation of the free people of color in the United States—a work in which the benevolent lady designs to take a practical part; and we hesitate not to say that we shall look with more confidence to her efforts in that department, than to those of any other single individual in the country. In addition to having a heart for the work, she, of all others, has the ability to command and combine the means for carrying it forward in a manner likely to be most efficient. She desires that some *practical* good shall result to the colored people of this country, by the publication of her book—that some useful institution shall rise up in the wake of *"Uncle Tom's Cabin."*—The good lady, after showing us, in the most child-like manner, any number of letters, in testimony of the value of her book, together with presents of various kinds, among the number the beautiful "Bronze Statue of a Female Slave," entered most fully into a discussion with us on the present condition and wants of *"the free colored people."*

Her style of conversation is free from the slightest tinge of affectation; she makes little account of emphasis, accentuation, pronunciation or rhetoric. The words are, evidently, subordinate to the thought—not the thought to the words. You listen to her, rather than to her language. While engaged in carrying out any particular branch of an argument, her whole mind seems turned within, and she seems not to think of the presence of any. But when the thought or argument is completely expressed, there is a lighting up of all the features; the eyes flash with especial brilliance. The feeling with which her manner inspired us, is not unlike that experienced when contemplating the ocean waves upon the velvet strand. You see them silently forming—rising—rolling—and increasing in speed, till, all at once, they are gloriously capped in sparkling beauty. Thus, wave after wave rolls in from the ocean: the mind fastened upon the beauty of the one, until disengaged by the still greater beauty of those succeeding. We could not feel other than at home in the presence of Mrs. Stowe, notwithstanding our reverence for her genius. She who had walked, with lighted candle, through the darkest and most obscure corners of the slave's soul, and had unfolded the secrets of the slave's lacerated heart, could not be a stranger to us; nor could we make ourselves such to her.

She was our friend and benefactress. Aye, and the friend of all mankind—one like Burns or Shakespeare, those favored ones of earth, to whom the whole book of humanity unfolds its ample pages, and from whom nothing is hid.

We looked around, while here, to see if we could find anything like a counterpart to little "Eva," (a "Topsy" we did not expect to find—that is a character for which we should look elsewhere—we think we have met with many in our day,) and lo! a dear little *"Eva"* stood at our elbow, in the person of a young daughter of Mrs. Stowe—a child from 8 to 10 years old, with a voice as tender and gentle, and eyes as soft, and as intensely spiritual as those which adorned the angelic creation in "Uncle Tom's Cabin." We said, "why you are little Eva!" the dear little girl answered with a beautiful meekness, and a turn of seriousness far beyond her years, "Oh! no, I'm not so good as she!"

Mrs. Stowe's plan for improving the condition of the free colored people will be made known in due season. For the present, it is sufficient to know that her attention is now most earnestly turned to this subject; and we have no question that it will result in lasting benefit to our class.

Frederick Douglass' Paper, March 4, 1853

TO HARRIET BEECHER STOWE

Rochester, March 8th, 1853

My Dear Mrs. Stowe:

You kindly informed me, when at your house, a fortnight ago, that you designed to do something which should permanently contribute to the improvement and elevation of the free colored people in the United States. You especially expressed an interest in such of this class as had become free by their own exertions, and desired most of all to be of service to them. In what manner, and by what means, you can assist this class most successfully, is the subject upon which you have done me the honor to ask my opinion.

Begging you to excuse the unavoidable delay, I will now most gladly comply with your request, but before doing so, I desire to express, dear Madam, my deep sense of the value of the services which you have already rendered my afflicted and persecuted people, by the publication of your inimitable book on the subject of slavery. That contribution to our bleeding cause, alone, involves us in a debt of gratitude which cannot be measured; and your resolution to make other exertions on our behalf excites in me emotions and sentiments, which I scarcely need try to give forth in words. Suffice it to say, that I believe you to have the blessings of your enslaved countrymen and countrywomen; and the still higher reward which comes to the soul in the smiles of our merciful Heavenly father, whose ear is ever open to the cries of the oppressed.

With such sentiments, dear Madam, I will at once proceed to lay before you, in as few words as the nature of the case will allow, my humble views in the premises. First of all, let me briefly state the nature of the disease, before I undertake to prescribe the remedy. Three things are notoriously true of us as a people. These are POVERTY, IGNORANCE AND DEGRADATION. Of course there are exceptions to this general statement; but these are so few as only to prove its essential truthfulness. I shall not stop here to inquire minutely into the causes which have produced our present condition; nor to denounce those whom I believe to be responsible for these causes. It is enough that we shall agree upon the character of the evil, whose existence we deplore, and upon some plan for its removal.

I assert then, that *poverty, ignorance* and *degradation* are the combined evil or, in other words, these constitute the social disease of the Free Colored people in the United States.

To deliver them from this triple malady, is to improve and elevate them, by which I mean simply to put them on an equal footing with their white fellow-countrymen in the sacred right to *"Life, Liberty* and the pursuit of happiness." I am for no fancied or artificial elevation, but only ask fair play. How shall this be obtained? I answer, first, not by establishing for our use high schools and colleges. Such institutions are, in my judgment, beyond our immediate occasions, and are not adapted to our present most pressing wants. High schools and colleges are excellent institutions, and will, in due season, be greatly subservient to our progress; but they are the result, as well as they are the demand of a point of progress, which we, as a people, have not yet attained. Accustomed, as we have been, to the rougher and harder modes of living, and of gaining a livelihood, we cannot, and we ought not to hope that, in a single leap from our low condition, we can reach that of *Ministers, Lawyers, Doctors, Editors, Merchants,* &c. These will, doubtless, be attained by us; but this will only be, when we have patiently and laboriously, and I may add successfully, mastered and passed through the intermediate gradations of agriculture and the mechanic arts. Besides, there are (and perhaps this is a better reason for my view of the case) numerous institutions of learning in this country, already thrown open to colored youth. To my thinking, there are quite as many facilities now afforded to the colored people, as they can spare the time, from the sterner duties of life, to avail themselves of. In their present condition of poverty, they cannot spare their sons and daughters two or three years at boarding schools or colleges, to say nothing of finding the means to sustain them while at such institutions. I take it, therefore, that we are well provided for in this respect; and that it may be fairly inferred from the past that the facilities for our education, so far as schools and colleges in the Free States are concerned, will increase quite in proportion with our future wants. Colleges have been open to colored youth in this country during the last dozen years. Yet few, comparatively, have acquired a classical education; and even this few have found themselves educated far above a living condition, there being no methods by which they could turn their learning to account. Several of this latter class have entered the ministry; but you need not be told that an educated people is needed to sustain an educated ministry. There must be a certain amount of cultivation among the people to sustain such a ministry. At present, we have not that cultivation amongst us; and therefore, we value, in the preacher, strong lungs, rather than high learning. I do not say that educated ministers are not needed amongst us.—Far from it! I wish there were more of them; but to increase their number is *not* the largest benefit you can bestow upon us.

You, dear Madam, can help the masses. You can do something for the thousands; and by lifting these from the depths of poverty and ignorance, you can make an educated ministry and an educated class possible. In the present circumstances, prejudice is a bar to the educated black minister among the whites; and ignorance is a bar to him among the blacks.

We have now two or three colored lawyers in this country; and I rejoice in the fact; for it affords very gratifying evidence of our progress. Yet it must be confessed that, in point of success, our lawyers are as great failures as are our ministers. White people will not employ them to the obvious embarrassment of their causes, and the blacks, taking their *cue* from the whites, have not sufficient confidence in their abilities to employ them. Hence, educated colored men, among the colored people, are at a very great discount. It would seem that education and emigration go together with us; for as soon as a man rises amongst us, capable, by his genius and learning, to do us great service, just so soon he finds that he can serve himself better by going elsewhere. In proof of this, I might instance the Russwurms—the Garnetts—the Wards—the Crummells and others—all men of superior ability and attainments, and capable of removing mountains of prejudice against their race, by their simple presence in the country; but these gentlemen, finding themselves embarrassed here by the peculiar disadvantages to which I have referred—disadvantages in part growing out of their education—being repelled by ignorance on the one hand, and prejudice on the other, and having no taste to continue a contest against such odds, they have sought more congenial climes, where they can live more peaceable and quiet lives. I regret their election—but I cannot blame them; for, with an equal amount of education, and the hard lot which was theirs, I might follow their example.

But, again, it has been said that the colored people must become farmers—that they must go on the land, in order to their elevation. Hence, many benevolent people are contributing the necessary funds to purchase land in Canada, and elsewhere, for them. That prince of good men, Gerrit Smith, has given away thousands of acres to colored men in this State, thinking, doubtless, that in so doing he was conferring a blessing upon them.[34] Now, while I do not undervalue the efforts which have been made, and are still being made in this direction, yet I must say that I have far less confidence in such efforts, than I have in the benevolence which prompts them. Agricultural pursuits are not, as I think, suited to our condition. The reason of this is not to be found so much in the occupation, (for it is a noble and ennobling one,) as in the people themselves. That is only a remedy, which can be applied to the case; and the difficulty in agricultural pursuits, as a remedy for the evils of poverty and ignorance amongst us, is that it cannot, for various reasons, be applied.

We cannot apply it, because it is almost impossible to get colored men to go on the land. From some cause or other, (perhaps the adage that misery loves company will explain,) colored people will congregate in the large towns and cities; and they will endure any amount of hardship and privation, rather than separate, and go into the country. Again, very few have the means to set up for themselves, or to get where they could do so.

Another consideration against expending energy in this direction is our want of self-reliance. Slavery more than all things else, robs its victims of self-reliance. To go into the western wilderness, and there to lay the foundation of future society, requires more of that important quality than a life of slavery has left us. This may sound strange to you, coming as it does from a colored man; but I am dealing with facts, and these never accommodate themselves to the feelings or wishes of any. They don't *ask*, but *take leave to be*. It is a fact then, and not less so because I wish it were otherwise, that the colored people are wanting in self-reliance—too fond of society—too eager for immediate results—and too little skilled in mechanics or husbandry to attempt to overcome the wilderness; at least, until they have overcome obstacles less formidable. Therefore, I look to other means than agricultural pursuits for the elevation and improvement of colored people. Of course, I allege this of the many. There are exceptions. Individuals among us, with commendable zeal, industry, perseverance and self-reliance, have found, and are finding, in agricultural pursuits, the means of supporting, improving and educating their families.

The plan which I contemplate will, (if carried into effect,) greatly increase the number of this class—since it will prepare others to meet the rugged duties which a pioneer agricultural condition must impose upon all who take it upon them. What I propose is intended simply to prepare men for the work of getting an honest living—not out of dishonest men—but out of an honest earth.

Again, there is little reason to hope that any considerable number of the free colored people will ever be induced to leave this country, even if such a thing were desirable. This black man—*un*like the Indian—loves civilization. He does not make very great progress in civilization himself but he likes to be in the midst of it, and prefers to share its most galling evils, to encountering barbarism. Then the love of the country, the dread of isolation, the lack of adventurous spirit, and the thought of seeming to desert their "brethren in bonds," are a powerful check upon all schemes of colonization which look to the removal of the colored people, without the slaves. The truth is, dear madam, we are *here,* and here we are likely to remain. Individuals emigrate—nations never. We have grown up with this republic, and I see nothing in her character, or even in the character of the American people as yet, which compels the belief that we must leave the United States. If then, we are to remain here, the question for the wise and good is precisely that you have submitted to me—namely: What can be done to improve the condition of the free people of color in the United States? The plan which I humbly submit in answer to this inquiry—and in the hope that it may find favor with you, and with many friends of humanity who honor, love and co-operate with you—is the establishment in Rochester, N. Y., or in some other part of the United States equally favorable to such an enterprise, of an INDUSTRIAL COLLEGE in which shall be taught several important branches of the mechanical arts. This college is to be opened to colored youth. I will pass over, for the present, the details of such an institution as I propose. It is not worth while that I should dwell upon these at all. Once convinced that something of the sort is needed, and the organizing power will be forthcoming. It is the peculiarity of your favored race that they can always do what they think necessary to be done. I can safely trust all details to yourself, and the wise and good people whom you represent in the interest you take in my oppressed fellow-countrymen.

Never having had a day's schooling in all my life I may not be expected to map out the details of a plan so comprehensive as that involved in the idea of a college. I repeat, then, I leave the organization and administration to the superior wisdom of yourself and the friends who second your noble efforts. The argument in favor of an Industrial College—a college to be conducted by the best men—and the best workmen which the mechanical arts can afford; a college where colored youth can be instructed to use their hands, as well as their heads; where they can be put into possession of the means of getting a living whether their lot in after life may be cast among civilized or uncivilized men; whether they choose to stay here, or prefer to return to the land of their fathers—

is briefly this: Prejudice against the free colored people in the United States has shown itself nowhere so invincible as among mechanics. The farmer and the professional man cherish no feeling so bitter as that cherished by these. The latter would starve us out of the country entirely. At this moment I can more easily get my son into a lawyer's office to learn law than I can into a blacksmith's shop to blow the bellows and to wield the sledge-hammer. Denied the means of learning useful trades we are pressed into the narrowest limits to obtain a livelihood. In times past we have been the hewers of wood and the drawers of water for American society, and we once enjoyed a monopoly in the menial enjoyments, but this is so no longer. Even these enjoyments are rapidly passing away out of our hands. The fact is—every day begins with the lesson, and ends with the lesson—the colored men must learn trades; and must find new employment; new modes of usefulness to society, or that they must decay under the pressing wants to which their condition is rapidly bringing them.

We must become mechanics; we must build as well as live in houses; we must make as well as use furniture; we must construct bridges as well as pass over them, before we can properly live or be respected by our fellow men. We need mechanics as well as ministers. We need workers in iron, clay, and leather. We have orators, authors, and other professional men, but these reach only a certain class, and get respect for our race in certain select circles. To live here as we ought we must fasten ourselves to our countrymen through their every day cardinal wants. We must not only be able to *black* boots, but to *make* them. At present we are unknown in the Northern States as mechanics. We give no proof of genius or skill at the county, State, or national fairs. We are unknown at any of the great exhibitions of the industry of our fellow-citizens, and being unknown we are unconsidered.

The fact that we make no show of our ability is held conclusive of our inability to make any, hence all the indifference and contempt with which incapacity is regarded, fall upon us, and that too, when we have had no means of disproving the infamous opinion of our natural inferiority. I have during the last dozen years denied before the Americans that we are an inferior race; but this has been done by arguments based upon admitted principles rather than by the presentation of facts. Now, firmly believing, as I do, that there are skill, invention, power, industry, and real mechanical genius, among the colored people, which will bear favorable testimony for them, and which only need the means to develop them,

I am decidedly in favor of the establishment of such a college as I have mentioned. The benefits of such an institution would not be confined to the Northern States, nor to the free colored people. They would extend over the whole Union. The slave not less than the freeman would be benefited by such an institution. It must be confessed that the most powerful argument now used by the Southern slaveholder, and the one most soothing to his conscience, is that derived from the low condition of the free colored people of the North. I have long felt that too little attention has been given by our truest friends in this country to removing this stumbling block out of the way of the slave's liberation.

The most telling, the most killing refutation of slavery, is the presentation of an industrious, enterprising, thrifty, and intelligent free black population. Such a population I believe would rise in the Northern States under the fostering care of such a college as that supposed.

To show that we are capable of becoming mechanics I might adduce any amount of testimony; dear madam, I need not ring the changes on such a proposition. There is no question in the mind of any unprejudiced person that the Negro is capable of making a good mechanic. Indeed, even those who cherish the bitterest feelings towards us have admitted that the apprehension that Negroes might be employed in their stead, dictated the policy of excluding them from trades altogether. But I will not dwell upon this point as I fear I have already trespassed too long upon your precious time, and written more than I ought to expect you to read. Allow me to say in conclusion, that I believe every intelligent colored man in America will approve and rejoice at the establishment of some such institution as that now suggested. There are many respectable colored men, fathers of large families, having boys nearly grown up, whose minds are tossed by day and by night with the anxious enquiry, "what shall I do with my boys?" Such an institution would meet the wants of such persons. Then, too, the establishment of such an institution would be in character with the eminently practical philanthropy of your trans-Atlantic friends. America could scarce object to it as an attempt to agitate the public mind on the subject of slavery, or to *dissolve the Union.* It could not be tortured into a cause for hard words by the American people, but the noble and good of all classes, would see in the effort an excellent motive, a benevolent object, temperately, wisely, and practically manifested.

Wishing, you, dear madam, renewed health, a pleasant passage, and safe return to your native land.

I am most truly, your grateful friend,

Frederick Douglass

Proceedings of the Colored National Convention Held in Rochester, July 6th, 7th and 8th, 1853, Rochester, 1853, pp. 33-38

A FEW WORDS MORE ABOUT LEARNING TRADES

In our edition of last week, we strove to impress upon the free colored people the great importance of learning trades; and we are happy to know that the article on that subject has been highly approved by many intelligent colored men in this city. The more we think upon the subject, the more strongly are we convinced that our hope of elevation and improvement, and, indeed, of our very existence, depends mainly upon, and will be in proportion to, the extent, we adopt mechanical, and abandon menial employments. One thing is settled, and that is, if we do not speedily abandon menial employments, they will speedily abandon us. They will pass into the hands of others, and will be firmly withheld from us. We shall soon have to say with Othello, our "occupation is gone." This is no idle declamation, indulged in, to excite or amuse, but words of sober truth and warning, which we sincerely hope will not pass unheeded. On this point the Colonization papers have told us many important and startling truths. The fact that we do not make the use of them which is intended shall be made of them, by those journals, does not impair their real value. We ought to turn them to account, in a manner to make Colonization papers scarce. Those papers and those societies which advocate our removal from this country, find the only apology for their existence and their efforts in the notorious facts of our poverty, our ignorance, and our degradation. Let these facts be removed, and there will be an end to Colonization papers and Colonization societies.

How shall this be done? is the question.—It is not certainly to be done by that "dastardly inactivity" which has characterized us for many years. Nor will it be done by plodding on in the footsteps of our fathers.— This course has brought us just where we are; and will lead us into a deeper degradation, and a more abject and helpless poverty than that to which it has already conducted us.

Will holding conventions, and passing strong resolutions do it? No—we think not. These, if put into practice, would help, no doubt. We think well of resolutions, and we believe much in conventions; but the history of our conventions and resolutions as a people, reflect little credit upon us. And this is partly because we have aimed to accomplish objects beyond our reach, and passed over practical schemes for our improvement. We have manifested any amount of opposition to menial employments, but have adopted no measures for learning our sons and daughters useful trades. We have had much to say, and very properly, about education. Our interest in education has not altogether been thrown away; but are there not men, many of them amongst us, who have strained every nerve to give their sons and daughters an education; and when this has been accomplished, have not those same sons and daughters returned home to renew their dependence upon the parental arm for support? Have those sons and daughters found employment suited to their acquirements? Can the daughters find schools to teach? or the sons find books to keep? Do abolitionists give them employment in their stores or counting-houses?—The answers to these questions are instructive; and for our part, we feel that the time has come to look them fully and squarely in the face.

The fact is, the means of living must precede education; or in other words, the education of the hands must precede that of the head. We can never have an educated class until we have more men of means amongst us. While the black man can do little more than keep soul and body together, while the whole struggle of life with him is barely to live, his home will and must be, the abode of ignorance. We have said that the colored people must learn useful trades, and it is well said. There is, however, a question behind that, to which this is no answer, and that question is, how are they to learn trades?—We admit that here is the difficulty—a difficulty which is by no means slight; yet it can be met successfully. Listen: the blacksmith will not teach a black boy a trade. Why?—Not because the black boy can't learn, but partly for the very opposite reason—he fears that by teaching one black boy, he will admit a host of sable competitors in his line, and will see the loaf pass from his mouth to theirs. He will not take a black boy as an apprentice, because he fancies it is not for his interest to do so. Well, if money will shut, money will open. Let such of our people who have money, and some have it despite their circumstances, make it for the interest of white master working men, to extend their art among the colored people, by taking colored apprentices. Let a fund be raised for this purpose; and it will be strange, indeed, if the money does not open the way to trades, as well as to learning. Twenty thousand *dollars* thus appropriated, would open, on a respectable scale, a grand workshop for colored youth, under competent white mechanics. Such a workshop (or workshops, for they might be multiplied to any extent) would soon make itself felt among the colored people, and among the white people. It would make us known at the County, State, and the National fairs.—Our workmanship—useful and ornamental—would be exhibited with that of our more favored fellow-countrymen. Master workmen in iron, wood, clay, and leather, would go out from the institution with diplomas far more valuable to us than those obtained from high schools or colleges. They would be the badge of independence and respectability.

In conclusion, we call upon the leading men and women in the Bethel Church, in the Zion Church, and in all the colored churches, to take up this matter. Consider its importance and practicability, and decide that something of the sort shall be done.—The leaders in these Churches have the ears of the colored people; we have neither their eyes nor their ears; we speak only to the few—they to the many. And we therefore leave the matter to them. Will they attend to it?

Frederick Douglass' Paper, March 11, 1853

TO GERRIT SMITH

Rochester, April 6th, 1853

My dear Friend:

Your note and the Land Reform proceedings came this morning, the latter too late for this week's issue. They shall appear in next week's paper.

I have received and have accepted an invitation from Lewis Tappan, Esqr., to make a speech at the May meeting of the American and Foreign Anti-Slavery Society in New York. I have done this not without consideration and having weighed every objection to it. My mind is made up. I shall not trouble you with my reasons for doing so here. I may have to give them hereafter. I am now suffering from my old bronchitis affection [sic], but hope to be all right for the May meeting.

That hundred dollars you kindly sent came in well. Where shall I look when that *fifty* is paid in? This may be looking most too far ahead, but I can't help it. The thought will come.

By the way, I have to thank you for just the most trim and gentlemanly suit of clothes I ever had on. I am saving them for the New York occasion.

Ward I see is to go to England. He is a strange genius and one that will take well in England, after its Canada training. But I won't trespass upon your precious time.

Ever your devoted friend,
Frederick Douglass

My friend Julia desires her love to you.

Gerrit Smith Papers, Syracuse University

THE BLACK SWAN, ALIAS MISS ELIZABETH GREENFIELD

How mean, bitter, and malignant is *prejudice against color!* It is the most brainless, brutal, and inconsistent thing of which we know anything. It can dine heartily on dishes prepared by colored hands? It can drink heartily from the glass filled by colored hands? It can ride languishingly behind horses driven by colored hands? It can snooze soundly under a razor guided by colored hands! Finally, it can go to Metropolitan Hall, and listen with delight to the enchanting strains of a black woman! if in all those relations there be conditions acknowledging the inferiority of black people to white. This brainless and contemptible creature, neither man nor beast, caused the following particular notice to be placed on the placard, announcing the Concert of "The Black Swan" in Metropolitan Hall, New York:

"PARTICULAR NOTICE.—No colored person can be admitted, as there is no part of the house appropriated for them."

We marvel that Miss Greenfield can allow herself to be treated with such palpable *disrespect;* for the insult is *to her,* not less than to her race.

She must have felt *deep humiliation* and depression while attempting to sing in the presence of an audience and under arrangements which had thus degraded and dishonored the people to which she belongs.— Oh! that she could be a *woman* as well as a songstress—brave and dauntless—resolved to fall or flourish with her outraged race—to scorn the mean propositions of the oppressor, and to refuse sternly to acquiesce in her own degradation. She is *quite mistaken* if she supposes that her success, as an artist depends upon her entire abandonment of self-respect. There are *generous hearts* enough in this country who, if she but lead the way, would extend to her the meed of praise and patronage commensurate with her merits. We warn her also, that this yielding, on her part, to the cowardly and contemptible exactions of the Negro haters of this country may meet her in a distant land in a manner which she little imagines.

Frederick Douglass' Paper, April 8, 1853

THE KEY TO UNCLE TOM'S CABIN [35]

American Slavery, like every other form of wickedness, has a strong desire just to be let alone; and slaveholders, above all other preachers, to whom we ever listened, insist most strongly on the duty of every man's minding his own business. They are sure that to drag slavery out of its natural darkness, will only rivet the fetters more firmly on their slaves; still, they have very strong reasons against coming to the light. "Let us declare," said a Carolina journal, some years ago, "that the subject of slavery *is* not and *shall* not be open to discussion within our borders—that the moment any preacher or private citizen shall attempt to enlighten us on that subject, his tongue shall be cut out and cast upon a dung hill!" Unlike Ajax, the cry is, give us but darkness, and slavery asks no more. "Mind your own business," said the late Mr. Clay to Mr. Mendenhall. *"Look at home,"* said the amiable *Mrs. Julia Gardner Ex-President John Tyler,* of Virginia, to the Duchess of Sutherland. Well, there is a good deal in the idea of one's minding his own business; and we are not sure that, if that idea were fully carried out, it would not abolish slavery.— Suppose every slaveholder should some day resolve to mind his own business, take care of his own concerns, be at the pains and industry of providing for his own wants with his own hands, or with the money obtained by his own energies—and suppose he should say to his slaves, "follow my example, mind your own business, don't look after mine, but look after your own business in your own way"—why, just here would be the end of slavery. Slaveholders preach to others this doctrine while they are themselves most grossly and scandalously intermeddling with the business of others to the utter neglect of their own.

It is noticeable, too, that the complaint of interference is never preferred against any of our sainted priesthood who bulwark the system with the gospel. These holy Doctors are held to be very properly employed. It is only your hot-headed men who think a *"n——r"* has rights as well as a white man—that a slave is as good as his master—who are supposed to need counsel to mind their own business.

But to return. Slavery dreads exposure. The light, which strengthens other systems, weakens slavery; and slaveholders know this very well. The wonder is, that, knowing it *so well,* they do not more skilfully manage their affairs. It is surprising that they allow such fiendish advertisements to find their way into their public journals—permit such bloody enactments to stain their statute books—and, publicly, commit such shocking atrocities as fill the pages of the *"Thousand Witnesses,"* and swell the volume of the *"Key"* to "Uncle Tom's Cabin." Some one should call attention to this unguarded point. How would it do, instead of advertising in the everywhere circulating newspaper for "blood-hounds to *hunt slaves,"* *"cash for Negroes,"* &c., to use small hand-bills for the purpose? These would not come North, telling their tales of misery on the one hand, and of deep wickedness on the other. Then, too, would it not be well to repeal most of the laws regulating the whipping, branding, ironing, shooting, stabbing, hanging and quartering, of slaves? Could not all these ends be attained without their being provided for in the statute book? Could not *"the spirit"* be retained without *"the letter?"* for it is *"the letter"* which, in this instance, is deadly—while *"the spirit"* of these laws is the life of the system of slavery. We should not be surprised if some such suggestions prevailed at the South; for slavery cannot bear to be looked at. The slaveholder must become a madman, and forget the eyes of just men and of a just God, when he burns his name into the flesh of a woman.

Bold and incorrigible as slaveholders, generally, are, they are, nevertheless, far from being indifferent to the good opinions of their fellowmen. They are seldom found willing to acknowledge themselves cruel, or wanting at all in the sentiments of humanity. On the contrary, none are more anxious than they to be regarded as kind and humane. Hence, they are ever anticipating objections to the slave system, by asserting the mildness of the treatment of their slaves, the excellency of their condition and the quiet of their minds. The best of them, however, would find the presence, for any considerable time, of a Northern man of anti-slavery principles on their plantations, watching the intercourse between themselves and their *contented* and *happy, un*paid laborers, very inconvenient and irksome! No. Masters should be seen apart from their slaves. They find it easier to commend slavery in its absence, than when confronted by its ugly features.

Willingly enough are these slaveholding gentlemen and ladies to be seen at Saratoga Springs, at Niagara, where they are arrayed in purple and fine linen, and are covered with silks, satins and broadcloth—their hands shining with gold, and their bosoms sparkling with diamonds. Their manner is so genteel—their conversation so winning—their smiles are full of kindness, that they easily make their way, win friends, and conceal their abominations. But bring them out from their hiding place—tear off the gold with which their sin is plated, and they stand out, by all the deductions of reason, morality, and religion, naked pirates before God and man, guilty of cruelty which might make a devil blush. Concealment, then, is the constant care of slaveholders. To see a slave speaking to a Northern man throws them into agony. So anxious are they to retain the secrets of the slave prison, that they denounce death against any in their midst who undertakes to reveal them.

But all efforts to conceal the enormity of slavery fail. The most unwise thing which, perhaps, was ever done by slaveholders, in order to hide the ugly features of slavery, was the calling in question, and denying the truthfulness of *"Uncle Tom's Cabin."* They had better have owned the "soft impeachment" therein contained—for the "Key" not only proves the correctness of every essential part of "Uncle Tom's Cabin," but proves more and worse things against the murderous system than are alleged in that great book. Since the publication of that repository of human horrors—*"The Testimony of a Thousand Witnesses"*—there has not been an exposure of slavery so terrible as the *Key* to *"Uncle Tom's Cabin."* Let it be circulated far and wide, at home and abroad; let young and old read it, think of it, and learn from it to hate slavery with unappeasable intensity. The book, then, will be not only a *Key* to "Uncle Tom's Cabin," but a key to unlock the prison-house for the deliverance of millions who are now pining in chains, crying, "How long! How long! O Lord God of Sabaoth! How long shall these things be?"

Frederick Douglass' Paper, April 29, 1853

THE PRESENT CONDITION AND FUTURE PROSPECTS OF
THE NEGRO PEOPLE, speech at annual meeting of the American
and Foreign Anti-Slavery Society, New York City, May, 1853

Mr. President, Ladies and Gentlemen:

The resolution upon which I propose to make a few remarks, respects the present condition and future prospects of the whole colored
people of the United States. The subject is a great one, and opens ample
scope for thought and feeling. I feel a diffidence in undertaking the consideration for two causes: first, my own incompetence to do it justice;
and the second is, the peculiar relation subsisting between me and the
audience I am to address. Sir, I am a colored man, and this is a white
audience. No colored man, with any nervous sensibility, can stand before
an American audience without an intense and painful sense of the disadvantages imposed by his color. He feels little borne up by that brotherly
sympathy and generous enthusiasm, which give wings to the eloquence,
and strength to the hearts of other men, who advocate other and more
popular causes. The ground which a colored man occupies in this country is, every inch of it, sternly disputed. Sir, were I a white man, speaking
for the rights of white men, I should in this country have a smooth sea
and a fair wind. It is, perhaps, creditable to the American people (and
I am not the man to detract from their credit) that they listen eagerly
to the report of wrongs endured by distant nations. The Hungarian, the
Italian, the Irishman, the Jew and the Gentile, all find in this goodly land
a home; and when any of them, or all of them, desire to speak, they find
willing ears, warm hearts, and open hands. For these people, the Americans have principles of justice, maxims of mercy, sentiments of religion,
and feelings of brotherhood in abundance. But for *my* poor people (alas,
how poor!), enslaved, scourged, blasted, overwhelmed, and ruined, it
would appear that America had neither justice, mercy, nor religion. She
has no scales in which to weigh our wrongs, and no standard by which
to measure our rights. Just here lies the grand difficulty of the colored
man's cause. It is found in the fact, that we may not avail ourselves of
the just force of admitted American principles. If I do not misinterpret
the feelings and philosophy of my white fellow-countrymen generally,
they wish us to understand distinctly and fully that they have no other
use for us whatever, than to coin dollars out of our blood.

Our position here is anomalous, unequal, and extraordinary. It is a
position to which the most courageous of our race can look without deep

concern. Sir, we are a hopeful people, and in this we are fortunate: but for this trait of our character, we should have, long before this seemingly unpropitious hour, sunk down under a sense of utter despair.

Look at it, sir. Here, upon the soil of our birth, in a country which has known us for two centuries, among a people who did not wait for us to seek them, but who sought us, found us, and brought us to their own chosen land, a people for whom we have performed the humblest services, and whose greatest comforts and luxuries have been won from the soil by our sable and sinewy arms—I say, sir, among such a people, and with such obvious recommendations to favor, we are far less esteemed than the veriest stranger and sojourner.

Aliens are we in our native land. The fundamental principles of the republic, to which the humblest white man, whether born here or elsewhere, may appeal with confidence in the hope of awakening a favorable response are held to be inapplicable to us. The glorious doctrines of your revolutionary fathers, and the more glorious teachings of the Son of God, are construed and applied against us. We are literally scourged beyond the beneficent range of both authorities, human and divine. We plead for our rights, in the name of the immortal Declaration of Independence, and of the written constitution of government, and we are answered with imprecations and curses. In the sacred name of Jesus we beg for mercy, and the slave-whip, red with blood, cracks over us in mockery. We invoke the aid of the ministers of Him who came "to preach deliverance to the captive," and to set at liberty them that are bound, and from the loftiest summits of this ministry comes the inhuman and blasphemous response, saying: if one prayer would move the Almighty arm in mercy to break your galling chains, that prayer would be withheld. We cry for help to humanity—a common humanity, and here too we are repulsed. American humanity hates us, scorns us, disowns and denies, in a thousand ways, our very personality. The outspread wing of American Christianity, apparently broad enough to give shelter to a perishing world, refuses to cover us. To us, its bones are brass, and its feathers iron. In running thither for shelter and succor, we have only fled from the hungry bloodhound to the devouring wolf, from a corrupt and selfish world to a hollow and hypocritical Church; and may I not add, from the agonies of earth to the flames of hell! Sir, this is strong language. For the sake of my people, I would to God it were extravagantly strong. But, Sir, I fear our fault here to-day will not be that we have pleaded the cause of the slave too vehemently, but too tamely; that we have not contemplated his wrongs with too much excitement, but with unnatural calmness and composure. For my part, I cannot speak as I feel on this subject. My language, though never so bitter, is less bitter than my experience. At best, my poor speech is, to the facts in the case, but as the shadow to the substance. Sir, it is known to you, and to many who hear me, that I am alike familiar with the whip and chain of slavery, and the lash and sting of public neglect and scorn; that my back is marked with the one, and my soul is fretted with the other. My neck is galled by both yokes—that imposed by one master, and that imposed by many masters. More than twenty years of my life were passed in slavery, and nearly fifteen years have been passed in nominal freedom. Mine has been the experience of the colored people of America, both slave and free. I was born a slave. Even before I made part of this breathing world, the scourge was plaited for my back, and the fetters were forged for my limbs. My earliest recollections are associated with the appalling thought that I was a slave—a slave for life. How that crushing thought wrung my young heart I shall never be able fully to tell. But of some things I can tell—some things which are incident to the free and to the slave people of this country. Give me leave, then, in my own language to speak freely all that can be uttered of the thoughts of my heart in regard to the wrongs of the people with whom I thus stand associated in the two conditions to which I have thus alluded; for when I have said all, "the half will not then have been told." Sir, it was once said by that greatest of modern Irish orators, Daniel O'Connell, (a man whose patriotism was equalled only by his love of universal freedom,) that the history of the Irish people might be traced like a wounded man through a crowd, by the blood. That is a most startling saying. I read it with a shudder soon after it was said, and felt, if this were true in relation to the Irish people, it was still more true in relation to the colored people of the United States. Our wrongs and outrages are as old as our country. They date back to its earliest settlement, and extend through two hundred and thirty years, and they are as numerous and as oft-repeated as the days of all those years. Even now, while I speak and you listen, the work of blood and sorrow goes on. Methinks I hear the noise of chains and the clang of the whip. There is not a day, not an hour in any day, not a minute in any hour of the day, that the blood of my people does not gush forth at the call of the scourge; that the tenderest ties of humanity are not sundered; that parents are not torn from children, and husbands from their wives, for the convenience of those who gain fortunes by the blood of their souls. But I do not propose to confine your attention to the details of slavery. They are harrowing to think of, and too shocking to fix the mind upon for any length of time. I rather wish to speak of the condition of the colored people of the United States generally. This people, free and slave, are rapidly filling up the number of four millions. They are becoming a nation, in the midst of a nation which disowns them, and for weal or for woe this nation is united. The distinction between the slave and the free is not great, and their destiny seems one and the same. The black man is linked to his brother by indissoluble ties. The one cannot be truly free while the other is a slave. The free colored man is reminded by the ten thousand petty annoyances with which he meets of his identity with an enslaved people, and that with them he is destined to fall or flourish. We are one nation, then. If not one in immediate condition, at least one in prospects. I will not argue that we are men of like passions with the rest of mankind: that is unnecessary. All know at any rate that we are capable at least of love and hate, friendship and enmity. But whatever character or capacity you ascribe to us, I am not ashamed to be numbered with this race. I am not ashamed to speak here as a Negro. Sir, I utterly abhor and spurn with all the contempt possible that cowardly meanness (I will not call it pride) which leads any colored man to repudiate his connection with his race. I cannot say, therefore, as was said recently by a distinguished colored man at a Convention in Cincinnati, that "he did not speak as a colored man," for, Sir, as a colored man I do speak; as a colored man I was invited here to speak; and as a colored man there are peculiar reasons for my speaking. The man struck is the man to cry out. I would place myself—nay, I am placed among the victims of American oppression. I view this subject from their stand-point, and scan the moral and political horizon of the country with their hopes, their fears, and their intense solicitude. Standing here, then, and judging from the events and indications of the past few years, the black man must see that a crisis has arrived in his relations with the American people. He is reminded that trials and hardships await him; that the times are portentous of storms which will try the strength of his bark. Sir, it is evident that there is in this country a purely slavery party; a party which exists for no other earthly purpose but to promote the interests of slavery. The presence of this party is felt everywhere in the republic. It is known by no particular name, and has assumed no definite shape, but its branches reach far and wide in the Church and in the State. This shapeless and nameless party is not intangible in other and more important respects. That party, Sir, has determined upon a fixed, definite, and comprehensive policy towards the whole colored population of the United States. What that policy is, it becomes us as Abolitionists, and especially does it become the colored people themselves to consider and understand fully. We ought to know who our enemies are, where they are, and what are their objects and measures. Well, Sir, here is my version of it; not original with me, but mine because I hold it to be true. I understand this policy to comprehend five cardinal objects. They are these: 1st. The complete suppression of all anti-slavery discussion; 2d. The expatriation of the entire free people of color from the United States; 3d. The unending perpetuation of slavery in this republic; 4th. The nationalization of slavery to the extent of making slavery respected in every State of the Union; 5th. The extension of slavery over Mexico and the entire South American States. Sir, these objects are forcibly presented to us in the stern logic of passing events—in the facts which are and have been passing around us during the last three years. The country has been and is now dividing on these grand issues. In their magnitude these issues cast all others into the shade, depriving them of all life and vitality. Old party lines are broken. Like is finding its like on either side of these great issues, and the great battle is at hand. For the present, the best representative of the slavery party in politics is the Democratic party. Its great head for the present is President Pierce, whose boast it is that his whole life has been consistent with the interests of slavery; that he is above reproach on that score. In his inaugural address he reassures the South on this point. The head of the slave power being in power, it is natural that the pro-slavery elements should cluster around the Administration, and this is rapidly being done. A fraternization is going on. The stringent Protectionists and the Free Traders strike hands. The supporters of Fillmore are becoming the supporters of Pierce. The Silver Gray Whig shakes hands with the Hunker Democrat, the former only differing from the latter in name.[36] They are of one heart, one mind, and the union is natural, and perhaps inevitable. Both hate Negroes, both hate progress, both hate the "Higher Law,"[37] both hate Wm. H. Seward, both hate the Free Democratic party, and upon these hateful bases they are forming a union of hatred. "Pilate and Herod are thus made friends." Even the central organ of the Whig party is extending its beggar-hand for a morsel from the table of Slavery Democracy; and when spurned from the feast by the more deserving, it pockets the insult; when kicked on one side, it turns the other, and perseveres in its importunities. The fact is, that paper comprehends the demands of the times. It understands the age and its issues.

It wisely sees that slavery and freedom are the great antagonistic forces in the country, and it goes to its own side. Silver Grays and Hunkers all understand this. They are, therefore, rapidly sinking all other questions to nothing, compared with the increasing demands of slavery. They are collecting, arranging, and consolidating their forces for the accomplishment of their appointed work. The keystone to the arch of this grand union of the slavery party of the United States is the Compromise of 1850. In that Compromise we have all the objects of our slaveholding policy specified. It is, Sir, favorable to this view of the designs of the slave power that both the Whig and the Democratic party bent lower, sunk deeper, and strained harder in their conventions, preparatory to the late presidential election, to meet the demands of the slavery party than at any previous time in their history. Never did parties come before the Northern people with propositions of such undisguised contempt for the moral sentiment and the religious ideas of that people. They virtually asked them to unite in a war upon free speech, upon conscience, and to drive the Almighty Presence from the councils of the nation. Resting their platforms upon the Fugitive Slave Bill, they boldly asked the people for political power to execute the horrible and hell-black provisions of that bill. The history of that election reveals with great clearness the extent to which slavery has shot its leprous distilment through the life-blood of the nation. The party most thoroughly opposed to the cause of justice and humanity triumphed, while the party suspected of a leaning towards liberty was overwhelmingly defeated—some say, annihilated. But here is a still more important fact, illustrating the designs of the slave power. It is a fact full of meaning, that no sooner did this Democratic leading party come into power than a system of legislation was presented to the Legislatures of the Northern States designed to put the States in harmony with the Fugitive Slave Law, and the malignant bearing of the National Government towards the colored inhabitants of the country. This whole movement on the part of the States bears the evidence of having one origin, emanating from one head, and urged forward by one power. It was simultaneous, uniform, and general, and looked to one end. It was intended to put thorns under feet already bleeding, to crush a people already bowed down, to enslave a people already but half free. In a word, it was intended to discourage, dishearten, and drive the free colored people out of the country. In looking at the recent Black Law of Illinois, one is struck with its enormity.[38] It would seem that the men who enacted that law had not only banished from their minds all sense of justice, but all sense of shame. It coolly proposes to sell the bodies and souls of the blacks to increase the intelligence and refinement of the whites; to rob every black stranger who ventures among them to increase their literary fund. While this is going on in the States, a pro-slavery Political Board of Health is established at Washington. Senators Hale, Chase and Sumner are robbed of a part of their senatorial dignity and consequence, as representing sovereign States, because they have refused to be inoculated with the slavery virus.[39] Among the services which a Senator is expected by his State to perform are many that can only be done efficiently by Committees; and in saying to these honorable Senators, You shall not serve on the Committees of this body, the slavery party took the responsibility of robbing and insulting the States that sent them. It is an attempt at Washington to decide for the States who shall be sent to the Senate. Sir, it strikes me that this aggression on the part of the slave power did not meet at the hands of the proscribed Senators the rebuke which we had a right to expect would be administered. It seems to me that an opportunity was lost; that the great principles of senatorial equality were left undefended at a time when its vindication was sternly demanded. But it is not to the purpose of my present statement to criticise the conduct of our friends. I am persuaded that much ought to be left to the discretion of anti-slavery men in Congress, and charges of recreancy should never be made but on the most sufficient grounds. For, of all the places in the world where an anti-slavery man needs the confidence and encouragement of friends, I take Washington to be that place. Let me now call attention to the social influences which are operating and coöperating with the slavery party of the country, designed to contribute to one or all of the grand objects aimed at by that party. We see here the black man attacked in his vital interests. Prejudice and hate are excited against him. Enmity is stirred up between him and other laborers. The Irish people, warm-hearted, generous, and sympathizing with the oppressed everywhere when they stand on their own green island, are instantly taught on arriving in this Christian country to hate and despise the colored people. They are taught to believe that we eat the bread which of right belongs to them. The cruel lie is told the Irish that our adversity is essential to their prosperity. Sir, the Irish American will find out his mistake one day. He will find that in assuming our avocation he also has assumed our degradation. But for the present we are the sufferers. The old employments by which we have heretofore gained our livelihood are gradually, and it may be inevitably, passing into other hands. Every

hour sees us elbowed out of some employment, to make room perhaps
for some newly arrived immigrants, whose hunger and color are thought
to give them a title to especial favor. White men are becoming house-
servants, cooks and stewards, common laborers and flunkeys to our
gentry, and for aught that I see, they adjust themselves to their stations
with a becoming obsequiousness. This fact proves that if we cannot rise
to the whites, the whites can fall to us. Now, Sir, look once more. While
the colored people are thus elbowed out of employment; while the enmity
of immigrants is being excited against us; while State after State enacts
laws against us; while we are hunted down like wild game, and oppressed
with a general feeling of insecurity, the American Colonization Society—
that old offender against the best interests, and slanderer of the colored
people—awakens to new life, and vigorously presses its scheme upon the
consideration of the people and the Government. New papers are started;
some for the North and some for the South, and each in its tone adapting
itself to its latitude. Government, State and National, is called upon for
appropriations to enable the Society to send us out of the country by
steam. They want steamers to carry letters and Negroes to Africa. Evidently this Society looks upon our "extremity as its opportunity," and
we may expect that it will use the occasion well. It does not deplore, but
glories in our misfortunes. But, Sir, I must hasten. I have thus briefly
given my view of one aspect of the present condition and future prospects
of the colored people of the United States. And what I have said is far
from encouraging to my afflicted people. I have seen the cloud gather
upon the sable brows of some who hear me. I confess the case looks black
enough. Sir, I am not a hopeful man. I think I am apt even to under-
calculate the benefits of the future. Yet, Sir, in this seemingly desperate
case, I do not despair for my people. There is a bright side to almost every
picture of this kind, and ours is no exception to the general rule. If the
influences against us are strong, those for us are also strong. To the inquiry, Will our enemies prevail in the execution of their designs? in my
God and in my soul I believe they *will not*. Let us look at the first object
sought for by the slavery party of the country, viz., the suppression of
anti-slavery discussion. They desire to suppress discussion on this subject,
with a view to the peace of the slaveholder and the security of slavery.
Now, Sir, neither the principal nor the subordinate objects here declared
can be all gained by the slave power, and for this reason: It involves the
proposition to padlock the lips of the whites, in order to secure the fetters
on the limbs of the blacks. The right of speech, precious and priceless,

cannot, will not be surrendered to slavery. Its suppression is asked for, as I have said, to give peace and security to slaveholders. Sir, that thing cannot be done. God has interposed an insuperable obstacle to any such result. "There can be *no peace,* saith my God, to the wicked." Suppose it were possible to put down this discussion, what would it avail the guilty slaveholder, pillowed as he is upon the heaving bosoms of ruined souls? He could not have a peaceful spirit. If every anti-slavery tongue in the nation were silent; every anti-slavery organization dissolved; every anti-slavery press demolished; every anti-slavery periodical, paper, book, tract, pamphlet or what not were searched out, gathered together, deliberately burnt to ashes, and their ashes given to the four winds of heaven, still, still the slaveholder could have *"no peace."* In every pulsation of his heart, in every throb of his life, in every glance of his eye, in the breeze that soothes and in the thunder that startles, would be waked up an accuser whose language is, "Thou art verily guilty concerning thy brother." Oh! Sir, I can say with the poet Cowper—and I speak from observation—

I would not have a slave to till my ground.

Again: The prospect, Sir, of putting down this discussion is anything but flattering at the present moment. I am unable to detect any signs of the suppression of this discussion. I certainly do not see it in this crowded assembly, nor upon this platform, nor do I see it in any direction. Why, Sir, look all over the North; look South, look at home, look abroad! Look at the whole civilized world! And what are all this vast multitude doing at this moment? Why, Sir, they are reading *Uncle Tom's Cabin,* and when they have read that, they will probably read *The Key to Uncle Tom's Cabin*—a key not only to the cabin, but I believe to the slave's darkest dungeon. A nation's hand, with that "Key," will unlock the slave-prison to millions. Then look at the authoress of *Uncle Tom's Cabin.* There is nothing in her reception abroad which indicates a declension of interest in the great subject which she has done so much to unfold and illustrate.[40] The sending of a princess on the shores of England would not have produced the same sensation. I take it, then, that the slavery party will find this item of their programme the most difficult of execution, since it is the voice of all experience that opposition to agitation is the most successful method of promoting it. Men will write. Men will read. Men will think. Men will feel. And the result of all this is, men will speak. And it were as well to chain the lightning as to repress the moral convictions and humane prompting of enlightened human nature. Herein, Sir, is our hope. Slavery cannot bear discussion. It is a matter of darkness; and as Junius said of the character of Lord Granby, "it can only pass without censure, as it passes without observation." The second cardinal object of this party, viz.: the expatriation of the free colored people of the United States, is a very desirable one to our enemies; and we read, in the vigorous efforts making to accomplish it, an acknowledgment of our manhood, and the danger to slavery arising out of our presence. Despite the tremendous pressure brought to bear against us, the colored people are gradually increasing in wealth, in intelligence, and in respectability. Here is the secret of the Colonization scheme. It is easily seen that just in proportion to the intelligence and respectability of the free colored race at the North is their power to endanger the stability of slavery. Hence the desire to get rid of us. But, Sir, the desire is not merely to get us out of this country, but to get us at a convenient and harmless distance from slavery. And here, Sir, I think I can speak as if by authority for the free colored people of the United States. The people of this republic may commit the audacious and high-handed atrocity of driving us out of the limits of their borders. They may virtually confiscate our property; they may invade our civil and personal liberty, and render our lives intolerable burdens, so that we may be induced to leave the United States; but to compel us to go to Africa is quite another thing. Thank God, the alternative is not quite so desperate as that we must be slaves here, or go to the pestilential shores of Africa. Other and more desirable lands are open to us. We can plant ourselves at the very portals of slavery. We can hover about the Gulf of Mexico. Nearly all the isles of the Caribbean Seas bid us welcome; while the broad and fertile valleys of British Guiana, under the sway of the emancipating Queen, invite us to their treasures, and to nationality. With the Gulf of Mexico on the South, and Canada on the North, we may still keep within hearing of the wails of our enslaved people in the United States. From the isles of the sea and from the mountain-tops of South America we can watch the meandering destiny of those we have left behind. Americans should remember that there are already on this continent, and in the adjacent islands, all of 12,370,000 Negroes, who only wait for the lifegiving and organizing power of intelligence to mould them into one body, and into a powerful nation. The following estimate of our numbers and localities is taken from one of the able reports of the British and Foreign Anti-slavery Society, carefully drawn up by its former Secretary, John Scoble, Esq.:

United States,	3,650,000	Dutch Colonies,	50,000
Brazil,	4,050,000	Danish Colonies,	45,000
Spanish Colonies,	1,470,000	Mexico,	70,000
S. American Republics,	1,130,000	Canada,	35,000
British Colonies,	750,000		
Haiti,	850,000	Total,	12,370,000
French Colonies,	270,000		

Now, Sir, it seems to me that the slavery party will gain little by driving us out of this country, unless it drives us off this continent and the adjacent islands. It seems to me that it would be after all of little advantage to slavery to have the intelligence and energy of the free colored people all concentrated in the Gulf of Mexico. Sir, I am not for going any where. I am for staying precisely where I am, in the land of my birth. But, Sir, if I must go from this country; if it is impossible to stay here, I am then for doing the next best, and that will be to go wherever I can hope to be of most service to the colored people of the United States. Americans, there is a meaning in those figures I have read. God does not permit twelve millions of his creatures to live without the notice of his eye. That this vast people are tending to one point on this continent is not without significance. All things are possible with God. Let not the colored man despair, then. Let him remember that a home, a country, a nationality, are all attainable this side of Liberia. But for the present the colored people should stay just where they are, unless they are compelled to leave. I have faith left yet in the wisdom and justice of the country, and it may be that there are enough left of these to save the nation. But there is a third object sought by the slavery party, namely, to render slavery a permanent system in this republic, and to make the relation of master and slave respected in every State in the Union. Neither part of this object can be accomplished. Slavery has no means within itself of perpetuation or permanence. It is a huge lie. It is of the Devil, and will go to its place. It is against nature, against progress, against improvement, and against the government of God. It cannot stand. It has an enemy in every bar of railroad iron, in every electric wire, in every improvement in navigation, in the growing intercourse of nations, in cheap postage, in the relaxation of tariffs, in common schools, in the progress of education, the spread of knowledge, in the steam engine, and in the World's Fair, now about to assemble in New York, and in everything that will be exhibited there. About making slavery respectable in the North, laws have been made to accomplish just that thing; the law of

'50 and the law of '93. And those laws, instead of getting respect for slavery, have begot distrust and abhorrence. Congress might pass slave-laws every day in the year for all time, if each one should be followed by such publications as *Uncle Tom* and the *Key*. It is not in the power of human law to make men entirely forget that the slave is a man. The freemen of the North can never be brought to look with the same feelings upon a man escaping from his claimants as upon a horse running from his owner. The slave is a man, and no slave. Now, Sir, I had more to say on the encouraging aspects of the times, but the time fails me. I will only say, in conclusion, greater is He that is for us than they that are against us; and though labor and peril beset the Anti-slavery movements, so sure as that a God of mercy and justice is enthroned above all created things, so sure will that cause gloriously triumph. [Great applause.]

Annual Report of the American and Foreign Anti-Slavery Society for 1853

THE CLAIMS OF OUR COMMON CAUSE, address of the Colored Convention held in Rochester, July, 1853, to the People of the United States

Fellow citizens:

Met in convention as delegates, representing the Free Colored people of the United States; charged with the responsibility of inquiring into the general condition of our people, and of devising measures which may, with the blessing of God, tend to our mutual improvement and eleva-tion; conscious of entertaining no motives, ideas, or aspirations, but such as are in accordance with truth and justice, and are compatible with the highest good of our country and the world, with a cause as vital and worthy as that for which (nearly eighty years ago) your fathers and our fathers bravely contended, and in which they gloriously triumphed—we deem it proper, on this occasion, as one method of promoting the honor-able ends for which we have met, and of discharging our duty to those in whose name we speak, to present the claims of our common cause to your candid, earnest, and favorable consideration.

As an apology for addressing you, fellow-citizens! we cannot announce the discovery of any new principle adapted to ameliorate the condition of mankind. The great truths of moral and political science, upon which we rely, and which we press upon your consideration, have been evolved and enunciated by you. We point to your principles, your wisdom, and to your great example as the full justification of our course this day. That "all men are created equal": that "life, liberty, and the pursuit of happiness" are the right of all; that "taxation and representation" should go together; that governments are to protect, not to destroy, the rights of mankind; that the Constitution of the United States was formed to establish justice, promote the general welfare, and secure the blessing of liberty to all the people of this country; that resistance to tyrants is obedience to God—are American principles and maxims, and together they form and constitute the constructive elements of the American government. From this elevated platform, provided by the Republic for us, and for all the children of men, we address you. In doing so, we would have our spirit properly discerned. On this point we would gladly free ourselves and our cause from all misconception. We shall affect no especial timidity, nor can we pretend to any great boldness. We know our poverty and weakness, and your wealth and greatness. Yet we will not attempt to repress the spirit of liberty within us, or to conceal, in any wise, our sense of the justice and the dignity of our cause.

We are Americans, and as Americans, we would speak to Americans. We address you not as aliens nor as exiles, humbly asking to be permitted to dwell among you in peace; but we address you as American citizens asserting their rights on their own native soil. Neither do we address you as enemies, (although the recipients of innumerable wrongs); but in the spirit of patriotic good will. In assembling together as we have done, our object is not to excite pity for ourselves, but to command respect for our cause, and to obtain justice for our people. We are not malefactors imploring mercy; but we trust we are honest men, honestly appealing for righteous judgment, and ready to stand or fall by that judgment. We do not solicit unusual favor, but will be content with roughhanded "fair play." We are neither lame or blind, that we should seek to throw off the responsibility of our own existence, or to cast ourselves upon public charity for support. We would not lay our burdens upon other men's shoulders; but we do ask, in the name of all that is just and magnanimous among men, to be freed from all the unnatural burdens and impediments with which American customs and American legislation have hindered our progress and improvement. We ask to be disencumbered of the load of popular reproach heaped upon us—for no better cause than that we wear the complexion given us by our God and our Creator.

We ask that in our native land, we shall not be treated as strangers, and worse than strangers.

We ask that, being friends of America, we should not be treated as enemies of America.

We ask that, speaking the same language and being of the same religion, worshipping the same God, owing our redemption to the same Savior, and learning our duties from the same Bible, we shall not be treated as barbarians.

We ask that, having the same physical, moral, mental, and spiritual wants, common to other members of the human family, we shall also have the same means which are granted and secured to others, to supply those wants.

We ask that the doors of the school-house, the workshop, the church, the college, shall be thrown open as freely to our children as to the children of other members of the community.

We ask that the American government shall be so administered as that beneath the broad shield of the Constitution, the colored American seaman, shall be secure in his life, liberty and property, in every State in the Union.

We ask that as justice knows no rich, no poor, no black, no white, but, like the government of God, renders alike to every man reward or punishment, according as his works shall be—the white and black man may stand upon an equal footing before the laws of the land.

We ask that (since the right of trial by jury is a safeguard to liberty, against the encroachments of power, only as it is a trial by impartial men, drawn indiscriminately from the country) colored men shall not, in every instance, be tried by white persons; and that colored men shall not be either by custom or enactment excluded from the jury-box.

We ask that (inasmuch as we are, in common with other American citizens, supporters of the State, subject to its laws, interested in its welfare liable to be called upon to defend it in time of war, contributors to its wealth in time of peace) the complete and unrestricted right of suffrage, which is essential to the dignity even of the white man, be extended to the Free Colored man also.

Whereas the colored people of the United States have too long been retarded and impeded in the development and improvement of their natural faculties and powers, even to become dangerous rivals to white men, in the honorable pursuits of life, liberty and happiness; and whereas, the proud Anglo-Saxon can need no arbitrary protection from open and equal competition with any variety of the human family; and whereas, laws have been enacted limiting the aspirations of colored men, as against white men—we respectfully submit that such laws are flagrantly unjust to the man of color, and plainly discreditable to white men; and for these and other reasons, such laws ought to be repealed.

We especially urge that all laws and usages which preclude the enrollment of colored men in the militia, and prohibit their bearing arms in the navy, disallow their rising, agreeable to their merits and attainments —are unconstitutional—the constitution knowing no color—are anti-Democratic, since Democracy respects men as equals—are unmagnanimous, since such laws are made by the many, against the few, and by the strong against the weak.

We ask that all those cruel and oppressive laws, whether enacted at the South or the North, which aim at the expatriation of the free people of color, shall be stamped with national reprobation, denounced as contrary to the humanity of the American people, and as an outrage upon the Christianity and civilization of the nineteenth century.

We ask that the right of pre-emption, enjoyed by all white settlers upon the public lands, shall also be enjoyed by colored settlers; and that the word *"white"* be struck from the pre-emption act. We ask that no appropriations whatever, state or national, shall be granted to the colonization scheme; and we would have our right to leave or to remain in the United States placed above legislative interference.

We ask that the Fugitive Slave Law of 1850, that legislative monster of modern times, by whose atrocious provisions the writ of *"habeas corpus,"* the "right of trial by jury," have been virtually abolished, shall be repealed.

We ask, that the law of 1793 be so construed as to apply only to apprentices, and others really owing service or labor; and not to slaves, who can *owe* nothing. Finally, we ask that slavery in the United States shall be immediately, unconditionally, and forever abolished.

To accomplish these just and reasonable ends, we solemnly pledge ourselves to God, to each other, to our country, and to the world, to use all and every means consistent with the just rights of our fellow men, and with the precepts of Christianity.

We shall speak, write and publish, organize and combine to accomplish them.

We shall invoke the aid of the pulpit and the press to gain them.

We shall appeal to the church and to the government to gain them.

We shall vote, and expend our money to gain them.

We shall send eloquent men of our own condition to plead our cause before the people.

We shall invite the co-operation of good men in this country and throughout the world—and above all, we shall look to God, the Father and Creator of all men, for wisdom to direct us and strength to support us in the holy cause to which we this day solemnly pledge ourselves.

Such, fellow-citizens are our aims, ends, aspirations and determinations. We place them before you, with the earnest hope, that upon further investigation, they will meet your cordial and active approval.

And yet, again, we would free ourselves from the charge of unreasonableness and self-sufficiency.

In numbers we are few and feeble; but in the goodness of our cause, in the rectitude of our motives, and in the abundance of argument on our side, we are many and strong.

We count our friends in the heavens above, in the earth beneath, among good men and holy angels. The subtle and mysterious cords of human sympathy have connected us with philanthropic hearts throughout the civilized world. The number in our own land who already recognize the justice of our cause, and are laboring to promote it, is great and increasing.

It is also a source of encouragement, that the genuine American, brave and independent himself, will respect bravery and independence in others. He spurns servility and meanness, whether they be manifested by nations or by individuals. We submit, therefore, that there is neither necessity for, nor disposition on our part to assume a tone of excessive humility. While we would be respectful, we must address you as men, as citizens, as brothers, as dwellers in a common country, equally interested with you for its welfare, its honor and for its prosperity.

To be still more explicit: We would, first of all, be understood to range ourselves no lower among our fellow-countrymen than is implied in the high appellation of *"citizen."*

Notwithstanding the impositions and deprivations which have fettered us—notwithstanding the disabilities and liabilities, pending and impending—notwithstanding the cunning, cruel, and scandalous efforts to blot out that right, we declare that we are, and of right we ought to be *American citizens*. We claim this right, and we claim all the rights and privileges, and duties which, properly, attach to it.

It may, and it will, probably, be disputed that we are citizens. We may, and, probably, shall be denounced for this declaration, as making an inconsiderate, impertinent and absurd claim to citizenship; but a very little reflection will vindicate the position we have assumed, from so unfavorable a judgment. Justice is never inconsiderate; truth is never impertinent; right is never absurd. If the claim we set up be just, true and right, it will not be deemed improper or ridiculous in us so to declare it. Nor is it disrespectful to our fellow-citizens, who repudiate the aristocratic notions of the old world that we range ourselves with them in respect to all the rights and prerogatives belonging to American citizens. Indeed, we believe, when you have duly considered this subject, you will commend us for the mildness and modesty with which we have taken our ground.

By birth, we are American citizens; by the principles of the Declaration of Independence, we are American citizens; within the meaning of the United States Constitution, we are American citizens; by the facts of history, and the admissions of American statesmen, we are American citizens; by the hardships and trials endured; by the courage and fidelity displayed by our ancestors in defending the liberties and in achieving the independence of our land, we are American citizens. In proof of the justice of this primary claim, we might cite numerous authorities, facts and testimonies,—a few only must suffice.

In the Convention of New York, held for amending the Constitution of that State, in the year 1821, an interesting discussion took place, upon a proposition to prefix the word *"white"* to male citizens. Nathan Sandford, then late Chancellor of the State, said:

"Here there is but one estate—*the people*—and to me the only qualification seems to be their virtue and morality. If they may be safely trusted to vote for one class of rulers, why not for all? The principle of the scheme is, that those who bear the burdens of the State, shall choose those that rule it."

Dr. Robert Clark, in the same debate, said:

"I am unwilling to retain the word *'white,'* because it is repugnant to all the principles and notions of liberty, to which we have heretofore professed to adhere, and to our 'Declaration of Independence,' which is a concise and just expose of those principles." He said "it had been appropriately observed by the Hon. gentleman from Westchester, (Mr. Jay,) that by retaining this word, you violate the Constitution of the United States."

Chancellor Kent supported the motion of Mr. Jay to strike out the word *"white."*

"He did not come to this Convention," said he, "to disfranchise any portion of the community."

Peter A. Jay, on the same occasion, said, "It is insisted that this Convention, clothed with all the powers of the sovereign people of the State, have a right to construct the government in a manner they think most conducive to the general good. If Sir, right and power be equivalent terms, then I am far from disputing the rights of this assembly. We have power, Sir, I acknowledge, not only to disfranchise every black family, but as many white families also, as we may think expedient. We may place the whole government in the hands of a few and thus construct an aristocracy. * * * * * * But, Sir, right and power are not convertible terms. No man, no body of men, however powerful, have a right to do wrong."

In the same Convention, Martin Van Buren said:

"There were two words which have come into common use with our revolutionary struggle—words which contained an abridgement of our political rights—words which, at that day, had a talismanic effect—which led our fathers from the bosom of their families to the tented field—which for seven long years of toil and suffering, had kept them to their arms, and which finally conducted them to a glorious triumph. They were *Taxation and Representation.* Nor did they lose their influence with the close of the struggle. They were never heard in our halls of legislation without bringing to our recollection the consecrated feelings of those who won our liberties, or, reminding us of everything that was sacred in principle."

Ogden Edwards without, said, "he considered it no better than robbery to demand the contributions of colored people towards defraying the public expenses, and at the same time to disfranchise them."

But we must close our quotations from these debates. Much more could be cited, to show that colored men are not only citizens, but that they have a right to the exercise of the elective franchise in the State of New York. If the right of citizenship is established in the State of New York, it is in consequence of the same facts which exist at least in every free State of the Union. We turn from the debates in the State of New York to the nation; and here we find testimony abundant and incontestible, that Free Colored people are esteemed as citizens, by the highest authorities in the United States.

The Constitution of the United States declares "that the citizens of each State shall be entitled to all the privileges and immunities of citizens in the United States."

There is in this clause of the Constitution, nothing whatever, of that watchful malignity which has manifested itself lately in the insertion of the word *"white,"* before the term *"citizen."* The word *"white"* was unknown to the framers of the Constitution of the United States in such connections—unknown to the signers of the Declaration of Independence —unknown to the brave men at *Bunker Hill, Ticonderoga* and at *Red Bank.* It is a modern word, brought into use by modern legislators, despised in revolutionary times. The question of our citizenship came up as a national question, and was settled during the pendency of the Missouri question, in 1820.

It will be remembered that that State presented herself for admission into the Union, with a clause in her Constitution prohibiting the settlement of colored citizens within her borders. Resistance was made to her admission into the Union, upon that very ground; and it was not until that State receded from her unconstitutional position, that President Monroe declared the admission of Missouri into the Union to be complete.

According to *Niles' Register,* August 18th, vol. 20, page 338-339, the refusal to admit Missouri into the Union was not withdrawn until the General Assembly of that State, in conformity to a fundamental condition imposed by Congress, had, by an act passed for that purpose, solemnly enacted and declared:

"That this State [Missouri] has assented, and does assent, that the fourth clause of the 26th section of the third article of their Constitution should never be construed to authorize the passage of any law, and that no law shall be passed in conformity thereto, by which any citizen of either of the United States shall be excluded from the enjoyment of any of the privileges and immunities to which such citizens are entitled, under the Constitution of the United States."

Upon this action by the State of Missouri, President Monroe proclaimed the admission of Missouri into the Union.

Here, fellow-citizens, we have a recognition of our citizenship by the highest authority of the United States; and here we might rest our claim to citizenship. But there have been services performed, hardships endured, courage displayed by our fathers, which modern American historians forget to record—a knowledge of which is essential to an intelligent judgment of the merits of our people. Thirty years ago, slavery was less powerful than it is now; American statesmen were more independent then, than now; and as a consequence, the black man's patriotism and bravery were more readily recognized. The age of slave-hunting had not then come on. In the memorable debate on the Missouri question, the meritorious deeds of our fathers obtained respectful mention. The Hon. Wm. Eustis, who had himself been a soldier of the revolution, and Governor of the State of Massachusetts, made a speech in the Congress of the United States, 12th December, and said:

"The question to be determined is, whether the article in the Constitution of Missouri, requiring the legislature to provide by law, 'that free negroes and mulattoes shall not be admitted into that State,' is, or is not repugnant to that clause of the Constitution of the United States which declares 'that the citizens of each State shall be entitled to all the privileges and immunities of citizens in the several States?' This is the question. Those who contend that the article is not repugnant to the Constitution of the United States, take the position that free blacks and mulattoes are not citizens. *Now I invite the gentlemen who maintain this to go with me and examine this question to its root.* At the early part of the revolutionary war, there were found in the middle and northern States, many blacks and other people of color, capable of bearing arms, a part of them free, and a greater part of them slaves. The freemen entered our ranks with the whites. The time of those who were slaves were purchased by the State, and they were induced to enter the service in consequence of a law, by which, on condition of their serving in the ranks during the war, they were made freemen. In Rhode Island, where their numbers were more considerable, they were formed under the same considerations into a regiment, commanded by white officers; and it is required in justice to them, to add that they discharged their duty with zeal and fidelity. The gallant defence of Red Bank, in which the black regiment bore a part, is among the proofs of their valor.

"Not only the rights but the character of those men do not seem to be understood; nor is it to me at all extraordinary that gentlemen from other States in which the condition, character, the moral facilities, and the rights of men of color differ so widely, should entertain opinions so variant from ours. In Massachusetts, Sir, there are among them who possess all the virtues which are deemed estimable in civil and social life. They have their public teachers of religion and morality—their schools and other institutions. On anniversaries which they consider interesting to them, they have their public processions, in all of which they conduct themselves with order and decorum. Now, we ask only, that in a disposition to accommodate others, their avowed rights and privileges be not taken from them. If their number be small, and they are feebly represented, we, to whom they are known, are proportionately bound to protect them. But their defence is not founded on their numbers; it rests on the immutable principles of justice. If there be only one family, or a solitary individual who has rights guaranteed to him by the Constitution, whatever may be his color or complexion, it is not in the power, nor can it be the inclination of Congress to deprive him of them. And I trust, Sir, that the decision on this occasion will show that we will extend good faith even to the blacks."—*National Intelligencer,* January 2, 1821.

The following is an extract from a speech of the Hon. Mr. Morrill, of New Hampshire, delivered in the United States Senate in the same month, and reported in the *National Intelligencer,* Jan. 11th, 1821:

"Sir, you excluded, not only the citizens from their constitutional privileges and immunities, but also your soldiers of color, to whom you have given patents of land. You had a company of this description. They have fought your battles. They have defended your country. They have preserved your privileges; but have lost their own. What did you say to them on their enlistment? 'We will give you a monthly compensation, and, at the end of the war, 160 acres of good land, on which you may settle, and by cultivating the soil, spend your declining years in peace and in the enjoyment of those immunities for which you have fought and bled.' Now, Sir, you restrict them, and will not allow them to enjoy the fruit of their labor. Where is the public faith in this case? Did they suppose, with a patent in their hand, declaring their title to land in Missouri, with the seal of the nation, and the President's signature affixed thereto, it would be said unto them by any authority, you shall not possess the premises? This could never have been anticipated; and yet this must follow, if colored men are not citizens."

Mr. Strong, of New York, said, in the same great debate, "The federal constitution knows but two descriptions of freemen: these are citizens and aliens. Now Congress can naturalize only aliens—i.e., persons who owe allegiance to a foreign government. But a slave has no country, and owes no allegiance except to his master. How, then, is he an alien? If restored to his liberty, and made a freeman, what is his national character? It must be determined by the federal constitution, and without reference to policy; for it respects liberty. Is it that of a citizen, or alien? But it has been shown that he is not an alien. May we not, therefore, conclude—nay, are we not bound to conclude that he is a citizen of the United States?"

Charles Pinckney, of South Carolina, speaking of the colored people, in Congress, and with reference to the same question, bore this testimony:

"They then were (during the Revolution) as they still are, as valuable a part of our population to the Union, as any other equal number of inhabitants. They were, in numerous instances, the pioneers; and in all the labors of your armies, to their hands were owing the erection of the greatest part of the fortifications raised for the protection of our country. Fort Moultrie gave at an early period the experience and untired valor of our citizens' immortality to American arms; and in the Northern States, numerous bodies of them were enrolled, and fought, side by side, with the whites, the battles of the Revolution."

General Jackson, in his celebrated proclamations to the free colored inhabitants of Louisiana, uses these expressions: *"Your* white fellow-citizens;" and again: *"Our* brave *citizens are united,* and *all* contention has ceased *among them."*

FIRST PROCLAMATION (*Extracts*)

HEADQUARTERS, 7th Military Dis't.,⎫
Mobile, Sept. 21st, 1814.   ⎬

To the Free Colored Inhabitants of Louisiana:

Through a mistaken policy you have heretofore been deprived of a participation in the glorious struggle for national rights, in which your country is engaged.

This no longer shall exist.

As sons of freedom, you are now called on to defend our most inestimable blessings. As *Americans,* your country looks with confidence to her adopted children for a valorous support. As fathers, husbands, and brothers, you are summoned to rally round the standard of the Eagle, to defend all which is dear to existence.

Your country, although calling for your exertions, does not wish you to engage in her cause without remunerating you for the services rendered.

In the sincerity of a soldier, and in the language of truth, I address you.—To every noble-hearted free man of color, volunteering to serve during the present contest with Great Britain, and no longer, there will be paid the same bounty in money and land now received by the white soldiers of the United States, viz: $124 in money, and 160 acres of land. The non-commissioned officers and privates will also be entitled to *the same* monthly pay and daily rations, and clothes, furnished *to any American soldier.*

The Major General commanding will select officers for your government from your white fellow-citizens. Your non-commissioned officers will be selected from yourselves. Due regard will be paid to the feelings of freemen and soldiers. As a distinct, independent battalion or regiment, pursuing the path of glory, you will, undivided, receive the applause and gratitude of *your* countrymen. Andrew Jackson,

Major Gen. Commanding.

Niles' Register, Dec. 3, 1814, *Vol.* 7, *p.* 205

SECOND PROCLAMATION

To the Free People of Color:

Soldiers! when on the banks of the Mobile I called you to take up arms, inviting you to partake the perils and glory of your *white* fellow-citizens, I expected much from you; for I was not ignorant that you possessed qualities most formidable to an invading enemy. I knew with what fortitude you could endure hunger and thirst, and all the fatigues of a campaign.

I knew well how you loved your native country, and that you, as well as ourselves, had to defend what *man* holds most dear—his parents, wife, children, and property. You have done more than I expected. In addition to the previous qualities I before knew you to possess, I found among you a noble enthusiasm which leads to the performance of great things.

Soldiers! the President of the United States shall hear how praiseworthy was your conduct in the hour of danger, and the representatives of the American people will give you the praise your exploits entitle you to. Your General anticipates them in applauding your noble ardor.

The enemy approaches—his vessels cover our lakes—*our brave citizens are united,* and all contention has ceased among them. Their only dispute is, who shall win the prize of valor, or who the most glory, its noblest reward.—By order, Thomas Butler, Aide-de-Camp.

Such, fellow-citizens, is but a sample of a mass of testimony, upon which we found our claim to be American citizens. There is, we think, no flaw in the evidence. The case is made out. We and you stand upon the same broad national basis. Whether at home or abroad, we and you owe equal allegiance to the same government—have a right to look for protection on the same ground. We have been born and reared on the same soil; we have been animated by, and have displayed the same patriotic impulses; we have acknowledged and performed the same duty; we have fought and bled in the same battles; we have gained and gloried in the same victories; and we are equally entitled to the blessings resulting therefrom.

In view of this array of evidence of services bravely rendered, how base and monstrous would be the ingratitude, should the republic disown us and drive us into exile!—how faithless and selfish, should the nation persist in degrading us! But we will not remind you of obligations—we will not appeal to your generous feelings—a naked statement of the case is our best appeal. Having, now, upon the testimony of your own great and venerated names completely vindicated our right to be regarded and treated as American citizens, we hope you will now permit us to address you in the plainness of speech becoming the dignity of American citizens.

Fellow-citizens, we have had, and still have, great wrongs of which to complain. A heavy and cruel hand has been laid uopn us.

As a people, we feel ourselves to be not only deeply injured, but grossly misunderstood. Our white fellow-countrymen do not know us. They are strangers to our character, ignorant of our capacity, oblivious of our history and progress, and are misinformed as to the principles and ideas that control and guide us as a people. The great mass of American citizens estimate us as being a characterless and purposeless people; and hence we hold up our heads, if at all, against the withering influence of a nation's scorn and contempt.

It will not be surprising that we are so misunderstood and misused when the motives for misrepresenting us and for degrading us are duly considered. Indeed, it will seem strange, upon such consideration, (and in view of the ten thousand channels through which malign feelings find utterance and influence,) that we have not even fallen lower in public estimation than we have done. For, with the single exception of the Jews, under the whole heavens, there is not to be found a people pursued with a more relentless prejudice and persecution, than are the Free Colored people of the United States.

Without pretending to have exerted ourselves as we ought, in view of an intelligent understanding of our interest, to avert from us the unfavorable opinions and unfriendly action of the American people, we feel that the imputations cast upon us, for our want of intelligence, morality and exalted character, may be mainly accounted for by the injustice we have received at your hands. What stone has been left unturned to degrade us? What hand has refused to fan the flame of popular prejudice against us? What American artist has not caricatured us? What wit has not laughed at us in our wretchedness? What songster has not made merry over our depressed spirits? What press has not ridiculed and condemned us? What pulpit has withheld from our devoted heads its angry lightning, or its sanctimonious hate? Few, few, very few; and that we have borne up with it all—that we have tried to be wise, though denounced by all to be fools—that we have tried to be upright, when all around us have esteemed us as knaves—that we have striven to be gentlemen, although all around us have been teaching us its impossibility—that we have remained here, when all our neighbors have advised us to leave, proves that we possess qualities of head and heart, such as cannot but be commended by impartial men. It is believed that no other nation on the globe could have made more progress in the midst of such an universal and stringent disparagement. It would humble the proudest, crush the energies of the strongest, and retard the progress of the swiftest. In view of our circumstances, we can, without boasting, thank God, and take courage, having placed ourselves where we may fairly challenge comparison with more highly favored men.

Among the colored people, we can point, with pride and hope, to men of education and refinement, who have become such, despite of the most unfavorable influences; we can point to mechanics, farmers, merchants, teachers, ministers, doctors, lawyers, editors, and authors against whose progress the concentrated energies of American prejudice have proved quite unavailing.—Now, what is the motive for ignoring and discouraging our improvement in this country? The answer is ready. The intelligent and upright free man of color is an unanswerable argument in favor of liberty, and a killing condemnation of American slavery. It is easily seen that, in proportion to the progress of the free man of color, in knowledge, temperance, industry, and righteousness, in just that proportion will he endanger the stability of slavery; hence, all the powers of slavery are exerted to prevent the elevation of the free people of color.

The force of fifteen hundred million dollars is arrayed against us; hence, the *press,* the pulpit, and the platform, against all the natural promptings of uncontaminated manhood, point their deadly missiles of ridicule, scorn and contempt at us; and bid us, on pain of being pierced through and through, to remain in our degradation.

Let the same amount of money be employed against the interest of any other class of persons, however favored by nature they may be, the result could scarcely be different from that seen in our own case. Such a people would be regarded with aversion; the money-ruled multitude would heap contumely upon them, and money-ruled institutions would proscribe them. Besides this money consideration, fellow-citizens, an explanation of the erroneous opinions prevalent concerning us is furnished in the fact, less creditable to human nature, that men are apt to hate most those whom they have injured most.—Having despised us, it is not strange that Americans should seek to render us despicable; having enslaved us, it is natural that they should strive to prove us unfit for freedom; having denounced us as indolent, it is not strange that they should cripple our enterprise; having assumed our inferiority, it would be extraordinary if they sought to surround us with circumstances which would serve to make us direct contradictions to their assumption.

In conclusion, fellow-citizens, while conscious of the immense disadvantages which beset our pathway, and fully appreciating our own weakness, we are encouraged to persevere in efforts adapted to our improvement, by a firm reliance upon God, and a settled conviction, as immovable as the everlasting hills, that all the truths in the whole universe of God are allied to our cause.

> Frederick Douglass,
> J. M. Whitfield,
> H. O. Wagoner,
> Rev. A. N. Freeman,
> George B. Vashon.

TO HON. GERRIT SMITH

Rochester, July 15th, 1853

My dear Sir:

May you soon recover your wonted health. The last tidings from you were encouraging. You were remembered at our Convention last week. We cannot forget you, when we think of our cause and its friends. You will be pleased to learn that the local effect of the Convention has been excellent. The current of feeling towards colored people has been wonderfully improved by the Convention. In truth, the talent and eloquence displayed took our opponents by surprise. It would have warmed your heart to have seen and heard on the occasion. I had been deeply concerned for the results of the Convention for weeks before it was held.

I now feel abundantly relieved. My best hopes have been surpassed. We had one Lady delegate—Mrs. Jeffrey of Geneva—strange to say we had the good sense to make no *fuss* about it. My friend Julia sends love to yourself and dear Mrs. Smith.

Truly and affectionately yours,

Frederick Douglass

I hope you will like my address to the people of the United States. It is somewhat tame, but perhaps it will reach some minds which a more spirited document would not.

F. D.

Gerrit Smith Papers, Syracuse University

TO HON. GERRIT SMITH

Rochester, Aug. 18, 1853

My dear Sir:

You, and your prospective career in Congress, are much talked about among our friends in the east. I had a long talk with a gentleman of much learning, belonging to the Boston bar (E. G. Lorin), who expressed the deepest interest in your success at Washington. But he expressed some solicitude for you, upon a point of which I had not before thought. It is a small point but he deemed it very important. I therefore take the liberty to mention it. He remarked that you might be so occupied with other subjects—the history, principles, and measures of Government—as not to be well instructed in parliamentary rules. I thought the remark a wise one, and asked him to write you. He modestly declined, but gave me leave to use his name, as I have done. Do get yourself the best manual of Parliamentary rules which the country affords—forget, for a little while, subjects of greater weight—shut yourself up—place me in the chair of the H.—surround yourself with a company of the most watchful and skilful parliamentary tacticians—and make yourself such a master of the rules of Congress, as to defy all the mantraps which they will surely set for your feet. Now just hear the impertinence of this runaway slave!! Ah! but he knows who he is talking to.

I am expecting a letter from you pretty soon about my late behavior at Boston—and yet I think [you] would not have blamed me had you been present. But give me a lecture—I have ears to hear. Indeed I am greatly desirous of keeping out of quarrels with Boston. Nevertheless, I think, on the score of downright bigotry and pride of position, Boston deserves just such a "going over" as you gave Mr. Quincy a few years ago. They talk down there, just as if the Anti-Slavery Cause belonged to them—and as if all Anti-Slavery ideas originated with them and that no man has a right to "peep or mutter" on the subject, who does not hold letters patent from them. I wish Goodell would take them in hand—it would do them good.

Very truly your friend

F. Douglass

Gerrit Smith Papers, Syracuse University

EDITORIAL CORRESPONDENCE

The friends of freedom in Elmira have recently had the pleasure of welcoming among them, several who have worn the bonds. I saw two of these—one a young woman from *Missouri,* or as she now calls it, *misery.* She was brought by her owners into this State, and emancipated by the intervention of anti-slavery friends in Elmira. *Julia*—for this is the young woman's name—had much to overcome in deciding to stay in New York. She desired to be free, and deeply wished to go back to Missouri. The struggle was severe. She had a beloved mother, and loving sisters, and the thought of never meeting them again on earth cost her young heart a pang, whose bitterness may easily be imagined by those who know the strength of a daughter's affection. She had beside this tie to bind her to Missouri, another of a still more solemn nature. She had, before leaving Missouri, promised to return with her owner. Her word had been given— aye, her word—and she could not see how with a good conscience she could remain here after having given her word to the contrary. The conflict in Julia's mind was intense on this point; and I doubt if she is yet quiet in regard to it. Here is a question for moral philosophers. Did Julia do right to break her promise in this case?

I am not very learned in such knowledge, and may not be qualified to give a very intelligent opinion upon the point in issue—Slaveholders and their minions North and South will brand her as false and faithless; and will point to her as another proof that the word of the slave cannot be relied upon. They will say, that the girl deceived her mistress, and "is tricky and *ungrateful,*" (the peculiar sins of Negroes, now-a-days,

North as well as South). That in order to get into a free State, she committed the sin of telling a lie. This is their view of the case; and the reader may ask, what is my view of it? I answer, I am glad that the young woman is free. I am glad that her bondage is ended, and that the power of the tyrant is broken. It is certain that Julia's course differs from that of "Uncle Tom;" and the question is, was she right in refusing to go back after giving her word that she would go back? My opinion is, *that Julia was right*. The reasons for this opinion are these:

1st. The promise to return to Missouri was not intelligently made—that is, it was made in ignorance.

2d. The promise was made under unnatural constraint—that is, in the fear, and under the power of her owners.

3d. The promise was a promise to do that which no human being can do without violating the laws of God. A promise to commit murder, or suicide, would have been quite as binding as a promise to plunge into the gulf of slavery.

A man has no right to murder himself; and if in his ignorance he promises or plans his own destruction, he does right to break that promise. A man has just as much right to murder himself as to enslave himself, and a promise to do either, being a promise to do evil, is not binding.

But who is to decide upon the character of slavery, and say whether it is or it is not evil? I answer, Julia. She is the proper person to decide, and she has decided properly, and I thank God for the result; may she use her freedom wisely, and spend the remainder of her days happily. She is surrounded by kind friends, who will be mothers and sisters to her.

Some of the pro-slavery fraternity found fault with Mr. Langdon, and other friends of the slave, for urging Julia to remain.—To me, it seems they would have been justified, even in using force to prevent her going back. But I am dwelling too long upon this matter. From Elmira I went to Corning, and held a meeting in the Methodist Church. I am particular to mention where meetings are held, because it gives the reader some notion of the progress of the anti-slavery cause. The time was, when it was not easy to get into the churches to plead the anti-slavery cause. That time, so far as my present field of labor is concerned, is past. The churches all over Allegheny are opening their doors, and ministers of the gospel are cheering on the friends of freedom! Let the feeling prevalent here become universal in the North, and the jubilee will not be far off. . . .

F. Douglass.

Frederick Douglass' Paper, September 23, 1853   Elmira, Sept. 19, 1853.

THE INDUSTRIAL COLLEGE

If any of our readers, and especially our colored readers, have become impatient for intelligence in regard to this proposed College, let them be consoled by the reflection, that great works of this kind require *time* as well as energy for their projection. Neither we nor the National Council, have lost sight of this important measure. It is now nearly twelve months since the hearts of our oppressed people were gladdened by the presentation of what they deemed a practical mode of escape from their present precarious, insecure, and painfully dependent position. This mode, or measure, is the establishment, in this country, for the benefit of our *caste*-stricken people, of an Institution which shall combine the double advantage of a good, *mental* education, with a practical knowledge of three or four of the best paying handicrafts. The subject of the establishment of this Institution was ably discussed and elaborately reported upon by a committee appointed for the purpose at the late National Convention of colored citizens, held in the city of Rochester last July; at that time the desirableness, and the feasibleness of the Industrial College were pretty generally admitted. Much confidence was placed in the practicability of such an establishment by the intimation which had been given, that Mrs. Harriet Beecher Stowe, had privately expressed herself quite favorable to the enterprise; and that she expected to aid materially in its establishment. In addition to this, the measure was received by the liberal press of the country, with the New York *Tribune* at its head, with the most gratifying marks of approval. Indeed, the only public opposition with which the idea met, strange to say, came from one distinguished as "An American Abolitionist." Writing to the editor of the *Anti-Slavery Advocate,* (R. D. Webb, Esq.,) he says:

"What, then, ought to be done with funds given for anti-slavery purposes? Just what the abolitionists have been doing for many years. Scatter arguments, appeals, entreaties; thunder at the doors of schools and colleges and churches; let there be no rest till slavery is abolished. All schemes of instruction, amelioration, etc., are delusive and cruel while slavery lasts. As well talk of painting and making water-tight the house while it is on fire, as combine instruction and slavery. It is a childish amusement for childish philanthropy, of which the world is full, even looking aside from the main trying question. Of course, schools will be more popular than emancipation with nine-tenths of the people one meets; because nine-tenths have not the habit of investigation, nor the natural sagacity that hits the nail on the head, and seizes things by the right handles. Emancipation will necessarily be instruction; but instruction is not necessarily emancipation.

"Prussia is a well instructed kingdom. This application of anti-slavery funds to the founding of colored schools would be like the mistake of British abolitionists in rejecting the counsel of Granville Sharp, when he walked the committee room begging Clarkson and the rest to strike at slavery and *not* the trade. I do not mean that the mistake can be so fatal, because in this case the main battle will still go on uninfluenced. But the awakening minds will get a dose of quietism, and the colored people a dose of humiliation when they need self-esteem.

"Let pro-slavery found schools. It will not fail to do that and abundance of such works. The harder we press them as abolitionists, the more of these works they will do. If these schools were harmless, not bad, I should object to them as not the highest good. It is good to distribute coals to the poor, but it is better to abolish the despotism that makes them poor. Let suffering be ameliorated, but above all let *wrong*, the cause of suffering, be *righted*. Nothing could be more beneficial to the cause of humanity than the discussion in all the English and American journals on the subject. It is a great legislative question, one of the most important that ever arises in the policy of nations."

This extract contains the philosophy of a whole class of abolitionists; and they have succeeded in making it appreciable in many directions. According to it, the nominally free colored people must not look to them for assistance in any matter aside from what is technically called, anti-slavery agitation. We are very significantly told that, for all means of amelioration and instruction, we must rely upon *pro*-slavery; always remembering that, those who *refuse* to help us at points where we *need* the help of friends, are much better friends to us than those who *really* help us. Well! if it must be so, so it must be; but may God forever save us from becoming so devoutly engaged in searching out the cause of disease as to become indifferent to the actual suffering of the afflicted. The *free colored people* of this country are, by the power of slavery and prejudice, converted into a *means* of perpetuating the enslavement of their brethren in the Southern States. As they are *poor, ignorant,* and *degraded,* in that proportion is the bondage of the race to which they belong, strengthened. While the slaveholder is able to plead that his slaves will bear a favorable comparison, in point of physical comforts, with the *free* colored man at the North—while he can say, "The emancipation which you ask for my slaves is, simply, emancipation from master *individual,* to master *society;*" and while he can plead that his dominion is *less* harsh and *more* beneficent than that of society, or any part of society, his conscience is shielded by impenetrable bulwarks.—"Give up your slaves," the agitator may say; "Educate your free," the *slaveholder* may say; "Give wages to your black laborers," the agitator may say; "Allow your black laborers to labor," the *slaveholder* may say; "Cease to kick them out of your work-shop; cease to drive them out of your stores."—Teach them useful trades, and compel them not to drag out the miserable existence of poverty, vice and ignorance, to which all menially employed people are almost inevitably doomed. If there is one proposition which commands our hearty and instant assent more than another, it is, that *"the free colored man's elevation is essential to the* slave *colored man's emancipation;"* and further, we shall need more than the recommendation of Mr. Webb, to receive any man as the especial friend of the slave who, while he is zealous in agitating the public mind on the subject of slavery, and would free the slave that is *"afar off,"* yet leaves the *semi*-slave at his own doors, to the care of his *pro*-slavery enemies. But, we took up our pen merely to assure our friends that the measure is not lost sight of nor abandoned. Plans are maturing for the energetic prosecution of the work. It is, however, but justice to say that our eminent and philanthropic friend, Mrs. Stowe, for reasons which she deems quite satisfactory, does not, at present, see fit to stand forth as the patron of the proposed institution. It is equally our duty to state that Mrs. Stowe desires the work to go forward in the hands of the National Council; and we doubt not she will, in the end, be found among the principal friends of the Institution. What is now wanted on our part, is united and energetic co-operation— the wisdom of our best and wisest men and women is necessary to the carrying out of this purpose. A better demonstration of self-help could not well be made by the colored people of this country than the starting of an Industrial College by themselves. The necessity for the measure is too *plain* to need an argument, and too *pressing* to be disregarded. The lesson of the passing hour, as well as of the future, is to the colored man, "Learn trades, or starve." A prosperous summer, a light winter, a successful gold excursion into California, may obscure this lesson for a time; but the landing of poverty-stricken thousands from the continent of Europe, at the wharves of New York, Philadelphia, and Baltimore—and the rapidity with which these thousands are displacing the colored man as a coachman, as a waiter, as a barber, as a whitewasher, as a bootblacker, as a steward, as a stevedore, as a wood-sawyer, tells in language more impressive than any we can command—the necessity for opening new channels of industry and new sources of support for our people.

Colored men! let no fancied inferiority, or want of comprehension lead you to distrust your own energies. If *Hungarians* understand their liberties—if *Irishmen, Italians* and *Frenchmen* may be presumed to understand their moral, physical and intellectual wants *for themselves,* we, too, may presume to understand and to properly appreciate our situation without either egotism or arrogance.—You will be called upon soon to take the initiatory step towards the establishment of an Industrial College. The plan for such a College is maturing—and we believe that the colored people themselves have only to set the example of beginning the work *in earnest,* in order to command the sympathy, the money, and the respect of all who wish well to our race.

Frederick Douglass' Paper, January 2, 1854

THE NEBRASKA CONTROVERSY—THE TRUE ISSUE

There is danger in the present struggle upon the Nebraska and Kansas bill,[1] that the cause of freedom may suffer a wound in the house of its friends. Concessions may be made under the pressure of the excitement of the moment which, in the after-coming calm, the friends of freedom may have cause to regret. It is all-important that the *true issue* should be kept in view, through all the meanderings of this grand controversy between slavery and freedom. In contending for the binding force of the odious compromise of 1820, the inference that the friends of freedom are willing to abide by that compromise, is admissible, if not irresistible.—By this very compact, the sacredness of which has become the burden of the speeches, petitions, addresses, resolutions, letters and editorials of the opponents of the Nebraska slavery extending bill, the largest, fairest and most eligible portion of the national domain, is by the plainest inference given up to the slave system.

This compromise of 1820 can only be insisted upon now, by the North, on the low ground of *"honor among thieves,"* or at best, as the least of two evils. It was a compromise at the first—has been ever since—and is now, and will be so long as it is permitted to exist—"not fit to be made." It was a demoralizing bargain, and has done more to debauch the moral sentiment of the nation than any other legislative measure we know of. In the face of the universality of the principles of justice, humanity and religion, it would localize and legalize a crime against humanity, only second in turpitude to murder itself. In no degree is that compromise less offensive to us, because it halts at positive avowal, and accomplishes what we allege of it by inference only. The inference in this instance is practically as mischievous as would have been a substantive declaration authorising the establishment of slavery, south of 36 deg. 30 min. To say that slavery should not be established north of this line, was equal to saying that it might be established south of it. So the South understood the bargain at the time, and so the North understood it at the time. There is no getting away from it. Whatever may be said of other compacts, this, at least, was a "covenant with death," and one which cannot be innocently perpetuated by this generation. Those who made it had no right to make it; and we who live after them, have no right to keep it. The fact that now a proposition comes from the slavery side for its repeal, shows the danger of ever making compacts with wrong. It is another illustration of thawing a deadly viper, instead of killing it. We regard this Missouri Compromise as scarcely fit to be made an incidental issue with the slave power. It may be owing to our ignorance of, and our want of experience in, matters of this sort—but to our unsophisticated apprehension, the friends of freedom have but little real concern for the Missouri Compromise, or any other compromise with the slave power of the country. Our cause is not helped, but hindered, by pleading such compromises.—That cause must fight its battles on broader and sounder principles than can be found in the narrow and rotten compromise of 1820. Liberty must stick no stakes, and draw no lines short of the outer circle of the republic. Liberty and justice, as laid down in the preamble of the U. S. Constitution, must be maintained in the outermost parts of the republic. The real issue to be made with the slave power, and the one which should never be lost sight of, is this: Slavery, like rape, robbery, piracy or murder, has no right to exist in any part of the world—that neither north or south of 36 deg. 30 min. shall it have a moment's repose, if we can help it. On this vantage ground, the friends of freedom are impregnable. On any other, they are easily put to flight. Slavery can beat us in talking of lines and compromises. Most plainly we are lame here, even though our side shall be better than theirs. They have more talkers and more backers than we; and what they lack in the goodness of their cause they make up in these.

It is true that the slave power is mean, dishonorable, treacherous, perfidious and guilty of any amount of low scoundrelism, in seeking to throw off the obligations of a bargain, after pocketing the consideration which induced them to assume those obligations, and it may be proper enough to tell the South so. But it is not the perfidy of the South, but *that* for which the South is perfidious, which we are to battle with.— Common honesty does not flourish among the traffickers in human flesh. Such creatures having broken faith with God, cannot be expected to keep faith with man. As with them, so with their shameless minions at the North. Slavery has corrupted them.—They are sold to slavery, and will do the work of slavery, despite of plighted faith or other considerations of that sort.

To us the attempt now being made in Congress to nullify the Missouri Compromise, is hateful, because it is designed to extend and perpetuate slavery. Herein is the essential wrong, and against the man-imbruting, labor-degrading, land-blasting, curse of curses, and crime of crimes, should all the batteries of freedom be directed. The struggle is one for ascendancy. Slavery aims at absolute sway, and to banish liberty from the republic. It would drive out the school-master, and install the slave-driver, burn the school-house, and erect the whipping-post, prohibit the Holy Bible and establish the bloody slave code, dishonor free labor with its hope of reward, and establish slave labor with its dread of the lash. This is the crusade of cruelty and blood-guiltiness which the friends of freedom are now called upon to resist, and not the perfidy or bad faith involved in repealing the rotten compromise of 1820.

The mere repeal of that compromise apart from such objects as are now contemplated, standing alone, is a thing to which the friends of freedom might, so far as we are able to see, properly assent. It is more irrepealable than any other human enactment. If slavery does not repeal it, freedom ought, and will in the end. The fact that its repeal is now sought in a fraudulent manner, and from the blackest of motives, and for the basest of purposes, should not make us lose sight of the real nature of the compromise itself, and hold it as a thing desirable.—While it exists, liberty fights slavery over a chain. A hand to hand struggle is more desirable. Let the two systems of free labor and slave labor meet, and decide the great question between them fairly, without congressional or executive interference, and freedom would have nothing to lose in such a contest.

If non-intervention were really to be hoped for from the passing of this Nebraska bill, slavery would gain nothing by it. Let but this general government cease to interfere in behalf of slavery. Let the compromises into which it has entered, be repealed, and slavery stand out, distinct from national politics, nakedly upon its own merits, and it would disappear like the dew before the brightness of the morning sun. Slavery is now protected under the shadow of the national government. The slaveholder has heretofore found his greatest security in pleading the past in support of his claims.—Old compromises, old understandings, old intentions, and so forth, have been his covert and refuge. Now let him destroy his covert and refuge, if he will, and the consequences be on his own head.

It may be well enough for Whigs and Democrats of the North who honor compromises with slavery, and even hate slavery, up to a given line to devote their time and talents to maintaining the Missouri Compromise, and to resisting on such ground the attempt to force slavery north of 36 deg. 30 min. But quite other and different work should engage the heads and hearts of the friends of universal freedom. These should take an aggressive attitude. The ground should be distinctly taken that slavery has no rightful existence anywhere—that it is a system of lawless violence, and its multitudinous crimes and horrors should be spread out before the world with such terrible truth as to make the traffickers in human flesh tremble and call for rocks and mountains to fall on them. The whole nature and character and workings of the system, which it is proposed to extend, should be presented in such a blaze of light, that the slaveholders themselves would wish to withdraw the hateful thing from controversy, and would, of themselves, gladly get south of any line to escape from the hated light.

Frederick Douglass' Paper, February 24, 1854

TO HON. CHARLES SUMNER

Rochester, February 27th, 1854

My Dear Sir:

All the friends of freedom, in every State, and of every color, may claim you, just now, as their representative. As one of your sable constituents, my dear Sir, I desire to thank you for your noble speech for freedom, and for your country, which I have now read twice over.[2] When Messrs. Chase, Wade, and Seward had spoken, I could not see what remained for you to say. The result shows that the world is larger than it looks to be from the little valley where I live. If I thought you were, or could be, dissatisfied with your speech, I should have to consider you a hard master, and a very unreasonable man.

It is sad to think that after all the efforts of your Spartan band, this wicked measure will pass. A victory now for freedom would be the turning point in freedom's favor. But "God dwells in eternity," and it may be time enough yet. Heaven preserve you and strengthen you.

Yours most truly and gratefully,

Frederick Douglass

Charles Sumner Papers, Harvard University

TO HON. GERRIT SMITH

Rochester, March 6, 1854

My dear Sir:

I am slowly recovering from my illness, and hope soon to be at work again. I am, with you, quite sorry that W. H. Seward's abolitionism is not of a more decided type; and that he annexes so many hard conditions to the freedom of the Slave, in the D[istrict] [of] C[olumbia].[3] Yet so anxious am I, to see emancipation there, I would see it almost at any price. And since we cannot have you, and such as you, to propose plans in Congress for Emancipation I am glad of even so much as Wm. H. Seward's plan. As to "indemnifying" slaveholders, that is by no means so repulsive to me since your great speech on the Nebraska Bill,[4] which speech by the way, I was reading but yesterday. I hope it will not be long before I shall see and hear you again, for I always feel the better for having seen and heard you. I am, dear Sir,

Yours as ever truly and affectionately,

Frederick Douglass

Gerrit Smith Papers, Syracuse University

TO HON. GERRIT SMITH

Rochester, March 13th, 1854 [probably]

My Dear Friend:

I am at home, and have your welcome notes. You have only to vote and speak the convictions of your head and heart to have my earnest, though feeble support. I knew you would vote against the *homestead bill,* as soon as I learned that the mean and wicked amendment of Mr. Wright had prevailed.[5] Thomas Davis is known to me, and I was prepared to hear that he voted right. His opinions have changed much since our first acquaintance, now more than twelve years, but his heart is, no doubt, as noble as ever.

There was a good chance on Wright's *"white"* amendment, to have recounted some of the patriotic services of the colored people, and to have made an argument in favor of their citizenship. But one man cannot say everything, and perhaps the time was not allowed. I brought together some facts on this point for the Colored Convention held here last summer,[6] which may prove convenient to you. I therefore take the liberty to send them. My friend Julia comes home nightly gratified, perhaps I ought to say, ecstatic with her visit to Washington.

Believe me always truly and gratefully your friend,

Frederick Douglass

Please write often.

Gerrit Smith Papers, Syracuse University

TO HON. GERRIT SMITH

Rochester, May 6th, 1854.

My dear Sir:

I am grateful for your notice of me in Congress.[7] How lost to all sense of right are your Brother Legislators, that in the face of your manly and Christian opposition, the abominable and proscriptive amendment was adopted. Of your speech on the Nebraska Bill, aside from all my admiration and love for the friend of my poor people, I must pronounce it the mightiest and grandest production, ever before delivered in the House or Senate of this nation. I am about leaving home for New York. I am glad to see you intend speaking at length on the post office and Pacific Railroad question. In haste, your faithful friend.

Frederick Douglass

Gerrit Smith Papers, Syracuse University

TO HON. GERRIT SMITH

Rochester, May 19, 1854.

My Dear Sir:

I am again at my post. I found the packet of your speech here on my return from New York. I am very glad to have them to dispose of. It is the best Anti-Slavery document for the times, extant. Is it not too bad that Anti-Slavery men should do up all the arguments in the Slavery side against you? I was sick of the dogmatic and canting superior honesty indulged in at New York by the speakers at the late meeting of the Am[erican] A[nti] S[lavery] Society. With some of them, the best evidence that a man can give of being a knave, is to profess to believe in the soundness of your views respecting the Constitution. With the manner of your opposition to the Kansas-Nebraska Bill, those who know you most and love you best are entirely satisfied. It would not look dignified or consistent to see Gerrit Smith either leading or following what at best must be pronounced a factious opposition. I hope Cutting's amendment [8] will fail, and if we must have the repeal of the Missouri restriction, let nothing be done to soften the harshness of the measure.

My faithful friend Julia desires best love.

Always yours truly,
Frederick Douglass

Gerrit Smith Papers, Syracuse University

THE END OF ALL COMPROMISES WITH SLAVERY— NOW AND FOREVER

Against the indignant voice of the Northern people—against the commonest honesty—against the most solemn warnings from statesmen and patriots—against the most explicit and public pledges of both the great parties—against the declared purpose of Pres't Pierce on assuming the reins of government—against every obligation of honor, and the faith of mankind—against the stern resistance of a brave minority of our representatives—against the plainest dictates of the Christian religion, and the voice of its ministers, the hell-black scheme for extending slavery over Nebraska, where thirty-four years ago it was solemnly protected from slavery forever, has triumphed. The audacious villainy of the slave power, and the contemptible pusillanimity of the North, have begotten this monster, and sent him forth to blast and devour whatsoever remains of liberty, humanity and justice in the land. The North is again whipt—driven to the wall. The brick is knocked down at the end of the row, by which the remainder are laid prostrate. The Republic swings clear from all her ancient moorings, and moves off upon a tempestuous and perilous sea. Woe! woe! woe to slavery! Her mightiest shield is broken. A bolt that bound the North and South together has been surged asunder, and a mighty barricade, which has intervened between the forces of slavery and freedom, has been madly demolished by the slave power itself; and for one, we now say, in the name of God, let the battle come. Is this the language of excitement? It may be; but it is also the language of truth. The man who is unmoved now, misconceives the crisis; or he is intensely selfish, caring nothing about the affairs of his country and kind. Washington, long the abode of political profligacy and corruption, is now the scene of the revelry of triumphant wickedness, laughing to scorn the moral sense of the nation, and grinding the iron heel of bondage into the bleeding heart of living millions. Great God in mercy, overrule this great wrath to thy praise!

But what is to be done? Why, let this be done: let the whole North awake, arise; let the people assemble in every free State of the Union; and let a great party of freedom be organized, on whose broad banner let it be inscribed, All compromises with slavery ended—The abolition of slavery essential to the preservation of liberty. Let the old parties go to destruction, whither they have nearly sunk the nation. Let their names be blotted out, and their memory rot; and henceforth let there be only a free party, and a slave party. The banner of God and liberty, and the bloody flag of slavery and chains shall then swing out from our respective battlements, and rally under them our respective armies, and let the inquiry go forth now, as of old, Who is on the Lord's side? Let the ministers of religion, all over the country, whose remonstrances have been treated with contempt—whose calling has been despised—whose names have been made a byword—whose rights as citizens have been insolently denied—and whose God has been blasphemed by the plotters of this great wickedness, now buckle on the armor of their master, and heartily strive with their immense power, to arrest the nation in its downward progress, and save it from the deep damnation to which it is sinking.

If ye have whispered truth, whisper no longer,
Speak as the tempest does, sterner and stronger.

The time for action has come. While a grand political party is form-ing, let companies of emigrants from the free States be collected together —funds provided—and with every solemnity which the name and power of God can inspire. Let them be sent out to possess the goodly land, to which, by a law of Heaven and a law of man, they are justly entitled.

Frederick Douglass' Paper, May 26, 1854

IS IT RIGHT AND WISE TO KILL A KIDNAPPER?

A kidnapper has been shot dead, while attempting to execute the fugi-tive slave bill in Boston.[9] The streets of Boston in sight of Bunker Hill Monument, have been stained with the warm blood of a man in the act of perpetrating the most atrocious robbery which one man can possibly commit upon another—even the wresting from him his very person and natural powers. The deed of blood, as of course must have been expected, is making a tremendous sensation in all parts of the country, and calling forth all sorts of comments. Many are branding the deed as "murder," and would visit upon the perpetrator the terrible penalty attached to that dreadful crime. The occurrence naturally brings up the question of the reasonableness, and the rightfulness of killing a man who is in the act of forcibly reducing a brother man who is guilty of no crime, to the horrible condition of a slave. The question bids fair to be one of important and solemn interest, since it is evident that the practice of slave-hunting and slave-catching, with all their attendant enormities, will either be pursued, indefinitely, or abandoned immediately according to the decision arrived at by the community.

Cherishing a very high respect for the opinions of such of our readers and friends as hold to the inviolability of the human life, and differing from them on this vital question, we avail ourselves of the present excite-ment in the public mind, calmly to state our views and opinions, in ref-erence to the case in hand, asking for them an attentive and candid perusal.

Our moral philosophy on this point is our own—never having read what others may have said in favor of the views which we entertain.

The shedding of human blood at first sight, and without explanation is, and must ever be, regarded with horror; and he who takes pleasure in human slaughter is very properly looked upon as a moral monster. Even the killing of animals produces a shudder in sensitive minds, uncalloused by crime; and men are only reconciled to it by being shown, not only its reasonableness, but its necessity. These tender feelings so susceptible to pain, are most wisely designed by the Creator, for the preservation of life. They are, especially, the affirmation of God, speaking through nature, and asserting man's right to live. Contemplated in the light of warmth of these feelings, it is in all cases, a crime to deprive a human being of life: but God has not left us solely to the guidance of our feelings, having endowed us with reason, as well as with feeling, and it is in the light of reason that this question ought to be decided.

All will agree that human life is valuable or worthless, as to the innocent or criminal use that is made of it. Most evidently, also, the possession of life was permitted and ordained for beneficent ends, and not to defeat those ends, or to render their attainment impossible. Comprehensively stated, the end of man's creation is his own good, and the honor of his Creator. Life, therefore, is but a means to an end, and must be held in reason to be not superior to the purposes for which it was designed by the All-wise Creator. In this view there is no such thing as an absolute right to live; that is to say, the right to live, like any other human right, may be forfeited, and if forfeited, may be taken away. If the right to *life* stands on the same ground as the right to *liberty,* it is subject to all the exceptions that apply to the right to liberty. All admit that the right to enjoy *liberty* largely depends upon the use made of that liberty; hence Society has erected jails and prisons, with a view to deprive men of their liberty when they are so wicked as to abuse it by invading the liberties of their fellows. We have a right to arrest the locomotion of a man who insists upon walking and trampling on his brother man, instead of upon the highway. This right of society is essential to its preservations; without it a single individual would have it in his power to destroy the peace and the happiness of ten thousand otherwise right minded people. Precisely on the same ground, we hold that a man may, properly, wisely and even mercifully be deprived of life. Of course life being the most precious is the most sacred of all rights, and cannot be taken away, but under the direst necessity; and not until all reasonable modes had been adopted to prevent this necessity, and to spare the aggressor.

It is no answer to this view, to say that society is selfish in sacrificing the life of an individual, or of many individuals, to save the mass of mankind, or society at large. It is in accordance with nature, and the examples of the Almighty, in the execution of his will and beneficent laws. When a man flings himself from the top of some lofty monument, against a granite pavement, in that act he forfeits his *right* to live. He dies according to law, and however shocking may be the spectacle he presents, it is no argument against the beneficence of the law of gravitation, the suspension of whose operation must work ruin to the well-being of mankind. The observance of this law was necessary to his preservation; and his wickedness or folly, in violating it, could not be excused without imperilling those who are living in obedience to it. The atheist sees no benevolence in the law referred to; but to such minds we address not this article. It is enough for us that the All-Wise has established the law, and determined its character, and the penalty of its violation; and however we may deplore the mangled forms of the foolish and the wicked who transgress it, the beneficence of the law itself is fully vindicated by the security it gives to all who obey it.

We hold, then, in view of this great principle, or rule, in the physical world, we may properly infer that other law or principle of justice is the moral and social world, and vindicate its practical application to the preservation of the rights and liberties of the race, as against such exceptions furnished in the monsters who deliberately violate it by taking pleasure in enslaving, imbruting and murdering their fellow-men. As human life is not superior to the laws for the preservation of the physical universe, so, too, it is not superior to the eternal law of justice, which is essential to the preservation of the rights, and the security, and happiness of the race.

The argument thus far is to the point, that society has the right to preserve itself even at the expense of the life of the aggressor; and it may be said that, while what we allege may be right enough, as regards society, it is false as vested in an individual, such as the poor, powerless, and almost friendless wretch, now in the clutches of this proud and powerful republican government. But we take it to be a sound principle, that when government fails to protect the just rights of any individual man, either he or his friends may be held in the sight of God and man, innocent, in exercising any right for his preservation which society may exercise for its preservation. Such an individual is flung, by his untoward circumstances, upon his original right of self defence. We hold, therefore, that when James Batchelder, the truckman of Boston, abandoned his useful employment, as a common laborer, and took upon himself the revolting business of a kidnapper, and undertook to play the bloodhound on the track of his crimeless brother Burns, he labelled himself the common enemy of mankind, and his slaughter was as innocent, in the sight of God, as would be the slaughter of a ravenous wolf in the act of throttling an infant. We hold that he had forfeited his right to live, and that his death was necessary, as a warning to others liable to pursue a like course.

It may be said, that though the right to kill in defence of one's liberty be admitted, it is still unwise for the fugitive slave or his friends to avail themselves of this right; and that submission, in the circumstances, is far wiser than resistance. To this it is a sufficient answer to show that submission is valuable only so long as it has some chance of being recognized as a virtue. While it has this chance, it is well enough to practice it, as it may then have some moral effect in restraining crime and shaming aggression, but no longer. That submission on the part of the slave, has ceased to be a virtue, is very evident. While fugitives quietly cross their hands to be tied, adjust their ankles to be chained, and march off unresistingly to the hell of slavery, there will ever be fiends enough to hunt them and carry them back. Nor is this all nor the worst. Such submission, instead of being set to the credit of the poor sable ones, only creates contempt for them in the public mind, and becomes an argument in the mouths of the community, that Negroes are, by nature, only fit for slavery; that slavery is their normal condition. Their patient and unresisting disposition, their unwillingness to peril their own lives, by shooting down their pursuers, is already quoted against them, as marking them as an inferior race. This reproach must be wiped out, and nothing short of resistance on the part of colored men, can wipe it out. Every slave-hunter who meets a bloody death in his infernal business, is an argument in favor of the manhood of our race. Resistance is, therefore, wise as well as just.

At this point of our writing, we meet with the following plea, set up for the atrocious wretch, "gone to his own place," by the Rochester *Daily American,* a Silver Grey paper.

"An important inquiry arises,—Who are the murderers of Batchelder? There are several. First, and most guilty, are Wendell Phillips, Theodore Parker, and their Fanueil Hall coadjutors. All just minds will regard their conduct as more atrocious than even that of the ruffians who shot and mangled the unfortunate officer. Cold, remorseless, and bloody as the cruel axe, they deliberately worked up the crowd to a murderous frenzy, and pointed out the path which led to murder. The guilt which rests upon the infuriated assassins is light compared with that which blackens the cowardly orators of Fanueil Hall.

"What had Batchelder done, that Phillips, Parker and their minions should steep their souls in his blood? Why did these men make his wife a widow,—his children fatherless, and send his unwarned spirit to the presence of God?"

This is very pathetic. The *widow* and the *fatherless* of this brutal truckman—a truckman who, it seems, was one of the swell-head bullies of Boston, selected for the office of Marshal or Deputy Marshal, solely because of his brutal nature and ferocious disposition.

We would ask Mr. Mann whether if such a wretch should lay his horney paws upon his own dignified shoulders, with a view to reduce him to bondage, he would hold, as a murderer, any friend of his, who, to save him from such a fate, shot down the brute?—There is not a citizen of Rochester worthy of the name, who would not shoot down any man in defence of his own liberty—or who, if set upon, by a number of robbers, would not thank any friend who interposed, even to the shedding of blood, for his release.—*The widow and orphans* are far better off with such a wretch in the grave, than on the earth. Then again, the law which he undertook to execute, has *no tears* for the *widows and orphans* of poor innocent fugitives, who make their homes at the North. With a hand as relentless as that of death, it snatches the husband from the wife, and the father from his children, and this for no crime.—Oh! that man's ideas of justice and of right depended *less* upon the circumstance of color, and *more* upon the indestructible nature of things. For a *white* man to defend his friend unto blood is praiseworthy, but for a *black* man to do precisely the same thing is crime. It was glorious for Patrick Henry to say, *"Give me liberty or give me death!"* It was glorious for Americans to drench the soil, and crimson the sea with blood, *to escape the payment of three-penny tax upon tea;* but it is crime to shoot down a monster in defence of the liberty of a black man and to save him from a bondage "one hour of which (in the language of Jefferson) is worse than ages of that which our fathers rose in rebellion to oppose." Until Mr. Mann is willing to be a slave—until he is ready to admit that human legislation can rightfully reduce him to slavery, by a simple vote—until he abandons the right of self defence—until he ceases to glory in the deeds of Hancock, Adams, and Warren—and ceases to look with pride and patriotic admiration upon the sombre pile at Bunker Hill, where the blood of the oppressor was poured out in torrents making thousands of *widows and orphans,* it does not look graceful in him to brand as *murderers* those that killed the atrocious *Truckman* who attempted to play the blood-hound on the track of the poor, defenceless BURNS.

Frederick Douglass' Paper, June 2, 1854

THE CLAIMS OF THE NEGRO ETHNOLOGICALLY CON-SIDERED, address delivered at Western Reserve College, July 12, 1854

Gentlemen, in selecting the Claims of the Negro as the subject of my remarks to-day, I am animated by a desire to bring before you a matter of living importance—a matter upon which action, as well as thought is required. The relation subsisting between the white and black people of this country is the vital question of the age. In the solution of this question, the scholars of America will have to take an important and controlling part. This is the moral battle field to which their country and their God now call them. In the eye of both, the neutral scholar is an ignoble man. Here, a man must be hot, or be accounted cold, or, perchance, something worse than hot or cold. The lukewarm and the cowardly, will be rejected by earnest men on either side of the controversy. The cunning man who avoids it, to gain the favor of both parties, will be rewarded with scorn; and the timid man who shrinks from it, for fear of offending either party, will be despised. To the lawyer, the preacher, the politician, and to the man of letters, there is no neutral ground. He that is not for us, is against us. Gentlemen, I assume at the start, that wherever else I may be required to speak with bated breath, here, at least, I may speak with freedom the thought nearest my heart. This liberty is implied, by the call I have received to be here; and yet I hope to present the subject so that no man can reasonably say, that an outrage has been committed, or that I have abused the privilege with which you have honored me. I shall aim to discuss the claims of the Negro, general and special, in a manner, though not scientific, still sufficiently clear and definite to enable my hearers to form an intelligent judgment respecting them.

The first general claim which may here be set up, respects the manhood of the Negro. This is an elementary claim, simple enough, but not without question. It is fiercely opposed. A respectable public journal, published in Richmond, Va., bases its whole defence of the slave system upon a denial of the Negro's manhood.

"The white peasant is free, and if he is a man of will and intellect, can rise in the scale of society; or at least his offspring may. He is not deprived by law of those 'inalienable rights,' 'liberty and the pursuit of happiness,' by the use of it. But here is the essence of slavery — that we do declare the Negro destitute of these powers. We bind him by law to the condition of the laboring peasant for ever, without his consent, and we bind his posterity after him. Now, the true question is, have we a right to do this? If we have not, all discussions about his comfortable situation, and the actual condition of free laborers elsewhere, are quite beside the point. If the Negro has the same right to his liberty and the pursuit of his own happiness that the white man has, then we commit the greatest wrong and robbery to hold him a slave—an act at which the sentiment of justice must revolt in every heart and Negro slavery is an institution which that sentiment must sooner or later blot from the face of the earth."—*Richmond Examiner*.

After stating the question thus, the *Examiner* boldy asserts that the Negro has no such right—BECAUSE HE IS NOT A MAN!

There are three ways to answer this denial. One is by ridicule; a second is by denunciation; and a third is by argument. I hardly know under which of these modes my answer to-day will fall. I feel myself somewhat on trial; and that this is just the point where there is hesitation, if not serious doubt. I cannot, however, argue; I must assert. To know whether a Negro is a man, it must first be known what constitutes a man. Here, as well as elsewhere, I take it, that the "coat must be cut according to the cloth." [It is not necessary, in order to establish the manhood of any one making the claim, to prove that such an one equals Clay in eloquence, or Webster and Calhoun in logical force and directness; for, tried by such standards of mental power as these, it is apprehended that very few could claim the high designation of *man*. Yet something like this folly is seen in the arguments directed against the humanity of the Negro. His faculties and powers, uneducated and unimproved, have been contrasted with those of the highest cultivation; and the world has then been called upon to behold the immense and amazing difference between the man admitted, and the man disputed. The fact that these intellects, so powerful and so controlling, are almost, if not quite as exceptional to the general rule of humanity, in one direction, as the specimen Negroes are in the other, is quite overlooked.]

Man is distinguished from all other animals, by the possession of certain definite faculties and powers, as well as by physical organization and proportions. He is the only two-handed animal on the earth—the only one that laughs, and nearly the only one that weeps. Men instinctively distinguish between men and brutes. Common sense itself is scarcely needed to detect the absence of manhood in a monkey, or to recognize its presence in a Negro. His speech, his reason, his power to acquire and to retain knowledge, his heaven-erected face, his habitudes, his hopes, his fears, his aspirations, his prophecies, plant between him and the brute creation, a distinction as eternal as it is palpable. Away, therefore, with all the scientific moonshine that would connect men with monkeys; that would have the world believe that humanity, instead of resting on its own characteristic pedestal—gloriously independent —is a sort of sliding scale, making one extreme brother to the ourang-ou-tang, and the other to angels, and all the rest intermediates! Tried by all the usual, and all the *un*usual tests, whether mental, moral, physical, or psychological, the Negro is a MAN—considering him as possessing knowledge, or needing knowledge, his elevation or his degradation, his virtues, or his vices—whichever road you take, you reach the same conclusion, the Negro is a MAN. His good and his bad, his innocence and his guilt, his joys and his sorrows, proclaim his manhood in speech that all mankind practically and readily understand.

A very recondite author says, that "man is distinguished from all other animals, in that he resists as well as adapts himself to his circumstances." He does not take things as he finds them, but goes to work to improve them. Tried by this test, too, the Negro is a man. You may see him yoke the oxen, harness the horse, and hold the plow. He can swim the river; but he prefers to fling over it a bridge. The horse bears him on his back—admits his mastery and dominion. The barnyard fowl know his step, and flock around to receive their morning meal from his sable hand. The dog dances when he comes home, and whines piteously when he is absent. All these know that the Negro is a MAN. Now, presuming that what is evident to beast and to bird, cannot need elaborate argument to be made plain to men, I assume, with this brief statement, that the Negro is a man.

The first claim conceded and settled, let us attend to the second, which is beset with some difficulties, giving rise to many opinions, different from my own, and which opinions I propose to combat.

There was a time when, if you established the point that a particular being is a man, it was considered that such a being, of course, had a common ancestry with the rest of mankind. But it is not so now. This is, you know, an age of science, and science is favorable to division. It must explore and analyze, until all doubt is set at rest. There is, therefore, another proposition to be stated and maintained, separately, which, in other days, (the days before the Notts, the Gliddens, the Agassiz, and Mortons, made their profound discoveries in ethnological science,) might have been included in the first.

It is somewhat remarkable, that, at a time when knowledge is so generally diffused, when the geography of the world is so well understood—when time and space, in the intercourse of nations, are almost annihilated—when oceans have become bridges—the earth a magnificent hall—the hollow sky a dome—under which a common humanity can meet in friendly conclave—when nationalities are being swallowed up—and the ends of the earth brought together—I say it is remarkable—nay, it is strange that there should arise a phalanx of learned men—speaking in the name of *science*—to forbid the magnificent reunion of mankind in one brotherhood. A mortifying proof is here given, that the moral growth of a nation, or an age, does not always keep pace with the increase of knowledge, and suggests the necessity of means to increase human love with human learning.

The proposition to which I allude, and which I mean next to assert, is this, that what are technically called the Negro race, are a part of the human family, and are descended from a common ancestry, with the rest of mankind. The discussion of this point opens a comprehensive field of inquiry. It involves the question of the unity of the human race. Much has and can be said on both sides of that question.

Looking out upon the surface of the Globe, with its varieties of climate, soil, and formations, its elevations and depressions, its rivers, lakes, oceans, islands, continents, and the vast and striking differences which mark and diversify its multitudinous inhabitants, the question has been raised, and pressed with increasing ardor and pertinacity, (especially in modern times,) can all these various tribes, nations, tongues, kindreds, so widely separated, and so strangely dissimilar, have descended from a common ancestry? That is the question, and it has been answered variously by men of learning. Different modes of reasoning have been adopted, but the conclusions reached may be divided into two—the one YES, and the other NO. *Which* of these answers is most in accord-

ance with facts, with reason, with the welfare of the world, and reflects most glory upon the wisdom, power, and goodness of the Author
of all existence, is the question for consideration with us? On which
side is the weight of the argument, rather than which side is absolutely proved?

It must be admitted at the beginning, that, viewed apart from the
authority of the Bible, neither the unity, nor diversity of origin of the
human family, can be demonstrated. To use the terse expression of the
Rev. Dr. Anderson, who speaking on this point, says; "It is impossible
to get far enough back for that." This much, however, can be done.
The evidence on both sides, can be accurately weighed, and the truth
arrived at with almost absolute certainty.

It would be interesting, did time permit, to give here, some of the
most striking features of the various theories, which have, of late, gained
attention and respect in many quarters of our country—touching the
origin of mankind—but I must pass this by. The argument to-day, is to
the unity, as against that theory, which affirms the diversity of human
origin.

The Bearings of the Question

A moment's reflection must impress all, that few questions have
more important and solemn bearings, than the one now under consideration. It is connected with eternal as well as with terrestrial interests. It
covers the earth and reaches heaven. The unity of the human race—
the brotherhood of man—the reciprocal duties of all to each, and of
each to all, are too plainly taught in the Bible to admit of cavil.—The
credit of the Bible is at stake—and if it be too much to say, that it must
stand or fall, by the decision of this question, *it is* proper to say, that
the value of that sacred Book—as a record of the early history of mankind—must be materially affected, by the decision of the question.

For myself I can say, my reason (not less than my feeling, and my
faith) welcomes with joy, the declaration of the Inspired Apostle, "that
God has made of one blood all nations of men for to dwell upon all
the face of the earth." But this grand affirmation of the unity of the
human race, and many others like unto it, together with the whole
account of the creation, given in the early scriptures, must all get a new
interpretation or be overthrown altogether, if a diversity of human origin
can be maintained.—Most evidently, this aspect of the question makes it
important to those, who rely upon the Bible, as the sheet anchor of

their hopes—and the frame work of all religious truth. The young minister must look into this subject and settle it for himself, before he ascends the pulpit, to preach redemption to a fallen race.

The bearing of the question upon Revelation, is not more marked and decided than its relation to the situation of things in our country, at this moment. *One seventh* part of the population of this country is of Negro descent. The land is peopled by what may be called the most dissimilar races on the globe. The black and the white—the Negro and the European—these constitute the American people—and, in all the likelihoods of the case, they will ever remain the principal inhabitants of the United States, in some form or other. The European population are greatly in the ascendant in numbers, wealth and power. They are the rulers of the country—the masters—the Africans, are the slaves— the proscribed portion of the people—and precisely in proportion as the truth of human brotherhood gets recognition, will be the freedom and elevation, in this country, of persons of African descent. In truth, this question is at the bottom of the whole controversy, now going on between the slaveholders on the *one* hand, and the abolitionists on the other. It is the same old question which has divided the selfish, from the philanthropic part of mankind in all ages. It is the question whether the rights, privileges, and immunities enjoyed by some ought not to be shared and enjoyed by all.

It is not quite two hundred years ago, when such was the simplicity (I will not now say the pride and depravity) of the Anglo Saxon inhabitants of the British West Indies, that the learned and pious Godwin, a missionary to the West Indies, deemed it necessary to write a book, to remove what he conceived to be the injurious belief that it was sinful in the sight of God to baptize Negroes and Indians. The West Indies have made progress since that time.—God's emancipating angel has broken the fetters of slavery in those islands, and the praises of the Almighty are now sung by the sable lips of eight hundred thousand freemen, before deemed only fit for slaves, and to whom even baptismal and burial rights were denied.

The unassuming work of *Godwin* may have had some agency in producing this glorious result. One other remark before entering upon the argument. It may be said, that views and opinions, favoring the unity of the human family, coming from one of lowly condition, are open to the suspicion, that *"the wish is father to the thought,"* and so, indeed, it may be.—But let it be also remembered, that this deduction from the weight of the argument on the one side, is more than counter-balanced by the pride of race and position arrayed on the other. Indeed, ninety-nine out of every hundred of the advocates of a diverse origin of the human family in this country, are among those who hold it to be the privilege of the *Anglo-Saxon* to enslave and oppress the African —and slaveholders, not a few, like the Richmond Examiner to which I have referred, have admitted, that the whole argument in defence of slavery, becomes utterly worthless the moment the African is proved to be equally a man with the Anglo-Saxon. The temptation therefore, to read the Negro out of the human family is exceedingly strong, and may account somewhat for the repeated attempts on the part of Southern pretenders to science, to cast a doubt over the Scriptural account of the origin of mankind. If the origin and motives of most works, opposing the doctrine of the unity of the human race, could be ascertained, it may be doubted whether *one* such work could boast an honest parentage. Pride and selfishness, combined with mental power, never want for a theory to justify them—and when men oppress their fellow-men, the oppressor ever finds, in the character of the oppressed, a full justification for his oppression. Ignorance and depravity, and the inability to rise from degradation to civilization and respectability, are the most usual allegations against the oppressed. The evils most fostered by slavery and oppression, are precisely those which slaveholders and oppressors would transfer from their system to the inherent character of their victims. Thus the very crimes of slavery become slavery's best defence. By making the enslaved a character fit only for slavery, they excuse themselves for refusing to make the slave a freeman. A wholesale method of accomplishing this result, is to overthrow the instinctive consciousness of the common brotherhood of man. For, let it be once granted that the human race are of multitudinous origin, naturally different in their moral, physical, and intellectual capacities, and at once you make plausible a demand for classes, grades and conditions, for different methods of culture, different moral, political, and religious institutions, and a chance is left for slavery, as a necessary institution. The debates in Congress on the Nebraska Bill during the past winter, will show how slaveholders have availed themselves of this doctrine in support of slaveholding. There is no doubt that Messrs. Nott, Glidden, Morton, Smith and Agassiz were duly consulted by our slavery propagating statesmen.

Ethnological Unfairness Towards the Negro

The lawyers tell us that the credit of a witness is always in order. Ignorance, malice or prejudice, may disqualify a witness, and why not an author? Now, the disposition everywhere evident, among the class of writers alluded to, to separate the Negro race from every intelligent nation and tribe in Africa, may fairly be regarded as one proof, that they have staked out the ground beforehand, and that they have aimed to construct a theory in support of a foregone conclusion. The desirableness of isolating the Negro race, and especially of separating them from the various peoples of Northern Africa, is too plain to need a remark. Such isolation would remove stupendous difficulties in the way of getting the Negro in a favourable attitude for the blows of scientific christendom.

Dr. Samuel George Morton may be referred to as a fair sample of American Ethnologists. His very able work *"Crania Americana,"* published in Philadelphia in 1839, is widely read in this country.—In this great work his contempt for Negroes, is ever conspicuous. I take him as an illustration of what had been alleged as true of his class.

The fact that Egypt was one of the earliest abodes of learning and civilization, is as firmly established as are the everlasting hills, defying, with a calm front the boasted mechanical and architectural skill of the nineteenth century—smiling serenely on the assaults and the mutations of time, there she stands in overshadowing grandeur, riveting the eye and the mind of the modern world—upon her, in silent and dreamy wonder—Greece and Rome—and through them Europe and America have received their civilization from the ancient Egyptians. This fact is not denied by anybody. But Egypt is in Africa. Pity that it had not been in Europe, or in Asia, or better still in America! Another unhappy circumstance is, that the ancient Egyptians were not white people; but were, undoubtedly, just about as dark in complexion as many in this country who are considered genuine Negroes; and that is not all, their hair was far from being of that graceful lankness which adorns the fair Anglo Saxon head. But the next best thing, after these defects, is a positive unlikeness to the Negro. Accordingly, our learned author enters into an elaborate argument to prove that the ancient Egyptians were totally distinct from the Negroes, and to deny all relationship between. Speaking of the "Copts and Fellahs," whom every body knows are descendants of the Egyptians, he says, *"The Copts, though now remarkably distinct from the people that surround them, derive from their remote ancestors some mixture of Greek, Arabian, and perhaps even Negro blood."* Now, mark the description given of the Egyptians in this same work: *"Complexion brown. The nose is straight, excepting the end, where it is rounded and wide; the lips are rather thick, and the hair black and curly."* This description would certainly seem to make it safe to suppose the presence of *"even* Negro blood." A man, in our day, with brown complexion, "nose rounded and wide, lips thick, hair black and curly," would, I think, have no difficulty in getting himself recognized as a Negro!!

The same authority tells us that the "Copts are supposed by *Neibhur, Denon* and others, to be the descendants of the ancient Egyptians"; and Dr. Morton adds, that it has often been observed that a strong resemblance may be traced between the Coptic visage and that presented in the ancient mummies and statues. Again, he says, the *"Copts can be, at most, but the degenerate remains, both physically and intellectually, of that mighty people who have claimed the admiration of all ages."* Speaking of the Nubians, Dr. Morton says, (page 26,)——

"The hair of the Nubian is thick and black—often curled, either by nature or art, and sometimes *partially frizzled,* but *never woolly."*

Again:——

"Although the Nubians occasionally present their national characters unmixed, they generally show traces of their social intercourse with the Arabs, and *even* with the Negroes."

*　　*　　*

The repetition of the adverb here *"even,"* is important, as showing the spirit in which our great American Ethnologist pursues his work, and what deductions may be justly made from the value of his researches on that account. In everything touching the Negro, Dr. Morton, in his "Crania Americana," betrays the same spirit. He thinks that the *Sphinx* was not the representative of an Egyptian Deity, but was a shrine, worshiped at by the degraded *Negroes* of Egypt; and this fact he alleges as the secret of the mistake made by Volney, in supposing that the Egyptians were real Negroes. The absurdity of this assertion will be very apparent, in view of the fact that the great Sphinx in question was the chief of a series, full two miles in length. Our author again repels the supposition that the Egyptians were related to Negroes, by saying there is no mention made of *color* by the historian, in relating the marriage of Solomon with Pharaoh's daughter; and with genuine American feeling, he says, such a circumstance as the marrying of an

European monarch with the daughter of a Negro would not have been passed over in silence in our day. This is a sample of the reasoning of men who reason from *prejudice* rather than from *facts*. It assumes that a *black skin* in the *East* excites the same prejudice which we see here in the West. Having denied all relationship of the Negro to the ancient Egyptians, with characteristic American assumption, he says, "It is easy to prove, that whatever may have been the hue of their skin, they belong to the same race with ourselves."

Of course, I do not find fault with Dr. Morton, or any other American, for claiming affinity with Egyptians. All that goes in that direction belongs to my side of the question, and is really right.

The leaning here indicated is natural enough, and may be explained by the fact, that an educated man in Ireland ceases to be an Irishman; and an intelligent black man is always supposed to have derived his intelligence from his connection with the white race. To be intelligent is to have one's Negro blood ignored.

There is, however, a very important physiological fact, contradicting this last assumption; and that fact is, that intellect is uniformly derived from the maternal side. Mulattoes, in this country, may almost wholly boast of Anglo Saxon male ancestry.

It is the province of prejudice to blind; and scientific writers, not less than others, write to please, as well as to instruct, and even unconsciously to themselves, (sometimes,) sacrifice what is true to what is popular. Fashion is not confined to dress; but extends to philosophy as well—and it is fashionable now, in our land, to exaggerate the differences between the Negro and the European. If, for instance, a phrenologist, or naturalist undertakes to represent in portraits, the differences between the two races—the Negro and the European—he will invariably present the *highest* type of the European, and the *lowest* type of the Negro.

The European face is drawn in harmony with the highest ideas of beauty, dignity and intellect. Features regular and brow after the Websterian mold. The Negro, on the other hand, appears with features distorted, lips exaggerated, forehead depressed—and the whole expression of the countenance made to harmonize with the popular idea of Negro imbecility and degradation. I have seen many pictures of Negroes and Europeans, in phrenological and ethnological works; and all, or nearly all, excepting the work of Dr. Prichard, and that other great work, Combs' Constitution of Man, have been more or less open to this objection. I think I have never seen a single picture in an American work, designed to give an idea of the mental endowments of the Negro, which did any thing like justice to the subject; nay, that was not infamously distorted. The heads of *A. Crummel, Henry H. Garnet, Sam'l R. Ward, Chas. Lenox Remond, W. J. Wilson, J. W. Penington, J. I. Gaines, M. R. Delany, J. W. Loguen, J. M. Whitfield, J. C. Holly,* and hundreds of others I could mention, are all better formed, and indicate the presence of intellect more than any pictures I have seen in such works; and while it must be admitted that there are Negroes answering the description given by the American ethnologists and others, of the Negro race, I contend that there is every description of head among them, ranging from the highest Indoo Caucasian downward. If the very best type of the European is always presented, I insist that *justice,* in all such works, demands that the very best type of the Negro should also be taken. The importance of this criticism may not be apparent to all;—to the *black* man it is very apparent. He sees the injustice, and writhes under its sting. But to return to Dr. Morton, or rather to the question of the affinity of the Negroes to the Egyptians.

It seems to me that a man might as well deny the affinity of the American to the Englishman, as to deny such affinity between the Negro and the Egyptian. He might make out as many points of difference, in the case of the one as in that of the other. Especially could this be done, if, like ethnologists, in given cases, only typical specimens were resorted to. The lean, slender American, pale and swarthy, if exposed to the sun, wears a very different appearance to the full, round Englishman, of clear, *blonde* complexion. One may trace the progress of this difference in the common portraits of the American Presidents. Just study those faces, beginning with *Washington;* and as you come thro' the *Jeffersons,* the *Adamses,* and the *Madisons,* you will find an increasing bony and wiry appearance about those portraits, & a greater remove from that serene amplitude which characterises the countenances of the earlier Presidents. I may be mistaken, but I think this is a correct index of the change going on in the nation at large—converting Englishmen, Germans, Irishmen, and Frenchmen, into Americans, and causing them to lose, in a common American character, all traces of their former distinctive national peculiarities.

Authorities as to the Resemblance of the Egyptians to Negroes

Now, let us see what the best authorities say, as to the personal appearance of the Egyptians. I think it will be at once admitted, that while they differ very strongly from the Negro, debased and enslaved, that difference is not greater than may be observed in other quarters of the globe, among people notoriously belonging to the same variety, the same original stock; in a word, to the same family. If it shall be found that the people of Africa have an African character, as general, as well defined, and as distinct, as have the people of Europe, or the people of Asia, the exceptional differences among them afford no ground for supposing a difference of race; but, on the contrary, it will be inferred that the people of Africa constitute one great branch of the human family, whose origin may be as properly referred to the families of Noah, as can be any other branch of the human family, from whom they differ. Denon, in his *'Travels in Egypt,'* describes the Egyptians, as of full, but "delicate and voluptuous forms, countenances sedate and placid, round and soft features, with eyes long and almond shaped, half shut and languishing and turned up at the outer angles, as if habitually fatigued by the light and heat of the sun; cheeks round; thick lips, full and prominent; mouth large, but cheerful and smiling; complexion dark, ruddy and coppery, and the whole aspect displaying—as one of the most graphic delineators among modern travelers has observed—the genuine African character, of which the *Negro* is the exaggerated and extreme representation." Again, Prichard says, (page 152,)—

"Herodotus traveled in Egypt, and was, therefore, well acquainted with the people from personal observation. He does not say anything directly, as to the descriptions of their persons, which were too well known to the Greeks to need such an account, but his indirect testimony is very strongly expressed. After mentioning a tradition, that the people of Colchis were a colony from Egypt, Herodotus says, that 'there was one fact strongly in favor of this opinion—the Colchians were *black* in complexion and *woolly* haired.'"

These are the words by which the complexion and hair of Negroes are described. In another passage, he says that

"The pigeon, said to have fled to Dodona, and to have founded the Oracle, was declared to be *black,* and that the meaning of the story was this: The Oracle was, in reality, founded by a female captive from the Thebaid; she was *black,* being an Egyptian." "Other Greek writers," says Pritchard, "have expressed themselves in similar terms."

Those who have mentioned the Egyptians as a *swarthy* people, according to Prichard, might as well have applied the term *black* to them, since they were doubtless of a chocolate color. The same author brings together the testimony of Eschylus and others as to the color of the ancient Egyptians, all corresponding, more or less, with the foregoing. Among the most direct testimony educed by Prichard, is, first that of Volney, who, speaking of the modern Copts, says:

"They have a puffed visage, swollen eyes, flat nose, and thick lips, and bear much resemblance to mulattoes."

Baron Larrey says, in regard to the same people:

"They have projecting cheek bones, dilating nostrils, thick lips, and hair and beard black and *crisp."*

Mr. Ledyard, (whose testimony, says our learned authority, is of the more value, as he had no theory to support,) says:

"I suspect the *Copts* to have been the *origin* of the *Negro* race; the nose and lips correspond with those of the Negro; the hair, wherever I can see it among the people here, is curled, *not* like that of the Negroes, but like the mulattoes."

Here I leave our learned authorities, as to the resemblance of the Egyptians to Negroes.

It is not in my power, in a discourse of this sort, to adduce more than a very small part of the testimony in support of a near relationship between the present enslaved and degraded Negroes, and the ancient highly civilized and wonderfully endowed Egyptians. Sufficient has already been adduced, to show a marked similarity in regard to features, hair, color, and I doubt not that the philologist can find equal similarity in the structures of their languages. In view of the foregoing, while it may not be claimed that the ancient Egyptians were Negroes,—viz:—answering, in all respects, to the nations and tribes ranged under the general appellation, Negro; still, it may safely be affirmed, that a strong affinity and a direct relationship may be claimed by the Negro race, to *that grandest of all the nations of antiquity, the builders of the pyramids.*

But there are other evidences of this relationship, more decisive than those alledged in a general similarity of personal appearance.

Language is held to be very important, by the best ethnologists, in tracing out the remotest affinities of nations, tribes, classes and families. The color of the skin has sometimes been less enduring than the speech of a people. I speak by authority, and follow in the footsteps of some of the most learned writers on the natural and ethnological history of man, when I affirm that one of the most direct and conclusive proofs of the general affinity of Northern African nations, with those of West, East and South Africa, is found in the general similarity of their language. The philologist easily discovers, and is able to point out something like the original source of the multiplied tongues now in use in that yet mysterious quarter of the globe. *Dr. R. G. Latham,* F. R. S., corresponding member of the Ethnological Society, New York—in his admirable work, entitled "Man and his Migrations"—says:

"In the languages of Abyssinia, the Gheez and Tigre, admitted, as long as they have been known at all, to be *Semitic,* graduate through the Amharic, the Talasha, the Harargi, the Gafat and other languages, which may be well studied in Dr. Beke's valuable comparative tables, into the Agow tongue, unequivocally indigenous to Abyssinia, and through this into the true Negro classes. But, unequivocal as may be the Semitic elements of the Berber, Coptic and Galla, their affinities with the tongues of Western and Southern Africa are more so. I weigh my words when I say, not *equally,* but *more;* changing the expression, for every foot in advance which can be made towards the Semitic tongues in one direction, the African philologist can go a yard towards the Negro ones in the other."

In a note, just below this remarkable statement, Dr. Latham says:

"A short table of the Berber and Coptic, as compared with the other African tongues, may be seen in the Classical Museum of the British Association, for 1846. In the Transactions of the Philological Society is a grammatical sketch of the Tumali language, by Dr. S. Tutshek of Munich. The Tumali is a truly Negro language, of Kordufan; whilst, in respect to the extent to which its inflections are formed, by internal changes of vowels and accents, it is fully equal to the Semitic tongues of Palestine and Arabia."

This testimony may not serve prejudice, but to me it seems quite sufficient.

Superficial Objections

Let us now glance again at the opposition. A volume, on the Natural History of the Human Species, by Charles Hamilton Smith, quite false in many of its facts, and as mischievous as false, has been published recently in this country, and will, doubtless, be widely circulated, especially by those to whom the thought of human brotherhood is abhorrent. This writer says, after mentioning sundry facts touching the dense and spherical structure of the Negro head:

"This very structure may influence the erect gait, which occasions the practice common also to the Ethiopian, or mixed nations, of carrying burdens and light weights, even to a tumbler full of water, upon the head."

No doubt this seemed a very sage remark to Mr. Smith, and quite important in fixing a character to the Negro skull, although different to that of Europeans. But if the learned Mr. Smith had stood, previous to writing it, at our door (a few days in succession), he might have seen hundreds of Germans and of Irish people, not bearing burdens of *"light* weight," but of *heavy* weight, upon the same vertical extremity. The carrying of burdens upon the head is as old as Oriental Society; and the man writes himself a blockhead, who attempts to find in the custom a proof of original difference. On page 227, the same writer says:

"The voice of the Negroes is feeble and hoarse in the male sex."

The explanation of this mistake in our author, is found in the fact, that an oppressed people, in addressing their superiors—perhaps I ought to say, their oppressors—usually assume a minor tone, as less likely to provoke the charge of intrusiveness. But it is ridiculous to pronounce the voice of the Negro feeble; and the learned ethnologist must be hard pushed, to establish differences, when he refers to this as one. Mr. Smith further declares, that

"The typical woolly haired races have never discovered an alphabet, framed a grammatical language, nor made the least step in science or art."

Now, the man is still living (or was but a few years since), among the Mandingoes of the Western coast of Africa, who has framed an alphabet; and while Mr. Smith may be pardoned for his ignorance of that fact, as an ethnologist, he is inexcusable for not knowing that the Mpongwe language, spoken on both sides of the Gaboon River, at Cape Lopez, Cape St. Catharine, and in the interior, to the distance of two or three hundred miles, is as truly a grammatically framed language as any extant. I am indebted, for this fact, to Rev. Dr. *M. B. Anderson,* President of the Rochester University; and by his leave, here is the Grammar—[holding up the Grammar.] Perhaps, of all the attempts ever made to disprove the unity of the human family, and to brand the Negro with natural inferiority, the most compendious and barefaced is the book, entitled *"Types of Mankind,"* by Nott and Glidden. One would be well employed, in a series of Lectures, directed to an exposure of the unsoundness, if not the wickedness of this work.

The African Race But One People

But I must hasten. Having shown that the people of Africa are, probably, one people; that each tribe bears an intimate relation to other tribes and nations in that quarter of the globe, and that the Egyptians may have flung off the different tribes seen there at different times, as implied by the evident relations of their language, and by other similarities; it can hardly be deemed unreasonable to suppose, that the African branch of the human species—from the once highly civilized Egyptian to the barbarians on the banks of the Niger—may claim brotherhood with the great family of Noah, spreading over the more Northern and Eastern parts of the globe. I will now proceed to consider those physical peculiarities of form, features, hair and color, which are supposed by some men to mark the African, not only as an inferior race, but as a distinct species, naturally and originally different from the rest of mankind, and as really to place him nearer to the brute than to man.

The Effect of Circumstances Upon the Physical Man

I may remark, just here, that it is impossible, even were it desirable, in a discourse like this, to attend to the anatomical and physiological argument connected with this part of the subject. I am not equal to that, and if I were, the occasion does not require it. The form of the *Negro*—[I use the term *Negro,* precisely in the sense that you use the term Anglo Saxon; and I believe, too, that the former will one day be as illustrious as the latter]—has often been the subject of remark. His flat feet, long arms, high cheek bones and retreating forehead, are especially dwelt upon, to his disparagement, and just as if there were no white people with precisely the same peculiarities. I think it will ever be found, that the *well* or *ill* condition of any part of mankind, will leave its mark on the physical as well as on the intellectual part of man. A hundred instances might be cited, of whole families who have degenerated, and others who have improved in personal appearance, by a change of circumstances. A man is worked upon by what *he* works on.

He may carve out his circumstances, but his circumstances will carve him out as well. I told a boot maker, in New Castle upon Tyne, that I had been a plantation slave. He said I must pardon him; but he could not believe it; no plantation laborer ever had a high instep. He said he had noticed, that the coal heavers and work people in low condition, had, for the most part, flat feet, and that he could tell, by the shape of the feet, whether a man's parents were in high or low condition. The thing was worth a thought, and I have thought of it, and have looked around me for facts. There is some truth in it; though there are exceptions, in individual cases.

[The day I landed in Ireland, nine years ago, I addressed] (in company with Father *Spratt,* and that good man who has been recently made the subject of bitter attack; I allude to the philanthropic *James Haughton, of Dublin*) [a large meeting of the common people of Ireland, on temperance. Never did human faces tell a sadder tale. More than five thousand were assembled; and I say, with no wish to wound the feelings of any Irishman, that these people lacked only a black skin and woolly hair, to complete their likeness to the plantation Negro. The open, uneducated mouth—the long, gaunt arm—the badly formed foot and ankle—the shuffling gait—the retreating forehead and vacant expression—and, their petty quarrels and fights—all reminded me of the plantation, and my own cruelly abused people.] Yet, *that* is the land of *Grattan,* of *Curran,* of *O'Connell,* and of *Sheridan.* [Now, while what I have said is true of the common people, the fact is, there are no more really handsome people in the world, than the educated Irish people. The Irishman educated, is a model gentleman; the Irishman ignorant and degraded, compares in form and feature, with the Negro!]

I am stating facts. If you go into Southern Indiana, you will see what climate and habit can do, even in one generation. The man may have come from New England, but his hard features, sallow complexion, have left little of New England on his brow. The right arm of the blacksmith is said to be larger and stronger than his left. The ship carpenter is at forty round shouldered. The shoemaker carries the marks of his trade. One locality becomes famous for one thing, another for another. Manchester and Lowell, in America, Manchester and Sheffield, in England, attest this. But what does it all prove? Why, nothing positively, as to the main point; still it raises the inquiry—May not the condition of men explain their various appearances? Need we go behind the vicissitudes of barbarism for an explanation of the gaunt, wiry, ape like appearance of some of the genuine Negroes? Need we look higher than a vertical sun, or lower than the damp, black soil of the Niger, the Gambia, the Senegal, with their heavy and enervating miasma, rising ever from the rank growing and decaying vegetation, for an explanation of the Negro's color? If a cause, full and adequate, can be found here, *why seek further?*

The Eminent Dr. *Latham,* already quoted, says that nine tenths of the white population of the globe are found between 30 and 65 degrees North latitude. Only about one fifth of all the inhabitants of the globe are white; and they are as far from the Adamic complexion as is the Negro. The remainder are—*what?* Ranging all the way from the brunette to jet black. There are the red, the reddish copper color, the yellowish, the dark brown, the chocolate color, and so on, to the jet black. On the mountains on the North of Africa, where water freezes in winter at times, branches of the same people who are *black* in the valley are *white* on the mountains. The Nubian, with his beautiful curly hair, finds it becoming frizzled, crisped, and even woolly, as he approaches the great Sahara. The Portuguese, white in Europe, is brown in Asia. The Jews, who are to be found in all countries, never intermarrying, are white in Europe, brown in Asia, and black in Africa. Again, what does it all prove? Nothing, absolutely; nothing which places the question beyond dispute; but it *does* justify the conjecture before referred to, that outward circumstances *may* have something to do with modifying the various phases of humanity; and that color itself is at the control of the world's climate and its various concomitants. It is the sun that paints the peach—and may it not be, that he paints the *man* as well? My reading, on this point, however, as well as my own observation, have convinced me, that from the beginning the Almighty, within certain limits, endowed mankind with organizations capable of countless variations in form, feature and color, without having it necessary to begin a new creation for every new variety.

A powerful argument in the favor of the oneness of the human family, is afforded in the fact that nations, however dissimilar, may be united in one social state, not only without detriment to each other, but, most clearly, to the advancement of human welfare, happiness and perfection. While it is clearly proved, on the other hand, that those nations freest from foreign elements, present the most evident marks of deterioration. Dr. JAMES McCUNE SMITH, himself a colored man, a gentleman and scholar, alleges—and not without excellent reason—that this, our own great nation, so distinguished for industry and enterprise, is largely indebted to its composite character. [We all know, at any rate, that now, what constitutes the very heart of the civilized world—(I allude to England)—has only risen from barbarism to its present lofty eminence, through successive invasions and alliances with her people.] The Medes and Persians constituted one of the mightiest empires that ever rocked the globe. The most terrible nation which now threatens the peace of the world, to make its will the law of Europe, is a grand piece of Mosaic work, in which almost every nation has its characteristic feature, from the wild Tartar to the refined Pole.

But, gentlemen, the time fails me, and I must bring these remarks to a close. My argument has swelled beyond its appointed measure. What I intended to make special, has become, in its progress, somewhat general. I meant to speak here to-day, for the lonely and the despised ones, with whom I was cradled, and with whom I have suffered; and now, gentlemen, in conclusion, what if all this reasoning be unsound? What if the Negro may not be able to prove his relationship to Nubians, Abyssinians and Egyptians? What if ingenious men are able to find plausible objections to all arguments maintaining the oneness of the human race? What, after all, if they are able to show very good reasons for believing the Negro to have been created precisely as we find him on the Gold Coast—along the Senegal and the Niger—I say, what of all this?—*"A man's a man for a' that."* I sincerely believe, that the weight of the argument is in favor of the unity of origin of the human race, or species—that the arguments on the other side are partial, superficial, utterly subversive of the happiness of man, and insulting to the wisdom of God. Yet, what if we grant they are not so? What, if we grant that the case, on our part, is not made out? Does it follow, that the Negro should be held in contempt? Does it follow, that to enslave and imbrute him is either *just* or *wise*? I think not. Human rights stand upon a common basis; and by all the reason that they are supported, maintained and defended, for one variety of the human family, they are supported, maintained and defended for *all* the human family; because all mankind have the same wants, arising out of a common nature. A diverse origin does not disprove a common nature, nor does it disprove a united destiny. The essential characteristics of humanity are everywhere the same. In the language of the eloquent *Curran,* "No matter what complexion, whether an Indian or an African sun has burnt upon him," his title deed to freedom, his claim to life and to liberty, to knowledge and to civilization, to society and to Christianity, are just and perfect. It is registered in the Courts of Heaven, and is enforced by the eloquence of the God of all the earth.

I have said that the Negro and white man are likely ever to remain the principal inhabitants of this country. I repeat the statement now, to submit the reasons that support it. The blacks can disappear from the face of the country by three ways. They may be colonized,—they may be exterminated,—or, they may die out. Colonization is out of the question; for I know not what hardships the laws of the land can impose, which can induce the colored citizen to leave his native soil. He was here in its infancy; he is here in its age. Two hundred years have passed over him, his tears and blood have been mixed with the soil, and his attachment to the place of his birth is stronger than iron. It is not probable that he will be exterminated; two considerations must prevent a crime so stupendous as that—the influence of Christianity on the one hand, and the power of self interest on the other; and, in regard to their dying out, the statistics of the country afford no encouragement for such a conjecture. The history of the Negro race proves them to be wonderfully adapted to all countries, all climates, and all conditions. Their tenacity of life, their powers of endurance, their malleable toughness, would almost imply especial interposition on their behalf. The ten thousand horrors of slavery, striking hard upon the sensitive soul, have bruised, and battered, and stung, but have not killed. The poor bondman lifts a smiling face above the surface of a sea of agonies, *hoping on, hoping ever.* His tawny brother, the Indian, dies, under the flashing glance of the Anglo Saxon. *Not* so the Negro; civilization cannot kill him. He accepts it—becomes a part of it. In the Church, he is an Uncle Tom, in the State, he is the most abused and least offensive. All the facts in his history mark out for him a destiny, united to America and Americans. Now, whether this population shall, by *Freedom, Industry, Virtue and Intelligence,* be made a blessing to the country and the world, or whether their multiplied wrongs shall kindle the vengeance of an offended God, will depend upon the conduct of no class of men so much as upon the Scholars of the country. The future public opinion of the land, whether anti-slavery or pro-slavery, whether just or unjust, whether magnanimous or mean, must redound to the honor of the Scholars of the country or cover them with shame. There is but one safe road for nations or for individuals. The fate of a wicked man and of a wicked nation is the same. The flaming sword of offended justice falls as certainly upon the nation as upon the man. God has no children whose rights may be safely trampled upon. The sparrow may not fall to the ground without the notice of His eye, and men are more than sparrows.

Now, gentlemen, I have done. The subject is before you. I shall not undertake to make the application. I speak as unto wise men. I stand in the presence of Scholars. We have met here to-day from vastly different points in the world's condition. I have reached here—if you will pardon the egotism—by little short of a miracle; at any rate, by dint of some application and perseverance. Born, as I was, in obscurity, a stranger to the halls of learning, environed by ignorance, degradation, and their concomitants, from birth to manhood, I do not feel at liberty to mark out, with any degree of confidence, or dogmatism, what is the precise vocation of the Scholar. Yet, this I *can* say, as a denizen of the world, and as a citizen of a country rolling in the sin and shame of Slavery, the most flagrant and scandalous that ever saw the sun, "Whatsoever things are true, whatsoever things are honest, whatsoever things are just, whatsoever things are pure, whatsoever things are lovely, whatsoever things are of good report, if there be any virtue, and if there be any praise, think on these things."

Pamphlet, Rochester, 1854

TO HON. GERRIT SMITH

Rochester, August 22, 1854

My dear Sir:

In this week's paper you will see that I ask your views on several points.[10] Do go into the matter there brought forward as fully as you can. I readily see that your point of look out, has been such during the session of Congress just closed, as to afford you special facilities for forming intelligent views on all the points respecting which I ask you to speak.

Knowing how completely your office has exposed you to the inflictions as well as the afflictions of correspondents, I have aimed to trouble you as little as possible. I wanted you to have all your precious time and strength for the great work in which you were engaged. I do not regret this prudence and hope you do not.

Now about your letter to your constituents: Laying aside all friendly partiality of which I am conscious, I pronounce it on every point except one an invulnerable and everyway satisfactory document. In every step of your Congressional movement, my heart and judgment have gone with you, except your remarks touching the annexation of Cuba.[11] Here I hesitated, and have finally come strongly to wish, such views were not yours. This much is due to frankness. You may ask why I have not said as much in my paper. I answer, I saw with shame and mortification deep and intense, that a swarm of hungry birds were picking at you, with no other apparent motive than to prove Gerrit Smith as weak as themselves. I did wish to show myself not of that class.

Some of this class of writers make you a great political sinner for resigning your seat in Congress.[12] What would have been lauded as highly democratic and magnanimous in others, is treachery and meanness in you. Giving up place and power at a point when that place was every hour becoming more honorable, and when that power was becoming more and more widely felt, should have given rise to other reflections than those with which you have been greeted. My dear Sir, while I do not see the wisdom of getting Cuba into the Union, with or without slavery, it is proper to say, that the avowal one way or the other, does not touch the anti-slavery integrity of any man. A warm personal friend of mine, Mr. Jennings of Cork, called on me this afternoon after having spent several months in Cuba, and told me that annexation would be an incalculable benefit to the slaves of Cuba. He instanced the terrible cruelties of slavery in Cuba, the enormous disproportion of males to females, the dreadful evils arising therefrom, and the total moral unfitness of the Cuban population to deal with the system of slavery. The entire absence of any thought there, of the sinfulness of slavery, made it, as he thought, desirable even to the slaves themselves to be brought under the American government. His argument made an impression on my mind at the time, but did not at all satisfy me that the slaves of Cuba would be better off, for being in this Union.

Always most truly yours,
Frederick Douglass

Gerrit Smith Papers, Syracuse University

OUR PLAN FOR MAKING KANSAS A FREE STATE

The momentous question, Shall Kansas be a Free State? continues to engage the thoughts, and to exercise the minds of the best friends of Freedom throughout the Republic. But we do not observe, among all the plans now submitted, having for their object the prevention of Slavery in that Eden-like country, one which we deem half so likely to accomplish that most desirable, and solemnly important object, as would be the one which we are now about to submit, were it but promptly put into execution.—This plan is, simply. the settlement, in the Kansas Territory, at the earliest possible period, a large and well-disciplined body of Free Colored People from the Northern States. There is nothing, confessedly, which slaveholders more dread than the presence of a numerous population of industrious, enlightened, and orderly Colored men—and just such a population as that, we believe, could be most easily flung into that much-coveted Territory.

Certain it is, that the Laws of the United States oppose no insurmountable barrier to settlements of that description. Even the infamous Nebraska Bill, mischievous in all its parts and particulars, has not closed this door against Colored Americans. The Homestead Bill, to be sure, denies them the rights of pre-emption.[18] But this injustice is so utterly base and scandalous, that we believe the common sense, honor and magnanimity of most of the white population of Kansas would render it inoperative and void. The Law permits a meanness which the honest people will not perpetrate. There is something so mean and so shocking about the crime of denying to a man the benefit of his own hard-earned improvements, that we doubt whether there is one in ten in the Territory who would possess the hardihood to commit the deed.

We say again, the coast is clear. Colored men, Colored Citizens—for such they really are—native born Citizens to boot, can emigrate to Kansas, and can safely occupy lands located therein. And the question is *Ought they not to do so?* We believe they ought to do so. Whether regarded from the point of duty to the Slave—its effect being to weaken the slave power—or from the point of duty to themselves—its effect being to increase their welfare, and to elevate their condition—*they ought to go* into that Territory as *permanent* settlers.

There is now no question, that Kansas is one of the finest countries in the world. The testimony on this point, from those who have resided there, and those who have traversed its fertile prairies, is uniform and conclusive. The climate, soil, and productions are precisely such as are adapted to develop the energies of Colored laborers, reared in the Middle and Northern States of the Union. To emigrate thither, is *far* better than to emigrate to Liberia, to the West Indies, or to Central America, and especially on account of its tendency to make Kansas a Free State. Let it be known, throughout the country, that one thousand Colored families, provided with all the needful implements of pioneers, and backed up by the moral influence of the Northern pepole, have taken up their abode in Kansas, and slaveholders, who are now bent upon blasting that fair land with Slavery, would shun it, as if it were infested by famine, pestilence, and earthquakes. They would stand as a wall of living fire to guard it. The true antidote, in that Territory, for *black slaves,* is an enlightened body of black freemen—and to that Territory should such freemen go.

To the question, Can this thing be accomplished? we answer—Yes! Three cities can, at once, be named, in which, if proper means be adopted, *nine hundred* of the *one thousand* families can be obtained in three months, who would take up their abode as permanent settlers in Kansas the coming spring. New York City and its vicinity could send three hundred families. Philadelphia and its vicinity would gladly spare three hundred families more. Cincinnati and vicinity could afford three hundred families for such a purpose; and Boston, with the aid of New England, could easily send the additional one hundred—making an army of One Thousand families. When once in Kansas, armed with spades, rakes and hoes, and other useful implements, they need not be driven out, without *"their own consent"*; and we doubt very much if any attempt would be made to dislodge them from their adopted homes. But, for fear of the worst, let one hundred families settle upon lands near the center of the Territory, and let the remaining nine hundred spread themselves out in a circle of twenty-five or fifty miles from the center; and let all go manfully and soberly to work, minding their own business, respecting the just rights of each other, and those of all settlers in the Territory, with whom they are brought in contact; and thus, we believe, Kansas may be secured for Liberty, without conflict, without bloodshed, and without Government interference. That the announcement of this plan, and the attempt to put it into execution, would call forth loud threats from the Lords of the lash may be expected. They have already threatened and resolved. They have talked of Bowie-knives and Revolvers; but to no purpose. Emigration is going on, and *will* go on. A principal recommendation of our plan, is, that it exactly meets the slaveholder on his own ground. The line of argument which establishes the right of the South to settle their black slaves in Kansas, is equally good for the North in establishing the right to settle black freemen in Kansas. The theory is, that the Territory acquired by the treasure of all the States, belongs alike and equally to all the States;—that the Missouri restriction was an odious, unjust, and unconstitutional discrimination against the South—not allowing such *Patriarchs* as Senator Badger to settle his black *Mammy* on Territory belonging as much to the *South,* as to the *North.*

Well! the South has repealed the restriction; and now, as they think, they occupy an equal footing with the Northern States, they can drive their scarred and fettered Negroes upon those fertile Prairies. The Law allows it, and the Court awards it.—What is done, is done. Repeal is out of the question. A platform on that single stick would not admit of foot-room for half a dozen. Since this is the case, if the North is wise, it will profit by the Southern argument. The Free States have as clear a right, certainly, to send into that Territory *black Freemen,* and to protect them there, as the Southern States have to send in black Slaves, and to hold them there. We should say to the South, Freedom is not less a Northern Institution, than Slavery is a Southern one; and since you have flung down the wall which separated the two, and have invited the conflict, Let it come, and God protect the Right!

We are not to listen to the argument that the settlement of Colored Freemen, virtually excludes the white slaveholder from the Territory of Kansas. Such an argument was addressed to the South, in behalf of the free, white working-man. They scouted it; and told the free, white working-man, if the presence of slaves offended him, he might keep *out* of the Territory. Very well; we avail ourselves again of a Southern argument; and we say, that, if the presence of *free* Negroes in Kansas is offensive to slaveholders, *let them keep out of it!*—that's all! "What is fair for the *Goose,* is fair for the *Gander!*" It is the boast of Douglas, that his Bill leaves Liberty and Slavery on terms of equality.

Again; when the day of election comes, and these people, with the other settlers of the territory, shall meet to determine what shall be the character of their institutions, we should like to see the argument based on the principle or doctrine of popular sovereignty[14] against their voting, and voting for whom they please. But even if debarred from voting, they would not be without influence, and there is no question on which side that influence would be wielded. The Nebraska bill says "every free white male inhabitant of the age of twenty-one years, who shall be an actual resident of said territory, and shall possess the qualifications hereinafter prescribed, shall be entitled to vote at the first election." This, of course, is entirely unconstitutional. For the Constitution of the United States makes no such discrimination on account of color in the exercise of any rights under it; and, deeming it so, the people might prefer to conform to the Constitution, at a point so important to popular sovereignty. We repeat that the Constitution of the United States makes no distinction among citizens on account of color, but says, "that the citizens of each State shall be entitled to all the privileges and immunities of citizens of the several States."

But again; while this otherwise wicked Nebraska bill mentions the kind of persons who may vote, it does not mention the sort who may not vote; at least it does not mention the color of the parties who shall not vote, but simply restricts the right *"of suffrage, and holding office, to citizens of the United States."* Now, under this, the public opinion of the neighborhood, agreeing thereto, the colored man might exercise the elective franchise at the very first election.—But whether voting or non-voting, their presence in the territory would, of itself, form a powerful barrier to the inflowing of a large slave and slaveholding population, and secure the territory to freedom and to free institutions.

But how shall we begin, (the South has already begun). Let an association of wealthy men be at once formed, having for its object the emigration of respectable free colored people to Kansas. Let them appoint two agents for each of the large cities named—men capable of inspiring confidence—and let the latter lay the subject of emigration to Kansas before the colored people, assuring such as are disposed to improve their fortunes by emigration, that they will be aided and protected in their rights in the territory. Let a fund be raised—say forty thousand dollars—(it will be a grand, benevolent investment)—to all such as are too poor to undertake the journey upon their own means. The first hundred families could soon be raised and put on their way; and the second and third would soon follow, and so on to the end of the chapter. Let the press of the North take hold of this idea and press it upon the public mind, and Kansas need not be a slave State, and your cities need not have an unequal share of the free colored people of the North. Meanwhile, let white free working men flock into the territory by thousands. There is room and work for all. Will the people of the North aid such a movement as is here contemplated? We believe they will, and will do so joyfully.—Those who are themselves going to Kansas may not have time or attention to bestow upon the plan for colonizing colored men in Kansas, but there are hundreds of thousands who, while they cannot go themselves, still look with the deepest interest upon that territory, and feel an abiding concern for the possible results of the struggle now going on with regard to its future character and destiny. Among these thousands are men of mind, and men of money, and men of heart. These men will give time, money, talents, influence, and dignity to the enterprise. The work to be done is to launch it; set it in motion. Get it once before the people, once on the waves of public opinion, and it will float itself. We broach the idea, and so much (very little we know) is done. We leave others to do the rest, promising, however, to lend a hand, a pen, a voice, or anything else we possess, to make the plan successful.

If it be said that there are all-sufficient means in operation to keep slavery out of Kansas, the answer is, slavery is already there—and there is reason to believe that while many good and true men are going to that territory who can neither be frightened nor bought into supporting slavery, there are others quite of a different stamp. Congress is not the only place to find doughfaces.—They are among the peoples as well as among the peoples' representatives; and some may seek to better their fortunes by availing themselves of the emigration societies now scattered over the country. Besides, the Southern slaveholders are generally hard to beat. When they set about an enterprise for slavery, they are "*dreadfully*" apt to succeed. It is, therefore, unwise in a conflict like this, where so much is at stake, and where the right is so clearly on our side, to omit any effort or neglect any plan to secure a victory for freedom—a victory which may decide the whole controversy with slavery forever.

We call now for judgment upon this plan. It is imperfectly presented, we know. The wise heads of the press may improve upon it; we ask that it be considered and tried.—We make no apology for the heading we have seen fit to put to this article. Stephen A. Douglas has given his plan for getting slavery into Kansas; and we see not why Frederick Douglass should not submit his plan for keeping slavery out of Kansas.

Friends of Freedom! what say you to meeting the enemy on this vantage ground? You can meet them and beat them in the way here indicated; and if you do not do it, the responsibility is yours.

Frederick Douglass' Paper, September 15, 1854

THE KANSAS-NEBRASKA BILL, speech at Chicago, October 30, 1854

Friends and Fellow Citizens:

A great national question, a question of transcendent importance—one upon which the public mind is deeply moved, and not my humble name—has assembled this multitude of eager listeners in Metropolitan Hall this evening. You have come up here in obedience to a humane and patriotic impulse, to consider of the requirements of patriotism and humanity, at an important crisis in the affairs of this nation.

In this patriotic and holy purpose, I hail your presence here with grateful, sincere, and heart-felt pleasure. I am anxious to address you on the great subject which has called you together—and will do so—but circumstances will justify me in saying a few words first of a personal nature.

I have the misfortune of being deemed an intruder by some of your fellow citizens.—My visit among you is thought to be untimely, and to savor of impudence, and the like. Upon this matter I have a word to say in my own defence. A man that will not defend himself is not fit to defend a good cause.

And first, ladies and gentlemen, I am not sure that a visit on my part to Chicago would at any time afford those who are now complaining of me any special pleasure. But, gentlemen, I am not ashamed of being called an intruder. I have met it a thousand times in a thousand different places, and I am quite prepared to meet it now—and here, as I have met it, at other times and in other places.

Every inch of ground occupied by the colored man in this country is sternly disputed. At the ballot box and at the altar—in the church and in the State—he is deemed an intruder. He is, in fact, seldom a welcome visitor anywhere. Marvel not, therefore, if I seem somewhat used to the charge of intrusiveness, and am not more embarrassed in meeting it. Men have been known to get used to conditions and objects which, at the first, seemed utterly repulsive and insufferable. And so may I.

One reason why I am not ashamed to be here is this: I have a right to be here and a duty to perform here. That right is a constitutional right, as well as a natural right. It belongs to every citizen of the United States. It belongs not less to the humblest than to the most exalted citizens. The genius of American institutions knows no privileged class or classes. The plebian and the (would be) patrician stand here upon a common level of equality, and the last man in the world who should complain of this is the earnest advocate of popular sovereignty.

I have a right to come into this State to prosecute any lawful business in a lawful manner. This is a natural right, and is a part of the supreme law of the land. By that law the citizens of each state are the citizens of the United States, with rights alike and equal in all the States. The only question of right connected with my case here respects my citizenship. If I am a citizen, I am clothed all over with the star spangled banner and defended by the American Constitution, in every State of the American Union. That constitution knows no man by the color of his skin. The men who made it were too noble for any such limitation of humanity and human rights. The word white is a modern term in the legislation of this country. It was never used in the better days of the Republic, but has sprung up within the period of our national degeneracy.

I claim to be an American citizen. The constitution knows but two classes: Firstly, citizens, and secondly, aliens. I am not an alien; and I am, therefore, a citizen. I am moreover a free citizen. Free, thank God, not only by the law of the State in which I was born and brought up but free by the laws of nature.

In the State of New York where I live, I am a citizen and a legal voter, and may therefore be presumed to be a citizen of the United States. I am here simply as an American citizen, having a stake in the weal or woe of the nation, in common with other citizens. I am not even here as an agent of any sect or party. Parties are too politic and sects are too sectarian, to select one of my odious class, and of my radical opinions, at this important time and place, to represent them. Nevertheless, I do not stand alone here. There are noble minded men in Illinois who are neither ashamed of their cause nor their company. Some of them are here tonight, and I expect to meet with them in every part of the State where I may travel. But, I pray, hold no man or party responsible for my words, for I am no man's agent; and I am no parties' agent; and I beg that my respected friends—the reporters—will be good enough to make a note of that. I have a very good reason for making this request—a reason which I may some day give to the world, but which I need not give now.

One other remark; and it shall be in regard to a matter about which you wish to hear at once. It touches the matter involved on my mission here. I wish not only to stand within my rights as a man, but to stand approved at the bar of propriety as a gentleman, when, as in this case, I can do so without the sacrifice of principle. It has been given out, I believe, by some friends and also by some of the enemies of the principles I am here to sustain that I have come into this State to confront in public debate, my distinguished namesake, the Hon. Stephen A. Douglas.

Fellow citizens, I wish to disclaim so much of this report as can possibly imply the slightest disrespect for the talents of your honorable Senator. His fame as an orator, and as a man of energy and perseverence, has not risen higher anywhere than in my own judgment. He is a man of the people. He came up from among them, and that by the native energy of his character and his manly industry. I am ever pleased to see a man rise from among the people. Every such man is prophetic of the good time coming. I have watched him during the past winter, when apparently overwhelmed with learning and eloquence, rise again, and with more than the tact and skill of a veteran, drive all before him. There is perhaps something in a name, and that may possibly explain the peculiar interest with which I have watched and contemplated the fortune of Mr. S. A. Douglas.

This feeling, I think, you will admit, is quite natural. No man likes to read in a newspaper of the hanging of a man bearing his own name.[15]

On the other hand, no man bearing the name of Douglas, would think less of his name, if this great nation should, in the abundance of goodness be pleased to place that name in the scroll of its Presidents; and this, notwithstanding the trite saying, that a rose by any other name would smell as sweet.

But the times, the times bid us to have done with names. Names have lost their significance, in more ways than one—deeds, not words, are the order of the day; names are valued so long as they are associated with honor, justice and liberty; and become execrable when associated with falsehood, treachery and tyranny?

It is alleged that I am come to this State to insult Senator Douglas. Among gentlemen, that is only an insult which is intended to be such, and I disavow all such intention. I am not even here with the desire to meet in public debate, that gentleman. I am here precisely as I was in this State one year ago—with no other change in my relations to you, or to the great question of human freedom, than time and circumstances have brought about. I shall deal with the subject in the same spirit now as then; approving such men and such measures as I look to the security of liberty in the land and with my whole heart condemning all men and measures as serve to subvert or endanger it.

If Hon. S. A. Douglas, your beloved and highly gifted Senator, has designedly, or through mistaken notions of public policy ranged himself, on the side of oppressors and the deadliest enemies of liberty, I know of no reason, either in this world or any other world, which should prevent me, or prevent any one else, from thinking so, or from saying so.

The people in whose cause I come here to-night, are not among those whose right to regulate their own domestic concerns, is so feelingly and eloquently contended for in certain quarters. They have no Stephen Arnold Douglas—no Gen. Cass, to contend at North Market Hall for their Popular Sovereignty. They have no national purse—no offices, no reputation, with which to corrupt Congress, or to tempt men, mighty in eloquence and influence into their service. Oh, no! They have nothing to commend them but their unadorned humanity. They are human—that's all—only human. Nature owns them as human—God owns them as human; but men own them as property!—Every right of human nature, as such, is denied them—they are dumb in their chains! To utter one groan, or scream, for freedom in the presence of the Southern advocate of Popular Sovereignty, is to bring down the frightful lash upon their quivering flesh. I knew this suffering people; I am acquainted with their sorrows; I am one with them in experience; I have felt the lash of the slave driver, and stand up here with all the bitter recollections of its horrors vividly upon me.

There are special reasons, therefore, why I should speak and speak freely. The right of speech is a very precious one, especially to the oppressed.

I understand that Mr. Douglas regards himself as the most abused man in the United States and that the greatest outrage ever committed upon him, was in the case in which your indignation raised your voices so high that his could not be heard. No personal violence, as I understand, was offered him. It seems to have been a trial of vocal powers between the individual and the multitude; as might have been expected, the voice of one man was not equal in volume to the voice of five hundred.

I do not mention this circumstance to approve it; I do not approve it; I am for free speech as well as for freemen and free soil; but how ineffably insignificant is this wrong done in a single instance, and to a single individual, compared with the stupendous iniquity perpetrated against more than three millions of the American people, who are struck dumb by the very men in whose cause Mr. Senator Douglas was here to plead. While I would not approve the silencing of Mr. Douglas, may we not hope that this slight abridgment of his rights may lead him to respect in some degree the rights of other men, as good in the eyes of Heaven, as himself.

Let us now consider the great question of the age; the only great national question which seriously agitates the public mind at this hour. It is called the vexed question; and excites alarm in every quarter of the country.

Efforts have been made to set it at rest.—Statesmen, and political parties, and churches have exerted themselves to settle it forever. They sought to bind it with cords; to resist it with revolutions, and bury it under platforms; but all to no purpose. The waves of the ocean still roll, and the earthquakes still shake the earth, and men's hearts still fail them for fear of those judgments which threaten to come upon the land.

Fellow Citizens: some things are settled, and settled forever—not by the laws of man, but by the laws of God; by the constitution of mankind; by the relations of things and by the facts of human experience.

It is, I think, pretty well settled, that liberty and slavery cannot dwell in the United States in peaceful relations; the history of the last five and twenty years settles that.

It is pretty well settled, too, that one or the other of these must go to the wall. The South must either give up slavery, or the North must give up liberty. The two interests are hostile, and are irreconcilable.—The just demands of liberty are inconsistent with the overgrown exactions of the slave power.

There is not a single tendency of slavery but is adverse to freedom. The one is adapted to progress, to industry, and to dignify industry. Slavery is anti-progressive—sets a premium on idleness, and degrades both labor and laborers. The fetters on the limbs of the slave, to be secure, must be accompanied with fetters on society as well. A free press and a free gospel, are as hostile as fire and gunpowder—separation or explosion, are the only alternatives.

No people in this country better understand this peculiarity than the slaveholders themselves. Hence the repeated violations of your Post Office laws in Southern towns and cities; hence the expurgations of Northern literature, and the barbarous outrages committed upon the persons of Northern travellers in the Southern States. Light and love, justice and mercy, must be guarded against in a community where the cruel lash is the law, and human lust is religion.

For a long time, it has been seen that the ideas and institutions of liberty, if allowed their natural course, would finally overthrow slavery.

That slaveholders themselves would after a while come to loathe it.

Selfishness combined with this knowledge has at length ultimated into the formation of a party, ranged under the very taking appellation of National—the greatest business of which is to hold at bay, and restrain, and if possible to extinguish in the heart of this great nation every sentiment supposed to be at variance with the safety of slavery.

This party has arisen out of the teachings of that great man of perverted faculties, the late John C. Calhoun. No man of the nation has left a broader or a blacker mark on the politics of the nation, than he. In the eye of Mr. Calhoun every right guaranteed by the American constitution, must be held in subordination to slavery. It was he who first boldly declared the self-evident truths of the declaration of independence, self-evident falsehoods.[16] He has been followed in this by Mr. Benton D. D. from Indiana.

The very spirit of Mr. Calhoun animates the slavery party of to-day. His principles are its principles, and his philosophy its philosophy. He looked upon slavery as the great American interest. The slavery party of to-day so esteem it. To preserve it, shield it, and support it, is its constant duty, and the object and aim of all its exertions. With this party the right of free men, free labor, and a free north are nothing. Daniel Webster never said a truer word than at Marshfield, in '48—"Why the North? There is no North!" But there is a South and ever has been a South controlling both parties, at every period of their existence.

The grand inauguration of this slavery party took place in the Summer of 1852.—That party was represented in both the great parties; and demanded as a condition of their very existence, that they should give their solemn endorsement, as a finality to the compromise measures of 1850. Abhorrent as were its demands, and arrogant and repulsive as was its manner of pressing them—that party was obeyed. Both conventions took upon them the mark of the beast; and called upon the whole North to do the same.—The Democratic party consented to be branded thus:

"That Congress has no power, under the constitution, to interfere with, or control the domestic institutions of the several States; and that such States are the sole and proper judges of everything appertaining to their own affairs, not prohibited by the constitution—that all efforts of the Abolitionists or others to induce Congress to interfere with the question of slavery, or to take incipient steps in relation thereto, are calculated to lead to the most alarming and dangerous consequences; and that all such efforts have an inevitable tendency to diminish the happiness of the people, and endanger the stability and permanency of the Union; and ought not to be countenanced by any friend of our political institution.

"*Resolved,* That the foregoing proposition covers and was intended to embrace the whole subject of the slavery agitation in Congress; and, therefore, the Democratic party of this Union, standing on this National platform, will abide by, and adhere to a faithful execution of the acts known as the compromise measures, settled by the last Congress—the act for reclaiming fugitives from service or labor included, which act being decided to carry out an express provision of the constitution, cannot, with fidelity, be repealed or be changed as to destroy or impair its efficacy.

"*Resolved,* That the Democratic party will resist all attempts at renewing, in Congress or out of it, the agitation of the slavery question, under whatever shape or color the attempt may be made."

Gentlemen: Such was the Democratic *mark,* and such was the Democratic *pledge.* It was taken in sight of all the nation, and in the sight of God, only two years ago. Has it kept that pledge? Does it stand acquitted to-day at the bar of public honor? or does it stand forth black with perfidy towards the North, while it wallows in the mire of deeper servility to the South? Has the Democratic party a single claim on your confidence, more than any notorious liar would have upon your credulity? Can you believe in a party that keeps its word, only as it has no temptation to break it? Is there a single man that can pretend to say that the Democrats —the Baltimore platform Democrats, have been true to their solemn declarations? Have they not renewed, and, in a manner to peril the cause of liberty—the agitation of slavery, which they solemnly promised to resist? Do you say they have not? Then there is no longer an intelligible proposition in the English language—nor is it possible to frame one.

But let me read to you the resolution imposed on the Whig National Convention, as the vital condition of its existence; and which was given to the world as the faith of that great organization, touching the matter of slavery. Here it is:

"That the series of acts, of the 31st Congress, known as the compromise, including the fugitive slave act, are received and acquiesced in by the Whig party of the United States, as a final settlement, in principle and substance, of the dangerous and exciting subjects which they embrace; and so far as the fugitive slave law is concerned, we will maintain the same, and insist upon its strict enforcement, until time and experience shall demonstrate the necessity of further legislation to guard against the evasion of the laws on the one hand, and the abuse of their powers on the other—not impairing their present efficacy—and deprecate all further agitation of the questions thus settled, as dangerous to our peace; and we will discountenance a continuance or renewal of such agitation, whenever, wherever, or however, the attempt may be made; and we will maintain this system as essential to the nationality of the Whig party, and the integrity of the Union."

Now, fellow-citizens: In those platforms, and in the events which have since transpired, it is easy to read the designs of the slave power. Something is gained when the plans and purposes of an enemy are discovered.

I understand the first purpose of the slave power to be the suppression of all anti-slavery discussion. Next, the extension of slavery over all the territories. Next, the nationalizing of slavery, and to make slavery respected in every State in the Union.

First, the right of speech is assailed, and both parties pledge themselves to put it down. When parties make platforms, they are presumed to put nothing into them, which, if need be, they may not organize into law. These parties on this presumption, are pledged to put down free discussion by law—to make it an offence against the law to speak, write, and publish against slavery, here in the free States, just as it now is an offence against the law to do so in the slave States. One end of the slave's chain must be fastened to a padlock in the lips of Northern freemen, else the slave will himself become free.

Now, gentlemen, are you ready for this?—Are you ready to give up the right of speech, and suppress every human and Christ-inspired sentiment, lest the conscience of the guilty be disturbed?

Our parties have attempted to give peace to slaveholders. They have attempted to do what God has made impossible to be done; and that is to give peace to slaveholders.—"There is no peace to the wicked, saith my God." In the breast of every slaveholder, God has placed, or stationed an anti-slavery lecturer, whose cry is *guilty,* guilty, guilty; "thou art verily guilty concerning thy brother."

But now let me come to the points of this great question which touch us most nearly to-night.

I take the case to be this: The citizens of this State are now appealed to, to give their sanction to the repeal of the law, by which slavery has been, during a period of thirty four years, restricted to the south of 36 deg. 30 min. of north latitude, in the territory acquired by the purchase of Louisiana.

This is but a simple and truthful statement of the real question.

The question is not, whether "popular sovereignty" is the true doctrine for the territories—it is not whether the chief agents in the repeal of that line, acted from good or bad motives; nor is it whether they are able or feeble men.

These are points of very little consequence in determining the path of duty in this case.

When principles are at stake, persons are of small account; and the safety of a Republic is found in a rigid adherence to principles. Once give up these, and you are a ship in a storm, without anchor or rudder.

Fellow-Citizens: The proposition to repeal the Missouri Compromise, was a stunning one. It fell upon the nation like a bolt from a cloudless sky. The thing was too startling for belief. You believed in the South, and you believed in the North; and you knew that the repeal of the Missouri Compromise was a breach of honor; and, therefore, you said the thing could not be done. Besides, both parties had pledged themselves directly, positively and solemnly against re-opening in Congress the agitation on the subject of slavery; and the President himself had declared his intention to maintain the national quiet. Upon those assurances you rested, and rested fatally.

But you should have learned long ago that "men do not gather grapes of thorns, nor figs of thistles." It is folly to put faith in men who have broken faith with God. When a man has brought himself to enslave a child of God, to put fetters on his brother, he has qualified himself to to disregard the most sacred of compacts—beneath the sky there is nothing more sacred than man, and nothing can be properly respected when manhood is despised and trampled upon. Now let us attend to the defence made before the people by the advocates of the Kansas-Nebraska bill.

They tell us that the bill does not open the Territories to slavery, and complain that they are misrepresented and slandered by those charging them with flinging open the Territories to slavery. I wish to slander no man. I wish to misrepresent no man. They point us to the bill itself as proof that no such opening of the Territories to slavery is contemplated, or intended by it. I will read to you from the bill itself, to see what is relied upon at this point:

"It being the true intent and meaning of this act not to legislate slavery into any Territory or State; *nor to exclude it therefrom,* but to leave the people thereof perfectly free to form and regulate their domestic institutions in their own way; subject only to the constitution of the United States."

One part of this declaration is true and carries the evidence of its truth on its face. It is true that it is no part of the true intent and meaning of the act to exclude slavery from any Territory or State. If its true intent and meaning had been otherwise, it would not have repealed the law, the only law, which had excluded slavery from those territories, and from those States which may be formed out of them. I repeat, this part of the bill needs no explanation. It is plain enough already. There is not a slave-holder in the land, however ardent an advocate of slavery extension he may be, who has ever complained that the true intent and meaning of the Kansas-Nebraska bill was to exclude slavery from the territories in question, or from any States which might be formed out of them. Slaveholders do not so understand the bill. Had they so understood it, they would never have gone in a *body* to sustain the bill. It is very significant that on this part of this "stump speech" in the declaration, the country is agreed, everybody understanding it alike, while on the other hand, the words in the bill, directly preceding it, are the subject of controversy. Why is this so? You are told that it is owing to the perversity of man's understanding. But this is not the answer. I will tell you why it is. The people, like the old rat, do not deny that the white dust they see here is meal—real and genuine meal—but under the meal they detect the treacherous form of the cat. Under that smooth exterior there are the sharp teeth and destructive claws, and hence they avoid, shun and detest it.

But again: it is claimed that the Nebraska bill does not open the territories to Slavery for another reason. It is said that Slavery is the creature of positive law, and that it can only exist where it is sustained by positive law—that neither in Kansas nor in Nebraska is there any law establishing Slavery, and that, therefore, the moment a slaveholder carries his slaves into those Territories they are free, and restored to the rights of human nature. This is the ground taken by General Cass. He contended for it in the North Market Hall, with much eloquence and skill. I thought, while I was hearing him on this point, that slaveholders would not be likely to thank him for the argument. Theoretically the argument is good, practically the argument is bad. It is not true that slavery cannot exist without being established by positive law. On the contrary, the instance cannot be shown where a law was ever made establishing slavery, where the relation of master and slave did not previously exist. The law is always an aftercoming consideration. Wicked men first overpower, and subdue their fellow-men to slavery, and then call in the law to sanction the deed.

Even in the slave States of America, slavery has never been established by positive law. It was not so established under the colonial charters of the original States, nor the constitution of the States. It is now, and always has been, a system of lawless violence.

On this proposition, I hold myself ready and willing to meet any defender of the Nebraska bill. I would not even hesitate to meet the author of that bill himself. I insist upon it that the very basis upon which this bill is defended, is utterly and entirely false as applied to the practice of slavery in this country. The South itself scouts the theory of Messrs. Douglas and Cass at this point, and esteem it simply as a gull-trap in which to catch the simple. They look upon it simply as a piece of plausible stump oratory, and censure it as such. But that slavery is not the tame creature of law, as alleged, I will not rely solely on my own declaration.

Senator Mason, of Virginia, the author of the Fugitive Slave bill, and one of the most influential members of the American Senate, during the debate on the Fugitive Slave bill in 1850, scouted such a basis for slavery, and confessed that no such existed. He said, and I quote his own words:

"Then again, it is proposed (by one of the opponents of the bill) as a part of the proof to be adduced at the hearing after the fugitive has been recaptured, that evidence shall be brought by the claimant to show that slavery is established in the State from whence the fugitive has absconded. Now, this very thing, in a recent case in the city of New York, was required by one of the judges of that State, which case attracted the attention of the authorities of Maryland, and against which they protested, because of the indignities heaped upon their citizens, and the losses which they sustained in that city. In that case, the Judge of the State Court required proof that slavery was established in Maryland, and went so far as to say that the only mode of proving it was by reference to the statute book. Such proof is required in the Senator's amendment; and if he means by this that proof shall be brought that slavery is established by existing laws, it is impossible to comply with the requisition, for no such proof can be produced, I apprehend, in any of the slave States. *I am not aware that there is a single State in which the institution is established by positive law.* On a former occasion, and on a different topic, it was my duty to endeavor to show to the Senate that no such law was necessary for its establishment; certainly none could be found, and none was required in any of the States of the Union."

There you have it. It cannot be shown that slavery is established by law even in the slaveholding States. But slavery exists there—and so may it exist in Nebraska and in Kansas—and I had almost said that this is well known to the very men who are now trying to persuade the people of the north that it cannot.

But there is another defence set up for the repeal of the Missouri restriction. It is said to be a patriotic defence, supported by patriotic reasons. It is the defence which Senator Douglas uses with much effect wherever he goes.

He says he wants no broad black line across this continent. Such a line is odious and begets unkind feelings between the citizens of a common country.

Now, fellow-citizens, why is the line of thirty-six degrees thirty minutes, a broad black line? What is it that entitles it to be called a *black line?* It is the fashion to call whatever is odious in this country, black.—You call the Devil black—and he may be, but what is there in the line of thirty-six degrees thirty minutes, which makes it blacker than the line which separates Illinois from Missouri, or Michigan from Indiana? I can see nothing in the line itself which should make it black or odious. It is a line, that's all.

If it is black, black and odious, it must be so not because it is a line, but because of the things it separates.

If it keeps asunder what God has joined together—or separates what God intended should be fused—then it may be called an odious line, a black line; but if on the other hand, it marks only a distinction—natural and eternal—a distinction, fixed in the nature of things by the Eternal God, then I say, withered be the arm and blasted be the hand that would blot it out.

But we are told that the people of the North were originally opposed to that line, that they burnt in effigy the men from the North who voted for it, and that it comes with a bad grace from the North now to oppose its repeal.

Fellow-citizens, this may do in the Barroom. It may answer somewhere outside of where the moon rises, but it won't do among men of intelligence.

Why did the North condemn the Missouri line? This it was: they believed that it gave slavery an advantage to which slavery had no right.

By establishing the Missouri Compromise line, slavery got all south of it. By repealing that line it may get all north of it. Now are any so blind as not to see that the same reasons for opposing the original line, are good against repeal.

Allow me to illustrate. Thirty-four years ago, a man succeeds in getting a decision unjustly, by which he comes in possession of one half of your farm. You protest against that decision, and say it is corrupt. But the man does not heed your protests. He builds his house upon it, and fences in his lands and warns you to keep off his premises. You cannot help yourself. You live by his side thirty-four years. You have lost the means of regaining your lost property. But just at this time there comes a new Judge, a Daniel, a very Daniel, and he reverses so much of the judgment by which you lost the first half of your farm, and makes another decision by which you may lose the other half.

You meekly protest against this new swindle. When the Judge in question, with great affectation of impartiality, denounces you as very difficult to please, and as flagrantly inconsistent.

Such, gentlemen, is the plain and simple truth in the matter.

By the Missouri Compromise, slavery—an alien to the Republic, and enemy to every principle of free Institutions, and having no right to exist anywhere—got one half of a territory rightfully belonging to Freedom.— You complained of that. Now a law is repealed whereby you may lose the other half also, and you are forbidden to complain.

But hear again:

It is said with much adroitness by the advocates of the Nebraska bill, that we are unnecessarily solicitous for the rights of Negroes, that if the people of the territories can be trusted to make laws for white men, they may be safely left to make laws for black men.

Now, gentlemen, this is a favorite point of the author of the Nebraska bill. Under its fair seeming front, is an appeal to all that is mean, cowardly, and vindictive in the breast of the white public. It implies that the opponents of the Nebraska bill feel a deeper concern for the Negroes as such, than for white men, that we are unnaturally sensitive to rights of the blacks, and unnaturally indifferent to the rights of the whites.

With such an unworthy implication on its face, I brand it as a mean, wicked and bitter appeal to Popular Prejudice, against a people wholly defenceless, and at the mercy of the public.

The argument of Senator Douglas at this point, assumes the absurd position that a slaveholding people will be as careful of the rights of their black slaves as they are of their own. They might as well say that wolves may be trusted to legislate for themselves, and why not for lambs, as to say that slaveholders may do so for themselves, and why not for their slaves?

Shame on the miserable sophistry, and shame on the spirit that prompted its utterance! There is nothing manly or honorable in either. Take another specimen of senatorial logic; a piece of the same roll to which I have just referred.

Senator Douglas tells you, that the people may be as safely left to make laws respecting slavery, as to regulate theft, robbery, or murder. Very well—so they may. There is no doubt about that; but as usual, the Hon. Senator fails to bring out the whole truth.—To bring out the whole truth here, is to cover him with shame.

To put the matter in its true light, let us suppose that in the Southern States of this Union, the people are so benighted as to practice and support "theft," "robbery," and "murder," but that in the other States that practice is loathed and abhorred.

Suppose, also, that up to a certain line in a territory belonging alike and equally to all the States, these wicked practices were prohibited by law; and then, suppose a grave Senator from a State where theft, robbery and murder are looked upon with horror, rising in his place in the national legislature and moving to repeal the line excluding "theft," "robbery" and "murder," and demanding that "theft," "robbery" and "murder," be placed upon the same footing with honesty, uprightness and innocence.—I say, suppose this, and you have a parallel to the conduct of Senator Douglas, in repealing the line of 36 deg. 30 min.

But the grand argument, and the one which seems to be relied upon as unanswerable and overwhelming, is this: The people of the territories are American citizens, and carry with them the right of self-government; that this Nebraska bill is based upon this great American principle of Popular Sovereignty, and that to oppose this principle, is to act as did King George towards the American colonies.

Let me answer this argument. It may not need an answer here in Chicago, for it has been answered here, and answered well.—Nevertheless, let me answer it again, and prove by the bill itself, that it is a stupendous shame with every motive to deceive without the power.

What is meant by Popular Sovereignty?—It is the right of the people to establish a government for themselves, as against all others. Such was its meaning in the days of the revolution. It is the independent right of a people to make their own laws, without dictation or interference from any quarter. A sovereign subject is a contradiction in terms, and is an absurdity. When sovereignty becomes subject, it ceases to be sovereignty. When what was future becomes the present, it ceases to be the future— and so with sovereignty and subjection, they cannot exist at the same time in the same place, any more than an event can be future and present at the same time. This much is clear.

Now the question is, does the Kansas-Nebraska bill give to the people of these territories the sovereign right to govern themselves? Is there a man here who will say that it does?

The author of the bill, in his stump speeches in the country, says that it does; and some men think the statement correct. But what say you, who have read the bill?

Nothing could be further from the truth, than to say that Popular Sovereignty is accorded to the people who may settle the territories of Kansas and Nebraska.

The three great cardinal powers of government are the Executive, Legislative and Judicial. Are these powers secured to the people of Kansas and Nebraska?

That bill places the people of that territory as completely under the powers of the federal government as Canada is under the British crown. By this Kansas-Nebraska bill the federal government has the substance of all governing power, while the people have the shadow. The judicial power of the territories is not from the people of the territories, who are so bathed in the sunlight of popular sovereignty by stump eloquence, but from the federal government.—The executive power of the territories derives its existence not from the overflowing fountain of popular sovereignty, but from the federal government. The Secretaries of the territories are not appointed by the sovereign people of the territories, but are appointed independently of popular sovereignty.

But is there nothing in this bill which justifies the supposition that it contains the principle of popular sovereignty? No, not one word. Even the territorial councils, elected, not by the people who may settle in the territories, but by only certain descriptions of people are subject to a double veto power, vested first in a governor, which they did not elect, and second in the President of the United States. The only shadow of popular sovereignty is the power given to the people of the territories by this bill to have, hold, buy and sell human beings. The sovereign right to make slaves of their fellowmen if they choose is the only sovereignty that the bill secures.

In all else, popular sovereignty means only what the boy meant when he said he was going to live with his uncle Robert. He said he was going there, and that he meant while there, to do just as he pleased, if his uncle Robert would let him!

I repeat, that the only seeming concession to the idea of popular sovereignty in this bill is authority to enslave men, and to concede that right or authority is a hell black denial of popular sovereignty itself.

Whence does popular sovereignty take rise? What and where is its basis? I should really like to hear from the author of the Nebraska bill, a philosophical theory, of the nature and origin of popular sovereignty. I wonder where he would begin, how he would proceed and where he would end.

The only intelligible principle on which popular sovereignty is founded, is found in the Declaration of American Independence, there and in these words: We hold these truths to be self-evident, that all men are created equal and are endowed by their Creator with the right of life, liberty and the pursuit of happiness.

The right of each man to life, liberty and the pursuit of happiness, is the basis of all social and political right, and, therefore, how brass-fronted and shameless is that impudence, which while it aims to rob men of their liberty, and to deprive them of the right to the pursuit of happiness—screams itself hoarse to the words of popular sovereignty.

But again: This bill, this Nebraska bill, gives to the people of the territories the right to hold slaves. Where did this bill get this right, which it so generously gives away? Did it get it from Hon. Stephen A. Douglas? Then I demand where he got that right?—Who gave it to him? Was he born with it? Or has he acquired it by some noble action? I repeat, how came he by it, or with it, or to have it? Did the people of this State, from whom he derived his political and legislative life, give him this right, the right to make slaves of men? Had he any such right?

The answer is, he had not. He is in the condition of a man who has given away that which is not his own.

But it may be said that Congress has the right to allow the people of the territories to hold slaves.

The answer is, that Congress is made up of men, and possesses only the rights of men, and unless it can be shown, that some men have a right to hold their fellow-men as property, Congress has no such right.

There is not a man within the sound of my voice, who has not as good a right to enslave a brother man, as Congress has. This will not be denied even by slaveholders.

Then I put the question to you, each of you, all of you, have you any such right?

To admit such a right is to charge God with folly, to substitute anarchy for order, and to turn earth into a hell. And you know it.

Now, friends and fellow-citizens, I am uttering no new sentiments at this point, and am making no new argument. In this respect there is nothing new under the sun.

Error may be new or it may be old, since it is founded in a misapprehension of what truth is. It has its beginnings and has its endings. But not so with truth. Truth is eternal. Like the great God from whose throne it emanates, it is from everlasting unto everlasting, and can never pass away.

Such a truth is man's right to freedom.—He was born with it. It was his before he comprehended it. The title deed to it is written by the Almighty on his heart, and the record of it is in the bosom of the eternal —and never can Stephen A. Douglas efface it unless he can tear from the great heart of God this truth. And this mighty government of ours will never be at peace with God until it shall, practically and universally, embrace this great truth as the foundation of all its institutions, and the rule of its entire administration.

Now, gentlemen, I have done. I have no fear for the ultimate triumph of free principles in this country. The signs of the times are propitious. Victories have been won by slavery, but they have never been won against the onward march of anti-slavery principles. The progress of these principles has been constant, steady, strong and certain. Every victory won by slavery has had the effect to fling our principles more widely and favorably among the people.—The annexation of Texas—the Florida war— the war with Mexico—the compromise measures and the repeal of the Missouri Compromise, have all signally vindicated the wisdom of that great God, who has promised to overrule the wickedness of men for His own glory—to confound the wisdom of the crafty and bring to naught the counsels of the ungodly.

Frederick Douglass' Paper, November 24, 1854

THE ANTI-SLAVERY MOVEMENT, lecture delivered before the
Rochester Ladies' Anti-Slavery Society, January, 1855

Ladies and Gentlemen:

Had I consulted my own health, or the advice of my physician, I
should have been elsewhere, and otherwise employed this evening. I am
not well, and have not been so for several weeks. I have usually come to
this platform to lecture on slavery—that darkest and hugest of all wrongs
—the vilest (in the language of John Wesley) that ever saw the sun. But
it has pleased the Rochester Ladies' Anti-Slavery Society to have presented
here, during the winter, almost every phase of that terrible wrong; and
I have, therefore, selected my topic in view of that fact. It will, probably,
amount to the same thing in the end.

Some one has, happily, said, that it matters very little which path the
traveller may take; he has but to go forward to go round the world. In
like manner it may be said, that it matters little which path of inquiry
a man may pursue, or which great moral or spiritual fact he may investigate; he has but to honestly persevere to find himself, at last, at the portals
of the whole universe of truth, and speedily walking amidst its golden
glories.

The subject of my lecture this evening is, the nature, character, and
history of the anti-slavery movement. I own that, were I here on any
ordinary occasion, to deliver a lecture on the question of slavery, I should
select topics of a more popular and stirring character than those I propose
to touch this evening. When I speak of the anti-slavery movement, I
mean to refer to that combination of moral, religious and political forces
which has long been, and is now, operating and cooperating for the abolition of slavery in this country, and throughout the world. I wish to speak
of that movement, to-night, more as the calm observer, than as the ardent
and personally interested advocate. For, while I am willing to have it
known, that every fibre of my soul is enlisted in the cause of emancipation, I would not have it thought that I am less capable than others, of
calmly and rationally contemplating the movement designed to accomplish that important and much desired end. In making this statement, I
am quite aware of the common impression concerning the mental abilities of my race. It has been said, that the variety of the human family, to
which I belong, excels less in the intellectual, than in the emotional characteristics of men; and the great leader of the anti-slavery movement in
our country allowed himself to say, in the columns of his paper, not long

ago, that "the anti-slavery movement, both religiously and politically, has transcended the ability of the sufferers from American slavery and prejudice, as a class, to keep pace with it, or to perceive what are its demands, or to understand the philosophy of its operations."[17] Notwithstanding such discouraging considerations, I presume to speak to you, to-night, on the subject selected. In doing so, I have one consolation, and that is, as I apprehend it, the anti-slavery movement is, after all, no cold abstraction, requiring a sharp and flinty intellect to analyze it. While it is a subject of surpassing dignity, and one upon which the wisest and best minds may be employed, it is, nevertheless, a subject upon which the humblest may venture to think and speak, without justly being exposed to the reproach of treading upon ground which should be trodden only by men of the "superior race."

One other word for my subject. A grand movement on the part of mankind, in any direction, or for any purpose, moral or political, is an interesting fact, fit and proper to be studied. It is such, not only for those who eagerly participate in it, but also for those who stand aloof from it—even for those by whom it is opposed. I take the anti-slavery movement to be such an one, and a movement as sublime and glorious, in its character, as it is holy and beneficent in the ends it aims to accomplish. At this moment, I deem it safe to say, it is properly engrossing more minds in this country than any other subject now before the American people. The late John C. Calhoun—one of the mightiest men that ever stood up in the American Senate—did not deem it beneath him; and he probably studied it as deeply, though not as honestly, as Gerrit Smith, or William Lloyd Garrison. He evinced the greatest familiarity with the subject; and the greatest efforts of his last years in the Senate had direct reference to this movement. His eagle eye watched every new development connected with it; and he was ever prompt to inform the South of every important step in its progress. He never allowed himself to make light of it; but always spoke of it and treated it as a matter of grave import; and, in this, he showed himself a master of the mental, moral, and religious constitution of human society. Daniel Webster, too, in the better days of his life, before he gave his assent to the Fugitive Slave Bill, and trampled upon all his earlier and better convictions—when his eye was yet single— he clearly comprehended the nature of the elements involved in this movement; and in his own majestic eloquence, warned the South, and the country, to have a care how they attempted to put it down. He is an illustration that it is easier to give, than to take good advice. To these two men—the greatest men to whom the nation has yet given birth—may be traced the two great facts of the present—the South triumphant, and the North humbled. Their names may stand thus: Calhoun and domination—Webster and degradation. Yet again. If to the enemies of liberty this subject is one of engrossing interest, vastly more so should it be such to freedom's friends. The latter, it leads to the gates of all valuable knowledge, philanthropic, ethical and religious; for it brings them to the study of man, wonderfully and fearfully made—the proper study of man through all time—the open book, in which are the records of time and eternity!

Of the existence and power of the anti-slavery movement, as a fact, you need no evidence. The nation has seen its face, and felt the controlling pressure of its hand. You have seen it moving in all directions, and in all weathers, and in all places, appearing most where desired least, and pressing hardest where most resisted. No place is exempt. The quiet prayer meeting, and the stormy halls of national debate, share its presence alike. It is a common intruder, and, of course, has got the name of being ungentlemanly. Brethren who had long sung, in the most affectionate fervor, and with the greatest sense of security,

Together let us sweetly live—together let us die,

have been suddenly and violently separated by it, and ranged in hostile attitude towards each other. One of the most powerful religious organizations (I allude to the Methodists) of this country, has been rent asunder, and its strongest bolts of denominational brotherhood started at a single surge. It has changed the tone of the Northern pulpit, and modified that of the press. A celebrated Divine, who, four years ago, was for flinging his own mother, or brother, into the remorseless jaws of the monster Slavery, lest he should swallow up the Union, now recognizes anti-slavery as a characteristic of future civilization. Signs and wonders follow this movement; and the fact just stated is one of them. Party ties are loosened by it; and men are compelled to take sides for or against it, whether they will or not. Come from where he may, or come for what he may, he is compelled to show his hand. What is this mighty force? What is its history? and what is its destiny? Is it ancient or modern, transient or permanent? Has it turned aside, like a stranger and a sojourner, to tarry for a night? or has it come to rest with us forever? Excellent chances are here for speculation; and some of them are quite profound. We might, for instance, proceed to inquire not only into the philosophy of the anti-slavery movement, but into the philosophy of the law, in obedience to which that movement started into existence. We might demand to know what is that law or power which, at different times, disposes the minds of men to this or that particular object—now for peace, and now for war—now for freedom, and now for slavery; but this profound question I leave to the Abolitionists of the superior class to answer. The speculations which must precede such answer, would afford, perhaps, about the same satisfaction as the learned theories which have rained down upon the world, from time to time, as to the origin of evil. I shall, therefore, avoid water in which I cannot swim, and deal with anti-slavery as a fact, like any other fact in the history of mankind, capable of being described and understood, both as to its internal forces, and its external phases and relations.

First, then, let us consider its history. About this there is much error, and little truth in many minds. Some who write and speak on the subject, seem to regard the anti-slavery movement as a recent discovery, brought out for the first time less than a quarter of a century ago. I cannot consent to view it thus. This movement is older and weightier than that. I would deprive William Lloyd Garrison of no honor justly his. All credit must forever redound to him as the man to whose earnest eloquence— more than to that of any other living man—we owe the revival of the anti-slavery movement in this country; but it is due to truth to say, he neither discovered its principles, originated its ideas, nor framed its arguments. These are all older than the preacher. It is an error to speak of this venerable movement as a new thing under the sun. The causes producing it, and the particles composing it, like the great forces of the physical world, fire, steam, and lightning, have slumbered in the bosom of nature since the world began. There are coal and iron, and lead, and copper, and silver, and gold, and precious gems in the hillsides, whereon the shepherd-boy sings, unconsciously, his evening song. They are all there, though he knows it not, awaiting the thoughtful discoverer, and the skillful workman to bring them forth in the varied and multitudinous forms of beauty, power, and glory, of which they are capable. And so it is with the elements of this history. They are prior to the present anti-slavery movement. Whence are these elements? I trace them to nature and to nature's God. From heaven come the rain, the snow, and the crystalizing blast, which pile up the glaciers; and from the same source come also those melting beams and softening breezes, which send down the thundering avalanche, to awe and astonish the hearts of man. What, though one passed by at the moment! shall he ascribe to his tiny tread the solemn crash, and the stunning reverberation? Rather let him stand, awe-struck, ascribing to God all the glory and honor for his wondrous works. It is a thought no less true, than consoling, that, in fitting out this globe for its mighty and mysterious voyage in time and space, the Great Mind who loosed it from its moorings, foresaw all its perils, and comprehended all its vicissitudes— and better still, bountifully provided for the moral, as well as for the physical safety of its passengers. In the very heart of humanity are garnered up, as from everlasting to everlasting, all those elementary principles, whose vital action constitutes what we now term the "anti-slavery movement." They are the treasures of our common store-house. The humblest may approach, enter, and be supplied with arms, to meet the ills that flesh is heir to. A thousand moral battles have been fought with them, and they are as good as ever. Ages of oppression, and iron-hearted selfishness, have rolled over them, and covered them with their blinding dust; but these have had no power to extinguish, or to destroy them. Occasional glimpses of these important principles have gladdened the eyes of good men, at different stages of the world's progress, who have wisely written down, to be read by after coming generations, their apprehensions of them. Noble testimonies of this sort may be found all along the way trodden by the race. They are the common inheritance of all men, without money and without price. In reading these ancient testimonies, some of them reaching back to the grand exodus of Israel, and some to the earliest days of our country, more than a century ago, one is filled with veneration for the vast accumulation, the mighty bulwark of judgment, of solemn conviction, of holy protest, reared for the defence of the rights of man.

The anti-slavery movement has little to entitle it to being called a new thing under the sun, in view of any just historical test. I know nothing original about it. Its ideas and arguments were already to the hand of the present workmen; the oldest abolitionist of to-day is but the preacher of a faith framed and practised long before he was born. The patriots of the American Revolution clearly saw, and with all their inconsistency, they had the grace to confess the abhorrent character of slavery, and to hopefully predict its overthrow and complete extirpation. Washington, and Jefferson, Patrick Henry, and Luther Martin, Franklin, and Adams, Madison, and Monroe, and a host of the earlier statesmen, jurists, scholars, and divines of the country, were among those who looked forward to this happy consummation. But, now, let us come to the sober record, and it will be seen that the anti-slavery movement in this country, is older than the Republic. In the records of the churches, especially, we find most important data, showing that the anti-slavery sentiment was national at the very beginning of the Republic, and that this sentiment got its fullest and most earnest expression through the churches at that time. The Methodist, Baptist, and Presbyterian churches of the country, stood upon radical anti-slavery ground. It will not be easy to find anywhere, in the records of any modern anti-slavery society, testimony more vital and stringent than is found in the proceedings of the Methodist church against slavery, nearly a hundred years ago; and the same is true of the Baptist churches of the South. The Methodist church vaulted up to the highest position occupied by the most ultra Abolitionists of to-day. It denied slavery all sanction, human and divine, against the laws of God, and against the laws of man. In 1780, that denomination said: "The Conference acknowledges that slavery is contrary to the laws of God, man and nature, and hurtful to society—contrary to the dictates of conscience, and true religion, and doing to others that we would not they should do unto us." In 1784, the same church declared, "that those who buy, sell, or give slaves away, except for the purpose to free them, shall be expelled immediately." In 1785, the Conference spoke even more stringently on the subject. It then said: "We hold in the deepest abhorrence the practice of slavery, and shall not cease to seek its destruction by all wise and proper means."

Still later, in 1801:—

"We declare that we are more than ever convinced of the great evil of African slavery, which still exists in these United States, and every member of the Society who sells a slave shall immediately, on full proof, be excluded from the Society. The Conferences are directed to draw up addresses, for the gradual emancipation of the slaves, to the Legislatures. Proper committees shall be appointed, out of the most respectable of our friends, for the conducting of the business. And the presiding elders, deacons, and travelling preachers, shall do all in their power to further the blessed undertaking. Let this be continued from year to year, till the desired end be accomplished."

So reads the record of the Methodist Episcopal Church of America, more than half a century ago. Here was an anti-slavery movement springing out of the very bosom of the church. In what did this movement differ from the present one? In this, and in this only, *as to time.* The first looked for the gradual abolition of slavery; and the other looks for immediate emancipation. Under the operation of the one doctrine, nearly sixty thousand slaves have been emancipated in Maryland, and as many in Virginia, and many more in the several Southern States, besides universal emancipation in the Northern States. The only new idea brought to the anti-slavery movement, by Mr. Garrison, is the doctrine of immediatism, as against gradualism, and thus far, it must be confessed, that fewer slaves have been emancipated under the influence of this doctrine, in this country, than under the old doctrine of gradual emancipation. So much as this is due to facts. Nevertheless, I would not give up a just principle because it has been slower of adoption than a principle less just. The doctrine of immediatism was not, however, original with Mr. Garrison. Dr. Hopkins, of Newport, R. I., had urged that doctrine upon the consideration of his slaveholding congregation before Mr. Garrison was born. That brave, old philanthropist met the slave-holder face to face with the stern demand of emancipation, *"without delay."* Dr. Hopkins was a strong reasoner, and an earnest reformer. The Abolitionist of to-day will lose nothing by perusing the anti-slavery works of their noble predecessor. The Methodist Episcopal Church, whose course on the slavery question I have been unfolding, was not singular in its position respecting slavery fifty years ago. Elizabeth Herrick, too, of England, as early as 1824, published a pamphlet in favor of immediate and unconditional emancipation. The Presbyterian Church, and the Methodist, stood on the same ground. In 1794, the General Assembly of that body, pronounced the following judgment on the character of slavery, and that of slaveholders:—

"1st Timothy, 1st chapter, 10th v.—'The law is made for manstealers.' 'This crime among the Jews exposed the perpetrators of it to capital punishment.'—Exodus xxi. 15. And the apostle here classes them with sinners of the first rank. The word he uses in its original import, comprehends all who are concerned in bringing any of the human race into slavery, or in retaining them in it. Stealers of men are all those who bring off slaves or freemen, and keep, sell, or buy them. 'To steal a freeman,' says Grotius, 'is the highest kind of theft.' In other instances we only steal human property, but when we steal or retain men in slavery, we seize those who, in common with ourselves, are constituted, by the original grant, lords of the earth."

A good deal has been said and written about harsh language, but I think it would be difficult to find, in the writings of any modern Abolitionist, language more severe than this held by a religious assembly. Slaveholders are declared to be sinners of the first rank, man-stealers, worthy of capital punishment, guilty of the highest kind of theft. Prior to this action of the Presbyterian General Assembly, the Baptist Church in Virginia had declared itself opposed to slavery, and was actively at work in the cause of emancipation in that State. My assertion can be verified by referring to Semple's History of the rise and progress of the Baptists of Virginia:—

"In the year 1783, a General Committee, composed of delegates from local associations, was instituted in Virginia, charged with 'considering matters that might be for the good of the whole Society.' It was especially the duty of this committee to be the medium through which the Baptists should address themselves to the Legislature, for redress of grievances, &c. At a meeting of this General Committee, March 7, 1788, delegates from four associations being present, among 'the religious political subjects' taken up was this:

" '3d. Whether a petition should be offered to the General Assembly, praying that the yoke of slavery may be made more tolerable. Referred to the next session.'

"I do not discover that in the next session anything was done; but at the meeting of August 8, 1789, delegates from seven associations being present, the subject was considered, and the account is thus given by Semple, in his History of the Rise and Progress of the Baptists of Virginia, p. 79. He says:

" 'The propriety of hereditary slavery was also taken up at this session, and after some time employed in the consideration of the subject, the following resolution was offered by Mr. Seland and adopted:

" 'Resolved, That slavery is a violent deprivation of the rights of nature, and inconsistent with a republican government, and, therefore (we) recommend it to our brethren, to make use of every legal measure to extirpate this horrid evil from the land; and pray Almighty God that our honorable Legislature may have it in their power to proclaim the great jubilee, consistent with the principles of good policy.'

"A fact like this could not be an isolated one; and there are incidental circumstances scattered in the history of those times which have come down to us, showing that the anti-slavery sentiment was widespread and effective.

"To it I presume is to be attributed the rise of the powerful anti-slavery party, which for some time existed among the Baptists of Kentucky, known as Emancipators. For accounts of this party, I must refer you to Benedict's History of the Baptists, (edition of 1813,) vol. 2; pages 231, 235, 245, 250. This edition of Benedict's contains other allusions to the subject of slavery, which are interesting. You will find some account of the Emancipators of Kentucky, in the first volume of the Baptist Memorial, edited by Dr. Babcock, under the head 'Kentucky Baptists.' The Rev. Dr. Peck, of Illinois, has lately furnished, for the *New York Recorder,* articles on the Emancipators, which I will send you, if we have spare copies.

"In the minutes of the Philadelphia Baptist Association, for the year 1789—the year of the passage of the above named resolution by the General Committee of Virginia—I find the following:—(See edition of the American Baptist Publication Society, edited by Rev. A. D. Gillette, p. 247.)

"'Agreeably to a recommendation in the letter from the Church at Baltimore, this Association declare their high approbation of the several Societies formed in the United States and Europe, for the gradual abolition of the slavery of the Africans, and for guarding against their being detained or sent off as slaves, after having obtained their liberty; and do hereby recommend to the churches as represent, to form similar Societies, to become members thereof, and exert themselves to obtain this important object.'"

I have the above from a distinguished Baptist, who has fully investigated the subject; and I must express my deep gratitude for the assistance that gentleman has rendered me in the collection of these valuable facts, which, though well known to the Baptists of the country, are yet quite unknown to the public generally. Not having at my command the books to which he refers, I have preferred to incorporate his letter to me as it stands.

It is hardly necessary, in this connection, to refer to the Society of Friends, in these early times. All who know anything of them, know that they were emancipationists. That venerable Society had made Abolitionism a fundamental religious duty, long before the oldest Abolitionist, now living, was on the stage. Wherever that Society obtained a footing in this country, the work of amelioration went on. Slaves were emancipated, and the condition of the free people of color was improved. The broad brim, and the plain dress, were a terror to slaveholders, and a praise to the slave. When running from slavery, only seventeen years ago, I had not transferred my confidence from the Quakers to the Abolitionists. I believed in them for what they had done, years ago, for my race; and when the Abolitionists, of modern times, have done as much for freedom as the early Friends, they will not have to complain that the confidence of the colored people has been withdrawn from them. I now deny, in view of the facts of this history, that any man, now living, has any business to lay claim to the anti-slavery movement, as a thing of his invention, or of his discovery. We, who now work, have inherited, derived, received this movement from the churches of earlier times. Good men, who wrought before us, laid the foundation upon which we are building. All along the pages of the holy Bible, from Moses to John, may be found the constructive principles upon which this movement is based; and the organizers of the present anti-slavery societies, found here an inexhaustible mine of material, ready to be fused into that solid bolt, with which they now shake the land. It was here that Godwin, and Sharpe, and Clarkson, and Wilberforce, and Fox, and Benezet, and Wesley, and Woolman, forged the magnificent, moral armory, with which they began the mighty struggle, and with which Lundy, Walker, Garrison, and Leavitt, and Elizur Wright, and William Goodell, and Beriah Green, and the Tappans, and Gerrit Smith, and Judge Jay, have nobly continued until now. Honor to the memory of the departed, and honor to those who remain.

But what was the condition of the anti-slavery movement twenty years ago, and how came it in that condition? It is much easier to answer the first, than to answer the last question. There were witnesses for freedom in the church, but the church had become comparatively dead on the subject. The friends continued to work, though with flagging zeal. The other churches had become complicated with slavery, and the slave was forgotten by those who were once his friends. Lundy was at work for an anti-slavery revival, when Mr. Garrison joined him, and raised the note of immediate emancipation. Alas! for human frailty! and alas! for the poor slave. Present efforts may promise much, but we cannot but remember that one anti-slavery generation nearly died out without leaving men to take their places, and so may the present. The country which had been deploring the existence of slavery, and deeply desiring its abolition, had become like the world. The price of human flesh had risen, and man stealers had become gentlemen. This brings me to notice the revival of the anti-slavery movement twenty-five years ago. The country was soon in a blaze, as all know; yet, nothing strange happened to the early advocates of a cause, new to be sure, but only new by the new zeal and fresh eloquence brought to its service. The plainer the truth, and the more obvious the justice of the demand made, the more stern and bitter is the opposition; and for this reason, the plainer the truth, the brighter the prospect of its realization. The enunciation, and persistent proclamation of anti-slavery principles twenty-five years ago, demonstrate this. Never was there a cause more just—never one more peaceful and harmless in its character—never truths more self-evident. Immediate and unconditional emancipation was proclaimed, as the right of the slave, and as the duty of the slave-holder. This demand was enforced in the name, and according to the law of the living God. No sword, no bayonet, the simple truth uttered in the love of it. That is all.

> *"Weapons of war we have cast from the battle*
> *Truth is our armor, our watchword is love;*
> *Hushed be the sword and the musketry's rattle,*
> *All our equipments are drawn from above."*

The slave-holder was not, then, an object of hate and of execration. Had he gone into an abolition meeting, he would have been heard with patience and courtesy in his own defence. Yet, at this point, how was this cause met? How was it met by the American people, and how was it met by the church, to which latter, indeed, the movement owes its origin in this country, as well as in England?

The facts of this history are too recent, too notorious, and too fresh in the minds of all to need minute narration; and even if this were not so, it would scarcely be necessary to dwell long upon this aspect of the subject. Find out what happened on the presentation of any new truth, or any truth, which an age had lost sight of or discarded, and you are masters of the facts which attended the anti-slavery revival. As with the mission of the Savior of mankind, so with the anti-slavery movement. The latter could say, "had ye believed Moses, ye would have believed me." The new gospel of liberty was tried as by fire. The old folly was attempted, of crucifying the body to quench the spirit—of killing men to kill their principles. There was much trial in those early days. Lovejoy, a noble martyr, in defence of a free press and a free gospel, weltered in his warm blood at Alton. A brother of his, as true an Abolitionist, is now a member of the Legislature of the State, which received this bloody baptism. Crandal perished in prison at Washington, for having, and carrying a few anti-slavery papers in his portmanteau.[18] The *National Era* is now published there, and has the largest circulation of any paper at the seat of Government. Mr. Garrison was dragged through the streets of Boston by a mob, and took refuge in the common jail;[19] and is now, comparatively, a popular man in that city, surrounded by friends, rich, and powerful.

But to drop the present, and to refer exclusively to the past. The country was like a savage drunkard, roused from his slumbers. Speaking and writing on the subject of slavery became dangerous. Mob violence menaced the persons and property of the Abolitionists, and their very homes became unsafe for themselves and their families. Boston, New York, and Philadelphia, Cincinnati, and Utica, were under mob law. Pennsylvania Hall was burned with fire, because it had given shelter to the hunted spirit of liberty for a few brief hours. As to the free colored people, a more than demoniacal hate was roused against them—assault and insult came down upon them without measure, and without mixture, and a wild and clamorous cry of blood! blood! came howling over all the broad savannahs of the South.

Then to side with truth is noble, when we share her wretched crust,
Ere her cause bring fame and profit, and 'tis prosperous to be just;
Then it is the brave man chooses, while the coward stands aside,
Doubting in his abject spirit, till his Lord is crucified;
And the multitude make virtue of the faith they had denied.

Someone has called the period to which I have been referring, "the martyr age of anti-slavery;" and not having been an actor in those scenes, I may properly admire—as who could do other than admire— the manly heroism displayed by the Abolitionists at this trying point of their experience.

Like true apostles, as they were, their faith in their principles knew no wavering. The heathen raged, and the people imagined a vain thing. Conventions were broken up, only to be held again; presses were demolished, to be erected again. The anti-slavery lecturer was pelted from one town only, to flee into another; and the new faith of the prophets waxed stronger and stronger. For every advocate struck down, ten new ones stood up. With them, obstacles were converted into facilities— hindrances into helps—curtailments into increase—and curses into blessings. If you will turn to the letters and speeches of that period, you will find that they burn with love to the *slave,* as a wronged, and bitterly abused fellow-man. His sorrows and sufferings were the burden of early anti-slavery eloquence. It was remembering the bondman as bound with him; and the thought that their suffering as freemen, was as nothing compared to that of their enslaved brother, which enabled the early Abolitionists of this country to preserve, and to make a deep impression on the hearts of men. Mr. Garrison had been so true to the slave, that when in England he was supposed to be, till seen, a veritable *Negro.* He was proud of it then, and spoke of it in proof of his faithfulness. I shall be pardoned if I say, he would scarcely consider this mission complimentary to him now. I have now glanced at the reception which the anti-slavery revival met at the hands of the world. Now, let us see how it was received by the Church. Besides the early anti-slavery position of the Church, to which I have already directed attention, there were special reasons for anticipating a better reception at the hands of the Church, than it had received at the hands of the cold and selfish world. The American Churches stood already committed to causes, analogous in their spirit and purpose to the anti-slavery cause. The heathen in Asia, Africa, and in the isles of the sea, were not only remembered by the Church, but were objects of special, earnest, and energetic exertion. Prayers, and contribution boxes, were abundant for these, to save them from the bondage of sin and superstition. Our Church sent bibles and missionaries "from the rivers to the ends of the earth." Under its outspread wings, were warmly sheltered the Missionary Society, the Tract Society, the Sabbath School Society, and innumerable sewing societies, composed of honorable women connected with the Church. These were all, apparently, animated by an honest desire to improve the condition of the human race, in other and distant lands. I say, therefore, it was both reasonable and natural to expect a better reception for the anti-slavery cause from the church than from the world.

And, yet again, there was something in the condition of the enslaved millions at our own doors, which appealed directly to the Church, supposing the heart of the Church to beat in unison with the heart of the Son of God. At the very outset of his mission among the children of men, he was careful to range himself on the side of the poor, the enslaved, and heart-broken victims of oppression.

"The spirit of the Lord is upon me," said the great one, who spake as never man spake, "because he hath anointed me to preach the Gospel to the poor. He hath sent me to bind up the broken-hearted—to preach deliverance to the captive, and recovery of sight to the blind; to set at liberty them that are bruised."

The Abolitionist could point to this sublime declaration of the Son of God, and then point to the millions of enslaved, captured, bruised, maimed, and heart-broken people, whose cries of anguish ascend to God continually—and this they did. They carried those bleeding and heart-broken millions—poor, helpless and forlorn—to the very altar of the Church; and cried, "men of Israel, help!" They described their physical suffering—their mental, moral debasement, and destitution; and said to the Church: "In the name of mercy open unto us." An angel of mercy, with benignant aspect, and streaming eyes, stood at the door of the Church, veiled in deep sorrow, imploring, entreating, in the name of God, and down-trodden man, for entrance; but those who held the key, repulsed her with iron bolts. The cry for mercy disturbed the worship—

and it drove the angel away, and went on praying. But this is not all. In imitation, perhaps, of the example set by the world, the Church not only rejected, but became an active persecutor of the anti-slavery movement. She sent forth some of her ablest champions to battle against it. The Holy Bible, which had furnished arguments against slave-holding seventy years ago, was found to contain now the best arguments for slavery.

So recently as the year 1850, she rained down millions of sermons, to prove it right to hunt slaves, and consign them to life-long bondage. The Methodist Church which, in its infancy and purity held so high a position, forgot her ancient testimonies; and led off, in a grand crusade, to put down the anti-slavery movement. It undertook to censure and silence such of its members as believed with John Wesley; that slavery is the sum of all villainies. In what striking, strange and painful contrast are the resolutions adopted at Cincinnati by the General Conference, in 1836, with those adopted by the same Conference in 1801. Here they are, preamble and all:—

"*Whereas* great excitement has prevailed in this country on the subject of modern abolitionism, which is reported to have been increased in this city, by the unjustifiable conduct of two members of the General Conference, in lecturing upon, and in favor of that agitating topic; and whereas such a course on the part of any of its members is calculated to bring upon this body the suspicion and distrust of the community, and to misrepresent its sentiments in regard to the point at issue; and whereas, in this aspect of the case, a due regard for its character, as well as just concern for the interests of the Church confided to its care, demand a full, decided, and unequivocal expression of the views of the General Conference in the premises; therefore,

"*Resolved,* 1st. By the delegates of the Annual Conference, in General Conference assembled, that they disapprove in the most unqualified sense of the conduct of the two members of the General Conference, who are reported to have lectured in this city recently, upon and in favor of that agitating topic.

"*Resolved,* 2d. By the delegates of the Annual Conference, in General Conference assembled, that they are decidedly opposed to Modern Abolitionism; and wholly disclaim any right, wish or intention to interfere in the civil and political relation between master and slave, as it exists in the States of this Union."

Here, then, was an entire change in the attitude of the Methodist Episcopal Church, on the subject of slavery. The traffickers in the bodies and souls of men were set at ease in her Zion; and the victims of the bloody lash were literally driven from her gates.

As went the Methodist Episcopal Church, so went the Baptist and Presbyterian Churches. They receded from their anti-slavery ground; despised the claims of the movement, which their earlier and holier precepts and example had called into being. The Churches which began their career in love for the oppressed, had now become the friends of the oppressor, and the bulwark of slavery.

Here arose that crisis in the anti-slavery movement, from the evil effects of which it has not yet recovered. It will never be forgotten. The conflict was terrible to all concerned, flinging the Church against man, and some of the advocates of emancipation against God. The Church stepped between the slave's chains, and the uplifted blow aimed to break them. The alternative presented was to oppose the Church, or abandon the slave! Here were religion and slavery on the one hand, and freedom and humanity on the other. The Church raised the cry of infidelity, and her opponents laughed at her forms and ceremonies, and poured contempt upon her prayers. The Church cherished her forms all the more for being assailed, and the advocates of emancipation clung the more to anti-slavery, because it was assailed by the Church, and thus unbelief and irreligion are seen thickest where this battle has raged hottest. The Church, by her professions, should have been the right arm and shield of this beneficent movement; but alas! she proved false to her trust, abandoned her right mission of striking down slavery, and attempted to strike down liberty. The slave, under the uplifted lash of the taskmaster, quivering with fear, and imploring mercy, could no longer look to the Church for succor. The buyers and sellers of men were welcomed to her bosom, and the slave, in his chains, was driven away.

Is it strange, then, that those who once loved, began now to loathe the Church? Is it strange, that their faith, in her regard for the souls of men, should wane when they saw her shameless contempt for the bodies of men? Could they believe that she loved God truly, who hated the image of God so intensely? Had the Church of this country welcomed this movement, as a long lost child, which had stayed away from its home, in the church—had she given to it the endorsement of her name, adopted it as her own, lent to it the aid of her coöperation, the influence of her example—had she given it the facilities of her widespread organization, the support of her press, and the might of her eloquence, the great battle of liberty would, long ere this, have been decided. The slave's chains would have been broken into a thousand fragments, and millions, now pining in bondage, would have been rejoicing in their liberty. Not only was here lost a splendid opportunity for blessing the world, but a golden opportunity was lost for bringing honor to the name of the Church, and reverence to her ministry. A new occasion, a new harvest, was given unto her, which she might have gathered and garnered up for the days of drought and moral famine, which have since rolled over her. An invincible army of sable soldiers, with ample means to scourge and drive back the allied host of infidelity and atheism now marching against her, were foolishly and wickedly left in chains. Three millions of joyful hearts, clapping their glad hands in freedom, ascribing their great deliverance from thraldom to the beneficent interposition of the Church of God, would have thundered into silence the clamor of scoffers, and made her name glorious throughout the world.

But she flung away the golden chance, and is now exposed not only to the assaults of sin, but on her hands, is a more solemn controversy. The attacks of unbelief are not so galling as the fire from the ramparts of justice and humanity. Not only has the slave been converted into an enemy of the Church, and taught to look elsewhere for succor and deliverance, but the sober thinking philanthropist has been led to raise the dangerous enquiry—Of what use to this sin-cursed world is a church, whose religion and gospel are the dread of the oppressed and the delight of the oppressor? This aspect of this history is of the profoundest significance and deserves to be pondered on. The usefulness, and the very existence of the Church, as an organization, are involved in the use made of this subject. Let the Church look to it. Organizations are strong, but there is something in the world much stronger than any human organization. The eternal spirit is mightier than all the external world; religion is greater than the form created to express it. Forms and organizations are but the *"mint,"* *"annis"* and *"cummin."* The weightier matters of the law are judgment, mercy and faith; and the latter are with the oppressed and enslaved everywhere. Forms and ceremonies may pass current for a time; but there is too much love among mankind for what is real, true and genuine, to endure always what is empty, hollow and hypocritical. It won't do for the Church to weep over the heathen abroad, and laugh over the heathen at home. It will not do to send Bibles and missionaries to India, with money wrung from the blood and sweat of the heathen of South Carolina and Georgia, to whom we prohibit, under pains and penalties, the privilege of learning to read the name of Almighty God! It will not do to save souls abroad, and enslave souls at home. Let the Church, then, look to it, for here is the source of her weakness, attracting, as well from the sky of truth, as from the clouds of error, the exterminating bolt and the devouring fire. Her new moons, appointed feasts, Sabbath days, solemn assemblies, are no atonement for refusing to do justice. She is under the law to cease to do evil, and learn to do well. She must seek justice and relieve the oppressed. In a word, she must abolish slavery, or be abolished by slavery. The voice of one crying in the wilderness, has the same lesson to-day as in the days of Jesus. The axe is laid at the root of the tree. Usefulness is the price of existence. Do or die, wear out or rust out, bring forth fruit or be cut down, is the law now and always. Men may go often, but they will not go always to an exhausted fountain; they will not long search for substance where they are only rewarded with shadows. If they do not find God and his eternal attributes among the solemn splendors of the Church, they will turn away from its altars and aisles, and go forth into the temple of God's creation, and strive to interpret for themselves the heavenly inscriptions of divine love.

Many who once stood with delight in the Church, apart from the world, go not up with the great congregation to worship now; and they tell us the Church must make peace with the slave before it can make peace with God. She must bring back the child of her early love, from the wandering exile into which she has driven it. She must return to her early testimonies, and teach the oppressor now, as at the beginning, to "break every yoke, and let the oppressed go free," and gather around her the affections of those who esteem mercy more than sacrifice.

Let us now turn away from the Church, and examine the anti-slavery movement in its branches, for divisions are here, as well as elsewhere. I will not enter into an examination of their causes. God forbid! that I should open here those bitter fountains. I may say, however, that the first grand division took place fourteen years ago, and on the very minor question—Shall a woman be a member of a committee in company with men? The majority said she should be; and the minority seceded. Thus was a grand philanthropic movement rent asunder by a side issue, having nothing, whatever, to do with the great object which the American Anti-Slavery Society was organized to carry forward. Before I would have stood in such an attitude, and taken the responsibility of dividing the ranks of freedom's army, I would have suffered my right arm to be taken off. How beautiful would it have been for that woman, how nobly would her name have come down to us in this history, had she said: "All things are lawful for me, but all things are not expedient!

While I see no objection to my occupying a place on your committee, I can for the slave's sake forego that privilege. The battle of Woman's Rights should be fought on its own ground; as it is, the slave's cause, already too heavy laden, had to bear up under this new addition; but I will not go further on that subject, except to characterize it as a sad mistake."

But I propose to speak of the different anti-slavery sects and parties, and to give my view of them very briefly. There are four principal divisions.

1st. The Garrisonians, or the American Anti-Slavery Society.

2d. The Anti-Garrisonians, or the American and Foreign Anti-Slavery Society.

3d. The Free Soil Party, or Political Abolitionists.

4th. The Liberty Party, or Gerrit Smith School of Abolitionists.

There are others, and among them those conscientious men and women, principally of the Society of Friends, who may be called *"free labor people"*—since their remedy for slavery is an abstinence from slave produce. This Society formerly published in Philadelphia a periodical, called "The Non-Slaveholder," and kept open a store for the sale of free labor goods; and besides this, it promoted the growth of free cotton in several of the more Southern States. This Society is still in existence, and is quietly doing its work.[20]

I shall consider, first, the Garrisonian Anti-Slavery Society. I call this the Garrisonian Society, because Mr. Garrison is, confessedly, its leader. This Society is the oldest of modern Anti-Slavery Societies. It has, strictly speaking, two weekly papers, or organs—employs five or six lecturers—and holds numerous public meetings for the dissemination of its views. Its peculiar and distinctive feature is, its doctrine of *"no union with slaveholders."* This doctrine has, of late, become its bond of union, and the condition of good fellowship among its members. Of this Society, I have to say, its logical result is but negatively, anti-slavery. Its doctrine, of "no union with slaveholders," carried out, dissolves the Union, and leaves the slaves and their masters to fight their own battles, in their own way. This I hold to be an abandonment of the great idea with which that Society started. It started to free the slave. It ends by leaving the slave to free himself. It started with the purpose to imbue the heart of the nation with sentiments favorable to the abolition of slavery, and ends by seeking to free the North from all responsibility of slavery, other than if slavery were in Great Britain, or under some other nationality.

This, I say, is the practical abandonment of the idea, with which that Society started. It has given up the faith, that the slave can be freed short of the overthrow of the Government; and then, as I understand that Society, it leaves the slaves, as it must needs leave them, just where it leaves the slaves of Cuba, or those of Brazil. The nation, as such, is given up as beyond the power of salvation by the foolishness of preaching; and hence, the aim is now to save the North; so that the American Anti-Slavery Society, which was inaugurated to convert the nation, after ten years' struggle, parts with its faith, and aims now to save the North. One of the most eloquent of all the members of that Society, and the man who is only second to Mr. Garrison himself, defines the Garrisonian doctrine thus:

"All the slave asks of us, is to stand out of his way, withdraw our pledge to keep the peace on the plantation; withdraw our pledge to return him; withdraw that representation which the Constitution gives in proportion to the number of slaves, and without any agitation here, without any individual virtue, which the times have eaten out of us, God will vindicate the oppressed, by the laws of justice which he has founded. Trample under foot your own unjust pledges, break to pieces your compact with hell by which you become the abettors of oppression. Stand alone, and let no cement of the Union bind the slave, and he will right himself."

That is it. "Stand alone;" the slave is to "right himself." I dissent entirely from this reasoning. It assumes to be true what is plainly absurd, and that is, that a population of slaves, without arms, without means of concert, and without leisure, is more than a match for double its number, educated, accustomed to rule, and in every way prepared for warfare, offensive or defensive. This Society, therefore, consents to leave the slave's freedom to a most uncertain and improbable, if not an impossible, contingency.

But, *"no union with slaveholders."*

As a mere expression of abhorrence of slavery, the sentiment is a good one; but it expresses no intelligible principle of action, and throws no light on the pathway of duty. Defined, as its authors define it, it leads to false doctrines, and mischievous results. It condemns Gerrit Smith for sitting in Congress, and our Savior for eating with publicans and sinners. Dr. Spring uttered a shocking sentiment, when he said, if one prayer of his would emancipate every slave, he would not offer that prayer. No less shocking is the sentiment of the leader of the disunion forces, when he says, that if one vote of his would emancipate every slave in this country, he would not cast that vote. Here, on a bare theory, and for a theory which, if consistently adhered to, would drive a man out of the world—a theory which can never be made intelligible to common sense—the freedom of the whole slave population would be sacrificed.

But again: "no union with slaveholders." I dislike the morality of this sentiment, in its application to the point at issue. For instance: A. unites with B. in stealing my property, and carrying it away to California, or to Australia, and, while there, Mr. A. becomes convinced that he did wrong in stealing my property, and says to Mr. B., "no union with property stealers," and abandons him, leaving the property in his hands. Now, I put it to this audience, has Mr. A., in this transaction, met the requirements of stringent morality? He, certainly, has not. It is not only his duty to separate from the thief, but to restore the stolen property to its rightful owner. And I hold that in the Union, this very thing of restoring to the slave his long-lost rights, can better be accomplished than it can possibly be accomplished outside of the Union. This, then, is my answer to the motto, "No union with slaveholders."

But this is not the worst fault of this Society. Its chief energies are expended in confirming the opinion, that the United States Constitution is, and was, intended to be a slave-holding instrument—thus piling up, between the slave and his freedom, the huge work of the abolition of the Government, as an indispensable condition to emancipation. My point here is, first, the Constitution is, according to its reading, an anti-slavery document; and, secondly, to dissolve the Union, as a means to abolish slavery, is about as wise as it would be to burn up this city, in order to get the thieves out of it. But again, we hear the motto, "no union with slave-holders;" and I answer it, as that noble champion of liberty, N. P. Rogers, answered it with a more sensible motto, namely—*"No union with slave-holding."* I would unite with anybody to do right; and with nobody to do wrong. And as the Union, under the Constitution, requires me to do nothing which is wrong, and gives me many facilities for doing good, I cannot go with the American Anti-Slavery Society in its doctrine of disunion.

But to the second branch of the anti-slavery movement. The American and Foreign Anti-Slavery Society has not yet departed from the original ground, but stands where the American Anti-Slavery Society stood at the beginning. The energies of this association are mainly directed to the revival of anti-slavery in the Church. It is active in the collection, and in the circulation of facts, exposing the character of slavery, and in noting the evidences of progress in the Church on the subject. It does not aim to abolish the Union, but aims to avail itself of the means afforded by the Union to abolish slavery. The Annual Report of this Society affords the amplest and truest account of the anti-slavery movement, from year to year. Nevertheless, I am somewhat against this Society, as well as against the American Anti-Slavery Society. It has almost dropped the main and most potent weapon with which slavery is to be assailed and overthrown, and that is speech. At this moment, when every nerve should be strained to prevent a reaction, that Society has not a single lecturing agent in the field.

The next recognized anti-slavery body is the Free Soil party, *alias*— the Free Democratic party, *alias*—the Republican party. It aims to limit and denationalize slavery, and to relieve the Federal Government from all responsibility for slavery. Its motto is, *"Slavery Local—Liberty National."* The objection to this movement is the same as that against the American Anti-Slavery Society. It leaves the slaves in his fetters—in the undisturbed possession of his master, and does not grapple with the question of emancipation in the States.

The fourth division of the anti-slavery movement is, the *"Liberty Party"*—a small body of citizens, chiefly in the State of New York, but having sympathizers all over the North. It is the radical, and to my thinking, the *only* abolition organization in the country, except a few local associations. It makes a clean sweep of slavery everywhere. It denies that slavery is, or *can* be legalized. It denies that the Constitution of the United States is a pro-slavery instrument, and asserts the power and duty of the Federal Government to abolish slavery in every State of the Union. Strictly speaking, I say this is the only party in the country which is an abolition party. The mission of the Garrisonians ends with the dissolution of the Union—that of the Free Soil party ends with the relief of the Federal Government from all responsibility for slavery; but the Liberty Party, by its position and doctrines, and by its antecedents, is pledged to continue the struggle while a bondman in his chains remains to weep. Upon its platform must the great battle of freedom be fought out—if upon any short of the bloody field. It must be under no partial cry of "no union with slaveholders;" nor selfish cry of "no more slavery extension;" but it must be, "no slavery for man under the whole heavens." The slave as a man and a brother, must be the vital and animating thought and impulse of any movement, which is to effect the abolition of slavery in this country. Our anti-slavery organizations must be brought back to this doctrine, or they will be scattered and left to wander, and to die in the wilderness, like God's ancient people, till another generation shall come up, more worthy to go up and possess the land.

One anti-slavery movement nearly died out fifty years ago, and I am not prepared to deny the possibility of a like fate for this one. The elements of discord and deterioration are already in it, and working their legitimate results. And yet I am not gloomy. Present organizations may perish, but the cause will go on. That cause has a life, distinct and independent of the organizations patched up from time to time to carry it forward. Looked at apart from the bones and sinews, and body, it is a thing immortal. It is the very essence of justice, liberty and love. The moral life of human society—it cannot die, while conscience, honor and humanity remain. If but one be filled with it, the cause lives. Its incarnation in any one individual man, leaves the whole world a priesthood, occupying the highest moral eminence—even that of disinterested benevolence. Whoso has ascended this height, and has the grace to stand there, has the world at his feet, and is the world's teacher, as of divine right. He may sit in judgment on the age, upon the civilization of the age, and upon the religion of the age; for he has a test, a sure and certain test, by which to try all institutions, and to measure all men. I say, he may do this, but this is not the chief business for which he is qualified. The great work to which he is called is not that of judgment. Like the Prince of Peace, he may say, if I judge, I judge righteous judgment; still mainly, like him, he may say, this is not his work. The man who has thoroughly embraced the principles of justice, love, and liberty, like the true preacher of Christianity, is less anxious to reproach the world of its sins, than to win it to repentance. His great work on earth is to exemplify, and to illustrate, and to engraft those principles upon the living and practical understandings of all men within the reach of his influence. This is his work; long or short his years, many or few his adherents, powerful or weak his instrumentalities, through good report, or through bad report, this is his work. It is to snatch from the bosom of nature the latent facts of each individual man's experience, and with steady hand to hold them up fresh and glowing, enforcing, with all his power, their acknowledgment and practical adoption. If there be but *one* such man in the land, no matter what becomes of abolition societies and parties, there will be an anti-slavery cause, and an anti-slavery movement. Fortunately for that cause, and fortunately for him by whom it is espoused, it requires no extraordinary amount of talent to preach it or to receive it when preached.

The grand secret of its power is, that each of its principles is easily rendered appreciable to the faculty of reason in man, and that the most unenlightened conscience has no difficulty in deciding on which side to register its testimony. It can call its preachers from among the fishermen, and raise them to power. In every human breast, it has an advocate which can be silent only when the heart is dead. It comes home to every man's understanding, and appeals directly to every man's conscience. A man that does not recognize and approve for himself the rights and privileges contended for, in behalf of the American slave, has not yet been found. In whatever else men may differ, they are alike in the apprehension of their natural and personal rights. The difference between abolitionists, and those by whom they are opposed, is not as to principles. All are agreed in respect to these. The manner of applying them is the point of difference.

The slave-holder himself, the daily robber of his equal brother, discourses eloquently as to the excellency of justice, and the man who employs a brutal driver to flay the flesh of his Negroes, is not offended when kindness and humanity are commended. Every time the abolitionist speaks of justice, the anti-abolitionist assents—says, yes, I wish the world were filled with the disposition to render to every man what is rightfully due him. I should then get what is due me. That's right; let us have justice. By all means, let us have justice. Every time the abolitionist speaks in honor of human liberty, he touches a chord in the heart of the anti-abolitionist, which responds in harmonious vibrations. Liberty—yes, that is very evidently my right, and let him beware who attempts to invade or abridge that right. Every time he speaks of love, of human brotherhood, and the reciprocal duties of man and man, the anti-abolitionist assents—says, yes, all right—all true—we cannot have such ideas too often, or too fully expressed. So he says, and so he feels, and only shows thereby that he is a man as well as an anti-abolitionist. You have only to keep out of sight the manner of applying your principles, to get them endorsed every time. Contemplating himself he sees truth with absolute clearness and distinctness. He only blunders when asked to lose sight of himself. In his own cause he can beat a Boston lawyer, but he is dumb when asked to plead the cause of others. He knows very well, whatsoever he would have done unto himself, but is quite in doubt as to having the same things done unto others. It is just here that lions spring up in the path of duty, and the battle once fought in heaven is refought on the earth. So, it is, so hath it ever been, and so must it ever be, when the claims of justice and mercy make their demand at the door of human selfishness. Nevertheless, there is that within which ever pleads for the right and the just.

In conclusion, I have taken a sober view of the present anti-slavery movement. I am sober, but not hopeless. There is no denying, for it is everywhere admitted, that the anti-slavery question is the great moral and social question now before the American people. A state of things has gradually been developed, by which that question has become the first thing in order. It has got to be met. Herein is my hope. The great idea of impartial liberty is now fairly before the American people. Anti-slavery is no longer a thing to be prevented. The time for prevention is past. This is great gain. When the movement was younger and weaker—when it wrought in a Boston garret to human apprehension, it might have been silently put out of the way. Things are different now. It has grown too abundant—its ramifications too extended—its power too omnipotent, to be snuffed out by the contingencies of infancy. A thousand strong men might be struck down and its ranks still be invincible. One flash from the heart-supplied intellect of Harriet Beecher Stowe could light a million camp fires in front of the embattled hosts of slavery, which, not all the waters of the Mississippi, mingled as they are, with blood, could extinguish. The present will be looked to by after coming generations, as the age of anti-slavery literature—when supply on the gallop could not keep pace with the ever growing demand—when a picture of a Negro on the cover was a help to the sale of a book—when conservative lyceums and other American literary associations began first to select their orators for distinguished occasions, from the ranks of the previously despised Abolitionists. If the anti-slavery movement shall fail now, it will not be from outward opposition, but from inward decay. Its auxiliaries are everywhere. Scholars, authors, orators, poets, and statesmen, give it their aid. The most brilliant of American poets volunteer in its service. Whittier speaks in burning verse, to more than thirty thousand, in the *National Era*. Your own Longfellow whispers, in every hour of trial and disappointment, "labor and wait." James Russell Lowell is reminding us, that "men are more than institutions." Pierpont cheers the heart of the pilgrim in search of liberty, by singing the praises of "the north star." Bryant, too, is with us; and though chained to the car of party, and dragged on amidst a whirl of political excitement, he snatches a moment for letting drop a smiling verse of sympathy for the man in chains. The poets are with us. It would seem almost absurd to say it, considering the use that has been made of them, that we have allies in the Ethiopian songs; those songs that constitute our national music, and without which we have no national music. They are heart songs, and the finest feelings of human nature are expressed in them. "Lucy Neal," "Old Kentucky Home," and "Uncle Ned," can make the heart sad as well as merry, and can call forth a tear as well as a smile. They awaken the sympathies for the slave, in which anti-slavery principles take root, grow and flourish. In addition to authors, poets, and scholars at home, the moral sense of the civilized world is with us. England, France, and Germany, the three great lights of modern civilization, are with us, and every American traveller learns to regret the existence of slavery in his country. The growth of intelligence, the influence of commerce, steam, wind, and lightning, are our allies. It would be easy to amplify this summary, and to swell the vast conglomeration of our material forces; but there is a deeper and truer method of measuring the power of our cause, and of comprehending its vitality. This is to be found in its accordance with the best elements of human nature. It is beyond the power of slavery to annihilate affinities recognized and established by the Almighty. The slave is bound to mankind, by the powerful and inextricable net-work of human brotherhood. His voice is the voice of a man, and his cry is the cry of a man in distress, and man must cease to be man before he can become insensible to that cry. It is the righteousness of the cause—the humanity of the cause— which constitutes its potency. As one genuine bank bill is worth more than a thousand counterfeits, so is one man, with right on his side, worth more than a thousand in the wrong. "One may chase a thousand, and put ten thousand to flight." It is, therefore, upon the goodness of our cause, more than upon all other auxiliaries, that we depend for its final triumph.

Another source of congratulation is the fact that, amid all the efforts made by the Church, the Government, and the people at large, to stay the onward progress of this movement, its course has been onward, steady, straight, unshaken, and unchecked from the beginning. Slavery has gained victories, large and numerous; but never, as against this movement—against a temporizing policy, and against Northern timidity, the slave power has been victorious; but against the spread and prevalence in the country, of a spirit of resistance to its aggression, and of sentiments favorable to its entire overthrow, it has yet accomplished nothing. Every measure, yet devised and executed, having for its object the suppression of anti-slavery, has been as idle and fruitless as pouring oil to extinguish fire. A general rejoicing took place, on the passage of "the Compromise Measures" of 1850. Those measures were called peace measures, and were afterwards termed by both the great parties of the country, as well as by leading statesmen, a final settlement of the whole question of slavery; but experience has laughed to scorn the wisdom of pro-slavery statesmen; and their final settlement of agitation seems to be the final revival, on a broader and grander scale than ever before, of the question which they vainly attempted to suppress forever. The Fugitive Slave Bill has especially been of positive service to the anti-slavery movement. It has illustrated before all the people the horrible character of slavery toward the slave, in hunting him down in a free State, and tearing him away from wife and children, thus setting its claims higher than marriage or parental claims. It has revealed the arrogant and over-bearing spirit of the slave States towards the free States; despising their principles—shocking their feelings of humanity, not only by bringing before them the abominations of slavery, but by attempting to make them parties to the crime. It has called into exercise among the colored people, the hunted ones, a spirit of manly resistance well calculated to surround them with a bulwark of sympathy and respect hitherto unknown. For men are always disposed to respect and defend rights, when the victims of oppression stand up manfully for themselves.

There is another element of power added to the anti-slavery movement of great importance; it is the conviction, becoming every day more general and universal, that slavery must be abolished in the South, or it will demoralize and destroy liberty in the North. It is the nature of slavery to beget a state of things all around it, favorable to its own continuance. This fact connected with the system of bondage, is beginning to be more fully realized. The slave-holder is not satisfied to associate with men in the Church or in the State, unless he can thereby stain them with the blood of his slaves. To be a slave-holder, is to be a propagandist from necessity; for slavery can only live by keeping down the undergrowth morality which nature supplies. Every new-born white babe comes armed from the Eternal presence, to make war on slavery. The heart of pity, which would melt in due time over the brutal chastisements it sees inflicted on the helpless, must be hardened. And this work goes on every day in the year, and every hour in the day.

What is done at home, is being done also abroad here in the North. And even now the question may be asked, have we at this moment a single free State in the Union? The alarm at this point will become more general. The slave power must go on in its career of exactions. Give, give, will be its cry, till the timidity which concedes shall give place to courage, which shall resist. Such is the voice of experience, such has been the past, such is the present, and such will be that future, which, so sure as man is man, will come. Here I leave the subject; and I leave off where I began, consoling myself and congratulating the friends of freedom upon the fact that the anti-slavery cause is not a new thing under the sun; not some moral delusion which a few years' experience may dispel. It has appeared among men in all ages, and summoned its advocates from all ranks. Its foundations are laid in the deepest and holiest convictions, and from whatever soul the demon, selfishness, is expelled, there will this cause take up its abode. Old as the everlasting hills; immovable as the throne of God; and certain as the purposes of eternal power against all hindrances, and against all delays, and despite all the mutations of human instrumentalities, it is the faith of my soul that this Anti-Slavery cause will triumph.

Ladies and gentlemen, I am not superstitious, but I recognize an arm stronger than any human arm, and an intelligence higher than any human intelligence, guarding and guiding this Anti-Slavery cause, through all the dangers and perils that beset it, and making even auxiliaries of enemies, and confounding all worldly wisdom for its advancement. Let us trust that arm—let us confide in that intelligence—in conducting this movement; and whether it shall be ours to witness the fulfilment of our hopes, the end of American slavery or not, we shall have the tranquil satisfaction of having faithfully adhered to eternal principles of rectitude, and may lay down life in the triumphant faith, that those principles will, ultimately, prevail.

The Anti-Slavery Movement. A lecture by Frederick Douglass, before the Rochester ladies' anti-slavery society, Rochester, 1855

SELF-ELEVATION—REV. S. R. WARD

The letter of our esteemed friend, Ward, published in another column, will well repay an attentive perusal. It will be seen that he is in London, attending to private business. It is said, that "distance lends enchantment to the view"; this declaration may hold good in some cases, but in that of brother Ward, it is completely at variance. For just such men as he, *are needed here on the battle ground,* to work faithfully in the cause of our elevation—our emancipation from every species of servitude.

It is needless to remark, that the views of Mr. Ward, so clearly set forth in this letter, elicit our hearty concurrences. We always admired his characteristic boldness and plainness of utterance. In this letter before us, these features stand out in bold relief. We do not confess to a very extravagant appreciation of the modesty of some of our brethren which precludes them from speaking the truth, at the risk of offending those who arrogate to themselves a position, wholly in conflict with their democratic theory of EQUALITY.

It is well known that we have called down upon our devoted head, the holy (?) horror of a certain class of Abolitionists, because we have dared to maintain our Individuality, and have opened our own eyes, and looked out of them, through another telescope. This has been the head and front of our offending. *This is the way,* we "have thrown our principles to the winds, and substituted policy therefor."

Every day brings with it renewed evidence of the truthfulness of the sentiment, now, in various quarters, gaining the confidence and sympathy of our oppressed People, THAT OUR ELEVATION AS A RACE, IS ALMOST WHOLLY DEPENDENT UPON OUR OWN EXERTIONS. If we are ever elevated, our elevation will have been accomplished through our own instrumentality. The history of other oppressed nations will confirm us in this assertion. No People that has solely depended upon foreign aid, or rather, upon the efforts of those, in any way identified with the oppressor, to undo the heavy burdens, ever stood forth in the attitude of Freedom. Some one, imbued with the spirit of human freedom, from among themselves, has arisen to lead them on to victory. *They* have dashed their fetters to the ground. We do not affirm that no oppressed nation has ever received aid from abroad, which proved conducive to its deliverance. Not at all; but we do say, that the oppressed nation itself, has always taken a prominent part in the conflict, and has not been merely employed by its help-meet or coadjutor, to light camp-fires, bring water to the sick and wounded, and do all the incidental drudgery of the warfare.

We look upon the past as a precedent for the future. Our oppressed people are wholly ignored, in one sense, in the generalship of the movement to effect our Redemption. Nothing is done—no, nothing, as our friend Ward asserts, to inspire us with the Idea of our Equality with the whites. We are a poor, pitiful, dependent and servile class of Negroes, *"unable to keep pace"* with the movement, to which we have adverted—not even capable of *"perceiving what are its demands, or understanding the philosophy of its operations!"* Of course, if we are "unable to keep pace" with our white brethren, in their vivid perception of the demands of our cause, those who assume the leadership of the Anti-Slavery Movement; if it is regarded as having *"transcended our ability,"* we cannot consistently expect to receive from those who indulge in this opinion, a *practical recognition of our Equality.* This is what we are contending for. It is what we have never received. It is what we must receive to inspire us with confidence in the self-appointed generals of the Anti-Slavery host, the Euclids who are *theoretically* working out the almost insoluble problem of our future destiny.

True, our assertions may be misconstrued into a "malicious" misrepresentation of the facts of the case. But we shall present the facts, nevertheless, for none of these things shall ever deter us from the utterance of the truth. Our friend Ward seems to understand, that for the candid expression of his opinion, in this matter, he sets himself up as a target; but *"there I have said it,"* he remarks; and he has said it opportunely, and said it well. He has even dared in his insolence, to peep into the headquarters of the American Garrisonianism, to look at the colored mail-wrappers, and waiters in general, who, we fear, will be kept in their "waiting" position, till they satisfy their superiors, that they are able to "keep pace" with them, and that they "understand" the illiberal policy of *their* "operation." This they can never do in their present secondary position, as understrappers. They must *develop their manhood,* and not be too *modest* to attempt such development. Finally, we would remark, that we need, as a people, unity of effort, to impart efficiency to any self elevation movement, we may institute. If we rise, we must rise together; if we fall, we must fall together. We want such men as Ward, and Garnet, and Crummell, *at home.* They *must* come and help us. We know, by experience, that it is very *pleasant* to be where one can inhale a pure atmosphere, and lift up the voice against oppression, wafted as it were to the skies, upon the gratulations of the sympathising multitude, but "any one can perform an agreeable duty." Come home, then, brethren, and help us perform the *"disagreeable duty,"* of telling the truth, and the whole truth, though its promulgation make enemies of "our best friends"; come with an invincible determination to bring your mighty energies to bear upon the redemption of our race, and our whole race, from every species of oppression, irrespective of the form it may assume, or the source whence it may emanate.

Yes! come home, brethren—for, although the Garrisonian host have taken an anti-color position the great mass of Abolitionists call for us now more loudly than ever. There never was a time when your services were more in requisition than now. The field is ripe for the harvest; come, then, for the laborers are few.

Frederick Douglass' Paper, April 13, 1855

TO HON. CHAS. SUMNER

Rochester, April 24, 1855

My dear Sir:

There were two points in your address,[21] which grated a little on my ear at the moment, and which I would have called to your attention immediately after its delivery in Rochester had opportunity permitted. The first claimed that Mr. Garrison originated the present Anti-Slavery movement—a claim which I do not regard as well grounded, and I think I have succeeded in showing this in a lecture recently delivered in Rochester and in several other places during the past winter. Mr. Garrison found the Anti-Slavery movement already in existence when he stepped to the side of Benjamin Lundy in Baltimore. The second point was your very guarded disclaimer touching the social elevation of the colored race. It seemed to me that considering the obstinate and persecuting character of American prejudice against color, and the readiness with which those who entertain it avail themselves of every implication in its favor, your remark on that point was unfortunate.

I may be a little sensitive on the subject of our social position. I think I have become more so of late, because I have detected, in some of my old comrades, something like a falling away from their first love, touching the recognition of the entire manhood and social equality of the colored people. I do not mean by this, that every colored man, without regard to his character or attainments, shall be recognized as socially equal to white people who are in these respects superior to him; but I do mean to say that the simple fact of *color* should not be the criterion by which to ascertain or to fix the social station of any. Let every man, without regard to color, go wherever his character and abilities naturally carry him. And further, let there be no public opinion already to repel any who are in these respects fit for high social position.

For my own individual part as a colored man, I have little of which to complain. I have found myself *socially* higher than I am placed politically. The most debased white man in New York is my superior at the ballot box, but not so in a social point of view. In the one case color is the standard of fitness or unfitness; in the other, character.

I thank you heartily, my dear Sir, for honoring me with the opportunity of dropping these suggestions for your perusal.

With the spirit and manner of your noble address, I was not only pleased but profoundly gratified, and I thank God that talents and acquirements so high as yours, are devoted to the service of my crushed and bleeding race.

Believe me, my dear Sir,
Your faithful and grateful friend,
Frederick Douglass

Charles Sumner Papers, Harvard University

THE DOOM OF THE BLACK POWER

The days of the Black Power are numbered. Its course, indeed, is onward, but with the swiftness of an arrow, it rushes to the tomb. While crushing its millions, it is also crushing itself.—The sword of Retribution, suspended by a single hair, hangs over it. That sword must fall. Liberty must triumph. It possesses an inherent vitality, a recuperative energy, to which its opposite is a stranger. It may to human appearances be dead, the enemy may rejoice at its grave, and sing its funeral requiem, but in the midst of the triumphal shout, it leaps from its well guarded sepulchre, asserts the divinity of its origin, flashes its indigant eye upon the affrighted enemy, and bids him prepare *for the last battle, and the grave*.

We were never more hopeful, than at the present time, of the final triumph of the great Principles which underlie the Abolition movement. We rest our hopes upon a consciousness of their inherent Righteousness. Truth is mighty, and will prevail. This is a maxim, which we do not regard as a mere rhetorical flourish. We are conscious that there is a black side to our picture. The developments of the Slave Power, are anything but pleasant to contemplate. The Present, with its inflexible realities, seems to be but an echo of the terribleness of the Past. We have lived through the one, we are now grappling with the other. We should not, as an oppressed People, grow despondent. Fear and despondency prevent us from working for the overthrow of our common enemy, with that hopeful spirit which causes us to keep our head above the waters, despite the raging of the elements. If we can at the present crisis, catch but one soft, low whisper of peace to our troubled souls, let us cling to it. Let us rejoice in Hope. The arm of the enemy will yet be paralyzed, and *with our withered arm made whole,* we'll rise in all the majesty and might of *Freemen,* and crush the crushers of the dangerous element of Abolitionism.

Whoever will contemplate the diversified phases of the Abolition Movement, from its inception to the present, will readily discern, that at no period of its history, has it presented so favorable an aspect as at the present. Truth is progressive. It ever has been; it always will be. Retrogression cannot be written on its brow. To the gaze of the world, error may appear, robed in the habiliments of gladness, and riding upon the wings of the wind. Truth may seemingly lag behind, and stop to rest upon the weeping willow. But the progress of the latter is sure and steady. The race is not to the swift; Error will soon lie down and die, but Truth will live forever. Let these reflections continually inspire us while battling with the oppressor.

Again: we should rejoice that the People are beginning to read, mark, and inwardly digest the truth. The attention of the masses is being directed to the enormity, the crushing cruelty, the ever-grasping cupidity of Slavery.—They begin to feel and know that Slavery is as relentless as the greedy grave, that its thirst for human blood can only be satiated for the time being; even a gift of nearly a half a million square miles only cools, *pro tempore,* the ardor of its ferocity. They have found out to their hearts' content, the utter inutility of attempting to compromise, or enter into any kind of contract with it, that so soon as compromises and contracts cease to conduce to its own aggrandizement, it spurns the compromise, and those who were gulled by it, and tramples on the contract. They have also found out that the Slavery question is one in which white men, as well as black men, are immediately interested, that Slavery invades the rights of man, irrespective of color and condition. They now begin to realize as Truth, that which a short time ago, they were wont to regard as the freak of disordered imaginations. Hence, the wolfish cry of *"fanaticism,"* has lost its potency; indeed the *"fanatics"* are looked upon as a pretty respectable body of People. Some consolation can be deduced from this reflection.

Another thought: we regard the present developments of the Slave Power as precipitating the era of its disastrous doom. It has overreached itself, in its efforts to abolish Freedom in the United States, and erect its black standard upon every hill-top and valley in the land. It never wore an aspect so repulsive, as it does to-day. It has made such a frightful noise of late, that the attention of the world is directed toward it. The passage of the Fugitive Slave Act, and the Nebraska Bill; the recent marauding movements of the oligarchy in Kansas,[22] all the ebullitions of its pent-up wrath, are fatal stabs in the monster side. The Anti-Slavery sentiment of the North, has been strengthened and increased by these developments; indeed, the Abolitionists have now a most potent ally in the Slave Power. Slaveholders are unconsciously performing good service in the cause of Liberty, by demonstrating in their conduct, the truthfulness of the sentiments advanced and advocated by Abolitionists. The Anti-Slavery men of the land have faithfully admonished the whole country, and held up the Slave Power, as an Oligarchy determined on swaying the sceptre of universal dominion. But they have been regarded fanatics, and enthusiasts, crying wolf, when there was no wolf, inciting peaceful citizens to Rebellion, turning the country upside down, striving to destroy the Union. These and a host of similar allegations have been brought against them.

But now the great masses of the People find out by experience, that the wolf is indeed among them. They see his red, glaring eyes, and they cry out, *"kill the wolf;* he must not be permitted to go any farther in his depredations; our eyes have been opened." Thanks to the Fugitive Slave and Nebraska Bills. They have sealed the doom of the Black Power.

Lastly, we behold that doom written in unmistakable characters, by the great Republican Movement, which is sweeping like a whirlwind over the Free States. We rejoice in this demonstration. It evinces the fact of a growing determination on the part of the North, to redeem *itself* from bondage, to bury party affinities, and predilections, and also the political leaders who have hitherto controlled them; to unite in one grand phalanx, and go forth, and whip the enemy. *We* cannot join this party, because we think it lacks vitality; it does not go far enough in the right direction; it gives aid and comfort to the Slaveholder, by its concessions, and its willingness to "let Slavery alone where it is"—This is the very place where it should be attacked. We cannot attack it very well where it is not. But we have in former articles commented at length on the inconsistency and absurdity of that phase of Anti-Slavery sentiment and action, denominated Free-Soilism. We are, however, hopeful that this Republican Party as it grows in numbers, will also grow *"in the knowledge of the Truth."* A few more pro-Slavery demonstrations, a few more presses thrown into the river, a few more northern ministers driven from the South and West, a few more recaptures of Fugitives, near Bunker Hill, and Plymouth Rock, causing the People to see the system in all its native ugliness, and hate it with indescribable intenseness, and all will be well. We have no fears of ultimate success. Let each man do his duty. Let him continue to *agitate* in the circle in which he moves. Let him not lose sight of his individual responsibility, for this gives tone and vigor to associated action. The Slave's complaint must be heard at the fireside, in the street, in the counting house, in the prayer meeting, in the conference room, from the pulpit, in synods, and associations, and conferences, and especially *at the Polls*. We must follow the oppressor whithersoever he goeth, irrespective of the form in which he may develop himself, or the habiliments he may assume. Use the proper means, fight with the right weapons, let there be no cessation of the warfare, no diversion from the *real cause of the battle,* and we shall yet witness the *end of the Black Power in America.*

Frederick Douglass' Paper, July 27, 1855

TO HON. GERRIT SMITH

Rochester, Aug. 14, 1855

My dear Friend:

It would have been quite compensation enough to know that the dedication of my Book[23] afforded you pleasure. That dedication was inserted to place you under obligations, not to discharge my obligations to you, but rather to couple my poor name with a name I love and honor, and have it go down on the tide of time with the advantage of that name. Nevertheless, I gratefully accept your draft for fifty dollars. I do not know, just yet, what use I shall make of it. I am ever disposed to prefer the useful to the ornamental, and shall no doubt find some useful purpose to which I may properly devote the money.

My family are well and join me in kind regards to you and yours.

I leave home tomorrow on a four weeks campaign through Niagara and Orleans counties. I shall try to uphold the great principles of freedom, as laid down by yourself and Mr. Goodell at the radical abolition convention.

Yours most truly,
Frederick Douglass

Gerrit Smith Papers, Syracuse University

THE TRUE GROUND UPON WHICH TO MEET SLAVERY

If one half of the time, talent and money, which has been spent in attempts to fix upon the Constitution of the United States, a pro-slavery interpretation, had been devoted to showing its anti-slavery character, and in pointing out the duty of the citizen and statesman to abolish slavery under the Constitution, the anti-slavery cause would be in a far more hopeful condition than it now is. Never, in our judgment, will the North be roused to intelligent and efficient action against slavery, until it shall become the settled conviction of the people, that slavery is anarchical, unconstitutional, and wholly incapable of legalization. While men admit that slavery can be lawful anywhere, they concede that it may be made lawful everywhere; the morality which concedes the legality of slavery in Missouri, is impotent as against slavery in Kansas or anywhere else.— Slavery cannot be legal and illegal at the same time. It cannot be constitutional and unconstitutional at the same time. Grant that the constitution recognizes the right of slaveholders to their slaves in any State of this Union; and all the laws of comity, good neighborhood, and good faith, require that the parties to the constitution should respect the slaveholder's right of property everywhere in the Union.—Free Soilism is lame, halt and blind, while it battles against the spread of slavery, and admits its right to exist anywhere. If it has the right to exist, it has a right to grow and spread. The slaveholder has the best of the argument the very moment the legality and constitutionality of slavery is conceded. There is much reason in the logic of the late John C. Calhoun. If slaves are property in the eye of the constitution of the United States, they are subject to the same condition of all other property contemplated in that instrument, and their owners are entitled to all the advantages of this property equally with other citizens in their property.—We repeat, slaves are property, or they are not property. They are persons, or they are beasts of burden. The constitution must recognize them as one or the other. It cannot regard them as men and regard them as things at the same time. If it regards them as things, legitimate objects of property, then the laws that govern the rights and privileges of property must prevail in respect to them. But if it regards them as persons, then all the thunders of the constitution may be launched at the head of him who dares to treat them contrary to the rights sacred to persons in the constitution.

Now, the question is, does the constitution, in any of its provisions, know any man as a slave? Does it know anything under the name and character of slavery? Is there a single word in the constitution about slaves, slaveholders or slavery? We utterly deny that there is one such word, sentence or syllable to be found in that instrument, and will thank any reader of our paper to point out any such, as he may even think, by any necessary implication, and contradict our assertion. But there is no such reference to recognition of slavery in the constitution.

The concession that the constitution recognizes and allows slavery in the slave States, is a most false, injurious, and hurtful concession.—The doctrine resulting from it, drives conscientious abolitionists from the ballot-box, reduces the masses—who would be practical abolitionists—into mere *"Free Soilers,"* and arms the slaveholder with almost the only available power this side of *revolution* to defeat the anti-slavery movement. Out of this needless concession has arisen the partial and impatient watchwords of Northern anti-slavery men. Instead of the immediate, unconditional, and universal abolition of slavery in this country, we have liberty national, and slavery sectional—"no more slave States"—"no slavery outside the slave States." Instead of walking straight up to the giant wrong and demanding its utter overthrow, we are talking of limiting it, circumscribing it, surrounding it with free States, and leaving it to die of inward decay. A theory more fanciful and false, for getting rid of slavery, it would be difficult to conceive of. There was far more plausibility in the old notion that the abolition of the foreign slave trade would be the abolition of slavery. Cut off the stream and the pond will dry up, thought our fathers and the history of slavery demonstrates their folly, by showing that slavery has become more and more powerful every hour after the abolition of the slave trade. Before that trade was abolished, the anti-slavery sentiment of the country was active and energetic, and withal, bearing most precious fruits in gradual emancipation. But the slave trade at an end, the conscience of the people began to be at rest, and slavery took a new and more vigorous growth, and has been growing ever since. By surrounding the slave States with free States, it is contended that the influence of the latter upon the former, will naturally undermine and eventually overthrow slavery in the slave States. Now, when will men reason in accordance with facts? When will they learn wisdom from the past, and reduce that wisdom to practice? The lesson taught by the facts of history, and the facts of the present, is, that the free States on the borders of slave States, are far more likely to be corrupted by slavery than to abolish slavery.—The influence of Maryland on Pennsylvania has resulted in the conversion of the latter into a slave State, in a very important sense, making her mob and burn the property of the abolitionists, and converting her very halls of justice into slave prisons.

The only way to put an end to the aggressions of slavery, is to put an end to slavery itself. While the system of slavery exists, it must, from its very nature, be aggressive. The safety of liberty requires the complete extinction of its opposite; and since the U. S. Constitution was established to secure the blessing of liberty, there is, therefore, a high constitutional, as well as moral obligation, resting upon the American people to abolish slavery. Liberty can never be national while slavery is sectional, for the reason that a thing cannot exist and non-exist at the same time. Down with slavery everywhere, and proclaim the law of liberty everywhere is the truest, wisest and best course, and the manifest duty of abolitionists now and always.

Frederick Douglass' Paper, August 24, 1855

THE NEW YORK *TRIBUNE*—"Unpalatable Counsel"—Our Political Rights and Duties

We call the attention of our readers, and those, especially, for whom the advice is intended, to the article from the *Tribune,* under the caption, "Unpalatable Counsel." We have read it very carefully, and have arrived, not without due reflection, at the conclusion, that it reflects no credit upon the source from which it emanates. We very much regret its appearance, in such a journal as the *Tribune,* at such a crisis. And we indignantly repudiate all such counsel, however sincere and well intended, as counsel not fit to be given, much less to be obeyed. As much as we respect the *Tribune,* for its recent fearless advocacy of the sublime interests of Freedom, we cannot consent to occupy the position of mere automata, to move as we are moved, and act as we are acted upon, by its editor, or anyone else, who may arrogate unto himself the prerogative of making out for us, the path in which we must walk, in order to reach the goal of our political aspirations.—All advice addressed to us as men, and couched in language as respectful as that employed in advising other men, will be received in a manly and respectful manner. But when our gratuitous counsellors presume to address us in a tone of assumed superiority, and arrogant complacency, reminding us continually of our *"moral debasement,"* and virtually informing us, that, in descending to the advocacy of our Rights as Men, they expose themselves to public odium, and "incur very general obloquy, and injure their political associations by so doing," we, with all due deference, must respectfully decline their proffered assistance, and request them, with such counsel, to keep at a respectful distance from us.

We earnestly hoped to secure the *co-operation* of the *Tribune,* in the struggle which we have initiated for the attainment of our political rights. Believing that our moral, social, religious, and political elevation, is very materially dependent upon our own elevation, is very materially dependent upon our own endeavors, and that we have too long already relied upon the strong arm of the white man, to accomplish that for us which must be accomplished, to a great extent, through our instrumentality, we were not satisfied with forever remaining the victims of that suicidal inertia which has hitherto distinguished us, but revived upon our own responsibility, the agitation of our political Rights, and met in a Conventional capacity, with the specific object in view, of *"agitating"* the question of the Elective Franchise, and of initiating and elaborating, if possible, some movement, which would extort the respect even from our enemies, for the abolition of the odious restriction, now shamelessly imposed upon us.—But the *Tribune* meets us upon the very threshold of the agitation, and with a gracious condescension, not wholly unappreciated, informs us that *"they"* (we) *"can help win their rights if they will, but not by jawing for them."* *Et tu Brute?*

But why does the editor of the *Tribune* object to *our* agitation of our Political Rights? Why object to our making at this crisis, the hateful *"property qualification,"* [24] so-called, a prominent theme of discussion? It is because we are rightfully made the victims of those "fictitious distinctions," which he would gladly see obliterated? Not at all. He candidly declares, that "the Blacks ought to enjoy the Right of Suffrage exactly as the Whites do;" and, furthermore, adds, "we condemn all Property Qualifications, but if such were at all justifiable, they would be quite as salutary in their application to Whites as to Blacks." The Property Qualification, imposed upon us, is a great and grievous wrong. We have a Right, then, to be redressed; the same Right, derived from the same source, as has Horace Greeley, to be redressed of any wrong of which he may consider himself the recipient. And this being the case, it logically follows, *that we have the same Right to advocate the redress of what we feel to be a grievance,* as he, or any other man, or set of men, within the broad range of the Universe.

But the editor of the *Tribune* must not be misapprehended. We would do him ample justice. He gives us to understand very clearly why he considers *"jawing for our Rights,"* detrimental to our interests, as a People. He remarks, with characteristic candor: "We have no hope that the wrong now prevailing on this point will be redressed for many weary years; and we see very clearly that present agitation for its overthrow will only result in exposing to popular odium the Whites engaged in it. Efforts to abolish this partial Property Qualification do not hasten the enfranchisement of the Blacks, but they strongly tend to the practical disfranchisement of the Whites who favor their claims. We did what we could for Equal Suffrage in 1846, with feeble hopes of success, but with a perfect consciousness that we incurred very general obloquy and injured our political associates by so doing. At the same time we provoked the implacable hostility of the Blacks by telling them in reply to their formal solicitation of our Counsel, that the Case of Equal Suffrage could only be damaged by their conspicuous advocacy, that they would serve it most by keeping themselves as much out of sight as possible. That was honest and wholesome advice, but it subjected us to a large measure of active, hearty hatred."

Now, if these declarations mean anything, they mean, first, that there should be no agitation at present, on this subject, by either "Blacks" or Whites; and this assertion is based upon the untenable assumption that men should not do their duty, for fear of incurring popular odium. Upon what Principle of Ethics, such a conclusion can find a legitimate basis, we are at a loss to determine. Surely, not upon the eternal Principle of

Right. "Let Justice be done, though the heaven should fall."—Whether or not, the present agitation of this question, will have a favorable bearing upon its prospective triumph, we should do our duty, and so should everyone who is conscious of the Divinity of his origin, and his responsibility to God. And, again, if such an objection were valid, it would prevent the advocacy of all those great Reforms, by defending which, the Editor of the *Tribune,* and others become the victims of popular odium. We could, for instance, affirm with equal propriety, that as there are those who have no hope that the "three and a half millions of slaves" will be redressed for many weary years, and we see very clearly that present agitation for the overthrow "of Slavery" "only results in exposing to popular odium, the Whites engaged in it," we should all cease "jawing about their Rights." This decision is in perfect accordance with the code of Ethics, laid down by the philosopher of the *Tribune.*

But, in the second place, we are told that "efforts to abolish this partial Property Qualification do not hasten the enfranchisement of the Blacks, but they strongly tend to the practical disfranchisement of the Whites who favor their claims." This declaration is closely allied to the old and hackneyed assertion, that the Abolitionists have retarded the emancipation of the slave, by their continued agitation of the Slavery question. It is not expedient, we are to understand, from this, and similar declarations, to make any effort to abolish this wrong; no effort, either on the part of black, or white men. We have but to remark, that "Whatever is right, is practicable." And therefore, men should do their duty, and leave the event with God.

We are not informed how, or in what manner, white men became disfranchised, while doing their duty in regard to our enfranchisement. And we would say just here, in reference to another remark, that if one's *"political associates"* can be injured by his doing his duty, and he incurs obloquy at their hands for so doing, they are not fit associates for any *honest* man.

But we are told that the Cause of Equal Suffrage is damaged by our *"conspicuous advocacy,"* and that we should *"keep as much out of sight as possible."* This is *"honest"* advice, very likely, but, owing, perhaps, to the obliquity of our mental and moral vision, we are not able to discern and appreciate its *"wholesome"* tendency. We must not advocate our own Cause, for fear of damaging it; and the whites cannot be expected to do so, for they will but *incur general obloquy, and injure their political associates.* Verily, then, are we left without an advocate of any sort. We cannot keep out of sight; being the aggrieved party, we would not, if we could. The Editor of the *Tribune* places altogether too low an estimate upon our character as men, if he expects from us *such* humility. Our advocates, some of them, at least, generally seem to lose sight of the fact, that we are, naturally, their equals, men, like unto themselves. And they, apparently, regard us as *supplicants for favor* at the hands of the State, or Nation. We ask no favors at the hands of our common country. Upon our merits, let us stand, or fall. Being American Citizens, we wish to be in possession of all the Rights of our fellow-citizens.

With regard to our people *"clamoring"* in an *"Ethiopian* Convention," we could remark that we are not aware that any such Convention has ever been held in this country. No such contemptuous thrusts at the deliberative bodies of Colored American Citizens, shall deter us from the right of peaceably assembling ourselves together; while, on the other hand, we are not insensible to the amount of good to be derived from colored men pursuing other avocations than those we have, to a great extent, been forced to monopolize. It is too true, that as a People, our aspirations have not been sufficiently elevated; and, it is also equally true, that we have been, and still are the victims of an ostracism as relentless as the grave, which has superinduced that comparative degradation, to which the *Tribune* ungenerously calls attention, as *"a consequence of our moral debasement."* And while we have never beheld in Mr. Greeley, the development of *"any peculiar regard"* for our afflicted people, we must confess, that he indulges now and then in certain unmanly expressions, which lead us to infer that even he is not altogether free from that "unjust and damaging prejudice" to which he alludes in connection with our more than *"skin-deep degradation."* A hint to the wise is sufficient. The editor of the *Baltimore Clipper* has the following thrust at Mr. G. which may serve to illustrate our meaning. He says:

"Mr. Greeley, the great leader of the Abolition party in the North, and who has so often appealed to the Declaration of Independence, for his claim that the Negroes should enjoy a social and political equality with the whites, in a recent letter from London, shows the hypocrisy of his pretensions, and his abhorrence of that equality which he has so repeatedly preached. He says:

" 'The English are not skillful in varnishing vice—at least I have seen no evidence of their tact in that line. I have endured the spectacle of men dancing with women when rather beery and smoking, but at last the sight of a dark and by no means elegant mulatto waltzing with a decent looking white girl, while puffing away at a rather bad segar, proved too much for my Yankee prejudice, and I started.' "

We conclude this long article, by calling upon our people to put forth every effort in carrying out the measures inaugurated at our State Convention, for our complete and equal enfranchisement. Let us develop our manhood, not by folding our arms together, and keeping out of sight, while all the oppressed Nations of the earth are *struggling* to be free, but let us ever remember "that they who would be free, themselves must strike the blow."

Frederick Douglass' Paper, September 28, 1855

THE NEW YORK *TRIBUNE*—"Its Unpalatable Counsel"— "A Particular Kind of Effort."

"*Frederick Douglass' Paper,* criticising our 'unpalatable counsel,' says of our strictures on agitation and convention-holding by Blacks in resistance to their disfranchisement:

" 'It is not expedient, we are to understand from this and similar declarations, to make any effort to abolish this wrong.'

"—Now as our article was written expressly to discourage a particular kind of 'effort' as mistaken and ineffective, and to commend another species of effort as far preferable and likely to be more effective, we submit that the above is unwarranted."—*Tribune.*

We "submit" that this declaration of the *Tribune,* does not, in the least, invalidate the force, or impair the truthfulness of the strictures alluded to, nor does it prove the inference deduced, at all unwarrantable. We repeat the assertion above quoted. It makes but very little difference with us, or with those with whom we are proud to be identified, what was, or was not the intention of the Editor of the *Tribune,* in giving to our oppressed, but rapidly rising People, the uncalled for thrust, which he has very significantly and appropriately designated *"unpalatable counsel".*

We distinctly affirm, and re-affirm, that, whatever may have been the "intention" of said counsel, the words employed in the expression of that intention, are of such a character as not only *"to discourage a particular kind of effort,"* but all effort, on our part, to abolish the specific wrong of which we complain, which complaint, the *Tribune,* in classic language, denominates *"jawing"* for our Rights. We go farther.—Mr. Greeley not only objects to the efforts of the colored People, to abolish the Property Qualification, but to *any effort, at present,* to say the least, on the part of our *white* fellow citizens, for its abolition. And he assigns his reasons for such objections, in the following paragraph:

"Yet we have no hope that the wrong now prevailing on this point will be redressed for many weary years; and we see very clearly that present agitation for its overthrow will only result in exposing to popular odium the Whites engaged in it. Efforts to abolish this partial Property Qualification do not hasten the enfranchisement of the Blacks, but they strongly tend to the practical disfranchisement of the Whites who favor their claims. We did what we could for Equal Suffrage in 1846, with feeble hopes of success, but with a perfect consciousness that we incurred very general obloquy and injured our political associates by so doing.—At the same time we provoked the implacable hostility of the Blacks by telling them, in reply to their formal solicitation of our counsel, that the cause of Equal Suffrage could only be damaged by their conspicuous advocacy—that they would serve it most by keeping themselves as much out of sight as possible. That was honest and wholesome advice, but it subjected us to a large measure of active, hearty hatred."

Now, after reading these candid declarations, were we not fully justified in making the inference which Mr. G. declares *"unwarranted?"* We were remarking, in the article to which he has reference, upon the specific wrong imposed upon us in this so-called Property Qualification; and, in view of what he had said in relation to our *"keeping"* ourselves *"as much out of sight as possible;"* on the subject the assertion, that *"efforts to abolish this Property Qualification do not hasten the enfranchisement of the Blacks,"* &c.; and then holding us up to the world as an *"indolent, improvident, servile, and licentious class,"* could we refrain from making the inference that Mr. G. thought it inexpedient for us to "make any effort to abolish this wrong?" True, he advises us to stop "clamoring against white oppression," and, with our axe upon our shoulder, go to clearing and buying farms, and leave white men to sit alone at their tables, acting upon the principle, that if eating meat (with them) make them offend, we will eat no more. But will he pretend that such a course of conduct on our part, could properly be regarded as an effort to abolish *the* wrong about which we are *"jawing"* and *"clamoring?"* Would it be regarded as such an effort on the part of the "licentious" class known as the Irish, whose right to "jaw" about their rights, *ad libitum,* the *Tribune* so zealously and righteously advocates? Does Mr. Greeley advise the Irish to cease "jawing about their rights," and "clamoring" against Know Nothing oppression; [25] keep themselves as much out of sight as possible; and, in order to get rid of the virulent prejudice of which they are the victims, and work out the problem of their further destiny, to bring corn and potatoes, the products of their own farms, to market? If he has ever given such advice, it has escaped our observations. If he has objected to their meeting in convention, and other public assemblages, for the purpose of "jawing" against their oppressors, we are not aware of it. Then why should American citizens be debarred the privilege of meeting in Conventions, if they desire it, for the purpose of calling public attention to any specific wrong, or indignity, which they feel too intolerable to be borne? Why should *we* be told to break up our Conventions, cease "jawing" and "clamoring," when others equally *"indolent, improvident, servile, and licentious,"* (all of which adjectives we reject as untruthful, and *"unpalatable,"*) are suffered to indulge, without animadversion, in similar demonstrations? In a word, why should we be sent to hoeing, and planting corn, to digging potatoes, and raising cabbages, as the *"preferable and more effective"* method of abrogating the unjust, anti-Republican, and disgraceful restriction imposed upon us, in the property qualification? We see no good reason for it; neither does Mr. Greeley. No one has been more prominent than he in advocating the right of women to "jaw" about their political, and other Rights. The laboring classes, too, while *"clamoring"* about oppression, receive from him, the most cordial demonstrations of sympathy. We are, however, only *colored* men in his estimation, and being an "anomalous class," we must be dealt with in an anomalous manner. If necessary to prevent the "practical disfranchisement" of our white brethren, we must even give up the right to assemble ourselves together; we must cease our conspicuous advocacy of our cause; we must be neither seen, nor heard; we must go out into the country. And if ever the time should arrive when the agitation in question will not be deemed impracticable; a time when the white man's advocacy of our right to vote without the dollars, like other men, will not expose them to "popular odium," and "injure" their "political associates," why, then, they will—think about it.

Now, we do not deny that as a class, the aspirations of the free colored portion of our citizens have not been of a character sufficiently elevated, to excite the admiration of Mr. Greeley. Perhaps, we should approach nearer the fact in the case, were we to affirm, that our aspirations have been high enough, but they have been crushed by a power, superior in strength, and apparently, in wickedness, if not in indolence and licentiousness. In our former article, we made little or no allusion to the wholesale allegations of indolence, &c., first concocted by Slaveholders to subserve their own interests, but now taken up by Mr. G. and levelled against us, in a manner calculated to excite their profound admiration, and their unaffected gratitude. We now simply deny that there is any foundation for his ungenerous and libellous accusations; for, if facts speak more loudly than words, and if *statistics* are of any consequence in this controversy, never were words made to speak more falsely, than the four *"unpalatable"* definitives, while standing in their present connection.

In conclusion, we call upon Mr. G. to read his article again, and to see whether or not he has discouraged any action on the part of the "free blacks," for the overthrow of the particular wrong adverted to.

Frederick Douglass' Paper, October 5, 1855

THE FINAL STRUGGLE

Among the varied and multitudinous array of opposition to the antislavery movement, no Abolitionist should abate his zeal, or relax his energy, but rather redouble his diligence, and resolve, if need be, to die upon the battle field, struggling for the victory. There is some consolation in the reflection, that the conflict will not, cannot, last forever. The hour which shall witness *the final struggle,* is on the wing. Already we hear the *booming* of the bell which shall yet toll the death knell of human slavery.

Liberty and Slavery cannot dwell together forever in the same country. There is not one iota of affinity existing between them. They hate each other, with a hatred which is unto Death. They ever have been, and they ever must remain, in a state of irreconcilable hostility. Before a union can be effected between them, the laws which govern the moral universe must be repealed. It is absurd in any one to expect to witness the spirit of Liberty being led, by the demon of Slavery, to the hymeneal altar.—As well expect the pains and sorrows of hell, to mingle, in happy unison, with the pleasures and the joys of heaven; the spirits of just men made perfect, with the spirits of the lost.

It is useless, then, to attempt to effect a union between them. No compromise can effect it. No legislation can change the inflexible law of adaptation, the eternal fitness of things. No compact can make that Right, which is wrong from its first principles to its crowning assumptions.

It is, then, perfectly apparent to every reflecting mind, that a crisis more critical than any which has preceded it, is pending. This crisis cannot much longer be delayed. It must come to pass as the legitimate result of the past and the present struggle for the mastery in which we behold these deadly enemies engaged. We may attempt to bind up the wounds of the respective hostile parties, with mollifying ointment, but this will not avert the impending hour. It must come, as sure as the laws of God cannot be trampled upon with impunity.

Then, as a nation, if we are wise, we will prepare for the last conflict, for that final struggle in which the enemy of Freedom must capitulate. Instead of indulging in delusive dreams of safety, the Slave Power should prepare for the era of its disastrous doom; it will be wise and consider its latter end.

The motto to be inscribed upon the banner of Freedom, in the last conflict is not, "No more Slave States," nor "No Slavery outside of the Slave States;" but no Slavery where it does exist; no Slavery in the Republic. We shall not be burdened or annoyed by unhallowed compromises, we shall make no contracts with the perfidious enemy. Not one word of concession or compromise, shall escape our lips, not one syllable of apology. Truth and Error, Liberty and Slavery, in a hand-to-hand conflict. This is what we want; this is what we will have. The utter extinction of Slavery, everywhere in our national domain; the subversion of the Black Power, wherever, in all our widespread territory, it dare lift its defiant head toward Heaven.

Again; in the final struggle, in order to be successful, there must exist a thorough organization of freemen, with the single issue presented, Liberty everywhere, Slavery nowhere; there must be unity of effort; every man who loves freedom, must array himself in her defence, whatever may have been his past political predilections. The magnet of Human Freedom, must be held high above the din of party tumult, and every man who is willing to peril his life, his fortune, and his sacred honor, in its defence, will ultimately be attracted to the magnet, whether Whig, or Democrat, or Freesoiler, or Abolitionist. This will form the great Abolition Party of the land. In fact, there must be, and there will be, but two Parties in the country; these will be known not as Whigs, nor as Democrats, nor as Republicans, so far as party names are concerned, but simply as the Anti-Slavery and Pro-Slavery parties of the country. All who are desirous of maintaining a sort of assumed neutrality on the question, as well as the most inveterate haters of the Abolition movement, will constitute the Pro-Slavery Party. Neither of these parties, in the last conflict, will be *wheedled* from the arena, by the presentation of incidental issues. Each party, forming a unit, and rallying under its own banner, will fight for the triumph of its respective Principles.

We do not fear the result of such a struggle. The sooner the last battle shall be fought, the sooner victory will perch upon the standard of the free. The Principles which form the basis of the Abolition movement, are as unchanging and as undying as their Eternal Author. They must triumph *for Heaven has nowhere promised to delegate his power to another*. Let us then prepare for the battle, and for victory. Already are the masses moving. The disintegration of the once powerful political Parties, is a cheering and significant sign of the times. The throne of the despot is trembling to its deep foundations. There is a good time coming. We yet shall make the welkin ring with the mighty hallelujahs of the free.

Frederick Douglass' Paper, November 16, 1855

THE REPUBLICAN PARTY—OUR POSITION

By reference to the article published in another column, from "The *Oneida Sachem,*" under the caption, "The Position of Parties," it will be observed, that the Editor of that Paper indulges in a train of well-intended criticism upon an editorial which appeared in a recent number of this journal, upon the various Phases of Anti-Slavery. He also expresses the apprehension that Mr. Douglass, "by keeping a certain number of men within the sphere of his influence, from voting in the only place where their votes will count against Slavery, will indirectly aid the cause which he deprecates."—He does not deny the correctness of our brief exposition of the Principles of the Republican Party, but attempts to defend them. He indirectly, if not directly, accuses us of retarding the cause of God and Humanity, by indulging in what he conceives to be an abstract proposition, thus standing in the way of the newly organized Party.

Our contemporary makes our incidental reference to the Abolition of

Slavery by Legislation, a subject of special criticism and condemnation; and in his query, "When or where has anybody in his sober senses declared for the doctrine of abolishing slavery by Legislation" either entirely ignores the existence of such men as Gerrit Smith, Wm. Goodell, Beriah Green, Lysander Spooner, and thousands of others, or accuses them of laboring under the doleful effects of mental hallucination.

Now, though we may not be regarded as "in our sober senses," we affirm what the Editor of the *Sachem* denies; viz. That Congress has power to abolish slavery in the States. And, as he expressly affirms that he believes *that every slave at the South* is held in defiance of the Constitution, we do not see how he can consistently remain with the Republican Party, and deny the Right of the General Government to abolish a so-called Institution, which is directly inimical to the objects for which the Government was established.

It may be well for us, however, to dispel an illusion, of which our respected contemporary, is, apparently, the victim. When we speak of abolishing Slavery by Legislation, we do not wish to be understood as affirming that it is the duty or prerogative of Congress to enact a specific law, in order to *make* Slavery illegal.—We have never asserted that Congress, or any other body of men, has any such power. Such an assertion would presuppose the present legality of Slavery. What we declare, is, first, *that Slavery has never been legalized, and never can be.* That, when the Constitution was adopted, there was no legal or constitutional Slavery in the States—that not a single State Constitution then in existence, recognized, authorized, or sanctioned Slavery. And, furthermore, that there could have been no constitutional authority in the several Legislatures to enact the statutes which were passed in obedience to the dicta of Slaveholders. In the second place, Slavery being illegal, and, of course, unconstitutional, *Congress is bound, constitutionally bound, to provide all necessary means in having this principle carried out in practice.*—And how so? Let us briefly examine. We affirm, what no man, "in his sober senses," will deny, that the Constitution, in declaring that "no person shall be deprived of liberty, without due process of Law," and that "the right of the people to be secure in their persons shall not be violated," prohibits Slavery. Again; this instrument in declaring that "the writ of Habeas Corpus shall not be suspended in time of peace," ("the writ that made Slavery impossible in England,") provides for the liberation of every slave in the land.—Furthermore, "The United States shall guaranty to every State in this Union, a republican form of government." The Federal

Government is then constitutionally bound to abolish Slavery in the States, for Slavery is directly in conflict with Republicanism. The moment the General Government carries out this provision of the Constitution, the equal rights of every citizen in the country, will be secured.

It seems very clear to us, not only that the Constitution prohibits Slavery, but also confers power on the Federal Government to abolish it. For, we read,

"Congress shall have power to make all laws which shall be necessary and proper for carrying into execution the foregoing powers, and all other powers vested by this Constitution in the Government of the United States, or in any department or officer thereof." (Art. I, Sec. 8, Clause 18.)

Much is said concerning the limited powers of the Federal Government; but certainly these powers are not so limited as to prevent it from performing what it is expressly required to perform. We must ever remember that if the Constitution calls upon the Federal Government, to "secure the blessings of Liberty"—"to establish justice"—"insure domestic tranquility"—"provide for the common defence," and "promote the general welfare," and the powers of the General Government are too limited to "interfere" with a "State Institution," which is a fruitful source of all manner of Despotism, of injustice, of wars, &c., &c., then the State Governments *virtually abolish the General Government,* as their powers are supreme, and the General Government *is a nullity.* Does the Editor of the *Sachem* deny this? But the Constitution of the United States is the supreme Law of the land, and *if Congress has any power at all, it has power to compel the execution of all the power vested by the Constitution in the Government of the United States.*—Hence, we affirm, that Congress has power to abolish Slavery in the States, such Slavery being illegal, and unconstitutional.

The editor of the *Sachem* remarks, that if an unconstitutional act is committed; if persons are deprived of life, liberty, or property, "without due process of law," in defiance of the Constitution, there must be a tribunal to which to appeal that the wrong may be righted. That tribunal is established by our Government. It is not Congress; it is not the President or his Cabinet—it is the "United States Supreme Court." We do not deny the power of the Supreme Court to abolish Slavery by a righteous decision, affirming the Unconstitutionality of Slavery, and applying the Habeas Corpus to slaves. But we *do* deny that Congress "in order to set the slaves in the Southern States at Liberty," would be obliged to "usurp the place" of the Supreme Court. Let Congress execute its own legitimate powers, without interfering with the Supreme Judiciary, let her establish courts in all the slaveholding States, and appoint Federal Judges who shall give the writ of Habeas Corpus to the slaves in the land—and, as it were, in an instant, the hideous monster would be throttled to death. Let her suppress the slave trade between the States, organize, arm, and discipline the slaves as militia, all of which she has power to do, and the "Institution" would be as a thing of yesterday. Now, if Congress has power to do these things, (and we defy any man to prove to the contrary,) she has power to abolish Slavery.

We do not, as our friend of the *Sachem* alleges, "complain of the Republican Party, because it has not proposed to exercise a power which the Constitution does not confer upon Congress;" but, believing as we do that Slavery anywhere in the country is unconstitutional (this the editor of the *Sachem* admits,) we *do* complain that this party admits its *Constitutional right to continue where it exists,* and proposes to let it there flourish as long as it is possible to do so; the Party will not consent to touch it so long as it restricts the sphere of its worse than barbarous operations, to certain localities. It dances to the music of Freedom National— Slavery, Sectional. Though the Constitution expressly declares that "*no* person shall be deprived of liberty without due process of law," and the right of the people to be secure in their persons," "shall not be violated," the Republican Party virtually declares to the country, and to the world, that it does not propose to interfere with the Constitutional Rights (?) of those traffickers in the blood of souls, who are daily depriving millions of men and women of their liberty, without due process of Law; but it will only strive to prevent the extension of Slavery. Now, we unhesitatingly declare that the slaveholder, *as such,* has no Right under the Constitution; for no man has a Right, either constitutionally, or otherwise, to deprive his fellow-man of liberty, except for crime, and then, only by "due process of law." Then, how can we accept the invitation of the *Sachem,* to join the Republican Party, *conceding, as it does, to the slaveholder* the "*Constitutional Right*" to rob his present and future victims, in the slave States. We can endorse no such Principle. Our motto is, *Onward*—not *Backward*. Were we to relinquish our present position on the Slavery question, and join the Republican Party, we should feel that we were retrograding, instead of advancing.

We believe that the Principles enunciated by Gerrit Smith, and Wm. Goodell, and other great men in the land, are just and Right, and we cannot forsake those principles, on the ground of their alleged impracticability. But at the same time we do not claim for this journal that it is the *only true* Anti-Slavery paper in the western part of this State, as the *Sachem* unjustly and uncharitably affirms. We believe that the Republican Party is Anti-Slavery as far as it goes; but believing that it does not go far enough in the right direction, we earnestly invite its members to take a higher position, make no concessions to the Slave Power, strike at Slavery *everywhere* in the country, and not wait for a pro-Slavery Supreme Court to proclaim the acceptable year, the year of Jubilee, throughout all the land, and unto *all* the inhabitants thereof.

Frederick Douglass' Paper, December 7, 1855

TO MRS. TAPPAN

Rochester, March 21st, 1856

Dear Madam:

The notice of the death of Miss Weems was already in my paper when your letter came. You will receive the dozen papers as you direct. You will be glad to know that Mr. Garnet is now in the United States and that you may learn more from him of one in whom you have taken so lively an interest. I have now been at home about one week—and am resting a little from my winter's labors. I have travelled this winter between four and five thousand miles, visited communities as far east as Bangor, and as far west as Cincinnati, delivered about seventy lectures, been in snowdrifts oft, but have reached this season, always very trying to my health, with nothing more serious than a sore throat which is now on the mend.

Please say to my good friend, your husband, that I am very glad that his mind is for the present especially directed to the subject of enquiry: how can the condition of the free colored people be best improved? I am yet of the opinion that nothing can be done for the free colored people remaining in their present employment. These employments— such as waiting at hotels, on steamboats, barbering in large cities, and the like—contribute to no solid character. They require servility, beget dependence, destroy self-reliance, and furnish leisure and temptation to every possible view—from smoking cigars to drinking whiskey. What we want is steady employment at respectable trades, or on the land. To this end if I had money I would establish an industrial school to begin with, where the education of the hands and heart should be the main feature. I have now five colored boys in my family—three my own children, and two adopted ones taken from the street. They have been with me nearly a year. They are good boys both—and may make good men—but if my paper should fail, they would be flung out of employment and I know not where they would find any other than those which would be sure to degrade them and perhaps ruin them. A small amount of money expended in this direction—I mean, in securing places for colored boys to learn trades—would bring good results. But I write in haste. I have not heard Mr. Finney, for I have scarcely spent a Sabbath in the city this winter. Two Sundays ago, I had the high pleasure of hearing [an] able discourse from Mr. Tappan's friend Mr. Boynton at Cincinnati. He made mention of the late tragedy in that city in his prayer in a manner wonderfully solemn and impressive. I hope to hear Mr. Finney on Sunday.

Yours with great respect,
Frederick Douglass

Frederick Douglass MSS, Henry P. Slaughter Collection

TO HON. GERRIT SMITH

Rochester, March 22d, 1856

Yes, my dear friend, I am at home, and am at home quite sick with my old throat disorder, of which I had hoped I was entirely rid, because it passed me by so gently last year. It is now, however, upon me, much after the old fashion, but less severely than formerly.

No, Mr. Smith, you are not down. Lies cannot put you down. Why, small as I am, it will take something bigger than big lies to put me down. With the smiles of God and the approval of my own conscience, even I can stand—and I have more faith in your ability to stand, than in my own. I am glad you gave 3000 dollars to the cause of freedom in Kansas, and I hope you will use your power in that country to shame the free State men out of this contemptible selfishness in excluding the free colored man out of that Territory. The dark spirit, that would forbid God's sable children in Kansas, would drive them off the footstool. It is the principle of slavery. I am anxious to see the call for the Syracuse Convention. Please make friendly mention of me to Mrs. Smith and to all your dear ones.

Yours truly always,
Frederick Douglass

Gerrit Smith Papers, Syracuse University

THE UNHOLY ALLIANCE OF NEGRO HATE AND ANTI-SLAVERY

No reform of greater dignity than the Anti-Slavery reform; no movement more beneficent in its purpose, or comprehensive in its scope, has claimed the attention and support of mankind, since the announcement on earth of the primary doctrines of "peace and good will," and the brotherhood of man. Slavery is said to be the sum produced by the addition of all villainies; hence the Anti-Slavery movement may be esteemed in its purposes as the sum of all virtues.

The command to love one another; to do as we would be done by, had been heard by men of the past, but their full import and application were not understood. Its moral grandeur was not perceived until the Anti-Slavery movement burst on the world, avowing as its mission "to curb the great, and raise the low"; embracing in its influence, men of all races and tongues; claiming an equality of manhood for the servile peasantry of Europe, the brown wanderers of Asia and America; lastly and more wonderful still, the ebon hued Negro, whose darkened brow was held to be the mark of God's displeasure, placing him beyond the pale of human sympathies, rendering him a lawful prey to the spoiler and the task master.

Attracted by ideas of such sublime and universal benevolence, the Anti-Slavery movement was received into the hearts, and baptised with the genius of such men as Sharpe, Clarkson, and Wilberforce of England, and at a later date, of Garrison, Rodgers, and other devoted American reformers.

Aided by the talents and unwavering self-devotion of its advocates, but more by its own intrinsic power, it commenced a career of triumphant progress, and is destined to encompass the earth, and fill all hearts with a conviction of the dignity and inviolable sacredness of humanity.

First, it touched the slave trade, which to that time had been deemed the most honorable as well as the most lucrative branch of commerce. Kings rivalled each other in its marts, and honored their subjects who had been successful in its prosecution. But this mighty interest· speedily succumbed to the onslaughts of the friends of freedom, and although not suppressed, is deemed piracy by all right thinking men, and is so pronounced by all civilized governments. This was but a partial triumph. It next attacked the institutions of slavery itself, and one by one the nations of the earth are rising up and casting out the foul devilism of slavery.

England from the magnitude of her sacrifices, may claim to lead the way in the onward march of the genius of universal emancipation, and the torch of freedom has passed from nation to nation, until the followers of the Arabian prophet, they who morning, noon and night bow their heads towards Mecca, and declare "there is no God, but God, and Mahomet is his Prophet," have, "for the glory of God," suppressed the slave traffic, and abolished slavery in their borders.

Slavery now finds no refuge among civilized men, except in the colonies of effete Spain, in semi-barbarous Brazil, and semi-Republican America. And here we rejoice to think that it cannot much longer continue, for if the North remains indifferent to the crime and disgrace of their complicity with slaveholding, that dark power will destroy itself, by the virulence of its defenders, who by their shameless outrages will compel Northern men in self-defence, to make common cause with the slave.

Of late years the political Economist has entered the field against slavery. Quitting the high moral ground of its innate and utter sinfulness, ceasing to exhort the people and "we are verily guilty concerning our brother," the Economist parades long columns of figures, to prove that slavery is unprofitable. Statements of the improvident modes of culture, and the wornout lands of the slave States, abound, and assertions of its blasting degrading effect upon the poor white laborers of the slave States, are made, and they are called on to rise up against its longer continuance.

We are pleased to see this. We would have every moral precept, every consideration of interest that influences men brought to bear against the accursed system. We are pleased that the whites are finding that they cannot degrade their black brother without sharing his degradation. But we grieve to find, that under the shelter of this mode of attack the fell spirit of Negro hate can hide itself.

Opposing slavery and hating its victims has come to be a very common form of Abolitionism. We see its development in the professedly free Constitutions of California and Kansas, claiming the support of the world as free States, and yet refusing to colored men a legal residence. They meet colored men on their thresholds, and say, "we care not how temperate and industrious you may be, how you accumulate wealth, or acquire knowledge, we want none* of you here." This is a government of white men. Prominent citizens of Kansas have declared their intention, to preserve the soil of Kansas, from the *accursed* presence of the African, *bond* or *free*.

Out on such Anti-Slavery as this. 'Tis the basest selfishness masquerading in the garb of an angel. Let it everywhere be marked and denounced, by those whose Anti-Slavery convictions admit the brotherhood of man; all else is false reform, and will curse more than it will bless.

In view of these facts, we need a new preaching of the Anti-Slavery evangel, directed to the hearts and consciences of men, and not their purses. The banner of pure Anti-Slavery must be borne aloft as of old, and men be called to its support in the name of God and humanity. This people must be taught that slavery is not only an economical blunder, but an outrage on humanity, and a sin against God.

Frederick Douglass' Paper, April 5, 1856

TO BENJAMIN COATES, ESQR.

Rochester, April 17th, 1856

My dear Sir:

Your two letters have reached me, and should have been sooner answered but for my absence from home when they arrived here. You have, my dear Sir, given me many and striking proofs of an honest desire to assist in changing the popular estimate in which my poor people are held, in this country. I hope and I believe, I am not wanting in gratitude to you for your unostentatious labors to this end, although I am not able to agree with you as to the wisdom of Colonization as a means to that end. You think I do not understand Colonization. Perhaps I don't. I am sure, however, that I understand and appreciate your earnest and disinterested endeavors to promote the welfare, happiness, and higher de-

*Original reads "some," obviously a printer's error.—*Ed.*

velopment of my unfortunate race—whether in Africa or America. This is to me a great satisfaction. I know you less as connected with Colonization than as connected with the improvement of the character and condition of the colored people here. I am not about to write you an argument against Colonization. You are already acquainted with the argument. It has been repeatedly pressed upon your attention far more ably than I am able to press it, and I know that when the truth strongly presented fails to convince, convincement is not likely to follow when the same truth is but feebly and imperfectly stated. Still I am almost compelled by your eloquent plea for Colonization, briefly to state my conviction touching the Colonization movement. I believe then, that the agitation of Colonization, has a direct tendency to divert attention from the great and paramount duty of abolition, and stands directly in the way of the latter, that it serves to deaden the national conscience when it needs quickening to the great and dreadful sin of slavery, that it furnishes an apology for delaying emancipation until the whole four millions can be sent to Africa, thus interposing a physical impossibility between the slave and his deliverance from chains, that it aims to extinguish the hope of ultimate elevation for the free Negro in this country, and to unsettle all his plans of progress here, that it robs his future in this country of all that can gladden his heart and nerve him to manly endeavor, that it serves to confirm existing prejudice as a thing natural and unsurmountable. Believing all this and more—however I may feel towards Liberia as an existing fact, I cannot do other than expose the Colonization movement. You have large views of the future of Africa. So have I. My heart can never be indifferent to any legitimate movement for spreading the blessings of Christianity and civilization in that country. But the effort must not be to get the Negroes out of this country but to get Christianity into that.

Please send me any names you may have to whom you think my Book or paper will be acceptable, and either shall be promptly sent as you shall direct. I am, my dear Sir,

Your true and grateful friend,

Frederick Douglass

William M. Coates Papers, Historical Society of Pennsylvania

THE SUFFRAGE QUESTION

The Legislature of the Empire State has adjourned, and the suffrage question remains in *statu quo*. The various Petitions presented to that body, praying for the abolition of the odious, anti-Democratic, and anti-Christian property-qualification clause, (a clause which is odious on account of its restrictive application,) were referred to a Committee of seven, who did not report thereon. Judge Foote, the Chairman of said Committee, and one other gentleman, were in favor of granting the prayer of the Petitioners. The remaining five were opposed. These wished us to remain in our present position, that they might have the opportunity of pointing to us as evidence of the inability of the colored man to rise above his degraded condition. We should, for certain reasons, be glad to know the political complexion of these five philanthropic Legislators.

We learn from reliable authority, that the Chairman of the Committee thought it best, under the circumstances, not to report, pro or con, on the Petitions. There would have been a majority and minority Report. But we would have been far better satisfied had the Committee reported. We should then have had the arguments of Judge Foote in our favor, and the influence of this distinguished gentleman might have operated favorably for our cause at the next session of the Legislature; for, like the importunate widow in the Gospel, we intend by our continual coming, *to weary* the Legislature into a recognition of our manhood, by abolishing the infamous restriction alluded to. And on the other hand we should have had the satisfaction of reading the arguments of those who practically deny the Democratic axiom, that Taxation and Representation should go together, and in its stead enunciate and enforce the absurd dogma, that Representation and a certain physical Conformation should go together.

But we are not at all disheartened. If our enemies suppose that we intend to give up the contest, they have made an egregious blunder.— *Nil desperandum* is still our motto, and we will never relinquish it. We will cling to it despite all opposition, for Right must be triumphant in the end.

During the past few years, public sentiment has undergone a change, favorable to the recognition of our claims as citizens. The injustice of the disabilities under which we labor, is becoming more and more apparent. The masses begin to look at the matter in its true light. The laboring

population begin now to realize their critical position; for the same aristocratic selfishness which thrusts us outside the pale of Humanity, will as
soon thrust them out, and the monopoly of the Elective Franchise be
enjoyed by the dyspeptic nabobs of the State. The same hand which is
laid upon us so heavily, will yet be laid upon them. And they would be
wise, to oppose *all* the proscriptive movements of the day, and oppose
them from Principle.

Finally, we call upon our oppressed brethren throughout the State to
remain firm and unshaken. Endure unto the end, and the battle is ours.
The enemy must inevitably capitulate.—There is about Truth an inherent
vitality, a recuperative energy, to which Error is a stranger. Let us, then,
press onward. Progression is the law of our being. We must sedulously
observe its every requirement, or pay the penalty; for the law is inflexible,
and cannot be violated with impunity. The mandate is, "go forward."
Who, then, will advance, in solid phalanx, to the battle? We have no
time for delay. Delays are dangerous.

Frederick Douglass' Paper, April 25, 1856

WHAT IS MY DUTY AS AN ANTI-SLAVERY VOTER?

There are, and have been, for the last dozen years, a band of conscientious men in this country, who have insisted upon casting their votes
at the Ballot-Box in a manner fully to indicate their earnest desire for the
abolition of Slavery. To these, the old Liberty Party of eight years ago,
furnished the required platform, and the natural channels of political co-
operation. Under the Banner of this party, with many, or with few, they
felt at home, and ready to fall or flourish. It was a noble party, and was
animated by a noble spirit. That party, as such, has almost vanished. Its
members are scattered, and its old armor has been borne off to a party
with another name, and of another spirit. Led by the Barnburners of New
York, it supported Martin Van Buren for the Presidency in 1848. Since
then, it has been in the wilderness, wandering in darkness. Active, to be
sure, but making little progress towards the great end which combined its
original elements. A portion of those who have filled the ranks of this
wandering army, are beginning to raise the enquiry which heads this
article.

The aggressive front of Slavery, openly declaring for the entire mastery of the country—the ready enrollment of the Democratic and Know Nothing parties in the boldest enterprises of Slavery—the shocking outrages perpetrated in Kansas—and the evident determination of the Slave Power to make slaveholding and slave-buying and selling, the law of the whole land—have suggested the propriety of giving up the more radical and comprehensive measures of Abolitionists at the Ballot-Box, and the adoption of some one measure, upon which a large and important party can be united and organized to meet the Slave Power.

It is against this suggestion that we propose to offer a few remarks—remarks which, though coming from an humble source, may yet be deemed entitled to consideration by some sincere enquirer for the right way.

1. The ultimate success of the Anti-Slavery movement depends upon nothing, under God, more than upon the soundness of its principles, the earnestness, stringency and faithfulness with which they are enforced, and the integrity, consistency and disinterestedness of those who stand forth as its advocates. The purity of the cause is the success of the cause. There can be very little necessity for sustaining this proposition by argument. We rely upon honesty, and not dishonesty, to uproot injustice and wrong. This element of power can be rallied and enlisted by its like—and only by its like.—"Men will not serve God if the Devil bid them"—and hence the necessity for purity and consistency in all who seek to leave the world better than they found it. The first duty of the Reformer is to be right. If right, he may go forward; but if wrong, or partly wrong, he is as an house divided against itself, and will fall. He will move, if he moves at all, like a man in fetters, and to no valuable purpose. To succeed against Slavery, the public must be brought to respect Anti-Slavery; and it cannot be respected unless consistent with itself, and its advocates are conscientiously consistent with it. The country must be made to feel the pulsation of an enlightened conscience, animating, supporting and directing that cause, before they will own it and bless it as a cause entitled to triumph.

2. That the National Republican party, around whose standard Abolitionists are now called upon to rally, does *not* occupy this high Anti-Slavery ground, (and what is worse, does not mean to occupy it,) is most painfully evident. From the hour that the old Liberty Party was swallowed up by the Van Buren Free Soil party in '48, the work of deterioration began, and has been continued until now. Instead of going upward,

the political Anti-Slavery sentiment has been going downward. The Buffalo platform in '48 was lower than that of the Liberty Party; and the Pittsburgh platform of '56, is lower than that of '52. But not only is this deterioration shown in the platform of the Pittsburgh Convention, recently adopted. It is painfully manifest in the spirit of the Convention itself. There was a spirit of cold calculation, of deliberate contriving, so to pair off the edge of Anti-Slavery truth, and so to arrange and dispose of Anti-Slavery principles, as to draw into the Republican ranks men of all parties and sentiments, except the men of the Administration party. No man could have been found in the Republican Convention, held in Pittsburgh four years ago, bold enough to have proposed a slaveholder— an actual man-stealer—to preside over that Convention of Anti-Slavery men. Such a proposition would have been scouted as an insult to the Anti-Slavery sentiment of the North. Then the tone of the speeches made on the occasion was lower and weaker than on any former occasion. The Anti-Slavery creed, after the filtration of this Convention, came out simply a measure to restore the restriction against Slavery to Kansas and Nebraska. Nothing said of the Fugitive Slave Bill—nothing said of Slavery in the District of Columbia—nothing said of the slave trade between States—nothing said of giving the dignity of the nation to Liberty— nothing said of securing the rights of citizens, from the Northern States, in the constitutional right to enter and transact business in the slave States. There is not a single warm and living position, taken by the Republican party, except freedom for Kansas. We need not ask Radical Anti-Slavery men if this is the natural and desirable tendency of the political Anti-Slavery sentiment of the country. They instinctively recoil from it, as destructive of the great purpose of the Anti-Slavery movement of the country. They can only be induced to follow after the Republican movement under the teachings of a plausible and sinuous political philosophy, which is the grand corrupter of all reforms. The substance of this philosophy is, that the one thing needful, the thing to precede all else, is a large party; and in order to do this, we are at liberty to abandon almost everything but a name. Parties of this kind serve certain leading ones who get into office by them; but they seldom advance the cause that gave them birth.

3. We hold that the true mode to prevent this falling away from Anti-Slavery truth and duty, and to save the Anti-Slavery movement from utter destruction, is to support candidates for the Presidency and Vice Presidency, of tried Anti-Slavery character, and of decided Anti-

Slavery principles. This is the true path of Anti-Slavery duty. The Anti-Slavery voters of the country must not allow themselves to be transferred from one political demagogue to another, until all vitality shall have departed from them. Nothing can be more certain, than that the habitual accommodation of Anti-Slavery men to the men opposed to them, has weakened the self-respect of the Anti-Slavery party, and awakened the contempt of their opponents. The slaveholders themselves, seeing how ready we are to chase shadows, and to fight men of straw, are perpetually leading us away from the main issue by these trifles.—We must show the slaveholders, and the country, that we are in earnest, and cannot be drawn away from our legitimate work. For this reason, we shall look to Syracuse, rather than to Philadelphia, for the candidates to be supported in the next Presidential election. With the party at Syracuse, principles are more precious than numbers—and hence our cause is more safe there than elsewhere.

4. But it is said that by casting our votes for a man who duly represents our Radical Anti-Slavery sentiments, in the coming Presidential election, we shall probably give the Government into the hands of the Democratic Party, and thereby establish Slavery in Kansas, thus depriving the North of a Free State, and adding its power to the Slave States—the better enabling the latter to perpetuate Slavery.—This is very evidently a grave argument, and cannot be lightly disposed of. It is meet that it should be duly considered. Suppose, then, that by voting as above, the result, which is possible, should occur—Slavery should be established in Kansas, and Kansas added to the Slave States. It then becomes us to estimate the loss which freedom would sustain, not as against the saving of Kansas to freedom, but as against the evils which would arise from the policy, which it is relied on, will save Kansas to freedom. This is the only consistent and certain method by which to arrive at the path of Duty in the premise. Looking at the matter from this point then, we hold, that great as would be the misfortune to liberty should Kansas be given to Slavery, tenfold greater would be the misfortune, should Kansas be saved by means which must certainly demoralize the Anti-Slavery sentiment of the North, and render it weak and inefficient for the greater work of saving the entire country to Liberty. Keep in mind the fact that our aim is the entire abolition of Slavery; that our work is not done till this is done; and that the real importance of establishing freedom in Kansas, is to be found in its effect to establish freedom in the country at large. We deliberately prefer the loss of Kansas to the loss of our Anti-

Slavery integrity. With Kansas saved, and our Anti-Slavery integrity gone, our cause is ruined. With Kansas lost, and our Anti-Slavery integrity saved, we have, at least, means left us with which to continue the war upon Slavery, and of final victory.

5. But this is arguing at great disadvantage, far greater than our position requires. We have granted more than there is any absolute necessity for granting. It is by no means certain that Kansas can be saved by the Republican Party, even with the votes of Abolitionists. Freedom in Kansas depends, less upon politics, than upon the Anti-Slavery sentiment of the North, and the Anti-Slavery integrity of those who settle that Territory from the North.—Dark indeed would be the prospect of freedom in Kansas, if it depended entirely upon the election of a Republican President for the next four years. If that is to decide the question, Slavery has very little to fear and everything to hope. Republican enthusiasm may predict the election of a Republican President, but the calmer reason of that party must pronounce it strongly improbable. With the South united, and the North divided, it is easy to see which side will be victorious at the Polls. Republicans will have an enemy to contend with at the North, which will require all its strength, flinging the South out of the question. Again we might claim that a strong vote for Radical Abolitionists would far more certainly help freedom in Kansas than a much stronger vote for the Republicans would do.

The whole Slave population of this country whether in States, Territories, dock yards, or on the high seas, must be emancipated. For this the true friends of the Slave must toil and hope, and for nothing less than this. It is short-sighted, as a matter of policy, to aim lower than this, and it is cruel to those bleeding millions to do so. Our God, our country and the slave, alike have called us to this great work, and we cannot come down from it to mingle in a less comprehensive or a less commanding struggle. Slavery is a sin now, a sin at all times, and a sin everywhere; and as we hold all human enactments designed to sustain it as of no binding authority, and utterly contrary to the Constitution of the United States, the coast is clear for an open, and direct war upon Slavery everywhere in the United States.—But should we not do one thing at a time?— Yes, one thing at a time; but let that thing be the abolition of Slavery. It is not doing one thing at a time, in any important sense, to limit the domain of Slavery, and to leave its continuance unlimited. It is not doing one thing at a time to establish Freedom for the white citizen in Kansas, and to hunt the black citizen from it, like a wolf; and if it is doing one thing at a time to do this, we hold that a strong vote for the Radical Abolition candidate is the best way to accomplish that one thing at a time.—"Freedom for all, or chains for all."

Frederick Douglass' Paper, April 25, 1856

TO GERRIT SMITH

Rochester, May 23, 1856

My Dear Sir:

I hope you are the better of your cold. If all be well I shall certainly meet you at Syracuse. I am released from my earlier appointments in Ohio.

Now I want your counsel. Your unceasing interest in me and in my paper, and in the cause to which it is devoted, makes it right that I should seek your counsel.

I am almost convinced that my paper cannot be sustained. I am now full fifteen hundred dollars in debt for it, and have on hand only six hundred dollars from my friend Julia Griffiths to pay my creditors. My paper is deep in its ninth year. I have done my part toward putting it on a permanent footing. I have failed, at least for the present. My credit is good and I might go on. But is it right and best? I am almost persuaded that it is not. The prospect is dark. My paper is dying of the disease which carried the *Model Worker* to its grave. It is opposed to the Republicans of fifty six as it was opposed to Free Soilers in forty eight. My paper is not Republican and therefore Republicans look coldly on it. It is not Garrisonian and therefore Garrisonians hate and spare no pains to destroy it. Meanwhile, the colored people do very little to support it. Now what shall be done? Shall the paper go down and be a total wreck—or shall it be saved—by being merged into the *Radical Abolitionist?* Cannot the *Radical Abolitionist* be made a weekly journal and some way be devised by which my subscription list be transferred to that of the *Abolitionist?* I am sick at the thought of the failure of my paper and humbled by the thought that no Negro has yet succeeded in establishing a press in the United States—but when a man cannot stand up he must fall down. I have struggled about nine years to establish such a press—and although I had when I began five or six thousand dollars I should not have now half that sum but for the success attending my lectures last winter and the sale of my Book. The nine years have almost gone. My children are growing up and increasing their demands upon me, and it becomes me to submit to the humiliation of failure rather than blindly go on till all is lost. I ask nothing for myself in this business. I do not even ask for a place in the paper but simply ask that you will help me to save my paper from positive failure by merging it into the *Radical Abolitionist*. I suggest this to your own private eye. While I do not ask any place in the *Radical Abolitionist* as an editor or assistant in case my paper is merged, yet it might be an element of strength to the concern to have me in some way connected with it.

I am, my dear friend, very truly yours,

Frederick Douglass

I lectured last night to the largest audience in Corinthian Hall which has assembled here during the past winter.

I hope you will not consider the foregoing an appeal to your pockets, for it honestly is not.

Personally I am quite "well off" in the world having health, and heart, a good house and lot, a little money, and a wide field of usefulness as a lecturer in the cause of freedom. *My Bondage and My Freedom* will sell, as long as I can lecture—so that I regard myself well provided for for the present.

Love to dear Mrs. Smith,

Again yours F. D.

Gerrit Smith Papers, Syracuse University

FREMONT AND DAYTON

The readers of our journal will observe that the honored names which, for some time, stood at the head of our columns, as its candidates for the president and vice-president of the United States, have been withdrawn and although no other names have been or shall be placed at the head of our columns, we deem it proper frankly to announce our purpose to support, with whatever influence we possess, little or much, John C. Fremont and William L. Dayton, the candidates of the Republican Party for the presidency and vice-presidency of the United States, in the present political canvass.

To a part of our readers, this announcement, considering our previous position, will be an unwelcome surprise. We have, hitherto, advocated to the best of our ability, a course of political action inconsistent with our present course. It is, therefore, eminently fit that we should accompany the foregoing announcement with something like a statement of reasons for our newly adopted policy.

1. A step so important as to lead to a separation in action, at least, between ourselves and of loved, honored, and tried friends, should not be hastily or inconsiderately taken. In full view of this truth, we have with much care examined and re-examined the subject of our political relations and duties regarding Slavery and the colored people of the United States. Our position, as well as the suggestion of wisdom just referred to, very naturally cause hesitation. The name of Gerrit Smith has long been synonymous with us as genuine, unadulterated Abolitionism. Of all men beneath the sky, we would rather see this just man made President. Our heart and judgment cling and twine around this man and his counsels as the ivy to the oak. To differ from him, and the beloved friends who may still intend to vote for him at the approaching election, is the result only of stern and irresistible conviction, the voice of which we cannot feel ourselves at liberty to disregard.

2. The time has passed for an honest man to attempt any defence of a right to change his opinion as to political methods of opposing Slavery. Anti-Slavery consistency itself, in our view, requires of the Anti-Slavery voter that disposition of his vote and his influence, which, in all the circumstances and likelihoods of the case tend most to the triumph of Free Principles in the Councils and Government of the nation. It is not to be consistent to pursue a course politically this year, merely because that course seemed the best last year, or at any previous time. Right Anti-Slavery action is that which deals the severest deadliest blow upon Slavery that can be given at that particular time. Such action is always consistent, however different may be the forms through which it expresses itself.

3. Again, in supporting Fremont and Dayton, we are in no wise required to abandon a single Anti-Slavery Truth or Principle which we have hitherto cherished, and publicly advocated. The difference between our paper this week and last week is a difference of Policy, not of Principle. Hereafter, as hitherto, we shall contend for every principle, and maintain [mutilated] the platform of the Radical Abolitionists. The unconstitutionality of Slavery, the illegality of Slavery, the Right of the Federal Government to abolish Slavery in every part of the Republic,

whether in States or Territories, will be as firmly held, and as sternly insisted upon, as hitherto. Nor do we wish, by supporting the Republican Candidate in the approaching election, to be understood as merging our individuality, body and soul, into that Party, nor as separating ourselves from our Radical Abolition friends in their present endeavors to enforce the great Principles of Justice and Liberty, upon which the Radical Abolition movement is based. Furthermore, we here concede, that upon Radical Abolition grounds, the final battle against Slavery in this country must be fought out—Slavery must be seen and felt to be a huge crime, a system of lawless violence, before it can be abolished. In our Paper, upon the Platform, at home and abroad, we shall endeavor to bring Slavery before the People in this hateful light; and by so doing, shall really be upholding the Radical Abolition Platform in the very ranks of the Republican Party.

4. Beyond all controversy, the commanding and vital issue with Slavery at the approaching Presidential election, is the extension or the limitation of Slavery. The malign purpose of extending, strengthening, and perpetuating Slavery, is the conclusion of the great mass of the slaveholders. The execution of this purpose upon Kansas, is plainly enough the business set down for the present by the friends of Slavery, North and South. And it cannot be denied that the election either of Buchanan or Fillmore would be the success of this malign purpose of the Slave Power. Other elements enter into the issue, such, for instance, as Northern or Southern ascendency of the Slave power in the Councils of the Nation, the continued humiliation of the Northern People, the reign of Terror at Washington, the crippling of the Anti-Slavery movement, and the security and preservation of Slavery from inward decay or outside destroying influences. The fact that Slaveholders had taken a united stand in favor of this measure, is, at least, an argument why Anti-Slavery men should take a stand to defeat them. The greatest triumphs of Slavery have been secured by the division of its enemies, one party insisting on attacking one point, and another class equally in earnest bending their energies in another direction. Were it in our power, the order of battle between Liberty and Slavery would be arranged differently. Anti-Slavery in our hands, at the ballot box, should be the aggressor; but it is not within our power, or within that of any other man, to control the order of events, or the circumstances which shape our course, and determine our conduct at particular times. All men will agree, that, generally speaking, the point attacked, is the point to be defended.

The South has tendered to us the issue of Slavery Extension; and to meet the Slave Power here, is to rouse its most devilish animosity. It is to strike hardest, where the Slaveholders feel most keenly. The most powerful blow that could be given at that point would in our judgment, be the election to the Presidency and Vice Presidency of the Republic the Candidates of the Republican Party.

5. Briefly, then, we shall support Fremont and Dayton in the present crisis of the Anti-Slavery movement, because they are, by position, and from the very nature of the organization which supports them, the admitted and recognized antagonists of the Slave Power, of gag-law, and of all the hellish designs of the Slave Power to extend and fortify the accursed slave system. We shall support them because they are the most numerous Anti-Slavery Party, and, therefore, the most powerful to inflict a blow upon, and the most likely to achieve a valuable victory over, the Slave Oligarchy. There is not a trafficker in the bodies and souls of men, from Baltimore to New Orleans, that would not crack his bloody slave whip with fiendish delight over the defeat of Fremont and Dayton. Whereas, on the other hand, the moral effect of the Radical Abolition vote, separated as it must be from the great Anti-Slavery body of the North, must, from the nature of the case, be very limited for good, and only powerful for mischief, where its effect would be to weaken the Republican Party. We shall support Fremont and Dayton, because there is no chance whatever in the present contest of electing better men than they. And we are the more reconciled to accepting them, by the fact that they are surrounded by a Party of progressive men. Take them, therefore, not merely for what they are, but for what we have good reason to believe they will become when they have lived for a time in the element of Anti-Slavery discussion. We shall support them by pen, by speech, by vote, because it is by no means certain that they can succeed in this State against the powerful combinations opposed to them without the support of the full and complete Abolition vote. Bitter indeed, would be the reproach, and deep and pointed would be the regret, if, through the Radical Abolitionists, victory should perch on the bloody standard of Slave Rule, as would be the case if Fremont and Dayton were defeated, and Buchanan and Breckenridge elected. For one, we are not disposed to incur this reproach, nor to experience this regret, and shall, therefore, vote for Fremont and Dayton. In supporting them, we neither dishonor our Principles nor lessen our means of securing their adoption and active application. We can reach the ears and heart of as

great a number within the ranks of the Republican Party as we could possibly do by remaining outside of those ranks. We know of no law applicable to the progress and promulgation of Radical Abolition Principles which would act less favorably towards our Principles inside the Party, than outside of it.

6. Another reason for supporting the Republican Party at the ballot-box and thus supporting the Anti-Slavery vote as a unit, is, that such action conforms exactly to the facts of our existing relations as citizens. There is now, evidently, but one great question of widespread and of all-commanding national interest; and that question is Freedom or Slavery. In reality, there can be but two Parties to this question; and for ourselves, we wish it to be with the natural division for Freedom, in form, as well as in fact.

7. It seems to us both the dictate of good morals and true wisdom, that if we cannot abolish Slavery in all the States by our votes at the approaching election, we ought, if we can, keep Slavery out of Kansas by our vote. To pursue any other policy is to abandon at present, practical advantage to Freedom in an assertion of more comprehensive claims, right enough in themselves, but which reason and fact assure us can only be attained by votes in the future, when the public mind shall have been educated up to those claims. We are quite well aware that to the foregoing, objections of apparent weight may be urged by those for whose conscientious convictions we cherish the profoundest respect. And although we do not propose to anticipate objections, but intend to meet them as they shall be presented in the progress of the canvass, we will mention and reply to one. Most plainly the greatest difficulty to be met with by a Radical Abolitionist in supporting Fremont and Dayton, is the fact that these Candidates have not declared and do not declare any purpose to abolish Slavery by legislation, in the States. They neither entertain nor declare any such purpose, and in this they are far from occupying the high Anti-Slavery position of the Radical Abolition Society. But let us not be unreasonable or impatient with the Republican Party. In considering this defect in the Anti-Slavery character and creed of the Republican Candidates, it should be borne in mind that they stand now in respect to this doctrine precisely where the Liberty Party stood ten years ago. The Right and duty of the Federal Government to abolish Slavery everywhere in the United States, is entirely true and deeply important; and yet, it must be confessed that this doctrine has been made appreciable but to a few minds, the dwellers in the moun-

tain peaks of the moral world, who catch the first beams of morning, long before the slumberers in the valleys awake from their dreams. This new doctrine, we think, may very properly be left to take its turn in the arena of discussion. Time and argument will do more for its progress, and its final adoption by the people, than can be done for it in the present crisis, by the few votes of the isolated Radical Abolitionists. In further extenuation or apology, it may be very properly urged, that while the Republican Party has not at this point adopted the Abolition creed, it has laid down principles and promulgated doctrines, which in their application, directly tend to the Abolition of Slavery in the States. But the conclusive answer to all who object upon this ground is the indisputable Truth, that neither in Religion nor Morals, can a man be justified in refusing to assist his fellow-men to accomplish a possible good thing, simply because his fellows refuse to accomplish some other good things which they deem impossible. Most assuredly, that theory cannot be a sound one which would prevent us from voting with men for the Abolition of Slavery in Maryland simply because our companions refuse to include Virginia. In such a case, the path of duty is plainly this; go with your fellow-citizens for the Abolition of Slavery in Maryland when they are ready to go for that measure, and do all you can, meanwhile, to bring them to whatever work of righteousness may remain and which has become manifest to your clearer vision. Such, then, is the conclusion forced upon us by the philosophy of the facts of our condition as a nation. A great crime against Freedom and Civilization is about to be perpetrated. The Slave Power is resolved to plant the deadly Upas, Slavery, in the virgin soil of Kansas. This great evil may be averted, and all the likelihoods of the case, the election of John C. Fremont and William L. Dayton, will be instrumental in averting it. Their election will prevent the establishment of Slavery in Kansas, overthrow Slave Rule in the Republic, protect Liberty of Speech and of the Press, give ascendency to Northern civilization over the bludgeon and blood-hound civilization of the South, and the mark of national condemnation on Slavery, scourge doughfaces from place and from power, and inaugurate a higher and purer standard of Politics and Government. Therefore, we go for Fremont and Dayton.

Frederick Douglass' Paper, August 15, 1856

TO HON. GERRIT SMITH

Rochester Aug. 31st, 1856

My dear friend:

I have not yet received your letter to Mr. Delevan except as it appeared in the *Albany Evening Journal*. You have not paid me the usual compliment of sending me an advance copy of your letter in this instance, though you have favored some of my neighbors. I have, however, got your letter and shall publish it unless you otherwise wish. My dear Sir, you must not strike my humble name from your list of those to whom you usually send your thoughts. You are not likely to write anything, or to speak anything which I shall not gladly lay before my readers. I cannot allow myself to think that the failure to send me your Delevan letter was intended as a rebuke to me for my support of Fremont, and yet it may be so. I should not complain if such it should prove, though I should deeply regret it. I have done what seemed to me right and proper to be done in this crisis, and can afford to be calm under the censure of those who cannot approve my course. I support Fremont as the best thing I can do *now,* but without losing sight of the great doctrines and measures, inseparable from your great name and character.

I am as ever, most truly yours,

Frederick Douglass

Gerrit Smith Papers, Syracuse University

TO HON. GERRIT SMITH

Rochester, Sept. 6, 1856

My dear friend:

I am just home from Ohio, where I have been lecturing, and find your kind letters for which please accept my thanks. What I think of your letter to our friend William Goodell, will be seen in my paper of yesterday. I had noticed your letter before your note reached me. Yes! I get it all around. Mr. Garrison tries his hand upon my case this week, the most skilful of them all. The *Liberator* and *Standard* seem more shocked at my apostacy from the Radical Abolition Society, than at Mr. May's apostacy from the American Society. They are tender with him, but harsh with me. I shall endeavor to be at the Jerry Rescue (1st Oct.) celebration and possibly in Syracuse at the Liberty Party meeting on the 17th Sept.

I am as ever, yours truly and affectionately,

Frederick Douglass

Gerrit Smith Papers, Syracuse University

THE DO-NOTHING POLICY

When will colored men learn to discard the do-nothing tactics, the "masterly inactivity," for which their course in the past has been distinguished? When the American People were almost to a man arrayed against us, when to present a petition from the colored citizens of a State would provoke a storm of violence upon the head of the individual who had the hardihood to present it, then the cry was we are powerless, we are bound hand and foot, and delivered to the spoiler. Now, when there is a more hopeful state of public sentiment; when the friends of impartial liberty may be counted by thousands; the cry is we must be quiet, we must not make ourselves be heard or felt in this contest, lest we injure the cause for which we pray. And we fold our hands and indolently gaze at the tremendous struggle going on in the nation, by which our rights will be determined.

This is a false position. Who of all the people in this country have the deepest stake in the contest for supremacy between slavery and freedom? The colored people. Who ought then to be the most active, the most vigilant and self sacrificing? The colored people. It is vain for us to expect to realize any degree of liberty and respect in our country, unless we are willing to bear our share in the struggle. What deprivation of right have the whites met with in Kansas, which is greater than the disabilities inflicted on colored men in nearly every state; yet we submit quietly, scarcely mustering enough of energy to make an annual and spasmodic protest against our wrongs, while they, forsaking the comforts and refinements of their homes, taking their lives in their hands, are contending bravely for their rights, and many of them are lying stark and stiff, under the soil of Kansas. We may learn a lesson of them; the man deprived of rights is the man to contend for them. The revolutionary worthies of our early history pledged their lives, their fortunes and their sacred honors, for the success of their cause and nobly have they redeemed their pledge. Are we prepared to make the same pledge, and having made it to redeem it as they did? If so the day of our emancipation is near at hand, even at the door.

No race on earth have greater incentives to exertion than we. Not only our equality as a race is denied, but we are even denied our rank as men; we are enslaved, oppressed, and even those most favorably disposed towards us, are so from motives more of pity than respect. For the first time since the dawn of history, is there a chance afforded us to prove our equal manhood. What a noble work is here before us then, to redeem an entire race from the obloquy and scorn of the world, and place it upon the same level with the rest of mankind. Generations unborn will envy us the felicity of having been born at a time when such noble work could be accomplished, when the foundations can be laid deep and strong for the future liberation of the race. The American people, with all their lack of justice, and cruel oppression of our people, are yet of that stock which admires and respects a sturdy contender for his own rights. Happily the strife we are called upon to enter is not, in the northern States, a war-like one. The republicans of France and of Italy, can achieve their freedom only by bloodshed, by the overthrow of their governments, and the slaughter of their enemies. With us the only hardship is, the industry and persistence with which our efforts must be made. The right of petition, the right of the press, and free speech, are left to us, and the use of these is all that is required for the acquisition of our rights in the northern States. Will we use them? Now while the masses of the people are loud in their professions of love for freedom —now while the slave power is measuring to their whites of the North, the same degree of oppression and violence to which we have so long been subjected—now while the waters of the political Siloam are stirred, have we enough of energy to step into its healing waters and be cured?

There are two States of the North in which we believe equal political rights are within the reach of their colored citizens, only needing a determined and united move on their part. New York is one of those States, Ohio, the other. The colored citizens of New York meet next month at Syracuse to confer together on the subject. If they are united, if they are resolved to use with unwavering energy the press, the orator, and the petition, they will gain all they desire. To meet and pass resolutions will do no good; but appoint reliable, energetic men to conduct the canvass, raise money to support them, and unite with them afterward in perfecting and executing the plans proposed, and all will be well. On the other hand, to float quietly with the current, allowing others to win and bestow the freedom which we lazily propose to enjoy, will go far to prove the charges of our enemies true, and sink us lower in the estimation of our white countrymen. The open sesame for the colored man is action! action!! action!!

Frederick Douglass' Paper, September 12, 1856

TO HON. GERRIT SMITH

Rochester, Dec. 16, 1856.

My dear Sir:

Please accept my thanks for your generous donation of twenty dollars. I am happy to know by this expressive sign that you still desire to see my paper afloat. You ought to, for you have watched over it with almost paternal interest. No, my dear Sir, I am not a member of the Republican party. I am still a radical abolitionist, and shall as ever, work with those whose Anti-Slavery principles are similar to your own. My English friends are just now dealing with me for my Jerry Rescue Resolutions.[26] They think you were altogether too tolerant of my abominable sentiments. I am writing an article, though not a formal reply, to strictures made upon those resolutions, yet a sort of embodiment of the sentiments uttered by me at the "Jerry rescue" celebration.

Please make my best respects to Mrs. Smith. Accept my sincere thanks for the donation of twenty dollars.

Yours always most truly,
Frederick Douglass

Gerrit Smith Papers, Syracuse University

PEACEFUL ANNIHILATION OF SLAVERY IS HOPELESS

While we feel bound to use all our powers of persuasion and argument; to welcome every instrumentality that promises to peacefully destroy that perpetual contemner of God's laws, and disturber of a nation's peace—Slavery; we yet feel that its peaceful annihilation is almost hopeless, and hence stand by the doctrines enunciated in those resolutions, and contend that the slave's right to revolt is perfect, and only wants the occurrence of favourable circumstances to become a duty. . . . We cannot but shudder as we call to mind the horrors that have ever marked servile insurrections—we would avert them if we could; but shall the millions forever submit to robbery, to murder, to ignorance, and every unnamed evil which an irresponsible tyranny can devise, because the overthrow of that tyranny would be productive of horrors? We say not. The recoil, when it comes, will be in exact proportion to the wrongs inflicted; terrible as it will be, we accept and hope for it. The slaveholder has been tried and sentenced, his execution only waits the finish to the training of his executioners. He is training his own executioners.

William Chambers, *American Slavery and Colour,* New York, 1857, p. 174

TO HON. GERRIT SMITH

20 April, '57.

My dear Sir:

The Bill sent to Mr. Green was by mistake. The five dollars of which he speaks is duly set to his credit, and the five you have now sent shall also be set to his credit. He shall not be troubled with a bill again. I am amazed as well as gratified at the strength of the vote in favor of a radical Abolition Personal Liberty Bill. I am sorry the Convention appointed here is given up, but your proposition for turning Republican Conventions into Abolition ones strikes me fair. We have turned Whigs and Democrats into Republicans and we can turn Republicans into Abolitionists. You have already gone a great way in that direction. I trace that magnificent show of hands in the Assembly directly to your speech and counsels. You cannot, however, expect that your disciples shall be quite as successful as yourself. I am better of my throat trouble.

Rosa joins me in love to Mrs. Smith.

> I am, dear Sir, always yours truly,
> Frederick Douglass

Gerrit Smith Papers, Syracuse University

THE DRED SCOTT DECISION, speech delivered before American Anti-Slavery Society, New York, May 11, 1857 [27]

Mr. Chairman, Friends, and Fellow Citizens:

While four millions of our fellow countrymen are in chains—while men, women, and children are bought and sold on the auction-block with horses, sheep, and swine—while the remorseless slave-whip draws the warm blood of our common humanity—it is meet that we assemble as we have done to-day, and lift up our hearts and voices in earnest denunciation of the vile and shocking abomination. It is not for us to be governed by our hopes or our fears in this great work; yet it is natural on occasions like this, to survey the position of the great struggle which is going on between slavery and freedom, and to dwell upon such signs of encouragement as may have been lately developed, and the state of feeling these signs or events have occasioned in us and among the people generally. It is a fitting time to take an observation to ascertain where we are, and what our prospects are.

To many, the prospects of the struggle against slavery seem far from cheering. Eminent men, North and South, in Church and State, tell us that the omens are all against us. Emancipation, they tell us, is a wild, delusive idea; the price of human flesh was never higher than now; slavery was never more closely entwined about the hearts and affections of the southern people than now; that whatever of conscientious scruple, religious conviction, or public policy, which opposed the system of slavery forty or fifty years ago, has subsided; and that slavery never reposed upon a firmer basis than now. Completing this picture of the happy and prosperous condition of this system of wickedness, they tell us that this state of things is to be set to our account. Abolition agitation has done it all. How deep is the misfortune of my poor, bleeding people, if this be so!

How lost their condition, if even the efforts of their friends but sink them deeper in ruin!

Without assenting to this strong representation of the increasing strength and stability of slavery, without denouncing what of untruth pervades it, I own myself not insensible to the many difficulties and discouragements that beset us on every hand. They fling their broad and gloomy shadows across the pathway of every thoughtful colored man in this country. For one, I see them clearly, and feel them sadly. With an earnest, aching heart, I have long looked for the realization of the hope of my people. Standing, as it were, barefoot, and treading upon the sharp and flinty rocks of the present, and looking out upon the boundless sea of the future, I have sought, in my humble way, to penetrate the intervening mists and clouds, and, perchance, to descry, in the dim and shadowy distance, the white flag of freedom, the precise speck of time at which the cruel bondage of my people should end, and the long entombed millions rise from the foul grave of slavery and death. But of that time I can know nothing, and you can know nothing. All is uncertain at that point. One thing, however, is certain; slaveholders are in earnest, and mean to cling to their slaves as long as they can, and to the bitter end. They show no sign of a wish to quit their iron grasp upon the sable throats of their victims. Their motto is, "a firmer hold and a tighter grip" for every new effort that is made to break their cruel power. The case is one of life or death with them, and they will give up only when they must do that or do worse.

In one view the slaveholders have a decided advantage over all opposition. It is well to notice this advantage—the advantage of complete organization. They are organized; and yet were not at the pains of creating their organizations. The State governments, where the system of slavery exists, are complete slavery organizations. The church organizations in those States are equally at the service of slavery; while the Federal Government, with its army and navy, from the chief magistracy in Washington, to the Supreme Court, and thence to the chief marshalship at New York, is pledged to support, defend, and propagate the crying curse of human bondage. The pen, the purse, and the sword, are united against the simple truth, preached by humble men in obscure places.

This is one view. It is, thank God, only one view; there is another, and a brighter view. David, you know, looked small and insignificant when going to meet Goliath, but looked larger when he had slain his foe. The Malakoff was, to the eye of the world, impregnable, till the hour it fell before the shot and shell of the allied army. Thus hath it ever been. Oppression, organized as ours is, will appear invincible up to the very hour of its fall. Sir, let us look at the other side, and see if there are not some things to cheer our heart and nerve us up anew in the good work of emancipation.

Take this fact—for it is a fact—the anti-slavery movement has, from first to last, suffered no abatement. It has gone forth in all directions, and is now felt in the remotest extremities of the Republic.

It started small, and was without capital either in men or money. The odds were all against it. It literally had nothing to lose, and everything to gain. There was ignorance to be enlightened, error to be combatted, conscience to be awakened, prejudice to be overcome, apathy to be aroused, the right of speech to be secured, mob violence to be subdued, and a deep, radical change to be inwrought in the mind and heart of the whole nation. This great work, under God, has gone on, and gone on gloriously.

Amid all changes, fluctuations, assaults, and adverses of every kind, it has remained firm in its purpose, steady in its aim, onward and upward, defying all opposition, and never losing a single battle. Our strength is in the growth of anti-slavery conviction, and this has never halted.

There is a significant vitality about this abolition movement. It has taken a deeper, broader, and more lasting hold upon the national heart than ordinary reform movements. Other subjects of much interest come and go, expand and contract, blaze and vanish, but the huge question of American Slavery, comprehending, as it does, not merely the weal or the woe of four millions, and their countless posterity, but the weal or the woe of this entire nation, must increase in magnitude and in majesty with every hour of its history. From a cloud not bigger than a man's hand, it has overspread the heavens. It has risen from a grain not bigger than a mustard seed. Yet see the fowls of the air, how they crowd its branches.

Politicians who cursed it, now defend it; ministers, once dumb, now speak in its praise; and presses, which once flamed with hot denunciations against it, now surround the sacred cause as by a wall of living fire. Politicians go with it as a pillar of cloud by day, and the press as a pillar of fire by night. With these ancient tokens of success, I, for one, will not despair of our cause.

Those who have undertaken to suppress and crush out this agitation for Liberty and humanity, have been most woefully disappointed. Many who have engaged to put it down, have found themselves put down. The agitation has pursued them in all their meanderings, broken in upon their seclusion, and, at the very moment of fancied security, it has settled down upon them like a mantle of unquenchable fire. Clay, Calhoun, and Webster each tried his hand at suppressing the agitation; and they went to their graves disappointed and defeated.

Loud and exultingly have we been told that the slavery question is settled, and settled forever. You remember it was settled thirty-seven years ago, when Missouri was admitted into the Union with a slaveholding constitution, and slavery prohibited in all territory north of thirty-six degrees of north latitude. Just fifteen years afterwards, it was settled again by voting down the right of petition, and gagging down free discussion in Congress. Ten years after this it was settled again by the annexation of Texas, and with it the war with Mexico. In 1850 it was again settled. This was called a final settlement. By it slavery was virtually declared to be the equal of Liberty, and should come into the Union on the same terms. By it the right and the power to hunt down men, women, and children, in every part of this country, was conceded to our southern brethren, in order to keep them in the Union. Four years after this settlement, the whole question was once more settled, and settled by a settlement which unsettled all the former settlements.

The fact is, the more the question has been settled, the more it has needed settling. The space between the different settlements has been strikingly on the decrease. The first stood longer than any of its successors.

There is a lesson in these decreasing spaces. The first stood fifteen years—the second, ten years—the third, five years—the fourth stood four years—and the fifth has stood the brief space of two years.

This last settlement must be called the Taney settlement. We are now told, in tones of lofty exultation, that the day is lost—all lost—and that we might as well give up the struggle. The highest authority has spoken. The voice of the Supreme Court has gone out over the troubled waves of the National Conscience, saying peace, be still.

This infamous decision of the Slaveholding wing of the Supreme Court maintains that slaves are within the contemplation of the Constitution of the United States, property; that slaves are property in the same sense that horses, sheep, and swine are property; that the old doctrine that slavery is a creature of local law is false; that the right of the slaveholder to his slave does not depend upon the local law, but is secured wherever the Constitution of the United States extends; that Congress has no right to prohibit slavery anywhere; that slavery may go in safety anywhere under the star-spangled banner; that colored persons of African descent have no rights that white men are bound to respect; that colored men of African descent are not and cannot be citizens of the United States.

You will readily ask me how I am affected by this devilish decision—this judicial incarnation of wolfishness? My answer is, and no thanks to the slaveholding wing of the Supreme Court, my hopes were never brighter than now.

I have no fear that the National Conscience will be put to sleep by such an open, glaring, and scandalous tissue of lies as that decision is, and has been, over and over, shown to be.

The Supreme Court of the United States is not the only power in this world. It is very great, but the Supreme Court of the Almighty is greater. Judge Taney can do many things, but he cannot perform impossibilities. He cannot bale out the ocean, annihilate the firm old earth, or pluck the silvery star of liberty from our Northern sky. He may decide, and decide again; but he cannot reverse the decision of the Most High. He cannot change the essential nature of things—making evil good, and good evil.

Happily for the whole human family, their rights have been defined, declared, and decided in a court higher than the Supreme Court. "There is a law," says Brougham, "above all the enactments of human codes, and by that law, unchangeable and eternal, man cannot hold property in man."

Your fathers have said that man's right to liberty is self-evident. There is no need of argument to make it clear. The voices of nature, of conscience, of reason, and of revelation, proclaim it as the right of all rights, the foundation of all trust, and of all responsibility. Man was born with it. It was his before he comprehended it. The *deed* conveying it to him is written in the center of his soul, and is recorded in Heaven. The sun in the sky is not more palpable to the sight than man's right to liberty is to the moral vision. To decide against this right in the person of Dred Scott, or the humblest and most whip-scarred bondman in the land, is to decide against God. It is an open rebellion against God's government. It is an attempt to undo what God has done, to blot out the broad distinction instituted by the *Allwise* between men and things, and to change the image and superscription of the everliving God into a speechless piece of merchandise.

Such a decision cannot stand. God will be true though every man be a liar. We can appeal from this hell-black judgment of the Supreme Court, to the court of common sense and common humanity. We can appeal from man to God. If there is no justice on earth, there is yet justice in heaven. You may close your Supreme Court against the black man's cry for justice, but you cannot, thank God, close against him the ear of a sympathising world, nor shut up the Court of Heaven. All that is merciful and just, on earth and in Heaven, will execrate and despise this edict of Taney.

If it were at all likely that the people of these free States would tamely submit to this demoniacal judgment, I might feel gloomy and sad over it, and possibly it might be necessary for my people to look for a home in some other country. But as the case stands, we have nothing to fear.

In one point of view, we, the abolitionists and colored people, should meet this decision, unlooked for and monstrous as it appears, in a cheerful spirit. This very attempt to blot out forever the hopes of an enslaved people may be one necessary link in the chain of events preparatory to the downfall and complete overthrow of the whole slave system.

The whole history of the anti-slavery movement is studded with proof that all measures devised and executed with a view to ally and diminish the anti-slavery agitation, have only served to increase, intensify, and embolden that agitation. This wisdom of the crafty has been confounded, and the counsels of the ungodly brought to nought. It was so with the Fugitive Slave Bill. It was so with the Kansas-Nebraska Bill; and it will be so with this last and most shocking of all pro-slavery devices, this Taney decision.

When great transactions are involved, where the fate of millions is concerned, where a long enslaved and suffering people are to be delivered, I am superstitious enough to believe that the finger of the Almighty may be seen bringing good out of evil, and making the wrath of man redound to his honor, hastening the triumph of righteousness.

The American people have been called upon, in a most striking manner, to abolish and put away forever the system of slavery. The subject has been pressed upon their attention in all earnestness and sincerity. The cries of the slave have gone forth to the world, and up to the throne of God. This decision, in my view, is a means of keeping the nation awake on the subject. It is another proof that God does not mean that we shall go to sleep, and forget that we are a slaveholding nation.

Step by step we have seen the slave power advancing; poisoning, corrupting, and perverting the institutions of the country; growing more and more haughty, imperious, and exacting. The white man's liberty has been marked out for the same grave with the black man's.

The ballot box is desecrated, God's law set at nought, armed legislators stalk the halls of Congress, freedom of speech is beaten down in the Senate. The rivers and highways are infested by border ruffians, and white men are made to feel the iron heel of slavery. This ought to arouse us to kill off the hateful thing. They are solemn warnings to which the white people, as well as the black people, should take heed.

If these shall fail, judgment, more fierce or terrible, may come. The lightning, whirlwind, and earthquake may come. Jefferson said that he trembled for his country when he reflected that God is just, and his justice cannot sleep forever. The time may come when even the crushed worm may turn under the tyrant's feet. Goaded by cruelty, stung by a burning sense of wrong, in an awful moment of depression and desperation, the bondman and bondwoman at the south may rush to one wild and deadly struggle for freedom. Already slaveholders go to bed with bowie knives, and apprehend death at their dinners. Those who enslave, rob, and torment their cooks, may well expect to find death in their dinner-pots.

The world is full of violence and fraud, and it would be strange if the slave, the constant victim of both fraud and violence, should escape the contagion. He, too, may learn to fight the devil with fire, and for one, I am in no frame of mind to pray that this may be long deferred.

Two remarkable occurrences have followed the presidential election; one was the unaccountable sickness traced to the National Hotel at Washington, and the other was the discovery of a plan among the slaves, in different localities, to slay their oppressors.[28] Twenty or thirty of the suspected were put to death. Some were shot, some hanged, some burned, and some died under the lash. One brave man owned himself well acquainted with the conspiracy, but said he would rather die than disclose the facts. He received seven hundred and fifty lashes, and his noble spirit went away to the God who gave it. The name of this hero has been by the meanness of tyrants suppressed. Such a man redeems his race. He is worthy to be mentioned with the Hoffers and Tells, the noblest heroes of history. These insurrectionary movements have been put down, but they may break out at any time, under the guidance of higher intelligence, and with a more invincible spirit.

The fire thus kindled, may be revived again;
The flames are extinguished, but the embers remain;
One terrible blast may produce an ignition,
Which shall wrap the whole South in wild conflagration.

The pathway of tyrants lies over volcanoes
The very air they breathe is heavy with sorrows;
Agonizing heart-throbs convulse them while sleeping,
And the wind whispers Death as over them sweeping.

By all the laws of nature, civilization, and of progress, slavery is a doomed system. Not all the skill of politicians, North and South, not all the sophistries of Judges, not all the fulminations of a corrupt press, not all the hypocritical prayers, or the hypocritical refusals to pray of a hollow-hearted priesthood, not all the devices of sin and Satan, can save the vile thing from extermination.

Already a gleam of hope breaks upon us from the southwest. One Southern city has grieved and astonished the whole South by a preference for freedom. The wedge has entered. Dred Scott, of Missouri, goes into slavery, but St. Louis declares for freedom. The judgment of Taney is not the judgment of St. Louis.

It may be said that this demonstration in St. Louis is not to be taken as an evidence of sympathy with the slave; that it is purely a white man's victory. I admit it. Yet I am glad that white men, bad as they generally are, should gain a victory over slavery. I am willing to accept a judgment against slavery, whether supported by white or black reasons—though I would much rather have it supported by both. He that is not against us, is on our part.

Come what will, I hold it to be morally certain that, sooner or later, by fair means or foul means, in quiet or in tumult, in peace or in blood, in judgment or in mercy, slavery is doomed to cease out of this otherwise goodly land, and liberty is destined to become the settled law of this Republic.

I base my sense of the certain overthrow of slavery, in part, upon the nature of the American Government, the Constitution, the tendencies of the age, and the character of the American people; and this, notwithstanding the important decision of Judge Taney.

I know of no soil better adapted to the growth of reform than American soil. I know of no country where the conditions for affecting great changes in the settled order of things, for the development of right ideas of liberty and humanity, are more favorable than here in these United States.

The very groundwork of this government is a good repository of Christian civilization. The Constitution, as well as the Declaration of Independence, and the sentiments of the founders of the Republic, give us a platform broad enough, and strong enough, to support the most comprehensive plans for the freedom and elevation of all the people of this country, without regard to color, class, or clime.

There is nothing in the present aspect of the anti-slavery question which should drive us into the extravagance and nonsense of advocating a dissolution of the American Union as a means of overthrowing slavery, or freeing the North from the malign influence of slavery upon the morals of the Northern people. While the press is at liberty, and speech is free, and the ballot-box is open to the people of the sixteen free States; while the slaveholders are but four hundred thousand in number, and we are fourteen millions; while the mental and moral power of the nation is with us; while we are really the strong and they are the weak, it would look worse than cowardly to retreat from the Union.

If the people of the North have not the power to cope with these four hundred thousand slaveholders inside the Union, I see not how they could get out of the Union. The strength necessary to move the Union must ever be less than is required to break it up. If we have got to conquer the slave power to get out of the Union, I for one would much rather conquer, and stay in the Union. The latter, it strikes me, is the far more rational mode of action.

I make these remarks in no servile spirit, nor in any superstitious reverence for a mere human arrangement. If I felt the Union to be a curse, I should not be far behind the very chiefest of the disunion Abolitionists in denouncing it. But the evil to be met and abolished is not in the Union. The power arrayed against us is not a parchment.

It is not in changing the dead form of the Union, that slavery is to be abolished in this country. We have to do not with the dead, but the living; not with the past, but the living present.

Those who seek slavery in the Union, and who are everlastingly dealing blows upon the Union, in the belief that they are killing slavery, are most woefully mistaken. They are fighting a dead form instead of a living and powerful reality. It is clearly not because of the peculiar character of our Constitution that we have slavery, but the wicked pride, love of power, and selfish perverseness of the American people. Slavery lives in this country not because of any paper Constitution, but in the moral blindness of the American people, who persuade themselves that they are safe, though the rights of others may be struck down.

Besides, I think it would be difficult to hit upon any plan less likely to abolish slavery than the dissolution of the Union. The most devoted advocates of slavery, those who make the interests of slavery their constant study, seek a dissolution of the Union as their final plan for preserving slavery from Abolition, and their ground is well taken. Slavery lives and flourishes best in the absence of civilization; a dissolution of the Union would shut up the system in its own congenial barbarism.

The dissolution of the Union would not give the North one single additional advantage over slavery to the people of the North, but would manifestly take from them many which they now certainly possess.

Within the Union we have a firm basis of anti-slavery operation. National welfare, national prosperity, national reputation and honor, and national scrutiny; common rights, common duties, and common country, are so many bridges over which we can march to the destruction of slavery. To fling away these advantages because James Buchanan is President, or Judge Taney gives a lying decision in favor of slavery, does not enter into my notion of common sense.

Mr. Garrison and his friends have been telling us that, while in the Union, we are responsible for slavery; and in so telling us, he and they have told us the truth. But in telling us that we shall cease to be responsible for slavery by dissolving the Union, he, and they have not told us the truth.

There now, clearly, is no freedom from responsibility for slavery, but in the Abolition of slavery. We have gone too far in this business now to sum up our whole duty in the cant phrase of "no Union with slave-holders."

To desert the family hearth may place the recreant husband out of the sight of his hungry children, but it cannot free him from responsibility. Though he should roll the waters of three oceans between him and them, he could not roll from his soul the burden of his responsibility to them; and, as with the private family, so in this instance with the national family. To leave the slave in his chains, in the hands of cruel masters who are too strong for him, is not to free ourselves from responsibility. Again: If I were on board of a pirate ship, with a company of men and women whose lives and liberties I had put in jeopardy, I would not clear my soul of their blood by jumping in the long boat, and singing out no union with pirates. My business would be to remain on board, and while I never would perform a single act of piracy again, I should exhaust every means given me by my position, to save the lives and liberties of those against whom I had committed piracy. In like manner, I hold it is our duty to remain inside this Union, and use all the power to restore to enslaved millions their precious and God-given rights. The more we have done by our voice and our votes, in times past, to rivet their galling fetters, the more clearly and solemnly comes the sense of duty to remain, to undo what we have done. Where, I ask, could the slave look for release from slavery if the Union were dissolved? I have an abiding conviction founded upon long and careful study of the certain effects of slavery upon the moral sense of slaveholding communities, that if the slaves are ever delivered from bondage, the power will emanate from the free States. All hope that the slaveholders will be self-moved to this great act of justice, is groundless and delusive. Now, as of old, the Redeemer must come from above, not from beneath. To dissolve the Union would be to withdraw the emancipating power from the field.

But I am told this is the argument of expediency. I admit it, and am prepared to show that what is expedient in this instance is right. "Do justice, though the heavens fall." Yes, that is a good motto, but I deny that it would be doing justice to the slave to dissolve the Union and leave the slave in his chains to get out by the clemency of his master, or the strength of his arms. Justice to the slave is to break his chains, and going out of the union is to leave him in his chains, and without any probable chance of getting out of them.

But I come now to the great question as to the constitutionality of slavery. The recent slaveholding decision, as well as the teachings of anti-slavery men, make this a fit time to discuss the constitutional pretensions of slavery.

The people of the North are a law abiding people. They love order and respect the means to that end. This sentiment has sometimes led them to the folly and wickedness of trampling upon the very life of law, to uphold its dead form. This was so in the execution of that thrice accursed Fugitive Slave Bill. Burns and Simms were sent back to the hell of slavery after they had looked upon Bunker Hill, and heard liberty thunder in Faneuil Hall. The people permitted this outrage in obedience to the popular sentiment of reverence for law. While men thus respect law, it becomes a serious matter so to interpret the law as to make it operate against liberty. I have a quarrel with those who fling the Supreme Law of this land between the slave and freedom. It is a serious matter to fling the weight of the Constitution against the cause of human liberty, and those who do it, take upon them a heavy responsibility. Nothing but absolute necessity, shall, or ought to drive me to such a concession to slavery.

When I admit that slavery is constitutional, I must see slavery recognized in the Constitution. I must see that it is there plainly stated that one man of a certain description has a right of property in the body and soul of another man of a certain description. There must be no room for a doubt. In a matter so important as the loss of liberty, everything must be proved beyond all reasonable doubt.

The well known rules of legal interpretation bear me out in this stubborn refusal to see slavery where slavery is not, and only to see slavery where it is.

The Supreme Court has, in its day, done something better than make slaveholding decisions. It has laid down rules of interpretation which are in harmony with the true idea and object of law and liberty.

It has told us that the intention of legal instruments must prevail; and that this must be collected from its words. It has told us that language must be construed strictly in favor of liberty and justice.

It has told us where rights are infringed, where fundamental principles are overthrown, where the general system of the law is departed from, the Legislative intention must be expressed with irresistible clearness, to induce a court of justice to suppose a design to effect such objects.

These rules are as old as law. They rise out of the very elements of law. It is to protect human rights, and promote human welfare. Law is in its nature opposed to wrong, and must everywhere be presumed to be in favor of the right. The pound of flesh, but not one drop of blood, is a sound rule of legal interpretation.

Besides there is another rule of law as well of common sense, which requires us to look to the ends for which a law is made, and to construe its details in harmony with the ends sought.

Now let us approach the Constitution from the standpoint thus indicated, and instead of finding in it a warrant for the stupendous system of robbery, comprehended in the term slavery, we shall find it strongly against that system.

"We, the people of the United States, in order to form a more perfect Union, establish justice, insure domestic tranquility, provide for the common defence, promote the general welfare, and secure the blessings of liberty to ourselves and our posterity, do ordain and establish this constitution for the United States of America."

Such are the objects announced by the instrument itself, and they are in harmony with the Declaration of Independence, and the principles of human well-being.

Six objects are here declared, "Union," "defence," "welfare," "tranquility," and "justice," and "liberty."

Neither in the preamble nor in the body of the Constitution is there a single mention of the term *slave* or *slave holder, slave master* or *slave state,* neither is there any reference to the color, or the physical peculiarities of any part of the people of the United States. Neither is there anything in the Constitution standing alone, which would imply the existence of slavery in this country.

"We, the people"—not we, the white people—not we, the citizens, or the legal voters—not we, the privileged class, and excluding all other classes but we, the people; not we, the horses and cattle, but we the people —the men and women, the human inhabitants of the United States, do ordain and establish this Constitution, &c.

I ask, then, any man to read the Constitution, and tell me where, if he can, in what particular that instrument affords the slightest sanction of slavery?

Where will he find a guarantee for slavery? Will he find it in the declaration that no person shall be deprived of life, liberty, or property, without due process of law? Will he find it in the declaration that the Constitution was established to secure the blessing of liberty? Will he find it in the right of the people to be secure in their persons and papers, and houses, and effects? Will he find it in the clause prohibiting the enactment by any State of a bill of attainder?

These all strike at the root of slavery, and any one of them, but faithfully carried out, would put an end to slavery in every State in the American Union.

Take, for example, the prohibition of a bill of attainder. That is a law entailing on the child the misfortunes of the parent. This principle would destroy slavery in every State of the Union.

The law of slavery is a law of attainder. The child is property because its parent was property, and suffers as a slave because its parent suffered as a slave.

Thus the very essence of the whole slave code is in open violation of a fundamental provision of the Constitution, and is in open and flagrant violation of all the objects set forth in the Constitution.

While this and much more can be said, and has been said, and much better said, by Lysander Spooner, William Goodell, Beriah Green, and Gerrit Smith, in favor of the entire unconstitutionality of slavery, what have we on the other side?

How is the constitutionality of slavery made out, or attempted to be made out?

First, by discrediting and casting away as worthless the most beneficent rules of legal interpretation; by disregarding the plain and common sense reading of the instrument itself; by showing that the Constitution does not mean what it says, and says what it does not mean, by assuming that the written Constitution is to be interpreted in the light of a secret and unwritten understanding of its framers, which understanding is declared to be in favor of slavery. It is in this mean, contemptible, underhand method that the Constitution is pressed into the service of slavery.

They do not point us to the Constitution itself, for the reason that there is nothing sufficiently explicit for their purpose; but they delight in supposed intentions—intentions nowhere expressed in the Constitution, and everywhere contradicted in the Constitution.

Judge Taney lays down this system of interpreting in this wise:

"The general words above quoted would seem to embrace the whole human family, and, if they were used in a similar instrument at this day, would be so understood. But it is too clear for dispute that the enslaved African race were not intended to be included, and formed no part of the people who framed and adopted this declaration; for if the language, as understood in that day, would embrace them, the conduct of the distinguished men who framed the Declaration of Independence would have been utterly and flagrantly inconsistent with the principles they asserted; and instead of the sympathy of mankind, to which they appealed, they would have deserved and received universal rebuke and reprobation.

"It is difficult, at this day, to realize the state of public opinion respecting that unfortunate class with the civilized and enlightened portion of the world at the time of the Declaration of Independence and the adoption of the Constitution; but history shows they had, for more than a century, been regarded as beings of an inferior order, and unfit associates for the white race, either socially or politically, and had no rights which white men are bound to respect; and the black man might be reduced to slavery, bought and sold, and treated as an ordinary article of merchandise. This opinion, at that time, was fixed and universal with the civilized portion of the white race. It was regarded as an axiom of morals, which no one thought of disputing, and everyone habitually acted upon it, without doubting, for a moment, the correctness of the opinion. And in no nation was this opinion more fixed, and generally acted upon, than in England; the subjects of which government not only seized them on the coast of Africa, but took them, as ordinary merchandise, to where they could make a profit on them. The opinion, thus entertained, was universally maintained on the colonies this side of the Atlantic; accordingly, Negroes of the African race were regarded by them as property, and held and bought and sold as such in every one of the thirteen colonies, which united in the Declaration of Independence, and afterwards formed the Constitution."

The argument here is, that the Constitution comes down to us from a slaveholding period and a slaveholding people; and that, therefore, we are bound to suppose that the Constitution recognizes colored persons of African descent, the victims of slavery at that time, as debarred forever from all participation in the benefit of the Constitution and the Declaration of Independence, although the plain reading of both includes them in their benificent range.

As a man, an American, a citizen, a colored man of both Anglo-Saxon and African descent, I denounce this representation as a most scandalous and devilish perversion of the Constitution, and a brazen misstatement of the facts of history.

But I will not content myself with mere denunciation; I invite attention to the facts.

It is a fact, a great historic fact, that at the time of the adoption of the Constitution, the leading religious denominations in this land were anti-slavery, and were laboring for the emancipation of the colored people of African descent.

The church of a country is often a better index of the state of opinion and feeling than is even the government itself.

The Methodists, Baptists, Presbyterians, and the denomination of Friends, were actively opposing slavery, denouncing the system of bondage, with language as burning and sweeping as we employ at this day.

Take the Methodists. In 1780, that denomination said: "The Conference acknowledges that slavery is contrary to the laws of God, man, and nature, and hurtful to society—contrary to the dictates of conscience and true religion, and doing to others that we would not do unto us."

In 1784, the same church declared, "that those who buy, sell, or give slaves away, except for the purpose to free them, shall be expelled immediately." In 1785, it spoke even more stringently on the subject. It then said: "We hold in the deepest abhorrence the practice of slavery, and shall not cease to seek its destruction by all wise and proper means."

So much for the position of the Methodist Church in the early history of the Republic, in those days of darkness to which Judge Taney refers.

Let us now see how slavery was regarded by the Presbyterian Church at that early date.

In 1794, the General Assembly of that body pronounced the following judgment in respect to slavery, slaveholders, and slaveholding.

"1st Timothy, 1st chapter, 10th verse: 'The law was made for man-stealers.' 'This crime among the Jews exposed the perpetrators of it to capital punishment.' Exodus, xxi, 15.—And the apostle here classes them with sinners of the first rank. The word he uses in its original import, comprehends all who are concerned in bringing any of the human race into slavery, or in retaining them in it. Stealers of men are all those who bring off slaves or freemen, and keep, sell, or buy them. 'To steal a freeman,' says Grotius, 'is the highest kind of theft.' In other instances, we only steal human property, but when we steal or retain men in slavery, we seize those who, in common with ourselves, are constituted, by the original grant, lords of the earth."

I might quote, at length, from the sayings of the Baptist Church and the sayings of eminent divines at this early period, showing that Judge Taney has grossly falsified history, but will not detain you with these quotations.

The testimony of the church, and the testimony of the founders of this Republic, from the declaration downward, prove Judge Taney false; as false to history as he is to law.   •

Washington and Jefferson, and Adams, and Jay, and Franklin, and Rush, and Hamilton, and a host of others, held no such degrading views on the subject of slavery as are imputed by Judge Taney to the Fathers of the Republic.

All, at that time, looked for the gradual but certain abolition of slavery, and shaped the constitution with a view to this grand result.

George Washington can never be claimed as a fanatic, or as the representative of fanatics. The slaveholders impudently use his name for the base purpose of giving respectability to slavery. Yet, in a letter to Robert Morris, Washington uses this language—language which, at this day, would make him a terror of the slaveholders, and the natural representative of the Republican party.

"There is not a man living, who wishes more sincerely than I do, to see some plan adopted for the abolition of slavery; but there is only one proper and effectual mode by which it can be accomplished, and that is by Legislative authority; and this, as far as my suffrage will go, shall not be wanting."

Washington only spoke the sentiment of his times. There were, at that time, Abolition societies in the slave States—Abolition societies in Virginia, in North Carolina, in Maryland, in Pennsylvania, and in Georgia —all slaveholding States. Slavery was so weak, and liberty so strong, that free speech could attack the monster to its teeth. Men were not mobbed and driven out of the presence of slavery, merely because they condemned the slave system. The system was then on its knees imploring to be spared, until it could get itself decently out of the world.

In the light of these facts, the Constitution was framed, and framed in conformity to it.

It may, however, be asked, if the Constitution were so framed that the rights of all the people were naturally protected by it, how happens it that a large part of the people have been held in slavery ever since its adoption? Have the people mistaken the requirements of their own Constitution?

The answer is ready. The Constitution is one thing, its administration is another, and, in this instance, a very different and opposite thing. I am here to vindicate the law, not the administration of the law. It is the written Constitution, not the unwritten Constitution, that is now before us. If, in the whole range of the Constitution, you can find no warrant for slavery, then we may properly claim it for liberty.

Good and wholesome laws are often found dead on the statute book. We may condemn the practice under them and against them, but never the law itself. To condemn the good law with the wicked practice, is to weaken, not to strengthen our testimony.

It is no evidence that the Bible is a bad book, because those who profess to believe the Bible are bad. The slaveholders of the South, and many of their wicked allies at the North, claim the Bible for slavery; shall we, therefore, fling the Bible away as a pro-slavery book? It would be as reasonable to do so as it would be to fling away the Constitution.

We are not the only people who have illustrated the truth, that a people may have excellent law, and detestable practices. Our Savior denounces the Jews, because they made void the law by their traditions. We have been guilty of the same sin.

The American people have made void our Constitution by just such traditions as Judge Taney and Mr. Garrison have been giving to the world of late, as the true light in which to view the Constitution of the United States. I shall follow neither. It is not what Moses allowed for the hardness of heart, but what God requires, ought to be the rule.

It may be said that it is quite true that the Constitution was designed to secure the blessings of liberty and justice to the people who made it, and to the posterity of the people who made it, but was never designed to do any such thing for the colored people of African descent.

This is Judge Taney's argument, and it is Mr. Garrison's argument, but it is not the argument of the Constitution. The Constitution imposes no such mean and satanic limitations upon its own benificent operation. And, if the Constitution makes none, I beg to know what right has anybody, outside of the Constitution, for the special accommodation of slaveholding villainy, to impose such a construction upon the Constitution?

The Constitution knows all the human inhabitants of this country as "the people." It makes, as I have said before, no discrimination in favor of, or against, any class of the people, but is fitted to protect and preserve the rights of all, without reference to color, size, or any physical peculiarities. Besides, it has been shown by William Goodell and others, that in eleven out of the old thirteen States, colored men were legal voters at the time of the adoption of the Constitution.

In conclusion, let me say, all I ask of the American people is, that they live up to the Constitution, adopt its principles, imbibe its spirit, and enforce its provisions.

When this is done, the wounds of my bleeding people will be healed, the chain will no longer rust on their ankles, their backs will no longer be torn by the bloody lash, and liberty, the glorious birthright of our common humanity, will become the inheritance of all the inhabitants of this highly favored country.

Two speeches by Frederick Douglass; one on West India emancipation, delivered at Canandaigua, Aug. 4th, and the other on the Dred Scott decision, delivered in New York, on the occasion of the anniversary of the American Abolition Society, May, 1857, Rochester, 1857

TO THE SECRETARY OF THE EDINBURGH NEW ANTI-SLAVERY ASSOCIATION

Rochester, N. Y., July 9, 1857

Dear Madam:

Your note of June third has been received. I beg in response to it, to thank the members of the Edinburgh New Anti-Slavery Association for the donation of five pounds in aid of the publication of my Anti-Slavery paper. Please assure the Association that I also feel deeply grateful for the kind cooperation extended to my zealous and untiring friend Miss Griffiths, who has labored very earnestly both here and in Great Britain to place my anti-slavery paper on a firm and permanent basis. I much fear that these exertions of hers have been greatly beyond her strength and that she is now seriously suffering the consequences of over-taxed powers. I am really indebted to Miss Griffiths for these voluntary and disinterested exertions and am deeply grateful to those dear people who aided and cheered her on in those exertions. I the more especially speak of the *disinterestedness* of Miss Griffiths because evil minded persons, I learn, have insinuated that Miss G. is receiving donations in my name for her own benefit. There is no truth in this insinuation or charge. All the donations made through her for the paper or for the Fugitive Fund come directly and unfailingly to those objects.

You need not be told that we have not the friendship of Mr. Garrison and his friends either in this country or in England. They have carried on the war against me with indelicate regard to the means. I am not sure that I am more obnoxious to them than is Miss Griffiths. Indeed they regard my repudiation of their religious or irreligious teaching as due to her influence. I am hated not as an apostate from the Anti-Slavery Cause, for all know that I am as faithful to that cause as I ever was, but I am an apostate from Garrisonism—an "ism" which comprehends opposition to the Church, the ministry, the Sabbath and the government as institutions in themselves considered and viewed apart from the question of Slavery. I am opposed to them at these points and could not lend my humble influence to the spread of such opinions in the name of the Slave or his cause. No persecution which I have received causes me any regret for the course I have felt it my duty to pursue.

I have nothing new (or that you will not get through public channels) to tell you about the present prospects of our cause. My speech at

New York which I hope may have met your eyes states my views of the present aspects of our cause. I am now at work less under the influence of hope than the settled assurance of faith in God, and the ultimate triumph of righteousness in the world. The cause of the slave is a righteous one, and I believe precious in the sight of Heaven. Though long delayed, it will triumph at last. Please excuse this short epistle. Write me whenever you may desire any information I can give.

I am, Dear Madam, with grateful regards to the Edinburgh New Anti-Slavery Association. With great respect,

Frederick Douglass

Frederick Douglass MSS., Frederick Douglass Memorial Home, Anacostia, D. C.

WEST INDIA EMANCIPATION, speech delivered at Canandaigua, New York, August 4, 1857

. . . . Friends and fellow-citizens: We have met here to-day to celebrate with all fitting demonstrations of joy and gladness, this the twenty-third anniversary of the inauguration of freedom as the ruling law of the British West Indies. The day and the deed are both greatly distinguished. They are as a city set upon a hill. All civilized men at least, have looked with wonder and admiration upon the great deed of justice and humanity which has made the first of August illustrious among all the days of the year. But to no people on the globe, leaving out the emancipated men and women of the West Indies themselves, does this day address itself with so much force and significance, as to the people of the United States. It has made the name of England known and loved in every Slave Cabin, from the Potomac to the Rio Grande, and has spread alarm, hatred, and dread in all the accursed slave markets of our boasted Republic from Baltimore to New Orleans.

Slavery in America, and slavery everywhere, never received a more stunning and killing condemnation.

The event we celebrate is the finding and the restoration to the broken ranks of human brotherhood, eight hundred thousand lost members of the human family. It is the resurrection of a mighty multitude, from the grave of moral, mental, social, and spiritual death, where ages of slavery and oppression, and lust and pride and cruelty, had bound them. Here they were instantly clothed with all the rights, responsibilities, powers, and duties, of free men and women.

Up to the morning of the first of August, 1834, these people were slaves, numbered with the beasts of the field, marked, branded, priced, valued, and ranged as articles of property. The gates of human brotherhood were bolted and barred against them. They were outside of both law and gospel. The love taught in the Bible, and the justice recorded in the Statute Book, did not embrace them: they were outside. Their fellow men had written their names with horses, sheep, and swine, and with horned cattle. They were not governed by the law, but the lash, they were not paid for their work, but whipped on to toil as the American slave now is. Their degradation was complete. They were slaves; and when I have said that, I have said all. The essence of wickedness, the intensified sum of all iniquity, the realization of the idea of a burning hell upon the earth, in which every passion is an unchained devil, let loose to deal out ten thousand pains, and horrors start up to view at the very mention of slavery!—It comprehends all that is foul, shocking, and dreadful. Human nature shudders, and turns pale at its presence, and flies from it as from a den of lions, a nest of scorpions, or an army of rattlesnakes. The very soul sickens, and the mind revolts at the thought of slavery, and the true man welcomes instant death in preference to being reduced to its degradation and ruin.

Yet such was the condition of our brothers and sisters in the British West Indies, up to the morning of the first of August, 1834. The wicked love of dominion by man over man, had made strong their fetters and multiplied their chains. But on the memorable morning which we are met to celebrate, one bolt from the moral sky of Britain left these blood-stained irons all scattered and broken throughout the West Indies, and the limbs they had bruised, out-stretched in praise and thanksgiving to God for deliverance. No man of any sensibility can read the account of that great transaction without emotions too great for utterance. There was something Godlike in this decree of the British nation. It was the spirit of the Son of God commanding the devil of slavery to go out of the British West Indies.

It said tyrant slave-driver, fling away your blood-stained whip, and bury out of sight your broken fetters and chains. Your accursed occupation is gone. It said to the slave, with wounds, bruises, and scars yet fresh upon him, you are emancipated—set free—enfranchised—no longer slaves, but British subjects, and henceforth equal before the British law!

Such, my friends, was the change—the revolution—the wondrous transformation which took place in the condition of the colored people in the British West Indies, twenty-three years ago. With the history of the causes, which led to this great consummation, you are perhaps already sufficiently acquainted. I do not intend in my present remarks to enter into the tedious details of this history, although it might prove quite instructive to some in this assembly. It might prove especially interesting to point out various steps in the progress of the British Anti-Slavery movement, and to dwell upon some of the more striking analogies between that and our movement in this country. The materials at this point are ample, did the limits of the hour permit me to bring them forward.

One remark in this connection I will make. The abolition movement in America, like many other institutions of this country, was largely derived from England. The defenders of American slavery often excuse their villainy on the ground that they inherited the system from England. Abolitionism may be traced to the same source, yet I don't see that it is any more popular on that account. Mr. Garrison applied British abolitionism to American slavery. He did that and nothing more. He found its principles here plainly stated and defined; its truths glowingly enunciated, and the whole subject illustrated, and elaborated in a masterly manner. The sin—the crime—the curse of slavery, were all demonstrated in the light of reason, religion, and morality, and by a startling array of facts. We owe Mr. Garrison our grateful homage in that he was among the first of his countrymen who zealously applied the British argument for abolition, against American slavery. Even the doctrine of immediate emancipation as against gradualism, is of English, not American origin. It was expounded and enforced by Elizabeth Herrick, and adopted by all the earnest abolitionists in England. It came upon the British nation like Uncle Tom's Cabin upon our land after the passing of the fugitive slave law, and it is remarkable that the highest services rendered the anti-slavery cause in both countries, were rendered by women. Elizabeth Herrick, who wrote only a pamphlet, will be remembered as long as the West India Emancipation is remembered, and the name of Harriet Beecher Stowe can never die while the love of freedom lives in the world.

But, my friends, it is not with these analogies and minute references that I mean in my present talk, to deal.

I wish you to look at West India Emancipation as one complete transaction of vast and sublime significance, surpassing all power of exaggeration. We hear and read much of the achievements of this nineteenth century, and much can be said, and truthfully said of them. The world has literally shot forward with the speed of steam and lightning. It has probably made more progress during the last fifty years, than in any five hundred years to which we can refer in the history of the race. Knowledge has been greatly increased, and its blessing widely diffused. Locomotion has been marvelously improved, so that the very ends of the earth are being rapidly brought together. Time to the traveler has been annihilated.

Deep down beneath the stormy surface of the wide, wide waste of waters, a pathway has been formed for human thought. Machinery of almost every conceivable description, and for almost every conceivable purpose, has been invented and applied; ten thousand discoveries and combinations have been made during these last fifty years, till the world has ceased to ask in astonishment "what next?" for there seems scarcely any margin left for a next. We have made hands of iron and brass, and copper and wood, and though we have not been able to endow them with life and soul, yet we have found the means of endowing them with intelligent motion, and of making them do our work, and to do it more easily, quickly and more abundantly than the hands in their palmiest days were able to perform it. I am not here to disparage or underrate this physical and intellectual progress of the race. I thank my God for every advance which is made in this direction.

I fully appreciate the beautiful sentiment which you farmers, now before me, so highly regard, "that he who makes two blades of grass grow where only one grew before," is a benefactor. I recognize and honor, as you do, all such benefactors. There is not the slightest danger that those who contribute directly to the world's wealth and ease will ever be forgotten by the world. The world loves its own. A hungry man will not forget the hand that feeds him, though he may forget that Providence which caused the bread to grow. Arkwright, Watt, Fulton, Franklin, Morse, and Daguerre, are names which will not fade from the memories of men. They are grand civilizers, but civilizers after their kind—and great as are their achievements, they sink to nothingness when compared with that great achievement which has given us the first day of August as a sacred day. "What shall it profit a man if he gain the whole world and lose his own soul?" We are to view this grand event in the light of this sublime enquiry.

"Men do not live by bread alone," said the great Redeemer. What is true of individual men, is also true of societies, and nations of men.

Nations are not held in their spheres, and perpetuated in health by cunning machinery. Railroads, steamships, electric wires, tons of gold and silver, and precious stones cannot save them. A nation may perish in the midst of them all, or in the absence of them all. The true life principle is not in them.

Egypt died in the sight of all her imposing wealth and her everlasting Pyramids. The polished stone is there, but Egypt is gone. Greece has vanished, her life disappeared as it were, in a trance of artistic beauty and architectural splendor. Great Babylon, the mother of harlots and the abominations of the earth, fell in the midst of barbaric wealth and glory. The lesson taught by the history of nations is that the preservation or destruction of communities does not depend upon external prosperity. Men do not live by bread alone, so with nations. They are not saved by art, but by honesty. Not by the gilded splendors of wealth, but by the hidden treasure of manly virtue. Not by the multitudinous gratification of the flesh, but by the celestial guidance of the spirit.

It is in this view that West India Emancipation becomes the most interesting and sublime event of the nineteenth century. It was the triumph of a great moral principle, a decisive victory, after a severe and protracted struggle, of freedom over slavery; of justice and mercy against a grim and bloody system of devilish brutality. It was an acknowledgment by a great nation of the sacredness of humanity, as against the claims of power and cupidity....

Now, my friends, how has this great act of freedom and benevolence been received in the United States. How has our American Christian Church and our American Democratic Government received this glorious new birth of National Righteousness.

From our professions as a nation, it might have been expected that a shout of joy and gladness would have shook the hollow sky, that loud hallelujahs would have rolled up to heaven from all our borders, saying, "Glory to God, in the highest, on earth peace and good will toward man. Let the earth be glad." "The Lord God omnipotent reigneth."

Alas, no such responsive note of rejoicing has reached my ear, except from a part of the colored people and their few white friends. As a nation, we are deaf, dumb, and blind to the moral beauty and transcendent sublimity of West India Emancipation. We have passed it by with averted eyes, regarding it rather as a reflection to be resented than as an example to be imitated. First, we looked for means of impeaching England's motives for abolishing Slavery, and not being able to find any such, we have made ourselves hoarse in denouncing emancipation as a failure.

We have not viewed the great fact in the light of a liberal philosophy, but have applied to it rules of judgment which were not intended to reveal its true character and make known its actual worth. We have taken a microscope to view the stars, and a fish line to measure the ocean's depths.

We have approached it as though it were a railroad, a canal, a steamship, or a newly invented mowing machine, and out of the fullness of our dollar-loving hearts, we have asked with owl-like wisdom, Will it pay? Will it increase the growth of sugar? Will it cheapen tobacco? Will it increase the imports and exports of the Islands? Will it enrich or ruin the planters? How will it effect Jamaica spirits? Can the West Indies be successfully cultivated by free labor? These and sundry other questions, springing out of the gross materialism of our age and nation, have been characteristically put respecting West India Emancipation. All our tests of the grand measure have been such as we might look for from slave-holders themselves. They all proceed from the slave-holders' side, and never from the side, of the emancipated slaves.

The effect of freedom upon the emancipated people of the West Indies passes for nothing. It is nothing that the plundered slave is now a freeman; it is nothing with our sagacious, economical philosophers, that the family now takes the place of concubinage; it is nothing that marriage is now respected where before it was a mockery; it is nothing that moral purity has now a chance to spring up, where before pollution was only possible; it is nothing that education is now spreading among the emancipated men and women, bearing its precious fruits, where only ignorance, darkness, superstition and idolatry prevailed before; it is nothing that the whipping post has given way to the schoolhouse; it is nothing that the church stands now where the slave prison stood before; all these are nothing, I say, in the eyes of our slavery-cursed country.

But the first and last question, and the only question which we Americans have to press in the premises, is the great American question (viz.) *will it pay?*

Sir, if such a people as ours had heard the beloved disciple of the Lord, exclaiming in the rapture of the apocalyptic vision, "And I saw another angel fly in the midst of heaven, having the everlasting gospel to preach to them that dwell on the earth, and to every nation, kindred, tongue, and people;" they, instead of answering, Amen Glory to God in the Highest, would have responded,—But brother John, *will it pay?* Can money be made out of it? Will it make the rich richer, and the strong stronger? How will it affect property? In the eyes of such people, there is no God but wealth; no right and wrong but profit and loss.

Sir, our national morality and religion have reached a depth of baseness than which there is no lower deep. They both allow that if men can make money by stealing men and women, and by working them up into sugar, rice, and tobacco, they may innocently continue the practice, and that he who condemns it is an unworthy citizen, and a disturber of the church. Money is the measure of morality, and the success or failure of slavery, as a money-making system, determines with many whether the thing is virtuous, or villainous, and whether it should be maintained or abolished. They are for Slavery where climate and soil are said to be for it, and are really not opposed to it anywhere, though as a nation we have made a show of opposition to it where the system does not exist. With our geographical ethics, and climatic religion, we have naturally sided with the slave-holders and women-whippers of the West Indies, in denouncing the abolition of slavery in the West Indies a failure.

Sir: As to what has been the effect of West India freedom upon the material condition of the people of those Islands, I am happy that there is one on this platform, who can speak with the authority of positive knowledge. Henry Highland Garnet has lived and labored among those emancipated people. He has enjoyed ample opportunity for forming an intelligent judgment in respect to all that pertains to the subject. I therefore most willingly leave this branch of the subject to him.

One remark, however, I will venture to make—and that is this: I take it that both the friends and the enemies of the emancipated have been too impatient for results. They seem to forget that although a nation can be born in a day, it can mature only in centuries—that though the fetters on the limbs can be broken in an instant, the fetters on the soul can wear off only in the ages.

Degradation, mental, moral, and physical, ground into the very bones of a people by ages of unremitting bondage, will not depart from that people in the course even of many generations.

West India freedom, though more than twenty-one years old, is yet but an infant. And to predicate its future on its present weakness, awkwardness, and improvidence now, is about as wise as to apply the same rule to your little toothless children. It has taken at least a thousand years to bring some of the leading nations of the earth from the point where the Negroes of the West Indies started twenty-three years ago, to their present position. Let considerations like these be duly weighed, and black man though I am, I do not fear the world's judgment.

Now, sir, I like these annual celebrations. I like them because they call us to the contemplation of great interests, and afford an opportunity of presenting salutary truths before the American people. They bring our people together, and enable us to see and commune with each other to mutual profit. If these occasions are conducted wisely, decorously, and orderly, they increase our respectability in the eyes of the world, and silence the slanders of prejudice. If they are otherwise conducted they cover us with shame and confusion. But, sir, these celebrations have been objected to by our slaveholding democracy; they do not think it in good taste. Slaveholders are models of taste. With them, propriety is everything; honesty, nothing. For a long time they have taught our Congress, and Senate, and Pulpits, what subjects should be discussed, and what objects should command our attention. Senator Sumner fails to observe the proscribed rules and he falls upon the Senate floor, stunned and bleeding beneath the ruffian blows of one of our southern models of propriety.[29] By such as these, and by their timid followers, this is called a *British* celebration.

From the inmost core of my soul I pity the mean spirits, who can see in these celebrations nothing but British feeling. The man who limits his admiration of good actions to the country in which he happens to be born, (if he ever was born,) or to the nation or community of which he forms a small part, is a most pitiable object. With him to be one of a nation is more than to be one of the human family. He don't live in the world, but he lives in the United States. Into his little soul the thought of God as our common Father, and of man our common Brother has never entered. To such a soul as that, this celebration cannot but be exceedingly distasteful.

But sarcasm aside, I hold it to be eminently fit that we keep up those celebrations from year to year, at least until we shall have an American celebration to take its place. That the event we thus commemorate transpired in another country, and was wrought out by the labors and sacrifices of the people of another nation, forms no valid objection to its grateful, warm, hearty, and enthusiastic celebration by us. In a very high sense, we may claim that great deed as our own. It belongs not exclusively to England and the English people, but to the lovers of Liberty and of mankind the world over. It is one of those glorious emanations of Christianity, which, like the sun in the Heavens, takes no cognizance of national lines or geographical boundaries, but pours its golden floods of living light upon all. In the great Drama of Emancipation, England was the theatre, but universal and everywhere applying principles of Righteousness, Liberty, and Justice were the actors. The great Ruler of the Universe, the God and Father of all men, to whom be honor, glory, and praise for evermore, roused the British conscience by his truth, moved the British heart, and West India Emancipation was the result. But if only Englishmen may properly celebrate this great concession to justice and liberty, then, sir, we may claim to be Englishmen, Englishmen in the love of Justice and Liberty, Englishmen in magnanimous efforts to protect the weak against the strong, and the slave against the slaveholder. Surely in this sense, it ought to be no disgrace to be an Englishman, even on the soil of the freest people on the globe.

But, Mr. Chairman, we celebrate this day on the broad platform of Philanthropy—whose country is the world, and whose countrymen are all mankind. On this platform we are neither Jews nor Greeks, strangers nor foreigners, but fellow citizens of the household of faith. We are the brothers and friends of Clarkson, Wilberforce, Granville, Sharpe, Richard Baxter, John Wesley, Thomas Day, Bishop Portius, and George Fox, and the glorious company of those who first wrought to turn the moral sense of mankind in active opposition to slavery. They labored for freedom not as Englishmen, but as men, and as brothers to men—the world over— and it is meet and right to commemorate and imitate their noble example. So much for the Anti-British objection.

I will now notice a special objection. It is said that we, the colored people, should do something ourselves worthy of celebration, and not be everlastingly celebrating the deeds of a race by which we are despised.

This objection, strange as it may seem, comes from no enemy of our people, but from a friend. He is himself a colored man, a high spirited and patriotic man, eminent for learning and ability, and to my mind, he has few equals, and no superior among us. I thank Dr. J. M'Cune Smith for this objection, since in the answer I may make to it, I shall be able to give a few of my thoughts on the relation subsisting between the white and colored people of this country, a subject which it well becomes us to consider whenever and wherever we congregate.

In so far as this objection to our celebrating the first of August has a tendency to awaken in us a higher ambition than has hitherto distinguished us, and to raise our aims and activities above the dull level of our present physical wants, and so far as it shall tend to stimulate us to the execution of great deeds of heroism worthy to be held in admiration and perpetual remembrance, for one, sir, I say amen to the whole of it. I am free to say, that nothing is more humiliating than the insignificant part we, the colored people, are taking in the great contest now going on with the powers of oppression in this land. I can stand the insults, assaults, misrepresentations, and slanders of the known haters of my race, and brave them all. I look for such opposition. It is a natural incident of the war, and I trust I am to a certain degree prepared for it; but the stolid contentment, the listless indifference, the moral death which reigns over many of our people, we who should be all on fire, beats down my little flame of enthusiasm and leaves me to labor, half robbed of my natural force. This indifference, in us, is outrageous. It is giving aid and comfort to the men who are warring against our very manhood. The highest satisfaction of our oppressors, is to see the Negro degraded, divested of public spirit, insensible to patriotism, and to all concern for the freedom, elevation, and respectability of the race.

Senator Toombs with a show of truth, lyingly said in Boston a year or two ago in defence of the slavery of the black race, they are mentally and morally inferior, and that if the whole colored population were swept from this country, there would be nothing in twenty years to tell that such a people had ever existed. He exulted over our assumed ignorance and over our destitution of valuable achievements. Of course the slaveholder uttered a falsehood, but to many it seemed to be a truth, and vast numbers of the American people receive it as a truth to-day, and shape their action accordingly.

The general sentiment of mankind is, that a man who will not fight for himself, when he has the means of doing so, is not worth being fought for by others, and this sentiment is just. For a man who does not value freedom for himself will never value it for others, nor put himself to any inconvenience to gain it for others. Such a man, the world says, may lie down until he has sense enough to stand up. It is useless and cruel to put a man on his legs, if the next moment his head is to be brought against a curb-stone.

A man of that type will never lay the world under any obligation to him, but will be a moral pauper, a drag on the wheels of society, and if he, too, be identified with a peculiar variety of the race he will entail disgrace upon his race as well as upon himself. The world in which we live is very accommodating to all sorts of people. It will co-operate with them in any measure which they propose; it will help those who earnestly help themselves, and will hinder those who hinder themselves. It is very polite, and never offers its services unasked.—Its favors to individuals are measured by an unerring principle in this: viz—respect those who respect themselves, and despise those who despise themselves. It is not within the power of unaided human nature to persevere in pitying a people who are insensible to their own wrongs, and indifferent to the attainment of their own rights. The poet was as true to common sense as to poetry when he said,

"*Who would be free, themselves must strike the blow.*"

When O'Connell, with all Ireland at his back, was supposed to be contending for the just rights and liberties of Ireland, the sympathies of mankind were with him, and even his enemies were compelled to respect his patriotism. Kossuth, fighting for Hungary with his pen long after she had fallen by the sword, commanded the sympathy and support of the liberal world till his own hopes died out. The Turks, while they fought bravely for themselves and scourged and drove back the invading legions of Russia, shared the admiration of mankind. They were standing up for their own rights against an arrogant and powerful enemy; but as soon as they let out their fighting to the Allies, admiration gave way to contempt. These are not the maxims and teachings of a cold-hearted world. Christianity itself teaches that a man shall provide for his own house. This covers the whole ground of nations as well as individuals. Nations no more than individuals can innocently be improvident. They should provide for all wants, mental, moral, and religious, and against all evils to which they are liable as nations. In the great struggle now progressing for the freedom and elevation of our people, we should be found at work with all our might, resolved that no man or set of men shall be more abundant in labors, according to the measure of our ability, than ourselves.

I know, my friends, that in some quarters the efforts of colored people meet with very little encouragement. We may fight, but we must fight like the Sepoys of India, under white officers. This class of Abolitionists don't like colored celebrations, they don't like colored conventions, they don't like colored Anti-Slavery fairs for the support of colored newspapers. They don't like any demonstrations whatever in which colored men take a leading part. They talk of the proud Anglo-Saxon blood, as flippantly as those who profess to believe in the natural inferiority of races.

Your humble speaker has been branded as an ingrate, because he has ventured to stand up on his own right, and to plead our common cause as a colored man, rather than as a Garrisonian. I hold it to be no part of gratitude to allow our white friends to do all the work, while we merely hold their coats. Opposition of the sort now referred to, is partisan opposition, and we need not mind it. The white people at large will not largely be influenced by it. They will see and appreciate all honest efforts on our part to improve our condition as a people.

Let me give you a word of the philosophy of reform. The whole history of the progress of human liberty shows that all concessions yet made to her august claims, have been born of earnest struggle. The conflict has been exciting, agitating, all-absorbing, and for the time being, putting all other tumults to silence. It must do this or it does nothing. If there is no struggle there is no progress. Those who profess to favor freedom and yet deprecate agitation, are men who want crops without plowing up the ground, they want rain without thunder and lightning. They want the ocean without the awful roar of its many waters.

This struggle may be a moral one, or it may be a physical one, and it may be both moral and physical, but it must be a struggle. Power concedes nothing without a demand. It never did and it never will. Find out just what any people will quietly submit to and you have found out the exact measure of injustice and wrong which will be imposed upon them, and these will continue till they are resisted with either words or blows, or with both. The limits of tyrants are prescribed by the endurance of those whom they oppress. In the light of these ideas, Negroes will be hunted at the North, and held and flogged at the South so long as they submit to those devilish outrages, and make no resistance, either moral or physical. Men may not get all they pay for in this world, but they must certainly pay for all they get. If we ever get free from the oppressions and wrongs heaped upon us, we must pay for their removal. We must do this by labor, by suffering, by sacrifice, and if needs be, by our lives and the lives of others.

Hence, my friends, every mother who, like Margaret Garner, plunges a knife into the bosom of her infant to save it from the hell of our Christian Slavery,[30] should be held and honored as a benefactress. Every fugitive from slavery who like the noble William Thomas at Wilkesbarre, prefers to perish in a river made red by his own blood, to submission to the hell hounds who were hunting and shooting him, should be esteemed as a glorious martyr, worthy to be held in grateful memory by our people.

The fugitive Horace, at Mechanicsburgh, Ohio, the other day, who taught the slave catchers from Kentucky that it was safer to arrest white men than to arrest him, did a most excellent service to our cause. Parker and his noble band of fifteen at Christiana, who defended themselves from the kidnappers with prayers and pistols, are entitled to the honor of making the first successful resistance to the Fugitive Slave Bill. But for that resistance, and the rescue of Jerry, and Shadrack,[31] the man-hunters would have hunted our hills and valleys here with the same freedom with which they now hunt their own dismal swamps.

There was an important lesson in the conduct of that noble Krooman in New York, the other day, who, supposing that the American Christians were about to enslave him, betook himself to the mast head, and with knife in hand, said he would cut his throat before he would be made a slave. Joseph Cinque on the deck of the Amistad, did that which should make his name dear to us. He bore nature's burning protest against slavery. Madison Washington who struck down his oppressor on the deck of the Creole, is more worthy to be remembered than the colored man who shot Pitcairn at Bunker Hill.

My friends, you will observe that I have taken a wide range, and you think it is about time that I should answer the special objection to this celebration. I think so too. This, then, is the truth concerning the inauguration of freedom in the British West Indies. Abolition was the act of the British Government. The motive which led the Government to act, no doubt was mainly a philanthropic one, entitled to our highest admiration and gratitude. The National Religion, the justice, and humanity, cried out in thunderous indignation against the foul abomination, and the government yielded to the storm. Nevertheless a share of the credit of the result falls justly to the slaves themselves. "Though slaves, they were rebellious slaves." They bore themselves well. They did not hug their chains, but according to their opportunities, swelled the general protest against oppression. What Wilberforce was endeavoring to win from the British Senate by his magic eloquence, the Slaves themselves were endeavoring to gain by outbreaks and violence. The combined action of one and the other wrought out the final result. While one showed that slavery was wrong, the other showed that it was dangerous as well as wrong. Mr. Wilberforce, peace man though he was, and a model of piety, availed himself of this element to strengthen his case before the British Parliament, and warned the British government of the danger of continuing slavery in the West Indies. There is no doubt that the fear of the consequences, acting with a sense of the moral evil of slavery, led to its abolition. The spirit of freedom was abroad in the Islands. Insurrection for freedom kept the planters in a constant state of alarm and trepidation. A standing army was necessary to keep the slaves in their chains. This state of facts could not be without weight in deciding the question of freedom in these countries.

I am aware that the rebellious disposition of the slaves was said to arise out of the discussions which the abolitionists were carrying on at home, and it is not necessary to refute this alleged explanation. All that I contend for is this: that the slaves of the West Indies did fight for their freedom, and that the fact of their discontent was known in England, and that it assisted in bringing about that state of public opinion which finally resulted in their emancipation. And if this be true, the objection is answered.

Again, I am aware that the insurrectionary movements of the slaves were held by many to be prejudicial to their cause. This is said now of such movements at the South. The answer is that abolition followed close on the heels of insurrection in the West Indies, and Virginia was never nearer emancipation than when General Turner kindled the fires of insurrection at Southampton.

Sir, I have now more than filled up the measure of my time. I thank you for the patient attention given to what I have had to say. I have aimed, as I said at the beginning, to express a few thoughts having some relation to the great interests of freedom both in this country and in the British West Indies, and I have said all that I meant to say, and the time will not permit me to say more.

Two speeches by Frederick Douglass; one on West India emancipation, delivered at Canandaigua, Aug. 4th, and the other on the Dred Scott decision, delivered in New York, on the occasion of the anniversary of the American Abolition Society, May, 1857, Rochester, 1857

TO JOHN BROWN

Rochester, Dec. 7, 1857[?]

My Dear Captain Brown:

I am very busy at home. Will you please come up with my son Fred and take a mouthful with me?   In haste, yours truly,

Frederick Douglass

Frederick Douglass MSS, Historical Society of Pennsylvania

THE TRUE ISSUE

It is enough to make a man's blood run cold now-o'-days to read the so-called anti-slavery papers of our country. The heartlessness displayed in dealing with the sin and crime which is eating out the very heart of all that is precious and worth struggling for, is absolutely shocking. While humanity, justice, and freedom are thawing the icy heart of Russia into life, and causing, even there, the iron hand of despotism to relax its terrible grasp upon the enslaved peasantry—while the "age and body of our time" would seem to cry aloud and spare not, against all forms of oppression—we of the United States are buried in stone-dead indifference to the only true and vital issue which freedom has any right to make with slavery.

We read of many issues with slavery just now. One is that slavery shall not commit any further aggressions upon the North; another, that slavery shall not have slaveholding Cuba added to her territory; another, that slavery shall not be established in Kansas; another, that the Dred Scott decision is not binding upon Congress; another, that the African slave trade shall not be re-opened; another, that the South shall not dissolve the Union, in case the Republican party shall elect its candidate to the Presidency in 1860. Shame, we say, everlasting shame upon all these miserable "shams." Following them the North has nearly lost sight of the only true and vital issue which can be made with slavery. What is that issue?

It is not, certainly, shall we humble the slave power? It is not, shall we give the broad Territories of the South-West to free white labor?—not whether the Dred Scott decision shall be adopted in whole or in part? not whether freedom and slavery shall live in peace side by side? but the great and all-commanding question, and the only question which should concern all earnest lovers of their country and of mankind, is, shall the four million slaves, now robbed of all their rights, and degraded to a level with brute beast, under the very droppings of the sanctuaries of religion and government, be restored to freedom and to progress? This, we take it, is the thing of all others to be kept before the American people —the thing of all others to be contended for. The true war cry is the complete and certain abolition of slavery. Anything in the way of anti-slavery, whether in theory or practice, which does not have this end in view, is clearly deceptive, false, and delusive—a "sham."

The whip-scarred millions, now toiling in bondage, have claims upon us, more powerful and telling, more authoritative and imperative, backed up by all the ties of nature, and nature's God, than any of the miserable appeals made to us in behalf of *"free white labor."* That sort of labor is, thank Heaven! already free. It can take care of itself. It has the ballot box and the sword, and needs no special protection. But *black labor* is in chains, under the merciless lash, sold on the auction block, crushed in spirit, and bleeding at heart. Upon its back rides an insolent and blood-thirsty aristocracy, and upon its heaving breast stands the cold, clammy, and blood-stained walls of the American Church, in which a hypocritical clergy mock God with sepulchral incantations from Sabbath to Sabbath, calling it divine worship. Methinks the very devils must grin, as these long robed divines perform their divine services, with their hearts crammed with hatred to the slave, and alive with affectionate interest in the salvation of the master.

Abolitionists! return to your principles! Come back, and do your first work over again. Make the slave first, midst, and last. Follow no longer the partial and side issues; strike for the abolition of slavery. William H. Seward has told us only what common sense has told us, that when this nation shall will the abolition of slavery, the way will be provided for its abolition. Our business is most plainly to stick to those doctrines and measures, and to labor in the promulgation of those facts and arguments, which tend directly and certainly to bring this nation, North and South, to favor the complete and certain abolition of slavery.

Douglass' Monthly, January, 1859

AFRICAN CIVILIZATION SOCIETY

"But I entreated you to tell your readers what your objections are to the civilization and christianization of Africa. What objection have you to colored men in this country engaging in agriculture, lawful trade, and commerce in the land of my forefathers? What objection have you to an organization that shall endeavor to check and destroy the African slave-trade, and that desires to co-operate with anti-slavery men and women of every grade in our own land, and to toil with them for the overthrow of American slavery?—Tell us, I pray you, tell us in your clear and manly style. 'Gird up thy loins, and answer thou me, if thou canst.' "—Letter from Henry Highland Garnet.

Hitherto we have allowed ourselves but little space for discussing the claims of this new scheme for the civilization of Africa, doing little more than indicating our dissent from the new movement, yet leaving our columns as free to its friends as to its opponents. We shall not depart from this course, while the various writers bring good temper and ability to the discussion, and shall keep themselves within reasonable limits. We hope the same impartiality will be shown in the management of the *Provincial Freeman,* the adopted organ of the African Civilization Society. We need discussion among ourselves, discussion to rouse our souls to intenser life and activity.—"Communipaw" did capital service when he gave the subtle brain of Wm. Whipper a little work to do, and our readers the pleasure of seeing it done. Anything to promote earnest thinking among our people may be held as a good thing in itself, whether we assent to or dissent from the proposition which calls it forth.

We say this much before entering upon a compliance with the request of our friend Garnet, lest any should infer that the discussion now going on is distasteful to us, or that we desire to avoid it. The letter in question from Mr. Garnet is well calculated to make that impression. He evidently enjoys a wholesome confidence, not only in the goodness of his own cause, but in his own ability to defend it.—Sallying out before us, as if in "complete steel," he entreats us to appear "in manly style," to *"gird up our loins,"* as if the contest were one requiring all our strength and activity. "Answer thou me if thou canst?"—As if an answer were impossible. Not content with this, he reminds us of his former similar entreaties, thus making it our duty to reply to him, if for no better reason than respect and courtesy towards himself.

The first question put to us by Mr. Garnet is a strange and almost preposterous one. He asks for our "objections to the civilization and christianization of Africa." The answer we have to make here is very easy and very ready, and can be given without even taking the trouble to observe the generous advice to "gird up our loins." We have not, dear brother, the least possible objection either to the civilization or to the christianization of Africa, and the question is just about as absurd and ridiculous as if you had asked us to "gird up our loins," and tell the world what objection Frederick Douglass has to the abolition of slavery, or the elevation of the free people of color in the United States! We not only have no objection to the civilization and christianization of Africa, but rejoice to know that through the instrumentality of commerce, and the labors of faithful missionaries, those very desirable blessings are already being realized in [the land of my fathers] Africa.

Brother Garnet is a prudent man, and we admire his tact and address in presenting the issue before us, while we cannot assent entirely to its fairness. *"I did not ask you for a statement of your preference of America to Africa."* That is very aptly said, but is it impartially said? Does brother Garnet think such a preference, in view of all the circumstances, a wise and proper one? Or is he wholly indifferent as to the preference or the other? He seems to think that our preferences have nothing to do with the question between us and the African Civilization Society, while we think that this preference touches the very bone of contention. The African Civilization Society says to us, go to Africa, raise cotton, civilize the natives, become planters, merchants, compete with the slave States in the Liverpool cotton market, and thus break down American slavery. To which we simply and briefly reply, "we prefer to remain in America;" and we do insist upon it, in the very face of our respected friend, that that is both a direct and candid answer. There is no dodging, no equivocation, but so far as we are concerned, the whole matter is ended. *You* go there, *we* stay here, is just the difference between us and the African Civilization Society, and the true issue upon which co-operation with it or opposition to it must turn.

Brother Garnet will pardon us for thinking it somewhat cool in him to ask us to give our objections to this new scheme. Our objections to it have been stated in substance, repeatedly. It has been no fault of ours if he has not read them.

As long ago as last September, we gave our views at large on this subject, in answer to an eloquent letter from Benjamin Coates, Esq., the real, but not the ostensible head of the African Civilization movement.

Meanwhile we will state briefly, for the benefit of friend Garnet, seven considerations, which prevent our co-operation with the African Civilization Society.

1. No one idea has given rise to more oppression and persecution toward the colored people of this country, than that which makes Africa, not America, their home. It is that wolfish idea that elbows us off the side walk, and denies us the rights of citizenship. The life and soul of this abominable idea would have been thrashed out of it long ago, but for the jesuitical and persistent teaching of the American Colonization Society. The natural and unfailing tendency of the African Civilization Society, by sending *"around the hat"* in all our towns and cities for

money to send colored men to Africa, will be to keep life and power in this narrow, bitter and persecuting idea, that Africa, not America, is the Negro's true home.

2. The abolition of American slavery, and the moral, mental and social improvement of our people, are objects of immediate, pressing and transcendent importance, involving a direct and positive issue with the pride and selfishness of the American people. The prosecution of this grand issue against all the principalities and powers of church and state, furnishes ample occupation for all our time and talents; and we instinctively shrink from any movement which involves a substitution of a doubtful and indirect issue, for one which is direct and certain, for we believe that the demand for the abolition of slavery now made in the name of humanity, and according to the law of the Living God, though long delayed, will, if faithfully pressed, certainly triumph.—The African Civilization Society proposes to plant its guns too far from the battlements of slavery for us. Its doctrines and measures are those of doubt and retreat, and it must land just where the American Colonization movement landed, upon the lying assumption, that white and black people can never live in the same land on terms of equality. Detesting this heresy as we do, and believing it to be full of all "deceivableness" of unrighteousness, we shun the paths that lead to it, no matter what taking names they bear, or how excellent the men who bid us to walk in them.

3. Among all the obstacles to the progress of civilization and of christianity in Africa, there is not one so difficult to overcome as the African slave trade. No argument is needed to make this position evident. The African Civilization Society will doubtless assent to its truth. Now, so regarding the slave trade, and believing that the existence of slavery in this country is one of the strongest props of the African slave trade, we hold that the best way to put down the slave trade, and to build up civilization in Africa, is to stand our ground and labor for the abolition of slavery in the U. S. But for slavery here, the slave trade would have been long since swept from the ocean by the united navies of Great Britain, France and the United States. The work, therefore, to which we are naturally and logically conducted, as the one of primary importance, is to abolish slavery. We thus get the example of a great nation on the right side, and break up, so far as America is concerned, a demand for the slave trade. More will have been done. The enlightened conscience of our nation, through its church and government, and its press, will be let loose against slavery and the slave trade wherever practiced.

4. One of the chief considerations upon which the African Civilization Society is recommended to our favorable regard, is its tendency to break up the slave trade. We have looked at this recommendation, and find no reason to believe that any one man in Africa can do more for the abolition of that trade, while living in Africa, than while living in America. If we cannot make Virginia, with all her enlightenment and christianity, believe that there are better uses for her energies than employing them in breeding slaves for the market, we see not how we can expect to make Guinea, with its ignorance and savage selfishness, adopt our notions of political economy. Depend upon it, the savage chiefs on the western coast of Africa, who for ages have been accustomed to selling their captives into bondage, and pocketing the ready cash for them, will not more readily see and accept our moral and economical ideas, than the slave-traders of Maryland and Virginia. We are, therefore, less inclined to go to Africa to work against the slave-trade, than to stay here to work against it. Especially as the means for accomplishing our object are quite as promising here as there, and more especially since we are here already, with constitutions and habits suited to the country and its climate, and to its better institutions.

5. There are slaves in the United States to the number of four millions.[32] They are stigmatized as an inferior race, fit only for slavery, incapable of improvement, and unable to take care of themselves. Now, it seems plain that here is the place, and we are the people to meet and put down these conclusions concerning our race. Certainly there is no place on the globe where the colored man can speak to a larger audience, either by precept or by example, than in the United States.

6. If slavery depended for its existence upon the cultivation of cotton, and were shut up to that single production, it might even then be fairly questioned whether any amount of cotton culture in Africa would materially affect the price of that article in this country, since demand and supply would go on together. But the case is very different. Slave labor can be employed in raising anything which human labor and the earth can produce. If one does not pay, another will. Christy says "Cotton is King," and our friends of the African Civilization movement are singing the same tune; but clearly enough it must appear to common sense, that "King Cotton" in America has nothing to fear from King Cotton in Africa.

7. We object to enrolling ourselves among the friends of that new Colonization scheme, because we believe that our people should be let

alone, and given a fair chance to work out their own destiny where they are. We are perpetually kept, with wandering eyes and open mouths, looking out for some mighty revolution in our affairs here, which is to remove us from this country. The consequence is, that we do not take a firm hold upon the advantages and opportunities about us. Permanent location is a mighty element of civilization. In a savage state men roam about, having no continued abiding place. They are "*going, going, going.*" Towns and cities, houses and homes, are only built up by men who halt long enough to build them. There is a powerful motive for the cultivation of an honorable character, in the fact that we have a country, a neighborhood, a home. The full effect of this motive has not hitherto been experienced by our people. When in slavery, we were liable to perpetual sales, transfers and removals; and now that we are free, we are doomed to be constantly harassed with schemes to get us out of the country. We are quite tired of all this, and wish no more of it.

To all this it will be said that Douglass is opposed to our following the example of white men. They are pushing East, West, North and South. They are going to Oregon, Central America, Australia, South Africa and all over the world. Why should we not have the same right to better our condition that other men have and exercise? Any man who says that we deny this right, or even object to its exercise, only deceives the ignorant by such representations.

If colored men are convinced that they can better their condition by going to Africa, or anywhere else, we shall respect them if they will go, just as we respect others who have gone to California, Fraser Island, Oregon and the West Indies. They are self-moved, self-sustained, and their success or failure is their own individual concern. But widely different is the case, when men combine, in societies, under taking titles, send out agents to collect money, and call upon us to help them travel from continent to continent to promote some selfish or benevolent end. In the one case, it is none of our business where our people go.—They are of age, and can act for themselves.—But when they ask the public to go, or for money, sympathy, aid, or co-operation, or attempt to make it appear anybody's duty to go, the case ceases to be a private individual affair, and becomes a public question, and he who believes that he can make a better use of his time, talents, and influence, than such a movement proposes for him, may very properly say so, without in any measure calling in question the equal right of our people to migrate.

Again it may be said that we are opposed to sending the Gospel to benighted Africa; but this is not the case. The *American Missionary Society,* in its rooms at 48 Beekman Street, has never had occasion to complain of any such opposition, nor will it have such cause. But we will not anticipate the objections which may be brought to the foregoing views. They seem to us sober, rational, and true; but if otherwise, we shall be glad to have them honestly criticised.

Douglass' Monthly, February, 1859

OUR RECENT WESTERN TOUR

It has not been many years since the West was contemplated by us as new and hard soil for anti-slavery labor, and when going thither, we set out, prepared for rough duty, resolutely determined to meet with calm front whatever in the shape of opposition might be flung in our pathway. In those days, it was common to meet with church doors bolted and barred against the cause of the slave, the minister warning his flock against the pestilent disturbers who were going about to turn the world upside down, to disorganize society, and break up the churches, destroy the revivals, turn the minds of the people from the claims of religion, to look after the mere temporal interests of men. It was common then, too, to meet with a cold and sullen indifference on the part of many, and a fierce and bitter spirit of persecution on the part of others.—The press was full of appeals to the basest passions against our cause, and poured out its scorn and contempt upon its advocates as either traitors or mad men. Brutal indignities met the anti-slavery lecturer, on stage coach, and at the hotels, and everywhere.—He was often compelled to get up his own meetings, hire a house, buy his candles, light up the house and ring the bell to call the people together, and sometimes after going to this trouble to get a meeting, he drew together only a few of the baser sort, who, stupefied with tobacco, or maddened by rum, would answer his arguments with bad eggs and brick bats. This state of things was not confined to the West alone. Within a dozen years, Mr. Garrison and the writer of this were mobbed, and their lives endangered in the civilized capital of Pennsylvania, for the utterance of simple abolition sentiments.[33]—In those days, friends were few, and enemies abundant. An Abolitionist was a proscribed man, and the proscription reached him in all the relations of life; his business was made to languish, and his social standing lowered, and his children pointed at in the streets as n——rs and "amalgamationists." The men who stood up in their isolation in those degenerate times, firm for God and Humanity, carried hearts in their bosoms and benignance in their faces, which shed hope even then upon the reigning moral desolation. It is good even now to get one of these *tried men* by the hand and talk with him about other days, when friends were few, and our cause covered with odium, and everywhere spoken against. Then Abolitionists loved each other with an ardor inspired by a common cause and a common persecution.

But times have changed very much of late. The Abolition lecturer speaks to a different audience, moves in a different atmosphere, and treads a less rugged pathway. The public sentiment has been gradually rising, the distance between the people and the Reformer has been steadily decreasing. The repellancy has become less and less strong, so that Abolitionism has become comparatively respectable, even in the West, where less anti-slavery labor has been performed than in the East. We, therefore, bring no discouraging news from the West—none from Michigan, none from Wisconsin, none from Illinois—the cause of freedom is onward and upward in them all. The work is not done; there is much more to be done, and will remain to be done, till the last yoke is broken and the last captive set free; but it is soul cheering to observe how much has been accomplished in spreading right views, sowing good seed, and the abundant fruit which has followed the labors already performed.

We think a Negro lecturer an excellent thermometer of the state of public opinion on the subject of slavery, much better than a white man. And for this reason, a hated opinion is not always in sight—a hated color is—and whatever of prejudice and pride, or other malign feeling may exist, are promptly called forth on the first appearance of a Negro. The Negro is the test of American civilization, American statesmanship, American refinement, and American Christianity. Put him in a rail car, in a hotel, in a church, and you can easily tell how far those around him have got from barbarism towards a true Christian civilization. We go about taking the measure of the times, scanning the field to ascertain the state of the contending moral forces, and the probabilities in favor of the final triumph of freedom over slavery.

We have, during the last seven weeks, visited Battle Creek, a fine flourishing young city in Michigan, where we met with a most hearty and cordial reception, by Abolitionists of all schools, Garrisonians, as well as others—Chicago, the home of Artemas Carter, L. C. Paine Freer, John Jones, H. O. Wagoner, and other long tried men—men who may always be relied upon to stand by the cause of God's poor in every emergency—men who stood by James H. Collins, now gone to his rest, in those days when he stood against the whole combined force of slavery; but we must not stop here to name the men.—Waukegan, Elgin, Belvidere, Rockford, Janesville, Freeport, Beloit, Princeton, (the home of Owen Lovejoy, brother to the noble Martyr,) Dixon, Mendota, Galesburg, Peoria, Bloomington, Ottawa, and Morris—towns in Illinois and Wisconsin—Jackson, Marshall, Albion, Ann Arbor and Detroit in Michigan, were all visited; and during our tour, we made nearly fifty speeches, a part of the time speaking twice a day, besides talking much of the time in rail cars and elsewhere.

We come home somewhat fatigued, but much gratified by what we have met with, seen, and heard during our journey. Those who came to hear us, were confessedly the most valuable and intelligent of the people in each community visited, just the class before whom it is of importance to get the claims of our people. And no matter what might be the subject of our discourses, whether before lyceums or elsewhere, slavery was really the thought uppermost in the minds of our hearers. Our own connection with slavery and identity with the oppressed, makes any good thing we are, under God, able to do, or say, tell in favor of the cause of our whole race.—Every town we visit, every audience we address, seem to regard us as the medium of an acquaintance with our enslaved people; and we have cause to rejoice when we see, as we have often seen during this and other tours through the country, a better feeling toward the colored man, a higher estimate of his qualities, and a deeper respect for his rights, as the results of our labors.

Our readers have already learned that we met with one incident of a slightly unpleasant character while at the American House at Janesville. The landlord, a rampant Democrat, wishing to signalize his devotion to the Dred Scott decision and to slavery generally by making an example of us, and for that purpose caused a table to be set at the extreme end of the dining room, with two hall doors and a street door opened directly upon it, where all the loafers of the bar room could come and feast their ill natured curiosity upon us, and indulge a morbid feeling of pleasure at our isolation. The table was covered with a dirty and ragged table cloth, and the whole appearance of the breakfast preparations made to resemble *"Negro fare"* on a slave plantation as nearly as it conveniently could. We, with our friends H. Ford Douglass and John Jones, who accompanied us, seeing that the whole thing was a premeditated attempt to degrade and insult us, paid our bill, and went to another hotel, where we were treated with the same consideration extended to other travelers. We made no noise, put on no airs, nor showed any marked sense of dissatisfaction, but simply told the landlord that we would pay our bill and leave, as we did not choose to gratify the feeling of prejudice and contempt which he had essayed to make us serve. We regret that this miserable affair has got into the papers at all, for it is every way exceptional, it being the only case of the kind we met with during our whole journey, the rule being all the other way; but since it has been made the subject of comment, we are thus particular to state the facts as they really are. We have been represented as imposing ourselves upon those who did not want us, forcing ourselves among white people, simply because when traveling we do not wish to be stowed away in a separate car from all other travelers, and when at hotels opened to the public, do not like to be set aside as a moral leper, unfit to be in the presence of other men. This is our offence, and our only offence. No one can say, either in or out of Rochester, that we ever took special pains to get into the society of white people, or of any other people. We have no prejudices nor preferences based upon color.

Our Democratic contemporary over the way thinks us too sensitive; that we should feel it no disgrace to sit apart from others at hotels. He is another instance of the philosophy and cool equanimity with which men can bear insults when offered to others. We hold that when at home, in one's own house, a man is at liberty to say who shall and who shall not come to his table, and to choose his own associates; but when he goes into a public hotel, his right of choice is qualified by the rights of other travelers, whose rights are equal to his. He has a right then to what he pays for, no more, no less. He may not say that the man with red hair shall not sit at the same table with him, nor that a man with a colored skin shall not sit at the same table with him; the right of the man with the red hair, and him of the black skin is as good as the right of any. Men who travel should leave their prejudices at home, and determine their conduct in the light of their just rights—rights which are equal, and which can only be forfeited by a violation of them in the persons of others. If guests have no right to set up their prejudices as the rule for the government of public houses, landlords have not.—They keep a public table, advertise to accommodate the public, and have no arbitrary right over the table. The table really belongs to those who pay for it, and equally to all who pay for it. Each person has a right to the knife, fork, and plate, and the good things before him, but he has no right to say who shall sit at the other end or the other side of the table, nor who shall sit next to him. Both landlord and guests ought to take *"pot luck"* in this respect. Strange as these common sense suggestions may appear now to some who may read them, they are certain to prevail in this country, and our visit to the West has done much to establish this conclusion. *"It's coming yet for a' that."*

Douglass' Monthly, April, 1859

THE KANSAS CONSTITUTIONAL CONVENTION

Few States, young or old, were ever blessed with a larger supply of constitutions, or of constitution makers, than the embryo State of Kansas. Since the moment she was handed over to the tender mercies of squatter sovereignty, she has been an inviting field to that class of statesmen who fancy they possess a special genius for organizing and shaping the destiny of new States. Constitutional lawyers and constitution makers have flocked to her borders from every section of our extended country, as to a field upon which to win glory for their skill, and perhaps something a little more substantial. New constitutions, new Governors, new political leaders, and new turns to political affairs there generally, have followed each other in rapid succession; and still that country has yet to be astonished by the discovery of a single Solon among all her statesmen. The whole machinery of Government, and all the wisdom of statesmanship, stand paralyzed in the presence of the *"Negro."* He balks every exertion, defeats every plan, and baffles all their wisdom. He is the rock of offence, the stone of stumbling, and the severest test of all their political skill. There have been in Kansas from the first, as in most other States, *apparently* two parties, essentially hostile one to the other in their estimate of the rights of the man of color, and the true policy of the State toward this particular variety of the human family. While, however, parties are nominally divided in Kansas, the cause of division does not thus far rise to the importance of a principle. *The Democrats have declared themselves our enemies, and the Republicans have not declared themselves our friends.* —The first would admit the black man into Kansas as a *slave,* and the other would seem to wish to exclude him as a *freeman;* one party would enslave him, and the other party would drive him from the face of all the earth over which they have power. Thus, while nominally and apparently at sword's point on the subject of Negroes, these parties, at heart, show but little difference. Neither party aims to be entirely just and humane to the black man. The Republican party has consented to the exclusion of the colored man from Oregon.[84] A more flagrant injustice and wrong could not well have been crowded into any constitution than in that of Oregon; yet Republican votes were given for that constitution. The far-famed Topeka constitution put the black man's rights in contempt, by putting them in question; and yet the party that framed and adopted that constitution claims to be the party of freedom and humanity, of honesty and decency. While they affirmed their own right to live in Kansas, and to live there in freedom, they submitted to the people the question as to whether colored men should have that right. Almost forty years ago, the State of Missouri was kept out of the Union on the ground that she had no right to exclude colored citizens from her borders, and a slaveholding President refused to proclaim her admission until she should blot out her wicked prohibitory law. This fact, stated in contrast with the statements of our statesmen and the character of our legislation of to-day, gives some idea of the distance we have drifted from the landmarks of liberty laid down by the fathers.

We have alluded thus to the animus of parties in Kansas at this time, because a new Constitutional Convention is about to undertake to supply that State with another constitution. In this Convention the Republican party has a clear majority of twelve members, and, of course, has the power to determine the character of whatever constitution shall be adopted by the Convention. We have observed, with some degree of alarm, that while there is no doubt that slavery will be prohibited, it is intimated that free Negroes are likely to be excluded. We have no doubt that an effort will be made to fasten this new wrong upon a people already meted, peeled and crushed beneath the terrible force of wrongs too numerous for specification, and we regret to say that there are indications that the effort will succeed.—The true policy of the Republican party is as plain as the sun in mid-heaven. That policy is to make a free State of Kansas, free to all the people of the country without distinction of any kind, for though such a course may excite the hatred of the slave power, it cannot excite contempt. The cruelty of dooming a whole race to exclusion from a State or Territory, needlessly branding them with inferiority, is a policy very little superior in humanity to slavery itself. The Republican party upon perpetrating such a wrong, would appear quite as devilish in spirit as the Democratic party itself. For the credit of humanity, let it be hoped that the Republican party in Kansas will step to the line of justice, and prove itself worthy of its name and professions in its present efforts of constitution making for that inchoate State.

Douglass' Monthly, August, 1859

PROGRESS OF SLAVERY

The friends of Emancipation in the United States have often cheered their spirits by dwelling upon the evidence of the progress of anti-slavery sentiments in the country. This is well. Reformers are human, and though capable of walking by faith, they naturally prefer to walk by sight. It is true that visible evidences of progress are sometimes deceptive; but upon the whole, men rely more firmly upon them, than upon what may turn out to be substantial progress, or may also turn out to be but the illusions of hope. To the strong eye of faith there is no darkness, no difficulties, no defeat, but the whole heavens are bathed in the golden light of victory. By this light we see the "heathen rage and the people imagine a vain thing;" we see the devices of the wicked confounded and brought to naught; we see the slave freed from his master, and all the powers of oppression broken and scattered. This is the true light, the true inspiration of the reformer. It has its foundation in the divinity of Truth, Justice, and Love—a divine, and therefore an eternal foundation against which not all the powers of sin and darkness can prevail. They who stand here, are delivered from the bondage of fear and the power of discouragement. Their objects, aims, and ends may be postponed, but never entirely defeated; and however unpromising the visible prospect, however dark the cloud, they see the complacent image of divinity, leading them on to ultimate victory. Of such faith as this the anti-slavery forces in America stand much in need just now. In the early days of the anti-slavery movement, when mobs were abundant, when rotten eggs and brick-bats were slavery's best arguments, there was faith in truth, faith in humanity, faith in the divineness and power of love. In the strength of this faith, the land was rocked from end to end, and the whole conclave of men-stealers were alarmed beyond measure and beyond pacification.

Very marked is the change and glaring is the contrast now presented. After a twenty years' conflict, the slaveholders are coolly estimating the value of their victories and felicitating themselves upon their security. Among the coolest and most devilish specimens of this complacency is that furnished in the recent valedictory speech of Mr. Stephens of Ga. He rejoices in the fact that *slavery* is stronger than it was sixteen years ago; cites the Dred Scott decision, anticipates five new slave States from Texas, revels in the abandonment of the slavery limitation doctrine of Rufus King and the Wilmot Proviso, and goes for the re-opening of the slave-trade with all its horrors. "Negro slavery," says Mr. Stephens, "is but in its infancy; it is a mere problem of our Government. Our fathers did not understand it. I grant that all the public men of the South were once against it; but they did not understand it. * * * The problem is yet unsolved. Ours is not only the best, but the only Government founded upon the principles of nature. Aristotle, and other ancient philosophers, had failed in their theories of Government. * * * All Government comes from the Creator. Statesmen never looked to the principles of graduation, but our Government is the only one founded on it; and our policy, and our institutions, and African slavery are founded on it. It is not for us to inquire into the great mysteries of nature, and it is most foolish to attempt to make things better than God made them."

In these diabolical statements and avowals we have the marrow of a speech which has been cited as expressing the cool and thoughtful conclusions of the leading minds of the slaveholding States. They let us into the sources of Southern repose, the tranquillity of tyrants, and are valuable as showing the progress of slavery. It will be seen that while Mr. Stephens refers with satisfaction to the Dred Scott decision, he admits the grounds of that decision to be false. All that gives that decision an air of plausibility is, that the founders of the Government were believers in the innocence of slavery, that Negroes had no rights. But Mr. Stephens denies the existence of this sentiment, and admits that at the beginning of the Government, the public men of the South were against slavery, and he excuses their opposition on the score of their ignorance of the character of the system.

It may be remarked in passing, that what is constantly denied by certain anti-slavery speakers and presses of the country, as to the state of public sentiment at the South on this subject, is now freely confessed by Mr. Stephens as being but the simple truth. The public men of the South, and of the whole country, were against slavery in the earlier days of the Republic. And yet the contrary is everywhere assumed, and we are called upon at the North to be of the same mind of our fathers in dealing with the question of slavery. Mr. Stephens is more honest than the Dred Scott decision—more honest in this particular than his Northern Democratic allies, and truer to history than our Garrisonian Abolitionists —all of whom insist that the vital element of the American Union was slavery.—Impossible is it to disguise the fact that slavery has made great progress, and has riveted itself more firmly in the Southern mind and heart, since the founding of the American Government. The whole moral atmosphere of the South has undergone a decided change for the worse.

"*Negro slavery,*" says man-stealer Stephens, is but in its infancy, (quite an aged infant, it being more than three hundred years old,) and according to him it is yet to astonish an admiring world by its marvelous benefits. He does not say that *slavery* itself is in its infancy, for, like murder and other terrible crimes, it has afflicted and cursed mankind in all ages. It is not peculiar to the Negro. All nations have had a taste of its bitter and poisonous fruits. Even the proud Saxon, who wields the bloody lash over the back of his black brother, has himself worn the fetter and the chain, and trembled at the voice of his Norman master. Mr. Stephens seems to be very religious as well as philosophical. He is a theologian as well as a statesman, and models the latter after the pattern of the former. In having a slaveholding God, he is not singular. The God of a proud and selfish tyrant, will be proud, selfish and tyrannical, the reflection, the image of a tyrant's own baseness. His appeal to the wisdom of such a God awakens no more reverent awe in us, than a like appeal to an ugly image in the jungles of Africa.

The grand defense of slavery in the South and in the North is the alleged inferiority of the Negro. There was a time when such inferiority granting that any such exists, would in the light of Christian ethics constitute an argument for kindness, charity, and for efforts directed to improve and strengthen the inferior race; but now, in our degeneracy, we see in the weakness of the Negro our best apology for robbing him of his liberty, crippling his energies, shutting out from him the light of knowledge, and making him a beast of burden. "Until," says our Christian Southern statesman, " 'the leopard can change his spots or the Ethiop his skin,' don't tell me that it is unlawful to hold slaves." As to the leopards, we have little concern. They are likely to take pretty good care of their spots; but the Ethiop is not so fortunately circumstanced. Inferior as he may be, and repellant as he may be to the white race, he is gradually changing his skin, or having it changed for him in all the slave States.

But we have referred to this speech as showing the onward march of slavery, and the sense of security which evidently prevails at the South as to the stability of the slave system. Once, nearly all public men at the South regarded the system as an evil and a curse; now they look upon it as a positive good and blessing, both to the white and the black race, the master and the slave. Formerly they regarded it as a transient system; now they regard it as permanent. Once they held it to be local; now, national. Once they defended it on grounds of expediency; now, on grounds of absolute right.

It is quite common to hear this state of mind at the South ascribed to the impertinent intermeddling of the Abolitionists of the North, and the free discussion there of the subject of slavery to which this intermeddling has given rise; but this is about as false as it is shallow and ridiculous. The argument is, that discussion has disclosed to the South the hidden beauties of slavery, and they who provoked discussion are responsible for this disclosure.

If a full discussion of the character of slavery in the South would tend to the establishment and permanence of slavery there, the lives of Abolitionists would no longer be in danger at the South. They would be held as the best friends of the slave system, the surest though unintentional supporters of Slavery. The boast that slavery has grown strong by discussion, is a lie, and none the less a lie because believed in and propagated by pro-slavery men at the North. Much truer is it that slavery has grown strong by the prohibition of all fair discussion of the subject in the South. How absurd is it to call that a discussion of a question, where an infuriated mob stand ready to cut out the tongue of any who dare speak on one side, and equally ready to shout applause to the most extravagant nonsense and blasphemy which may be uttered on the other side. And yet this is just the kind of discussion which slavery has allowed at the South, and which, according to Mr. Stephens of Georgia, and his doughface admirers at the North, has left slavery stronger than sixteen years ago. Let but the right of speech be once established in the slave States; let but the dumb millions be allowed to speak—nay, let only the smothered conscience of the poor white people of the South but leap forth, and we shall see where slavery will stand in the judgment of the Southern people. At present, discussion is all on one side. Neither press, pulpit, nor platform, dare speak out but in favor of slavery; and yet the notion has got abroad even here at the North, that slavery is in some way helped by discussion. Those who boast of the good effects of the discussion of slavery, are the men who imprison, shoot, and stab, and warn away from the South those who venture to discuss it; and where slavery loses this kind of defense, as in certain parts of Missouri and Kentucky, there it is looked upon as the monster of horrors that it really is.

Douglass' Monthly, August, 1859

THE BALLOT AND THE BULLET

"He has preached both the ballot and the bullet as the means by which slavery is to be destroyed and men have refused to employ either the one or the other, and the preacher has become discouraged. Let him discard both the ballot and the bullet, and as the best agent for the enfranchisement of man wield the sword of the spirit which divides Truth from Error, which separates between the Right and the Wrong. Then, when the weapon falls from his hand in death, he will be able to say with a cheerful tone and exulting heart, 'By this have I conquered.' "

The advice given above is addressed to our friend Gerrit Smith, by the *Anti-Slavery Bugle,* an organ of the non-voting theory. It sounds to us very much like nonsense, but may strike others differently. If the anti-slavery cause has failed, the ballot and the bullet are as little to blame for it as is the so-called *"sword of the spirit,"* which simply means, in the columns of the *Bugle,* telling men to do that which Garrisonians will not do themselves. They tell the Government to pass laws for the abolition of slavery, but will not themselves vote for such a law. They tell their State Legislatures to pass Personal Liberty Bills, but will not themselves vote for such men as will pass such bills. They denounce pro-slavery voting, but will not themselves cast an anti-slavery vote. Their cry is "no union with slaveholders," and yet they equally, with others, help to support the Government and consume the produce of the slave. Their money goes equally with others into the national treasury, and into the pockets of slave-drivers. While they "discard" both the ballot and the bullet, they seem to give no better proof of vitality and power than those who discard neither. Far be it from us to undervalue the power of truth when honestly addressed to the hearts and consciences of men; but truth to be efficient must be uttered in action as well as in speech.

If speech alone could have abolished slavery, the work would have been done long ago. What we want is an anti-slavery Government, in harmony with our anti-slavery speech, one which will give effect to our words, and translate them into acts. For this, the ballot is needed, and if this will not be heard and heeded, then the bullet. We have had cant enough, and are sick of it. When anti-slavery laws are wanted, anti-slavery men should vote for them; and when a slave is to be snatched from the hand of a kidnapper, physical force is needed, and he who gives it proves himself a more useful anti-slavery man than he who refuses to give it, and contents himself by talking of a "sword of the spirit."

Douglass' Monthly, October, 1859

CAPT. JOHN BROWN NOT INSANE

One of the most painful incidents connected with the name of this old hero, is the attempt to prove him insane.[35] Many journals have contributed to this effort from a friendly desire to shield the prisoner from Virginia's cowardly vengeance. This is a mistaken friendship, which seeks to rob him of his true character and dim the glory of his deeds, in order to save his life. Was there the faintest hope of securing his release by this means, we would choke down our indignation and be silent. But a Virginia court would hang a crazy man without a moment's hesitation, if his insanity took the form of hatred of oppression; and this plea only blasts the reputation of this glorious martyr of liberty, without the faintest hope of improving his chance of escape.

It is an appalling fact in the history of the American people, that they have so far forgotten their own heroic age, as readily to accept the charge of insanity against a man who has imitated the heroes of Lexington, Concord, and Bunker Hill.

It is an effeminate and cowardly age, which calls a man a lunatic because he rises to such self-forgetful heroism, as to count his own life as worth nothing in comparison with the freedom of millions of his fellows. Such an age would have sent Gideon to a mad-house, and put Leonidas in a strait-jacket. Such a people would have treated the defenders of

Thermopylae as demented, and shut up Caius Marcus in bedlam. Such a marrowless population as ours has become under the debaucheries of Slavery, would have struck the patriot's crown from the brow of Wallace, and recommended blisters and bleeding to the heroic Tell. Wallace was often and again as desperately forgetful of his own life in defense of Scotland's freedom, as was Brown in striking for the American slave; and Tell's defiance of the Austrian tyrant, was as far above the appreciation of cowardly selfishness as was Brown's defiance of the Virginia pirates. Was Arnold Winkelried insane when he rushed to his death upon an army of spears, crying "make way for Liberty!" Are heroism and insanity synonyms in our American dictionary? Heaven help us! when our loftiest types of patriotism, our sublimest historic ideals of philanthropy, come to be treated as evidence of moon-struck madness. Posterity will owe everlasting thanks to John Brown for lifting up once more to the gaze of a nation grown fat and flabby on the garbage of lust and oppression, a true standard of heroic philanthropy, and each coming generation will pay its installment of the debt. No wonder that the aiders and abettors of the huge, overshadowing and many-armed tyranny, which he grappled with in its own infernal den, should call him a mad man; but for those who profess a regard for him, and for human freedom, to join in the cruel slander, "is the unkindest cut of all."

Nor is it necessary to attribute Brown's deeds to the spirit of vengeance, invoked by the murder of his brave boys. That the barbarous cruelty from which he has suffered had its effect in intensifying his hatred of slavery, is doubtless true. But his own statement, that he had been contemplating a bold strike for the freedom of the slaves for ten years, proves that he had resolved upon his present course long before he, or his sons, ever set foot in Kansas. His entire procedure in this matter disproves the charge that he was prompted by an impulse of mad revenge, and shows that he was moved by the highest principles of philanthropy. His carefulness of the lives of unarmed persons—his humane and courteous treatment of his prisoners—his cool self-possession all through his trial—and especially his calm, dignified speech on receiving his sentence, all conspire to show that he was neither insane or actuated by vengeful passion; and we hope that the country has heard the last of John Brown's madness. The explanation of his conduct is perfectly natural and simple on its face. He believes the Declaration of Independence to be true, and the Bible to be a guide to human conduct, and acting upon the doctrines of both, he threw himself against the serried ranks of American oppression, and translated into heroic deeds the love of liberty and hatred of tyrants, with which he was inspired from both these forces acting upon his philanthropic and heroic soul. This age is too gross and sensual to appreciate his deeds, and so calls him mad; but the future will write his epitaph upon the hearts of a people freed from slavery, because he struck the first effectual blow.

Not only is it true that Brown's whole movement proves him perfectly sane and free from merely revengeful passion, but he has struck the bottom line of the philosophy which underlies the abolition movement. He has attacked slavery with the weapons precisely adapted to bring it to the death. Moral considerations have long since been exhausted upon slaveholders. It is in vain to reason with them. One might as well hunt bears with ethics and political economy for weapons, as to seek to "pluck the spoiled out of the hand of the oppressor" by the mere force of moral law. Slavery is a system of brute force. It shields itself behind *might*, rather than right. It must be met with its own weapons. Capt. Brown has initiated a new mode of carrying on the crusade of freedom, and his blow has sent dread and terror throughout the entire ranks of the piratical army of slavery. His daring deeds may cost him his life, but priceless as is the value of that life, the blow he has struck, will, in the end, prove to be worth its mighty cost. Like Samson, he has laid his hands upon the pillars of this great national temple of cruelty and blood, and when he falls, that temple will speedily crumble to its final doom, burying its denizens in its ruins.

Douglass' Monthly, November, 1859

TO THE ROCHESTER *DEMOCRAT AND AMERICAN*

Canada West, Oct. 31, 1859.

Mr. Editor:

I notice that the telegraph makes Mr. Cook (one of the unfortunate insurgents at Harper's Ferry, and now in the hands of the thing calling itself the Government of Virginia, but which in fact is but an organized conspiracy by one party of the people against the other and weaker,) denounce me as a coward—and to assert that I promised to be present at the

Harper's Ferry insurrection. This is certainly a very grave impeachment, whether viewed in its bearings upon friends or upon foes, and you will not think it strange that I should take a somewhat serious notice of it. Having no acquaintance whatever with Mr. Cook, and never having exchanged a word with him about the Harper's Ferry insurrection, I am induced to doubt that he could have used the language concerning me which the wires attribute to him. The lightning, when speaking for itself, is among the most direct, reliable and truthful of things; but when speaking for the terror-stricken slaveholders at Harper's Ferry, it has been made the swiftest of liars. Under their nimble and trembling fingers, it magnified seventeen men into seven hundred—and has since filled the columns of the New York *Herald* for days with interminable contradictions. But, assuming that it has told only the simple truth, as to the sayings of Mr. Cook in this instance, I have this answer to make to my accuser: Mr. Cook may be perfectly right in denouncing me as a coward. I have not one word to say in defence or vindication of my character for courage. I have always been more distinguished for running than fighting—and, tried by the Harper's Ferry insurrection test, I am most miserably deficient in courage—even more so than Cook, when he deserted his old brave captain, and fled to the mountains. To this extent Mr. Cook is entirely right, and will meet no contradiction from me or from anybody else. But wholly, grievously, and most unaccountably wrong is Mr. Cook, when he asserts that I promised to be present in person at the Harper's Ferry insurrection. Of whatever other imprudence and indiscretion I may have been guilty, I have never made a promise so rash and wild as this. The taking of Harper's Ferry was a measure never encouraged by my word or by my vote, at any time or place; my wisdom or my cowardice has not only kept me from Harper's Ferry, but has equally kept me from making any promise to go there. I desire to be quite emphatic here—for of all guilty men, he is the guiltiest who lures his fellow-men to an undertaking of this sort, under promise of assistance, which he afterwards fails to render. I therefore declare that there is no man living, and no man dead, who if living, could truthfully say that I ever promised him or anybody else, either conditionally or otherwise, that I would be present in person at the Harper's Ferry insurrection. My field of labor for the abolition of slavery has not extended to an attack upon the United States arsenal. In the teeth of the documents already published, and of those which hereafter may be published, I affirm no man connected with that insurrection, from its noble and heroic leader down, can connect my name with a single broken promise of any sort whatever. So much I deem it proper to say negatively.

The time for a full statement of what I know, and of *all* I know, of this desperate but sublimely disinterested effort to emancipate the slaves of Maryland and Virginia, from their cruel taskmasters, has not yet come, and may never come. In the denial which I have now made, my motive is more a respectful consideration for the opinions of the slave's friends, than from my fear of being made an accomplice in the general *conspiracy* against Slavery. I am ever ready to write, speak, publish, organize, combine, and even to conspire against Slavery, when there is a reasonable hope for success. Men who live by robbing their fellow-men of their labor and liberty, have forfeited their right to know anything of the thoughts, feelings, or purposes of those whom they rob and plunder. They have by the single act of slaveholding voluntarily placed themselves beyond the laws of justice and honor, and have become only fitted for companionship with thieves and pirates—the common enemies of God and of all mankind. While it shall be considered right to protect oneself against thieves, burglars, robbers and assassins, and to slay a wild beast in the act of devouring his human prey, it can never be wrong for the imbruted and whip-scarred slaves, or their friends, to hunt, harass and even strike down the traffickers in human flesh. If anybody is disposed to think less of me on account of this sentiment; or because I may have had a knowledge of what was about to occur, and did not assume the base and detestable character of an informer, he is a man whose good or bad opinion of me may be equally repugnant and despicable. Entertaining this sentiment, I may be asked, why I did not join John Brown—the noble old hero whose one right hand has shaken the foundation of the American Union, and whose ghost will haunt the bed-chambers of all the born and unborn slaveholders of Virginia through all their generations, filling them with alarm and consternation! My answer to this has already been given, at least, impliedly given: "The tools to those that can use them." Let every man work for the abolition of Slavery in his own way. I would help all, and hinder none. My position in regard to the Harper's Ferry insurrection may be easily inferred from these remarks, and I shall be glad if those papers which have spoken of me in connection with it would find room for this brief statement.

I have no apology for keeping out of the way of those gentlemanly United States Marshals, who are said to have paid Rochester a somewhat protracted visit lately, with a view to an interview with me. A government recognizing the validity of the *Dred Scott* decision, at such a time as this, is not likely to have any very charitable feelings towards me; and if I am to meet its representatives, I prefer to do so, at least, upon equal terms. If I have committed any offence against Society, I have done so on the soil of the State of New York, and I should be perfectly willing *there* to be arraigned before an impartial jury; but I have quite insuperable objections to being caught by the hands of Mr. Buchanan, and *"bagged"* by Gov. Wise. For this appears to be the arrangement. Buchanan does the fighting and hunting, and Wise *"bags"* the game.

Some reflections may be made upon my leaving on a tour to England, just at this time. I have only to say, that my going to that country has been rather delayed than hastened by the insurrection at Harper's Ferry. All knew that I had intended to leave here in the first week of November.

Frederick Douglass

Reprinted in New York *Herald*, November 4, 1859

TO MY AMERICAN READERS AND FRIENDS

Dear Readers and Friends:

About to leave my post as Editor for a long contemplated visit and lecturing tour in Great Britain, which may detain me many months from my Editorial duties, the peculiar circumstances of the occasion seem to justify me in saying to you a few parting words. In ordinary conditions, considering the rapidity, safety and certainty with which a journey is now made to Europe—almost converting the two continents into one—a simple voyage from America to Great Britain would not seem to warrant a very ceremonious and formal parting, or to require apology or explanation.

In any circumstances however, I should be most freely pardoned by all right feeling men and women, if while looking around upon the scores of kind and earnest friends who, during the last eighteen years, have cheered and sustained me by their sympathy and co-operation, in my humble labors to promote the emancipation and elevation of my people, I should let fall a tearful word at the thought of parting, and breathe one heart prayer that the cause of justice and benevolence, the bond of our friendship, may continue to fill their hearts and command their best

exertions for its ultimate triumph. Neither the long experience of part-
ings and meetings, nor the calmness borrowed from philosophy, avail me
anything, as I say to my friends and readers, farewell. Even the delightful prospect of renewing the *bonds-fraternal* formed in Great Britain and
Ireland, during my visit to those countries fourteen years ago, fails to
shield me from the keen edge of regret at leaving the friends here, in
the present state of the Anti-Slavery question. Dark and perilous as is the
hour—maddened and vengeful as is the slave power—the infuriated demon of Slavery never seemed to me more certain of extirpation than now.
At the present moment, Slavery seems to have gained an advantage. The
audacity of the attack made upon it by that stern old hero, who looks
death full in the face with a steady eye and undaunted heart, while pierced
with bayonet wounds and covered with sabre gashes, has created for the
moment, perhaps, a more active resistance to the cause of freedom and
its advocates; but this is transient. The moment of passion and revenge
will pass away, and reason and righteousness will all the more, for this
sudden shock, roll their thundering appeal to the ear and heart of this
guilty nation.

The Christian blood of Old John Brown will not cease to cry from
the ground long after the clamors of alarm and consternation of the
dealers in the bodies and souls of men will have ceased to arrest attention.
Men will soon begin to look away from the plot to the purpose—from the
effect to the cause.—Then will come the reaction—and the names now
covered with execration will be mentioned with honor, as noble martyrs
to a righteous cause. Yes, sad and deplorable as was the battle of Harper's
Ferry, it will not prove a total loss to the cause of Liberty. The sharp
crack of the rifles there, proclaiming Liberty to the Captive, cruelly left in
bondage by our boasted Religion and Law, may rouse a dead Church and
dumb Ministry to the duty of putting away this dark and dangerous sin.
The silent heights of the Alleghanies, leaning in grandeur against the
pure blue sky, will hereafter look down and speak to the slave with a
loving and wooing voice. The benumbed conscience of the nation will be
revived and become susceptible of right impressions. The slaveholders of
Virginia and the South generally, are endeavoring to make the impression that the Negroes summoned to the standard of freedom by John
Brown, viewed the effort to emancipate them with indifference. An eye
witness, and a prominent actor in the transactions at Harper's Ferry,
now at my side, tells me that this is grossly aside from the truth. But
even if the contrary were shown, it would afford small comfort to the

slaveholders. The slaves were sensible enough not to shout before they gained the prize, and their conduct was creditable to their wisdom. The brief space allowed them in freedom, was not sufficient to bring home to them in its fullness the real significance of the occasion. All the efforts to disparage the valor of the colored insurgents are grounded in the fears of the slaveholders, not in the facts of the action. They report many dead insurgents, and few killed among those who opposed them. I have at last seen one man among the insurgents reported killed, who is still alive and bids fair to live yet many years. On many accounts, were the thing possible, I should be glad to use the event at Harper's Ferry, and the state of feeling it has produced, before the American people. But there is work abroad as well as at home. Efforts will be made in England as well as in America to turn the Harper's Ferry insurrection to the account of Slavery. I may, for a time, be useful there, in resisting and counteracting these efforts.

It will probably be charged, by those who delight in any pretext for aspersing me, that I go to England to escape the demands of justice for my alleged complicity with the Harper's Ferry insurrection. I am not ashamed of endeavoring to escape from such justice as might be rationally expected by a man of color at the hands of a slaveholding court, sitting in the State of Virginia. I am not a favorite in that State, and even if acquitted by the court, with my knowledge of slaveholding magnanimity and civilization, I could scarcely hope to re-cross the slaveholding border with my life. There is no more dishonor in trying to keep out of the way of such a court, than there would be in keeping out of the way of a company of hungry wolves.—Nevertheless, it is only due to truth to state, that for more than a year past I have been making arrangements *not* to go to Harper's Ferry, but to England. This has been known alike to both friends and foes. My going, too, has been delayed, rather than hastened, by the occurrence of that outbreak.—The fact of my known intention to visit England in November, and my published lecturing engagements in different parts of the State of New York, plainly show that no man had any right to expect my personal co-operation elsewhere. I am, however, free to confess that I deem England a safer asylum for me than any afforded by the President of the United States. I have once before found shelter and protection in a monarchy, from the slavehunters of this Republic, and am indebted not to democratic humanity or justice for the liberty I have enjoyed during the last dozen years, and amid all the atrocities under the Fugitive Slave Bill in America—but to humane British men and women who bought my body and bones with British gold, and made me a present to myself—a free, an unsolicited gift. In other words, they gave me back the body originally given me by my Creator, but which had been stolen from me under the singularly just and generous laws of a republican slave State! I thank God that there is at least one Christian country on this globe where a colored man as well as a white man may rest secure from the fury and vengeance of alarmed and terrified slaveholders, the meanest tyrants that ever cursed the earth by their cruelty, or insulted Heaven by their blasphemous arrogance.

Almost ever since the Harper's Ferry disturbance, I have been assured that U. S. Marshals, in strong force, have been in search of me at different points, but chiefly at Rochester. A government which refuses to acknowledge—nay, denies that I can be a citizen, or bring a suit into its courts of justice—in a word, brands me as an outlaw in virtue of my blood, now professes a wish to try me for being a traitor and an outlaw! To be a traitor, two conditions are necessary: First—one must have a government; secondly—he must be found in armed rebellion against that government. I am guilty of neither element of treason. The American government refuses to shelter the Negro under its protecting wing, and makes him an outlaw. The government is therefore quite unreasonable and inconsistent. Allegiance and protection are said to go together, and depend upon each other. When one is withdrawn, the other ceases. But I think Mr. Buchanan is not only unreasonable and inconsistent in his design upon me, but a little cowardly withal. The plan seems to be to strike where his blows are likely to meet the least resistance. It cannot be that I am worthy of the extra attention paid me by the government. The Rochester *Union* very properly raises the inquiry as to why I am especially singled out—Am I more involved than others whose names have been mentioned in connection with the name of dear Old Ossawattomie Brown?—The eagerness to get hold of me, while the other and more popular men happened to be equally compromised, are merely threatened shows that my color, as well as my alleged crime, enters into the calculations of the government, and that it professes to arrest first those who can be arrested easiest. In this it acts with its usual cowardice.

But really, dear readers, I am much too highly honored by the importance given me in connection with this Harper's Ferry affair. My relation to it is far less important than friends or enemies seem to suppose. A letter sent for publication elsewhere, and which I hope will be inserted here, will give you a pretty clear idea of my true relation to that transaction.

In conclusion, I hope to be able to continue the regular publication of my paper during my absence, and to keep in correspondence with those who shall continue to stand by my little anti-slavery sheet. If this shall be done, (and I have very little doubt it will be,) I shall take my old post again, and do battle as of yore.

Douglass' Monthly, November, 1859

THE CONSTITUTION OF THE UNITED STATES: IS IT PRO-SLAVERY OR ANTI-SLAVERY? speech delivered in Glasgow, Scotland, March 26, 1860

... I proceed to the discussion. And first a word about the question. Much will be gained at the outset if we fully and clearly understand the real question under discussion. Indeed, nothing is or can be understood till this is understood. Things are often confounded and treated as the same, for no better reason than that they resemble each other, even while they are in their nature and character totally distinct and even directly opposed to each other. This jumbling up things is a sort of dust-throwing which is often indulged in by small men who argue for victory rather than for truth. Thus, for instance, the American Government and the American Constitution are spoken of in a manner which would naturally lead the hearer to believe that the one is identical with the other; when the truth is, they are as distinct in character as is a ship and a compass. The one may point right and the other steer wrong. A chart is one thing, the course of the vessel is another. The Constitution may be right, the Government wrong. If the Government has been governed by mean, sordid, and wicked passions, it does not follow that the Constitution is mean, sordid, and wicked. What, then, is the question? I will state it. But first let me state what is not the question. It is not whether slavery existed in the United States at the time of the adoption of the Constitution; it is not whether slaveholders took part in framing the Constitution; it is not whether those slaveholders, in their hearts, intended to secure certain advantages in that instrument for slavery; it is not whether the American Government has been wielded during seventy-two years in favour of the propagation and permanence of slavery; it is not whether a pro-slavery interpretation has been put upon the Constitution by the American Courts—all these points may be true or they may be false, they may be accepted or they may be rejected, without in any wise affecting the real question in debate. The real and exact question between myself and the class of persons represented by the speech at the City Hall[36] may be fairly stated thus:—1st, Does the United States Constitution guarantee to any class or description of people in that country the right to enslave, or hold as property, any other class or description of people in that country? 2nd, Is the dissolution of the union between the slave and free States required by fidelity to the slaves, or by the just demands of conscience? Or, in other words, is the refusal to exercise the elective franchise, and to hold office in America, the surest, wisest, and best way to abolish slavery in America?

To these questions the Garrisonians say Yes. They hold the Constitution to be a slaveholding instrument, and will not cast a vote or hold office, and denounce all who vote or hold office, no matter how faithfully such persons labour to promote the abolition of slavery. I, on the other hand, deny that the Constitution guarantees the right to hold property in man, and believe that the way to abolish slavery in America is to vote such men into power as will use their powers for the abolition of slavery. This is the issue plainly stated, and you shall judge between us. Before we examine into the disposition, tendency, and character of the Constitution, I think we had better ascertain what the Constitution itself is. Before looking for what it means, let us see what it is. Here, too, there is much dust to be cleared away. What, then, is the Constitution? I will tell you. It is no vague, indefinite, floating, unsubstantial, ideal something, coloured according to any man's fancy, now a weasel, now a whale, and now nothing. On the contrary, it is a plainly written document, not in Hebrew or Greek, but in English, beginning with a preamble, filled out with articles, sections, provisions, and clauses, defining the rights, powers, and duties to be secured, claimed, and exercised under its authority. It is not even like the British Constitution, which is made up of enactments of Parliament, decisions of Courts, and the established usages of the Government. The American Constitution is a written instrument full and complete in itself. No Court in America, no Congress, no President, can add a single word thereto, or take a single word therefrom. It is a great national enactment done by the people, and can only be altered, amended, or added to by the people. I am careful to make this statement here; in America it would not be necessary. It would not be necessary here if my assailant had showed the same desire to set before you the simple truth, which he manifested to make out a good case for himself and friends. Again, it should be borne in mind that the mere text, and only the text, and not any commentaries or creeds written by those who wished to give the text a meaning apart from its plain reading, was adopted as the Constitution of the United States. It should also be borne in mind that the intentions of those who framed the Constitution, be they good or bad, for slavery or against slavery, are to be respected so far, and so far only, as we find those intentions plainly stated in the Constitution. It would be the wildest of absurdities, and lead to endless confusion and mischiefs, if, instead of looking to the written paper itself, for its meaning, it were attempted to make us search it out, in the secret motives, and dishonest intentions, of some of the men who took part in writing it. It was what they said that was adopted by the people, not what they were ashamed or afraid to say, and really omitted to say. Bear in mind, also, and the fact is an important one, that the framers of the Constitution sat with closed doors, and that this was done purposely, that nothing but the result of their labours should be seen, and that that result should be judged of by the people free from any of the bias shown in the debates. It should also be borne in mind, and the fact is still more important, that the debates in the convention that framed the Constitution, and by means of which a pro-slavery interpretation is now attempted to be forced upon that instrument, were not published till more than a quarter of a century after the presentation and the adoption of the Constitution.

These debates were purposely kept out of view, in order that the people should adopt, not the secret motives or unexpressed intentions of any body, but the simple text of the paper itself. Those debates form no part of the original agreement. I repeat, the paper itself, and only the paper itself, with its own plainly-written purposes, is the Constitution. It must stand or fall, flourish or fade, on its own individual and self-declared character and objects. Again, where would be the advantage of a written Constitution, if, instead of seeking its meaning in its words, we had to seek them in the secret intentions of individuals who may have had something to do with writing the paper? What will the people of America a hundred years hence care about the intentions of the scriveners who wrote the Constitution? These men are already gone from us, and in the course of nature were expected to go from us. They were for a generation, but the Constitution is for ages. Whatever we may owe to them, we certainly owe it to ourselves, and to mankind, and to God, to maintain the truth of our own language, and to allow no villainy, not even the villainy of holding men as slaves—which Wesley says is the sum of all villainies—to shelter itself under a fair-seeming and virtuous language. We owe it to ourselves to compel the devil to wear his own garments, and to make wicked laws speak out their wicked intentions. Common sense, and common justice, and sound rules of interpretation all drive us to the words of the law for the meaning of the law. The practice of the Government is dwelt upon with much fervour and eloquence as conclusive as to the slaveholding character of the Constitution. This is really the strong point, and the only strong point, made in the speech in the City Hall. But good as this argument is, it is not conclusive. A wise man has said that few people have been found better than their laws, but many have been found worse. To this last rule America is no exception. Her laws are one thing, her practice is another thing. We read that the Jews made void the law by their tradition, that Moses permitted men to put away their wives because of the hardness of their hearts, but that this was not so at the beginning. While good laws will always be found where good practice prevails, the reverse does not always hold true. Far from it. The very opposite is often the case. What then? Shall we condemn the righteous law because wicked men twist it to the support of wickedness? Is that the way to deal with good and evil? Shall we blot out all distinction between them, and hand over to slavery all that slavery may claim on the score of long practice? Such is the course commended to us in the City Hall speech. After all, the fact that men go out of the Constitution to prove it pro-slavery, whether that going out is to the practice of the Government, or to the secret intentions of the writers of the paper, the fact that they do go out is very significant. It is a powerful argument on my side. It is an admission that the thing for which they are looking is not to be found where only it ought to be found, and that is in the Constitution itself. If it is not there, it is nothing to the purpose, be it wheresoever else it may be. But I shall have more to say on this point hereafter.

The very eloquent lecturer at the City Hall doubtless felt some embarrassment from the fact that he had literally to *give* the Constitution a pro-slavery interpretation; because upon its face it of itself conveys no such meaning, but a very opposite meaning. He thus sums up what he calls the slaveholding provisions of the Constitution. I quote his own words:—"Article 1, section 9, provides for the continuance of the African slave trade for 20 years, after the adoption of the Constitution. Art. 4, section 9, provides for the recovery from other States of fugitive slaves. Art. 1, section 2, gives the slave States a representation of three-fifths of all the slave population; and Art. 1, section 8, requires the President to use the military, naval, ordnance, and militia resources of the entire country for the suppression of slave insurrection, in the same manner as he would employ them to repel invasion." Now any man reading this statement, or hearing it made with such a show of exactness, would unquestionably suppose that the speaker or writer had given the plain written text of the Constitution itself. I can hardly believe that he intended to make any such impression. It would be a scandalous imputation to say he did. And yet what are we to make of it? How can we regard it? How can he be screened from the charge of having perpetrated a deliberate and point-blank misrepresentation? That individual has seen fit to place himself before the public as my opponent, and yet I would gladly find some excuse for him. I do not wish to think as badly of him as this trick of his would naturally lead me to think. Why did he not read the Constitution? Why did he read that which was not the Constitution? He pretended to be giving chapter and verse, section and clause, paragraph and provision. The words of the Constitution were before him. Why then did he not give you the plain words of the Constitution? Oh, sir, I fear that that gentleman knows too well why he did not. It so happens that no such words as "African slave trade," no such words as "slave representation," no such words as "fugitive slaves," no such words as "slave insurrections," are anywhere used in that instrument. These are the words of that orator, and not the words of the Constitution of the United States. Now you shall see a slight difference between my manner of treating this subject and that which my opponent has seen fit, for reasons satisfactory to himself, to pursue. What he withheld, that I will spread before you: what he suppressed, I will bring to light: and what he passed over in silence, I will proclaim: that you may have the whole case before you, and not be left to depend upon either his, or upon my inferences or testimony. Here then are the several provisions of the Constitution to which reference has been made. I read them word for word just as they stand in the paper, called the United States Constitution, Art. 1, sec. 2. "Representatives and direct taxes shall be apportioned among the several States which may be included in this Union, according to their respective numbers, which shall be determined by adding to the whole number of free persons, including those bound to service for a term of years, and excluding Indians not taxed, three-fifths of all other persons; Art. 1, sec. 9. The migration or importation of such persons as any of the States now existing shall think fit to admit, shall not be prohibited by the Congress prior to the year one thousand eight hundred and eight, but a tax or duty may be imposed on such importation, not exceeding ten dollars for each person; Art. 4, sec. 2. No person held to service or labour in one State, under the laws thereof, escaping into another shall, in consequence of any law or regulation therein, be discharged from such service or labour; but shall be delivered up on claim of the party to whom such service or labour may be due; Art. 1, sec. 8. To provide for calling for the militia to execute the laws of the Union, suppress insurrections, and repel invasions." Here, then, are those provisions of the Constitution, which the most extravagant defenders of slavery can claim to guarantee a right of property in man. These are the provisions which have been pressed into the service of the human fleshmongers of America. Let us look at them just as they stand, one by one. Let us grant, for sake of the argument, that the first of these provisions, referring to the basis of representation and taxation, does refer to slaves. We are not compelled to make that admission, for it might fairly apply to aliens—persons living in the country, but not naturalized. But giving the provisions the very worst construction, what does it amount to? I answer—It is a downright disability laid upon the slaveholding States; one which deprives those States of two-fifths of their natural basis of representation. A black man in a free State is worth just two-fifths more than a black man in a slave State, as a basis of political power under the Constitution. Therefore, instead of encouraging slavery, the Constitution encourages freedom by giving an increase of "two-fifths" of political power to free over slave States. So much for the three-fifths clause; taking it at its worst, it still leans to freedom, not to slavery; for, be it remembered that the Constitution nowhere forbids a coloured man to vote. I come to the next, that which it is said guaranteed the continuance of the African slave trade for twenty years. I will also take that for just what my opponent alleges it to have been, although the Constitution does not warrant any such conclusion. But, to be liberal, let us suppose it did, and what follows? why, this—that this part of the Constitution, so far as the slave trade is concerned, became a dead letter more than 50 years ago, and now binds no man's conscience for the continuance of any slave trade whatever. Mr. Thompson is just

52 years too late in dissolving the Union on account of this clause. He might as well dissolve the British Government, because Queen Elizabeth granted to Sir John Hawkins to import Africans into the West Indies 300 years ago! But there is still more to be said about this abolition of the slave trade. Men, at that time, both in England and in America, looked upon the slave trade as the life of slavery. The abolition of the slave trade was supposed to be the certain death of slavery. Cut off the stream, and the pond will dry up, was the common notion at that time.

Wilberforce and Clarkson, clear-sighted as they were, took this view; and the American statesmen, in providing for the abolition of the slave trade, thought they were providing for the abolition of slavery. This view is quite consistent with the history of the times. All regarded slavery as an expiring and doomed system, destined to speedily disappear from the country. But, again, it should be remembered that this very provision, if made to refer to the African slave trade at all, makes the Constitution anti-slavery rather than for slavery, for it says to the slave States, the price you will have to pay for coming into the American Union is, that the slave trade, which you would carry on indefinitely out of the Union, shall be put an end to in twenty years if you come into the Union. Secondly, if it does apply, it expired by its own limitation more than fifty years ago. Thirdly, it is anti-slavery, because it looked to the abolition of slavery rather than to its perpetuity. Fourthly, it showed that the intentions of the framers of the Constitution were good, not bad. I think this is quite enough for this point. I go to the "slave insurrection" clause, though, in truth, there is no such clause. The one which is called so has nothing whatever to do with slaves or slaveholders any more than your laws for the suppression of popular outbreaks has to do with making slaves of you and your children. It is only a law for suppression of riots or insurrections. But I will be generous here, as well as elsewhere, and grant that it applies to slave insurrections. Let us suppose that an anti-slavery man is President of the United States (and the day that shall see this the case is not distant) and this very power of suppressing slave insurrection would put an end to slavery. The right to put down an insurrection carries with it the right to determine the means by which it shall be put down. If it should turn out that slavery is a source of insurrection, that there is no security from insurrection while slavery lasts, why, the Constitution would be best obeyed by putting an end to slavery, and an anti-slavery Congress would do that very thing. Thus, you see, the so-called slave-holding provisions of the American Constitution, which a little while ago looked so formidable, are, after all, no defence or guarantee for slavery whatever. But there is one other provision. This is called the "Fugitive Slave Provision." It is called so by those who wish to make it subserve the interest of slavery in America, and the same by those who wish to uphold the views of a party in this country. It is put thus in the speech at the City Hall:—"Let us go back to 1787, and enter Liberty Hall, Philadelphia, where sat in convention the illustrious men who framed the Constitution—with George Washington in the chair. On the 27th of September, Mr. Butler and Mr. Pinckney, two delegates from the State of South Carolina, moved that the Constitution should require that fugitive slaves and servants should be delivered up like criminals, and after a discussion on the subject, the clause, as it stands in the Constitution, was adopted. After this, in the conventions held in the several States to ratify the Constitution, the same meaning was attached to the words. For example, Mr. Madison (afterwards President), when recommending the Constitution to his constituents, told them that the clause would secure them their property in slaves." I must ask you to look well to this statement. Upon its face, it would seem a full and fair statement of the history of the transaction it professes to describe and yet I declare unto you, knowing as I do the facts in the case, my utter amazement at the downright untruth conveyed under the fair seeming words now quoted. The man who could make such a statement may have all the craftiness of a lawyer, but who can accord to him the candour of an honest debater? What could more completely destroy all confidence in his statements? Mark you, the orator had not allowed his audience to hear read the provision of the Constitution to which he referred. He merely characterized it as one to "deliver up fugitive slaves and servants like criminals," and tells you that that provision was adopted as it stands in the Constitution. He tells you that this was done "after discussion." But he took good care not to tell you what was the nature of that discussion. He would have spoiled the whole effect of his statement had he told you the whole truth. Now, what are the facts connected with this provision of the Constitution? You shall have them. It seems to take two men to tell the truth. It is quite true that Mr. Butler and Mr. Pinckney introduced a provision expressly with a view to the recapture of fugitive slaves: it is quite true also that there was some discussion on the subject—and just here the truth shall come out. These illustrious kidnappers were told promptly in that discussion that no such idea as property in man should be admitted into the Constitution. The speaker in question might have told you, and he would have told you but the simple truth, if he had told you that the proposition of Mr. Butler and Mr. Pinckney—which he leads you to infer was adopted by the convention that framed the Constitution—was, in fact, promptly and indignantly rejected by that convention. He might have told you, had it suited his purpose to do so, that the words employed in the first draft of the fugitive clause were such as applied to the condition of slaves, and expressly declared that persons held to "servitude" should be given up; but that the word "servitude" was struck from the provision, for the very reason that it applied to slaves. He might have told you that that same Mr. Madison declared that that word was struck out because the convention would not consent that the idea of property in men should be admitted into the Constitution. The fact that Mr. Madison can be cited on both sides of this question is another evidence of the folly and absurdity of making the secret intentions of the framers the criterion by which the Constitution is to be construed. But it may be asked—if this clause does not apply to slaves, to whom does it apply?

I answer, that when adopted, it applies to a very large class of persons—namely, redemptioners—persons who had come to America from Holland, from Ireland, and other quarters of the globe—like the Coolies to the West Indies—and had, for a consideration duly paid, become bound to "serve and labour" for the parties to whom their service and labour was due. It applies to indentured apprentices and others who had become bound for a consideration, under contract duly made, to serve and labour, To such persons this provision applies, and only to such persons. The plain reading of this provision shows that it applies, and that it can only properly and legally apply, to persons "bound to service." Its object plainly is, to secure the fulfilment of contracts for "service and labour." It applies to indentured apprentices, and any other persons from whom service and labour may be due. The legal condition of the slave puts him beyond the operation of this provision. He is not described in it. He is a simple article of property. He does not owe and cannot owe service. He cannot even make a contract. It is impossible for him to do so. He can no more make such a contract than a horse or an ox can make one. This provision, then, only respects persons who owe service, and they only can owe service who can receive an equivalent and make a bargain. The slave cannot do that, and is therefore exempted from the operation of this fugitive provision. In all matters where laws are taught to be made the means of oppression, cruelty, and wickedness, I am for strict construction. I will concede nothing. It must be shown that it is so nominated in the bond. The pound of flesh, but not one drop of blood. The very nature of law is opposed to all such wickedness, and makes it difficult to accomplish such objects under the forms of law. Law is not merely an arbitrary enactment with regard to justice, reason, or humanity. Blackstone defines it to be a rule prescribed by the supreme power of the State commanding what is right and forbidding what is wrong. The speaker at the City Hall laid down some rules of legal interpretation. These rules send us to the history of the law for its meaning. I have no objection to such a course in ordinary cases of doubt. But where human liberty and justice are at stake, the case falls under an entirely different class of rules. There must be something more than history—something more than tradition. The Supreme Court of the United States lays down this rule, and it meets the case exactly—"Where rights are infringed—where the fundamental principles of the law are overthrown—where the general system of the law is departed from, the legislative intention must be expressed with irresistible clearness." The same court says that the language of the law must be construed strictly in favour of justice and liberty. Again, there is another rule of law. It is—Where a law is susceptible of two meanings, the one making it accomplish an innocent purpose, and the other making it accomplish a wicked purpose, we must in all cases adopt that which makes it accomplish an innocent purpose. Again, the details of a law are to be interpreted in the light of the declared objects sought by the law. I set these rules down against those employed at the City Hall. To me they seem just and rational. I only ask you to look at the American Constitution in the light of them, and you will see with me that no man is guaranteed a right of property in man, under the provisions of that instrument. If there are two ideas more distinct in their character and essence than another, those ideas are "persons" and "property," "men" and "things." Now, when it is proposed to transform persons into "property" and men into beasts of burden, I demand that the law that contemplates such a purpose shall be expressed with irresistible clearness. The thing must not be left to inference, but must be done in plain English. I know how this view of the subject is treated by the class represented at the City Hall. They are in the habit of treating the Negro as an exception to general rules. When their own liberty is in question they will avail themselves of all rules of law which protect and defend their freedom; but when the black man's rights are in question they concede everything, admit everything for slavery, and put liberty to the proof. They reverse the common law usage, and presume the Negro a slave unless he can prove himself free. I, on the other hand, presume him free unless he is proved to be otherwise. Let us look at the objects for which the Constitution was framed and adopted, and see if slavery is one of them. Here are its own objects as set forth by itself:—"We, the people of these United States, in order to form a more perfect union, establish justice, ensure domestic tranquillity, provide for the common defence, promote the general welfare, and secure the blessings of liberty to ourselves and our posterity, do ordain and establish this Constitution for the United States of America." The objects here set forth are six in number: union, defence, welfare, tranquillity, justice, and liberty. These are all good objects, and slavery, so far from being among them, is a foe of them all. But it has been said that Negroes are not included within the benefits sought under this declaration. This is said by the slaveholders in America—it is said by the City Hall orator—but it is not said by the Constitution itself. Its language is "we the people;" not we the white people, not even we the citizens, not we the privileged class, not we the high, not we the low, but we the people; not we the horses, sheep, and swine, and wheel-barrows, but we the people, we the human inhabitants; and, if Negroes are people, they are included in the benefits for which the Constitution of America was ordained and established. But how dare any man who pretends to be a friend to the Negro thus gratuitously concede away what the Negro has a right to claim under the Constitution? Why should such friends invent new arguments to increase the hopelessness of his bondage? This, I undertake to say, as the conclusion of the whole matter, that the constitutionality of slavery can be made out only by disregarding the plain and common-sense reading of the Constitution itself; by discrediting and casting away as worthless the most beneficent rules of legal interpretation; by ruling the Negro outside of these beneficent rules; by claiming everything for slavery; by denying everything for freedom; by assuming that the Constitution does not mean what it says, and that it says what it does not mean; by disregarding the written Constitution, and interpreting it in the light of a secret understanding. It is in this mean, contemptible, and underhand method that the American Constitution is pressed into the service of slavery. They go everywhere else for proof that the Constitution is pro-slavery but to the Constitution itself. The Constitution declares that no person shall be deprived of life, liberty, or property without due process of law; it secures to every man the right of trial by jury, the privilege of the writ of habeas corpus—that great writ that put an end to slavery and slave-hunting in England—it secures to every State a republican form of government. Any one of these provisions, in the hands of abolition statesmen, and backed up by a right moral sentiment, would put an end to slavery in America. The Constitution forbids the passing of a bill of attainder: that is, a law entailing upon the child the disabilities and hardships imposed upon the parent. Every slave law in America might be repealed on this very ground. The slave is made a slave because his mother is a slave. But to all this it is said that the practice of the American people is against my view. I admit it. They have given the Constitution a slaveholding interpretation. I admit it. They have committed innumerable wrongs against the Negro in the name of the Constitution. Yes, I admit it all; and I go with him who goes farthest in denouncing these wrongs. But it does not follow that the Constitution is in favour of these wrongs because the slaveholders have given it that interpretation. To be consistent in his logic, the City Hall speaker must follow the example of some of his brothers in America—he must not only fling away the Constitution, but the Bible. The Bible must follow the Constitution, for that, too, has been interpreted for slavery by American divines. Nay, more, he must not stop with the Constitution of America, but make war upon the British Constitution, for, if I mistake not, that gentleman is opposed to the union of Church and State. In America he called himself a Republican. Yet he does not go for breaking down the British Constitution, although you have a Queen on the throne, and bishops in the House of Lords.

My argument against the dissolution of the American Union is this: It would place the slave system more exclusively under the control of the slaveholding States, and withdraw it from the power in the Northern States which is opposed to slavery. Slavery is essentially barbarous in its character. It, above all things else, dreads the presence of an advanced civilisation. It flourishes best where it meets no reproving frowns, and hears no condemning voices. While in the Union it will meet with both. Its hope of life, in the last resort, is to get out of the Union. I am, therefore, for drawing the bond of the Union more closely, and bringing the Slave States more completely under the power of the Free States. What they most dread, that I most desire. I have much confidence in the instincts of the slaveholders. They see that the Constitution will afford slavery no protection when it shall cease to be administered by slaveholders. They see, moreover, that if there is once a will in the people of America to abolish slavery, there is no word, no syllable in the Constitution to forbid that result. They see that the Constitution has not saved slavery in Rhode Island, in Connecticut, in New York, or Pennsylvania; that the Free States have increased from one up to eighteen in number, while the Slave States have only added three to their original number. There were twelve Slave States at the beginning of the Government: there are fifteen now. There was one Free State at the beginning of the Government: there are eighteen now. The dissolution of the Union would not give the North a single advantage over slavery, but would take from it many. Within the Union we have a firm basis of opposition to slavery. It is opposed to all the great objects of the Constitution. The dissolution of the Union is not only an unwise but a cowardly measure—15 millions running away from three hundred and fifty thousand slaveholders. Mr. Garrison and his friends tell us that while in the Union we are responsible for slavery. He and they sing out "No Union with slaveholders," and refuse to vote. I admit our responsibility for slavery while in the Union, but I deny that going out of the Union would free us from that responsibility. There now clearly is no freedom from responsibility for slavery to any American citizen short of the abolition of slavery. The American people have gone quite too far in this slaveholding business now to sum up their whole business of slavery by singing out the cant phrase, "No union with slaveholders." To desert the family hearth may place the recreant husband out of the presence of his starving children, but this does not free him from responsibility. If a man were on board of a pirate ship, and in company with others had robbed and plundered, his whole duty would not be performed simply by taking the longboat and singing out "No union with pirates." His duty would be to restore the stolen property. The American people in the Northern States have helped to enslave the black people. Their duty will not have been done till they give them back their plundered rights. Reference was made at the City Hall to my having once held other opinions, and very different opinions to those I have now expressed. An old speech of mine delivered fourteen years ago was read to show—I know not what. Perhaps it was to show that I am not infallible. If so, I have to say in defence, that I never pretended to be. Although I cannot accuse myself of being remarkably unstable, I do not pretend that I have never altered my opinion both in respect to men and things. Indeed, I have been very much modified both in feeling and opinion within the last fourteen years. When I escaped from slavery, and was introduced to the Garrisonians, I adopted very many of their opinions, and defended them just as long as I deemed them true. I was young, had read but little, and naturally took some things on trust. Subsequent experience and reading have led me to examine for myself. This has brought me to other conclusions. When I was a child, I thought and spoke as a child. But the question is not as to what were my opinions fourteen years ago, but what they are now. If I am right now, it really does not matter what I was fourteen years ago. My position now is one of reform, not of revolution. I would act for the abolition of slavery through the Government—not over its ruins. If slave-holders have ruled the American Government for the last fifty years, let the anti-slavery men rule the nation for the next fifty years. If the South has made the Constitution bend to the purposes of slavery, let the North now make that instrument bend to the cause of freedom and justice. If 350,000 slaveholders have, by devoting their energies to that single end, been able to make slavery the vital and animating spirit of the American Confederacy for the last 72 years, now let the freemen of the North, who have the power in their own hands, and who can make the American Government just what they think fit, resolve to blot out for ever the foul and haggard crime, which is the blight and mildew, the curse and the disgrace of the whole United States.

Pamphlet, Howard University Library.

TO MY BRITISH ANTI-SLAVERY FRIENDS

Dear Friends:—You will have learned ere this the cause of my sudden departure from Great Britain to the United States, and will be glad to know that up to this date no harm has befallen me, or is likely to befall me, on account of the troubles in this country during the Autumn of last year. I am in Rochester, N. Y., at my office daily, walking the streets openly, known to be in the country by our slaveholding Government officials; yet, either because they are too busy in election-eering for a new President, or because they have no definite proof of my complicity in the Harper's Ferry insurrection, or because they dread the difficulty of taking me from Rochester, they allow me for the present to go unmolested, and do not even call me to Washington to give evidence before the Committee of the American Senate to trace out the ramifications of the John Brown plot.[37]—The Committee has thus far proved an entire failure. It has elicited nothing on the subject beyond the statements and disclosures of noble old John Brown himself. Nothing has really been added to the honest declaration of motives, plans and purposes, made by the brave old man to the alarmed and vindictive slaveholders, after he was overpowered and completely in their cruel hands. He spoke to them from the open gate of death in which he stood, and his words were solemn, searching and truthful. Of all the witnesses thus far summoned, none have given any other coloring to the Harper's Ferry affair than was given by the man who originated and attempted to carry out that uprising against slavery. One reason, perhaps, why I have not been compelled to appear before the Committee, is the doubt which has arisen as to the constitutional power of a purely legislative body, like the American Senate, to exercise a function so entirely judicial in its character as that of enforcing the attendance of witnesses, and compelling them to testify. In this respect our Senate differs from your House of Lords, of which it is in some respects a copy. It is not judicial. Nevertheless, I am yet liable to be called upon at any moment to go before this body, for while there is evidently no written constitutional grant of power of this sort to the Senate, the long exercise of the power unquestioned, makes it in some degree authoritative and conclusive. While I have no desire to go to Washington to testify before the Committee, the danger of violence toward me there would be light compared with what it would have been when the country was deeply and fiercely excited by the trials of the insurgents, and the reign of terror everywhere prevailing at the South. Yet, if summoned, I should hesitate before placing myself on slaveholding soil. Not even a white man with anti-slavery opinions is safe in the slave States. I am an offender both by color and conduct. I have done too much to give slaveholding a bad name, to be readily forgiven, or allowed to escape unharmed. I shall therefore see to it that I am not drawn into a slave State if I can help it, and my present conviction is that I can help it.

Very many of you, my kind, good friends, could not assent to the wisdom of my returning to this country, and regretted my determination to do so; but all of you sympathized with me in the sentiment which led me so suddenly to break off my anti-slavery work among you, and in the face of perils by sea and land, to fly to my sorrow-stricken family. My presence nowhere else, after the long months of anxiety, sickness, sorrow and death which have intervened, could be so sacredly beneficial as *at home*. My wife, my children, and the condition of my business affairs, all needed me; and although I ran some risk and suffered much during the voyage from a severe fall, caused by a sudden and unexpected motion of the ship, I do not regret having returned. For all your kindness, hospitality, sympathy, aid and co-operation while a stranger and sojourner among you, my heart overflows with the warmest gratitude. Especially do I remember the many touching marks of sympathy with me in the loss of my dearly beloved daughter, whose death was all the more painful because resulting, no doubt, from overanxiety for the safety of her father, and deep sorrow for the death of dear old John Brown, upon whose knee she had often sat only a few months before.

I am still intending to resume my tour in the Fall. All Ireland and the south of England remain to be visited, and I hope to enter upon my duties as early as the month of October.

On looking into the accounts of my weekly anti-slavery paper, and finding that its receipts had fallen much below its current expenses, I at first decided to discontinue its publication until after my return from Europe, for I then thought of leaving home for England about the first of this month. I have now, however, determined to continue its publication, and employ the interval between the present month and the time of my leaving the U. S., in enlarging its circulation, collecting outstanding subscriptions, and otherwise securing its permanence and increasing its usefulness.—The paper is as much needed as ever. Even in the event of the election of a Republican President, which I still hopefully anticipate, the real work of abolitionizing the public mind will still remain, and every pen, press and voice now employed will then, as now, be needed to carry forward that great work. The Republican party is, as I have often said in conversation with you, only negatively anti-slavery. It is opposed to the *political power* of slavery, rather than to slavery itself, and would arrest the spread of the slave system, humble the slave power, and defeat all plans for giving slavery any further guarantee of permanence. This is very desirable, but it leaves the great work of abolishing slavery, and giving freedom to the four millions now groaning in the chains and under the lash of slavery, still to be accomplished. The triumph of the Republican party will only open the way for this great work. While life, and health, and strength endure, I hope under God to be found faithfully and earnestly devoting whatever of power and skill I possess to this object—an object which I am glad to know is deeply dear to your hearts, and to the promotion of which you gladly extend your aid and sympathy.

I have nothing to add on the present aspect of anti-slavery affairs here to what will be found in the other columns of the *Monthly*, except to say, that I have never known the slaves to be escaping from slavery more rapidly than during the several weeks I have been at home. Ten have found food, shelter, counsel and comfort under my roof since I came home, and have been duly forwarded where they are beyond the reach of the slave-hunter. God speed the year of Jubilee the wide world o'er!

Yours, truly,   F.D.

Rochester, May 26, 1860.

Douglass' Monthly, June, 1860

THE CHICAGO NOMINATIONS

The nomination of Mr. Lincoln has taken the people of this part of the Country by surprise. The popular feeling in favor of Mr. Seward was nowhere stronger, or more earnest, than in this part of the State. The people felt that he had a stronger claim upon his party than any other man, having done more to give that party shape, and to systematise the elements composing it, and to furnish it with ideas, than any other man in the nation.

The Republican party is justly proud of Mr. Seward, proud of his history, proud of his talents, and proud of his attainments as a statesman, and it is not without strong feeling that it sees him shoved aside to make room for a man whose abilities are untried, and whose political history is too meagre to form a basis on which to judge of his future.

Still there does not appear to be the slightest disposition, on the part of Mr. Seward's friends to be factional under their disappointment, but they acquiesce in the decision of the Convention, with a grace which speaks much in praise of the party discipline in the Republican ranks.

There are a few of the more radical men, who regard Mr. Seward's defeat as a sort of political "judgment" upon him for his late speech in the Senate.[38] To them, that speech was so full of concession to the slave power, so clear a bid for the nomination at Chicago, and so nearly sunk the progressive statesman in the political trimmer, that they are well content with his defeat.

The road to the Presidency does not lead through the swamps of compromise and concession any longer, and Mr. Seward ought to have made that discovery, before John Brown frightened him into making his last great speech. In that speech he stooped quite too low for his future fame, and lost the prize that tempted the stoop after all. He had far better have lost it while standing erect.

Mr. Lincoln is a man of unblemished private character; a lawyer, standing near the front rank at the bar of his own State, has a cool, well balanced head; great firmness of will; is perseveringly industrious; and one of the most frank, honest men in political life. He cannot lay claim to any literary culture beyond the circle of his practical duties, or to any of the graces found at courts, or in diplomatic circles, but must rely upon his "good hard sense" and honesty of purpose, as capital for the campaign, and the qualities to give character to his administration. His friends cannot as yet claim for him a place in the front rank of statesmanship, whatever may be their faith in his latent capacities. His political life is thus far to his credit, but it is a political life of fair promise rather than one of rich fruitage.

It was, perhaps, this fact that obtained for him the nomination. Our political history has often illustrated the truth that a man may be too great a statesman to become President. The failure of Webster, Clay and Silas Wright in the Presidential race, is in point here, and the success of Harrison, Polk, Taylor and Pierce, tends to prove the same proposition.

If, therefore, Mr. Lincoln possesses great capacities, and is yet to be proved a great statesman, it is lucky for him that a political exigency moved his party to take him on trust and before his greatness was ripe, or he would have lost the chance. But when once elected it will be no longer dangerous for him to develop great qualities, and we hope that in taking him on a "profession of his faith," rather than on the recommendations of his political life, his party will witness his continual "growth in grace," and his administration will redound to the glory of his country, and his own fame.

As to his principles, there is no reason why the friends of Mr. Seward should not heartily support him. He is a radical Republican, and is fully committed to the doctrine of the "irrepressible conflict." [39] In his debates with Douglas, he came fully up to the highest mark of Republicanism, and he is a man of will and nerve, and will not back down from his own assertions. He is not a compromise candidate by any means. Mr. Bates was to have played that part, with Horace Greeley for prompter. But the Chicago Convention did not fall into the melting mood. Greeley "piped unto them but they would not dance;" he mourned unto them, but they did not "lament," and his "betweenity" candidate fell flat between the two stools of Somewhere and Nowhere. Mr. Greeley has the greatest passion for making political nominations from the ranks of his enemies of any man in America. His candidates are like the frogs bred along the Nile; the head begins to croak and show signs of life while the body is yet plain mud. So Mr. Greeley is forever digging up some man for a candidate, whose head just begins to appear, while his whole body is yet enveloped in pro-slavery mud, and we are glad he was defeated.

The Presidential contest, this fall, is likely to be rather sharply defined. If Mr. Douglas is put on the course, the old personal rivalry between him and Mr. Lincoln will render the campaign especially spicy.

Illinois will form a sort of pivot, around which the waves of the political sea will sweep and dash with great force.

The nomination of Bell and Everett[40] will tend to divert strength from the Democracy, and give advantage to Lincoln, but will have no great influence on the general result. Slavery propagandism, whether led by the vigorous and impulsive "little giant," or by the more staid and conservative Bell, will be the great enemy which the Republican party must meet.

For ourselves, we are sorry that the hosts of freedom could not have been led forth upon a higher platform, and have had inscribed upon their banners, "Death to Slavery," instead of "No more Slave States." But the people will not have it so, and we are compelled to work and wait for a brighter day, when the masses shall be educated up to a higher standard of human rights and political morality.

But as between the hosts of Slavery propagandism and the Republican party—incomplete as is its platform of principles—our preferences cannot hesitate.

While we should be glad to co-operate with a party fully committed to the doctrine of "All rights to all men," in the absence of all hope of rearing up the standard of such a party for the coming campaign, we can but desire the success of the Republican candidates.

It will be a great work accomplished when this Government is divorced from the active support of the inhuman slave system. To pluck executive patronage out of the hands of the pliant tools of the whip and the chain; to turn the tide of the National Administration against the man-stealers of this country and in favor of even a partial application of the principles of justice, is a glorious achievement, and we hope for its success.

To save a prospective empire, yet to be planted in the Great West, from the desecrating foot prints of inhuman oppression, and open these mountain slopes and river bottoms, to a hardy, industrious, and enlightened population of freemen, who are sure to follow the "Star of Empire" toward the Pacific, marching to the inspiring songs of "Free labor and free men," is a consummation devoutly to be wished—a vision of prospective good, inspiring to the patriot.

It is a sad fact that the people of this country are, as yet, on a plane of morality and philanthropy far below what the exigencies of the cause of human progress demands. It is to be regretted that they will not come up to the glorious work of striking the shackles from four million slaves at a single blow—but even though they persist in approaching the blood-cemented Bastille of oppression, by the slow processes of a cautious siege, rather than by the more brave and inspiring march of a storming party, we are compelled to submit for the present, and take with gratitude the little good thus proffered.

Douglass' Monthly, June, 1860

TO HON. CHARLES SUMNER

Rochester, N. Y., June 9th, 1860
My Dear Sir:

I wish I could tell you how deeply grateful I am to you, and to God, for the speech you have now been able to make in the United States Senate.[41] You spoke to the Senate and the nation, but you have another and a mightier audience. The civilized world will hear you, and rejoice in the tremendous exposure of the meanness, brutality, blood guiltiness, hell black iniquity and barbarism of American Slavery. As one who has felt the horrors of this stupendous violation of all human rights, I venture thus far to trespass upon your time and attention. My heart is full, sir, and I could pour out my feelings at length, but I know how precious is your time. I shall print every word of your speech.

Yours with most grateful regards,
Frederick Douglass

Charles Sumner Papers, Harvard University

TO JAMES REDPATH, ESQ.

Rochester, June 29, 1860

My Dear Sir:

Your kind note, inviting me to meet with yourself and other friends on the 4th of July, at North Elba, came into my hands only yesterday. Had it reached me only a day or two earlier, I certainly should have complied with it. Very gladly would I assemble with you and the others on that revolutionary day, to do honor to the memory of one whom I regard as the man of the nineteenth century. Little, indeed, can you and I do to add lustre to his deathless fame. The principles of John Brown, attested by a life of spotless integrity and sealed by his blood, are self-vindicated. His name is covered with a glory so bright and enduring, as to require nothing at our hands to increase or perpetuate it. Only for our own sake, and that of enslaved and imbruted humanity must we assemble. To have been acquainted with John Brown, shared his counsels, enjoyed his confidence, and sympathized with the great objects of his life and death, I esteem as among the highest privileges of my life. We do but honor to ourselves in doing honor to him, for it implies the possession of qualities akin to his.

I have little hope of the freedom of the slave by peaceful means. A long course of peaceful slaveholding has placed the slaveholders beyond the reach of moral and humane considerations. They have neither ears nor hearts for the appeals of justice and humanity. While the slave will tamely submit his neck to the yoke, his back to the lash, and his ankle to the fetter and chain, the Bible will be quoted, and learning invoked to justify slavery. The only penetrable point of a tyrant is the *fear of death*. The outcry that they make, as to the danger of having their *throats cut* is because they deserve to have them *cut*. The efforts of John Brown and his brave associates, though apparently unavailing, have done more to upset the logic and shake the security of slavery, than all other efforts in that direction for twenty years.

The sleeping dust, over which yourself and friends proposed to meet on the 4th, cannot be revived; but the noble principles and disinterested devotion which led John Brown to step serenely to the gallows and lay down his life will never die. They are all the more potent for his death.

Not anxiously are the eyes and hearts of the American slaves and their friends turned to the lofty peaks of the Alleghanies. The innumerable glens, caves, ravines and rocks of those mountains, will yet be the hiding-places of hunted liberty. The eight-and-forty hours of John Brown's school in Virginia taught the slaves more than they could have otherwise learned in a half-century. Even the mistake of remaining in the arsenal after the first blow was struck, may prove the key to future successes. The tender regard which the dear old man evinced for the life of the tyrants—and which should have secured him his life—will not be imitated by future insurgents. Slaveholders are as insensible to magnanimity as to justice, and the measure they meter must be meted to them again. My heart is with you.

Very truly,

Fred'k Douglass

The Liberator, July 27, 1860

TO WILLIAM STILL

Rochester, July 2d, 1860

. . . You hold up before me the glorious promises contained in the sacred Scriptures. These are needed by none more than by those who have presumed to put themselves to the work of accomplishing the abolition of Slavery in this country. There is scarcely one single interest, social, moral, religious, or physical, which is not in some way connected with this stupendous evil. On the side of the oppressor there is power, now as in the earlier days of the world. I find much comfort in the thought that I am but a passenger on board of this ship of life. I have not the management committed to me. I am to obey orders, and leave the rest to the great Captain whose wisdom is able to direct. I have only to go on in His fear and in His spirit, uttering with pen and tongue the whole truth against Slavery, leaving to Him the honor and the glory of destroying this mighty work of the devil. I long for the end of my people's bondage, and would give all I possess to witness the great jubilee; but God can wait, and surely I may. If He, whose pure eyes cannot look upon sin with allowance, can permit the day of freedom to be deferred, I certainly can work and wait. The times are just now a little brighter; but I will walk by faith, not by right, for all grounds of hope founded on external appearance, have thus far signally failed and broken down under me. Twenty years ago, Slavery did really *seem* to be rapidly hastening to its fall, but ten years ago, the Fugitive Slave Bill, and the efforts to enforce it, changed the whole appearance of the struggle. Anti-slavery in an abolition sense has been ever since battling against heavy odds, both in Church and State. Nevertheless, God reigns, and we need not despair, and I for one do not. I know, at any rate, no better work for me during the brief period I am to stay on the earth, than is found in pleading the cause of the down-trodden and the dumb.

Since I reached home, I have had the satisfaction of passing nearly a score [of fugitive slaves] on to Canada, only two women among them all. The constant meeting with these whip-scarred brothers will not allow me to become forgetful of the four millions still in bonds.

William Still, *The Underground Railroad,* Philadelphia, 1872, p. 598

TO GERRIT SMITH

Rochester, July 2d, 1860

My dear Friend:

I am glad to receive your note of this morning and sincerely thank you for your draft for twenty dollars, being the second twenty you have sent me since I got home. Did I see my way to keep the weekly going, I would gladly retain the draft. I am as deeply grateful to you as if I retained it. During the last six months my weekly has been running behind its income at the rate of from $25 to $30 per week. On finding its low condition when I got home, I at once decided to *stop* on the first of June, and said as much in the paper. But during the first week in June there was, owing to the appeal made to the readers and friends of the paper, such an improvement in the receipts that I ventured to assure its readers that the paper would be continued. Since then, however, the receipts have fallen nearly to nothing while the expenses stand at forty-five and fifty dollars per week. Under these circumstances I see nothing for me but to let the paper go down.

You may well believe that after nearly thirteen years of effort to put the paper on a permanent basis and make it an established anti-slavery instrumentality, that I am now very sorry to give up the struggle. There is no escape and I submit. I shall hereafter only publish my monthly paper.

I shall look with interest for your letter in the *"Principia."* [42] I cannot support Lincoln, but whether there is life enough in the Abolitionists to name a candidate, I cannot say. I shall look to your letter for light on the pathway of duty.

I am still intending to return to England in September, and whether I go or not you may expect a call from me at Peterboro. Did our friend George L. Stearns from Boston call upon you ten days ago? I took the liberty to tell him I knew you would be glad to see him. I had a call on Friday from Rev. Samuel Green. His cheerful spirit after the long years of missionary toil, speaks well for a life of labor and usefulness. Thirty-two years among the heathen has left him yet hale and strong. I was surprised to find that he had not yet seen you. I saw much in Mr. Green to remind me of his great brother at Whitesboro. Please remember me kindly to dear Mrs. Smith, and believe me always very sincerely your grateful friend.

Frederick Douglass

Gerrit Smith Papers, Syracuse University

THE REPUBLICAN PARTY

It cannot be denied that the anti-slavery sentiment in the Northern States is the vital element of the Republican party. To make that party indifferent to that sentiment, and to place it in opposition to it—assuming for the party a character opposed to anti-slavery agitation, opposed to Negro equality, to Negro advancement, to Negro suffrage, to Negro citizenship, and to Negro emancipation—is not only treason against the slave and the black man, but a fatal attack upon the very life of the party itself. Nothing is plainer than that the Republican party has its source in the old Liberty Party, which, beginning twenty years ago with but a handful of members, (among the most able and distinguished of whom was Myron Holly, a citizen of this town,) it increased in eight years from ten thousand to sixty thousand, as simply and strictly an anti-slavery or Abolition party. In 1848 it fused with the Free Soil party, and was all the life that party had, aside from the hope of place, power and spoils. Out of this Free Soil party has come the Republican party, and it is thus in its origin, history and pretensions, the anti-slavery party of the country, and must live or die as the abolition sentiment of the country flourishes or fades. For the members or leaders of this party to attempt now to create a new character for it, to make it a mere negation in the politics of the country, is to deprive it of more than half its dignity, and render it as despicable as the Bell and Everett party, the main boast of which is, that it has no political principles whatever, and that it needs none. We repeat, anti-slavery positive opposition to slavery is the main and all-sustaining element of the Republican party.

It is true that opposition to slavery is supported by different reasons: One man is opposed to slavery because it is an expensive and a non-remunerative system of labor, impoverishing the States and the communities where it is established. Another opposes it because it creates in the slave States an aristocratic class, who despise labor, who, living upon compulsory toil themselves, naturally look with contempt upon all others who, unlike themselves, work as all men must work for an honest living. A third reason is found for opposing slavery in the fact that those whose interests are mainly involved in the slave system, have endeavored, and with great success, to make the sentiments, ideas, principles and practices of slavery dominant and controlling over the whole country. They have sought to make themselves the masters of the United States, as they have succeeded in making themselves the masters of the slaves in the slave States, to give to the free States the manners and morals of the slave States, and to make themselves permanently the governing class of the country. Another motive for opposing or seeming to oppose slavery, is found in the fact that white men have an aversion to blacks, and that introducing the blacks into a new territory, practically amounts to the exclusion of the whites from that territory. Motives of this character, with others even less honorable to human nature, no doubt exert an influence and form an element in the great tide of opposition to slavery, and all contribute to the general probabilities of the success of the Republican party in electing its Presidential candidates this Fall. But the great and vital opposition to slavery, that which gives life and power to all other forms of opposition to the slave system, however ignored or denounced by Republicans and others, arises out of the fact that the slave is a man, clothed by the eternal God with the full dignity of manhood—a being of moral and intellectual powers, rights, duties, and responsibilities, and that to enslave him, to make of him, as slavery must, a beast of burden, strip him of his rights, shut against him the golden gates of knowledge, load him with chains, separate him from his wife, sell his children, cover his back with stripes, and doom him to unending slavery, is a most atrocious and revolting crime against nature and nature's God, to be immediately repented of and abolished forever. Without this mighty conviction—this just estimate of the nature and character of slavery itself, as a system of warfare upon all rights, and as the stupendous auxiliary of all wrong and violence—all other motives for opposing slavery and its extension would naturally decay and die out. That abolition element, that which sees a brother in the blackest slave, and feels with him the sting of the slave-driver's lash, as bound with him, is the main support of the Republican party. All else is weak, and standing alone is worthless.

Among the statesmen of the Republican party, none seem to understand this better than Senator Sumner. He has dared to recognize the Negro as a man, and as a man to hold him up before the Senate and the nation as a wronged and imbruted human being—one in whose degradation the whole of humanity is insulted and degraded. He has denounced the cherished institution of human fleshmongers as a system of brutal barbarism, and poured down upon it a holy torrent of moral indignation, sufficient to loose the tongue and fire the hearts of all who shall go forth this Fall to do battle for the Republican cause.—Let all such read, study and appropriate that speech—follow its lead before the people.—Banish the miserable twadde about standing for the rights of *white men,* about *white equality,* which nobody calls in question or purposes to endanger, and take your stand upon the eternal principle of justice and human nature. Teach the people for once in a political campaign the sacredness of human rights, the brotherhood of man, and expose to all the living light of day the foul and terrible abomination of Southern slavery, and your Republican party will deserve success, which is better even than success itself. The present campaign must either strengthen or weaken the abolition element of the country, and it is for Republicans to say which it shall be.

Of one thing we are unfeignedly glad, and that is, that no professions of loyalty to the South, no pledges to carry out that foul and merciless abomination of the Fugitive Slave Law, no expression of contempt for the rights of Negroes, no bowing or cringing to the popular prejudice against color, will win for the Republican party the support of genuine pro-slavery men, or avert from the party the odium of being the advocate and defender of the Negro as a man and a member of society. The interests of the party, as well as whatever principle and character it has, call upon the members of it to step promptly to the side of Charles Sumner, and assume towards the whole system of slavery the solid and commanding attitude taken by him in his great speech in the American Senate, and which the Massachusetts Legislature has so nobly backed up in a series of resolutions, which we elsewhere publish in our present number.[43]

Douglass' Monthly, August, 1860

THE DEMOCRATIC PARTY

This political organization is now hopelessly divided and broken up. During the last twenty years of its existence, its constant aim has been to discourage all anti-slavery tendencies in the country, to exalt and strengthen the slave power and to make the rapacious traffickers in the bodies and souls of men the permanent rulers and law-givers of the land. It has been regarded at the North and at the South as the natural ally of slavery, and its life has fully justified the estimate placed upon its character. If the Negro should discriminate between the various organized forces of this country against him, he would point to the Democratic party as pre-eminent in unscrupulous malignity and heartless cruelty. Attracting to itself all that is low, vulgar, coarse, brutal and mobocratic in the nation, it has poured down upon the Negro all these elements of wrath and poison. The vital element of the party has been hatred of Negroes and love of spoils. With a name altogether attractive to the masses, and a long period of uninterrupted strength and prosperity, its leaders and managers, like all others thus conditioned, began to think the party immortal. In every division of opinion, in all the contests of factions, the quarrels of greedy and aspiring candidates, hitherto the party has at the trial hour been found united and strong. The Whig party crumbled under the sturdy blows of the Abolitionists, and went to its own place, having outlived its usefulness eight years ago; but the Democratic party stood firm and united, impressing its enemies, as well as its friends, with the idea of its firmness and indivisibility. The illusion is now dispelled. Babylon has fallen. In sight of the whole nation, she has been doubly rent in twain, and utterly demoralized. The details of these transactions[44] are known to our readers, and we need not stay to recapitulate them. We wish only to send up a jubilee shout over the fact that the wisdom of the crafty has been confounded, that the counsels of the wicked have been brought to naught, and that the Democratic party, the bitter and malignant persecutor of our sable race, has fallen mortally wounded in the house of its friends in Baltimore. The condition of the scattered factions who still cling to the name of the party, makes it almost certain that Abraham Lincoln and Hannibal Hamlin will be President and Vice President of the United States in 1861.

Douglass' Monthly, August, 1860

THE PROSPECT IN THE FUTURE

The future of the anti-slavery cause is shrouded in doubt and gloom. The labors of a quarter of a century, instead of culminating in success, seem to have reached a point of weary hopelessness, so far as Radical Abolitionists are concerned. The great work of enlightening the people as to the wicked enormities of slavery, is well-nigh accomplished, but the practical results of this work have disappointed our hopes. The grim and bloody tragedies of outrage and cruelty are rehearsed day by day to the ears of the people, but they look on as coolly indifferent as spectators in a theatre. The dangers to our common country produce as little emotion as the revelation of the wrongs of our common humanity. They assent to all the horrid truths which reveal the inhuman secrets of the gloomy prison house, but are not moved to action. They commend the iron-linked logic and soul-born eloquence of Abolitionists, but never practice the principles laid bare by the one, or act upon the emotions called up by the other. An able advocate of human rights gratifies their intellectual tastes, pleases their imaginations, titillates their sensibilities into a momentary sensation, but does not move them from the downy seat of inaction. They are familiar with every note in the scale of abstract rights, from the Declaration of Independence to the orations of Charles Sumner, but seem to regard the whole as a grand operatic performance, of which they are mere spectators. You cannot relate a new fact, or frame an unfamiliar argument on this subject.—Reason and morality have emptied their casket of richest jewels into the lap of this cause, in vain. Religion has exhausted her volleyed thunders of denunciation upon the head of this gigantic crime, but it stands unmoved and defiant. She has poured out floods of the tears of love and sympathy before this people, but their hearts have never been so melted as to produce an appropriate response to her divine ardor. Art, literature and poetry have all expended their treasures to arouse the callous hearts of the American people to the duty of letting the oppressed go free, and yet four millions struggle out their lives in blood-rusted chains. Europe is rocking and heaving with the struggle for liberty, while America is comparatively indifferent under a system of bondage more terrible than Europe has known for centuries. Garibaldi lands on the coast of Sicily with a few hundred men, as the forlorn hope of Italian freedom, and a brave and generous and appreciating people flock to his standard, and drive the tyrant of Naples from his bloody throne. John Brown takes up arms against a system of tyranny more cruel and barbarous than that of the murderer of Palermo, and is hung on a Virginia gallows, while thirty millions of people, whose civil catechism is the Declaration of Independence, look on unmoved to interference.

What is the explanation of this terrible paradox of passing history? Are the people of this country of an inferior race? Are they lacking in physical courage? Do they fail to appreciate the value of liberty? Our history, if we shall confine its revelations to the descendants of the Anglo-Saxon, the Teutonic, or the Celtic races, answers all these questions in the negative. This conglomerate people, made up from the crossing of all these races, have shown great courage and patriotism in defending *their own freedom,* but have utterly failed in the magnanimity and philanthropy necessary to prompt respect for the rights of another and a weaker race than those mentioned above. It is not because we fail to appreciate or lack the courage to defend our own rights that we permit the existence of slavery among us, but it is because our patriotism is intensely selfish, our courage lacks generosity, and our love of liberty is circumscribed by our narrow and wicked selfhood, that we quietly permit a few tyrants to crush a weak people in our midst. Whoever levies a tax upon our Bohea or Young Hyson, will find the whole land blazing with patriotism and bristling with bayonets the next morning. Let the mightiest maritime nation on the globe but impress a few Yankee sailors, and our merchant ships will be punctured with port holes, and manned with sailors who fight like heroes. Let any power on earth claim sovereignty over a single rood of the scraggy pine woods of Maine, or a foot of the drifted sand of some island on our western border, and Congress will burst forth with such a flood of pyrotechnic oratory as to stir our warlike blood to the tune of battle. But millions of a foreign race may be stolen from their homes, and reduced to hopeless and inhuman bondage among us, and we either approve the deed, or protest as gently as "sucking doves." Our courage, our love of liberty, our statesmanship, our literature, our ethics, and our religion, are all most intensely and wickedly selfish. Our national character fails to present a single fulcrum for the lever of justice or humanity. We only ask to be permitted to enjoy our own heritage, and on this condition are content to see others crushed in our midst. Ours is the philosophy of Cain. When God and humanity cry out against the oppression of the African, we coolly ask what of it? "Am I my brother's keeper?" If his blood cry to us for redress, we say, "let it cry; it is not our blood." If his children are stolen and enslaved, we look on and say "they are not our children; don't you see their noses are flat and their hair curls." If his daughters are debauched, our blood remains cool, for they are neither our daughters nor sisters. If his wife is stolen, we have nothing to do so long as our wives are protected by law. If the way to heaven is open to the white man, and we have a chance to "land our souls in glory," we are sublimely indifferent to the fact that the Bible and the Gospel are withheld from the Negro, and go on shouting our amens, and singing our anthems so loud that nobody but God can hear his wail of agony above the din of our voiceful, but heartless piety. Heaven help the poor slave, whose only hope of freedom is in the selfish hearts of such a people!—Nor can heaven help him, except by moving him to help himself. The motive power which shall liberate the slave must be looked for in slavery itself—must be generated in the bosom of the bondman. Outside philanthropy never disenthralled any people. It required a Spartacus, himself a Roman slave and gladiator, to arouse the servile population of Italy, and defeat some of the most powerful armies of Rome, at the head of an army of slaves; and the slaves of America await the advent of an African Spartacus.

There is one element of American character which has as yet never been fairly appealed to in behalf of the slave. Our philanthropy melts itself away into maudlin tears at the story of his wrongs. Our sense of justice kicks the beam when his master's cotton bales are in the adverse scale. Our religion whines and snivels over his sufferings, but cannot leave its formal devotions long enough to bind up its wounds. Our politics bellow in his behalf on the stump, but only employ his cause as a stalking horse for party effect, and to carry self-seekers into power. But there is a latent element in our national character which, if fairly called into action, will sweep anything down in its course. The American people admire courage displayed in defense of liberty, and will catch the flame of sympathy from the sparks of its heroic fire.—The strength of this trait of character has been long manifest in the reception of the patriots who have been cast upon our shores from the wrecks of European revolutions; and when some African Eunus or Salvius shall call the servile population of the South to arms, and inspire them to fight a few desperate battles for freedom, the mere animal instincts and sympathies of this people will do more for them than has been accomplished by a quarter of a century of oratorical philanthropy. We can never cease to regret that an appeal to the higher and better elements of human nature is, in this case, so barren of fitting response. But so it is, and until this people have passed through several generations of humanitarian culture, so it will be.—In the meantime the slave must continue to suffer or rebel, and did they know their strength they would not wait the tardy growth of our American sense of justice.

To the Negro-hating conservative this language sounds harsh and vengeful, no doubt. But that same law-and-order conservative reads of the glorious deeds of Garibaldi and the Sicilian insurrectionists, with a shout of responsive enthusiasm springing to his lips, and rejoices at the downfall of the tyrants of Naples. The cruelties inflicted by the brutal police of Francis II, are reproduced every week on hundreds of plantations in America, and a people far outnumbering the Sicilians are crushed under the heel of a democracy which is far heavier than that of any crowned and booted Bourbon. Why should we shout when a tyrant is driven from his throne by Garibaldi's bayonets,[45] and shudder and cry peace at the thought that the American slave may one day learn the use of bayonets also?

Douglass' Monthly, August, 1860

TO ELIZABETH CADY STANTON

Rochester, Aug. 25, 1860

Dear Mrs. Stanton:

I am much obliged by your letter. I have been in a half and half condition about attending that Worcester convention[46] ever since I got the call signed by Messers Foster and Peirpont. Of course your letter has taken something from one half and added it to the other. I am now strongly inclined to go. The only cause of hesitation is that the difference between myself and Mr. Garrison might render me an unaccepted member to some who may come from that side of the house, Mr. Foster himself, included. I have always believed in Stephen Foster and never lifted my voice against him or against Mr. Garrison until compelled to do so in self-defense. I may call to see you on my way to Syracuse next week, and talk matters over with you. Thank you for your kind invitation. In haste. Yours very truly.

                                                        Frederick Douglass

Elizabeth Cady Stanton Papers, Library of Congress

GOING TO ENGLAND GIVEN UP

When called home, while in the midst of our anti-slavery labors in England, by a sad bereavement in our family, a few months ago, we cherished the hope of being able to resume our work in that country as early as next month. This hope is now given up. It has been relinquished with much reluctance. We breathe freer on British soil than elsewhere. Nowhere more than in England have our humble efforts for the freedom and elevation of our people been more warmly and heartily appreciated and supported than among the noble men and women of the British Isles. From the time that we went among them first, fifteen years ago, until now, we have been sustained in our labors by their generous sympathy, material aid and co-operation in every time of need. Were we to consult our own pleasure, our freedom from insult, proscription, social ostracism and oppression on account of color, we should be back to England in the next steamer. But we have something better than personal ease and security to live for, and that is the cause of our enslaved and oppressed people. That cause seems to make it our duty to stay here for the present. A Presidential canvass is pending, and the public mind is peculiarly awake. He who speaks now may have an audience. We wish to avail ourselves of the opportunity to strike while the iron is hot. Our Presidential and other elections are times for the education of the people in their moral and political duties. Mind is active; opinions and principles clash; truth with error meets in stern debate before all the people.—In this grand strife we mean to take our humble part. There is an audience for us, and we are bound to address it, and do our part in flinging before the peoples the principles of justice and liberty which alone can exalt the nation, and without the observance and practice of which nations, like individuals, must plunge headlong into destruction.

Besides the Presidential election now in progress, we have an additional reason for remaining at our post for the present. A proposition is now before the people of the State of New York to change the Constitution in such a manner as to place colored citizens on a footing of equality with others in the exercise of the right of suffrage.[47] The people have to vote yea or nay for this change. Of course, all that is malignant in the public mind will be hurled against the Negro and his friends in the coming contest. At such a time the black man has peculiar claims to be heard in his own behalf, and he who has any influence should remain and exert it in bringing the State to the great measure of justice now proposed.

We fully recognize the importance of keeping the subject of slavery before the British public. British influence must go one way or the other for slavery or against it. The cause of the slave cannot afford to lose that influence; and in order to retain it, the subject of slavery must be kept before the British people in some other shape than as furnishing cotton for the mills of Manchester. This work will now be done by men already on the ground. Rev. G. B. Cheever has already entered vigorously on his mission, and we think he is destined to make a powerful impression especially upon the religious classes of the country. He has the ability to speak with authority respecting the position and influence of the American churches on the question of slavery, and just that sort of testimony is needed more than any other in England. The anti-slavery sentiment of England is exposed to no influence more dangerous than that exerted by American pro-slavery divines who visit that country.

With the labors of Dr. Cheever and the efforts of the many excellent anti-slavery associations organized by our ever faithful friend and coadjutor, Mrs. Dr. Crofts, we may hope that the anti-slavery sentiment of Great Britain will be much strengthened. To the associations mentioned, very much of English anti-slavery life may now be ascribed They kindled anew the expiring flame of anti-slavery, and kept the cause alive where it might otherwise have died out. We earnestly hope that these societies will continue their exertions. The good that they do may seem small to them; but the poor bondman flying for liberty, whom they assist, and the truth they enable us to bring before the American people, make them important and indispensable auxiliaries.

Douglass' Monthly, September, 1860

DALLAS AND DELANY

Some of our American journals, to whom *black* in anything else than in the human heart, is a standing offense, are just now "taking on" very ruefully about what they are pleased to call a flagrant insult offered to the American Minister, Mr. G. M. Dallas, by Lord Brougham, at a meeting of the International Statistical Society, held in London. Small pots boil quick, and soon dry up; but they do boil terribly while they are at it. It would hardly be safe to say whereunto our present wrath would carry us, were we not somewhat restrained and held down by the onerous burdens of electing our President for the next four years. As an American, and being of the popular complexion, we are rather glad to see this sensitiveness. The most disgusting symptoms sometimes raise hopes for the recovery of the patient, and it may be so in this case. The startling offense of the venerable and learned Lord Brougham, was that he ventured to call the attention of Mr. Dallas, the American Minister Plenipotentiary, to the fact that a *"Negro"* was an acting member of the meeting of the International Statistical Society. This was the offense.—There was no mistaking the point. It struck home at once. Mr. Dallas felt it. It choked him speechless. He could say nothing. The hit was palpable. It was like calling the attention of a man, vain of his personal beauty, to his ugly nose, or to any other deformity.—Delany, determined that the nail should hold fast, rose, with all his blackness, right up, as quick and as graceful as an African lion, and received the curious gaze of the scientific world. It was complete. Sermons in stones are nothing to this. Never was there a more telling rebuke administered to the pride, prejudice and hypocrisy of a nation. It was saying: Mr. Dallas, we make members of the International Statistical Society out of the sort of men you make merchandise of in America. Delany, in Washington, is a *thing;* Delany, in London, is a *man.* You despise and degrade him as a beast; we esteem and honor him as a gentleman. Truth is of no color, Mr. Dallas, and to the eye of science a man is not a man because of his color, but because he is a man and nothing else. To our thinking, there was no truth more important and significant brought before the Statistical Society. Delany's presence in that meeting was, however, something more than a rebuke to American prejudice. It was an answer to a thousand humiliating inquiries respecting the character and qualifications of the colored race. Lord Brougham, in calling attention to him, performed a most noble act, worthy of his life-long advocacy of the claims of our hated and slandered people. There was doubtless something of his sarcastic temper shown in the manner of his announcement of Delany; but we doubt not there was the same genuine philanthropic motive at the bottom of his action, which has distinguished him through life. A man covered with honor, associated with the history of his country for more than a half century, conspicuous in many of the mightiest transactions of the greatest nation of modern times, between eighty and ninety years old, is not the man to indulge a low propensity to insult.— He had a better motive than the humiliation of Dallas. The cause of an outraged and much despised race came up before him, and he was not deterred from serving it, though it should give offense.

But why should Americans regard the calling attention to their characteristic prejudice against the colored race as an insult? Why do they go into a rage when the subject is brought up in England? The black man is no blacker in England than in America.—They are not strangers to the Negro here; why should they make strange of him there?—They meet him on every corner here; he is in their corn-fields, on their plantations, in their houses; he waits on their tables, rides on their carriages, and accompanies them in a thousand other relations, some of them very intimate. To point out a Negro here is no offense to anybody. Indeed, we often offer large rewards to any who will point them out. We are so in love with them, that we will hunt them; and of all men, our Southern brethren are most miserable when deprived of their Negro associates. Why then should we be offended by being asked to look at a Negro in London? We look at him in New York, and Mr. Dallas has often been called to look at the Negro in Philadelphia.

The answer to these questions may be this: In America the white man sees the Negro in that condition to which the white man's prejudice and injustices assigns him. He sees him a proscribed man, the victim of insult and social degradation. In that condition he has nothing against him. It is only when the Negro is seen *without* these limitations that his presence raises the wrath of your genuine American Christian. When poor, ignorant, hopeless and thoughtless, he is rather an amusement to his white fellow-citizens; but when he bears himself like a man, conscious of the God-like characteristics of manhood, determined to maintain in himself the dignity of his species, he becomes an insufferable offense. This explains Mr. Dallas, and explains the American people. It explains also the Negroes themselves.

It is often asked why the Negroes do not rise above the generally low vocations in which they are found? Why do they consent to spend their lives in menial occupations?—The answer is, that it is only here that they are not opposed by the fierce and bitter prejudice which pierces them to the quick the moment they attempt anything higher than is considered *their place* in American society. Americans thus degrade us, and are only pleased with us when so degraded. They tempt us on every side to live in ignorance, stupidity and social worthlessness, by the negative advantage of their smiles; and they drive us from all honorable exertion by meeting us with hatred and scorn the instant we attempt anything else. Had Mr. Delany been a poor, mean, dirty, ignorant Negro, incapable of taking an honorable place among gentlemen and scholars, Mr. Dallas could have turned the specimen to the account of his country. But the article before him was a direct contradiction to his country's estimate of Negro manhood. He had no use for him, and was offended when his attention was called to him.

There was still another bitter ingredient in the cup of the American minister. Men can indulge in very mean things when among mean men, and do so without a blush. They can even boast of their meanness, glory in their shame when among their own class, but who, when among better men, will hang their heads like sheep-stealing dogs the moment their true character is made known. To hate a Negro in America is an American boast, and is a part of American religion. Men glory in it. But to turn up your nose against the Negro in Europe is not quite so easy as in America, especially in the case of a Negro morally and intellectually the equal of the American Minister.

Douglass' Monthly, September, 1860

THE PRESIDENTIAL CAMPAIGN OF 1860, speech at celebration of West India Emancipation, August 1, 1860

Mr. President:—I thank you very sincerely for the kind and cordial welcome you have been pleased, on behalf of this vast audience, to extend to me, and also for the words of sympathy with me in the experiences through which I have passed since our last meeting in this place. I esteem it a high privilege, especially in view of the many vicissitudes and exciting incidents of the past twelve months, to join you again in appropriate recognition of this anniversary of freedom. It is now twenty-six years since the justice and humanity of England represented in the British Parliament and throne, abolished and put an end to slavery in the British West Indies forever. No greater demonstration of philanthropy has occurred during the present century. It astonished the world by its grandeur. Men could hardly believe that humanity could so succeed against the selfishness of property.—The transition for the slaves emancipated was a most wonderful experience. In all our emancipations in the United States, we have had nothing so sudden and so startling as this. The slaves were eight hundred thousand chattels yesterday; they were eight hundred thousand free men and women the next day. It was a trying event. It tested the mettle of slaves as well as masters, and the behavior of the former proved them worthy of their newly gained freedom. Emancipation had been looked for and prayed for by the scarred and mutilated bondman; but even *they* must have found it hard to believe that they were now forever free. Yet, in the doubt, and in the assurance, and in the great joy of the occasion, their behavior was equally orderly and beautiful.

Many of the old slave-drivers anticipated the event with the gloomiest forebodings. Knowing how well they had deserved vengeance, they shuddered at the thought of its possible approach. Guilty men! they read human nature wrong. They who study mankind with a whip in their hands, will always go wrong. They see but one side of everything about them, and that is the worst side. They only *see without,* the qualities they feel within themselves. Pride, self-love, cruelty, brutality and revenge had been cultivated with all the approved instruments of torture on the plantation. These qualities they knew and well understood; but they did not see the higher elements of human nature. According to their dismal fears and predictions, the Islands were to be desolated. The white inhabitants were to be slaughtered. Fire and sword were to be let loose, and neither age nor sex were to be spared.

It is one of the glories of the occasion and the event, that every such prediction and objection was refuted by the grand result. Not even the most unscrupulous and eager slanderers of the Negro race have been able to sustain a charge of violence against the emancipated bondmen. Peace, joy and gratitude combined to sanctify and hallow the glorious advent of liberty.

We meet here to-day, as we met here last year, to honor this high and brilliant example of British justice towards a people everywhere spoken against. The event is worthy the attention of all men, but to the American people it addresses itself with tenfold power and force as an example fit to be honored and imitated. The First of August is, and of right ought to be, the great abolition day for all the friends of freedom. In regard to England, a very significant and gratifying fact may be stated. Notwithstanding all the years of clamor against the results of emancipation, England has steadily persisted in its abolition policy.

The abolition of slavery in the West Indies is now, as at the beginning, esteemed by every true-hearted Britain as the chief glory of his country. And well it may be.—It was the result of the very best elements of cultivated human nature. The labor, the zeal, the earnestness, and the perseverance employed in bringing the British people to see slavery in its true character, and to bring them to act for its abolition, were never excelled by those of any other great reformatory movement. The people there talk to this day of the mighty enthusiasm that rocked the land, and every man is proud to say that he had a hand in the great work. The British public, though weighed down and staggering under a heavy weight of taxation, bore, without a murmur, the additional burden of twenty millions sterling. If there was any complaint at all, it was that the masters got it instead of the slaves. How striking and humiliating is the contrast in respect to slavery, between England and America, the mother and the daughter! If the merits of republican institutions, as against those of a monarchy, were made to depend upon the character and history of the American Republic, monarchical institutions would most certainly bear off the palm. The British monarchy, self-moved and self-sustained, emancipated, set free, and clothed with the dignity of citizenship, nearly a million slaves at a single stroke of the pen, and then began to exert, and continues to exert her great moral influence to make her noble example felt throughout the world.

It is really amazing how far into the regions of darkness and sorrow this knowledge of British feeling has penetrated. The most ignorant slave on the banks of the Red River has by some means or other come to learn that the English are the friends of the African race. Her ships are on the gold coast; they are in the Gulf of Mexico, and along the coast of the Brazils in search of slave pirates, only secure from arrest when they hoist the American flag. While the British monarchy thus employs its powers, how is it with our so-called Christian Protestant Republic? The story is soon told. Four millions clank their fetters at the very doors of our churches and our Government. The slave trade, long ago abolished by the humanity of your revolutionary fathers, is now openly defended, and is secretly carried on, with the evident connivance of the Government in various ports of the South. The policy of limiting slavery, which comes down to us from the founders of the government, has been set aside by the Dred Scott decision. Free colored men, who, in the better days of the Republic, were regarded and treated as American citizens, have been made aliens and enemies in the land of their birth. Slave-hunting, which had died out under the quiet influence of a partial civilization, has now, in the middle of the nineteenth century, been thoroughly revived. Thus, while the British Government, with far less pretension to liberty than we, is wielding the mighty power and influence which her position and greatness give her, for the promotion of liberty and humanity throughout the world—the American Government is worse than winking at the slave trade, and slavers are fitted out in sight of our business men's prayer meetings. It is evidently the design of the Slave Power of this Republic to fasten the terrible curse of human bondage upon every quarter of this continent.

But England is not the only nation whose conduct stands in marked and striking contrast with our own. There stands Russia, grim and terrible, half way between barbarism and civilization—a conglomeration of many races, darkened by ages of wide-spread cruelty and blood—governed by a despotism, cold and hard as granite—supremely indifferent to the good or ill opinion of mankind—with no freedom of tongue, no freedom of press—yet even she proves herself more just and wise in her day and generation than we. She knows enough, and is wise enough to make friends of her own household. The car of emancipation is advancing gloriously in that country; the shouts of millions, headed by the Emperor Alexander himself, go up in joy over the freedom of the Russian serf.

But with us how different is the spectacle! Slavery is everywhere the pet monster of the American people. All our political parties, and most of our churches, kneel with humility at its accursed shrine of tears and blood! Each party vies with the other in its zealous self-abasement and servile devotion. In our politics, as well as in our religion, he who refuses to join in the worship of whips, and in acknowledgment of the charity of chains, is stigmatized as a blasphemer, and an enemy to the State. We read, the Chaldean monarch set up an image of gold for his subjects to worship. That was bad enough, and one may rejoice that there was virtue enough in the three Hebrews to refuse to kneel. But bad as the image was as an object of worship, the thing itself was not undesirable. But our object of worship is in itself revolting. A vulture feeding on a living and quivering human heart, tearing it to pieces with his remorseless talons and bloody beak, would be an appropriate symbol of the object of our national devotion. For where under the whole heavens can there be found any system of wrong and cruelty to compare with our slavery? Who has measured its vast extent, found its limits, or sounded the depths of its wickedness? Language fails to describe it, and the human mind, though winged with a fancy outflying the lightning, fails to overtake and comprehend this huge and many-headed abomination. I know slavery as well as most men. I was born in it, as most of you know; but though I have been a victim to what has broken the spirit and cowed into servility many a better man than myself, I have not yet been able to convey even *my* limited sense of the ten thousand wrongs of slavery. I have spoken and written much on the subject during the last twenty years, and have been at times accused of exaggeration; and yet I can say, with truth, that I have fallen far short in describing the pains and woes, and in painting the unbroken stream of sorrow and sighing mercilessly poured down upon the sable millions doomed to life-long bondage in this boasted free country. Slavery has been denounced as the sum of all villainies. The language is well chosen. But who can grapple with a thing so huge as the sum of all villainies? The idea is too large and dreadful for the imagination. The warp and woof of slavery is yet to be unraveled.—Each bloody thread must yet be disentangled and drawn forth, before men will thoroughly understand and duly hate the enormity, or properly abhor its upholders and work its abolition. This is the work still to be done. After all the books, pamphlets and periodicals—after all the labors of the Abolitionists at home and abroad—we have still to make the American people acquainted with the sin and crime of our slave system.

In this good work, let me acknowledge the sentiment of gratitude which you and I feel on this occasion to Hon. Charles Sumner, of Massachusetts. It is more than empty praise to say that we recognize him as the Wilberforce of America. He has brought to the right side of the discussion a quenchless zeal, and an irresistible earnestness. His large culture and eminent talents have been industriously applied to the work of placing before the world the monstrous crime and withering barbarism of our country. For this great service, I embrace this occasion to thank him, in my own name, and in the name of our whole people. Many other noble men have spoken and have spoken well. We thank them all—we appreciate them all; but among them all, none has uttered the feelings of the black man so well; none have hurled at slavery such a succession of moral thunder-bolts as he. Were Mr. Sumner only a non-extensionist, we might not mention his name for special honor on this memorable day. But the brave Senator from Massachusetts takes rank with a higher order of men, and is engaged in a sublimer work. The principles which he enunciates, the doctrines which he maintains, with an eloquence unmatched in the American Senate, and unsurpassed out of it, compel us to rank him with the Sharpes, the Clarksons, the Buxtons, and the Broughams of England—the great men whose mighty efforts have given us and our people the event we have met this day to celebrate. Like them, Charles Sumner is an Abolitionist. Owing to a difference in the civilization of the two countries, Mr. Sumner has suffered as they did not, for the faithful utterance of his opinions. His sacred blood has stained the Senate floor. Assassin blows have fallen upon him; and yet we have him still with us, in all the strength, fertility and grandeur of his well-stored intellect. Four years of painful anxiety have been dispelled by the sight of his rising, as he has risen, with redoubled zeal, and with powers of action and utterance augmented, quickened and intensified. His assailants and would-be murderers were not spared, as I almost wish they had been, to experience the mortification of seeing the noble Senator rise, as if from the very grave to which they had aimed to consign him. They have both ceased from the earth, and Mr. Sumner looks in vain around the Senate hall to find any to imitate the example of his dead assassins. A mighty change has been going on in Washington during these last four years. The Massachusetts Senator could well indulge in what he calls the easy victory of charity towards his fallen foes.

But there is a charity which falls upon the head of the wrong-doers like coals of living fire. Such charity was deserved, and such was meted out to the haughty slave-masters of the Senate. I would have given a great deal to have looked upon them during the execration. A man more politic than Mr. Sumner might have broken the ominous silence of four years in a tone better suited to the taste of those who are just now desiring the success of the Republican party with principles or without principles. But Mr. Sumner is better than his company. He not only talks of the irrepressible conflict, but nobly flings himself into it with all the ardor of his great soul, and becomes himself a part of it. I hail him with a full heart, as a man of the right metal. Let us thank God and take courage, that such a man in this hour of pro-slavery truckling, backed up by the Legislature of such a State, bravely stands up in the highest council of the nation the champion of liberty and equal rights to all men of whatever class, clime, condition or color.

Friends, I shall not detain you to-day with any history of West India Emancipation.—Elsewhere, and on other occasions, I have done this at length. Nor shall I stop to justify emancipation by an appeal to its material results. The chief objection that we have ever heard against it, is, that when free, and left to decide the question for himself, the black man will not work. This objection comes from those who have as little taste for work under a tropical sun as the Negroes. A kind and humane lady in England, who took an earnest interest in emancipation, when told that the Negroes of Jamaica were lazy and would not work, answered the objection by saying she was glad that after working so long and hard under cruel task masters, the poor people could now take a little time to rest.—This charge of special indolence I have met on other occasions, and shall not repeat my refutation of it here. My work is nearer home. This is a free day—a day for free speech—and all things touching the cause of human freedom are in order here to-day.—Subjects of discourse are abundant, and invite us on every side. Our Democratic Republic is just now undergoing one of its periodical political convulsions. It is engaged in the quadrennial business of electing its King. We are a strange people. We flatter ourselves that the people govern, and that the government is directly and immediately responsible to the people. And so, indeed, it seems in theory; but the matter is quite different in practice. In this respect we are even in the rear of old England and our neighbors across the lakes. We have a less responsible Government than either. It should be distinguished from all other Governments as *the irresponsible Government.*

By the Constitution of the United States our King reigns over us for the term of four years. It seems a short term; but experience shows that it is quite long enough for the perpetration of almost innumerable mischiefs, and to thwart and defeat the most beneficent measures. Our King is armed with mighty powers, the veto power among them. He is Commander-in-Chief of the army and navy.—During his reign he can exercise his power as rigorously as any of the crowned heads of Europe, and do so with greater impunity. I assert fearlessly, that while Americans are ever boasting of the sovereignty of the people, there is no Government on the earth which can be administered in more open violation of the principles of freedom, or in more flagrant contempt for the rights and wishes of the people, than the American Government during a Presidential term. Commanding the purse, the sword and the patronage of the Government, and being safely installed in the Presidential chair, with a Cabinet of his own selection about him, the President is thereafter beyond the reach of the people. You cannot get at him. He is above inquiry, and therefore above impeachment and below assassination. The limits set to his term of office protect him. Any hardened old sinner, such as now reigns over us, once in office, may luxuriate in corruption and tyranny to his heart's content, (if such men have hearts and can feel content). Mr. Buchanan has been reveling in rascality from the very commencement of his reign. He began with the Dred Scott decision, advanced to the Lecompton Constitution, and has improved like a young bear from bad to worse ever since. We boast of our self-government. What superlative nonsense! It has no existence except one day in four years. The first Minister in England, who is in fact the ruler of the country, may be outvoted and compelled to resign his office any day in the year. The House of Commons, or any member of it, may call him to account upon the first appearance of misconduct in the direction of public affairs. All is different here. Once well mounted, with the reins of Government in his fists, the Presidential rider may force in his spurs, lay on the whip, draw the blood at every blow, and defy the national animal to throw him off. We have been kicking and tossing about very wildly since we felt Mr. Buchanan in the saddle; but there the old fellow sits as calm as a summer morning. The rulers over yonder, who have crowns annexed to them, must look out for their heads. Conspiracies, revolutions and assassinations are more than possible to them, as Louis Napoleon himself can tell you. But here we have a political safety valve. Freedom to choose a new ruler one day in four years, compensates for all the tyranny, injustice and corruption, inaugurated and submitted to during the Presidential term.—Schemes of villainy may be set in motion during such a term, which may cling to the country and curse it for ages. You have no remedy. You must bear it for four years, and then possibly take another a little more dishonest and tyrannical than his predecessor.— What better was Fillmore and the Fugitive Slave Bill, than Tyler and Texas? What better is Buchanan with Lecompton and bribery, than

Pierce with his shameless and violent measures for making Kansas a slave State? From bad to worse all the time.—The lesson which each gives his successor, is, steal all you can during your term, enrich yourself and your friends, for behave well or ill, you are sure to go out of office with as many curses as coppers. One scripture at least is followed by these Christian gentlemen. Make to yourselves friends of the mammon of unrighteousness. After each election one host of incompetent kin folks takes the place of another; and hence the offices of Government are constantly kept in green and incompetent hands. Such is the machine, and such are its workings. It looks well on paper. It sounds well on the stump, but its works testify trumpet tongued against it.

Well, we are about to try our hand again. A new political crisis is upon the country. The Presidential track is crowded with aspirants. A frightful number of patriots are modestly consenting to assume the burden of Presidential honors. Instead of the five loaves and two fishes—the usual number of political principles—we have five parties and no principles in the present canvass. And yet, since the organization of Government, there has been no election so exciting and interesting as this. The elements are everywhere deeply stirred, and nowhere are they more deeply stirred than at the South. Our political philosophers call the present contest a sectional strife: as if there could be conscious antagonism between two pieces of land not even separated by a stream of fresh water; as if the stately oaks and elms of New York had all at once become offended with the noble pines of North Carolina; as if the wheat, rye and oats of the North had all at once conceived a deadly hatred towards the rice, cotton and tobacco of the sunny South; or as if the bleak and cold granite hills of New Hampshire had declared open war against the hot and feverish rice swamps of Georgia, or the sugar plantations of Louisiana.

The irrepressible conflict has no such explanation. The present strife is one of sentiments, ideas and systems. It respects not so much the rights of labor, the rights of capital, as the rights of man. Under all the deceptive phrases of the political speech of the times, the real meaning of the contest forces itself into view, and defies all arts of concealment. Slavery is the real issue—the single bone of contention between all parties and sections. It is the one disturbing force, and explains the confused and irregular motion of our political machine. All other issues died ten years ago. This is the only living one. Every thoughtful man who goes to the ballot box this fall will go there either to help or to hinder slavery, or with the idea of neither helping nor hindering slavery. In any case, slavery is the object. Taking broad abolition ground, as I hope many of us do, we have much to regret, as well as much to congratulate ourselves upon in the present state of the abolition question, and in the relations and prospects of the political parties in reference to that question.

It is sad to think that after a struggle so long and perilous, marked by the blood and tears of martyrs, we are still confronted by the slave system, unconquered, unsubdued, fierce, greedy, turbulent, and more rampant than ever. But such is the fact. Twenty years ago, slaveholders and their advocates and abettors contented themselves with asking to be let alone. The people of the North were told to mind their own business, that slavery was purely a local system, one with which the North had nothing to do. If it were a curse, it was the curse of the South, and the South would bear it alone. If it were a blessing, it belonged alone to the South.—Very different is the tone of the Slave Power to-day. Now, slavery seems to be the only *national* interest, and the whole power of the Federal Government is invoked to fortify and perpetuate the system on pain of a dissolution of the Union and civil war.

How has this altered state of the question been brought about? Through what blunder on the part of the Abolitionists themselves has this advantage been given to the enemies of justice and freedom? Without question, one great and deplorable mistake has been committed by the opponents of slavery, and that mistake explains to some extent the present proud and arrogant behavior of the defenders of the huge abomination.—We have allowed them to prepare and make the issues of all our late elections, and to decide the character of the controversy before the people. Instead of basing ourselves firmly and immovably on the principle of immediate, unconditional emancipation, as the right of the slave, and as the duty of the masters, and being the aggressors, we have been defending outposts and allowing them to be the aggressors. We have permitted them the advantage of selecting the ground and stipulating the conditions. The result has been that we have been constantly battling against slavery where it does not exist, and conceding rights and privileges where it does exist.—Carefully guarding the slave system within its present limits, the slaveholders have now impudently demanded the right to extend the evil over all the land.

In attestation of what I have now affirmed, let me give a few pages in our national history. You are familiar with the facts, and still it is well to revive them and keep them before the public mind. I wish to impress upon your minds how the anti-slavery sentiment of the country has been abused and deadened—how the anti-slavery cause has been subverted—how the whole abolition movement, or *train,* (to use a railroad phrase,) has been switched off the abolition track to that of non-extension. The deep game by which this was accomplished was brought to light sixteen years ago.

In the year 1844, while all that was honest and upright in the country was sighing over the atrocious scourge and the deep disgrace and scandal of America; while we were sedulously teaching the infant lips of the Republic to denounce the existence of slavery as a curse; to abolish the hateful thing forever—the slaveholders, with an audacity half sublime, openly flung into the Presidential canvass an imperative demand for the annexation of Texas, a country as large as the French empire.—There was no concealment of the motives for this measure. The slaveholders told the country and the world just what they wanted with Texas. Mr. John C. Calhoun, then Secretary of State under John Tyler, was, as all know, the leading spirit in this bold enterprise and the part he took in it showed his satanic sagacity. His policy still lives, and his spectre now leads the infernal hosts of slavery and the slave trade. Texas was in debt, like most other slave countries. She wanted money and wanted credit. Two ways were open to her by which she could get both. England was willing to assist her, on condition that she would abolish her slavery; and America would assist her, provided she would make her slavery perpetual.

Again you have the Monarchy for freedom and the model Republic for slavery and chains. Mr. Calhoun at Washington, and Mr. Everett at London, both pressed the claims of this barbarism against the humanity and civilization of Europe. Mr. Calhoun told the British Government, in the name of the whole American people, that Texas was desired as a means of propping up slavery, and that America could not permit Texas to come under the anti-slavery policy of England. This bold and skillful maneuver of the slaveholders worked admirably. It sent Mr. Van Buren in silence to Kinderhood, Henry Clay to the shades of Ashland, and James K. Polk, a man unknown to fame, to the Presidential chair. Mr. Van Buren was moderately opposed to annexation; Mr. Clay was against it at the North, and for it at the South; and Mr. Polk for it North and South alike. This decided the conflict. Mr. Polk was triumphantly elected, and you all know what followed. The war with Mexico, with all its waste of blood and treasure, was the bitter fruit of annexation; for, as all know,

Texas was a revolted province of Mexico.—She had revolted in part because of the humane laws of Mexico for the abolition of slavery. In taking her we took her debts, her quarrels, her slavery, and all the disgrace and scandal attaching to her name. Hers was the bad reputation of criminals, slaveholders and cut throats.

The people of the North are and have ever been a strangely hopeful and confiding people. They have always presumed upon the good disposition and good intentions of their Southern brethren. I remember well, when a man would have been laughed at as a simpleton or frowned at as a fanatic if he ventured to whisper a danger of the annexation of Texas. Up to the very year in which the perfidious deed was consummated, scarcely anyone at the North believed that Texas could be annexed. Even after it was done, we went on hoping. Some went on so far as to tell the people that as Texas had been voted in, she could be voted out. Boston took the lead in denouncing the perfidy of forcing the old members of the Confederacy into this fellowship, without their consent or consultation. Others of the hopeful class said the South had got Texas, but the victory would be rendered barren by making the largest part of it into free States. Deluded and infatuated men!—They did not know the rapacious spirit and fatal skill at work against them. Disappointed and defeated, they nevertheless maintained the same hopeful and confiding tone in regard to the Territories acquired from Mexico after the war.

The Abolitionists who refused to vote for Mr. Clay—the man who was either for or against, or neither for nor against the annexation of Texas—were, during the interval between 1844 and 1848, placed in a trying position before the people of the North. They were kept under a galling fire of all the Whig guns of the country. They were charged with defeating Mr. Clay, by voting for James G. Birney, electing Mr. Polk, and annexing Texas. The thing was, to be sure, only a *lie*; but having the advantage of being well stuck to, it produced a visible effect upon the abolition party. Voting directly for the abolition of slavery declined. The leaders of the party began to look for available candidates outside of the abolition ranks. Abolition lecturers were supplanted by merely Free Soil lecturers. Abolition newspapers, one after another, faded from view, and Free Soil papers took their places. The Buffalo Convention of 1848, being the first confluence of the abolition sentiment with the old corrupt political elements of the country, was higher toned in its anti-slavery than any Convention since held. The abolition element has by no means kept pace with the growth of the non-extension party. The

National Conventions, held successively in Pittsburgh, Philadelphia and Chicago, have formed a regular gradation of descent from the better utterances of '48 at Buffalo, till at last good readers have been puzzled to find *even* a *fibre,* to saying nothing of a plank of abolition in the platform adopted at Chicago. We have constantly been acquiescing in present attainments of slavery, and only battle against its future acquisitions. We hear nothing now of no more slave States. We hear nothing of the abolition of slavery in the District of Columbia. We hear nothing of the repeal of the Fugitive Slave Law; and even the Declaration of Independence, declaring all men free and equal, came near being voted down in the Chicago Convention, and was admitted at last only on the strength of the eloquence of Geo. W. Curtis, who warned the Convention against rejecting it.[48]

This declaration is one of the disheartening features of the times. The facts wear anything but a cheering aspect to those of us who looked hopefully to the speedy abolition of slavery by moral and political action; and yet our cause is not lost, nor is it powerless. The abolition idea is still abroad, and may yet be made effective. It has no powerful party committed distinctly to its realization, but has a party distinctly committed to a policy which the people generally think will do certain preliminary work essential to the overthrow of slavery. While I see with others, and our noble friends Gerrit Smith and William Goodell among them, that the Republican party is far from an abolition party, I cannot fail to see also that the Republican party carries with it the anti-slavery sentiment of the North, and that a victory gained by it in the present canvass will be a victory gained by that sentiment over the wickedly aggressive pro-slavery sentiment of the country. I would gladly have a party openly combined to put down slavery at the South. In the absence of such a party, I am glad to see a party in the field against which all that is slaveholding, malignant and Negro-hating, both at the North and the South, is combined. I know of no class of men whose instincts as to men and measures touching slavery are more to be depended upon than those of the slaveholders. There are gradations in all things, and reforms among them. A man need not to be a William Lloyd Garrison or a William H. Seward in order to get himself recognized as an enemy to slavery. The slaveholders know that the day of their power is over when a Republican President is elected. The mobs gotten up to put down the Republican Conventions at Baltimore, Alexandria and Wheeling, the threats of violence offered to Cassius M. Clay and his Republican associates in Kentucky, and the threats of a dissolution of the Union in case of the election of Lincoln, are tolerable endorsements of the anti-slavery tendencies of the Republican party; and for one, Abolitionist though I am, and resolved to cast my vote for an Abolitionist, I sincerely hope for the triumph of that party over all the odds and ends of slavery combined against it. I do not accord with those who prefer the defeat of the Republican party from a fear that it will serve slavery as faithfully as the Democratic party, or either branch of it. To do anything of the kind would be to cut its own thread of existence.

If the Republican party shall arrest the spread of slavery; if it shall exclude from office all such in the slave States who know only slavery as master and law-giver, who burn every newspaper and letter supposed to contain anti-slavery matter, who refuse to hand a black man a letter from the Post Office because he is of the hated color, and will put men into office who will administer them justly and impartially; if it will send ministers and other agents to foreign courts who will represent other interests than slavery, and will give a colored citizen of a free State a pass-port as any other citizen—place the honor of the nation on the side of freedom, encourage freedom of speech and of the press, protect Republican principles and organizations in the slave States—that party, though it may not abolish slavery, will not have existed in vain. But if, on the other hand, it shall seek first of all to make itself acceptable to slaveholders—do what it can to efface all traces of its anti-slavery origin—fall to slave-catching—swear by the Dred Scott decision, and perpetuate slavery in the District of Columbia—it will disappoint the hopes of all its heart friends, and will be deserted, shunned and abhorred as the other parties now are and its place will be taken by another and better party, organized on higher ground and animated by a nobler spirit. Bad as the moral condition of this country is, and powerful as may be the influence of prejudice, the sun of science and civilization has risen too high in the heavens for any party to stand long on the mean, narrow and selfish idea of a "white man's party." This is an age of universal ideas. Men are men, and governments cannot afford much longer to make discriminations between men in regard to personal liberty.—Surely the Republican party will not fall into the mistake or the crime of competing with the old parties in the old wornout business of feeding popular malignity, by acts of discrimination against the free colored people of the United States. I certainly look to that party for a nobler policy than that avowed by some connected with the Republican organization.

How stands the case with the two wings of the so-called Democratic party? What is the difference between Douglas and Breckinridge? I will tell you: Breckinridge believes that the Supreme Court has decided that the slaveholder has a right to carry his slaves into any Territory belonging to the U. S., and that while Congress is bound to protect the slaveholders in this right, there is no power either in Congress, or in any such Territory, to prohibit the relation of master and slave. Mr. Douglas does not believe that the Supreme Court has so decided, but avows himself ready to abide by the decision as soon as the Court shall so decide. The difference between the two, is the difference between two obedient servants of the same master.—One thinks himself already sent, and the other holds himself ready upon the moment of receiving orders. Mr. Douglas, addressing the slaveholders, says:—I am your humble, obedient servant. I stand by the Dred Scott decision; and if that, or any other decision of the Supreme Court establishes slavery in the Territories, I am for it also. I am ready, upon a knowledge of this fact, to send all the moonshine I now hold, about the right of the people to govern themselves, to the winds.—The difference between Douglas and Breckinridge is, therefore, simply the difference between *now* and *then*—a difference which seems wide before the election, but which will vanish immediately after the election, let who will attain the Presidency—for there can be no doubt as to how the Supreme Court, with a majority of slaveholders, will decide the question, if it has not already decided.

In view of this state of the case, it is scarcely worth while to do more than denounce the humbug with which Mr. Douglas is just now seeking to win your votes. By a peculiar use of words, he confounds *power* with *right* in such a manner as to make the *power* to do wrong the *right* to do wrong. By his notion of human rights, everything depends upon the majority. It is not a bit more absurd and monstrous to say that the first settlers in a Territory have the right to protect murder, than that they have the right to protect slavery. The right to do the one is just as good as the right to do the other. The right of the slaveholder is precisely the right of the highway robber. The one says your money or your life, and the other says your liberty or your life, and both depend upon superior force for their existence.

I say nothing here and now about the Bell and Everett party. A party without any opinion need have no opinion expressed of it. If a party is of a mind to be blind and dumb, it cannot be surprised at being considered deaf as well. There is doubt now that there is any such party in existence, since the leaders of it have been endeavoring to sell the party out. It is a question who holds the bill of sale in this State—Mr. Brooks or Mr. Douglas. But could such a party as the Bell and Everett party, made up of the old effete Know Nothing elements, succeed in gaining power, there is nothing in its character to inspire a single ray of hope for the slave or humanity, but in addition to Negro hate, we should have an equally abominable hate toward foreigners.

Of the Houston and Stockton party, (the South Americans,) we may say just what has been said of the Bell and Everett party, and that is *as much as nothing*. It is impossible to distinguish between the two factions. On the great question of slavery they stand together, and may be relied upon in any emergency for slavery.

I alluded at the beginning to the exciting vicissitudes and incidents of the past year.—Three months after our last anniversary, there appeared upon the theatre of American life a man whose character and deeds dazzled, astonished and bewildered the whole nation.—A knowledge of him flashed across the oceans and continents like a splendid meteor. For a time, the whole civilized world stood amazed and gazing. There was that peculiarity in him, which in all the ages had awakened the reverence of men, the sage not less than the simple—a human soul illuminated with divine qualities in such high degree as to raise the question, was he our brother?—a man of like passions with ourselves. His behavior was so unusual that men did not know what to make of him. It was thought that the race of such men had become extinct. Men had read of them, as beings belonging to another age. They could not believe that any such man could now be on the earth, and not until they were startled by the reality could they admit the possibility. We have not yet recovered from the wonder with which this man's deeds filled us. His character is yet the study of great minds. Poets, statesmen and philosophers study him as the astronomers the heavenly bodies. He was as a comet, whose brightness overspread half the sky, and men, timid men, thought that a second visit might fire the earth. I need not tell you who this strange man was. You have anticipated me.

You know that I allude to the hero of Harper's Ferry. The ablest and best men of the land have spoken of John Brown, and have confessed their inability to do him justice.—The *Tribune* never said a truer thing than when it said the time had not come to pronounce judgment upon the character and deeds of John Brown. Our land is too fat with the lost sweat and warm blood of slaves driven to toil and death; our civilization is yet too selfish and barbarous; our statesmen are yet too narrow, base and mobocratic; our press is yet too venal and truckling; our religion is too commercial, too much after the pattern of the pride and prejudices of our times, to understand and appreciate the great character who sacrificed himself for the hated Negroes of this country. With the statesmanship, civilization and Christianity of America, the Negro is simply a piece of property, having no rights which white men are required to respect; but with John Brown and his noble associates, *the Negro is a man,* entitled to all the rights claimed by the whitest man on the earth. Brave and glorious old man! Yours was the life of a true friend of humanity, and the triumphant death of a hero.—The friends of freedom shall be nerved to the glorious struggle with slavery by your example; the hopes of the slave shall not die while your name shall live, and after ages shall rejoice to do justice to your great history.

Douglass' Monthly, September, 1860

REPUBLICAN OPPOSITION TO THE RIGHT OF SUFFRAGE

The World, a newly established and widely circulated Republican daily paper, published in New York, is opposed to the repeal of the law which requires that colored citizens be seized and possessed of two hundred and fifty dollars worth of real estate as a condition of exercising the elective franchise. For this opposition it gives the following reasons:

"It is undesirable that the two races should exist in close proximity. So long as they are intermingled in the same community with us, it is our duty to promote their welfare by all rational methods; but while our laws afford them the same protection which they do to us, they must be content with the present restrictions in the exercise of the elective franchise.—It is not philanthropy, but demagogism, that proposes anything different. Though this is a Republican measure, we hope Republicans will have the moral courage and political independence to vote it down."

Against the hopes of *The World, we* hope that Republicans will have the "moral courage," and the magnanimity to vote for equal rights. We know of no injustice more needless, mean and contemptible, than that which imposes a property qualification for voting on the colored citizens of this State. We are few in numbers, exposed to peculiar insults and hardships, on account of popular prejudice skillfully kept alive by all the wealth and power of slavery, acting through all the channels of social influence. These, one would think, were quite enough to repress our upward tendency as a people, without the State saddling our right of suffrage with an odious property qualification, imposed upon no other classes of people in the State. We submit to *The World,* whether it is not mean and base in the extreme to require of a black man a higher qualification for voting than is required of a white man? Of all the people of this State, colored people have the fewest means of acquiring property. Nearly all lucrative and respectable employments are closed against us, and in the face of this undeniable fact, the great and generous State of New York imposes on us the necessity of having and owning two hundred and fifty dollars worth of real property, more than it imposes upon any other class of its citizens. This gross injustice, this contemptible meanness does not well become a State so free and otherwise noble as the State of New York, and we hope that the year 1860 will see this feature of our State Constitution blotted out. As to the *"proximity of the two races," The World* may be right or it may be wrong; we won't stay to discuss whether *"close proximity"* of the two races is desirable or not. "Close proximity" already exists, and in all the likelihood of the case will continue to exist. The question is not whether proximity is desirable, but whether it shall be distinguished by justice and magnanimity, or by unfairness, injustice and meanness.

We do not understand *The World* as wishing to oppress us. It very kindly expresses an interest in our welfare, and even goes the length of making it the white man's duty to promote the black man's welfare. This is kind and amiable, and we like the manifestation of such kindness. Though as a colored man, while profoundly grateful for such a disposition to take care of us, we must say we should be far more grateful for something like a fair and an equal chance to take care of ourselves, and to promote our own happiness. Much trouble would be saved our dear white friends if they would once allow us this right, and we should get on quite as well besides. *The World* says that the laws afford colored people the same protection that it does whites. This sounds well, and in the sense of *The World* it is true; but the statement is a queer one, when used in an argument for the continuance of a law of the State imposing a burden on black men of two hundred and fifty dollars more than upon white men. We think it will be difficult for the world to make out a case of saneness here.

But it is a mockery to talk about protection in a Government like ours to any class in it denied the elective franchise. The very denial of that right strips them of "protection," and leaves them at the mercy of all that is low, vulgar, cruel and base in the community. The ballot box and the jury box both stand closed against the man of color, and open to every other man. These are the acknowledged safeguards of the people's liberty. The white people of this country would wade knee deep in blood before they would be deprived of either of these means of protection against power and oppression. How immeasurably hateful and mean, then, is it to mock us with this talk about same protection, while you are expressing the hope that the Republican party will vote to continue our exclusion, and to deny us equal admission to the ballot box of the State? What is *The World* afraid of? Does it fear that with equal protection Negro blood would prove more than a match for Anglo-Saxon blood in the race of improvement? Does it apprehend the departure of the reins of Government out of the hands of the white race, and for this reason is in favor of continuing extra weight and an additional disability upon the Negro? *The World* is too large for such unmanly and discreditable fears. Once for all, we only ask for our people fair play, equal and exact justice in this matter of suffrage and all others, and we hope that the people of this State, of all political parties, Republicans, Democrats, and National Union men, will yet see that this policy of justice towards us is the only wise and proper one to adopt toward the colored citizens of this great State and nation.

Douglass' Monthly, October, 1860

THE ABOLITION MOVEMENT RE-ORGANIZED

It is now more than a quarter of a century since a small band of philanthropic men and women, whose minds were inspired by a tender pity for the then two million slaves, and a sublime faith in the final triumph of Truth and Justice, met in the city of Philadelphia, under the disapproving frown of a hard-hearted and an united nation.[49] They calmly faced many fierce and manifest perils to person, property and reputation, and boldly avowed their purpose to seek forever thereafter the complete, immediate and unconditional abolition of slavery throughout the United States, by moral and political means alone. Time has rolled on since the declaration of that noble purpose, and many changes have been wrought out, both in respect of the reformers themselves, and of the nation to be reformed. Some who took part in the Philadelphia meeting, and gave their names to its heroic declaration of principles and objects, have grown old, have outlived the sublime faith which then nerved them to the conflict. Some have completely betrayed the cause they professed to love; others have become worn out in the service—their voices are silent, and their pens rarely move—and a few only remain full of faith and abundant in works until this day. Some, in the hope of serving the cause of the slave, and others with the hope of serving themselves, have fused with the pro-slavery churches and masses of the country, and have become a part and parcel of those masses, no longer distinguished from those masses in either anti-slavery words or works. All along the course through our pro-slavery wilderness, moral graves appear, wherein have fallen those who were unable to endure to the end. Much has been done. Great words have been uttered—great deeds performed—but the abolition of slavery, the end to be attained, is not yet. Wearily and sadly the slaves wait in their cruel chains. Of those who witnessed the inauguration of the anti-slavery movement, and hailed it as their deliverer, very few remain on the earth, and a new generation of bondmen have taken the place which death, more merciful than American religion, had made vacant. From two millions and a half, the slaves have increased to three millions, three millions and a half, and now they have passed beyond the number of four millions. Every bright morning sun, every opening flower, every dawning prospect of joyous nature, beholds the victims of bondage increased, their hardships multiplied, and their sufferings augmented. Human flesh is beaten to repress the upward tending human spirit, and human blood ranks higher in the Christian slave markets of America than ever.—Slave ships, by the connivance, if not by the encouragement of Government, loaded to the gunwales with naked men and women destined for the slave market, land their human cargoes on our Southern coast, at convenient distances to suit purchasers. The horrors of the slave trade are thoroughly revived. Fifty slave ships are known to be fitted out annually in the port of New York.[50] Africa bleeds from an hundred ports. Attracted by the smell of our Christian ships, rising from those who breathe disease and death from beneath their suffocating hatchways, the hungry shark makes the voyage from the west coast of Africa to the river mouths of America, finding provision all the way in the sick, dead and dying, flung over to save the rest. The slave trade, indeed, is again upon us with all its ancient horrid features, made more glaring by the slight and insufficient means opposed to its progress. We see the pure foaming billows of the deep stained with blood, and hear the moan of the dying captive rising above the hoarse sound of the sea.

Here, then, are the two revolting evils—slavery and the slave trade. They tower alone, gigantic and monstrous, overtopping every other form of iniquity, cursing the land with tears and the sea with blood. Their abolition was decreed, but they are not abolished. They have been assaulted, but they are yet defiant. They have been smitten a thousand times, yet they flourish. Why have they not fallen? Why has the resistance to them become impotent and spiritless?

Various answers may be given to these questions, but the all-comprehensive answer, the one which includes all others, is, that the American people have no earnest *wish* to put down slavery or the slave trade. This may be learned from our press, our pulpit, and our political parties, from the best of them as well as from the worst of them. The power to put away the evil is present, but the will to do it is absent. The church tells us that the abolition of slavery belongs to the Government, and the people, who are the Government, repudiate the obligation, because they have no will to perform the task it imposes. The effect of all anti-slavery effort thus far is this: It has filled the whole North with a sentiment opposed to slavery. Sentimental Abolitionism is abundant. It may well be met with in the pulpit, sometimes in the religious newspapers, and more frequently still we meet it in the meetings of the Republican party; yet among them all there is neither will nor purpose to abolish slavery. The Republican party, with all the professions of anti-slavery men attached to it, has no such *will,* no such *purpose.*

The very best that can be said of that party is, that it is opposed to *forcing slavery into any Territory of the United States where the white people of that Territory do not want it.* That party is not pledged, as we understand it, against the admission of slave States into the Union, nor in favor of abolishing slavery in the District of Columbia. It is simply opposed to allowing slavery to go where it is not at all likely to go, and that is, as we have said, where the people are opposed to it. A party may be better than its pledges, and a candidate may do more than he promises; but experience furnishes too many examples to the contrary to make it safe to build hopes upon such a foundation. Even the sentiment of the Republican party, as expressed by its leaders, have become visibly *thin* and *insipid* as the canvass has progressed. It promises to be about as good a Southern party as either wing of the old Democratic party. Its candidate is for slave-hunting at the North, and slaveholding at the South. He would catch a Negro while running for his liberty, or shoot him down while fighting for it. Mr. Seward, around whom the best anti-slavery hopes of the party have hitherto centred, seems to have fallen in love with the idea of making the Republican party the white man's party, and to regard the Negro only as a pitiable outcast from American society— an element which cannot be "*assimilated*" with white America. We do not mean to combat this idea here, but refer to it simply as one of the multitudinous proofs of the non existence of any serious design to abolish slavery on the part of the Republican organization. For further discussion of this topic, we commend the reader to the letter of "J. C. H." in our other columns.

The American Anti-Slavery Society has ceased to occupy the ground upon which it was originally started. It no longer seeks the abolition of slavery by the use of the ballot box. It hates slavery, and denounces the system of slavery with a hearty earnestness, but it can do nothing towards abolishing slavery through the machinery of the American Government, for it is conscientiously opposed to voting. The only body now in existence which is in favor of voting for the abolition of slavery, is that very small body in the State of New York which has just nominated Gerrit Smith as its candidate for the Presidency.[51] This body is too small to affect more than the preservation of the abolition integrity of its members. For this it is well worthy of respect; but everyone must see that that party, both in respect to men and means, falls far short of meeting the demands of the hour. In its doctrines, principles and objects, it is well based and strong; but principles, doctrines and objects imply something else.—There a.e any number of good principles and doctrines in the Declaration of Independence, and in the United States Constitution; but what is really wanted is an organization which shall labor to put those principles into practice. Now the Liberty Party has scarcely a paper in which to print the names of its candidates, and has not a single lecturer to publish its doctrines before the people. Doctrines and principles do not avail much in such circumstances. So much for the Liberty Party as a means for the abolition of slavery.

Next, there is the "Church Anti-Slavery Society."[52] It stands upon a narrow basis, too narrow for our ideas of an effective anti-slavery organization. Such an organization should not be limited by sectarianism in any shape, but should be as broad as humanity, and free as the wings of eternal truth. But we do not make this our chief objection to it. Our objection is that it has little more than a mere *paper* life. It is not out in the highways and hedges—not in the wilderness, or on the mountain side, with the startling cry of repentance. It is for the salvation of the church rather more than for the destruction of slavery. Like the Liberty Party, its life is spent within itself. It has no press, no agents, no auxiliaries. An association for the abolition of slavery, which does not extend itself by such means, is usually considered not much more than dead.

The history of the anti-slavery struggle thus far shows that after seven years of earnest, efficient and united labor, by which popular attention was arrested to the subject, and much right feeling generated, the anti-slavery forces of the country became divided; that those who had, during the period of the greatest hardships and perils of the cause, embraced each other as friends and brothers worthy of confidence, esteem and honor for their works' sake, began to accuse and denounce each other as traitors to that cause, and as personal enemies. This fratricidal conduct has continued, bringing new divisions and parties into the field, till at length there is little of associated effort left to carry on the work of popular anti-slavery agitation.

It is hardly necessary to stop in this place to ascertain who are responsible for these divisions, or to attach blame to those through whose errors and faults they may have come. Our business is the immediate and unconditional abolition of slavery in every State and Territory covered by the Constitution of the United States, and in our judgment that business requires a union of effort on the part of all those who desire to see this great and glorious object accomplished.

With such views and feelings, we rejoice to see a call for a great Convention soon to be held in Worcester, Mass., having in view the reorganization of the anti-slavery forces. At the head of this movement we find our old and esteemed friend Stephen S. Foster, a man of inflexible will and of high moral principle, and one of the ablest speakers in the anti-slavery ranks. The great object of Mr. Foster's efforts now is to re-unite the scattered anti-slavery elements of the country, and produce one solid abolition organization, who will use all the powers of the Federal as well as State Governments of the country for the abolition of slavery.

We shall attend that Convention, and do all we can to promote the noble objects which it has in view. The old proverb, "united we stand, divided we fall," has been fully and painfully illustrated by our anti-slavery experience, and it is quite time that we had learned its lesson of wisdom. Moral enterprises, not less than political and physical ones, require union of feeling, union of aim, union of effort. Too long, we think, has this important truth been underestimated. Why should the friends of abolition stand longer divided? Why should they not come together, and do their utmost to establish an abolition organization upon which all may honorably stand and labor together for the extirpation of the common evil of the country? We know not what will be the fate of Mr. Foster's effort. It may fail, as many other good things have, for the time, failed; but it need not fail, and if Abolitionists are true to themselves and their cause, it will not fail.

Douglass' Monthly, October, 1860

EQUAL SUFFRAGE

The movement in favor of "Equal Suffrage" in this State is almost exclusively in the hands of the colored people themselves. Neither Republicans nor Abolitionsts seem to care much for it. If we succeed in repealing the odious and unjust imposition of a property qualification upon us, we shall be more indebted, we fear, to the supineness of our enemies, than to the activity and zeal of our friends. A few only of the latter appear to give any attention to the subject; but we earnestly hope that on the day of election, some true man will be found, from sunrise to sunset, standing at every poll in the State, with a full supply of tickets in favor of Equal Suffrage, urging everybody to vote on the side of Justice and Liberty. It is quite time that this great wrong should be blotted from the Constitution of this great and free State, too great, we trust, to oppress even the weakest of her citizens. Read the Address on this subject,[53] which we send out in the present number, and act upon its principles and suggestions.

Douglass' Monthly, November, 1860

THE LATE ELECTION

Our last monthly paper announced the probable election of Abraham Lincoln and Hannibal Hamlin, the Republican candidates for President and Vice President of the U. S. What was then only speculation and probability, is now an accomplished fact. Pennsylvania, in her State election of October, it is true, had made this result, to a degree, certain; but there were efforts and appliances resorted to by the enemies of the Republican party, which could not fail to cause doubt and anxiety in the minds of the most sanguine.—The deed is, however, now done, and a new order of events connected with the great question of slavery, is now fairly opening upon the country, the end whereof the most sagacious and far-sighted are unable to see and declare. No preceding election resembles this in its issues and parties, and none resembles it in the effects it has already produced, and is still likely to produce. It was a contest between sections, North and South, as to what shall be the principles and policy of the national Government in respect to the slave system of the fifteen Southern States. The broadest assertion of a right of property in man, holding such property equally innocent, sacred and legal under the Constitution, as property in houses, lands, horses, sheep, and horned cattle, and like the latter entitled to Congressional protection in all the Territories, and by parity of reasoning, in all the States of the American Union. The Southern candidate for the Presidency, Mr. Breckinridge, fully represented this broad assertion of what Lord Mansfield well declared to be so opposed to nature, that nothing short of positive law could support it, and Brougham denounced as the "wild and guilty fantasy" of property in man. Mr. Lincoln, the Northern Republican candidate, while admitting the right to hold men as slaves in the States already existing, regards such property as peculiar, exceptional, local, generally an evil, and not to be extended beyond the limits of the States where it is established by what is called positive law. We thus simply state the issue, more for the benefit of our trans-Atlantic friends and readers, than for those at home, who have heard and read little else during the last three or four months. The clamor now raised by the slaveholders about "Northern aggression," "sectional warfare," as a pretext of dissolving the Union, has this basis only: The Northern people have elected, against the opposition of the slaveholding South, a man for President who declared his opposition to the further extension of slavery over the soil belonging to the United States. Such is the head and front, and the full extent of the offense, for which "minute men" are forming, drums are beating, flags are flying, people are arming, "banks are closing," "stocks are falling," and the South generally taking on dreadfully.

By referring to another part of our present monthly, our respected readers will find a few samples of the spirit of the Southern press on the subject. They are full of intrigue, smell of brimstone, and betoken a terrific explosion. Unquestionably, "secession," "disunion," "Southern Confederacy," and the like phrases, are the most popular political watch words of the cotton-growing States of the Union. Nor is this sentiment to be entirely despised. If Mr. Lincoln were really an Abolition President, which he is not; if he were a friend to the Abolition movement, instead of being, as he is, its most powerful enemy, the dissolution of the Union might be the only effective mode of perpetuating slavery in the Southern States—since if it could succeed, it would place slavery beyond the power of the President and his Government. But the South has now no such cause for disunion. The present alarm and perturbation will cease; the Southern fire-eaters will be appeased and will retrace their steps.—There is no sufficient cause for the dissolution of the Union. Whoever lives through the next four years will see Mr. Lincoln and his Administration attacked more bitterly for their pro-slavery truckling, than for doing any anti-slavery work. He and his party will become the best protectors of slavery where it now is, and just such protectors as slaveholders will most need. In order to defeat him, the slaveholders took advantage of the ignorance and stupidity of the masses, and assured them that Lincoln is an Abolitionist. This, Mr. Lincoln and his party will lose no time in scattering to the winds as false and groundless. With the single exception of the question of slavery extension, Mr. Lincoln proposes no measure which can bring him into antagonistic collision with the traffickers in human flesh, either in the States or in the District of Columbia. The Union will, therefore, be saved simply because there is no cause in the election of Mr. Lincoln for its dissolution. Slavery will be as safe, and safer, in the Union under such a President, than it can be under any President of a Southern Confederacy. This is our impression, and we deeply regret the facts from which it is derived.

With an Abolition President we should consider a successful separation of the slave from the free States a calamity, greatly damaging to the prospects of our long enslaved, bruised and mutilated people; but under what may be expected of the Republican party, with its pledges to put down the slaves should they attempt to rise, and to hunt them should they run away, a dissolution of the Union would be highly beneficial to the cause of liberty.—The South would then be a Sicily, and the North a Sardinia. Mr. Lincoln would then be entirely absolved from his slave-hunting, slave-catching and slave-killing pledges, and the South would have to defend slavery with her own guns, and hunt her Negroes with her own dogs. In truth, we really wish those brave, fire-eating, cotton-growing States would just now go at once outside the Union and set up for themselves, where they could be got at without disturbing other people, and got away from without encountering other people. Such a consummation was "one devoutly to be wished." But no, cunning dogs, they will smother their rage, and after all the dust they can raise, they will retire within the Union and claim its advantages.

What, then, has been gained to the anti-slavery cause by the election of Mr. Lincoln? Not much, in itself considered, but very much when viewed in the light of its relations and bearings. For fifty years the country has taken the law from the lips of an exacting, haughty and imperious slave oligarchy. The masters of slaves have been masters of the Republic. Their authority was almost undisputed, and their power irresistible. They were the President makers of the Republic, and no aspirant dared to hope for success against their frown. Lincoln's election has vitiated their authority, and broken their power. It has taught the North its strength, and shown the South its weakness. More important still, it has demonstrated the possibility of electing, if not an Abolitionist, at least an *anti-slavery reputation* to the Presidency of the United States. The years are few since it was thought possible that the Northern people could be wrought up to the exercise of such startling courage. Hitherto the threat of disunion has been as potent over the politicians of the North, as the cat-o'-nine-tails is over the backs of the slaves. Mr. Lincoln's election breaks this enchantment, dispels this terrible nightmare, and awakes the nation to the consciousness of new powers, and the possibility of a higher destiny than the perpetual bondage to an ignoble fear.

Another probable effect will be to extinguish the reviving fires of the accursed foreign slave trade, which for a year or two have been kindled all along the Southern coast of the Union. The Republican party is under no necessity to pass laws on this subject. It has only to enforce and execute the laws already on the statute book. The moral influence of such prompt, complete and unflinching execution of the laws, will be great, not only in arresting the specific evil, but in arresting the tide of popular demoralization with which the successful prosecution of the horrid trade in naked men and women was overspreading the country. To this duty the Republican party will be prompted, not only by the conscience of the North, but by what perhaps will be more controlling party interests.

It may also be conceded that the election of Lincoln and Hamlin, notwithstanding the admission of the former that the South is entitled to an efficient Fugitive Slave Law, will render the practice of recapturing and returning to slavery persons who have heroically succeeded, or may hereafter succeed in reaching the free States, more unpopular and odious. than it would have been had either Douglas, Bell or Breckinridge.been elected. Slaves may yet be hunted, caught and carried back to slavery, but the number will be greatly diminished, because of the popular disinclination to execute the cruel and merciless Fugitive Slave Law. Had Lincoln been defeated, the fact would have been construed by slaveholders, and their guilty minions of the country, as strong evidence of the soundness of the North in respect to the alleged duty of hounding down and handing over the panting fugitive to the vengeance of his infuriated master. No argument is needed to prove this gain to the side of freedom.

But chief among the benefits of the election, has been the canvass itself. Notwithstanding the many cowardly disclaimers, and miserable concessions to popular prejudice against the colored people, which Republican orators have felt themselves required, by an intense and greedy desire of success, to make, they have been compelled also to recur to first principles of human liberty, expose the baseless claim of property in man, exhibit the hideous features of slavery, and to unveil, for popular execration, the brutal manners and morals of the guilty slave-masters.— The canvass has sent all over the North most learned and eloquent men to utter the great truths which Abolitionists have for twenty years been earnestly, but unsuccessfully endeavoring to get before the public mind and conscience. We may rejoice in the dissemination of the truth by whomsoever proclaimed, for the truth will bear its own weight, and bring forth its own fruit.

Nevertheless, this very victory threatens and may be the death of the modern Abolition movement, and finally bring back the country to the same, or a worse state, than Benj. Lundy and Wm. Lloyd Garrison found it thirty years ago. The Republican party does not propose to abolish slavery anywhere, and is decidedly opposed to Abolition agitation. It is not even, by the confession of its President elect, in favor of the repeal of that thrice-accursed and flagrantly unconstitutional Fugitive

Slave Bill of 1850. It is plain to see, that once in power, the policy of the party will be only to seem a little less yielding to the demands of slavery than the Democratic or Fusion party,[54] and thus render ineffective and pointless the whole Abolition movement of the North. The safety of our movement will be found only by a return to all the agencies and appliances, such as writing, publishing, organizing, lecturing, holding meetings, with the earnest aim not to prevent the extension of slavery, but to abolish the system altogether. Congress should be at once memorialized for the abolition of slavery in the District of Columbia, and the slave trade between the States. The same zeal, activity, energy and earnestness should be displayed in circulating petitions, as in the earlier stages of the movement. We have the pen, voice and influence of only one man, and that man of the most limited class; but with few or many, in whatever vicissitudes which may surround the cause, now or hereafter, we shall join in no cry, and unite in no demand less than the complete and universal *abolition* of the whole slave system. Slavery shall be destroyed.

Douglass' Monthly, December, 1860

EQUAL SUFFRAGE DEFEATED

The late election, so far as the State of New York is concerned, has features of discouragement, as well as the opposite. The disposition made of the question of Equal Suffrage[55] was inconsistent with every profession and principle of the triumphant party, and must surprise the enemies of equal rights as much as it certainly disappoints the expectations of colored citizens, who supposed that this constitutional brand of inferiority (by which colored men must have two hundred and fifty dollars of real property before they can vote, while all others vote on their simple manhood) would be erased from the organic law, which it has so long disgraced, simultaneously with the triumph of the great Republican party. All parties had reason to believe this would be done, if the State were not carried for Fusion or the slavery party. It would have been done had faith in its principles equalled the declarations of the members of the Republican party. They professed to believe in the Declaration of American Independence, and inserted the fundamental principle of equality which it contains, into their platform of principles at Chicago, but deserted that principle at the first moment they were called upon to give it life and form in the fundamental law of the State.—Had the Republican party been as true to the sacred cause of liberty and equality, as the Democratic party always proves itself to slavery and oppression, the invidious and odious discrimination against our equal citizenship would have been blotted out, and the colored voters of the State would have had some reason for the enthusiasm with which they have shouted their praises of the Republican party. While the Democrats at the polls never failed to accompany their State and national tickets with one against the proposed amendment, Republicans—many of them—refused to touch a ticket in favor of the amendment, and this, too, while white men, native and foreign, were brought to the polls so drunk, that they needed support on both sides while depositing their votes, and whose only political principle seemed to be injustice to the Negro. We know whereof we affirm, for we stood at the polls all day, doing our best for Equal Suffrage.

The moral effect of this defeat of justice and equality will be to fix more deeply in the public mind the popular contempt and scorn with which the rights and feelings of colored citizens are regarded, and invite their brutal manifestations wherever the colored man appears. For when men degrade and oppress the weak, every act of that character tends to strengthen the malignant motive which incites to such action. The vote on the property qualification is in its nature a re-affirmation of the slavery-engendered contempt for the rights of black men, and is a fresh license to all who are mean enough (and their name is legion) to insult the man of color wherever they meet him. They are men who are brave enough to trip up a man on crutches, push a blind man off the side-walk, or flog a man when his hands are tied, but too base and cowardly to contend with one who has an equal chance of defense with themselves. The black man, excluded alike from the jury box and the ballot box, is at the mercy of his enemies. The blow is a heavy and damaging one.—Every intelligent colored man must feel it keenly. It was given without any rational cause. No decent man could assign a motive for his vote against us, without casting his eyes to the ground, or looking up with a blush of mingled shame and malignity. Not even the desire to stand well with the South could be pleaded. All knew that the election of Lincoln would destroy all the conciliating power which this new injustice to the Negro might exert in that quarter, so that even this base and contemptible motive could not be pleaded. No, it was an act of unmitigated pride and prejudice, intended to depress and degrade a class which, of all others in the State, need the ballot box as a means of self-elevation and popular regard. Had the colored people been a large and powerful body in the State, it might, with some show of reason, been contended that they would become controlling if allowed to vote on equal terms with others; but any pretense of this kind would have stamped the objector as a fool. Everybody knew that the scattered colored population of the State, voting wherever their interest or conscience might lead, would in no wise affect harmfully the policy of the State. We do not even wring from this vote the poor consolation that anybody was afraid of our influence or power. The victory over us is simply one of blind ignorance and prejudice, hardly less destitute of manly intelligence than the kick of an ass. It was the vote of drunken Irishmen, and ignorant Dutchmen, controlled by sham Democrats, whose Democracy consists not in equal and exact justice to all, but in the right of brute power to trample upon the weak and defenceless. We saw the kind of men by whom the deed was done in Rochester. They were the tools of the Negro-hating Democracy of this city, many of whom would sell their votes for a glass of whiskey. It is impossible to feel degraded by injustice from such a quarter.

But what will the colored people and their friends do now that the day has gone against them? Will the question of Equal Suffrage be allowed to sleep? We trust not. Our opponents need hope for no such thing. Our cause is just, wise, and proper, and must not be dropped. We are defeated rather by the supineness of our friends, than by the strength and activity of our enemies. We were overshadowed and smothered by the Presidential struggle—over laid by Abraham Lincoln and Hannibal Hamlin. The black baby of Negro Suffrage was thought too ugly to exhibit on so grand an occasion. The Negro was stowed away like some people put out of sight their deformed children when company comes. We were told by some of our Republican friends to keep still—make no noise— they would do the work. Now, the fox is out of the well, and the goat is in it. Cunning dogs, you are not done with us yet. We are going to follow you as the woman followed the unjust judge. You must and will eventually settle this question, and all others in respect to the colored people of this State, in harmony with the great principles at the basis of the American Government—the professed principles of the great Republican party of the State and nation.

Douglass' Monthly, December, 1860

SPEECH ON JOHN BROWN, delivered in Tremont Temple, Boston, December, 1860

Mr. President, Ladies and Gentlemen:—I occupied considerable attention this morning, and I do not feel called upon to take up much of the time this evening. There are other gentlemen here from whom I desire to hear, and to whom, I doubt not, you wish to listen.

This is a meeting to discuss the best method of abolishing slavery, and each speaker is expected to present what he regards as the best way of prosecuting the anti-slavery movement. From my heart of hearts I endorse the sentiment expressed by Mr. Phillips, of approval of all methods of proceeding against slavery, politics, religion, peace, war, Bible, Constitution, disunion, Union—[laughter]—every possible way known in opposition to slavery is my way. But the moral and social means of opposing slavery have had a greater prominence, during the last twenty-five years, than the way indicated by the celebration of this day—I mean the John Brown way. That is a recent way of opposing slavery; and I think, since it is in consequence of this peculiar mode of advocating the abolition of slavery that we have had a mob in Boston today,[56] it may be well for me to occupy the few moments I have in advocating John Brown's way of accomplishing our object. [Applause]

Sir, we have seen the number of slaves increase from half a million to four millions.—We have seen, for the last sixty years, more or less of resistance to slavery in the U. S. As early as the beginning of the U. S. Government, there were abolition societies in the land. There were abolition societies in Virginia, abolition societies in Maryland, abolition societies in South Carolina, abolition societies in Pennsylvania. These societies appealed to the sense of justice, appealed to humanity, in behalf of the slave. They appealed to the magnanimity of the slaveholders and the nation; they appealed to the Christianity of the South and of the nation, in behalf of the slave. Pictures of slavery were presented.—The ten thousand enormities daily occurring in the Southern States were held up—men sold on the auction-block—women scourged with a heavy lash—men tied to the stake and deliberately burned, the blood gushing from their nose and eyes, asking rather to be shot than to be murdered by such slow torture. The facts of these charges have been flung before the public by ten thousand eloquent lips, and by more than ten thousand eloquent pens.—The humanity, the common human nature of the country has been again and again appealed to. Four millions have bowed before this nation, and with uplifted hands to Heaven and to you, have asked, in the name of God, and in the name of humanity, to break our chains! To this hour, however, the nation is dumb and indifferent to these cries for deliverance, coming up from the South; and instead of the slaveholders becoming softened, becoming more disposed to listen to the claims of justice and humanity—instead of being more and more disposed to listen to the suggestions of reason, they have become madder and madder, and with every attempt to rescue the bond-man from the clutch of his enslaver, his grip has become tighter and tighter, his conscience more and more callous. He has become harder and harder, with every appeal made to his sense of justice, with every appeal made to his humanity, until at length he has come even to con-front the world with the pretension that to rob a man of his liberty, to pocket his wages, or to pocket the fruits of his labor without giving him compensation for his work, is not only right according to the law of nature and the laws of the land, but that it is right and just in sight of the living God. Doctors of Divinity—the Stuarts and the Lords, the Springs, the Blagdens, the Adamses, and ten thousand others all over the country—have come out in open defense of the slave system. Not only is this the case, but the very submission of the slave to his chains is held as an evidence of his fitness to be a slave; it is regarded as one of the strong-est proofs of the divinity of slavery, that the Negro tamely submits to his fetters. His very non resistance—what would be here regarded a Christian virtue—is quoted in proof of his cowardice, and his unwillingness to suffer and to sacrifice for his liberty.

Now what remains? What remains? Sir, it is possible for men to trample on justice and liberty so long as to become entirely oblivious of the principles of justice and liberty. It is possible for men so far to trans-gress the laws of justice as to cease to have any sense of justice. What is to be done in that case?—You meet a man on the sidewalk, in the morn-ing, and you give him the way. He thanks you for it. You meet him again, and you give him the way, and he may thank you for it, but with a little less emphasis than at first. Meet him again, and give him the way, and he almost forgets to thank you for it. Meet him again, and give him the way, and he comes to think that you are conscious either of your in-feriority or of his superiority; and he begins to claim the inside of the walk as his right.—This is human nature; this is the nature of the slave-holders. Now, something must be done to make these slaveholders feel the injustice of their course. We must, as John Brown, Jr.—thank God that he lives and is with us to-night! [applause]—we must, as John Brown, Jr., has taught us this evening, reach the slaveholder's conscience through his fear of personal danger. We must make him feel that there is death in the air about him, that there is death in the pot before him, that there is death all around him. We must do this in some way. It can be done. When you have a good horse, a kind and gentle horse, a horse that your wife can drive, you are disposed to keep him—you wouldn't take any money for that horse. But when you have one that at the first pull of the reins takes the bit in his teeth, kicks up behind, and knocks off the dasher-board, you generally want to get rid of that horse. [Laughter.]— The Negroes of the South must do this; they must make these slaveholders feel that there is something uncomfortable about slavery—must make them feel that it is not so pleasant, after all, to go to bed with bowie-knives, and revolvers, and pistols, as they must. This can be done, and will be done—[cheers]—yes, I say, *will* be done. Let not, however, these suggestions of mine be construed into the slightest disparagement of the various other efforts, political and moral.

I believe in agitation; and it was largely this belief which brought me five hundred miles from my home to attend this meeting. I am sorry— not for the part I humbly took in the meeting this morning—but I am sorry that Mr. Phillips was not there to look that Fay in the face. ["Hear!"] I believe that he, and a few Abolitionists like him in the city of Boston, well-known, honorable men, esteemed among their fellow-citizens—had they been there to help us take the initiatory steps in the organization of that meeting, we might, perhaps, have been broken up, but it would have been a greater struggle, certainly, than that which it cost to break up the meeting this morning. [Applause.]

I say, sir, that I want the slaveholders to be made uncomfortable. Every slave that escapes helps to add to their discomfort. I rejoice in every uprising at the South. Although the men may be shot down, they may be butchered upon the spot, the blow tells, notwithstanding, and cannot but tell. Slaveholders sleep more uneasily than they used to. They are more careful to know that the doors are locked than they formerly were. They are more careful to know that their bowie-knives are sharp; they are more careful to know that their pistols are loaded. This element will play its part in the abolition of slavery. I know that all hope of a general insurrection is vain. We do not need a general insurrection to bring about this result. We only need the fact to be known in the Southern States generally, that there is liberty in yonder mountains, planted by John

Brown. [Cheers.]—The slaveholders have but to know, and they do now know, but will be made to know it even more certainly before long—that from the Alleghanies, from the State of Pennsylvania, there is a vast broken country extending clear down into the very heart of Alabama—mountains flung there by the hand and the providence of God for the protection of liberty—[cheers]—mountains where there are rocks, and ravines, and fastnesses, dens and caves, ten thousand Sebastopols piled up by the hand of the living God, where one man for defense will be as good as a hundred for attack. There let them learn that there are men hid in those fastnesses, who will sally out upon them and conduct their slaves from the chains and fetters in which they are now bound, to breathe the free air of liberty upon those mountains. Let, I say, only a thousand men be scattered in those hills, and slavery is dead. It cannot live in the presence of such a danger. Such a state of things would put an end to planting cotton; it would put an end not only to planting cotton, but to planting anything in that region.

Something is said about the dissolution of the Union under Mr. Lincoln or under Mr. Buchanan. I am for a dissolution of the Union —decidedly for a dissolution of the Union! Under an abolition President, who would wield the army and the navy of the Government for the abolition of slavery, I should be for the union of these States. If this Union is dissolved, I see many ways in which slavery may be attacked by force, but very few in which it could be attacked by moral means. I see that the moment you dissolve the union between the South and the North, the slave part going by itself and doing so peaceably—as the cry is from the *Tribune* and the Albany *Evening Journal,* and other such papers, that it shall do[57]—establishing an independent government—that very moment the feeling of responsibility for slavery in the North is at an end. But men will tell us to mind our own business. We shall care no more for slavery in the Carolinas or in Georgia than we care for kingcraft or priestcraft in Canada, or slavery in the Brazils or in Cuba. My opinion is that if we only had an anti-slavery President, if we only had an abolition President to hold these men in the Union, and execute the declared provisions of the Constitution, execute that part of the Constitution which is in favor of liberty, as well as put upon those passages which have been construed in favor of slavery, a construction different from that and more in harmony with the principles of eternal justice that lie at the foundation of the government—if we could have such a government, a government that would force the South to behave herself, under those circumstances I should be for the continuance of the Union. If, on the contrary—no *if* about it—we have what we have, I shall be glad of the news, come when it will, that the slave States are an independent government, and that you are no longer called upon to deliver fugitive slaves to their masters, and that you are no longer called upon to shoulder your arms and guard with your swords those States—no longer called to go into them to put down John Brown, or anybody else who may strike for liberty there.—[Applause.] In case of such a dissolution, I believe that men could be found at least as brave as Walker, and more skillful than any other filibusterer, who would venture into those States and raise the standard of liberty there, and have ten thousand and more hearts at the North beating in sympathy with them. I believe a Garibaldi would arise who would march into those States with a thousand men, and summon to his standard sixty thousand, if necessary, to accomplish the freedom of the slave. [Cheers.]

We need not only to appeal to the moral sense of these slaveholders; we have need, and a right, to appeal to their fears. Sir, moral means are good, but we need something else. Moral means were very little to poor John Thomas on the banks of the Wilkesbarre river, in Pennsylvania, when the slave-catchers called upon him to provide them with a breakfast at the hotel, that while in the act of serving them with their beef-steak they might fall upon him and return him to slavery.—They did fall upon him; they struck him down; but, recovering himself, he ran and plunged into the Wilkesbarre. There he stood, up to his shoulders, and the slave-catchers gathered on the banks—and the moral suasion people of that vicinity gathered also on the banks—they looked indignantly on the slave-catchers. But the slave-catchers did not heed the cries of indignation and shame; they fired their revolvers until the river about that man was red with his blood, and no hand was lifted to strike down those assassins.— They went off, indeed, without their victim, but they supposed he was dead. Sir, what was wanted at that time was just what John Brown, Jr., has told us to-night—a few resolute men, determined to be free, and to free others, resolved, when men were being shot, to shoot again. Had a few balls there whistled, as at Christiana, about the heads of the slave-catchers, it would have been the end of this slave-catching business there. There is no necessity of permitting it. The only way to make the Fugitive Slave Law a dead letter is to make a few dead slave-catchers. [Laughter and applause.] There is no need to kill them either—shoot them in the legs, and send them to the South living epistles of the free gospel preached here at the North. [Renewed laughter.]

But, Sir, I am occupying too much time.—["Go on!" Go on!"] I see a friend on my right, whose voice to-night I have not heard for many years. These troublous times in which we live, and have been living for a few years past, make that voice doubly dear to me on this occasion; and I seize this occasion, as the first that has happened to me in at least six to eight years, to say that I rejoice, most heartily rejoice, in the privilege— for a privilege I esteem it—not only of hearing Mr. Phillips's voice, but of standing on a platform with him in vindication of free speech. [Applause.] But I hope to speak in Boston on Friday. I, therefore, will not prolong my remarks further. I thank you for this hearing. [Applause.]

Douglass' Monthly, January, 1861

A PLEA FOR FREE SPEECH IN BOSTON, delivered in Music Hall, Boston, Massachusetts, December 10, 1860

Boston is a great city and Music Hall has a fame almost as extensive as Boston. Nowhere more than here have the principles of human free-dom been expounded. But for the circumstances already mentioned, it would seem almost presumptuous for me to say anything here about these principles. And yet, even here, in Boston, the moral atmosphere is dark and heavy. The principles of human liberty, even if correctly appre-hended, find but limited support in this hour of trial. The world moves slowly, and Boston is much like the world. We thought the principle of free speech was an accomplished fact. Here, if nowhere else, we thought the right of the people to assemble and to express their opinion was se-cure. Dr. Channing had defended the right, Mr. Garrison had practically asserted the right, and Theodore Parker had maintained it with steadiness and fidelity to the last.

But here we are to-day contending for what we thought was gained years ago. The mortifying and disgraceful fact stares us in the face, that though Faneuil Hall and Bunker Hill monument stand, freedom of speech is struck down. No lengthy detail of facts is needed. They are already notorious; far more so than will be wished ten years hence.

The world knows that last Monday a meeting assembled to discuss the question: "How shall Slavery be Abolished?" The world also knows that that meeting was invaded, insulted, captured by a mob of gentlemen, and thereafter broken up and dispersed by the order of the mayor, who refused to protect it, though called upon to do so. If this had been a mere outbreak of passion and prejudice among the baser sort, maddened by rum and hounded on by some wily politician to serve some immediate purpose,—a mere exceptional affair,—it might be allowed to rest with what has already been said. But the leaders of the mob were gentlemen. They were men who pride themselves upon their respect for law and order.

These gentlemen brought their respect for the law with them and proclaimed it loudly while in the very act of breaking the law. Theirs was the law of slavery. The law of free speech and the law for the protection of public meetings they trampled under foot, while they greatly magnified the law of slavery.

The scene was an instructive one. Men seldom see such a blending of the gentlemen with the rowdy, as was shown on that occasion. It proved that human nature is very much the same, whether in tarpaulin or broadcloth. Nevertheless, when gentlemen approach us in the character of lawless and abandoned loafers,—assuming for the moment their manners and tempers,—they have themselves to blame if they are estimated below their quality. No right was deemed by the fathers of the Government more sacred than the right of speech. It was in their eyes, as in the eyes of all thoughtful men, the great moral renovator of society and government. Daniel Webster called it a homebred right, a fireside privilege. Liberty is meaningless where the right to utter one's thoughts and opinions has ceased to exist. That, of all rights, is the dread of tyrants. It is the right which they first of all strike down. They know its power. Thrones, dominions, principalities, and powers, founded in injustice and wrong, are sure to tremble, if men are allowed to reason of righteousness, temperance, and of a judgment to come in their presence. Slavery cannot tolerate free speech. Five years of its exercise would banish the auction block and break every chain in the South. They will have none of it there, for they have the power. But shall it be so here?

Even here in Boston, and among the friends of freedom, we hear two voices: one denouncing the mob that broke up our meeting on Monday as a base and cowardly outrage; and another deprecating and regretting the holding of such a meeting, by such men, at such a time. We are told that the meeting was ill-timed, and the parties to it unwise.

Why, what is the matter with us? Are we going to palhate and excuse a palpable and flagrant outrage on the right of free speech, by implying that only a particular description of persons should exercise that right? Are we, at such a time, when a great principle has been struck down, to quench the moral indignation which the deed excites, by casting reflections upon those on whose persons the outrage has been committed? After all the arguments for liberty to which Boston has listened for more than a quarter of a century, has she yet to learn that the time to assert a right is the time when the right itself is called in question, and that the men of all others to assert it are the men to whom the right has been denied?

It would be no indication of the right of speech to prove that certain gentlemen of great distinction, eminent for their learning and ability, are allowed to freely express their opinions on all subjects—including the subject of slavery. Such a vindication would need, itself, to be vindicated. It would add insult to injury. Not even an old-fashioned abolition meeting could vindicate that right in Boston just now. There can be no right of speech where any man, however lifted up, or however humble, however young, or however old, is overawed by force and compelled to suppress their honest sentiments.

Equally clear is the right to hear. To suppress free speech is a double wrong. It violates the right of the hearer as well as those of the speaker. It is just as criminal to rob a man of his right to speak and hear as it would be to rob him of his money. I have no doubt that Boston will vindicate this right. But in order to do so, there must be no concessions to the enemy. When a man is allowed to speak because he is rich and powerful, it aggravates the crime of denying the right to the poor and humble.

The principle must rest upon its own proper basis. And until the right is accorded to the humblest as freely as to the most exalted citizen, the government of Boston is but an empty name, and its freedom a mockery. A man's right to speak does not depend upon where he was born or upon his color. The simple quality of manhood is the solid basis of the right—and there let it rest forever.

Liberator, December 14, 1860

Reference Notes
to Biography of Frederick Douglass

THE UNIVERSAL REFORMER

1. *The North Star,* July 14, 1848.
2. *Ibid.,* Mar. 10, 1848. Douglass attended the Woman's State Temperance Convention in 1852 at Rochester and joined in the discussion. (See *The Lily,* May, 1852, especially p. 42.) In May, 1853, he was present at the organizational meeting of the New York State Woman's Temperance Society, and "closed the affair in the happiest manner." (*The Una,* June 1, 1853, p. 75.)
3. *The North Star,* July 14, 1848; Jan. 26, 1849.
4. *The North Star,* Nov. 9, 1849; *Frederick Douglass' Paper,* Aug. 15, 1856.
5. *The North Star,* Apr. 7, 1849.
6. *Liberator,* Oct. 22, 1858; Rochester *Daily American,* Oct. 5-6, 1858.
7. Lucy N. Colman in *Liberator,* Oct. 22, 1858.
   Douglass declared that capital punishment "instead of repressing and preventing the horrid crime of murder ... really serves by shocking and blunting the finer and better feelings of human nature, to undermine respect for human life, and leads directly to the perpetuation of the crime which it would extinguish." It was necessary, went the resolutions, to develop the criminal's "higher nature," hence Douglass called for "a thorough reform in our criminal laws—basing them on the truly Christian principle of love and good will towards man—and to reject forever the cold blooded and barbarous principle of retaliation." (*Liberator,* Oct. 22, 1858.)
8. *The North Star,* Mar. 9, 1849.
9. Elizabeth Cady Stanton, Susan B. Anthony, Mathilda Joslyn Gage, editors, *History of Woman Suffrage,* New York, 1881, vol. I, pp. 70-71.
10. *The Woman's Journal,* Apr. 14, 1888, p. 116; Stanton, Anthony, Gage, *op. cit.,* vol. I, p. 73.
    Years later a tablet was erected commemorating the occasion. It read:
    > On this spot stood the Wesleyan Chapel
    > Where the first Woman's Rights Convention
    > in the World's History was held
    > July 19 and 20, 1848
    > Elizabeth Cady Stanton
    > moved this resolution
    > which was seconded by Frederick Douglass
    > That it was the duty of the women
    > of this country to secure to themselves
    > their sacred right
    > to the elective franchise.
11. *The Woman's Journal,* Apr. 14, 1888.

12. Stanton, Anthony, Gage, *op. cit.*, vol. I, p. 86; *The North Star*, Aug. 11, 1848. Mrs. Stanton and Lucretia Mott had proposed Douglass as the chairman of the meeting, but the women of Rochester had opposed the suggestion and elected Abigail Bush, a local resident, to the office.

13. Harriet Jane Robinson, *Massachusetts in the Woman Suffrage Movement*, Boston, 1881, p. 25. The Rochester *Daily American* of Dec. 16, 1850, referred to the "She-Socialists" who had been prominent in the convention.

14. Susan B. Anthony to Gerrit Smith, Dec. 25, 1855, Gerrit Smith Papers, Syracuse University; *Frederick Douglass' Paper*, Oct. 30, 1851; Douglass to Gerrit Smith, June 14, 1853, Gerrit Smith Papers, Syracuse University.

15. Lucretia Mott to Elizabeth Cady Stanton, Oct. 3, 1848, Elizabeth Cady Stanton Papers, Library of Congress.

16. Douglass to Gerrit Smith, July 15, 1853, Gerrit Smith Papers, Syracuse University.

17. *Douglass' Monthly*, Nov., 1860; S. S. Foster to Gerrit Smith, Aug. 25, 1860.

DOUGLASS AND THE NEGRO CONVENTION MOVEMENT

1. "Public Warning to Cincinnati Negroes and commentary on their reaction," *Journal of Negro History*, vol. VIII, July, 1923, pp. 331-32.

2. Eighteen delegates were from Pennsylvania, four from New York, one from Connecticut, two from Rhode Island, seven from Maryland, three from Delaware, three from Virginia, and one each from New Jersey and Ohio.

3. Sixteen delegates met in Philadelphia in June, 1831; 29 delegates met again in Philadelphia in June, 1832; 56 delegates convened in Philadelphia in June, 1833; 40 delegates from seven states met in New York City in June, 1834; the 1835 convention met in June in Philadelphia, and the next national convention met in June, 1836, in New York City.

4. Bella Gross, *Clarion Call: The History and Development of the Negro Convention Movement in the United States from 1817 to 1840*, New York, 1947, pp. 40-41.

5. *Journal of Negro History*, vol. I, July, 1916, pp. 323-38.

6. *Minutes of the National Convention of Colored Citizens, Buffalo, New York, August, 1843*, pp. 8, 10, 13-15; W. M. Brewer, "Henry Highland Garnet," *Journal of Negro History*, vol. XIII, Jan., 1928, pp. 44-46.

7. *Minutes of the National Convention of Colored Citizens, Buffalo, New York, August, 1843*, pp. 24, 37-39; *Herald of Freedom*, (Concord) Sept. 1, 1943.

8. *Proceedings of the National Convention of Colored People, And their Friends held in Troy, N. Y. . . . October, 1847*, pp. 31-32. Other members of the committee on Abolition who signed the report were Alexander Crummel, John Lyle, and Thomas Van Rensselaer.

9. Zita Dyson, "Gerrit Smith's Efforts in behalf of the Negroes in New York," *Journal of Negro History*, vol. III, Oct., 1918, pp. 354-59.

10. *The North Star*, Jan. 14, 1848. The Committee on a National Press consisted of J. McCune Smith, G. B. Wilson, and Wm. H. Topp.

11. *Proceedings of the National Convention of Colored People, And their Friends held in Troy, N. Y. . . . October, 1847*, pp. 7-8.

12. *The North Star*, Jan. 14, 1848.

13. *The North Star*, Sept. 19, 1848; *Liberator*, Oct. 20, 1848.

14. *Report of Proceedings of Colored National Convention, Held at Cleveland, Ohio, on Wednesday, September 6, 1848,* Rochester, 1848, pp. 8, 12.

15. Cleveland *True Democrat,* Sept. 11, 1848; Gerrit Smith to Chas. B. Ray, Nov. 11, 1848, *Model Worker,* Dec. 29, 1848, reprinted in leaflet form, the Gerrit Smith Papers, Syracuse University.

16. *The North Star,* Aug. 17, 1849.

17. *Anti-Slavery Bugle,* Aug. 18, 1849. For a British reaction to the plan, see *London Inquirer,* reprinted in *The North Star,* Nov. 23, 1849.

18. W.R.G. to Douglass, Nov. 4, 1849, in *The North Star,* Nov. 16, 1849.
    Douglass wrote bitterly in *The North Star* of Oct. 26, 1849: "*The Impartial Citizen,* edited by a colored man, did not even notice it. *The Ram's Horn,* has been dumb over it. Very few of our public men have, as yet, given to the idea the slightest encouragement."

19. "Many of the colored people, unfortunately, are bitter sectarians," commented the *Anti-Slavery Bugle* on Aug. 18, 1849, "and Mr. Garnet has done his worst to array this class in hostility to the eloquent Fugitive."
    Garnet also attacked Douglass for having told the Negro people that "we have no country." Douglass replied: "In making the declaration, we meant only to exhibit forcibly the glaring fact that the colored man is denied the rights and privileges of an American citizen, by the American government; and that, in this respect, he is an outlaw in the land. . . . If any colored man wants to know whether he has a country, let him go to Charleston, South Carolina, under the protection of the American Constitution, and his country will be limited to a prison. That the colored people have a right to a country here, we have ever affirmed; and Mr. Garnet will never succeed in trying to make the colored people, nor any other enlightened people, believe the contrary." (*The North Star,* Aug. 17, 1849.)

20. *The North Star,* Oct. 26, Nov. 19, 1849.

21. Fred Landon, "The Negro Migration to Canada after 1850," *Journal of Negro History,* vol. V, Jan., 1920, p. 22.

22. *Proceedings of the Colored National Convention Held in Rochester, July, 1853.* Although written by Douglass, the "Address" was also signed by J. M. Whitfield, H. O. Wagoner, Rev. A. N. Freeman, and George B. Vashon.

23. *New York Tribune,* July 9, 1853.

24. *Minutes and Proceedings of the First Annual Convention of the People of Colour,* . . . Philadelphia, 1831, pp. 6-9; *Liberator,* Aug. 20, Nov. 26, Dec. 3, 1831, Jan. 12, July 6, 1833.

25. *Liberator,* May 11, June 15, 1833.

26. See Charles L. Reason, "The Colored People's Industrial College: What Some of the Builders have Thought," *Autographs for Freedom,* Rochester, 1854, pp. 13-15.

27. *Frederick Douglass' Paper,* Mar. 4, 1853.

28. Douglass to Harriet Beecher Stowe, Mar. 8, 1853, *Proceedings of the Colored National Convention Held in Rochester, July 6th, 7th and 8th, 1853,* Rochester, 1853, pp. 33-38.
    In July, 1851, after she had published five installments of *Uncle Tom's Cabin* in the *National Era,* Harriet Beecher Stowe wrote to Douglass asking him to assist her in gathering information about life on a cotton plantation which she could use in her novel. The main part of her letter was devoted to a long

defense of the church against the charge of many Abolitionists, Douglass among them, that it was pro-slavery. We do not know if Douglass answered the letter. (See Charles Edward Stowe, *The Life of Harriet Beecher Stowe*, Boston and New York, 1890, pp. 149-53.)

29. *Proceedings of the Colored National Convention Held in Rochester, July, 1853,* pp. 17-22.

30. *New York Tribune,* July 12, 1853.

31. Douglass to Gerrit Smith, July 15, 1853, Gerrit Smith Papers, Syracuse University; *Rochester Democrat,* reprinted in *Liberator,* July 22, 1853.

32. *Frederick Douglass' Paper,* Aug. 19, 1853, Oct. 2, 9, 16, 1853; *Chicago Tribune,* Oct. 5, 14, 1853.

33. *Frederick Douglass' Paper,* Aug. 19, 26, 1853. See also *Arguments, Pro and Con on the Call for a National Emigration Convention, to be held in Cleveland, Ohio, August, 1854, by Frederick Douglass, W. J. Watkins, and J. M. Whitfield.*

34. Louis R. Mehlinger, "The Attitude of the Free Negro Toward African Colonization," *Journal of Negro History,* vol. I, 1916, pp. 299-30.
    There were three groups at the emigration convention: one led by Martin R. Delaney favored going to the Niger Valley in Africa; another under J. M. Whitfield favored Central America, and James Theodore Holly of Canada sponsored the movement to Haiti. The leaders of the groups were commissioned to go to these countries to see what they could accomplish in carrying out their plans. Little of concrete value emerged from the enterprises.

35. *Frederick Douglass' Paper,* Jan. 2, 1854, carried the following announcement from the editor: "It is, however, but justice to say that our eminent and philanthropic friend, Mrs. Stowe, for reasons which she deems quite satisfactory, does not, at present, see fit to stand forth as the patron of the proposed institution. It is equally our duty to state that Mrs. Stowe desires the work to go forward in the hands of the National Convention."

36. "Communipaw" in *Frederick Douglass' Paper,* Jan. 9, 1854. The article was written by Dr. James McCune Smith; Douglass to Mrs. Tappan, Mar. 21, 1856, Douglass *Mss.,* Henry P. Slaughter Collection.

37. *Proceedings of the Colored Convention Held in Franklin Hall, Sixth Street, Below Arch, Philadelphia, October 16th, 17th and 18th, 1855,* Salem, New Jersey, 1856.

ANTI-SLAVERY ACTIVITY IN ROCHESTER

1. Douglass to Mrs. Tappan, Mar. 21, 1856, Douglass *Mss.,* Henry P. Slaughter Collection.

2. "Lecture No. 1 Delivered in Corinthian Hall, Rochester, N. Y., on Sunday Evening, Dec. 1st, 1850," *The North Star,* Dec. 5, 1850.

3. *Oration, . . . Delivered in Corinthian Hall, Rochester, July 5, 1852,* Rochester, 1852, p. 19.

4. Douglass to H. C. Warner, Esq., *The North Star,* Mar. 30, 1849. "No one," observed the *Liberator* in reprinting the letter, "who begins to read the following admirable and manly letter of Mr. Douglass, will fail to finish it." (*Liberator,* Oct. 6, 1848.)
   See also Dixon Wecter, editor, *The Love Letters of Mark Twain,* New York, 1949, p. 127.

5. *The North Star*, Nov. 9, 1849.

6. See E. O. Preston, Jr., "The Genesis of the Underground Railroad," *Journal of Negro History*, vol. XVIII, Apr., 1933, pp. 144-70; William Siebert, *The Underground Railroad*, New York, 1898.

7. *The North Star*, Dec. 3, 1847.

8. Horace McQuire, "Two Episodes of Anti-Slavery Days," *Publications of the Rochester Historical Society*, Rochester, N. Y., vol. IV, 1925, p. 219; Jane Marsh Parker, *Rochester*, Rochester, N. Y., 1884, pp. 257-58; Dorn, *op cit., p.* 79; Amy Post, "The Underground Railroad," in William Peck, editor, *Semicentennial History of Rochester*, Rochester, 1924, p. 458; Douglass to Anna H. Richardson, July 2, 1860, in William Still, *The Underground Railroad*, Philadelphia, 1872, p. 598.

9. *United States Statutes at Large*, vol. IX, p. 462; Marion Gleason McDouglass, *Fugitive Slaves*, Boston, 1891, pp. 87-90.

10. *The North Star*, Apr. 12, 1850.

11. *New York Tribune*, Aug. 23, 1850; *Anti-Slavery Standard*, Aug. 29, Sept. 5, 1850; *Syracuse Daily Standard*, Aug. 29, 1850.

12. Jane Marsh Parker, *Rochester*, p. 257; *Boston Atlas*, Oct. 15, 1850.

13. A. E. Dorn, in her study of the anti-slavery movement in Rochester, writes of the effects of the Fugitive Slave Act on the Negro population: "The character of the Negro population of Rochester changed considerably due to the passage of the new Fugitive Slave Law of 1850. Before 1850 there had been 114 members of the colored Baptist Church but after the law came into effect 112 of this number were forced to leave the town on account of this law. The fact that so many from this one group had to leave indicates that there must have been a large number of fugitives, who realized that they had to leave or be captured, and a great number who were simply afraid that they would be taken for fugitives because the law was so severe." ("A History of the Anti-Slavery Movement in Rochester and Vicinity," M.A. thesis, University of Buffalo, p. 77.)

14. *New York Herald*, Aug. 12, 1852; *Frederick Douglass' Paper*, June 9, 1854.

15. About thirty Negroes and two white men were arrested and charged with treason and with levying war against the government of the United States. The defense was conducted so brilliantly by John M. Read and Thaddeus Stevens that all the defendants were acquitted. (*The History of the Trial of Castner Hanway for Treason, by a Member of the Philadelphia Bar*, Philadelphia, 1852.)

16. The following hastily scribbled note sent by Douglass to Samuel D. Porter in Sept., 1851, probably refers to the three fugitives who had been involved in the Sadsbury affair: "There are three men now at my house who are in great peril. I am unwell, I need your advice. Please come at once." The note was signed "D.F." (Samuel D. Porter Papers, University of Rochester.)

17. Amy Hamner Croughton, "Anti-Slavery Days in Rochester," *Publications of the Rochester Historical Society*, Rochester, N. Y. vol. XV, 1936, pp. 133-34.

18. *Frederick Douglass' Paper*, Nov. 24, 1854. Douglass usually served as vice-president of the annual celebrations, with Smith as president.

19. *bid.*, May 27, 1852; *The Anti-Slavery Reporter*, July 1, 1858, pp. 167-68; *Douglass' Monthly*, May, 1859, Dec., 1861; William C. Nell to Garrison, Feb. 9, 1852, *Liberator*, Mar. 5, 1852.

20. Benjamin Quarles estimates that in ten years "Douglass personally helped approximately four hundred fugitives gain their freedom." ("The Public Life of Frederick Douglass," unpublished Ph.D. thesis, University of Wisconsin, 1938, p. 118.)

21. William C. Nell to Garrison, Feb. 19, 1852, *Liberator,* Mar. 5, 1852.

22. *Frederick Douglass' Paper,* May 19, 1854, June 19, 1857; *The Anti-Slavery Reporter,* July 1, 1858, p. 168; *Annual Report of the American Anti-Slavery Society, for the year Ending May 1, 1860,* New York, 1861, p. 49; *Douglass' Monthly,* June, 1860; Douglass to Anna H. Richardson, July 2, 1860, Still, *op cit.,* p. 598.

23. Dorn, *op. cit.,* p. 78.

24. *The Anti-Slavery Reporter,* July 1, 1858, p. 168.

25. Sarah H. Bradford, *Scenes in the Life of Harriet Tubman,* Auburn, New York, 1869, p. 233.
   In December, 1851, Harriet Tubman brought a party of eleven, including her brother and his wife, to Canada. Douglass may have met her on this occasion, for he wrote in his autobiography: "On one occasion, I had eleven fugitives at the same time under my roof." (*Life and Times of Frederick Douglass,* pp. 329-30; Earl Conrad, *Harriet Tubman,* Washington, 1943, pp. 45-46.)

26. *The North Star,* Oct. 26, 1849.

27. Douglass to S. D. Porter, Jan. 12, 1852, Samuel D. Porter Papers, University of Rochester.

THE SPLIT WITH THE GARRISONIANS

1. *Sixteenth Annual Report of the Massachusetts Anti-Slavery Society,* Boston, 1848, p. 42.

2. See *The North Star,* June 16, 1848, report of the New England Anti-Slavery Convention. In June, 1848 Douglass was elected vice-president of the New England Anti-Slavery Society.

3. Douglass to Oliver Johnson, *Anti-Slavery Bugle,* Oct. 6, 1849; *Liberator,* Nov. 26, 1841.

4. *The North Star,* Feb. 11, 1848. Douglass met Brown again late in 1848. He visited Springfield in October and November, 1848, and, after his return to Rochester "alluded prominently to his recent interview with Mr. John Brown of Springfield," in a speech to a group of Negro people. (*The North Star,* Nov. 17, 24, Dec. 8, 1848.)

5. *Life and Times of Frederick Douglass,* pp. 338-39. In this account Douglass states that the interview took place in 1847.

6. *Ibid.,* pp. 340-41; *The North Star,* Feb. 9, 1849; *Liberator,* June 8, 1849.

7. *The North Star,* Aug. 10, 1849; *Frederick Douglass' Paper,* Nov. 28, 1856; *Liberator,* July 27, 1860. *See also* William Chambers, *American Slavery and Colour,* New York, 1857, p. 174. For an analysis of militant abolitionism, see Herbert Aptheker, "Militant Abolitionism," *Journal of Negro History,* vol. XXVI, Oct., 1941, pp. 413-84.

8. *Liberator,* Nov. 26, Dec. 3, 1841; *Anti-Slavery Standard,* Feb. 24, 1842.

9. *The North Star,* Mar. 30, 1849.

10. *Report of a Public Meeting at Finsbury Chapel, Moorefields, to Receive Frederick Douglass . . .,* 1846, p. 6.

11. For a detailed analysis of Douglass' position on the Constitution and the Union, see his speeches, *The Constitution of the United States: Is it Pro-Slavery or Anti-Slavery*, Halifax, 1860, and *The Anti-Slavery Movement*, Rochester, 1855.

12. Douglass privately informed Stephen S. Foster and Samuel J. May of his new beliefs early in the spring of 1851. (Douglass to Gerrit Smith, May 21, 1851, Gerrit Smith Papers, Syracuse University.) In his letter to the *Liberator* of May 16, 1851, May wrote that Douglass' announcement of his changed sentiments was "not unexpected."

13. *The North Star*, May 15, 1851, reprinted in *Liberator*, May 23, 1851, and in *Frederick Douglass' Paper*, Dec. 9, 1853.

14. Douglass to Frederick May Holland, reprinted in *Open Court*, vol. IX, Mar. 7, 1895, p. 415; *The North Star*, May 15, 1851, reprinted in *Liberator*, May 23, 1851, and *Frederick Douglass' Paper*, Dec. 9, 1853.

15. Douglass to Gerrit Smith, May 21, 1851, Gerrit Smith Papers, Syracuse University; *Liberator*, July 4, 1851.

16. N. Farmer in *Liberator*, Jan. 2, 1852; *Frederick Douglass' Paper*, Feb. 5, 26, 1852.

17. Douglass to Gerrit Smith, May 15, 1852, Gerrit Smith Papers, Syracuse University; *Frederick Douglass' Paper*, May 20, 1852; Wendell Phillips to Elizabeth Pease, Dec. 4, 1852, *Anti-Slavery Letters*, Boston Public Library.

18. *Frederick Douglass' Paper*, Aug. 12, 1853.

19. *Ibid.*, Aug. 19, 1853. This issue contained a reprint of the original article which had appeared in the weekly three months before.

20. Robert Purvis to Garrison, Sept. 12, 1853, Anti-Slavery Letters to Garrison, Boston Public Library; William C. Nell to Garrison, Aug. 19, 1853, *Liberator*, Sept. 2, 1853. Nell claimed that Douglass refused to print one of his letters.

21. *Anti-Slavery Standard*, Sept. 3-24, 1853; *Liberator*, Sept. 2-16, Nov. 18, 1853.

22. Garrison to S. J. May, Sept. 23, 1853, Garrison *Mss.*, Boston Public Library. Douglass copied the idea for his paper, calling the column "Den of Villainy." In March, 1853, when he inaugurated the feature, he wrote: "The idea of such a department in our paper, is borrowed from one to whom we gladly acknowledge ourselves debtors for many others equally good, and that is to William Lloyd Garrison." (*Frederick Douglass' Paper*, Mar. 11, 1853.) Ironically enough, in a few months Douglass was to find himself quoted in Garrison's unique department.

23. J.T.C. in *Liberator*, Nov. 18, 1853.

24. *Liberator*, Nov. 18, 1853.

25. *Anti-Slavery Standard*, Sept. 24, 1853.

26. The question, however, had been privately discussed. In Jan., 1852, Samuel D. Porter had warned Douglass that Rochester was "full of scandalous reports" concerning his relations with Miss Griffiths. Douglass had emphatically denied that there was anything in these relations that should cause him to feel ashamed, and expressed resentment that his close friend had given even slight credence to the rumors. (Douglass to Samuel D. Porter, Jan. 12, 1852, Samuel D. Porter Papers, University of Rochester.)

27. *Liberator*, Dec. 2, 15, 1853. Garrison maintained that he "could bring a score of unimpeachable witnesses in Rochester" to prove his charge. *Liberator*, Dec. 17, 1853.

28. In reprinting these articles, Douglass wrote: "If I have not published, hereto-fore, the articles from the *Freeman, Standard* and *Liberator,* it was from the laudable wish to avoid a controversy which seemed to be pregnant only of mis-chief, and unwholly uncalled for.—From the beginning, however, I have de-signed to give my adversaries a fair hearing before my readers, whenever I should feel it worth while to reply to their lucubrations.—This intention is now fulfilled to the letter."

29. Oliver Johnson to Garrison, Dec. 10, 1853, Anti-Slavery Letters to Garrison, Boston Public Library.

30. *Report of a Public Meeting at Finsbury Chapel, Moorefields, to Receive Frederick Douglass . . .,* 1846, p. 14.

31. For a detailed picture of the split in the churches over slavery, see W. H. Sweet, *The American Churches and Slavery.*

32. William G. Allen to Gerrit Smith, London, Jan. 24, 1854, Gerrit Smith Papers, Syracuse University.

33. *Chicago Daily Tribune,* reprinted in *Frederick Douglass' Paper,* Jan. 13, 1854; *Frederick Douglass' Paper,* Dec. 30, 1853. See also James B. Vashon's letter to Douglass, Dec. 17, 1853, *Ibid.,* Jan. 13, 1854.

34. Susan B. Anthony to Garrison, Dec. 13, 1853, Anti-Slavery Letters to Garrison, Boston Public Library. The entire section of Miss Anthony's letter dealing with this question went: "We were all surprised & shocked at the appearance of Anna Douglass' letter in the Liberator. *Anna did* not to my certain knowledge, intend that letter to cover all the *essentials* of the Liberator's charge—for she declared to Amy Post, who happened to call there about the time it was con-cocted by Frederic & Julia; that she would *never* sign a paper that said, Julia had not *made her trouble.* Said she, *Garrison is right*—it is Julia *that has made* Frederic hate all his old friends—Said she, I don't care anything about her being in the *office*—but I won't have her in my house."

35. *Saturday Visitor,* reprinted in *Liberator,* Jan. 13, 1854; James B. Vashon to Douglass, Dec. 17, 1853, *Frederick Douglass' Paper,* Jan. 13, 1854

36. *Saturday Visitor,* reprinted in *Liberator,* Jan. 13, 1854.

37. Anti-Slavery Letters to Garrison, Boston Public Library.

38. Garrison to Samuel J. May, Mar. 21, Sept. 28, 1860; Garrison to his wife, Feb. 17, 1857; Garrison to Samuel J. May, Sept. [?], 1857, Garrison *Mss.,* Boston Public Library. Garrison was especially infuriated by Julia Griffiths' efforts to raise funds in England for Douglass' paper on the ground that he was "the Christian champion who is nobly battling our 'infidel' abolitionism." (Garrison to Samuel J. May, Mar. 21, 1856, Garrison *Mss.,* Boston Public Library.) For evidence on which Garrison's charge was based, see *The Anti-Slavery Reporter,* Apr. 1, 1857, pp. 80-82.

39. *The Constitution of the United States: Is it Pro-Slavery or Anti-Slavery,* Halifax, 1860, p. 3.

40. *Douglass' Monthly,* June, 1861.

41. *The Nation,* vol. LII, p. 391. Garrison's son was not nearly so generous to Douglass. In the same issue of *The Nation* (p. 388), he recalled the controversy between his father and the Negro leader and spoke of "Mr. Douglass' animus toward those to whom he owed everything but his native talent for oratory. . . ." It was precisely this attitude on the part of Garrison and a number of his

associates during the 'forties and 'fifties that had so much to do with provoking the controversy.

42. Douglass to Oliver Johnson, 1885, Douglass Papers, Frederick Douglass Memorial Home, Anacostia, D. C.

ANTI-SLAVERY POLITICAL ACTION

1. Negroes could vote in Maine, New Hampshire, Vermont, Massachusetts and Rhode Island, since there was nothing in the constitutions of these states which forbade colored people from exercising the suffrage. In New York, under the constitution adopted in 1821, a Negro had to own real estate worth two hundred and fifty dollars and had to be a citizen of the state for three years.

2. Charles H. Wesley, "The Participation of Negroes in Anti-Slavery Political Parties," *Journal of Negro History*, vol. XLII, 1945, pp. 39-45.

3. William Goodell, *Slavery and Anti-Slavery*, New York, 1853, p. 475.

4. Henry Wilson, *History of the Rise and Fall of the Slave Power in America*, vol. II, pp. 109-11; Wesley, *op cit.*, p. 51; *The North Star*, June 23, Aug. 4, 1848.

5. *The North Star*, July 7, 1848.

6. Quoted by T. C. Smith, *The Liberty and Free Soil Parties in the Northwest*, New York, 1897, pp. 126-28.

7. *The North Star*, June 16, July 21, 1848.

8. Wilson, *op. cit.*, vol. II, pp. 114-49. Douglass referred later to the convention as one of the most important events which led directly to emancipation. (*Life and Times of Frederick Douglass*, pp. 282-83.)

9. Oliver Dyer, *Phonographic Report of the Proceedings of the National Free Soil Convention at Buffalo, New York, August 9th and 10th, 1848*, New York, 1848, p. 21. Among those present at the convention were other Negro leaders such as Samuel R. Ward, Henry Highland Garnet, Charles L. Remond, and Henry Bibb. Douglass said there were "other colored gentlemen" also present. (*The North Star*, Aug. 11, 1848.)

10. *The North Star*, Aug. 18, 1848.

11. *The North Star*, Sept. 1, 29, 1848.

12. *Ibid.*, Aug. 18, Nov. 10, 1848.

13. "Campaign of 1848," *Free Soil Songs for the People*, Boston, 1848, front cover.

14. *Liberator*, Jan. 19, 1849.

15. Wesley, *op cit.*, p. 44.

16. T. C. Smith, *op. cit.*, pp. 160-61. Free Soil papers in the West cried: "Fight on! Work on and keep working."

17. Douglass to Gerrit Smith, May 15, 1851, Gerrit Smith Papers, Syracuse University.

18. Buffalo *Commercial Advertiser*, reprinted in *Frederick Douglass' Paper*, Oct. 30, 1851. See also Douglass to F. Gorton, B. E. Hecock, N. H. Gardner, etc. Oct., 1851), *Ibid.* In an appeal to the workingmen of the United States from the working classes of Glasgow there appeared the remark: "As a matter of self-interest, we conceive that any community within the Union who are unable to discern the representative powers of Frederick Douglass, are wholly at fault. In all earnestness our opinion of him is, that he would do honor to the most gifted legislative assembly in the world, and from such statement you may pos-

sibly draw your own conclusions as to what interests we would confide to his care, were it in our power to honor such an one with our suffrages either in matters municipal or parliamentary." (*The North Star*, Jan. 16, 1851.)

19. Douglass to Gerrit Smith, Feb. 19, 1852, Gerrit Smith Papers, Syracuse University; *Frederick Douglass' Paper*, Apr. 8, 1852.

20. Gerrit Smith Papers, Syracuse University.

21. *Frederick Douglass' Paper*, Aug. 20, 1852; Frederic May Holland, *Frederick Douglass*, pp. 210-12.

22. *New York Herald*, Aug. 12, 1852; *Frederick Douglass' Paper*, Aug. 20, 1852.

23. *The Anti-Slavery Reporter*, Oct., 1852, No. 1, p. 6.

24. *Frederick Douglass' Paper*, Aug. 20, Sept. 10, 1852.

25. Douglass to Gerrit Smith, Oct. 21, 1852, Gerrit Smith Papers, Syracuse University.
   Actually the candidates of the Liberty Party were William Goodell and S. M. Bell of Virginia. A committee of Liberty Party men had been appointed to ask Hale and Julian certain questions with the understanding that the party's support hinged on their answers. They asked whether a political party should regard itself as organized for the purpose of securing equal rights to all, and "whether you believe that slavery, so far as capable of legislation is a naked piracy, around which there can be no legal covering." Hale and Julian ignored the questions, so the Liberty Party met again in Syracuse on September 30 and made the nominations referred to above. Douglass was one of the vice-presidents of the convention, but he did not remove the names of Hale and Julian from the masthead of his paper.

26. *Liberator*, reprinted in *Frederick Douglass' Paper*, Nov. 19, 1852; Douglass to Samuel J. May[?], Nov. 10, 1852, Frederick Douglass *Mss.*, New York Historical Society; Douglass to Gerrit Smith, Nov. 6, 1852, Gerrit Smith Papers, Syracuse University.

27. Douglass to Gerrit Smith, Aug. 18, 1853, Gerrit Smith Papers, Syracuse University; *New York Tribune*, Aug. 19, 1854.

28. Douglass to Gerrit Smith, Aug. 22, 1854, Gerrit Smith Papers.

29. *New York Tribune, Massachusetts Spy, Cincinnati Commercial*, reprinted in *Frederick Douglass' Paper*, Aug. 4, 1854; *Syracuse Standard*, reprinted in *Liberator*, Aug. 25, 1854. See also *Liberator*, July 14, 1854.

30. *Philadelphia Argus* reprinted in *Frederick Douglass' Paper*, Aug. 4, 1854. The *Norfolk Daily News* commented: "The n——r statesmen of the North, we learn, are to be brought forward for Congress . . . if the presence of the Honorable Frederick Douglass in Washington will purge that noxious atmosphere of its poisons, chloride of lime will no longer be needed in the purlieu. . . ."

31. *Frederick Douglass' Paper*, Aug. 4, 1854.

32. *Ibid.*, Sept. 15, 1854; Frederic May Holland, *op. cit.*, pp. 233-37.

33. *Frederick Douglass' Paper*, July 27, 1855; Frederick Douglass, *The Anti-Slavery Movement*, Rochester, 1855, p. 35.

34. Douglass to Gerrit Smith, Mar. 27, 1855, Gerrit Smith Papers, Syracuse University; *The American Jubilee*, Apr., 1855; *Anti-Slavery Bugle*, reprinted in *The Anti-Slavery Advocate*, June, 1855, No. 33, p. 269.

35. *Proceedings of the Convention of Radical Political Abolitionists Held at Syracuse, N. Y., June 26, 27, and 28, 1855*, New York, 1855. Copy in Library of Congress.

36. Douglass to Gerrit Smith, Aug. 14, 1855, Gerrit Smith Papers, Syracuse University; *New York Herald*, Sept. 13, 17, 27, 1855; *D.A.S. Alexander, A Political History of the State of New York*, New York, 1906, vol. II, p. 216.

37. *Radical Abolitionist*, Dec., 1855 (copy in library of Cornell University); *Frederick Douglass' Paper*, Nov. 16, 1855.
   Gerrit Smith was the chief sponsor of the Radical Abolitionist Party as he was of the Liberty Party. He financed its organs, *The American Jubilee* which was published in March and April, 1855, and *The Radical Abolitionist* which replaced it and appeared from August, 1855, to December, 1859.

38. *Frederick Douglass' Paper*, Apr. 25, 1856; *Radical Abolitionist*, Apr., 1856.

39. Garrison to Samuel J. May, Mar. 21, 1856, Garrison *Mss.*, Boston Public Library. Garrison expressed pity for Smith. "It is really sad to see so good a man as Gerrit Smith befooled in this manner," he added in his letter to May.

40. *Radical Abolitionist*, July, 1856. While in Syracuse Douglass also addressed the Republican State Convention and made the same point. "You are called Black Republicans," he declared. "What right have you to that name. Among all the candidates you have selected, or talked of, I haven't seen or heard a single black one." *Syracuse Daily Standard*, May 29, 1856.

41. Wesley, *op. cit.*, pp. 70-71; *New York Morning Express*, May 30, 1856. James A. Woodburn, in his *Political Parties and Party Problems in the United States*, states that the Radical Abolitionists "nominated Gerrit Smith for president and Frederick Douglass for vice-president." (New York, 1924, p. 249.) James Ford Rhodes also makes this statement. (*History of the United States*, New York, 1900, vol. II, p. 186n.) Both base it on the report in the *New York Herald*.

42. The Liberty Party and the Radical Abolition Party were scheduled to meet together in Syracuse on September 17. Douglass looked forward to the meeting hoping they would definitely fuse. On August 8 he wrote in his paper that he was glad to see that "the radical friends of the slave 'still live'; that they are determined to carry their convictions of the utter unlawfulness and sinfulness of Slavery to the ballot-box." "The issue presented by the Republicans, for the restriction of the evil is too narrow," he added. (*Frederick Douglass' Paper*, Aug. 8, 1856, reprinted in *Liberator*, Sept. 5, 1856.)

43. *Frederick Douglass' Paper*, June 20, 1856, reprinted in *Liberator*, Sept. 5, 1856; *Frederick Douglass' Paper*, Aug. 15, 1856.

44. See the editorials "The Republican Party," "A Brief Response To Our Assailants," "Can An Abolitionist vote for Fremont," "To Colored Voters," "The Present Hour and Our Duty," *Frederick Douglass' Paper*, Aug. 29, Sept. 12, Oct. 3, 24, 1856.

45. Douglass to Gerrit Smith, Apr. 30, 1847, Gerrit Smith Papers, Syracuse University.

46. "No, my Dear Sir," he wrote to Smith on Dec. 16, 1856, "I am not a member of the Republican Party. I am still a radical Abolitionist." (Gerrit Smith Papers, Syracuse University.)

47. *Radical Abolitionist*, Oct., 1857.

48. A report in the *Gerrit Smith Banner*, a publication issued during the campaign, reveals some of the enthusiasm of the radical Abolitionists: "Already the 'Gerrit Smith movement' is producing a great commotion among the class who make politics a trade. Their craft is in danger." (*Gerrit Smith Banner*, Oct. 18, 1858.)

49. Henry Highland Garnet to Gerrit Smith, Sept. 10, 1858, Gerrit Smith Papers, Syracuse University; *Frederick Douglass' Paper*, July 8, 1859. (Copy in Wisconsin State Historical Society.)

DOUGLASS AND JOHN BROWN

1. Douglass delivered the lecture, "Self-Made Men," many times after 1859. The text quoted here is from a copy of the speech in the Rochester Public Library.
2. *John Brown—An Address by Frederick Douglass at the Fourteenth Anniversary of Storer College, Harper's Ferry, West Virginia*, May 30, 1881; *Life and Times of Frederick Douglass*, pp. 339-41.
   There is no discussion of Brown's relations with Douglass in the recent study by James C. Malin, *John Brown and the Legend of Fifty-Six*, published by the American Philosophical Society. In a letter to the writer, Feb. 6, 1947, Professor Malin writes: "You ask about Frederick Douglass. I did not find anything that struck me as particularly important which relates him to my field of investigation."
3. *Life and Times of Frederick Douglass*, p. 341.
4. On Nov. 15, 1856, Elizabeth Cady Stanton wrote that in December she expected to see Brown at Rochester where he would be "on a visit to Frederick Douglass." (T. Stanton and H. S. Blatch, *Elizabeth Cady Stanton*, New York, 1901, vol. II, p. 69.)
5. J. M. Parker, "Reminiscences of Frederick Douglass," *Outlook*, vol. LI, Apr. 6, 1895, p. 553; F. B. Sanborn, *The Life and Letters of John Brown*, Boston, 1885, p. 434. Brown probably stayed a little more than two weeks at Douglass' home. There are, however, conflicting reports on this question. Richard J. Hinton says he was at Douglass' home "for three weeks," and Douglass says he "remained for about a month." (Richard J. Hinton, *John Brown and His Men*, New York, 1899, p. 165; *Life and Times of Frederick Douglass*, p. 385.)
6. Douglass to John Brown, Feb. 27, 1858, Sanborn, *op. cit.*, pp. 443, 451-52.
7. John Brown's diary, Apr. 14, 1858, Ralph Volney Harlow, *Gerrit Smith*, New York, 1939, p. 339.
8. *New York Herald*, Oct. 27, 1859; Anonymous, "John Brown and His Friends," *Atlantic Monthly*, vol. XXX, July, 1872, pp. 50-61; *Life and Times of Frederick Douglass*, p. 387.
9. Franklin B. Sanborn, *Recollections of Seventy Years*, Boston, 1909, p. 138; *Atlantic Monthly*, vol. XXX, July, 1872, pp. 55ff. Douglass' daughter wrote to her father on Feb. 2, 1859, concerning Brown's exploits in running off slaves from Missouri: "Old Brown will have to keep out of sight for a little while. The Governor of Missouri has a reward of $3,000 for his capture." (Douglass Mss., Frederick Douglass Memorial Home, Anacostia, D. C.)
10. Horace McQuire, "Two Episodes of Anti-Slavery Days," *Publications of the Rochester Historical Society*, Rochester, N. Y., vol. IV, 1925, pp. 219-20.
11. On Aug. 9, 1867, Douglass wrote to Gerrit Smith: "I wish to say distinctly that John Brown never declared nor intimated to me that he was about to embark in a grand or unqualified insurrection; that the only insurrection he proposed was the escaping of slaves and their standing for their lives against any who should pursue them. For years before, Captain Brown's long entertained plan was to go to the mountains in the Slave States and invite the Slaves to flee there. . . . Three or four weeks previous to his invasion of Harper's Ferry Captain

Brown requested me to have an interview with him at Chambersburg, Pa. I did it and in this interview he had determined upon that invasion instead of carrying out his old plan of going into the mountains. . . . I do not suppose that any of his friends at the North knew of it." (Frederick Douglass *Mss.*, Frederick Douglass Memorial Home, Anacostia, D. C.) The last sentence would seem to indicate that Douglass was the first person outside of his band to whom Brown told his plan for attacking Harper's Ferry.

12. Sanborn, *Life and Letters of John Brown*, pp. 536-38; *Life and Times of Frederick Douglass*, p. 387. Douglass brought with him a letter to Brown containing twenty-five dollars from Mrs. J. N. Gloucester, a prosperous Negro woman in Brooklyn. (Sanborn, *Life and Letters of John Brown*, p. 538.)

13. *Life and Times of Frederick Douglass*, p. 390. Douglass' meeting with Brown lasted for three days. (Douglass to F. B. Sanborn, Apr. 15, 1885, Sanborn, *Life and Letters of John Brown*, p. 538.)

14. Sanborn, *Life and Letters of John Brown*, p. 541n. A copy of the letter to Douglass was found among the papers of John Brown captured at the farm Brown had rented early in the summer.

15. Sanborn, *Recollections of Seventy Years*, p. 153. Only a brief, unimportant letter from Brown to Douglass was found by Brown's captors. No other material involving Douglass was discovered among his papers at the farm.

16. Amy Hamner-Croughton, "Anti-Slavery Days in Rochester," *Publications of the Rochester Historical Society*, Rochester, N. Y., vol. XV, 1936, p. 143. Letters from Brown and a copy of the "Provisional Constitution" Brown had drawn up while at Douglass' home were in the desk. After the message was received they were removed.

17. Washington *Evening Star*, Feb. 21, 1895.

18. *New York Herald*, Oct. 20, 1859; *Liberator*, Dec. 23, 1859; Hamner-Croughton, *op. cit.*, p. 144.

19. *Life and Times of Frederick Douglass*, p. 379; *New York Herald*, Oct. 22, 1859.

20. See also Rochester *Democrat*, Oct. 26, 1859, and Rochester *Union*, Oct. 25, 1859, reprinted in *New York Herald*, Oct. 28, 1859.

21. *New York Herald*, Nov. 4, 1859.

22. As late as 1919 several of the surviving members of Brown's family, Henry Thompson, Salmon Brown, Annie Brown Adams, and Sarah Brown, told Oswald Garrison Villard that they had always believed that Douglass had failed "to live up to his obligations." (Oswald Garrison Villard, *John Brown*, New York, 1943, pp. 323, 627.)

23. Douglass to Rochester *Democrat*, reprinted in *New York Herald*, Nov. 4, 1859.

24. ". . . It is only truth to state," Douglass wrote in the Nov., 1859, issue of **his** monthly, "that for more than a year past I have been making arrangements **not** to go to Harper's Ferry, but to England."

25. Douglass to John C. Underwood, Nov. 14, 1866, John C. Underwood Collection, Library of Congress, Manuscript Division. Douglass to Elizabeth Keckly, Oct. 29, 1867, Elizabeth Keckley, *"Behind the Scenes or Thirty Years a Slave and Four Years in the White House,"* New York, 1886, p. 319.

26. *Douglass' Monthly*, Nov., 1859.

27. *Douglass' Monthly*, Dec., 1859.

28. Henry Wilson, *History of the Rise and Fall of the Slave Power in America,* vol. II, p. 606.

29. Douglass to James Redpath, June 29, 1860, *Liberator,* July 27, 1860.

THE EVE OF THE CIVIL WAR

1. *The Anti-Slavery Reporter,* Dec. 1, 1859, p. 276.

2. *The Anti-Slavery Advocate,* vol. II, No. 42, June 1, 1860, pp. 393-94.
Douglass entered into a heated debate with George Thompson over the interpretation of the Constitution of the United States as it related to the anti-slavery movement. See *Lecture on the Constitution of the United States by Mr. Thompson Delivered in the City Hall, Glasgow, February 27th, 1860, London Emancipation Committees Tracts, No. 5,* London, 1860; *Lecture by Mr. Douglass in Reply to Mr. Thompson, Delivered in the Queen's Rooms,* Glasgow, Mar. 26, 1860, and *Mr. Thompson's Rejoinder, A Lecture Delivered in the City Hall, Glasgow, April 3rd, 1860.* All the speeches were published in the Tract No. 5 issued by the London Emancipation Committee. A copy of the pamphlet is in the Boston Public Library.

3. Rosetta Douglass to Gerrit Smith, Apr. 11, 1860, Gerrit Smith Papers, Syracuse University; *Douglass' Monthly,* June, 1860, "To My British Anti-Slavery Friends." Douglass also had planned to visit France. After the American minister, Dallas, refused his application for a passport on the ground that he was not a citizen of the United States, the French minister at London granted Douglass a permit. Before he could cross the channel, the news arrived of his daughter's death. (See *Douglass' Monthly,* Sept., 1860; F. M. Holland, *Frederick Douglass,* p. 277.)

4. *Douglass Monthly,* June, 1860.

5. Another resolution adopted by the convention read: "*Resolved,* That for the Abolitionists to vote for a candidate like Abraham Lincoln, who stands ready to execute the accursed Fugitive Slave Law, to suppress insurrections among slaves, to admit new slave States, and to support the ostracism, socially and politically, of the black man of the North is to give the lie to their professions; to expose their hypocrisy to the world; and to do what they can, to put far off, the day of the slave's deliverance." (*The Principia,* Sept. 15, 1860; *Douglass' Monthly,* October, 1860.)

6. The initial meeting was held in Boston on May 29, 1860. Douglass was present and agreed to the calling of the second meeting. (*The Principia,* Sept. 15, 1860.)

7. Douglass to Elizabeth Cady Stanton, Aug. 25, 1860, Elizabeth Cady Stanton Papers, Library of Congress. Two weeks later, however, he wrote to Smith: "The more I think of the Worcester Convention the more [I] feel the importance of your attending it." (Douglass to Gerrit Smith, Sept. 7, 1860, Gerrit Smith Papers, Syracuse University.
Douglass' fears that a conflict would arise between himself and the Garrisonians were justified. George Howland, a Garrisonian, criticized Douglass in his report of the convention published in the *Liberator.* Douglass replied with a letter to the *Liberator* referring to Howland's "ill-mannered charge." He added an editorial to the discussion which closed: "The ranks of genuine Abolitionists—men who really desire to effect the abolition of slavery—are quite too *few* and *thin* to court strife or division among themselves. . . ." (*Douglass' Monthly,* Nov., 1860.)

8. *Douglass' Monthly,* Nov., 1860. The convention also adopted a resolution recommending the organization of "a Political Association, to be known as the Union

Democratic Party of the United States" which would have as its program the principle that "the Constitution, rightly interpreted, is entirely and unequivocally on the side of freedom." A "National Political Education Committee" was appointed to carry the resolution into effect. Douglass was chosen a member of the committee.

9. *Douglass' Monthly*, Oct., 1860. Douglass was probably referring to the fact that on Jan. 10, 1849, Lincoln had introduced a bill in Congress requiring the municipal authorities of Washington and Georgetown "to arrest and deliver up to their owners, all fugitive slaves escaping into said District." It had been introduced as a concession in the scheme of ridding the District of both the slave trade and slavery.

10. *Life and Times of Frederick Douglass*, p. 265.

11. *Douglass' Monthly*, Nov., 1860. According to a letter of Hamilton Fish of Sept. 21, 1860, "the Gerrit Smith element of opposition to the Republicans" was negotiating with the anti-Republican fusion groups in New York State and demanding that "Fred Douglass must be one of the names" of the electors on the fusion ticket. While there is little evidence that such negotiations were under way, the letter would seem to indicate that as late as September 21, Douglass was not campaigning for the Republicans. Hamilton Fish was a leading Republican in New York and would have known of Douglass' activities for his party if he had been campaigning for Lincoln. (Hamilton Fish to Sidney Laurence, Sept. 21, 1860, *Hamilton Fish Letterbooks*, pp. 26-27. Library of Congress, Manuscript Division.)

12. In 1837 the Negroes of New York City sent petitions to the State Legislature appealing for "an alteration of the constitution, so as to extend the right of voting to all male citizens of the state, on the same term, without distinction of color." Nine years later the question was submitted to the voters, but was rejected by a three to one majority. In 1860 the legislature again submitted the question of equal suffrage to the voters to decide upon it at the time of the presidential election. (See Emil Olbrich, *The Development of Negro Suffrage to 1860*, Madison, Wisconsin, 1901, pp. 30 ff., 126-28.)

13. *Brooklyn Daily Times*, reprinted in *The Principia*, Oct. 20, 1860.

14. James McCune Smith to Gerrit Smith, Sept. 29, 1860, Gerrit Smith Papers, Syracuse University. The tract was signed by James McCune Smith, James P. Miller, and John J. Zuille. (See *The Principia*, Oct. 20, 1860.)

15. The vote was 337,984 against ratification to 197,503 for. The vote for equal suffrage was greater by 112,097 over that cast in 1846 while the negative vote was greater by 113,648. In 1846 the majority against equal suffrage was 138,930 and in 1860 it was 140,481. (*The Principia*, Feb. 16, 1861.)

Douglass was bitter at the Republicans for failing to take a strong stand in favor of equal suffrage. "The black baby of Negro Suffrage was thought too ugly to exhibit on so grand an occasion," he wrote. ". . . We were told by some of our Republican friends to keep still—make no noise—they would do the work. Now, the fox is out of the well, and the goat is in it." (*Douglass' Monthly*, Dec., 1860.)

16. *Douglass' Monthly*, Dec., 1860.

17. For an analysis of conditions following Lincoln's election, See Philip S. Foner, *Business and Slavery*, pp. 224-84.

18. *Boston Evening Transcript*, Dec. 3, 1860; *New York Tribune*, Dec. 6, 1860; *Liberator*, Dec. 7, 1860. "The mob," wrote James Redpath, "was incited, and

chiefly composed of merchants, traders with the South—nearly all of whom have uncollected debts there, and many of them mortgages on slaves."

19. *Douglass' Monthly,* Jan., 1861; Douglass to Mrs. Livermore, Apr. 19, 1886, Douglass *Mss.,* Frederick Douglass Memorial Home, Anacostia, D. C.

20. *Liberator,* Dec. 4, 1860.

21. *Douglass' Monthly,* Feb., Mar., 1861.

22. *Douglass' Monthly,* Apr., 1861.

23. *Anti-Slavery Standard,* Aug. 19, 1847; *Frederick Douglass' Paper,* Nov. 16, 1855.

24. *Douglass' Monthly,* Jan., 1861. James Redpath, a former associate of John Brown and general agent of the Haitian Bureau of Emigration, claimed that he had been responsible for converting Douglass from "an energetic opponent of emigration . . . into a friend of Hayti." (James Redpath to Hon. M. Plesance, Secretary of State, Republic of Haiti, June 8, 1861, "Letters and Reports of James Redpath, General Agent of Emigration to Hayti," pp. 91-3. Library of Congress, Manuscript Division.)

25. *Douglass' Monthly,* May, 1861.

Reference Notes

to Writings and Speeches of Frederick Douglass

PART I

1. On Jan. 29, 1850, Henry Clay introduced a series of resolution which he believed would provide the basis for the settlement of "all questions of controversy . . . arising out of the institution of slavery, upon a fair, equitable, and just basis." His "comprehensive scheme of adjustment" proposed that California be admitted as a state with her free-state constitution: that Congress provide territorial governments for New Mexico and Utah, without restriction as to slavery, but without authorizing slaveholders to take their slaves there; that Texas be granted a sum of money for the payment of her public debt; that slavery should not be abolished in the District of Columbia without the consent of Maryland, but that the slave trade in the District should be prohibited; that a more effective fugitive slave law should be enacted, and that Congress had no power to prohibit or obstruct the trade in slaves between the slaveholding states.

These resolutions were referred to a select committee of thirteen of which Clay was made chairman, and its report was basically the proposals advanced by its chairman.

2. On Mar. 4, 1850, Calhoun's speech to the Senate was read by Mr. Mason of Virginia. He predicted that "if something is not done to arrest it, the South will be forced to choose between abolition and secession." No compromise plan, he declared, could save the Union. Only if the North did justice to the South could it be saved; "to do justice by conceding to the South an equal right in the acquired territory, and to do her duty by causing the stipulations relative to fugitive slaves to be faithfully fulfilled; to cease the agitation of the slavery question, and to provide for the insertion of a provision in the Constitution, by an amendment, which will restore to the South, in substance, the power she possessed of protecting herself, before the equilibrium between the sections was destroyed by the action of the government."

Three days after Calhoun's speech was delivered, on Mar. 7, 1850, Daniel Webster addressed the Senate in favor of Clay's compromise measures. He admitted that Northerners had not lived up to their obligations to return fugitive slaves, asserted that there could be no peaceful secession and argued that Congressional prohibition in the territories was useless since a law of nature had settled "beyond all terms of human enactment, that slavery cannot exist in California or New Mexico."

Webster was highly praised by conservatives throughout the North, but was roundly condemned in anti-slavery circles. (For an analysis of his speech and the reaction to it, see H. D. Foster, "Webster's Seventh of March Speech," *American Historical Review,* vol. XXVII, Jan., 1922, pp. 245-70.)

3. In 1832 a slave fled from Maryland to Pennsylvania. Five years later, Edward Prigg, an agent, seized her and returned her to her owner. Prigg was indicted on the charge of kidnapping in the York County Court, under a Pennsylvania

statute of 1826 relating to fugitive slaves. After the Supreme Court of Pennsylvania had upheld the action, the State of Maryland prosecuted a writ of error to the Supreme Court of the United States. The unanimous opinion of the Court, written by Mr. Justice Story, declared the Pennsylvania statute of 1826 unconstitutional because the Federal Fugitive Slave Act of 1793 superseded all state legislation on the subject.

The Supreme Court decision aroused great dissatisfaction in many northern states as a result of which Personal Liberty Laws were adopted by several states forbidding their officers to perform any duties under the Congressional act of 1793 or to use state jails or prisons for holding fugitive slaves.

4. On Mar. 11, 1850, Seward spoke in the Senate in opposition to Clay's compromise plan. He denounced the proposal for more stringent fugitive slave laws and caused a sensation with the statement: "The Constitution regulates our stewardship; the Constitution devotes the domain (*i.e.* the territories not formed into states) to union, to justice, to defence, to welfare, and to liberty. But there is a higher law than the Constitution, which regulates our authority over the domain, and devotes it to the same noble purposes."

5. A northern politician over-anxious to please the South was called a "Doughface." The term is believed to have been invented by John Randolph of Roanoke.

6. Senator Mason introduced his Fugitive Slave Bill into Congress on Jan. 23, 1850, in the form of amendments to the compromise plan. It provided that fugitive slaves could be seized by their master or agent, and be brought before any United States judge, commissioner, clerk, marshal, postmaster, or collector of customs. If proof sufficient to satisfy these officials existed, the owner or agent would receive a certificate which "shall be a sufficient warrant for taking and removing such fugitive from service or labor to the State or Territory from which he or she fled." Any one obstructing such action would be arrested and fined $1,000 for each violation of provisions in the law.

7. See *Life and Writings of Frederick Douglass*, Vol. I, p. 416.

8. On June 10, 1850, the London *Times* reprinted the account in the New York *Globe* of the attack upon Douglass in New York City, under the heading "Equality in New York." The next day the *Times* devoted a long editorial to the subject, declaring that "blind, unreasoning antipathy, was the cause of the outrage, and deemed by the Americans a sufficient excuse for it. We in England who happily have never been subjected to influences which could lead us to a state of mind so unjust, or so likely to lead to acts thus flagrantly opposed to the dictates of justice and benevolence, can hardly find words that sufficiently express our astonishment as well as sorrow on witnessing so strange a distortion of the moral vision among a people justly celebrated for their sagacity, and for the fervour of their piety. We marvel indeed to see the dictates of a religion which they as well as ourselves believe and obey utterly forgotten when this wild and senseless antipathy comes into play; and we are irresistibly impelled to ask, what command of morality or religion can be deemed sacred by these people, when those which result from the first principles of their faith—which are among the most imperative of those enforced by their laws, and sanctioned by the first precepts of their morality, are thus scouted and contemptuously neglected and opposed." (London *Times*, June 11, 1850.)

9. Douglass gave seven lectures during the course.

10. Douglass is referring to the Compromise of 1850.

11. Douglass is referring to attacks on anti-slavery meetings and to the case of James Hamlet, a fugitive slave, working as a porter in New York City. Late in

Sept., 1850, after the passage of the compromise measures, he was arrested, tried before the United States Commissioner, and ordered sent back to his former owner in Baltimore. He left behind him a wife and two children. The incident aroused great indignation in New York, and his freedom was purchased by a group of New York merchants. Hamlet was returned to New York on Oct. 8, 1850. (See Philip S. Foner, *Business and Slavery: The New York Merchants and the Irrepressible Conflict,* Chapel Hill, 1941, pp. 35-36.)

12. The lectures were published as a pamphlet bearing the title, *Lectures on American Slavery. By Frederick Douglass Delivered at Corinthian Hall, Rochester, N. Y.,* Buffalo, 1851.

13. For Henry Clay's speech in the Senate in behalf of measures to transport free Negroes to Liberia, see Carl Schurz, *Life of Henry Clay,* Boston and New York, 1899, vol. II, p. 378.

 An editorial entitled "The African Race" appeared in the New York *Tribune* of Jan. 17, 1851, which asserted that the Negro "cannot flourish surrounded by and mixed up with whites. His only sure resource against debasement is separation." It concluded with the hope that Negroes "will come to realize that colonization is the means whereby oppressed Races and communities renew their youth and strength."

14. Gerrit Smith was the financial backer of the *Liberty Party Paper,* a weekly journal edited and published in Syracuse by John Thomas. At the end of four months of existence the paper had fewer than seven hundred subscribers. Smith thereupon suggested that it be merged with *The North Star.* The merger took place on June 5, 1851.

15. *The National Era* was published weekly in Washington, D. C., under the editorship of Dr. George Bailey and with Amos A. Phelps and John G. Whittier as corresponding editors. While an anti-slavery paper, it did not confine itself to discussions of slavery but also contained literary pieces and news articles of general interest. In 1851 it had seventeen thousand subscribers and was a flourishing journal.

 Garrison denounced *The National Era* as a perfect example of "milk-and-water" abolitionism; "for that journal is so politic, adroit, and careful not to give offence, in its management of the Abolition question, that it has no more claim to be considered anti-slavery than scores of other journals which make no pretention on that score. That the *Era* has seventeen thousand subscribers is demonstrative evidence that it is not a radical sheet. If it were, in spite of its undeniable ability, its subscription list would be a very lean one; if it were, it could not be published three weeks consecutively in the city of Washington." (*The National Era,* April 22, 1852, vol. VI, no. 277, p. 67.) The *Era* denied that it was an enemy to "the South and to Southern Institutions," and called itself "the uncompromising opponent of Slavery, and of every man, North and South, who upholds it or seeks to extend it." (*The National Era,* July 28, 1853, vol. VII, no. 343, p. 117.)

16. In his address Smith welcomed the American Anti-Slavery Society to Central New York. (See *The Liberator,* May 16, 1851.)

17. Smith proposed the motto: "All Rights for All!" It was carried as the motto of *Frederick Douglass' Paper* directly under the name of the journal.

18. At the eighteenth annual meeting of the American Anti-Slavery Society at Syracuse, New York, a resolution was submitted by Rev. Samuel J. May, recommending that the *National Anti-Slavery Standard,* the *Pennsylvania Freeman,* the *Anti-Slavery Bugle* and *The North Star* should be recognized as of-

ficial organs of the Society. Garrison opposed this motion on the ground that the *Bugle* was a Liberty Party paper and should not be considered with the other papers. This led to a resolution that no paper which did not assume that the Constitution was a pro-slavery document should receive support.

During the discussion Douglass stated that he had come to the conclusion that "the Constitution might be consistent in the details with the noble purpose avowed in its preamble." He also said that "his opinions had recently changed materially in relation to the duty of political action and intimated that he would no longer oppose it." Whereupon Garrison is reported to have said, "There is roguery somewhere." He then moved that *The North Star* also be stricken from the list, and this was approved. (See *The Liberator,* Apr. 4, 1851, Jan. 13, 27, 1854; *Frederick Douglass' Paper,* Jan. 13, 1854.)

19. *Life and Writings of Frederick Douglass,* Vol. I, pp. 352, 361.

20. In Aug., 1850, William L. Chaplin and others were arrested by Washington police, on Maryland soil, for taking part in the escape of two slaves, the property of Robert Toombs and Alexander H. Stephens. Chaplin was kept in jail at Rockville, Maryland, until December; was subsequently indicted in the District of Columbia on a charge of assault with intent to kill, and in Maryland he was indicted on seven counts: three for assault with intent to murder, two for assisting slaves to escape, and two for larceny of slaves. Bail was fixed at $6,000 in the District and $19,000 in Maryland.

With the aid of Gerrit Smith, Lewis Tappan, W. H. Seward, and others, Chaplin's bail was secured and he was released from jail. Smith served as treasurer of the Chaplin fund, and contributed $10,000 to the movement to free Chaplin.

21. Daniel, a fugitive slave, was arrested in Buffalo, where the federal commissioner remanded him to his claimant. The case came before Judge Conkling in the United States District Court at Auburn. Judge Conkling pointed out in his decision that Daniel had escaped on Aug. 25, 1850, and that the Fugitive Slave Act had been adopted on Sept. 18, 1850, hence it would be applying an *ex post facto* principle to have Daniel restored to his master under this law. He, therefore, granted him a writ of habeas corpus, and Daniel, after his release from prison in Buffalo, fled to Canada. (For the entire text of Judge Conkling's decision, see New York *Tribune,* Sept. 2, 1851.)

22. In the early dawn of Sept. 11, 1851, an attack was made upon a Negro family in Christiana, Pennsylvania, to arrest some alleged fugitive slaves. The Negroes in the neighborhood came to the family's defense and a battle took place in which Edward Gorsuch, a Maryland slave owner, was killed and his son wounded. Castner Hanway, a Quaker—because he refused to assist in capturing the fugitives—was tried for treason but acquitted. In a speech early in November, 1851, Joshua R. Giddings hailed the fact that the Negroes had "stood up manfully in the defense of their God-given rights and shot down the miscreants, who had come with the desperate purpose of taking them again to the land of slavery." (W. U. Hensel, *The Chrisiana Riot and the Treason Trials of 1851,* Lancaster, Pa., 1911, p. 55.)

23. Soon after Indiana became a state, laws were passed discouraging immigration of free Negroes, forbidding their entrance into and residence in the state, unless heavy bonds for good behavior and support were forthcoming; denying all Negroes the right of testimony against a white person; cutting them off from any share in the public school fund, and excluding them entirely from the public schools. Most of these laws became a dead letter, but in remodeling the

State Constitution in 1851, the pro-slavery element in the state pushed for the adoption of these laws as part of the State Constitution. They were incorporated as the "Thirteenth Article," and provided generally for banishing "Negroes" and "mulattoes" from the state, fining heavily any who might employ them, and instructing the legislature to pass the necessary laws for their colonization beyond the state.

24. During his tour in the United States in 1849 Father Mathew was invited by Governor Lumpkin to visit Georgia in furtherance of the temperance cause. But when the Governor learned that his name had been associated with that of Daniel O'Conell in the famous Anti-Slavery Appeal from Ireland to Irish in America, he wrote to Father Mathew asking him if he entertained the same sentiments on the subject of slavery. Father Mathew assured the Governor that he had come to America for the sole purpose of advocating "the high and holy cause of temperance . . . being firmly resolved not to interfere in the slightest degree with the institutions of this mighty republic." Nevertheless, the invitation was withdrawn. At the same time Douglass wrote: "Thus it is likely that Father Mathew, in trying to meet the views of the North, without offending the South, will find himself deserted by both. This is exactly the treatment he deserves for seeking to be neutral in the cause of human freedom. May he profit by the experience." (*The North Star,* Dec. 14, 1849.)

Even earlier than this Father Mathew had aroused the anger of the Abolitionists by refusing to speak with Garrison and Phillips at a West Indies Emancipation meeting. "I have as much as I can do," he wrote to Garrison, "to save men from the slavery of intemperance without attempting to overthrow any other kind of slavery." (Rev. Patrick Rogers, *Father Theobold Mathew: Apostle of Temperance,* Dublin, 1943, pp. 126-28.)

25. N. Farmer's article appeared in *The Liberator* of Jan. 2, 1852. It was a long denunciation of Douglass for the latter's attack upon George Thompson.

26. William Henry, a fugitive slave from Missouri commonly known throughout the city of Syracuse as Jerry, had been working for some time in that city as a cooper. On Oct. 1, 1851, Jerry was arrested by Henry W. Allen, deputy United States Marshal, and brought before Joseph F. Sabine, commissioner of the United States Circuit Court. The city was crowded with visitors to the Onondaga County Fair and at the same time a Liberty Party convention was being held. A crowd attacked Sabine's office, and managed to get Jerry away. He was recaptured and the hearing resumed on the same day. Led by Gerrit Smith, Rev. Samuel J. May, C. A. Wheaton, and Rev. J. W. Loguen, a Negro minister, the crowd again forcibly rescued Jerry from deputy Marshall Allen. After a few days in hiding, he was taken to Kingston, Ontario.

Every October 1 the Abolitionists of Syracuse and vicinity celebrated the anniversary of the "Jerry Rescue." Until 1859 Gerrit Smith presided at these anniversary celebrations.

27. These words were used by William Lloyd Garrison in the first issue of *The Liberator.*

28. At the request of the Union Safety Committee of New York City, formed by conservative merchants, the clergymen of New York agreed to set aside Dec. 12, 1850, as a day on which sermons would be delivered upholding the Compromise of 1850, especially the Fugitive Slave Act. Practically all the sermons advised acquiescence on the part of the people to the law and denounced the "higher law" doctrine. The sermons were published and distributed by the Union Safety Committee. (See the pamphlets, *The Law-Abiding Conscience and the Higher*

Law Conscience, with Remarks on the Fugitive Slave Question, New York, 1850; John C. Lord, *The Higher Law in its Application to the Fugitive Slave Bill,* New York, 1851, and Philip S. Foner, *Business and Slavery,* pp. 56-58.)

29. Winfield Scott (1786-1866) was the Whig candidate and Franklin K. Pierce (1804-1869) the Democratic Party candidate for President.

30. Gerrit Smith was elected to Congress as the representative from the twenty-second Congressional district of New York. He had been nominated on an independent ticket. Smith spent eight months in Congress, and then resigned his seat.

31. Winfield Scott, the Whig candidate, was overwhelmingly defeated by Franklin Pierce in the electoral college. Pierce carried every state but four, but his popular majority was small, less than 50,000 out of 3,100,000 votes.

32. See p. 79 of present volume.

33. The name finally chosen was *Frederick Douglass' Paper.*

34. On Aug. 1, 1846, Gerrit Smith wrote to Rev. Theodore S. Wright, Rev. Charles B. Ray, and Dr. J. McCune Smith asking them to prepare a list of the colored men in certain counties eligible to receive a deed of land from him. The following conditions were attached to the offer: no person younger than twenty-one or older than sixty should be included, nor any person well-off and already an owner of land, and no drinker of intoxicating liquor. One hundred and twenty thousand acres of land were distributed by Smith to three thousand Negroes in New York. (See *An Address to the Three Thousand Colored Citizens of New York who are the Owners of One Hundred and Twenty Thousand Acres of Land, in the State of New York, Given to them by Gerrit Smith, Esq. of Peterboro,* New York, 1846.)

35. Harriet Beecher Stowe wrote the volume entitled *The Key to Uncle Tom's Cabin* to defend the veracity of her great novel, *Uncle Tom's Cabin.* It consisted of a mass of supporting data, court decisions, newspaper clippings, church proceedings, etc. It did not, however, consist of materials she had used when she wrote *Uncle Tom's Cabin.*

36. The Hunkers was the conservative faction of New York's Democratic Party in the 1840's who opposed the Abolitionists and deprecated anti-slavery agitation. By 1853-1855 the distinction between Hunkers and Barnburners, the more progressive wing of the Democratic Party in New York, was replaced by the terms "Hards" and "Softs." Most of the Hunkers became "Hards."

The Silver Grays was the name given to the conservative minority of the Whig Party in New York who, approving of the conciliatory policies of President Fillmore, bolted the Whig State Convention of 1850 in New York when the delegates endorsed the anti-slavery views of William H. Seward. They were so called because of the color of the hair of Francis Granger, leader of the bolters. After this incident the conservative anti-Abolitionist Whigs were known as Silver Grays or Cotton Whigs.

37. The "higher law" doctrine was an appeal to conscience as being superior in authority to the laws of Congress. It originated in the debate on the Compromise of 1850 when Senator Seward declared that the proposed Fugitive Slave Act might be constitutional, but there was a "higher law" than the Constitution.

38. The reference is to an act passed by the Illinois legislature in 1853 which provided that anyone aiding a Negro, bond or free, to secure settlement in Illinois was to be fined not less than $100 or more than $500 and was to be imprisoned

in the county jail not longer than a year. The Negro was to be fined $50 if he stayed in the state for ten days with the purpose of continuing his residence. Upon failure to pay his fine he would be arrested and be advertised for ten days by the sheriff and then sold to the person who would pay the fine and costs for the shortest term of service. During this period the temporary owner was to work the Negro at his own pleasure. The prosecuting witness was to receive half the fine imposed. The law was called by its opponents "An Act to establish slavery in this State." (See Mason McCloud Fishback, "Illinois Legislation on Slavery and Free Negroes, 1818-1865," *Transactions of the Illinois State Historical Society for the year 1904*, p. 428.)

39. In Jan., 1853, in the arrangement of the Senate Committees, Hale of New Hampshire, Sumner of Massachusetts, and Chase of Ohio, were excluded from the committee list upon the express ground that they were "outside of any healthy political organization in this country." A resolution protesting this action was defeated in the Massachusetts legislature.

40. For a description of Harriet Beecher Stowe's reception in England, see Forrest Wilson, *Crusader in Crinoline: The Life of Harriet Stowe*, Philadelphia, 1941, pp. 362-85.

PART II

1. The measure, designed by Stephen A. Douglas, provided for the organization of two new territories, Kansas and Nebraska. It set aside the Missouri Compromise of 1820 and authorized the settlers themselves to decide for or against slavery on the principle of popular sovereignty. Introduced in the Senate on Dec. 4, 1853, the bill aroused extremely bitter debate in both houses. President Pierce signed the measure on May 30, 1854.

2. The reference is to Sumner's great speech delivered on Feb. 21, 1854, against the Nebraska Bill. (For the text of the speech, see *The Works of Charles Sumner*, Boston, 1875, vol. III, pp. 277-332.)

3. In his speech in the Senate on Feb. 17, 1854, opposing the Nebraska Bill, Seward argued that if Congress had no authority over slavery in the territories it had none over it in the District of Columbia. He suggested that in line with the principle of popular sovereignty advocated by Stephen A. Douglas, the question of the existence of slavery within the District be submitted to its inhabitants. (See George E. Baker, ed., *The Works of William H. Seward*, Boston, 1884, vol. IV, p. 458.)

4. Gerrit Smith made several speeches against the Nebraska Bill, the most famous being delivered on Apr. 6, 1854. (See *Speeches of Gerrit Smith in Congress*, New York, 1855, pp. 113-215.)

5. The amendment referred to limited grants of land under the Homestead Act to white persons. It was introduced in the House by Daniel B. Wright, Democratic representative from Mississippi.

6. See pp. 29-31.

7. In the course of his speech in Congress, May 3, 1854, supporting the motion to strike out the word "white" from the bill granting donations of land to actual settlers in New Mexico, Gerrit Smith said: "I would, sir, that that noble man, Frederick Douglass, could be allowed to stand up here, and pour out the feelings of his great heart in his rich, and mellow, and deep voice. I refer to him, sir, because I regard him as the man of America. He was held in actual bondage

until he was twenty-one years old. Then he escaped from his tormentors. He was never at school a day in his life; and now he is confessedly one of the ablest public speakers and writers in this country. I feel sure, sir, that could he be heard, he would be able to bring the Committee to repent of its purpose (if such is its purpose) to retain the word 'white.' " (*Speeches of Gerrit Smith in Congress*, p. 228.)

8. On Mar. 21 and 27, 1854, Francis B. Cutting, Democratic representative from New York City, moved in the House that the Nebraska Bill be referred to the Committee of the Whole on the state of the Union. He also proposed that the people of the territories be permitted "to mould their own municipal regulation and their own domestic institutions in their own manner. . . ." The bill, he argued, should not alter the status of slavery in these territories by Congressional edict. "Leave the institution of slavery to those who are to live under it." (*Congressional Globe,* 33rd Cong., 1st Sess., Part I, pp. 701-03, 759-64.)

9. The reference is to the slaying in Boston of James Batchelder, a truckman, during the attack of a crowd seeking to release Anthony Burns, a fugitive slave held in the Court House. Burns had escaped from Richmond in February, 1854, and was hiding in Boston. He was arrested on May 24, 1854. The next morning he was about to be delivered to his master, when Richard H. Dana, Jr., who happened to be in the court-room, secured an adjournment of the hearing for two days.

Many conventions were being held in Boston at this time, and when the story reached the ears of the Abolitionists, they determined to prevent Burns' return to slavery. During an attack on the Court House to free Burns, James Batchelder, a truckman serving as a United States Marshal, was killed.

President Pierce ordered out federal troops to force Burns' return to his master, and an army carried him down State Street and flung him, manacled, into the hold of a vessel bound for Virginia.

10. The questions asked Smith were: "1st. Of the present posture of the Anti-Slavery question generally; 2dly. What hope, if any, may be predicated of the present Congress; 3dly. The nature, character, and extent of influence exerted in Congress, by the Anti-Slavery members of the House; 4thly. Who are the most effective supporters of Slavery there and the means of their efficiency; 5thly. Your impressions concerning the character, learning, ability, of members generally, and anything touching the House of Representatives, which may serve to give the public an insight into the proceedings of that body." (*Frederick Douglass' Paper,* Aug. 25, 1854.) For Gerrit Smith's answers, see *Speeches of Gerrit Smith in Congress,* pp. 401-12.

11. Smith spoke in Congress in favor of annexing Cuba to the United States even if slavery were not first abolished in that country. Slavery in America, he contended, was better than under Spain since American slavery encountered and was modified by a higher civilization. In addition, annexation of Cuba would end her connection with the slave trade. (See *Speeches of Gerrit Smith in Congress,* pp. 387-91.)

12. On Aug. 7, 1854, Gerrit Smith resigned his seat in Congress. The only explanation he gave was in a printed letter addressed to his successor in the House, H. C. Goodwin, in which he stated that he resigned because of the "pressure of my far too extensive private business." Abolitionists generally criticized Smith for his action, arguing that he had accepted a sacred trust when he entered Congress, and that he had no right to permit personal considerations to interfere with his work for the cause.

13. In 1841 the general pre-emption law was passed; it gave the pre-emption right (the right of pre-empting their claims in advance of the land sale so that they would not be obliged to bid for them against speculators) to all squatters who should take up locations upon the surveyed public lands. In 1853 and 1854 the right of pre-emption on unsurveyed lands was extended to a number of states, but the bill of 1854 was so amended as to limit its grant of land to white persons. Gerrit Smith, who had spoken in favor of the bill when it was first introduced, voted against it when this amendment was adopted. "If my fellow land-reformers," he wrote Douglass, explaining his vote, "with whom I have, as long, toiled for the success of our land-reform doctrines, shall be aggrieved by my vote, I shall be sorry. Nevertheless, I can never regret my vote. I was a *man* before I was a *land-reformer*. . . . The curse of God is upon the bill, or there is no God. There is no God, if we have liberty to insult and outrage any portion of His children." (*Speeches of Gerrit Smith in Congress*, p. 94.)

14. The principle of popular sovereignty was set forth clearly for the first time by Lewis Cass in a letter to A. O. P. Nicholson, Dec. 24, 1847, in which he declared that he was "in favor of leaving the people of any territory which may hereafter be acquired the right to regulate it [slavery] themselves, under the general principles of the Constitution." (For an extended analysis of the meaning of the principle, see Stephen A. Douglas, *Popular sovereignty in the territories. The dividing line between federal and local authority*, New York, 1859.)

15. The allusion is to the hanging of Stephen A. Douglas in effigy in Chicago and many other communities, from Iowa to Maine, during the debates in Congress on the Nebraska Bill.

16. On Jan. 12, 1838, Calhoun declared in the Senate: "Many in the South once believed it [slavery] was a moral and political evil. That folly and delusion are gone. We see it now in its true light and regard it as the most safe and stable basis for free institutions in the world." (R. K. Cralle, ed., *The Works of John C. Calhoun*, New York, 1854-1856, vol. III, p. 180.)

17. William Lloyd Garrison made this statement in Dec., 1853, in the course of his controversy with Douglass. (See *The Liberator*, Dec. 16, 1853; *National Anti-Slavery Standard*, Dec. 24, 1853.)

18. Dr. Reuben Crandall went to Washington in 1835 to lecture on the natural sciences. While engaged in this work, he received some packages, wrapped in newspapers, among which were a few copies of the *Emancipator* and the *Anti-Slavery Reporter*. These papers were circulated unwittingly by someone who obtained them from Dr. Crandall, and led to the latter's arrest. Dr. Crandall was forced to remain in jail for nearly eight months before he was brought to trial and acquitted.

19. In 1835 the English Abolitionist, George Thompson, came to the United States on a lecture tour. On Oct. 21, the Boston Female Anti-Slavery Society held a meeting, at which a mob of several thousand persons assembled, expecting to tar-and-feather Thompson. The latter, however, had been warned, and the crowd, searching for a victim, seized Garrison, dragged him with a rope around his neck through the street, and would probably have lynched him if Mayor Theodore Lyman had not intervened. Garrison spent the night in the Leverett Street jail and in the morning left the city for several weeks.

20. The Free Produce Movement was the attempt to strike at the slaveholding system by a boycott upon the products of slave labor. Since free produce societies

had a membership of only about fifteen hundred, most of whom were Quakers, and probably not more than five or six thousand people tried to purchase free labor goods, it is obvious that the movement could not be very successful. Douglass, however, strongly endorsed the free produce cause, considering it as rendering an important moral impetus to the struggle against slavery. (See Ruth Ketring Neuerinberger, "The Free Produce Movement: A Quaker Protest Against Slavery," *Historical Papers of the Trinity College Historical Society*, Series XXV, Duke University Press, 1942.)

21. For the text of the lecture entitled, "The Necessity, the Practicability and the Dignity of the Anti-Slavery Enterprise," see *The Works of Charles Sumner*, vol. IV, pp. 1-51. See also Douglass' editorial on Sumner's speech in *Frederick Douglass' Paper*, June 1, 1855.

22. After the passage of the Kansas-Nebraska Act, settlers from the North and the South poured into Kansas. The slaveowners organized bands of ruffians recruited from the riff-raff elements of western Missouri to invade Kansas and assist in establishing slavery in the territory. In elections for a delegate to Congress in Nov., 1854, and for a territorial legislature in Mar. 1855, the pro-slavery forces through the use of illegal voting and the terroristic tactics of the "Border Ruffians" from Missouri carried both contests. The free-soil element refused to recognize the legislature friendly to the slave power, established their own assembly, drew up a constitution and asked for admission into the Union. By 1856 actual civil war existed in Kansas as the "Border Ruffians" raided Lawrence and other towns, stole horses, and in general molested free-state families. The free-soil men retaliated in kind.

23. Douglass' *My Bondage and My Freedom* was dedicated to Gerrit Smith. The dedication read:

To
Honorable Gerrit Smith
as a slight token of
Esteem for his Character
Admiration for his Genius and Benevolence,
Affection for his Person, and
Gratitude for his Friendship,
and as
a Small but most Sincere Acknowledgement of
His Pre-Eminent Services in behalf of the Rights and Liberties
of an
Afflicted, Despised and Deeply Outraged People,
by Ranking Slavery with Piracy and Murder,
and by
Denying it Either a Legal or Constitutional Existence,
This Volume is Respectfully Dedicated,
By His Faithful and Firmly Attached Friend.

Rochester, N. Y.   *Frederick Douglass*

24. The first constitution of the state of New York, adopted April 20, 1777, required a property qualification of all male inhabitants, without reference to color. After 1821, when the constitution was amended, the property qualification was abolished for white voters. No Negro, however, could vote unless he was worth $250 in real estate. In 1846 the question of equal suffrage was submitted to the voters who rejected it by a three to one majority, 223,834 against the proposal and 85,306 for it. The Negro people in New York, however, continued the struggle to eliminate the property qualification, and it was in

reference to this struggle that the *Tribune* article was written. It acknowledged that "the Blacks ought to enjoy the Right of Suffrage exactly as the Whites do," but declared that there was little possibility of redressing the wrong "for many weary years." ". . . We see very clearly," it added, "that present agitation for its overthrow will only result in exposing to popular odium the Whites engaged in it. Efforts to abolish this partial Property Qualification do not hasten the enfranchisement of the Blacks, but they strongly tend to the practical disfranchisement of the Whites who favor their claims."

25. The American (or Know-Nothing) Party was founded in 1849 as a secret patriotic society known as the Order of the Star Spangled Banner. Members were sworn not to reveal its secrets, hence their answer to all questions concerning the movement was, "I know nothing about it," thus giving the organization its popular name, The Know-Nothing Party. Its members were pledged to vote only for native-born Americans, to agitate for a twenty-one-year probationary period preceding naturalization and to combat the Catholic Church. The movement grew enormously after 1852, but declined a few years later.

26. The resolutions referred to contained an attack on the Radical Abolitionists for their failure to support the Republican candidates in the election of 1856, and the assertion by Douglass that the peaceful annihilation of slavery was no longer possible. (See Syracuse *Daily Standard*, Oct. 2, 1856.)

27. Dred Scott, a slave, was brought by his master, Dr. Emerson, into the Louisiana Territory above the line where slavery was legally prohibited. Here Dred lived a number of years, married and raised a family. Eventually Dred Scott and his family were brought back to the slave state of Missouri. After Dr. Emerson's death, they were sold to a New Yorker, Sanford, whom they eventually sued for their freedom.

The case was decided by the Supreme Court on Mar. 6, 1857. Chief Justice Taney, writing the majority decision, held that the Missouri Circuit Court had no jurisdiction over the case since the Scotts were not and could never be citizens within the meaning of the Constitution, and therefore had no right to sue in a Federal Court. Taney argued that when the Constitution was adopted, Negroes were regarded as persons of an inferior order, and not as "citizens," and they were not intended to be included by the constitutional provision giving to citizens of different states the right to sue in Federal Courts.

Instead of resting the matter here, the Chief Justice went on to express an opinion not vital to the case. In this opinion, Taney upheld the right of slaveowners to take their slaves to any territory of the United States and to hold them there in bondage no matter what Congress or the territorial legislature said to the contrary. Dred Scott, he declared, had not become free by residence in a territory covered by the Missouri Compromise, since Congress had no constitutional power to enact the Missouri Compromise.

In a powerful dissenting opinion, Justice Curtis of Massachusetts attacked the majority decision of the Court.

28. On Nov. 7, 1856, "an extensive scheme of Negro insurrection" was discovered in Lavoca, De Witt, and Victoria counties in the southeastern part of Texas. A week later a plot was disclosed in St. Mary Parish, Louisiana. Conspiracies were also discovered in Obion, Tennessee; Fulton, Kentucky; New Madrid, and Scott counties, Missouri. In December conspiracies were discovered in nearly all of the southern states. (See Herbert Aptheker, *American Negro Slave Revolts*, New York, 1943, pp. 345-50; Harvey Wish, "The slave insurrection panic of 1856," *Journal of Southern History*, vol. V, pp. 208-14; *Annual Report of the American Anti-Slavery Society*, New York, 1856, pp. 76-79.)

29. On May 22, 1856, two days after Senator Sumner delivered his speech, "The Crime against Kansas," he was accosted at his desk by Representative Preston S. Brooks (1819-1857) of South Carolina who denounced him for having uttered "a libel on South Carolina, and Mr. Butler, who is a relative of mine." Brooks then struck Sumner a blow on the head with his heavy walking stick. Pinioned by his desk, Sumner could not rise till he had wrenched the desk from its fastenings. In this condition, he was beaten until he fell bleeding and unconscious to the floor. Three and a half years passed before Sumner was sufficiently recovered to return to the Senate. Meanwhile he had been re-elected by the almost unanimous vote of the Massachusetts legislature.

A special investigating committee of the House reported in favor of the expulsion of Brooks, but the report on a strictly party vote failed to receive the necessary two-thirds majority. Brooks, however, resigned after a speech in his own justification and was unanimously re-elected by his constituents. In the North he was fiercely denounced for his cowardly attack, but in the South he was hailed as a hero, and was presented with a number of gold-headed canes and a gold-handled cowhide.

30. In Jan., 1856, the Garner family, slaves of Archibald K. Gaines of Kentucky, escaped and found refuge in Cincinnati. They were pursued and attacked. Before the group was captured, Margaret Garner killed one of her children, and severely wounded two others "to save them all from Slavery by death." She was tried on a murder charge in Cincinnati and found guilty, but due to jurisdictional difficulties was returned to slavery in Kentucky. (For a detailed account of this story, see *Annual Report of the American Anti-Slavery Society,* New York, 1856, pp. 44-47.)

31. In Feb., 1851, Shadrach, a Negro waiter in Boston, was arrested on the complaint of John de Bree of Norfolk, Virginia, and was charged with having escaped from the South in May, 1850. Before the case was decided, a body of Negroes, led by Lewis Hayden, broke into the prison, seized Shadrach, and dispatched him to Canada.

32. New York City was commonly referred to at this time as "the prolongation of the South," where "ten thousand cords of interests are linked with the Southern Slaveholder." (For an analysis of these connections, see Philip S. Foner, *Business and Slavery,* Chapter I.)

33. The reference is to the address by Francis Preston Blair, entitled, *The Destiny of the Race on This Continent,* published in 1859. Blair advanced a plan to invite free colored people to colonize in Central America.

34. In 1857 Oregon applied for admission as a state into the Union with a constitution excluding free people of color from the state. On Feb. 11, 1859, a bill was reported from the Committee on Territories recommending Oregon's admission, but a minority report protested its admission with a constitution discriminating against people of color. The issue was debated for several months in the Senate, but on May 18, the bill providing for Oregon's admission was adopted by a vote of 35 to 17, several Republicans voting for it.

35. In Oct., 1859, John Brown, heading a band of eighteen, five of whom were Negroes, tried to capture the federal arsenal and armory at Harpers Ferry, Virginia. Part of a more ambitious undertaking whose ultimate end was the emancipation of slaves throughout the South, the raid proved unsuccessful. Colonel Robert E. Lee led a detachment of United States marines, and captured Brown and a number of his followers. Amid considerable excitement throughout the world, they were tried for treason and found guilty. Brown's counsel

attempted to raise the plea of his alleged insanity as a reason why the Governor of Virginia should show him clemency, but John Brown absolutely refused "to avail himself of this possible means of escape from the hangman. Not even to save his life would he consent to have the sacrifices already made minimized, and his entire twenty years' war upon slavery written down as the mere mania of a lunatic." (Oswald Garrison Villard, *John Brown,* New York, 1943, pp. 506-07.) In Dec., 1859, Brown was hanged at Charles Town.

36. The speech referred to was delivered by George Thompson in the City Hall, Glasgow, on Feb. 27, 1860. It was a fairly bitter attack on Douglass' interpretation of the Constitution. (See *Lecture on the Constitution of the United States by Mr. Thompson Delivered in the City Hall, Glasgow, February 27th, 1860.* London Emancipation Committees Tracts, No. 5, London, 1860, and *The Anti-Slavery Advocate,* London, Apr. 2, 1860, vol. II, no. 40, pp. 317-21. Copies of both are in the Boston Public Library.)

37. The Thirty-Sixth Congress assembled three days after the execution of John Brown. A resolution was immediately offered by Senator John M. Mason for the appointment of a committee to investigate every aspect of the affair at Harpers Ferry. The resolution was unanimously adopted, and a Senate Committee was appointed.

38. In an effort to placate the conservatives and assure his nomination as the Republican candidate for President, Seward, early in 1860, tried to live down his reputation of radicalism. He had originally endorsed Hinton Rowan Helper's *The Impending Crisis,* but in the edition printed in Jan., 1860, his endorsement was deleted. And in late Feb., 1860, in a speech in the Senate upon a bill for the admission of Kansas, Seward scrupulously avoided the "higher law" and "irrepressible conflict" doctrines. Nor did he demand, as formerly, that the Supreme Court rescind the Dred Scott decision. "Differences of opinion," he said, "even on the subject of slavery, are with us political, not social or personal differences. There is not one disunionist or disloyalist among us all. We are altogether unconscious of any process of dissolution going on among us or around us. We have never been more patient, and never loved the representatives of other sections more than now." (*Congressional Globe,* 36th. Cong., 1st. Sess., p. 913.)

39. In a speech in Rochester in the fall of 1858, Seward said: "Our country exhibits, in full operation, two radically different political systems; the one resting on the basis of servile or slave labor, the other on the basis of voluntary labor of freemen. . . . Hitherto, the two systems have existed in different States, but side by side, within the American Union. These antagonistic systems are continually coming into closer contact, and collision results. Shall I tell you what this collision means? They who think it is accidental, unnecessary, the work of interested, or fanatical agitators, and therefore ephemeral, mistake the case altogether. It is an irrepressible conflict between opposing and enduring forces; and it means that the United States must and will, sooner or later, become either entirely a slave-holding nation, or entirely a free-labor nation." Frederick W. Seward, *Seward at Washington, 1846-1861,* New York, 1891, p. 351.)

40. The Constitutional Union Party met in convention at Baltimore on May 9, 1860, and nominated John Bell for President and Edward Everett for Vice President. They ran on a platform that no political principles be recognized other than "the Constitution of the country, the Union of the States, and the enforcement of the laws."

41. The reference is to Sumner's great speech, "The Barbarism of Slavery," delivered in the Senate on June 4, 1860, in opposition to the bill providing for the admission of Kansas into the Union as a state. In the course of this four-hour speech, Sumner presented a merciless refutation of the defenses of slavery, and an elaborate analysis of the slave codes and the conduct of the slaveowners.

42. *The Principia*, edited by William Goodell and published by Samuel Wilde, began publication on Nov. 19, 1859, in New York City, and lasted until Feb. 6, 1852, when Wilde died. (For the correspondence between Gerrit Smith and William Goodell, see issues for Sept. 29-Oct. 27, 1860.)

43. The Massachusetts legislature passed a series of resolutions thanking Sumner "for his recent manly and earnest assertion of the right of free discussion on the floor of the United States Senate," approving "the thorough, truthful and comprehensive examination of slavery embraced in his recent speech," and declaring that "the stern morality of that speech, its logic and its power, command our entire admiration, and that it expresses with fidelity the sentiments of Massachusetts upon the questions therein discussed." (*See Twenty-Eighth Annual Report of the American Anti-Slavery Society for the year ending May 1, 1861*, New York, 1861, pp. 111-12.)

44. The Democratic national convention met in Charleston on May 23, 1860. A committee on resolutions and platform was appointed, and, on May 27, presented a majority and minority report. The former asserted that Congress had no power to abolish slavery in the Territories, and that the Territorial legislature could neither abolish slavery in the Territories nor prohibit the introduction of slaves therein, nor destroy or impair the right of property in slaves by any legislation. The principal minority report reaffirmed the Cincinnati platform of 1856, declared that all rights of property were judicial, and that the Democratic Party pledged itself to defer to the Supreme Court on the subject.

After long and heated debate, the minority report was carried, by a vote of 165 to 138. Thereupon most of the delegations from the lower South, led by William L. Yancey of Alabama, left the convention hall. The remaining delegates adjourned and made arrangements to reassemble at Baltimore. Here in June they named Stephen A. Douglas for President. The southern "bolters" also met in Baltimore and nominated John C. Breckenridge for President.

45. Giuseppe Garibaldi (1807-1882) led his victorious expedition to Sicily and Naples in 1860 and with his thousand "red shirts" overthrew the Bourbon monarchy and made possible the accession of these states to a United Italy. The movement culminated in the establishment of the Kingdom of Italy under the Piedmontese dynasty.

46. The call was signed by John Pierpont and Stephen S. Foster and went in part:
"An adjourned meeting of the Political Anti-Slavery Convention which met in the city of Boston on the 29th of May last, will be held in the city of Worcester, on Wednesday and Thursday, the 19th and 20th of Sept. next, at 10 o'clock A.M.

"The object of this Convention is to consider the propriety of organizing a *Political Party* upon an Anti-Slavery interpretation of the U.S. Constitution, with the avowed purpose of abolishing slavery in the States, as well as Territories of the Union. At its former meeting, resolutions setting forth the great principles of liberty and equality which must underlie and permeate a political movement, were introduced, and discussed, but without taking action upon them, the Convention adjourned to meet in the city of Worcester, at the call of the President and Chairman of the Business Committee. . . ." (*Douglass' Monthly,* Sept., 1860.)

47. The New York State Legislature submitted the issue of eliminating the property qualification for Negro voters to be voted on at the time of the Presidential election of 1860.

48. At the Republican convention in Chicago, J. R. Giddings proposed an amendment to a series of resolutions reported by Judge William Jessup, reaffirming the principles of the Declaration of Independence. When this was voted down, Giddings retired from the convention. But George W. Curtis took up the issue, and asked the delegates if they were prepared to appear before the country as a party which had voted down the Declaration of Independence, and which refused to reassert its basic principle "that all men are created equal" and were "endowed by their creator with certain inalienable rights; among these are Life, Liberty and the Pursuit of Happiness." His amendment was adopted amid shouts of approval.

49. On Dec. 4, 1833, a National Anti-Slavery Convention opened at the Adelphi Building in Philadelphia. Beriah Green of the Oneida Institute in New York was elected President, and Lewis Tappan and John G. Whittier were designated secretaries. The convention continued for three days, and established the American Anti-Slavery Society. A constitution and a Declaration of Principles were also adopted. In the Declaration the delegates pledged themselves to carry on ceaseless activity "to overthrow the most execrable system of slavery that has ever been witnessed upon earth to deliver our land from its deadliest curse, to wipe out the foulest stain which rests upon our national escutcheon, and to secure to the colored population of the United States all the rights and privileges which belong to them as men and Americans. . . ."

50. During the months from Jan., 1859, to Aug., 1860, it was conservatively estimated, close to one hundred vessels left New York City for the slave trade. The empire city after 1857 gained the dubious honor of being "the greatest slave-trading mart in the world," and, in fact, "the very depot of this nefarious traffic." (See Philip S. Foner, *Business and Slavery,* pp. 164-68.)

51. At the Radical Abolition National Convention, held in Syracuse, Aug. 29, 1860, Gerrit Smith was nominated for President and William Goodell for Governor of New York. Douglass was chosen one of the Presidential electors. (For the proceedings of that convention, see *The Principia,* Sept. 15, 1860.)

52. Douglass is referring to the American and Foreign Anti-Slavery Society.

53. The address was entitled, "The Suffrage Question in Relation to Colored Voters in the State of New York." It was signed by James McCune Smith, chairman, and James P. Miller and John J. Zuille for the New York City and County Suffrage Committee of Colored Citizens.

54. On Sept. 23, 1860, a committee of fifteen, appointed at a Grand Mass Meeting in New York City, announced that it had drawn up a fusion ticket consisting of eighteen Douglas, ten Bell, and seven Breckenridge electors. Thus the separate anti-Republican parties were united into a single Union electoral ticket for New York State. (For a discussion of the fusion movement, see Philip S. Foner, *Business and Slavery,* pp. 172-80.)

55. The proposal for equal suffrage was defeated by a majority of 140,481 votes— 337,984 against the proposal and 197,503 for it.

56. At a meeting in Tremont Temple, Boston, on Dec. 3, 1860, to commemorate the anniversary of John Brown's execution, the commercial interests hired

ruffians to invade the hall and break up the proceedings. Douglass was attacked by the mob and though he "fought like a trained pugilist," he was thrown "down the staircase to the floor of the hall." Six days later, at the Music Hall in the same city, another mob attempted to keep Douglass from lecturing. (See Boston *Evening Transcript,* Dec. 3, 6, 1860.)

57. Three days after Lincoln's election, Horace Greeley published an editorial in his New York *Tribune* in which he wrote: "If the cotton States shall decide that they can do better out of the Union than in it, we insist on letting them go in peace . . . whenever a considerable section of our Union shall resolve to go out, we shall resist all coercive measures designed to keep it in. We hope never to live in a republic whereof one section is pinned to the residue by bayonets." (See also New York *Tribune,* Nov. 16, 19, 24, 1860.) "The *Tribune* policy," writes Ralph Ray Fahrney, "not only encouraged the further alienation of Southern loyalty, but it discouraged the formation of public sentiment in the North favorable to the maintenance of the Union." (*Horace Greeley and the Tribune in the Civil War,* Cedar Rapids, Iowa, 1936, p. 49.)

During this same period, Thurlow Weed proposed in the Albany *Evening Journal* that concessions be granted to the South to keep the southern states in the Union. He also advocated peaceful secession and denounced any plan to keep the seceded states in the Union by force. (See Howard Cecil Perkins, ed., *Northern Editorials on Secession,* New York, 1942, pp. 107, 199, 300; Glyndon G. Van Deusen, *Thurlow Weed,* New York, 1947, pp. 267-70.)

INDEX